MW01674294

Embracing Business Sustainability Through Innovation and Creativity in the Service Sector

Pankaj Kumar Tyagi
Chandigarh University, India

Vipin Nadda
University of Sunderland, UK

Vishal Bharti
Chandigarh University, India

Ebru Kemer
Niğde Ömer Halisdemir University, Turkey

IGI Global
PUBLISHER of TIMELY KNOWLEDGE

A volume in the Advances in Business Strategy and Competitive Advantage (ABSCA) Book Series

Published in the United States of America by
IGI Global
Business Science Reference (an imprint of IGI Global)
701 E. Chocolate Avenue
Hershey PA, USA 17033
Tel: 717-533-8845
Fax: 717-533-8661
E-mail: cust@igi-global.com
Web site: http://www.igi-global.com

Copyright © 2023 by IGI Global. All rights reserved. No part of this publication may be reproduced, stored or distributed in any form or by any means, electronic or mechanical, including photocopying, without written permission from the publisher. Product or company names used in this set are for identification purposes only. Inclusion of the names of the products or companies does not indicate a claim of ownership by IGI Global of the trademark or registered trademark.

Library of Congress Cataloging-in-Publication Data

Names: Tyagi, Pankaj Kumar, 1979- editor.
Title: Embracing business sustainability through innovation and creativity in the service sector / Pankaj Tyagi, Vipin Nadda, Vishal Bharti, and Ebru Kemer, editors.
Description: Hershey, PA : Business Science Reference, [2023] | Includes bibliographical references and index. | Summary: "This book provides an in-depth understanding of various dimensions of business sustainability through innovation and creativity in the service sector"-- Provided by publisher.
Identifiers: LCCN 2022031050 (print) | LCCN 2022031051 (ebook) | ISBN 9781668467329 (hardcover) | ISBN 9781668467336 (paperback) | ISBN 9781668467343 (ebook)
Subjects: LCSH: Service industries--Technological innovations. | Service industries--Environmental aspects. | Sustainable development.
Classification: LCC HD9983.5 .E43 2023 (print) | LCC HD9983.5 (ebook) | DDC 338/.064--dc23/eng/20220805
LC record available at https://lccn.loc.gov/2022031050
LC ebook record available at https://lccn.loc.gov/2022031051

This book is published in the IGI Global book series Advances in Business Strategy and Competitive Advantage (ABSCA) (ISSN: 2327-3429; eISSN: 2327-3437)

British Cataloguing in Publication Data
A Cataloguing in Publication record for this book is available from the British Library.

All work contributed to this book is new, previously-unpublished material. The views expressed in this book are those of the authors, but not necessarily of the publisher.

For electronic access to this publication, please contact: eresources@igi-global.com.

Advances in Business Strategy and Competitive Advantage (ABSCA) Book Series

Patricia Ordóñez de Pablos
Universidad de Oviedo, Spain

ISSN:2327-3429
EISSN:2327-3437

Mission

Business entities are constantly seeking new ways through which to gain advantage over their competitors and strengthen their position within the business environment. With competition at an all-time high due to technological advancements allowing for competition on a global scale, firms continue to seek new ways through which to improve and strengthen their business processes, procedures, and profitability.

The **Advances in Business Strategy and Competitive Advantage (ABSCA) Book Series** is a timely series responding to the high demand for state-of-the-art research on how business strategies are created, implemented and re-designed to meet the demands of globalized competitive markets. With a focus on local and global challenges, business opportunities and the needs of society, the **ABSCA** encourages scientific discourse on doing business and managing information technologies for the creation of sustainable competitive advantage.

Coverage

- Adaptive Enterprise
- Competitive Strategy
- Core Competencies
- Innovation Strategy
- Strategic Management
- Economies of Scale
- Foreign Investment Decision Process
- Business Models
- Value Creation
- Ethics and Business Strategy

IGI Global is currently accepting manuscripts for publication within this series. To submit a proposal for a volume in this series, please contact our Acquisition Editors at Acquisitions@igi-global.com or visit: http://www.igi-global.com/publish/.

The Advances in Business Strategy and Competitive Advantage (ABSCA) Book Series (ISSN 2327-3429) is published by IGI Global, 701 E. Chocolate Avenue, Hershey, PA 17033-1240, USA, www.igi-global.com. This series is composed of titles available for purchase individually; each title is edited to be contextually exclusive from any other title within the series. For pricing and ordering information please visit http://www.igi-global.com/book-series/advances-business-strategy-competitive-advantage/73672. Postmaster: Send all address changes to above address. © © 2023 IGI Global. All rights, including translation in other languages reserved by the publisher. No part of this series may be reproduced or used in any form or by any means – graphics, electronic, or mechanical, including photocopying, recording, taping, or information and retrieval systems – without written permission from the publisher, except for non commercial, educational use, including classroom teaching purposes. The views expressed in this series are those of the authors, but not necessarily of IGI Global.

Titles in this Series

For a list of additional titles in this series, please visit: http://www.igi-global.com/book-series/advances-business-strategy-competitive-advantage/73672

Challenges and Opportunities for Aviation Stakeholders in a Post-Pandemic World
Salim Kurnaz (Suleyman Demirel University, Turkey & Kazimiero Simonaviciaus University, Lithuania) Antonio Rodrigues (Instituto Superior de Gestão, Portugal) and Dorothea Bowyer (Western Sydney University, Australia)
Business Science Reference • © 2023 • 314pp • H/C (ISBN: 9781668468357) • US $260.00

Handbook of Research on Business Model Innovation Through Disruption and Digitalization
Erik Stavnsager Rasmussen (University of Southern Denmark, Denmark) and Nicolaj Hannesbo Petersen (UCL University College, Denmark)
Business Science Reference • © 2023 • 425pp • H/C (ISBN: 9781668448953) • US $325.00

Strategic Management and International Business Policies for Maintaining Competitive Advantage
Ailson J. De Moraes (Royal Holloway University of London, UK)
Business Science Reference • © 2023 • 340pp • H/C (ISBN: 9781668468456) • US $250.00

Opportunities and Challenges of Business 5.0 in Emerging Markets
Sumesh Dadwal (Northumbria University, UK) Pawan Kumar (Lovely Professional University, India) Rajesh Verma (Lovely Professional University, India) and Gursimranjit Singh (Lovely Professional University, India)
Business Science Reference • © 2023 • 315pp • H/C (ISBN: 9781668464038) • US $250.00

Rapid Innovation and Development in the Global Cannabis Market
Pfano Mashau (University of KwaZulu-Natal, South Africa) and Jabulani Nyawo (University of KwaZulu-Natal, South Africa)
Business Science Reference • © 2023 • 352pp • H/C (ISBN: 9781668463468) • US $250.00

Analyzing International Business Operations in the Post-Pandemic Era
Bryan Christiansen (The Christiansen Foundation, USA) and John D. Branch (University of Michigan, USA)
Business Science Reference • © 2023 • 309pp • H/C (ISBN: 9781668437490) • US $250.00

Intellectual Capital as a Precursor to Sustainable Corporate Social Responsibility
Bartolomé Marco-Lajara (University of Alicante, Spain) Patrocinio Zaragoza-Sáez (University of Alicante, Spain) and Javier Martínez-Falcó (University of Alicante, Spain & Stellenbosch University, South Africa)
Business Science Reference • © 2023 • 291pp • H/C (ISBN: 9781668468159) • US $250.00

IGI Global
PUBLISHER of TIMELY KNOWLEDGE

701 East Chocolate Avenue, Hershey, PA 17033, USA
Tel: 717-533-8845 x100 • Fax: 717-533-8661
E-Mail: cust@igi-global.com • www.igi-global.com

Table of Contents

Detailed Table of Contents

The purpose of the study reported on in this chapter was to explore and attempt to answer the primary research question: To what extent can embracing business sustainability through digital transformation, implemented via unified communication and collaboration (UC&C) technologies, impact innovation and productivity in the global automotive sector? This will be presented against the background of embracing business sustainability through innovation and creativity in the service sector. Apart from creativity, collaboration, and generating savings featured in the subtitle of the chapter, changing work practices were also identified as a factor impacting innovation.

Digitalization of financial services has stimulated regulatory and regulatory concerns, technological progress, new capacities and client expectations, and has exposed the sector to competition. A dramatic, expensive, and risky turning moment challenged the conventional banking industry's viability. However, some safety and ethical difficulties still exist when it comes to the adaptation of business sustainability. Global transformation, harmonization, and convergence will be expanded, turning financial services into intelligent services in the services sector. The editorial argues that for digital transformation, we must first expand our understanding of the interactions and interrelationships that contribute to knowledge, creativity, and value creation among society's participants. Cybersecurity is a modern topic that is becoming a major concern owing to the epidemic in the industrial and service sectors. This research exposes cybersecurity strategy, formulation, management, sustainability issues, and organizational and corporate culture management in digital transformation.

Organizations need to innovate to stay relevant, for example, through the innovative work behavior of employees. Previous studies highlighted how different innovative phases may require other leadership behavior. In the present study, the authors aim to discover which type of transformational leadership behaviour best encourages employees in which innovative phase, both from the perspective of the manager and the employee. They conducted interviews with 42 leaders and 43 followers within four innovative companies in the e-tailing sector. They use thematic analysis and quantisization of the data.

The results show that not every subcomponent of transformational leadership has the same influence on each phase of innovative work behavior, nor with the same magnitude. The most prevalent relationship is between intellectual stimulation and idea generation. They report specific actions by leaders that promote innovative work behavior in followers.

Artificial intelligence in human resources plays an important and crucial role in the 21st century. It is helpful in gathering, analysing, and presenting data in such a way that is more helpful for the HR professional to use. As technological advancements happen in the era, artificial intelligence helps to fulfil organisational demands as well as employee demands. Artificial intelligence eases the work of HR as well as effectively provides efficient work. Therefore, the present study explores the implementation of artificial intelligence in human resource functions. It further explores the various benefits and challenges of artificial intelligence in human resource functions. Finally, the study concludes that the work of artificial intelligence can be used in all areas of the HR functions. No doubt in the initial stage of artificial intelligence implementation the HR professionals and organization can face some challenges, but after its successful implementation, it is considered the best tool for HR functions.

Airbnb is a platform allowing a peer-to-peer accommodation option for people sharing their own extra space. As simple it sounds, there are many challenges behind its implementation. It is crucial to look at both sides of the coin to understand not only what it brings but what it causes as well. Airbnb is a comparatively new phenomenon of the modern times and changes the traditional tourist behaviour as well as accommodation situation in the market. Initially, the general perception was that Airbnb is not a threat to the traditional accommodation as it attracts completely new customers. It is a big part of sharing economy and brings both advantages and disadvantages. The sharing economy is a new dimension of economy, and the classic structure is rapidly changing. It is a sustainable form of service provision and contributes to inclusive destination development. On the other hand, as Airbnb lies in providing accommodation by non-commercial residents, there is an overall lack of control of whether the host is reliable and if it is secure.

Preface

With the ever-increasing pressure and rivalry in the global business environment, businesses must develop sustainable practices that set them apart from the competition. Innovation and creativity are critical aspects of business that must be implemented in all areas for companies to not only survive but thrive.

Embracing Business Sustainability Through Innovation and Creativity in the Service Sector provides comprehensive research about sustainable business through innovation and creativity in the service sector and aims to contribute to the knowledge of various sustainable business practices. Covering key topics such as tourism, hospitality, wealth creation, and entrepreneurship, this premier reference source is ideal for business owners, managers, industry professionals, researchers, scholars, academicians, practitioners, instructors, and students.

The brief about various chapters is as follows.

The first chapter provides insight as to how Grameen Bank has gained a significant position in the global microfinance sphere that ensure the presence of poor in the mainstream financial scenario. The Grameen Bank microfinance concept has been adopted in over 40 countries and has had significant success in a variety of societies. This bank has served 9.44 million clients and 2,568 branches, GB provides services in 81,678 villages, covering more than 93 percent of the total villages in Bangladesh. To get lone from the GB, rural women must be extremely poor. This bank intention is to remove poverty and unemployment through the business and make them self-economic sustainably. GB does not only work in Bangladesh it also working developing countries. GB drawn global attention because of its aims and easy money lending mechanism to the rural poor people for making themselves financially strong and diminish the rate of poverty and unemployment.

The second chapter is about digitally sustaining the rural intangible cultural heritage. Conservation of intangible cultural heritage is important for any rural tourism destination. The rich intangible cultural heritage can be preserved using advanced digital technologies for future generations. Digital technologies provide the means of documenting, recovering, and presenting different components of the intangible cultural heritage of a rural destination. However, one of the challenges is finding appropriate forms, together with efficient methods, to document the ephemeral aspects of rural intangible heritage. Another barrier is finding effective ways to communicate the knowledge inextricably linked to people or communities. This chapter outlines state-of-the-art models, projects, and technical practices that have advanced the digitization lifecycle for intangible cultural heritage resources. The chapter further aims to identify the advancements and gaps in the existing conventions and to envision opportunities for transmitting embodied knowledge in intangible heritage.

The third chapter highlights the recruitment crisis in the British hospitality industry: a case for more sustainable practices. The scarce supply of labour and of a competent workforce in the hospitality sector has been researched and debated for decades. Although the sector is important to the UK economy contributing £130 billion pounds to the Gross Domestic Product, the inability of the sector to attract and retain the best talent remains an age-old problem. This paper is a commentary of the current debate on the recruitment crisis based on an examination of the most recent academic literature. The research finds that although many recommendations have been proffered by researchers to solve these problems the issues and mistakes made by hospitality employers appear to remain the same. Possible best practice solutions are explored. Reviews of scholarly journals, books and materials from the domains of marketing, human resources, hospitality management and organisational behaviour were used to find evidence about the current trends of thought, research findings and best practices in this field. The chapter concludes with three conceptual models that summarise the critical issues and possible solutions.

The fourth chapter is aimed to explore the role of knowledge management practices in promoting creativity and innovation in the service sector concerning the banking industry. The study assumes knowledge as an intangible internal asset and innovation as a way to develop sustainable strategic capabilities that are difficult to imitate. This quantitative study tested five proposed hypotheses on 437 responses collected from banking employees through the PLS-SEM method. Light indicated that knowledge sharing, application, and protection directly contributed to firm innovation, whereas knowledge creation encounters complete mediation through employee creativity. The study combines RBV and KM perspectives in developing long-term strategic capability and strengthens the evolutionary view of economists that new knowledge is based on existing knowledge, conforming the effect of knowledge protection to knowledge sharing. The study develops a knowledge management framework incorporating working/operational knowledge protection as one of the main dimensions of the knowledge management process.

The fifth chapter is about fostering creativity and innovation: tourism and hospitality perspective. This sector is the most progressive and fastest-growing not nationally, even globally. The tourism and hospitality sector fosters growth, prospers the hosts, and also offers immense potential for employment in various sections. Innovation is a decisive process for the well-being of an organization. With economic crises after COVID-19 and the slow recovery that continues, we believe that a solution can be improving the capacity to research and innovate to achieve sustainable development. The purpose of this chapter is to develop a meaningful debate on the creativity and innovations in the forms of new ideas, methods, and technology to better meet the evolving requirement of the organization and workforce sustainability. Further, exploring the future needs and circumstances rather than simply finding some responses to the situation, this chapter highlights challenges and prospects related to achieving creativity and innovation for business sustainability in tourism and hospitality.

The sixth chapter relates to the innovative practices in sustainable ecotourism promotion and impacts: changes through dynamic leadership. Sustainable Ecotourism, its promotion, its impacts have a bearing on the world considering the fact that tourism, travel and hospitality moved the millions around the world ensured a way of life for the local communities, governments and businesses. But what is that drives Sustainable Ecotourism in a way it happens; is it the destination, the product on offer or anything else? It is the people, may be the community, may be one individual, who provides a phenomenal direction and ensures all others follow in the right spirit. The Chapter is a tribute to four Indians who have contributed to Sustainable Ecotourism Leadership and ensured for various products that have helped in Ecotourism promotion and impacted the lives of the communities they have served and still continue. The work of these Leaders has been mapped to two frameworks, which itself will provide ample food for thought for the multitudes to adopt and move forward.

The seventh chapter focus on the green innovation in tourism businesses. Today, while all countries worldwide emphasize the significance of environmental awareness, among the sector areas, the tourism sector is the one that should focus on this matter most. The current study aimed, with examples from the tourism industry, to reveal the perspective of tourism businesses on green innovation practices, their practices, and the results obtained. After giving information about the "innovation concept, scope, and types" in general, this study provided fundamental explanations about the "green innovation concept, scope, and types" and dealt with the concept of green innovation in tourism businesses. Finally, the current study that provided general information about "tourism environmental awareness certificates" assessed the tourism sector by presenting examples of green innovation applications.

The eight chapter is about the application of artificial intelligence and robotics in tourism and hospitality marketing. Rapid technological developments have affected business areas and caused differences in products and services. The tourism and hospitality industry has also been affected by these rapid developments, and the use and importance of new technologies have increased. In this context, this research aims to evaluate the use of artificial intelligence and robotic technologies in the field of tourism marketing with data obtained from secondary data. As a result of the research, it has been determined that artificial intelligence and robotic technology applications in the tourism sector offer personalized and new opportunities for tourists in their travel decisions. Within the scope of the research, it has been suggested that these opportunities offered through big data are important in reducing operating costs and ensuring personnel productivity and competitive advantage. Therefore, using artificial intelligence in tourism marketing positively contributes to the systematic analysis of customer information.

The ninth chapter provides insight about technological innovations in tourism businesses: a study on contemporary trends. Technological innovations are bringing major breakthroughs and radical changes in the way businesses function. These technological innovations are helping all the industries to smoothen their functions and provide better experiences to the customers. Tourism industry also witnessing tremendous improvements in technological innovations. The article aims to study the different types of technologies which have emerged in recent times in tourism businesses. This study is conceptual in nature and uses various secondary sources for data collection along with the study of various cases to comprehend the usage of technology. The study concludes in supporting the statement made by world's largest and nodal tourism organization "United Nations World Tourism Organization" that technology and digitization are emerging, disrupting and affecting our lives in such a way that augurs the begging of next generation industrial revolution.

The tenth chapter relates to management of innovation: theories and practice. Innovation management is a prime concept of making changes and innovations in the business to make the business globally famous. The conceptual understanding of the innovative strategies has been covered in this book. Besides this, the discussion of key elements and the challenges a company might face to implement innovation has been discussed here. Identification and discussion, including the application of the innovation, have been covered here. The impact of the implementation of innovation-based managerial theories as well as practices has also been evaluated within the study to develop a critical understanding of business proceedings.

The eleventh chapter focus on central bank digital currency, poverty reduction and the United Nations sustainable development goal. It examines the role of central bank digital currency for poverty reduction and sustainable development. In the paper, I argue that a CBDC can eliminate poverty by first increasing financial inclusion which then gives poor people access to affordable credit and other basic financial services which they can use to improve their welfare, thereby enabling them to rise above poverty. This argument is valid only if a central bank digital currency is specially designed to incorporate features that increase financial inclusion for poor banked and unbanked adults. The argument may not apply to cases where a CBDC is not designed to increase financial inclusion as is the case in developed countries.

The twelfth chapter's purpose is to explore and attempt to answer the primary research question: To what extent can embracing business sustainability through digital transformation, implemented via Unified Communication and Collaboration (UC&C) technologies, impact innovation and productivity in the global automotive sector? This will be presented against the background of embracing business sustainability through innovation and creativity in the service sector. Apart from creativity, collaboration and generating savings featured in the subtitle of the chapter, changing work practices were also identified as a factor impacting on innovation.

The thirteenth chapter is about cybersecurity strategy, formulation, management, and sustainability issues in digital transformation and sustainability. Digitalization of financial services has stimulated regulatory and regulatory concerns, technological progress, new capacities and client expectations, and has exposed the sector to competition. A dramatic, expensive, and risky turning moment challenged the conventional banking industry's viability. However, some safety and ethical difficulties still exist when it comes to the adaptation of business sustainability. Global transformation, harmonization, and convergence will be expanded, turning financial services into intelligent services in the services sector. The editorial argues for digital transformation., we must first expand our understanding of the interactions and interrelationships that contribute to knowledge, creativity, and value creation among society's participants. Cybersecurity is a modern topic that is becoming a major concern owing to the epidemic in the industrial and service sectors. This research exposes cybersecurity strategy, formulation, management, sustainability issues, and organizational and corporate culture management in digital transformation.

The fourteenth chapter relates to transformational leadership and innovative work behavior of employees: two sides of the story. Organizations need to innovate to stay relevant, for example through the innovative work behavior of employees. Previous studies highlighted how different innovative phases may require other leadership behavior. In the present study we aim to discover which type of transformational leadership behaviour, best encourages employees in which innovative phase, both from the perspective of the manager, and the employee. We conducted interviews with 42 leaders and 43 followers within four innovative companies in the e-tailing sector. We use thematic analysis and quantisization of the data. The results show that not every subcomponent of transformational leadership has the same influence on each phase of innovative work behavior, nor with the same magnitude. The most prevalent relationship is between intellectual stimulation and idea generation. We report specific actions by leaders that promote innovative work behavior in followers.

The fifteenth chapter analysis artificial intelligence in human resource management: the next generation of technology for business excellence. Artificial intelligence in human resources plays an important and crucial role in today's time of the 21st century. It is helpful in gathering, analysing and presenting data in such a way that is more helpful for the HR professional to use. As technological advancements happen in the era, artificial intelligence helps to fulfil organisational demands as well as employee demands. Artificial intelligence eases the work of HR as well as effectively provides efficient work. Therefore, the present study explores the implementation of artificial intelligence in human resource functions. It further explores the various benefits and challenges of artificial intelligence in human resource functions. Finally, the study concludes that the work of artificial intelligence can be used in all areas of the HR functions. No doubt in the initial stage of artificial intelligence implementation the HR professionals and organization can face some challenges but after its successful implementation, it is considered the best tool for HR functions.

The sixteenth chapter is "Airbnb in the Local Neighbourhood: Innovation vs. Disruption." Airbnb is a platform allowing peer-to-peer accommodation option for people sharing their own extra space. As simple it sounds, there are many challenges behind its implementation. It is crucial to look at both sides of the coin to understand not only what it brings but what it causes as well. Airbnb is a comparatively new phenomenon of the modern times and changes the traditional tourist behaviour as well as accommodation situation in the market. Initially, the general perception was that Airbnb is not a threat to the traditional accommodation as it attracts completely new customers. It is a big part of sharing economy and brings both advantages and disadvantages. Sharing economy is a new dimension of economy and the classic structure is rapidly changing. It is a sustainable form of service provision and contributes to inclusive destination development. On the other hand, as Airbnb lies in providing accommodation by non-commercial residents, there is an overall lack of control whether the host is reliable and if it is secure.

The seventeenth chapter helps to understand the management of service in small hotel by self-service technology adoption: the customers' perspective from Thailand. Modern technology creating customer experience. Its algorithm could remember, predict, and provide customize needs of customers. The self-service technology (SST) is a service innovation that communicates with users through either the internet-based social media or applications. Yet, the hotels in Thailand are like other businesses that applied SST. Howbeit, the employees could better communicate, create human relationship, and understand profoundly of customer needs than technology. Therefore, the adoption technology in hotel especially small hotels must be efficient and effective. This study aims to assess the SST components that serve the small hotel customers' needs, and evaluate electronic service quality and technology adoption leading to satisfaction and repurchase intention. This study mainly used quantitative method by structural equation modelling. The scope of study are customers who had experienced using small hotel in Nakhon Ratchasima Province in Thailand. Nakhon Ratchasima is the fifth biggest province in Thailand and one of the top destinations of Thai people.

On behalf of all the authors, we hope that you enjoy this book and that it will enhance your quest to develop in your field of endeavour.

Vipin Nadda
University of Sunderland, UK

Chapter 1
Grameen Bank as an Economic Stabilizer for the Rural Banking Sector in Bangladesh

Md Hussin Alam
https://orcid.org/0000-0002-0652-3334
University of Wroclaw, Poland

ABSTRACT

Grameen Bank has gained a significant position in the global microfinance sphere that ensures the presence of the poor in the mainstream financial scenario. The Grameen Bank microfinance concept has been adopted in over 40 countries and has had significant success in a variety of societies. This bank has served 9.44 million clients and 2,568 branches. GB provides services in 81,678 villages, covering more than 93% of the total villages in Bangladesh. In order to get a loan from the GB, rural women have to be extremely poor. This bank's intention is to remove poverty and unemployment through the business and make them economically self-sustainable. GB works in Bangladesh and developing countries. GB has drawn global attention because of its aims and easy money lending mechanism to the rural poor people for making themselves financially strong and diminishing the rate of poverty and unemployment.

INTRODUCTION

Bangladeshi society was an example of deprived poor society where a large faction of the society was highly deprived of having basic necessities of life. In early seventies, after the independence from Pakistan, Bangladeshi society was facing huge influx of refugees that caused shortage of food in Bangladesh. Society was suffering from famine and also economic involvement. Muhammad Yunus came up with the idea of micro-credit facility at the very minimal level as he believed that the situation of poor can only be improved through the micro-credit provision that's why he invented a system of social collateral. This mechanism worked very effectively inculcating socially and financially excluded section of the society. The mechanism tried to gather those who are completely unable to participate in any small economic activity. This social collateral is actually an amalgamation of solidarity and peer pressure, it is a simple

DOI: 10.4018/978-1-6684-6732-9.ch001

Copyright © 2023, IGI Global. Copying or distributing in print or electronic forms without written permission of IGI Global is prohibited.

system to make all the factions of the society activated and participate in the economic activities in order to create income sources which would work to include them into the society on a broader perspective. Everyone was eligible to participate in this new micro-credit system that was exclusively design for the excluded people of the Bangladeshi society not on the basis of financial status but also on gender level because, women were also eligible to receive loans in a form of a group. The first loan given to one woman, the next member will receive a loan when the first one is able to follow the repayment scheme and in this way, a collective pressure on the whole group was retained. This mechanism has always been the key factor in the success of Grameen model of micro-credit and its repayment.

Grameen, micro-credit was not the main concern of global economic policies and public concern but when this idea was picked by Yunus in order to include most of the poor and unprivileged population of the society into main economic sphere then this idea gained popularity. He claimed that poverty and deprivation would be easily handled and eradicate through the Grameen micro-credit model. Yunus predicted that this mechanism could end poverty from generations and poverty could only be found in museum and this claim rose the excitement. Micro-credit was never been utilized in that specific mode in which Yunus built and implemented, he said that this could easily reduce the gap between different excluded people who are deprived of investment and opportunities to earn money and be a part of society. Yunus promised to bring capitalism down to the poor through self-help send individual entrepreneurship by giving them small loans with the proper system of repayment.

Grameen Bank has gained a significant position in the global microfinance sphere that ensure the presence of poor in the mainstream financial scenario. The Grameen Bank microfinance concept has been adopted in over 40 countries and has had significant success in a variety of societies. This bank has served 9.44 million clients and 2,568 branches, GB provides services in 81,678 villages, covering more than 93 percent of the total villages in Bangladesh (Grameen bank website, Oct-2021).

HISTORY OF GRAMEEN BANK

In 1976, Dr. Muhammad Yunus, a then university Professor of Economics, started a project by lending an amount of $27 to forty-two poor persons in a village named 'Jobra' near to his university. Yunus found that in order to survive, these people used to take loans from the local informal money lenders with difficult loan terms. He was not in favor of charity and thought that if these people get access to credit, they might 'increase their profitability, or diversify their economic activities, in ways that would allow them to raise their incomes' (Hulme, 2008) . Dr. Yunus paid the money from his own pocket as no bank was ready to provide these poor people with loans as they were perceived as not creditworthy (Yunus, 2004).

After several years, in 1983, this project was transformed into a formal bank called Grameen Bank. It was 'established as a specialised bank with its own charter to work exclusively with the poor' (Dowla, 2006). The huge success of Grameen Bank attracted the Governments and the NGOs of several countries around the world. This unique model was applied by many countries. Because of its huge success in the poverty alleviation in many countries of the world, Professor Yunus and his Grameen Bank jointly owned the Nobel Peace Prize in the year of 2006.

Rather than using the financial collaterals, Grameen Bank believes in using social collateral (Bernasek, 2003). Generally, these loans are not given to individuals rather these are given to groups of five to ten members (Mainsah et al., 2004). This total process of loan providing and recovering depends on trust, relationship and network. In other words, Grameen Bank runs its activities through using a concept called 'social capital' (Dowla, 2006). According to (Yunus, 2004), Grameen Bank follows certain principles in its operation. Firstly, it believes that poor people do not create poverty rather poverty is generated by the institutions and the policies surrounding these people. So, there is a need for a proper change in these policies. Secondly, the bank believes that the problem of poverty cannot be solved through charity, rather charity creates dependency. In order to fight against poverty, the inner energy and creativity of human beings should be utilised. Thirdly, the bank believes that poor people have equal ability like any other people in the society. Their under-utilised capacity needs to be utilised. Fourthly, Grameen bank does not follow the traditional banking style where the people who have more, get more credits. In this bank, the person who has less, gets more credit. Fifthly, the bank has the trust that the poor people always pay back. Sixthly, it is more important to lend to women than to men as women can bring more benefits to the families. (Hossain, 2013).

Bangladesh got her independence in 1971 after a devastating war. The post war economy was suffering from lack of infrastructure and massive poverty, especially in the rural areas.Getting the loan from Grameen Bank depends on a collective effort. It was discussed earlier that these loans are not given to the individuals rather these are generally given to a group of five members. As a result, the loan repayment almost becomes a collective effort. Peer pressure acts as an important factor in this case. As mentioned earlier, the loan is given to the group and the member who is the neediest, gets the loan first. The group leader gets the loan at the end. A group can remain eligible for further loans only when their past repayment record is good. (Hossain, 2013).

Todd (1996), by making a comparison between the Grameen Bank borrowers and non-borrowers in a district of Bangladesh called Tangail, found that the rate of poverty was significantly lower in case of the borrowers. Empirical research also highlighted that Grameen loans helped in women's empowerment. It was found that the women who borrowed money from Grameen Bank have a greater control over the loan activities and many of these women purchased lands in their own names (Bornstein, 1996 and Bernasek, 2003). Over the years the Grameen model became very popular and was applied in many countries in the world. (Hossain, 2013). But in its own country, Bangladesh, the bank faced huge criticisms also. The bank was blamed for providing loans with interest to the extreme poor. The bank's policy was attacked by the Marxist critics as well as the Islamic critics for this reason. The Marxists complained that giving a loan to the poor and taking interest from them ultimately follows the oppressing model of capitalism. The poor people are getting exploited when they are made bound to repay the loan with interest. Even the top-level politicians of Bangladesh have criticised the bank's policy for taking interest from the poor people. Even then the Grameen model remained popular among many economists and a part of the civil society. The international exposure of Dr. Muhammad Yunus helped the bank to deal with these criticisms. The bank was also criticised by the religious leaders for empowering women. In Bangladesh, the rural society is relatively traditional where women have a backward position. Grameen Bank's emphasis on women made them powerful and important in many ways. Many rural religious leaders criticised this effort of Grameen Bank vehemently for this reason. Grameen's approach of banking has been criticized for determination of interest rate charges, because the interest of Grameen is higher (20 percent) than the conventional banking (10-15 percent) in Bangladesh. However, there is a fear about the issue of further installment of the loan (which depend on the capability of borrowers to pay back the loan). This requirement leaves poor borrowers in the same financial situation; that is, the poor may hide their inability to add value to the received loans for the fear of not receiving subsequent loans. As a result, needy people can only use the money for survival rather than to make profit in order to pay the high interests on their loan. (Hussain et al, 2001)

Over the years, Grameen Bank has become a huge organisation. It has expanded its operation throughout Bangladesh. Moreover, it has extended its operation in many ways by investing in several development projects. In fact, most of these projects proved to be very innovative and successful while leads ultimately towards the economic development of the Bangladesh. (Hossain, 2013). The birth of Grameen was a resonance of myth in a tiny village of Bangladesh, which breaks the idea about ``poverty is an indispensable fact of life''. The age of Grameen is about 25 years but its activities are extending everywhere in the world, irrespective of the characteristics of economies (i.e. developed or developing). Grameen is very successful in eliminating rural poverty in Bangladesh and in many developing countries, but its unique characteristics enable it to function anywhere in the world. However, there are some advantages/opportunities existing for Grameen operation in the developed world, which seemingly enhance Grameen's implementation in the developed world including Europe. (Hussain et al, 2001).

The Grameen Bank became an independent bank in October 1983, as a well-known financial institution that distributes small loans to the poorest of the rural poor area. Muhammad Yunus provided small loan of $27 to 42 families to open business, that they could make products for sale without the heavy interest obligations that come with traditional lending procedures (BBC News, 2006). Yunus believed that expanding the availability of such loan payments to a bigger population would boost business and assist to relieve Bangladesh's widespread extreme poverty. He developed the Grameen Bank principles based on his believe (Wahid, 1999). Grameen Bank meaning is "Village bank "in Bangla. Grameen bank were the first services in Jobra village, Chittagong, Bangladesh (1976). The Bank initiative was expanded to the Tangail District in 1979, with help from Bangladesh Bank. The GB was success to maintain all requirements to get Bangladesh's government approved as a separate financial institution. As a result, 1983 Bangladesh's government has approved GB as an independent bank (world bank, 2021). In 2005, the bank had loaned over US$4.7 billion to the poor, and by the end of 2008, it had loaned over US$7.6 billion (Grameen Bank,2021). In 2017, the bank has over 2,600 branches and nine million debtors, with a repayment rate of 99.6%. The bank is present in 97 percent of Bangladesh's villages. Grameen Bank is expanding into developed countries also like Grameen America had 19 locations in eleven US cities as of 2017. It had a nearly 100,000-strong female-dominated loan bank (Betters, 2016). Additionally, all GB employees must complete a twelve-month intensive training program in information technology, accounting, administration, leadership, and strategic planning.

Although most of financial institutions, which provide credit based on security resources, but Grameen Bank provides loans without any type of security. Grameen Bank has been effective in resolving information asymmetry problems that are common in rural financial markets. Social respect is used to replace security in this bank. If they create groups of five persons, the poor can acquire small loans from Grameen Bank. Each group member receives a separate loan, but they are mutually responsible for all five credits. The majority of Grameen Bank loans are women, who are the poorest social category in rural areas. Grameen Bank loan recoverability has significantly improved the quality of financial return to women. GB has been providing facility to access microcredits for poor micro-entrepreneur, so that, they can have the credentials and credibility to grab market opportunities. This bank also worked to promote women empowerment. GB as an inspiration for the global microloans sector. Grameen bank same model (Grameen foundation) are working developing and developed countries like Bangladesh, India, Colombia, Mexico, Nigeria, South Africa, Turkey, Yemen, Jordan, Egypt, Ghana, Kenya, Bolivia, USA and Canada.

GOALS OF GRAMEEN BANK

Barrett Hazeltine (2003) has described GB goals on the article Grameen bank planning implementation, those goals are.:

- Banking facility should be extended to the deprived faction of the society.
- To stop money lenders exploitation to the poor
- To provide job and self-employment options for the majority of Bangladesh's poor and unemployed population, particularly in rural areas.
- Organize disadvantaged women in a way that understands and meets their financial and employment requirements.
- To create awareness of a new concept known as low income, credit & investment, more income, more savings, and more investment.

In order to get lone from the GB rural women have to be extremely poor. This bank intention is to remove poverty and unemployment through the business and make them self-economic sustainably. GB does not only work in Bangladesh it also working developing countries. GB drawn global attention because of its aims and easy money lending mechanism to the rural poor people for making themselves financially strong and diminish the rate of poverty and unemployment. This idea was creative and effective because its specialty was its organizational commitment and contribution to the exempted vulnerable people isolated from the structured credit system which focused on material collateral by collective liability where an individual can have access to credit but in party repayment. GB have social and financial precondition that allowed poor to have loans for the improvement of their life standards and quality. Most of the developmental financial institution were failed to contribute to rural development and credit availability for the societal development then at that instance, Grameen bank attracted the domestic attention as well as international attention as it can be named as the phenomenal development in Bangladeshi social and financial sector.

Model of Grameen Bank

Table 1. Model of Grameen Bank

Number		
1	Group	5 members (self-formed and group approved all loans request
2	Center	4 to 8 groups
3	Center meeting	weekly
4	Center manger	Grameen bank employee
5	Center chief	A member (Female)
6	Loan request and saving deposit	At center
7	Loan distribution	At bank branch
8	Training	Training program available on the center
9	If one member default, then no more loan to group	
10	Group members collectively responsible for loan	

Source: Muhammad Yunus, The world of three zeros

Rural women as the money creditors because they were not supposed to use loans badly as compare to the men moreover, they were more reliable than man when it comes to the repayment.

Five people in a group, who were collectively responsible for each other's loans in order to create social guarantee and activate mutual screening proces.

- The centers in the specific areas where at least 30 women (six cells) met each week, the reason was to meet, apply and repay at the same time.
- It was mandatory for each client to make micro saving each week so, the financial discipline would be created, and financial guarantee can be achieved. In this way a social conduct and responsibility could be easily maintained.
- He preferred to recruit and trained young graduates to eliminate the possibility of corruption.

Grameen Bank in USA (Grameen America)

Grameen America (GA) adopted Grameen model for poverty and unemployment reduction. GA was encountered institutional challenges of adopting this model from the perspective of developing nations juxtaposed with that of developed countries (Asif Kalam, 2021). Kamal also mentioned that the microfinance institutions (MFIs) implementing the Grameen model have been forerunners in the field of community finance in the context of industrialized economies and tackled the dual logics of community development and sustainability which may seem rather challenging to reconcile and hence confronted institutional complexities. In this theoretical backdrop, the nature of institutional challenges of adopting the Grameen model in the UK and the USA and why GA has been able to overcome such challenges was explored.

Grameen America founded by Muhammad Yunus in January 2008. More than 40 million people live in poverty in the United States. The federal government defines poverty as a family of four living on $25,100 or less a year. Many of these families are often working at minimum wage jobs. That is why Grameen bank move to America as a nonprofit microfinance organization dedicated to helping women who live in poverty build small businesses to create better lives for their families. The organization offers microloans, training, and support to transform communities and fight poverty in the United States. Grameen America has invested over $1.9 billion in more than 142,500 low-income women entrepreneurs" (www.grameenamerica.org) On the other hand, GA declared program, which will offer loan capital, financial training, asset and credit building tools to Black women entrepreneurs, aims to expand to $1.3 billion in loans to more than 80,000 Black women entrepreneurs(grameenamerica.org, May 13, 2021).

Grameen America Policy

According to Asif Kalam, (2021) Grameen America policy implications:

- Members should be allowed to self-select each other from tightly knit communities enabling the social collateral process to be effective.
- Weekly meetings should be made mandatory to facilitate dialogue and enhance discipline.
- Savings mobilization should be made compulsory with specified minimal contributions as it may be helpful for loan recovery and instilling discipline into borrowers.
- There should be a gender focus on female borrowers as findings suggest that this may have beneficial effects on loan recovery and outreach.
- Outreach should be predominantly based on the Grameen principle of "going to clients" or direct approach.
- Client training methods should focus on internal procedures and be used as way of augmenting discipline.
- Regulatory distortions should be minimized to facilitate the lending process including homes visits or community-based outreach.
- The nature of problem framing, and organizational identity should resonate well with that of the parent organization as this may be important for attaining procedural legitimacy.
- Significant changes in organizational identity may be contemplated in order to overcome regulatory impediments. GA's organizational aspiration to become a credit union is an example of this which if successful will help it to mobilize funds and help towards operational self-sufficiency.
- It would require broader policy changes such as enhancement of welfare to work incentives for MFIs (microfinance institution) to successfully recruit indigenous clients.

Compare Grameen Bank and Brac Bank in Bangladesh

Yunus suggested that microfinance for micro-enterprises is a way out for the poverty reduction, in 1990, United Nations arranged a series of global summits for the purpose of poverty reduction, gender equality, education and other social issues. A microcredit summit arranged by US based group RESULTS, but it was taken as global summit, it declared the notion of Microcredit is a human right and various head of the state endorsed it. This summit decided to launch US$21.6 billion for 150 million household for enabling them to stand with their own business and better livelihood. It also supplemented the idea of

Grameen Bank model of microfinance the socially and financially excluded people throughout the world. Few NGOS are working in Bangladesh to reduce poverty and help for the women. One of them is BRAC.

BRAC (Bangladesh Rural Advancement Committee) nearly doing similar work in Bangladesh as like Grameen bank. BRAC, Bangladesh is an NGO, which has started business in 1972 after the independence of Bangladesh. It is one of the largest NGO in the world, employs over 100000 people in 64 districts of Bangladesh as well as has spread its business in America, Africa, and Asia. It is self-financed by different organization that includes dairy products and food projects (Brac.net, 2021). It maintains offices more than 14 countries including UK and USA. Since the activities of the two banks are the same, so researcher compare two bank interest rate and property.

COMPARISON

Author of this thesis referring that unemployment and poverty are two products of unsustainable development of a society and for poverty reduction, government and other organizations have the responsibility to address the situation. Social Business would encourage vigorous economic activities and it ultimately generates more employment opportunities; this helps in better functioning of the state's economy on the contrary, high level of unemployment hinders the growth of domestic economy. This can be reduced by encouraging and facilitating overseas employment, in this manner, foreign exchange reserves, state economic functions and unsustainable growth can be evidently observed in a state societal and economic sphere. For economic boost, government duty is to adopt more vigorous and sustainable strategies, Social Business policy could be able to revitalize and rebuild a country's financial and developmental scenario, more investment in every sector is greatly important to achieve this objective as when the inclusion of investments, all the sectors ultimately need more people to work but not only government but all the other influential actors of the society should take the responsibility and work for the resolution of many prevalent social issues like unemployment. Author of this chapter also describe about outside of country working (Overseas working). Overseas working are also a significant solution of the unemployment problem but domestic job market must also be rebuilt and modified according to the international standards. Social Business employment training programs like driving, computer typing, handicraft bamboo basket training and sewing machine work are the best option as it not only makes domestic modern market and profitable but it also generates international attention because trained and well-acquainted workforce can easily make its place in international work sphere. Unemployed youth of the country is another bigger concern for the government but by providing them information, training, consultant services and financial assistance, they would become a great asset for organizations and state economic stability. This action not only beneficial for increasing overseas employment opportunities for the domestic employee's community but it helps government to introduce friendly and supportive public policies for infrastructure development and investment friendly regulatory reforms that surely expands the potential for self or small businesses like dairy, livestock or poultry breeding. Agriculture could be easily enhanced and advanced to meet the export requirements and provide with the best output of greater number of employment opportunities along with the increased national income.

Even in the context of rapid GDP growth, job creation has been moderate. In a comparative note on the international front, Bangladesh's pace of job creation over this period has not been as dramatic. But that, as indicated by 7, employment growth in Bangla was undermined based on the rate of GDP growth between 2003 and 2003. Compared to the regional peers, the work of the Anglicans has grown to a considerable height - at 3,900 years. And even in front of Vietnam, 4 but they have followed behind Pakistan and Nepal. However, dealing with low staff may seem like a challenge in a low-wage, low-wage worker like Bangladesh. As a result, given that few workers could afford to be unemployed, most of the workers would not be expected to respond quickly to low GDP. Nevertheless, the answer could come in large part through the limited working hours and the type of work, which is expressed through a series of working hours and prices (Amin et al., 2003).

Social business wants to promote inclusive development in rural village. Subsequently, the cultural aspect of promoting prosperity is a worthy issue. Bangladeshi looks at the cultural development of all races and minorities and their languages; in promoting the rights and aspirations of women and children as sewing groups; and on the socio-economic development of the disadvantaged communities including street children, people with disabilities, and people living in backward areas (Ali et al., 2017).

Additionally, social business rural development program is one of the key programs for rural women and rural area. Social business rural development program has been spent more than US $ 1 billion for road upgrades, soler electricity, buildup local library, Grameen school and other links to rural development sites as well as developing shopping malls, offices, rural health clinics. This included constructing small wood bridges for water pipes when needed on rural roads. This was accomplished under a special program called social business rural development projects. Social business rural development projects were the empowerment of rural women by providing them with shops in rural area. Rural area shops are owned and operated by rural women. This has brought about a kind of rural social change as these women now have more economic power and are enjoying the respect of men. Social business motivated rural women in farming area.

Before move on farming area, author of the thesis will describe why rural women want to do social business farming. A higher proportion of women's farming than men could explain greater differences in women. When farming is left out, the difference in women in working hours is reduced, with women and men in production spending more time at work, though women in services work fewer hours than men (Mahmud & Otsuka, 2017).

The lower hourly rate of labor for women compared to men in the non-agricultural sector suggests two things. First, women may not be able to fully access long-term careers, but they do make small events, considering many of the problems of the labor market. Studies show that women face significant barriers to mobility and distance to work, and the availability of opportunities within equal spaces. Employers should provide safer and more segregated women while working for female employees, and this may place an additional burden on business and reduce incentives to recruit women (Mahtab & Islam, 2017).

Furthermore, women may not have a social network to provide information on available jobs; the vast majority of employees take over and do work happens in informal ways. On the other hand, women may prefer this job allowing shorter work hours to handle all the economic tasks and household chores. Except for shorter hours, a very small proportion of women who work less than 35 hours a week agree to be willing and available to work overtime (Mahtab & Islam, 2017).

Although, the expected operating hours (subject to a review of the review) are the same as those of the LFP. Marriage and the number of young children, as well as the educational weight and share of the workforce, are important choices for working hours. Thus, marriage has to do with female workers but has to do with that of men, since married men are often the biggest seller in the house (Glinik et al., 2018). As a result, the increase in the number of infants continues to reduce the number of hours provided to women, while this has little effect on male labor.

Rural women work hard as the researcher see women work in the fishing sector, by providing training through distance learning services, e-learning would help to boost the women members of a family in fish farming. E-learning digital materials would greatly help women and girls living in rural Bangladesh who are unable to buy the study material for the traditional educational process. Bangladesh's teaching has been focused on program learning due to the lack of experimental and technological assets. Instructors aren't able to change the traditional teaching system. Low level of English language skills between students and instructors is another factor that adds to the unfriendly disposition. The present development and investment system of the country cannot generate new employment opportunities to satisfy its demand. In other terms, the development plan was to expand the scope and reach of state involvement in productive activities on the premise that the income and expenditure that had enriched the private sector for so long could now be reinvested for the good of everyone. That is why social business has been taken rural development initiative.

The Grameen Bank started to diversify in the late 1980s when it started attending to unutilized or underutilized fishing ponds, as well as irrigation pumps like deep tubewells. In 1989, these diversified interests started growing into separate organizations, as the fisheries project became Grameen Motsho (Grameen Fisheries Foundation) and the irrigation project became Grameen Krishi (Grameen Agriculture Foundation). Over time, the Grameen initiative has grown into a multi-faceted group of profitable and non-profit ventures, including major projects like Grameen Trust and Grameen Fund, which runs equity projects like Grameen Software Limited, Grameen CyberNet Limited, and Grameen Knitwear Limited. The success of the Grameen model of microfinancing has inspired similar efforts in a hundred countries throughout the developing world and even in industrialized nations, including the United States. (Yunus, 2007).

In early 2006 Yunus, along with other members of the civil society including Professor Rehman Sobhan, Justice Muhammad Habibur Rahman, Dr Kamal Hossain, Matiur Rahman, Mahfuz Anam and Debapriya Bhattchariya, participated in a campaign for honest and clean candidates in national elections. He considered entering politics in the later part of that year. On 11 February 2007, Yunus wrote an open letter, published in the Bangladeshi newspaper Daily Star, where he asked citizens for views on his plan to float a political party to establish political goodwill, proper leadership and good governance. In the letter, he called on everyone to briefly outline how he should go about the task and how they can contribute to it. (Yunus, 2007).

Yunus finally announced the foundation of a new party tentatively called Citizens Power (Nagorik Shakti) on 18 February 2007. There was speculation that the army supported a move by Yunus into politics. On 3 May, however, Yunus declared that he had decided to abandon his political plans following a meeting with the head of the interim government, Fakhruddin Ahmed (Yunus, 2007).

REFERENCES

Allen, F., Demirgüç-Kunt, A., Klapper, L. F., & Martinez Peria, M. S. (2012). *The foundations of financial inclusion: Understanding ownership and use of formal accounts*. Policy Research Working Paper, 6290.

Ali, I., Hatta, Z. A., & Azman, A., & Islam. (2017). Microfinance as a development and poverty alleviation tool in rural Bangladesh: A critical assessment. *Asian Social Work and Policy Review*, *11*(1), 4–15.

Amin, S., Rai, A. S., & Topa, G. (2003). Does microcredit reach the poor and vulnerable? Evidence from Northern Bangladesh. *Journal of Development Economics*, *70*, 59–82.

Kamal, A. (2021). *The Grameen model and its applicability in developed countries*. University of London and Kings College London Press.

Mahmud, M., Otsuka, K., Sawada, Y., Tanaka, M., & Tanaka, T. (2017). *Women empowerment in Bangladesh: Household decisions under development of non-farm sectors and microfinance institutions*. JICA-RI Working Paper, 154.

Barclays. (2010). *Banking for billions, report on improving access to financial services and expanding microfinance*. Available at: www.newsroom.barclays.com/Media-Library/Banking-for-Billions-report-165f.aspx

Basu, P., & Srivastava, P. (2005). Exploring possibilities: Micro finance and rural credit access for the poor in India. *Economic and Political Weekly*, *40*(17), 1747–1756.

Benjamin, L., Sass Rubin, J., & Zielenbach, S. (2004). Community development financial institutions: Current issues and future prospects. *Journal of Urban Affairs*, *26*(2), 177–195. doi:10.1111/j.0735-2166.2004.00196.x

Benjamin, M. P., Jr. (1994). *Credit Schemes For Microenterprises: Motivation, Design, and Viability* [PhD dissertation]. Georgetown University.

Bernasek, A. (2003). Banking on social change: Grameen Bank lending to women. *International Journal of Politics Culture and Society*, *16*(3), 369–385. doi:10.1023/A:1022304311671

Carbo, S., Gardener, E. P. M., & Molyneux, P. (2005). *Financial Exclusion*. Palgrave Macmillan. doi:10.1057/9780230508743

CDFA. (2005). *Inside Out: The State of Community Development Finance 2004*. CDFA.

Dowla, A. (2006). In credit we trust: Building social capital by Grameen Bank in Bangladesh. *Journal of Socio-Economics*, *35*(1), 102–122. doi:10.1016/j.socec.2005.12.006

Dowla, A. U. (1998). *Micro Leasing: The Grameen Bank Experience*. St. Mary's College of Maryland.

Glinik, M., Poandl, E. M., & Mueller, C. (2019). Searching for the ideal business model: Challenges for start-ups. *ISPIM Conference Proceedings*, 1-11.

Grameen Annual Report, . (2005). *Grameen Bank scholarship program*. Grameen Bank.

Grameen Bank. (2004). Opening Speech by Muhammed Yunus. *30th Zonal Manager Conference*. Grameen Ban.

Grameen Bank. (2005). Opening Speech by Muhammed Yunus. *30th Zonal Manager Conference*. Grameen Bank.

Grameen Shikka Bartta, . (2009). *Five highest scholars' faces from the children of GB members in 2009*. Grameen Bank.

Grameen Shikka Bartta, . (2014). *Talented children stories*. Grameen Bank.

Grameen Shakka Bartta. (2006). *Grammen Shikka Activities*. Grameen Shikka.

Grameen Shikka Bartta. (2019). *Arsenic mitigation program in Bangladesh*. Grameen Shikka.

Grameen Shikka Bartta. (2008). *Proud mothers from the borrowers of GB*. Department Administration, Grameen Bank.

Grameen Shikka Bartta. (2009). *Proud mothers from the borrowers of GB*. Department Administration, Grameen Bank.

Grameen Shikka Bartta. (2014). *Grameen Bank talented Scholars*. Department Administration, Grameen Bank.

Hashemi, S. M. (1997). Building up Capacity for Banking with the Poor: The Grameen Bank of Bangladesh. In H. Schneider (Ed.), *Microfinance for the Poor?* (pp. 109–128). OECD.

Honohan, P. (2004). *Financial sector policy and the poor.* World Bank Working Paper No. 43.

Hossain, D. M. (2013). Social Capital and Microfinance: The Case of Grameen Bank, Bangladesh. *Middle East Journal of Business, 8*(4).

Hulme, D. (2008). *The story of the Grameen Bank: From subsidised microcredit to market-based microfinance.* Brooks World Poverty Institute Working Paper, (60).

Hulme, D., & Mosley, P. (1996). *Finance Against Poverty*. Routledge.

Hussain, M., Maskooki, M., & Gunasekaran, A. (2001). Implications of Grameen banking system in Europe: Prospects and prosperity. *European Business Review, 13*(1), 26–41.

Khandker, S. R., Khalily, B., & Khan, Z. (1995). *Grameen Bank: Performance and Sustainability.* Discussion Paper No. 306. World Bank.

Leyshon, A., & Thrift, N. (1995). Geographies of financial exclusion: Financial abandonment in Britain and the United States. *Transactions of the Institute of British Geographers, NS, 20*(3), 312–341.

Mahtab, N., Islam, M.D., Ahmed, S., & Ahmed, S.U. (2017). Social business and its sustainability: A case study on 'Aponjon 'Project of D. Net, Bangladesh. *International Journal of Economics, Commerce and Management, 5*(7).

Mainsah, E., Heuer, S. R., Kalra, A., & Zhang, Q. (2004). Grameen Bank: Taking capitalism to the poor. *Chazen Web Journal of International Business, 1*, 28.

Mehrotra, N., Puhazhendhi, V., Nair, G.G., & Sahoo, B.B. (2009). *Financial Inclusion- An Overview*. Department of Economic Analysis and Research, NABARD.

Morduch, J. (1999). The role of subsidies in microfinance: Evidence from the Grameen Bank. *Journal of Development Economics, 60*(1), 229–248.

Rahman, A. (1999). Micro-credit Initiatives for Equitable and Sustainable Development: Who Pays? *World Development, 27*(1), 67–82.

Rangarajan, C. (2008). *Report of the Committee on Financial Inclusion*. Government of India.

Sharma, M. (2008). *Index of financial inclusion*. Working Paper 215, Indian Council for Research on International Economic Relations.

Villis, U., Strack, R., Bruysten, S., & Yunus, M. (2013). *The Power of Social Business: Lessons from Corporate Engagements with Grameen*. Available at: http://socialbusinesspedia.com/CaseStudy Report_PDF/BCG_Report_2013.pdf

Wahid, A. N. M. (1999). The Grameen Bank and women in Bangladesh. *Challenge*, *42*(5).

World Bank. (2006). *World Bank World Development Indicators*. World Bank.

World Bank. (2008). Finance for All - Policies and Pitfalls in Expanding Access. World Bank Policy Research Report.

Yaron, J., Benjamin, M., & Piprek, G. (1997). *Rural Finance: Issues, Design, and Best Practices*. World Bank.

Yunus, M. (2004). Grameen Bank, microcredit and millennium development goals. *Economic and Political Weekly*, 4077–4080.

Yunus, M. (2010). *Seven principles of social business*. Available at: www.yunuscenter.ait.asia/social-business

Yunus, M., Dalsace, F., Menasce, D., & Faivre-Tavignot, B. (2015). Reaching the Rich World's Poorest consumers. *Harvard Business Review*, *3*(1), 46–53.

Chapter 2
Digitally Sustaining:
The Rural Intangible Cultural Heritage

Aditya Ranjan
https://orcid.org/0000-0003-1304-5489
Bakri Chhap Agro Tourism and Natural Products Pvt. Ltd., India

Priya Chaturvedi
https://orcid.org/0000-0002-9875-661X
Jiwaji University, India

ABSTRACT

Conservation of intangible cultural heritage is important for any rural tourism destination. The rich intangible cultural heritage can be preserved using advanced digital technologies for future generations. Digital technologies provide the means of documenting, recovering, and presenting different components of the intangible cultural heritage of a rural destination. However, one of the challenges is finding appropriate forms, together with efficient methods, to document the ephemeral aspects of rural intangible heritage. Another barrier is finding effective ways to communicate the knowledge inextricably linked to people or communities. This chapter outlines state-of-the-art models, projects, and technical practices that have advanced the digitization lifecycle for intangible cultural heritage resources. The chapter further aims to identify the advancements and gaps in the existing conventions and to envision opportunities for transmitting embodied knowledge in intangible heritage.

INTRODUCTION

Tourism illustrates an example in the experience economy where participants on both the supply and demand sides of an offering novel experience value from their participation (Paul & Roy, 2017). Tourist attractions are very important to tourism because they provide reasons for a wide range of tourists and locals to visit. Hence tourist destinations must be inventive and provide distinctive and thrilling experiences to stand out in an increasingly competitive market (Lund et al., 2022). Consequently, an added value strategy for destination marketing is the experience that comes from using a good or service, with

DOI: 10.4018/978-1-6684-6732-9.ch002

Copyright © 2023, IGI Global. Copying or distributing in print or electronic forms without written permission of IGI Global is prohibited.

advantages for both tourists and the destination (Pine II & Gilmore, 2011). The intangible cultural heritage of a destination offers a unique opportunity to provide destination-specific experiences and end tourist search for authenticity, influences their perceptions, and motivates tourists to visit such destination (Lund et al., 2022; Rudan & Stipanović, 2021). The intangible cultural heritage symbolizes the pinnacle of human cultural heritage and is an essential and valuable part of the tourism sector (Ranjan & Chaturvedi, 2022; Zhang et al., 2018). However, the intangible heritage of a destination needs to be preserved prior to destination marketing. Particularly in historical destinations that are in decline or stagnation, where economic rebirth is essential for their revival, tourism growth offers a solid economic reason for the preservation of intangible heritage assets (Paul & Roy, 2017).

The United Nations Educational, Scientific and Cultural Organization (UNESCO) convention for the Safeguarding of the Intangible Cultural Heritage in 2003 was the first global platform highlighting the significance of preserving indigenous and traditional cultural heritage (Melis & Chambers, 2021). Since then, there has been a significant increase in the volume of research and digital approach to conserve and preserve the intangible cultural heritage of a community (Hou et al., 2022). Identifying, preserving, and conserving intangible cultural heritage enables rural communities and researchers to explore cultural authenticity and facilitates a thorough understanding of local rural culture (Zhang & Lee, 2022). Such initiatives strengthen the competitiveness of intangible cultural heritage within the larger context of cultural heritage tourism and generate social and economic benefits for the various stakeholders (Yang Zhang & Lee, 2022). Additionally, to increase the competitiveness of a destination, intangible cultural heritage serves as experiential products that cater to specific niche audiences, such as special interest tourists (Chen, 2022). On the other hand, it is well known that the relationship between tourism and heritage conservation is polarised, with strong complementarities and equally intense conflicts (Paul & Roy, 2017). In addition to various discourses, cultural practices can be considered part of intangible cultural heritage (Zhang & Lee, 2022). Hence, several scholars have shown an incompatibility between tourism and historical conservation, leading to a conflict between preserving the intangible cultural heritage and unjustifiable transformations pushed by market forces linked to tourism growth.

The concept of intangible cultural heritage piqued scientific curiosity due to its inherent adaptability, transformational power, and dynamism (Zhang et al., 2018). Communities' role in intangible cultural heritage identification, conservation, protection, and reproduction is codified institutionally, examined academically, and practiced through community-based endeavors. Additionally, the discussion surrounding intangible cultural heritage has given growing importance to all factors that indisputably connect it to human activities and perceptions (Giglitto et al., 2022). It carries a cultural memory representing national diversity and the collective cultural memory of generations across the nation (Xie, 2022). However, it is a fact that a significant portion of our intangible cultural heritage is currently being lost (Shuai & Yu, 2021). The loss of intangible cultural heritage can be attributed to several factors, including urbanization, migration, and changes in the natural environment (Tzima et al., 2020). One reason is that insufficient attention is being paid to intangible cultural assets since, for many people today, the concept of intangible cultural heritage is still quite abstract (Xie, 2022).

Because intangible cultural heritage is about people, it is inherently unstable, dynamic, and contentious and must rely on intricate social processes and political manoeuvres to "remain alive" (Giglitto et al., 2022). Foremost, the unintended learning of young community members results in abandoned intangible cultural heritage and hence, no successors, which directly causes the loss of many materials (Xie, 2022). In addition, the globalization of the economy has placed the preservation of intangible cultural heritage in a precarious position, threatening its very existence (Shuai & Yu, 2021). Additionally, it is elementary for memories and symbols of intangible cultural heritage to be ignored and forgotten with time, particularly certain aspects of oral cultural heritage (Xie, 2022). As a result, intangible cultural heritage remains confined to inaccessible and backward regions, exacerbating their precarious situation while retarding their development.

However, the rich intangible cultural heritage can be preserved using advanced digital technologies for future generations (Skublewska-Paszkowska et al., 2022). Digital technologies provide the means of documenting, recovering, and presenting different components of the intangible cultural heritage of a rural destination. However, one of the challenges is finding appropriate forms, together with efficient methods, to document the ephemeral aspects of rural intangible heritage. Nevertheless, traditional methods for digitizing intangible heritage currently concentrate on primary storage media such as audio and video recordings, which are practical documentation tools (Selmanović et al., 2020). More recently, methods for documenting intangible cultural heritage have started to explore more modern technologies. Another barrier is finding effective ways to communicate the intangible cultural heritage knowledge inextricably linked to people or communities. Hence, this chapter outlines state-of-the-art models, projects, and technical practices that have advanced the digitization lifecycle for intangible cultural heritage resources. The review focuses on several critical but less studied tasks within digital archiving, computational encoding, conceptual representation, and interactive engagement with intangible cultural elements. The chapter further aims to identify the advancements and gaps in the existing conventions and to envision opportunities for transmitting embodied knowledge in intangible heritage.

BACKGROUND

Intangible cultural heritage has been shown to be very important to the tourism industry (Melis & Chambers, 2021). The concept of "intangible cultural heritage" stands in contrast to "tangible cultural heritage," both of which are subsumed under the umbrella term "cultural heritage" (Xie, 2022). Cultural heritage is how society, customs, and values work together and can be traced back thousands of years (Giudici et al., 2013). The term "intangible cultural heritage" refers to the various traditional cultural expressions that have been passed down from generation to generation by the members of all different ethnic communities and are regarded as an essential component of their cultural heritage, tangible heritage, and places connected to such traditional cultural expressions (Giglitto et al., 2022; Ranjan & Chaturvedi, 2022). Convention for the Safeguarding of the Intangible Cultural Heritage of 2003 defines intangible cultural heritage as "the practices, representations, expressions, knowledge, skills as well as the instruments, objects, artifacts and cultural spaces associated in addition to that the communities, groups, and, in some cases, individuals recognize as part of their cultural heritage" (Skublewska-Paszkowska et al., 2022). The intangible cultural heritage refers to oral traditions and expressions such as language, performing arts, social customs, festivals, and habits connecting to nature and the external world, as well as traditional skills and other types of knowledge that are hard to quantify (UNESCO, 2003).

Intangible cultural heritage is the accumulated knowledge of countless individuals acquired through their work and experience. It is inextricable from the folk owners and inheritors, on whom it is dependent for transmission from one generation to the next. As a result, intangible cultural heritage, and the community that it belongs to are inseparably intertwined. Since intangible cultural heritage includes physical objects and locations related to traditional cultural expressions, it is an important insignia of a country's history and culture (Xie, 2022). Hence, the survival of intangible cultural heritage depends on people from different cultures learning to appreciate one another's ways of living and working together to preserve them (Isa et al., 2018). Intangible cultural heritage consists not just of many discourses but also of cultural practices, which are carried out by practitioners of intangible cultural heritage in the framework of a particular cultural tradition and involving their inherited traditional knowledge, skills, society, and the natural environment (Zhang & Lee, 2022). The intangible cultural heritage exhibits characteristics such as regionalism, distinctiveness, dynamism, activeness, inheritance, mobility, comprehensiveness, nationalism, and many others (Zhang et al., 2018). Communities' vital involvement in intangible cultural heritage identification, protection, and reproduction is institutionalized, researched academically, and regularly put into practice through community-based activities that may or may not include digital technologies (Giglitto et al., 2022). Hence, all ethnic groups' folk production and way of life are the foundation of intangible cultural heritage, which is a living culture.

It is necessary to point out that the current definition of intangible cultural heritage is not intended to be definitive. In some countries, regional variations are used, such as traditional plays and sports, animal husbandry traditions, pilgrimage traditions, and locations of recollection are also elements of intangible cultural heritage (Skublewska-Paszkowska et al., 2022). Intangible cultural heritage also comprises human actions or motions that may be witnessed, felt, heard, smelled, or tasted when they are carried out or exist, as well as such heritage that cannot be experienced when such actions or motions are no longer carried out or exist (Isa et al., 2018). The main focus of intangible cultural heritage is on the intangible aspects of cultural expressions like spirit, artistry, and creativity rather than the tangible aspects of cultural expressions like buildings or artifacts that have been created by humans, as is the case with global cultural heritage (Zhang et al., 2018).

There is a linkage between intangible and tangible cultural heritage to understand and interpret tangible cultural heritage (Ranjan & Chaturvedi, 2022). The physical or tangible cultural heritage develops shape and continues to gain significance within a larger intangible cultural heritage framework (Giudici et al., 2013). The future sustainability of intangible cultural heritage is ensured through mutual respect for a community's way of life, fostered by understanding intangible cultural legacy among various societies (Isa et al., 2018). The intangible cultural heritage can be seen as a framework for the social and ecological environments and the overall environment it interacts with. The explanation is that intangible cultural heritage can establish these connections with tangible heritage, creating a framework for tangible material interpretation (Giudici et al., 2013). Hence, safeguarding under the intangible cultural framework has evolved from a concept limited to a single industry to one that advocates for participation from across a wide range of societal sectors to encourage increased engagement and participation (Yan & Chiou, 2021).

RURAL INTANGIBLE CULTURAL HERITAGE

Rural regions are distinct locations that attempt to build tourism based on their distinctive traits and authenticity, as well as the characteristics of rural landscapes (Rudan & Stipanović, 2021). The concept of rural intangible cultural heritage refers to what cultures regard to be a part of their cultural history at present. The intangible cultural heritage of a rural community is the result of centuries or millennia of ingrained social customs, norms, rituals, and beliefs (Giudici et al., 2013). Rural intangible cultural heritage involves human acts or motions that can be seen, touched, perceived, inhaled, or heard when performed or existing but cannot be experienced when no longer performed or existing (Isa et al., 2018). Rural intangible cultural heritage comprises traditional music and dance, oral traditions, social practices, rituals and festive events, knowledge and practices concerning nature and the universe, and traditional craftsmanship (Skublewska-Paszkowska et al., 2022). Farmers in rural areas where there is a wide variety of traditional practices and cultural norms rely heavily on this medium to disseminate information and skills amongst their peers (Daskon & McGregor, 2012). Additionally, it results in the accumulation of skills that can be used to support their livelihoods.

Rural intangible cultural heritage has various qualities, including its dynamic nature, inherent fragility, personal connection to its creators and bearers, and the sense of self-identification experienced by communities, groups, and individuals (Lenzerini, 2011). The past and future can never contain the intangible cultural heritage of rural areas. Rural cultural history is thought to include historical and cultural expressions that are no longer practiced. Hence, the Convention for the Safeguarding of Intangible Cultural Heritage excludes historical phrases that are no longer used from its definition of intangible cultural heritage. Hence, the intangible cultural heritage is also known as "living heritage" (Giudici et al., 2013). The intangible cultural heritage is passed down from generation to generation and is constantly generated by communities in response to their environment, interactions with nature, and history. Hence, rural intangible cultural heritage also provides a sense of continuity and identity to the rural community. Moreover, when the local community is proud of their intangible cultural heritage, it helps these heritages to gradually become a crucial element of the integrated tourist offer in rural destinations (Rudan & Stipanović, 2021).

It is now well established that tourists' primary purpose for visiting a particular rural destination is to experience the intangible cultural heritage that fulfills their cultural interests and demands (Rudan & Stipanović, 2021). Exploring, experiencing, and utilizing intangible cultural heritage have become essential components of developing rural tourism at a destination because local culture is often the source of a rural destination's unique and attractive qualities (Garau, 2015). Rudan & Stipanović (2021) mention that the experiences that rural tourism products offer can only be provided within the unique physical or spital contexts that make up those rural destinations. Most tourists visiting a rural destination do so to immerse themselves in the region's rich tangible and intangible cultural heritage. According to Cheer et al. (2013), rural intangible cultural heritage is an additional cultural asset that the rural destination possesses and which has the potential to provide tourists with authentic and immersive rural cultural experiences (including traditional festivals, folk activities, etiquette and traditions, and power systems, among other things). Hence, a well-preserved intangible cultural heritage could serve as a valuable resource for the growth of rural tourism development (Ma et al., 2021). Intangible cultural heritage, such as traditional values and traditions, serve as unique tourist attractions that produce economic benefits while sustaining household subsistence activities (MacDonald & Jolliffe, 2003).

NEED FOR SUSTAINING RURAL INTANGIBLE CULTURAL HERITAGE

Cultural realms that integrate know-how processes that are anecdotal, oral, embodied, shared, and constantly evolving in adaptation to their varied audiences are examples of rural intangible cultural heritage (Lenzerini, 2011). The intangible cultural heritage has developed over the long course of human history (Sun et al., 2021). However, it is currently facing an increasingly severe crisis due to the growth of the modern economy, the acceleration of urbanization, and the transformation of productive patterns and lifestyles. It has resulted in many intangible cultural heritages losing their space for development and younger generations losing interest in passing on intangible cultural heritage, which has already led to the extinction of some intangible cultural heritages and is putting others in danger (Sun et al., 2021). Moreover, intangible heritage is now subject to more significant threats due to globalization and ongoing change, including natural disasters and pandemics (Hou et al., 2022).

As a process with "tangible" and "intangible" or "material" and "non-material" properties, intangible cultural heritage tourism development involves several components, including decision-makers, tourists, tourist amenities, activity locations, and events (Qiu & Zhang, 2021). Culture and tradition are frequently well-preserved across generations in rural areas, and heritage is actively protected during economic turbulence (Rudan & Stipanović, 2021). However, traditional music, dance, and folklore are some of the most sought-after resources in intangible cultural heritage tourism study (Qiu & Zhang, 2021). As such, the other components of intangible cultural heritage are diminishing from the cultural values of the rural people. It is typical for experiences and stories to be forgotten or conveyed incorrectly, and the introduction of new civilizations often eradicates previously existing cultures. Moreover, rural areas are not immune to the transformative power of changes in residents' daily life (improved living standards before the economic catastrophe brought on by the coronavirus pandemic) and tourism activities (Rudan & Stipanović, 2021). Because of this, it is indispensable to ensure that the non-material aspects of culture are preserved for future generations.

Intangible cultural heritage conservation and preservation have evolved from a single-industry concept to one that necessitates collaboration across different spheres of society in order to foster more engagement and broader participation (Yan & Chiou, 2021). The government initiatives in many countries to preserve intangible cultural heritage predominantly focus on other rural development works, and these initiatives generate a gap between the preservation initiatives and the rural population. Hence, getting people interested in and creative about intangible cultural heritage conservation is essential to get them to participate in intangible cultural heritage safeguarding work (Yan & Chiou, 2021). Moreover, it is necessary to build a relationship between locals and intangible cultural heritage so that intangible cultural heritage conservation can keep doing its social functions. Hence, while assuring long-term intangible cultural heritage conservation of resource bases, promoting sustainable development, and raising the standard of the tourism offering, developing products for the tourism industry in rural areas must consider the region's distinct characteristics (Rudan & Stipanović, 2021).

As a direct result of archaeological discoveries, many past artifacts were utilized to preserve the intangible cultural heritage, and in some cases, at least in distorted forms. Moreover, the preservation of intangible cultural heritage is much more complicated because intangible aspects of cultural life are handed down from one generation to generation. The spiritual-level memories of intangible cultural heritage provide aesthetic, technical, and creative significance in their own right, but they are vulnerable to being obliterated by the onslaught of contemporary ideas (Zhang et al., 2018). Hence, action is urgently needed, especially if stakeholders preserve vulnerable rural populations' living cultures (Hou et al., 2022). In addition to positive implications, the growth of tourism and economic and technological advancements bring about changes in lifestyle and productivity that may result in the eradication or commercialization of certain information, skills, and customs (Starčević et al., 2022).

PRESERVING RURAL INTANGIBLE CULTURAL HERITAGE

There is a growing social and cultural movement on a global scale to preserve and protect intangible cultural heritage (Yan & Chiou, 2021). Techniques for recording intangible heritage have recently started to look into more modern technologies (Selmanović et al., 2020). Countries, communities, and people all have unique preservation needs and use a wide range of strategies to conserve intangible cultural heritage. The literature on the preservation of intangible cultural heritage can be broadly categorized as theoretical or empirical research (Zhang et al., 2018). The term "preservation" describes the modern practice of storing and maintaining the cultural heritage of a place for the benefit of future generations in contexts such as museums, libraries, laboratories, culture centers, classrooms, and archives (Skublewska-Paszkowska et al., 2022). Intangible cultural heritage is constantly evolving in time and location; hence, it is essential to create comprehensive, accurate, and systematic records of such heritage that are valuable, vulnerable, and historically significant (Zhang et al., 2018). Currently, conventional techniques for digitizing intangible heritage rely on inexpensive storage mediums, such as audio and video recordings, which are helpful for documentation (Selmanović et al., 2020). Various known methods of preserving intangible cultural heritage include conservation, documentation, protection, reconstruction, restoration, dissemination, and spreading (Skublewska-Paszkowska et al., 2022).

The term "conservation" refers to the practice of extending the lifespan of cultural assets while simultaneously increasing the transmission of important intangible cultural heritage information and values. Any communicable material used to describe, clarify, or provide instructions for specific characteristics of intangible cultural heritage, such as its components, assembly, installation, maintenance, and use, is considered documentation. The process of documentation is associated with the act of storing a variety of different kinds of information related to intangible cultural heritage. The term "protection" refers to steps taken to prevent intangible cultural heritage from being damaged, destroyed, or suffering other types of loss. The process of reconstructing intangible cultural heritage elements in order to have a better understanding of those objects involves visualizing them. The integration and replacement of non-original pieces, reconstruction, retouching, and infilling are all parts of the restoration process, which is a series of operations that includes these steps. The dissemination process involves depicting and visualizing tangible and intangible cultural heritage elements through the application of contemporary technology. The purpose of spreading is to contact as many potential recipients as possible within or beyond the community to familiarise them with intangible cultural heritage.

However, these techniques are insufficient to describe intangible cultural heritage's minute details. In addition, with time, analog technologies are subject to a natural deterioration in the quality of the documented intangible cultural heritage (Skublewska-Paszkowska et al., 2022). In contrast, modern digital technologies are accessible, user-friendly, and efficient, and new media facilitates the production, transmission, and reception of intangible cultural heritage in various formats (Tzima et al., 2020). The usage of digital technologies has influenced the evolution of the preservation and sharing of rural intangible cultural heritage. Thus, digital technologies help with intangible cultural heritage documentation processes and make the acquisition and collection of intangible cultural heritage data safer and less likely to change.

The current consensus amongst industry professionals is that intangible cultural heritage preservation and development exist in a mutually exclusive and dialectical relationship (Zhang et al., 2018). Hence, creating a digital version of the intangible cultural heritage can, to some extent, effectively encourage the development of the intangible cultural heritage and help produce a human interaction between them (Ranjan & Chaturvedi, 2022). The use of digital tools has made it even more important to draw attention to the unique characteristics of intangible cultural heritages in terms of location, activity, and historical accumulation while discussing the legacy of cultural memory they represent. For example, it is also thought that with digital technologies, museums can be converted into hybrid spaces, opening new possibilities for producing high-quality, user-friendly rural cultural experiences (Tzima et al., 2020). When it comes to managing the complex interplay between established cultural and ecological frameworks and the perpetual evolution of tour operators and travel agencies, digital tools are indispensable. Hence, the digitization of tourist attractions solves the preservation demands of inheritance and evolution of intangible cultural heritage and boosts tourist attractors' competitiveness and service capability (Zhang et al., 2018). The digitized information might subsequently be made available to the public in an easy-to-understand format, considerably enhancing the experience and realism for tourists.

DIGITAL INNOVATIONS FOR SUSTAINING RURAL INTANGIBLE CULTURAL HERITAGE

As the world's economies become more intertwined and digital technology continues to advance at a dizzying rate, it has become imperative that safeguards be put in place to ensure the digital preservation of the inheritors of the community's intangible cultural heritage (Isa et al., 2018). Digitization and the applications of information and communications technology have been recognized as effective ways to preserve rural intangible cultural heritage while simultaneously providing significant resources (Hou et al., 2022). The intangible cultural heritage information can be stored using a diverse range of technologies, including those that deal with text, analog data, and two-dimensional data (2D) (Skublewska-Paszkowska et al., 2022). The digital preservation of representative inheritors of intangible cultural heritage requires conducting interviews with their inheriting representatives, recording and organizing them and projects via image, audio, video, and other modern technical means, and then cataloguing and recording the collected information (Hou et al., 2022). These preservation methods adhere to the established digital technological standards and guidelines. Information about the inheritors of intangible cultural heritage can be collected and edited digitally and then stored digitally, allowing for its management and use in a digital format.

Additionally, several academicians have argued that digitizing rural intangible cultural heritages should help build cultural spaces incorporating the meanings of people, places, and things (Vaughan, 2016). This situation necessitates a combination of different 3D technologies that improve comprehension of the rural intangible cultural heritages and adds fresh perspectives to the research. Several forms of 3D digital technology are used in fieldwork on intangible cultural heritage elements, such as 3D scanning, 3D modelling, Virtual Reality (VR), and Augmented Reality (AR), frequently used to perform virtual presentations of monuments and ancient artifacts (Skublewska-Paszkowska et al., 2022). Moreover, digital technologies like the Internet, big data, the Internet of Things, cloud computing, artificial intelligence, and 5G, which are constantly developing, see new advancements every day in the information age (Gao et al., 2021). Beyond the realm of communications, the adoption of 5G has the potential to foster innovation and the development of new enterprises and services, in addition to enhancing and accelerating the connectivity of rural destinations (Istanti, 2021).

Figure 1. Digital innovations for sustaining rural intangible cultural heritage

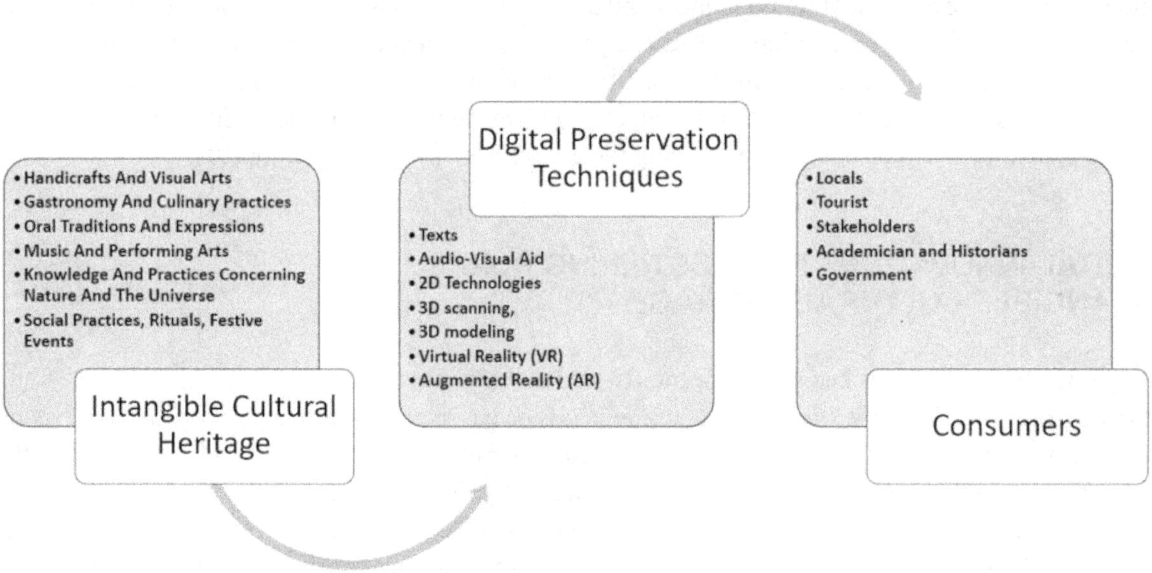

RURAL HERITAGE KINESTHETICS

Traditional rural intangible cultural heritage archives were generally stored in standard formats, due to which archival contents are typically sorted depending on a single dimension, like a visual representation, object focus, or linear progression (Hou et al., 2022). However, much work has been done recently to try and capture the living dynamics, with the human body serving as a primary rural intangible cultural heritage location. The embodied aspect of rural intangible cultural heritage encompasses not only bodily knowledge but also that which resides in and is enacted via the body (Craig et al., 2016). Some of the most common ways that people communicate and process their mindfulness is through movement and gesture. Sometimes they also serve as intermediaries in more complex interaction processes like exchanging information between humans and their environments or developing new knowledge. Thus, Motion Capture (MoCap) technologies, which capture and save movement, have grown in popularity as a means of archiving rural intangible cultural heritage data (Hou et al., 2022). With MoCap, data collecting can go "beyond the frame and within the volume," making it possible for there to be a sense of a human presence in a simulated cultural heritage environment (Chalmers et al., 2021). Mechanical, magnetic, and optical capture are the most common types of MoCap techniques; these use camera-based, sensor-based, or hybrid systems to provide the highest possible levels of precision and information harvesting.

Making live schemas in digital archiving can accommodate living actions' vigorous and fragile dynamics that transcend the use of digital powers more than placing multimedia collections online (Vaughan, 2016). Similarly, cultural heritage is often generated by interpreting several manifestations incorporating both material and performative approaches, even if performance can be transmitted through practice and perpetuated through dynamic documentation (Hou et al., 2022). Furthermore, it is commemorated through the ever-evolving recreations of its unique creators and cultural owners (Lenzerini, 2011). Because of the considerable multimedia collection and metadata sources available in digital archives, new modelling methodologies, such as 3D digitization, allow for a fresh take on rural intangible cultural heritage (Hou et al., 2022). Similarly, digital scenic area planning aims to digitally import intangible cultural heritage to realize the digital preservation and inheritance of intangible cultural heritage and the sustainable development of the rural tourism industry. Such a process integrates and utilizes natural and cultural resources, cultivates a diversified heritage tourism product system, and creates a 3D visualization of a cultural tourism scenic area with integrated functions of history exploration, culture display, art creation, leisure, and vacation (Zhang et al., 2018).

RURAL HERITAGE DENOMINATION

Intangible heritage is a cultural realm that encompasses anecdotal, oral, embodied, shared, and evolving know-how (Lenzerini, 2011). Therefore, it is as essential to mediate between digitizers and specific rural intangible cultural heritage holders as it is to upgrade the communication paradigms with the general public towards a kind of interactive transmission that prioritizes knowledge generation (Hou et al., 2022). The documentation of human endeavor, whether in the cultural, scientific, or social realms, relies heavily on narratives (Meghini et al., 2021). It is important to note that intangible and embodied knowledge is passed on in many ways, not just through poses, gestures, or moves in a particular order but also through people, places, and things, as well as rituals and traditional notes. Traditions and folklore are rural intangible cultural heritage components that are particularly challenging to simulate (Hou et al., 2022). So, an interconnected network of multimodal entities is a significant part of putting actions into context within a conceptual space. However, they may help generalize some ideas into a concept called cultural exchange and catalogued. Carboni & de Luca (2016) suggested using Multi-Entity Bayesian Networks (MEBNs), a probabilistic framework, to look at dance moves based on more information. Through the physical evidence such rural intangible cultural heritage carries, they may be able to point to media and documents that encode motion or pose. One example is *Drammar*, which provides a unified paradigm incorporating the vocabulary necessary for the long-term archiving and labelling of dramatic media items as collections of living creatures (Hou et al., 2022). Similarly, Narrative Ontology (NOnt) offers a contemporary method of representing crafts knowledge concerned with storytelling within the rural intangible cultural heritage domain. OWL 2 DL and SWRL are used to implement this vocabulary extension for CIDOC CRM, FRBRoo, and OWL Time (Meghini et al., 2021).

RURAL HERITAGE AUGMENTATION

Virtual environments have the potential to serve as a tool for conducting in-depth research and analysis on environments that are protected as Intangible Cultural Heritage (Selmanović et al., 2020). Visualization is a critical component of rural intangible cultural heritage embodiment and is essential to enabling new levels of cognition, knowledge, and analytics. Visualization is a critical component of embodiment and is essential to enabling new levels of cognition, knowledge, and analytics. Digital media and rapidly evolving virtual technologies have consistently argued in favor of enhancing the entire experience of cultural conversations (Hou et al., 2022). The study of cultural user experience (CUX), which enhances visitors' interactions with cultural items, has gained significant traction in GLAM (Galleries,

Libraries, Archives, and Museums) and rural heritage research. Virtual technologies, such as reality (VR), augmented reality (AR), mixed reality (XR), and extended reality (XR), which are constantly improving, have significantly boosted CUX by bringing creativity and flexibility to the interfaces. With the CUX justifications in mind, interactive digital storytelling (IDS) becomes an essential technique. The ultimate objective of IDS is to create a state of engagement that can prompt personal resonance through the narrative content. IDS advocates for a curated mix of technologies and perception channels to convey experience characteristics. It also stressed adapting stories to fit the attention span of today's digital natives, who are used to receiving information in bite-sized chunks and are not always willing to sit through lengthy videos.

Embodiment, which is created through visualization, hypermedia, and many senses, is crucial in creating an engaging visiting experience in rural areas. The Virtual Dance Museum is one example that serves as a revolutionary paradigm for preserving the intangible cultural heritage by displaying dressed-up folk dance performances of a 3D character in various virtual interfaces, such as an online 3D environment, a VR head-mounted display, and mobile-based augmented reality (Hou et al., 2022). A sensation of the embodiment is produced when physical environments are integrated via virtual means (VR/XR). It provides a multidimensional experience for the users and aids in pedagogical knowledge production. The iLLE (immersive learning level editor) is one example that develops an in-situ learning framework for life-sized reconstructions of intangible cultural heritage distribution and practical knowledge education by utilizing real-time embodied interactions and enhancing them with real-world visual and aural input (Kenderdine et al., 2021).

RURAL HERITAGE EDUTAINMENT

Entertainment has long been recognized as a driving force in educational apps to create an environment that encourages active learning (Hou et al., 2022). The concept of edutainment, or the merging of educational and entertaining content, has also attracted attention in preserving rural intangible cultural heritage. The audience's emotional, intellectual, physical, and social selves are all activated by a memorable and satisfying experience, leaving a lasting imprint that can be used to spread culture (Lo et al., 2019). The research was conducted to test the efficacy of using multimedia presentations of cultural history in a natural classroom setting, and educators found that using this approach increased students' interest and motivation levels (Rizvic et al., 2019). Serious games are a new trend in the digital world that aims to improve engagement and interaction between users and has become well-known for their role in creating immersive virtual settings for rural cultural education (Ibrahim & Ali, 2018). Andreoli et al. (2017) have summarised a model for making and assessing cultural heritage games that immerse players and encourage teamwork.

Education and the ease of acquiring new information have been the primary drivers behind the growth of both the technological and cultural heritage industries. Edutainment focusing on performance-based instruction and evaluation has benefited from the rise of virtual and immersive methods. For instance, to facilitate the transmission of folk traditions, the i-Treasures project has published a 3D visualization sensorimotor learning framework and implemented it with seven body-motion-game prototypes. Such an example shows how gaming vernaculars have created an awareness of cultural history by challenging established modes of communication. To evoke the reader's sense of motion, some attempted to establish a physical connection between the characters. Taking things in a different direction, Vosinakis et al. (2018) implemented a multi-user 3D environment in the gaming setting of *Ancient Agora of Athens*, an ancient site situated beneath the northwest slope of the Acropolis. This game went beyond merely depicting real-world objects and actions by giving them abstract representations in the form of NPCs (non-player characters), who may have meaningful conversations with the players. This innovative tool demonstrated the feasibility of enhancing intangible cultural heritage serious games with the addition of context-specific, tailored information. It also points toward creating a heritage setting incorporating historical narratives, contemporary conversations, routine activities, rituals, and more.

Human motion recognition algorithm improvements have opened up several paths that can improve data integration and help deal with the problem of scattered intellectuals and the growing size of living archives (Hou et al., 2022). Still, this kind of intelligence is only helpful if the proper training has been completed. The key to communicating cultural heritage, which includes the phenomenological design of spatial definitions, acoustic landscape, shaping of movement, and social presence, is constructing an interactive and interpretive digital experience. Most of the innovative design elements of intangible cultural heritage come from intangible cultural heritage products, both old and new. For example, appearance modelling, decorative elements, composition form, and color application are all taken from intangible cultural heritage products (Xie, 2022). Such a paradigm encourages sentient interaction in digital manifestations while conjuring the past. Visitors can therefore recall, sense, and imagine interactions with the heritage. Massive multimedia archives have the potential to act as instruments to enable new exploits for public involvement and contexts to connect them, provided they are appropriately translated into finely curated materials. While several initiatives have begun to investigate the potential of gamification to preserve intangible cultural materials, much more research has to be done (Hou et al., 2022).

CHALLENGES IN DIGITALLY SUSTAINING RURAL INTANGIBLE CULTURAL HERITAGE

Due to the constraints and difficulties of acquiring information about rural intangible cultural heritage, the digital theoretical and technical system of quick and decisive inheritance of rural destination information has some challenges (Gao et al., 2021). Recent years have seen a cognitive shift in the focus of research away from intangible cultural heritage preservation and toward intangible cultural heritage tourism development, primarily due to a greater emphasis on intangible cultural heritage preservation and inheritance at a tourist destination (Zhang et al., 2018). Today's archivists have access to various tools that allow them to create digital copies of documents. These tools include scanning, photography, three-dimensional volumetric photogrammetry, and filmmaking techniques. On the other hand, several of these have developed into indispensable tools for material-based intangible cultural heritage archives. Unfortunately, limited initiatives have provided sufficient assistance for the systematic encoding, documenting, representation, and display of the dynamic nature of intangible cultural heritage. Hence, It is challenging to put back together the lost concrete, ethereal, tacit, and fleeting information (Hou et al., 2022).

In recent years, more and more digital efforts have been made to conserve and share rural intangible cultural heritage assets. However, many of them were limited to choreographic documentation or working with object orientation. Because of this, rural intangible cultural heritage's living and physical aspects are rarely meaningfully portrayed in its representation. Virtual reality, augmented reality, and mixed reality all hold great promise, especially for incorporating physical activities into learning about intangible cultural heritage (Ibrahim & Ali, 2018). At the same time, gamification for intangible heritage content is not studied as much as it could be, but some projects are looking into it (Hou et al., 2022). Some practical applications have shown promise for enhancing rural intangible cultural heritage serious games with personalized intelligence (Andreoli et al., 2017). It also points to creating a legacy setting incorporating historical narratives, conversations, contemporary practices, norms, and rituals. Proper solutions are needed for the portability of equipment and interoperability of different platforms before such technologies may scale outside the laboratories. A further difficulty in creating serious games is making them highly user-friendly for their intended audience. When cultural resources are rationalized and connected to well-designed game reactions, serious games become excellent instructional tools (Hou et al., 2022). Otherwise, they risk causing player dissatisfaction and a rapid exodus of active players.

The growth of digital infrastructure in rural areas has led to an increase in available data and information. Intangible heritage data collection is non-standard and incomplete due to hardware limitations in remote areas and quality differences in the meaning of intangible cultural heritage among the people. A lack of knowledge about digital rural development is a significant barrier for locals, and the new methods of live-captured archives have made it harder to get to them in terms of programming and ideas. A major obstacle to protecting intangible cultural property is the absence of digital technical personnel, modern rural data processing personnel, and information service personnel in rural areas, which is exacerbated by the immense wealth gap between rural and urban areas. Moreover, employing big data technologies across the entire preservation process of intangible cultural heritage, including data collection, administration, sharing, analysis, application, and security, to draw valuable insights from enormous amounts of data and apply them to rural heritage preservation and development practice presents problems for rural destinations. As an excellent answer to this problem, the dimension of human movement is encouraged to force more intuitive and universal searches into the archives (Hou et al., 2022). Moreover, the creation and use of data on rural intangible cultural resources should be incorporated into the national strategy for information development (Gao et al., 2021). It is essential to encourage the widespread adoption of digital technology at rural destinations and speed up the digital transformation of the rural tourist industry chain.

CONCLUSION

Increased collaborative efforts to preserve and make use of intangible cultural heritage have helped to ensure the long-term sustainability of these cultural practices (Yan & Chiou, 2021). Moreover, the rapid advancement of technology in recent years demonstrates its utility in daily life, and this trend has fuelled an increase in the number of initiatives for digital preservation in the intangible cultural heritage domain (Isa et al., 2018). However, difficulties with the digital preservation of the intangible cultural legacy necessitate substantial initiatives to prevent the heritage from eroding and nearing extinction. To encourage the preservation of rural intangible cultural heritage, it is necessary to specify what is at risk whenever intangible cultural heritage is threatened (Zhang & Lee, 2022). In order to save distinct cultural genes, cultural customs, and national memories, intangible cultural heritage tourism attractions need to conserve and inherit the heir and authentically present living environment through particular geographical environments (Zhang et al., 2018).

Communities' vital involvement in intangible cultural heritage identification, protection, and reproduction is institutionalized, researched academically, and regularly put into practice through community-based activities that may or may not include digital technologies (Giglitto et al., 2022). In order to ensure the long-term and systematic preservation of rural intangible cultural heritage information and skills, it is necessary to digitize such knowledge (Isa et al., 2018). It is essential to stimulate the weak links of rural information infrastructure to encourage the digital preservation of the intangible cultural heritage of rural destinations (Gao et al., 2021). Improved regulations and procedures and more comprehensive planning could pave the way for the construction of such digital structures. However, to avoid over-commercialization, artificialization, and urbanization, as well as actions that arbitrarily modify rural intangible cultural heritage in the guise of inheritance and innovation, stakeholders must prevent the overloading and damaging exploitation of intangible cultural heritage owing to tourism development (Zhang et al., 2018).

REFERENCES

Andreoli, R., Corolla, A., Faggiano, A., Malandrino, D., Pirozzi, D., Ranaldi, M., Santangelo, G., & Scarano, V. (2017). A framework to design, develop, and evaluate immersive and collaborative serious games in cultural heritage. *Journal on Computing and Cultural Heritage*, *11*(1), 1–22. doi:10.1145/3064644

Carboni, N., & de Luca, L. (2016). Towards a conceptual foundation for documenting tangible and intangible elements of a cultural object. *Digital Applications in Archaeology and Cultural Heritage*, *3*(4), 108–116. doi:10.1016/j.daach.2016.11.001

Chalmers, A., Parkins, J., Webb, M., & Debattista, K. (2021). Realistic Humans in Virtual Cultural Heritage. *International Conference on Emerging Technologies and the Digital Transformation of Museums and Heritage Sites*, 156–165. 10.1007/978-3-030-83647-4_11

Cheer, J. M., Reeves, K. J., & Laing, J. H. (2013). Tourism and traditional culture: Land diving in vanuatu. *Annals of Tourism Research*, *43*(xx), 435–455. doi:10.1016/j.annals.2013.06.005

Chen, Z. (2022). Visualizing experiencescape–from the art of intangible cultural heritage. *Current Issues in Tourism*, *25*(4), 559–578. doi:10.1080/13683500.2021.1892040

Craig, C. J., JeongAe, Y., & Zou, Y. (2016). *The narrative nature of embodied knowledge: A cross-study analysis of teaching, learning, and living*. Academic Press.

Daskon, C., & McGregor, A. (2012). Cultural Capital and Sustainable Livelihoods in Sri Lanka's Rural Villages: Towards Culturally Aware Development. *The Journal of Development Studies*, *48*(4), 549–563. doi:10.1080/00220388.2011.604413

Gao, X., Guo, X., & Lo, T. (2021). Digital infrastructure - A potential method for rural revitalization through digitization of rural information. *Projections - Proceedings of the 26th International Conference of the Association for Computer-Aided Architectural Design Research in Asia, CAADRIA 2021*, *2*, 699–708.

Garau, C. (2015). Perspectives on cultural and sustainable rural tourism in a smart region: The case study of Marmilla in Sardinia (Italy). *Sustainability (Switzerland)*, *7*(6), 6412–6434. doi:10.3390u7066412

Giglitto, D., Ciolfi, L., & Bosswick, W. (2022). Building a bridge: Opportunities and challenges for intangible cultural heritage at the intersection of institutions, civic society, and migrant communities. *International Journal of Heritage Studies*, *28*(1), 74–91. doi:10.1080/13527258.2021.1922934

Giudici, E., Melis, C., Dessì, S., & Francine Pollnow Galvao Ramos, B. (2013). Is intangible cultural heritage able to promote sustainability in tourism? *International Journal of Quality and Service Sciences*, *5*(1), 101–114. doi:10.1108/17566691311316275

Hou, Y., Kenderdine, S., Picca, D., Egloff, M., & Adamou, A. (2022). Digitizing Intangible Cultural Heritage Embodied: State of the Art. *Journal on Computing and Cultural Heritage*, *15*(3), 1–20. doi:10.1145/3494837

Ibrahim, N., & Ali, N. M. (2018). A conceptual framework for designing virtual heritage environment for cultural learning. *Journal on Computing and Cultural Heritage*, *11*(2), 1–27. doi:10.1145/3117801

Isa, W. M. W., Zin, N. A. M., Rosdi, F., & Sarim, H. M. (2018). Digital preservation of intangible cultural heritage. *Indonesian Journal of Electrical Engineering and Computer Science*, *12*(3), 1373–1379. doi:10.11591/ijeecs.v12.i3.pp1373-1379

Kenderdine, S., Yip, A., Oliver, C., Pather, N., Sammut, C., Djokic, T., Marcus, N., & Ong, A. (2021). Designing Multi-disciplinary Interactive Virtual Environments for Next-Generation Immersive Learning Experiences: Case Studies and Future Directions in Astrobiology, Anatomy and Cultural Heritage. In Creative and Collaborative Learning through Immersion (pp. 49–67). Springer.

Lenzerini, F. (2011). Intangible cultural heritage: The living culture of peoples. *European Journal of International Law*, *22*(1), 101–120. doi:10.1093/ejil/chr006

Lo, P., Chan, H. H. Y., Tang, A. W. M., Chiu, D. K. W., Cho, A., See-To, E. W. K., Ho, K. K. W., He, M., Kenderdine, S., & Shaw, J. (2019). Visualising and revitalising traditional Chinese martial arts: Visitors' engagement and learning experience at the 300 years of Hakka Kungfu. *Library Hi Tech*, *37*(2), 269–288. doi:10.1108/LHT-05-2018-0071

Lund, N. F., Holst-Beck, P., Pine, B. J. II, & Leask, A. (2022). Hamlet Live : The 7 I's Experiential Strategy Framework for heritage visitor attractions. *Journal of Heritage Tourism*, *17*(2), 125–141. doi: 10.1080/1743873X.2021.1951277

Ma, X., Wang, R., Dai, M., & Ou, Y. (2021). The influence of culture on the sustainable livelihoods of households in rural tourism destinations. *Journal of Sustainable Tourism*, *29*(8), 1235–1252. doi:10.1080/09669582.2020.1826497

MacDonald, R., & Jolliffe, L. (2003). Cultural rural tourism: Evidence from Canada. *Annals of Tourism Research*, *30*(2), 307–322. doi:10.1016/S0160-7383(02)00061-0

Meghini, C., Bartalesi, V., & Metilli, D. (2021). Representing narratives in digital libraries: The narrative ontology. *Semantic Web*, *12*(2), 241–264. doi:10.3233/SW-200421

Melis, C., & Chambers, D. (2021). The construction of intangible cultural heritage: A Foucauldian critique. *Annals of Tourism Research*, *89*, 103206. doi:10.1016/j.annals.2021.103206

Paul, S. K., & Roy, S. (2017). Tourism-based heritage conservation in Murshidabad: An appraisal. *Journal of Heritage Tourism*, *12*(2), 139–154. doi:10.1080/1743873X.2016.1159685

Pine, J. B. II, & Gilmore, J. H. (2011). *The experience economy*. Harvard Business Review Press., doi:10.1163/9789004495012_003

Qiu, Q., & Zhang, M. (2021). Using content analysis to probe the cognitive image of intangible cultural heritage tourism: An exploration of Chinese social media. *ISPRS International Journal of Geo-Information*, *10*(4), 240. Advance online publication. doi:10.3390/ijgi10040240

Ranjan, A., & Chaturvedi, P. (2022). Digital Technologies and the Intangible Cultural Heritage of the Rural Destination. In *Disruptive Innovation and Emerging Technologies for Business Excellence in the Service Sector* (pp. 196–218). IGI Global. doi:10.4018/978-1-7998-9194-9.ch010

Rizvic, S., Boskovic, D., Okanovic, V., Sljivo, S., & Zukic, M. (2019). Interactive digital storytelling: Bringing cultural heritage in a classroom. *Journal of Computers in Education*, *6*(1), 143–166. doi:10.100740692-018-0128-7

Rudan, E., & Stipanović, C. (2021). Music in the tourism offering of rural regions (the case of eastern croatia). *European Countryside*, *13*(3), 685–696. doi:10.2478/euco-2021-0036

Selmanović, E., Rizvic, S., Harvey, C., Boskovic, D., Hulusic, V., Chahin, M., & Sljivo, S. (2020). Improving Accessibility to Intangible Cultural Heritage Preservation Using Virtual Reality. *Journal on Computing and Cultural Heritage*, *13*(2), 1–19. Advance online publication. doi:10.1145/3377143

Shuai, H., & Yu, W. (2021). Discussion on the application of computer digital technology in the protection of intangible cultural heritage. *Journal of Physics: Conference Series*, *1915*(3), 032048. Advance online publication. doi:10.1088/1742-6596/1915/3/032048

Skublewska-Paszkowska, M., Milosz, M., Powroznik, P., & Lukasik, E. (2022). 3D technologies for intangible cultural heritage preservation—Literature review for selected databases. *Heritage Science*, *10*(1), 1–24. doi:10.118640494-021-00633-x PMID:35003750

Starčević, K., Vojinović, Ž., & Glavaš, J. (2022). Intangible cultural heritage and their influence on financial results in rural tourism. *Ekonomika Poljoprivrede*, *69*(2), 483–496. doi:10.5937/ekoPolj2202483S

Sun, C., Chen, H., & Liao, R. (2021). Research on incentive mechanism and strategy choice for passing on intangible cultural heritage from masters to apprentices. *Sustainability (Switzerland)*, *13*(9), 5245. Advance online publication. doi:10.3390u13095245

Tzima, S., Styliaras, G., Bassounas, A., & Tzima, M. (2020). Harnessing the potential of storytelling and mobile technology in intangible cultural heritage: A case study in early childhood education in sustainability. *Sustainability (Switzerland)*, *12*(22), 1–22. doi:10.3390u12229416

UNESCO. (2003). *Intangible Heritage - 2003 Convention*. https://ich.unesco.org/en/intangible-heritage-domains-00052

Vaughan, L. (2016). Performance, practice and presence: Design parameters for the living archive. *Performing Digital: Multiple Perspectives on a Living Archive*, 51–62. doi:10.4324/9781315599960

Vosinakis, S., Avradinis, N., & Koutsabasis, P. (2018). Dissemination of Intangible Cultural Heritage Using a Multi-agent Virtual World. Lecture Notes in Computer Science, 10754, 197–207. doi:10.1007/978-3-319-75789-6_14

Xie, J. (2022). Innovative Design of Artificial Intelligence in Intangible Cultural Heritage. *Scientific Programming, 2022*(1). doi:10.1155/2022/6913046

Yan, W. J., & Chiou, S. C. (2021). The safeguarding of intangible cultural heritage from the perspective of civic participation: The informal education of chinese embroidery handicrafts. *Sustainability (Switzerland), 13*(9), 4958. Advance online publication. doi:10.3390u13094958

Zhang, Y., Han, M., & Chen, W. (2018). The strategy of digital scenic area planning from the perspective of intangible cultural heritage protection. *EURASIP Journal on Image and Video Processing, 2018*(1), 130. Advance online publication. doi:10.118613640-018-0366-7

Zhang, Y., & Lee, T. J. (2022). Alienation and authenticity in intangible cultural heritage tourism production. *International Journal of Tourism Research, 24*(1), 18–32. doi:10.1002/jtr.2478

Chapter 3
The Recruitment Crisis in the British Hospitality Industry:
A Case for More Sustainable Practices

Wendy C. Sealy
https://orcid.org/0000-0001-6256-9866
University of Chichester, UK

Paula Jenkins
University of Chichester, UK

Alice Jalley
University of Chichester, UK

ABSTRACT

The scarce supply of labour and of a competent workforce in the hospitality sector has been researched and debated for decades. Although the sector is important to the UK economy contributing £130 billion pounds to the gross domestic product, the inability of the sector to attract and retain the best talent remains an age-old problem. This chapter is a commentary of the current debate on the recruitment crisis based on an examination of the most recent academic literature. The research finds that although many recommendations have been proffered by researchers to solve these problems, the issues and mistakes made by hospitality employers appear to remain the same. Possible best practice solutions are explored. Reviews of scholarly journals, books, and materials from the domains of marketing, human resources, hospitality management, and organisational behaviour were used to find evidence about the current trends of thought, research findings, and best practices in this field. The chapter concludes with three conceptual models that summarise the critical issues and possible solutions.

DOI: 10.4018/978-1-6684-6732-9.ch003

Copyright © 2023, IGI Global. Copying or distributing in print or electronic forms without written permission of IGI Global is prohibited.

INTRODUCTION

The hospitality industry plays a significant role in economic and social development in the UK. The industry employs 3.2 million people, produces £130 billion of economic activity and generates £39 billion in taxation for the UK government (UK Hospitality, 2018). The hospitality industry comprise that part of the services sector represented by pubs, bars, cruise ships, restaurants, catering companies, guests houses, branded hotel chains, travel agencies, tour operators, airlines, event agencies and visitor attractions. In the next 10 years the industry is projected to produce around 72 million jobs (Ghani *et al.*, 2022). However, globally, the hospitality industry continues to suffer from the challenge of attracting and retaining high quality talent resulting in poor organisational performance and the lack of sustainable growth. Research into turnover rates in the industry revealed that turnover in the hotel industry is double the national average compared to all other industries (Malek, Klein, and DiPietro, 2018). This chapter examines why it is still difficult to recruit and retain hospitality employees.

The issue of recruitment and retention of hospitality staff is nothing new and has been the topic of research and debate for decades (Ohlin & West, 1994; Iverson & Deery, 1997; Pratton, 2003; Lashley & Chapman,1999). Employee retention has been identified as one of the biggest challenges in the 21st century, particularly in the hospitality industry (Ghani *et a*l., 2022). So critical is the situation in the UK that some hospitality businesses are forced to close several days a week losing up to £21 billion in trade (McAlister, 2022). The decision to leave the EU has exacerbated the situation in the UK and has resulted in 200,000 circa hospitality workers leaving the country (Financial Times, 2022). The UK no longer allows free movement of labour from the EU. Employers must use the Points Based System (Tier 2) to recruit non-UK workers but this is costly. Tier 2 requires the employer to sponsor an employee at a cost of £1,476, and each employee is then required to pay for a Certificate of Sponsorship at a fee of £199. The application for a visa would cost the employee around £575 although this may be paid for by the employer. When all the costs are factored in, it is estimated that employing an overseas worker cost an employer as much as £3,250 excluding the standard administrative and legal costs and any relocation fees. The decision to leave the EU has lessened the pool of workers that would ordinarily be available to work in the hospitality industry. The problem with Tier 2 is that unless you are highly skilled and earning over £20,000 annually you are unlikely to gain sufficient points to qualify for the visa (www.gov.uk/skilled-worker-visa/if-you-work-in-healthcare-or-education). Applicants usually need to have degrees or higher-level qualifications, should have spent time living in the UK prior to applying and need to pass an English sufficiency test. Tier 2 would be more suitable for highly skilled imported labour as the cost of the visa would probably deter those seeking low skilled jobs. However, the recruitment crisis, though exacerbated by Brexit, does not have its roots there. Besides, even if there were pools of migrant labour available, being highly dependent on migrant labour can create conflicts and competition between migrants and locals for jobs and in the work place. A predominant migrant work force in one organisation could create cultural problems and have an effect on the marketing and brand management of the company. A hospitality business is a product of its destination environment and should reflect the culture and essence of the place. It is therefore important that this essence is represented by a balance in the employees that are hired.

The negative image and reputation of the sector in the UK is an often-cited primary cause for the recruitment problem. According to Nachmias (2017), the industry is struggling to recruit skilled workers due to low pay, low prestige, poor or no benefits, limited career advancement opportunities, poor treatment of workers and the seasonality of jobs. According to a 2022 survey of 55 event management students at a post 1992 university in the UK, students perceive the industry as an avenue for low and poor paying jobs, perceiving it as 'waitressing', 'poorly treated staff', 'long hours, lots of work and low pay. In the same survey 71.4% of students also stated that poor work experience in the sector during their studies led them to not want to work in the hospitality industry. Students reported that poor treatment and bad working conditions during volunteering and placement was the major cause (Nadda, Arnott, Sealy & Delaney, 2022). Ghani *et al.,* (2022) suggests retention issues are due to lack of career growth and development, low levels of job satisfaction, poor work environment and long working hours. The wellbeing and attitudes of staff is highly important and low morale can affect an employee's ability to produce high quality customer service which can affect the business' competitive advantage (Ghani *et al.*, 2022).

Employment opportunities in hospitality are varied ranging from unskilled porter type roles to highly skilled managerial roles. However, the majority of staff employed in the sector are generally regarded as semi or unskilled. Employers in the industry value the more generic soft skills such as the ability to follow instructions, willingness to learn, and ability to be flexible and adaptive (Hospitality Training Foundation, 2000). Employers are also very sceptical of qualifications, as they do not view these as a guarantee of the skills they require, some claiming that they prefer people with the right work ethic instead (Sealy, 2023). Generally, the education levels in the sector are low (Rasheed, Okumus, Weng, Hameed & Nawaz, 2020) and not all hospitality managers are trained to manage talent, even when holding degrees in the field. The sector has a reputation for poor leadership and training. Most organisations would train employees in basic customer service and interaction but managers/owners are reluctant to invest in training due to high staff turnover rates or simply because of a lack of time to do so (Poulson, 2007). Inadequately trained staff jeopardises service quality, and can demean and embarrass employees, yet anecdotal evidence overwhelmingly suggests training is poor in the sector but an employee can still be disciplined for their inability to perform despite their lack of training (*Ibid*). Training and development affects job satisfaction and organisational performance which in turn affect profits. Research indicates that 70% of managers in this sector are poorly trained or untrained leading to a lack of quality leadership (DiPietro and Condly, 2007). The fact that organizations would rather incur the cost of recruiting new people than the more sustainable and cheaper option of retaining the talent they already have is mindboggling (Cicerale, 2020). Hospitality managers remain ignorant of proper forecasting, staffing, recruitment strategies and talent management (Ghani, *et al* 2022). Forecasting and planning is very difficult in the sector due to uncertainty in demand and requires very skilled data driven managers. Lack of proper forecasting and planning results in casual work and '0' hour contracts as a mitigation strategy to manage the risk of uncertainty but these are a major turn-off to prospective employees.

Hospitality employers also depend on the emotional labour of workers, including face-to-face contact with the public and the ability to produce a positive emotional state in another person which activates the feel-good hormones, 'pheromones', which are central to the visitor experience and essential for business networking and repeat customers. Front-line hospitality workers are basically 'actors' who must appear personable, enthusiastic and friendly at all times despite how they may be feeling on the inside. Because the work is physically and emotionally intense due to high levels of personal and positive interactions with guests, staff are required to be physically and mentally fit and to have high levels of emotional intelligence which can make the work exhausting. Front-of-the-house workers have to deal with the administrative tasks but also with unreasonable requests or 'hard to please' or abusive customers while still maintaining a pleasant demeanour and positive emotions. Insincere emotions and the need to please in this very 'customer first' sector can cause stress to build up leading to emotional exhaustion. Several industry professionals suffer from emotional and physical burnout and may move onto other professions as a result (Wang, 2020).

The industry in the UK is renowned for gender discrimination with several roles being feminised such as 'bar maid', 'housekeeper' etc; and poor career advancement, particularly for women. Calinaud, Kokkranikal & Gebbels (2021) argue that gender forms the basis for the division of labour, employee hiring, promotions and how rewards are distributed in hospitality organisations. The industry image is also tarnished by high levels of unprofessionalism some of which occurs through conjugal relationships between staff, particularly between management and their subordinates, creating a climate for nepotism, favouritism (Seger-Guttmann & Medler-Liraz, 2018) and unfair practices such as wrongful dismissal, victimization and the sexual harassment of female workers (Lopa & Gong, 2020). The sector is also known for fear management such as bullying. Women are particularly vulnerable to bullying in the hospitality sector but also men (Bohle, Knox, Noone, McNamara, Rafalski, Quinlan, 2017). Some researchers even suggest that bullying is part of the culture in many hospitality organisations with Boyle *et al* (2017) explaining that bullying and abuse is normalised behaviour behind-the-scenes in kitchens and other back-of-the-house areas where the behaviour is not subjected to disciplinary action. They further explained that this is the result of poor leadership and management within the organisation and total disregard for socially sustainable practices.

Research and anecdotal evidence suggest that work pressure precipitate aggression and bullying. Long hours, irregular and unsociable work hours, job and income insecurity, weak unions and ineffective industrial relations contribute to workplace abuse *(ibid).* Very often the fear of retribution and job insecurity along with weak unions makes it difficult for workers to lodge complaints (*Ibid*). Hospitality managers have a lot of power, usually due to the fact that many own the company or they have been appointed through some form of favouritism or nepotism. Workers therefore see leaving as the best option rather than filing a grievance that may also tarnish their reputation. Managers that own their companies may view the business as a 'lifestyle business' or a 'lifestyle job' - a job or business that pays for his/her lifestyle – (Sealy, 2020) and therefore would not necessarily make employee satisfaction and retention a priority. Poor treatment of employees and the lack of fair and just systems to complain leads to service sabotage where a disgruntled employee misbehaves intentionally to counter the imbalance in power by sabotaging the service encounter with a "deliberate" and carefully orchestrated course of action that can negatively impact the service or the reputation of the organisation (Lai, Sun & Chu, 2020). Some examples of service sabotage would be 'go-slows', 'sick-outs' (large numbers of staff calling-in sick at the same time during peak busy periods) or rudeness to customers. Service sabotage is a secretive plan designed to hurt the business. Whatever form it takes 'service sabotage' like 'industrial sabotage' cost employers money and can tarnish their reputation resulting in the permanent loss of customers or the loyalty of travel agents and tour operators.

Numerous studies have demonstrated a skills deficiency in the sector which exacerbates the recruitment crisis. A 2015 survey by the Association of American Colleges and Universities showed that 91% of employers agree that critical thinking skills, written and oral communication skills, teamwork, ethical decision-making, the ability to apply knowledge in a real-world setting and an ability to solve complex problems is more important than a degree (Mainga, Daniel, & Alamil, 2022). Ninety-six percent (96%) of employers agree that all college/university students should learn how to solve problems with different-minded people showing the importance of inter-cultural skills. At the 2022 Confex Conference of the events industry in the UK, employers made it clear that they needed people who had high levels of intellectual reasoning and who could interpret data and manipulate numbers. But high-level skills come with high levels of pay and the industry is notorious for poor pay. Colleges and universities in the UK focus more on vocational studies to attract students from different backgrounds rather than on developing critical thinking, intellectual or numerical skills. The dearth in skilled labour contributes to toxic working environments and means that people are often placed in positions that they are not qualified for.

The COVID-19 pandemic has also influenced recruitment and retention. More than one in ten UK hospitality workers left the industry in 2020 (Evans, 2021). Employees' priorities have changed since the pandemic and now work-life balance, flexibility and mental health are priorities (Charlton, 2021). Employees are wanting more flexible, hybrid virtual-working models and the opportunity to work from home for three days a week (Charlton, 2021). The hospitality industry has been infamously known for its long, unsocial hours and burnt-out employees due to the emotional labour endured in the industry (Kotera *et al.,* 2021). However, the pandemic has changed employees' mindsets and they no longer want to work in those conditions which is making recruiting and retaining staff difficult. However, working from at home may be difficult to organised in this 'customer-facing- industry. It is clear that what is needed is better forecasting, planning, management and recruitment of talent underpinned by appropriate management training and development programmes.

A recent resourcing and talent planning report by the CIPD (Chartered Institute of Personnel Development) (2022) reveals that rather than taking a strategic approach to workforce planning, by looking at internal capability, both permanent and contingent, there seems to be more of a 'knee jerk' reaction to the current recruitment and retention problem. Organisations are increasing pay and/or benefits (6 weeks leave, wellbeing levies etc) to address recruitment difficulties while ignoring poor work conditions. CIPD also suggest that what is needed are strategies to retain critical skills and that more dynamic, innovative, strategic and modern recruitment processes are needed to develop, upskill and retain employees. Developing an attractive employee value proposition especially for those in different life stages and promoting the uniqueness of the employer brand and culture seem to be the fewer chosen actions despite sound evidence that these are increasingly important post pandemic to potential recruits. Poon (1988) argued that success in the hospitality industries will increasingly depend upon innovativeness and its capacity to anticipate and to respond creatively to changes taking place in the international tourism marketplace. There is some evidence of creative and innovative approaches to recruitment and retention in the sector. The paper now turns attention to examples of these more modern and innovation solutions from the academic and corporate literature.

Best Practices

Several studies have concluded that the key to employee recruitment and retention is employee satisfaction comprising a sustainable positive work environment; growth opportunities for career advancement; sustainable & effective communications; and sustainable & effective recruitment and selection practices (Ghani, Zada, Memon, Ullah, Khattak, Han, Ariza-Montes, Araya-Castillo, 2022). To achieve these, researchers (Charlton, 2021; Ghani *et al.*, 2022; Frye *et al.*, 2020; Monaco and Smith, 2007; CIPD, 2022) have posited the importance of putting employees at the centre of a company's vision and strategic planning. A hospitality company's employees are its USP, and it is what makes a company unique by creating a competitive advantage. People are part of a product dimension that cannot be duplicated by competitors. It is the employee that creates the experience, not the company itself. For an industry that depends on repeat customers employees are a central force in driving profitability and are critical to a company gaining or maintaining a sustainable advantage over competitors. A high staff turn-over therefore negatively impacts a company's competitiveness, profitability and drives marketing, recruitment and training costs up making the company less sustainable. Ghani *et al.* (2022) suggests that hospitality businesses should be focusing on motivating and caring for their employees through modern HR practices. These HR practices would involve evaluation, regular feedback, continuous support, and sustainable career development (Ghani *et a*l., 2022). Overall, importance must be put on understanding employees needs and developing a supportive, creative, and forward-thinking environment in which employees want to stay and grow; but the industry must be willing to change and implement more modern HR practices.

Working with Millennials

The managing director of Edwards and Finn (Asksuite, 2021) stated that to successfully attract employees to jobs in the hospitality industry, the industry will need to start offering working from home and flexible time in job offers. Being offered mental health resources in the workplace could also attract employees as it has been found that 50% of employers reported an increase in the use of available company mental health resources since the pandemic began (Charlton, 2021). Recent research also notes that the new generation of worker, 'Generation Y', 'the Millennials', have different perceptions and attitudes about working preferences and job satisfaction from previous generations (Frye *et al.*, 2020). The millennial is not willing to tolerate abusive customers or managers or poor working conditions. They hold their management to high standards, they want good working environments, relationships with their managers and challenging work and are less motivated by money (*Frye et al.*, 2020). This workforce has been raised to feel special and entitled. They expect more freedom and does not appreciate the rigid leadership styles inherited from the era of the manufacturing-based economy (Bodenhausen & Curtis, 2016). The top-down, bureaucratic management and leadership style may not be effective with this younger generation of employees (Gursoy, Maier & Chi, 2008). Instead, they want to be included in decision-making, being valued for their knowledge, skills, and competencies. Thus, they bring these same values of inclusion and entitlement into the workplace (Monaco and Smith, 2007). Generation 'Y' expect fast career progression, good pay, job security, a positive work culture and supportive managers (Dutta & Mishra, 2021). Millennials are also very innovative and forward thinking and they embrace the use of technology, having grown up as digital natives. Currently employers, particularly those who had to work their way up the ladder, have been struggling to understand what Generation 'Y' workers look for in a work environment (Frye *et al.*, 2020) and this may be contributing to the high turnover levels.

Making employees feel valued and listened too is important and satisfied employees appear to be more committed to their employer (Frye *et al.,* 2020). Retention schemes that could be introduced to improve employee satisfaction include, internal marketing communications which involves treating employees as though they are customers (Frye *et al*., 2020; Marriott, 2022) so that they make a powerful emotional connection to the business and develop a passion for the brand vision (Mitchell, 2002). Internal marketing communications reduces employee turnover and opens a channel for participative management which then also results in decreasing recruiting and training costs (Arnett et al., 2002). Resources that would be used to employ new staff can be redirected to improving the skills of current employees and low turnover results in less stress for existing employees (Arnett *et al.*, 2002).

Employer Branding

Employers need to be proactive with workforce planning and develop compelling offerings to attract and retain a diverse group of employees. CIPD (2022) suggests that pay increases are not sustainable nor can employers continue to afford continued pay increases so must explore more realistic and long-term options. Employer branding is an important tool when recruiting. Increasingly firms are using employer branding to attract the best talent. The theory is based on the economic foundations of competitive advantage and scarce resources and is used as a means to attract the best talent. As a branded employer it forms an image that the organisation is a good place to work (Backhaus and Tikoo, 2004). Employer branding involves promoting, both within and outside the firm, a clear view of what makes a firm different and desirable as an employer (Sarabdeen, El-Rakhawy & Khan, 2020). Sarabdeen, El-Rakhawy & Khan explains that employer branding is based on the 'Recourse Based View' theory that an organisation can achieve a sustainable competitive advantage through internal resources such as human assets to create a rare and non-substitutable resource for a competitive edge. Table 1 shows the different dimensions of employer branding and how each can be achieved (Backhause and Tikoo, 2004).

Table 1. How employer branding can help recruitment

Employer branding points	What employers need to offer
Organisational Identity	- Company's values and morals (PWC, 2011). - Empowered employees (Duncan, 2019). - Open communication (Duncan, 2019). - Trans media storytelling (Roxo, 2020).
Organisational Culture	- Feedback and encouragement (PWC, 2011). - Vertical career progression (PWC, 2011). - Varied and interesting culture (PWC, 2011). - Participative management/empowerment (Marriott, 2020).
Employer Brand Associations	- Millennials are attracted to employer brands that they admire as consumers (PWC, 2011). - Eco-Friendly values and practices. - Good community relations (Andersson, Gustaf & Zalamans,2012).
Employer Image	- A good reputation (PWC, 2011).
Employer Attraction	- Management training programmes (Four Seasons, 2022). - International opportunities (PWC, 2011). - Good benefits package (PWC, 2011). - Well-designed uniforms and grooming (Emirates, 2022). - Diversity/equal opportunities (PWC, 2011). - Travel and transfer opportunities in international companies (Marriott, Sheraton, Intercontinental). - Overseas training opportunities. - Perks (5 start hotels stays, generous peridium) (Emirate Airlines). - Culturally diverse workforce (Emirate Airlines). - Generous benefits package. - Medical & dental insurance. - Educational allowances. - Workmen compensation. - Tax free allowances. - Study leave. - Spa treatments.
Employee Productivity	- Flexible working hours (Charlton, 2021). - Job shares. - Hybrid working (Charlton, 2021). - Work/life balance (PWC, 2011). - Cash and non-cash incentives - Profit sharing/ Bonus (Almond Beach Resorts. Bougainvillea Beach Resorts – Barbados). - Child care support.

Artificial Intelligence

More research is needed into the role of artificial intelligence (AI) while avoiding the potential pitfalls. AI is affecting the way companies engage with staff and customers. However, it is important that the hospitality industry uses technology to enhance its services and does not fall prey to dehumanising the personal touch. It can be argued that through continually evolving smart technologies and tools, managers will be free of tasks deemed difficult, mundane or less exciting and will instead be able to focus on tasks that are perceived to be more stimulating and focussing more on the personal touch and 'high touch services', leading to a combination of reduced staffing costs, improved staff satisfaction and happier guests and customers. The question arises whether this development can substitute for the human touch in this very socially interactive industry. Certainly, technology could help with labour intensive tasks such as luggage-carrying robots, front desk robots for check-in and concierge robots for booking tours and services (Avgeli, Dahlan, Bakir, & Wickens, 2020). Robotics could possibly make the industry less emotionally exhausting. Tourism and hospitality companies also use robots for the provision of information, cleaning, room service orders, delivering items, serving food and drinks and entertaining guests etc (Ivanov, Seyitoğlu, & Markova, 2020). Service robots are also used in restaurants and bars to take orders, drones food delivery, museums and attractions, airport check-in and in hotels in yield management etc.

A fully automated hotel has just opened in Japan, the Henn-na Hotel, which is staffed exclusively by robots who speak multiple languages and greet and help the customers at the front desk. Other innovations include robotic arms which are in charge of storing guests' luggage, and the rooms are accessed by facial recognition systems (Zlatanov, & Popesku, 2019). Robotics can eliminate a range of laborious tasks but provide opportunities for a wider range of general skills for human interaction and personnel to deal with non-routine activities to support and educate guests in operating the robots, and to monitor the operations. Artificial intelligence is helping hotels make better informed decisions that can increase efficiency, manage risk, reduce human error and optimize performance. It is helping businesses to optimise performance in hotel operations, revenue management, the booking experience, and can take customer service to a higher level of personalisation. Robotics, including virtual and augmented reality could make hospitality operations easier and more sustainable, reducing the need for human employees. AI is being used by top hotel brands like Hilton and Marriott but it is not known to what extent AI is being used across the sector. Unfortunately, the scientific literature on the subject is scarce. Its impact, effectiveness and capabilities need to be explored further with research.

The use of artificial intelligence (AI), augmented and virtual reality along with other technologies can provide opportunities for advance learning and training particularly those jobs that require high levels of specialisation, sensitivity, discretion, judgment, and quick decision-making (Tracey & Swart, 2019). AI could make training and education more accessible for employees and cheaper for employers. It could provide individuals with substantial up-to-date and innovative content that could advance careers and make jobs less mundane. A major challenge might be how to process and disseminate vast amounts of information. Moreover, the growing resources and content will become increasingly informed by and shaped from a global perspective for more inclusive and diverse solutions from all over the world (*Ibid*). Employers would be wise, however, to implement a comprehensive cost-benefits analysis to ensure that the customer expectations and experience is not compromised by robotics.

Community Engagement

Hospitality businesses, through their respective associations, or unilaterally can resolve the labour shortage through more innovative approaches to community engagement by incorporating corporate social responsibility values into their business strategy. Businesses can engage with schools, colleges and universities within their immediate communities to promote the mirage of opportunities available for work in the sector. Businesses can provide schools with hosted day out opportunities so that students can engage and sample what it feels like to work in the sector and to observe the working environment first-hand. University students, in the immediate region, could be provided with part-time jobs, placements, internships and projects that are meaningful and contribute to their learning and readiness for work. They should be made to feel special and feel a sense of belonging so that they become emotionally attached to the organisation. The role of such initiatives would be to equip students with skills and attributes (knowledge, attitudes and behaviour) that employers claim are lacking in graduates. The goal should be to equip students with in-depth knowledge of their subject as well as generic skills which would result in improved employability (Andersson, Gustaf & Zalamans,2012).

Training and Developing Managers to Manage Talent

Attracting the right talent to an organisation with the right knowledge, skills and personality fit are of strategic importance in most businesses. With low unemployment in the UK and a tight labour market for many skills as economies emerge from the global pandemic, organisations need to ensure that they attract and retain the best employees possible; but this does not happen by accident. Based on the authors' research, work experience and consultancy experience with hospitality companies the authors now offer local and regional employers' executive short courses to support managers in the development and retention of talent. These courses (table 2) consider employee branding, workforce planning, sources of employees in the labour market, efficient and effective resourcing approaches, managing induction and the probationary period and developing new talent. The reader may be interested to know that one of our clients in the Holiday Park sector are currently offering this course as part of their 'aspiring leaders' development programme to grow and retain talent.

Table 2. Management training and development for innovative talent management

Key Concepts for Training & Development	*Content*
Resourcing and Talent Development	- Employee branding. - Workforce planning and job analysis. - The labour market and new 'war for talent'. - Changing world and work and skills for the future. - The changing demographics of the workforce. - Hybrid and remote working-the implications. - Traditional and contemporary approaches to resourcing. - Attracting the right talent pool. - What is our EVP? - Role descriptions. - Selecting the best candidates for the role. - Employment law considerations. - Induction and the probationary period. - The role of the line manager in talent development.
Fundamentals for A Successful Resourcing and Talent Development Strategy	- Systematic planning. - Efficiency and effectiveness. - The digital opportunity in attracting and sourcing talent. - Diversity and inclusivity. - Measurements of success. - Links with reward, employee development and performance management practices.
Designing and Managing an Effective Recruitment Campaign	- The business case to recruit. - Establishing the best process to meet the business needs. - Attracting a talent pool. - Screening in and out. - Communicating with candidates and stakeholders. - Successful onboarding. - Community engagement.
Evaluating the process and implementing improvements	- Measurements of success. - Process review and improvement.

Sources: (CIPD, 2022, Green, 2019; Canlas & Williams, 2022; Sarabdeen, El-Rakhawy & Khan, 2011; PWC, 2011; Duncan, 2019; Roxo, 2020; Marriott, 2019)

Table 3. Summary of recruitment and retention issues and further solutions

Problem	Solution
Long hours	- Flexible working hours (Charlton, 2021). - Realistic job previews (Bonn, 1992). - Opportunity to work from home (Charlton, 2021). - Artificial Intelligence.
Low pay	- Have a good benefits package (PWC, 2011). - Introduce performance-based incentives. - Hazzard pay or penalty pay for jobs done during unsociable hours (Richardson, 2008). - Profit sharing (Almond Beach Resorts Barbados).
Limited career progression	- Have better work experience opportunities for students to understand how the industry works (Richardson, 2008). - Give feedback to employees. - Management training programmes (Four Seasons, 2022). - Create structured career paths (Robertson, 2008). - Mentoring schemes - Policies and procedures to address gender discrimination. - Study leave.
Bad image and reputation	- Educate the public on the different roles within the hospitality industry (Asksuite, 2021). - Employer branding (Backhause and Tikoo, 2004). - Improve work experience opportunities (Richardson, 2008).
Exploitation of staff	- Offer work/life balance (Charlton, 2021). - Flexible, hybrid virtual-working models (Charlton, 2021). - Mental health support services (Charlton, 2021). - Marriott Hotels 'TakeCare Program' – physical wellbeing, mental and emotional health, career development, financial planning, team building, recognition (Marriott International, 2019). - Artificial Intelligence applications.
Low morale	- Good relationships with managers and colleagues (Frye et al., 2020). - Ensure employees feels valued and listened too (Frye et al., 2020). - Internal marketing (Mitchell, 2002). - HR practices including, regular feedback, appraisals, continuous support, and sustainable career. development (Ghani et al., 2022). - Participative management – Empowerment (Marriott, International, 2019).

DISCUSSION, CONCLUSION, AND GOING FORWARD

Table 3 conceptualises the most critical factors affecting recruitment and retention of hospitality workers and possible solutions. Despite the wealth of research and literature on good recruitment and retention practices in the hospitality industry there is evidence to show that the textbook advice is not being followed across all hospitality sectors, even in large firms (Kilibarda and Fonda, 1997). While this is probably due to low levels of education held by hospitality managers and the emphasis on profits and the bottom-line than on employee satisfaction, more research needs to be done on employers' current attitudes and approach towards recruitment and retention, particularly post pandemic. Unfortunately, hospitality managers are not always quick to embrace innovation and accept change.

The three priorities for the sector to tackle is the deep-seated perception of hospitality as a sector of low-paid work, low status, long, often anti-social hours, poor people management and poor conditions of work. Added to that, is the widely held view that there is now a precariousness working in this sector as it has proved to be highly susceptible to volatility in the external environment with pandemics and government economic responses, inflation pressures and cost of living increases at a time when there are more attractive employment options available. Employers also need to focus on branding and organisational culture, the employee value proposition, and talent attraction and retention strategies including employee development, career progression opportunities and cultivating a deep sense of organisational belonging (Canlas & Williams, 2022) of the utmost urgency.

The perception and attitudes towards the hospitality industry must change to attract a high calibre of employees, especially graduates, who will bring key skills and talent to the industry. Hospitality employers must change their approach to recruitment and retention of employees and make strategic human resources management an integral part of their long-term strategic business planning. It appears that unless the industry can offer higher wages and improve career paths and provide better working conditions for its employees at all levels, the industry will continue to lose talent. Research has shown that resolving the issues related to salary levels, relationships with managers, career paths and better working conditions are the remedies to solve this problem. With hospitality degrees now requiring students to undertake industry experience as a part of their degree, it is vital that these work placements are productive. The educational institutions and industry must collaborate to ensure that the experience students are receiving while on work placement or volunteering are of a high quality (Richardson, 2008).

Employers need to be honest in their job advertisements about the hard 'slog' of the industry, put more effort into employer branding and connect with educational institutions whilst also connecting with the new generation of workers and invest in their internal marketing and branding to retain employees. The industry must take responsibility and reflect on its own practices and be willing to change and embrace more modern management practices. It must implement modern and ethical HR practices and focus on training and developing its management employees. Policies to eradicate ongoing phenomenon such as nepotism, favouritism and gender discrimination must be the focal point of all institutions large or small in order to attract first-class talent. The industry continues to attract bad press in the UK which is indeed unfortunate; but; the fact is that the hospitality industry can be fun, creative and incredibly rewarding and this needs to be communicated and made realistic to the future generation of workers for the industry to become more sustainable. There are also wider pools of labour available to the hospitality industry such as underrepresented groups like disabled persons, LGBTQ, seniors, retirees, ethnic minorities, travellers/gypsy etc for a more balanced, diverse and culturally enriched workplace that reflects the destination and product brand. A diverse workforce could bring together new ideas, innovation and new thinking styles that could give a company a sustainable competitive advantage (Sarabdeen, El-Rakhawy & Khan, 2011). Looking into these pools of labour could be a short-term or even a long-term fix to this ongoing phenomenon.

Hospitality is a deeply relational human sector that revolves around the human experience. Improving HR capabilities and strategic HR knowledge and expertise are key to enabling a higher level of strategic thinking about the workforce, better quality evidence-based decision making which informs quality HR strategy execution and congruent and fully aligned HR practices, processes and policies (Green, 2019). There are some examples of good practice working towards this within the sector and this is demonstrated above, but, should be investigated further with field-based research and the findings shared on academic and industry platforms. It would, however, be useful to know the extent to which the strategies above are being used, the sectors that use them and their effectiveness. Another set of research could compare and contrast the experiences of small and medium sized businesses with large corporations. The experiences of hospitality employers in developed and undeveloped countries could also be researched to see if the same issues exist.

REFERENCES

Andersson, G., Gustaf, O., & Zalamans, D. (2012). Community engagement by an academic tourism department. Advances in Food. *Hospitality and Tourism*, *2*(1), 52–75.

Arnett, D. B., Laverie, D. A., & McLane, C. (2002). Using job satisfaction and pride as internal-marketing tools. *The Cornell Hotel and Restaurant Administration Quarterly*, *43*(2), 87–96. doi:10.1177/001088040204300209

Asksuite. (2021). *The Recruitment Challenge in The Hospitality Industry*. https://www.youtube.com/watch?v=yghavmrG2Kg

Avgeli, V., Dahlan, M. A., Bakir, A., & Wickens, E. (2020). 4IR impacts on tourism education and industry. Journal on Tourism & Sustainability, 4 (1), 06–15.

Backhaus, K., & Tikoo, S. (2004). Conceptualizing and researching employer branding. *Career Development International*, *9*(5), 501–517. doi:10.1108/13620430410550754

Bodenhausen, C., & Curtis, C. (2016). Transformational leadership and employee involvement: Perspectives from millennial workforce entrants. *Journal of Quality Assurance in Hospitality & Tourism*, *17*(3), 371–387.

Bohle, P., Knox, A., Noone, J., Mc Namara, M., Rafalski, J., & Quinlan, M. (2017). Work organisation, bullying and intention to leave in the hospitality industry. *Employee Relations*, *39*(4), 446–458. doi:10.1108/ER-07-2016-0149

Brien, A. (2004). December. Do I want a job in hospitality? Only till I get a real job. In *Proceedings of the New Zealand tourism and hospitality research conference* (35-42). Wellington, New Zealand: Victoria University of Wellington.

Calinaud, V., Kokkranikal, J., & Gebbels, M. (2021). Career advancement for women in the British hospitality industry: The enabling factors. *Work, Employment and Society*, *35*(4), 677–695. doi:10.1177/0950017020967208

Canlas, A., & Williams, M. (2022). Meeting belongingness needs: An inclusive leadership practitioner's approach. *Advances in Developing Human Resources*, *24*(4), 225–241. doi:10.1177/15234223221118953

Charlton, E. (2021). *4 things workers want implemented by their bosses' post-pandemic*. World Economic Forum. https://www.weforum.org/agenda/2021/05/employers-pandemic-covid-19-mental-health/.r

Cicerale, V. (2020). Turnover rates in the hospitality industry and the factors contributing to employee loss or retention. *Hospitality Graduate Student Scholarship*. https://scholarsarchive.jwu.edu/hosp_graduate/5

CIPD. (2022). *Resourcing and talent planning report 2022*. Chartered Institute of Personnel and Development. https://www.cipd.co.uk/Images/resourcing-and-talent-planning-report-2022-1_tcm18-111500.pdf

Dipietro, R. B., & Condly, S. J. (2007). Employee turnover in the hospitality industry: An analysis based on the CANE model of motivation. *Journal of Human Resources in Hospitality & Tourism*, *6*(1), 1–22. doi:10.1300/J171v06n01_01

Duncan, R. D. (2019). Why the 'identity' of your organization really matters. Forbes. https://www.forbes.com/sites/rodgerdeanduncan/2019/10/03/why-the-identity-of-your-organization-really-matters/?sh=41396be15892

Dutta, D., & Mishra, S. K. (2021). Predictors of applicant attraction among Gen-X and millennials: Evidence from an emerging economy. *International Journal of Manpower*, *42*(8), 1479–1499. doi:10.1108/IJM-04-2020-0169

Evans, C. (2021). *Covid and jobs: Why are hospitality workers leaving the industry?* BBC News. https://www.bbc.co.uk/news/uk-wales-57241370

Ferris, K., Cameron, D., Jenkins, A., & Marson, J. (2018). The consequences of the BREXIT vote on management attitudes to recruitment in the hospitality industry. *Business Law Review*, *39*(4).

Financial Times. (2022). *UK hospitality industry loses nearly 200,000 overseas workers*. https://www.ft.com/content/027ea2e9-d6c3-4a18-a735-87f92ace95a4

Frye, W. D., Kang, S., Huh, C., & Lee, M. J. M. (2020). What factors influence Generation Y's employee retention in the hospitality industry? An internal marketing approaches. *International Journal of Hospitality Management*, *85*, 102352. doi:10.1016/j.ijhm.2019.102352

Ghadeer, M., Badr, E., & Aboul-Ela, G. (2016). Employer branding: What constitutes An Employer of choice? *The Journal of Business and Retail Management Research*, *11*(1), 154–166.

Ghani, B., Zada, M., Memon, K. R., Ullah, R., Khattak, A., Han, H., Ariza-Montes, A., & Araya-Castillo, L. (2022). Challenges and strategies for employee retention in the hospitality industry: A review. *Sustainability*, *14*(5), 2885. doi:10.3390u14052885

Green, K. (2019). *Competitive People Strategy How to attract, develop and retain the staff you need for business success*. Kogan Page.

Gursoy, D., Maier, T. A., & Chi, C. G. (2008). Generational differences: An examination of work values and generational gaps in the hospitality workforce. *International Journal of Hospitality Management*, *27*(3), 448–458. doi:10.1016/j.ijhm.2007.11.002

Hospitality, U. K. (2018). *UK Hospitality Workforce Commission 2030 report: The changing face of hospitality September 2018*. https://www.youthemployment.org.uk/dev/wp-content/uploads/2018/09/UK-Hospitality-Workforce-Commission-2030.pdf

Hospitality Training Foundation. (2000). *Getting the basics right in the hospitality industry: integrating the basic skills standards into the occupational standards of the Hospitality Training Foundation.* https://www.worldcat.org/title/1166630477 https://www.gov.uk/skilled-worker-visa/if-you-work-in-healthcare-or-education

Ivanov, S., Seyitoğlu, F., & Markova, M. (2020). Hotel managers' perceptions towards the use of robots: A mixed-methods approach. *Information Technology & Tourism*, *22*(4), 505–535. doi:10.100740558-020-00187-x

Iverson, R. D., & Deery, M. (1997). Turnover culture in the hospitality industry. *Human Resource Management Journal*, *7*(4), 71–82. doi:10.1111/j.1748-8583.1997.tb00290.x

Kilibarda, P., & Fonda, N. (1997). Random Selection. *People Management*, *3*(24).

Kotera, Y., Adhikari, P., & Sheffield, D. (2021). Mental health of UK hospitality workers: Shame, self-criticism, and self-reassurance. *Service Industries Journal*, *41*(15-16), 1076–1096. doi:10.1080/02642069.2020.1713111

Lai, M., Sun, L. H., & Chu, H. E. (2020). Emotional labor and service sabotage in the hospitality industry: The mediating role of emotional exhaustion. *Journal of Tourism and Hospitality Management*, *8*(1), 120–132.

Lashley, C., & Chapman, A. (1999). Labour turnover: Hidden problem, hidden cost. *Hospitality Review*, *1*(1), 49–54.

Lopa, J., & Gong, Z. (2020). Sexual harassment of hospitality interns. *Journal of Hospitality & Tourism Education*, *32*(2), 88–101.

Mainga, W., Daniel, R. M., & Alamil, L. (2022). Perceptions of employability skills of undergraduate business students in a developing country: An exploratory study. *Higher Learning Research Communications*, *12*(1), 28–63. doi:10.18870/hlrc.2022.v12i1.1257

Malek, K., Kline, S. F., & DiPietro, R. (2018). The impact of manager training on employee turnover intentions. *Journal of Hospitality and Tourism Insights*, *1*(3), 203–219. doi:10.1108/JHTI-02-2018-0010

Marriott International. (2019). *Marriott International Announces Expanded Wellbeing Certification Program.* https://news.marriott.com/news/2019/09/18/marriott-international-announces-expanded-wellbeing-certification-program

McAlister, J. (2022). *Record Staff Shortages Causing Hospitality to Lose £21 billion in trade.* https://www.bighospitality.co.uk/Article/2022/06/23/record-staff-shortages-causing-hospitality-to-lose-21bn-in-trade

Mitchell, C. (2002). Selling the brand inside. Harvard Business Review. Available at: https://hbr.org/2002/01/selling-the-brand-inside

Nachmias, S. (2017). *Students' Attitude Towards Hospitality Education: An Anglo-Cypriot Critical Study.* http://irep.ntu.ac.uk/id/eprint/30577/1/8398_Nachmias.pdf

Nadda, V., Arnott, I., Sealy, W., & Delaney, E. (2022). *Employability and Skills Development in the Sports, Events & Hospitality Industries.* IGI Global. doi:10.4018/978-1-7998-7781-3

Ohlin, J. B., & West, J. J. (1994). An analysis of the effect of the fringe benefit offerings on the turnover of hourly workers in the hotel industry. *International Journal of Hospitality Management, 12*(4), 323–336. doi:10.1016/0278-4319(93)90049-F

Poon, A. (1988). Innovation and the future of Caribbean tourism. *Tourism Management, 9*(3), 213-220.

Pratton, J.D. (2003). The training and retention of chefs. *International Journal of Contemporary Hospitality Management, 15*(4), 237-242.

PWC. (2011). *Millennials at work Reshaping the workplace*. Available at: https://www.pwc.com/co/es/publicaciones/assets/millennials-at-work.pdf

Rasheed, M. I., Okumus, F., Weng, Q., Hameed, Z., & Nawaz, M. S. (2020). Career adaptability and employee turnover intentions: The role of perceived career opportunities and orientation to happiness in the hospitality industry. *Journal of Hospitality and Tourism Management, 44*, 98–107. doi:10.1016/j.jhtm.2020.05.006

Richardson, S. (2008). Undergraduate tourism and hospitality students' attitudes toward a career in the industry: A preliminary investigation. *Journal of Teaching in Travel & Tourism, 8*(1), 23–46. doi:10.1080/15313220802410112

Roxo, P. (2020). Transmedia storytelling as a potential employer branding strategy: Participatory culture and recruitment. *U. Porto Journal of Engineering, 6*(1), 66–77. doi:10.24840/2183-6493_006.001_0007

Sarabdeen, El-Rakhawy, & Khan. (2011). Employer branding in selected companies in UAE. *Communications of IBIMA*.

Sealy, W. (2020). A commentary on risk and resilience in the hospitality, tourism, aviation and events Industry: Responses to COVID–19 and lessons learned. *Journal on Tourism & Sustainability., 4*(1), 82–93.

Sealy, W. (2023). Working Paper: The good, the bad & the ugly of event management initiatives in a regional business school.

Seasons, F. (2022). *Jobs at Four Seasons LTD*. https://jobs.fourseasons.com/home/working-at-fs/

Seger-Guttmann, T., & Medler-Liraz, H. (2018). Hospitality service employees' flirting displays: Emotional labor or commercial friendship? *International Journal of Hospitality Management, 73*, 102–107. doi:10.1016/j.ijhm.2018.02.008

Testa, M. R., & Sipe, L. (2012). Service-leadership competencies for hospitality and tourism management. *International Journal of Hospitality Management, 31*(3), 648–658. doi:10.1016/j.ijhm.2011.08.009

Tracy, B., & Swart, M. P. (2019). Training and development research in tourism and hospitality: A perspective paper. *Tourism Review, 75*(1), 256–259. doi:10.1108/TR-06-2019-0206

Wang, C.-J. (2020). Managing emotional labour for service quality: A cross-level analysis among hotel employees. *International Journal of Hospitality Management, 88*, 102396. doi:10.1016/j.ijhm.2019.102396

Zlatanov, S., & Popesku, J. (2019). Current Applications of Artificial Intelligence in Tourism and Hospitality. Paper presented at Sinteza 2019 - International Scientific Conference on Information Technology and Data Related Research. doi:10.15308/Sinteza-2019-84-90

Chapter 4
Role of Knowledge in Creativity and Innovation in the Service Sector:
An Example From the Banking Sector in a Developing Nation

Salinda Weerasinghe
Queensland University of Technology, Australia

Darshana Sedera
Southern Cross University, Australia

ABSTRACT

The present study aimed to explore the role of knowledge management practices in promoting creativity and innovation in the service sector concerning the banking industry. The study assumes knowledge as an intangible internal asset and innovation as a way to develop sustainable strategic capabilities that are difficult to imitate. This quantitative study tested five proposed hypotheses on 437 responses collected from banking employees through the PLS-SEM method. Light indicated that knowledge sharing, application, and protection directly contributed to firm innovation, whereas knowledge creation encounters complete mediation through employee creativity. The study combines RBV and KM perspectives in developing long-term strategic capability and strengthens the evolutionary view of economists that new knowledge is based on existing knowledge, conforming the effect of knowledge protection to knowledge sharing. The study develops a knowledge management framework incorporating working/operational knowledge protection as one of the main dimensions of the knowledge management process.

DOI: 10.4018/978-1-6684-6732-9.ch004

Copyright © 2023, IGI Global. Copying or distributing in print or electronic forms without written permission of IGI Global is prohibited.

INTRODUCTION

Trust, solidarity, and scale economics have always been the defining characteristics of the good banking business (Central Bank of Sri Lanka, 2020). The banking industry was relatively quiet, and the market was incredibly steady at its beginnings, possibly up until the beginning of the 20th century, therefore, there was little competition among the existing rivals (Melewar & Navalekar, 2002). This environment has been turned upside down by globalization and ICT development, and the banking industry structure has also made them more vulnerable to new international competition. As a result of the sanctions and ongoing financial restructuring requirements brought on by the worldwide shifts, banking management has grown extremely complicated, and financial compliances have become crucial. Melewar & Navalekar, (2002) observed that many financial institutes that were resilient long before are struggling now to survive due to the loss of their identity in business competencies. So, developing long-term competencies has become a challenge for many banks. Many extent studies claim that creativity and innovation are two close connected groundbreaking concepts on which firms' strategic capabilities develop and that work together for excellent business performance, especially in industries like banking and finance due to their high volatility and competitiveness (Chaubey & Sahoo, 2021; Saulais & Ermine, 2012; S. Zhao et al., 2020). With that, many firms questioned how firms develop creativity and innovation competencies that are unable to copy, difficult to imitate, and that ensure long-term stability and business resilience.

These questions are at the heart of resource base theory and are the focus of the study. Past literature shows that creativity and innovation have long been connected to knowledge. We defined knowledge as a dynamic human activity of defending one's convictions on reality (Nonaka, 1994). Bulut et al., (2022); Yang & Rui, (2009) stated that knowledge is the heart of creativity and innovation. So, many historical studies argue that firm innovation would not happen or significantly delayed without the firm knowledge (Weerasinghe & Dedunu, 2020b, 2020a). Hence, firm knowledge is recognized as a strategic asset and, a core and dynamic competency that led to competitiveness, value creation, creativity, and innovation (Geisler & Wickramasinghe, 2015; Grant, 1991; Gurteen, 1998; Y. Liu et al., 2019; Muthuveloo et al., 2017). However, Gurteen, (1998) pointed out the main challenge we confront today is to build effective systems that support us in making knowledge productive. Hence, the study attempted to explore how proper knowledge management improves employee creativity and firm innovation.

Many studies have contributed significantly to the literature exploring business firms' knowledge, creativity, and innovation. See knowledge, creativity & innovation (Astuti et al., 2022; Gurteen, 1998); creativity and knowledge management (Saulais & Ermine, 2012); knowledge collecting behavior and firm creativity (Giustiniano et al., 2016); knowledge and product creativity (Yang & Rui, 2009). (Martins et al., 2004) discuss cultural models (D. Liu & Zeinaly, 2020) role of IT, and the artificial intelligence approach (Botega & da Silva, 2020) to stimulate firm innovation and creativity. What has been learned from the careful observation of the above studies is that all have discussed knowledge, creativity, and innovation concerning manufacturing industries, however, Bulut et al., (2022) argue that examining creativity and innovation in the service sector compared to the manufacturing sector is difficult due to the fact that first, measuring the output of innovation with an economical method, in the service sector, is difficult and vague, second service sector innovation depends less on technology, then lower formality but high incrementality. Further, existing studies do not provide a clear picture of what knowledge management functions (knowledge creation (KC), sharing (KS), application (KA), and protection(KP)) are important in promoting the creativity and innovation of firms, especially in the service sector, therefore the present study proposes to explore the role of knowledge management process in promoting creativity and innovation in the service sector concerning the banking industry which one of the vibrant and volatile industries in Sri Lanka.

We used resource base theory to explain how creativity and innovation become a firm's internal intangible resources, and how that intangible resource base develops long-term distinctive capabilities. Second, we used the knowledge management perspective to explain how knowledge management practices facilitate firms' creativity and innovation. Thus, we integrate two theories to show how the interplay of these competitive theories develops long-term sustainability. We found that KC continuously happens in banks through staff training, experiments, research & development, and networking with external institutes. We illustres how the continuous sharing of knowledge makes employees update and develop a strong platform for innovation. Moreover, we found the banks which update their SOPs/ work manual/ working process regularly, applies previously learned lessons, replicate successful experiments, make use of employee's knowledge can create a solid foundation for internal research and firm innovation. Further, we could confirm the evolutionary theory of innovation which states that new knowledge is based on existing knowledge. Accordingly, the present study mainly significance to the policy makers and industry professionals to understand how knowledge management support firm innovation especially in the banking sector, therefore the paper will be a groundwork for the many future studies that aim to explore contrition of knowledge practices to firm performance. Thus, the current study targets academics, professionals and practitioners who have innate interest about this management concepts.

THEORY AND HYPOTHESIS

The study combines the Resource Based View (RBV) and Knowledge Management Perspective to explore the role of knowledge to promote creativity and innovation. According to the RBV, firm resources are unevenly dispersed and imperfectly transportable among firms, therefore the resource difference among firms is obvious (Helfat & Peteraf, 2003). As a result, the distinctive position created by firms in relation to their rivals is founded on complex firm-specific resources (Caiazza et al., 2015), which includes all tangible and intangible assets tied to the firm semi-permanently (Wernerfelt, 1984). Muñoz-Pascual & Galende, (2017) argues that intangible resources are most significant from a competitive standpoint than other forms of resources as they are invisible and challenging to duplicate. In the present knowledge era, knowledge-based competencies are now dominant as fixed and tangible assets no longer provide a sustainable foundation for completive advantage (Sharratt & Usoro, 2003). As per Barney, (1991), resources bring long-term competitive advantages when it possesses four key attributes; value, rare, inimitable, and organizational support. Figure 1 explains how these four key attributes support firm to develop sustainable competitive advantages.

Figure 1. Strategic capability

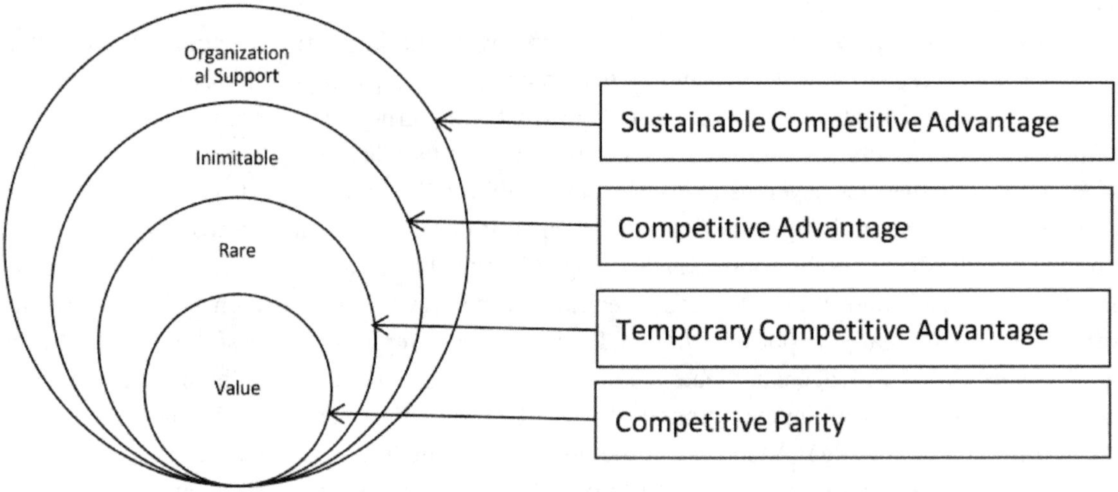

According to Johnson (2010), a resource only becomes valuable if it improves the firm's return or lowers its costs; nevertheless, it is unlikely to be a competitive advantage when it is readily accessible. If all firms possess a similar valuable resource base, the competitive base becomes equal and the firm's survival is threatened (Johnson et al., 2010). This competitive parity changes into a short competitive advantage when the firm's resource is distinctive and difficult for others to find (Riordan & Chris, 2006). The company gains a competitive edge when rivals recognize how expensive and difficult it is to copy, acquire, or substitute; this advantage only lasts as long as the company supports its continued growth and development (Johnson et al., 2010). Achieving a lasting competitive edge is fairly simple when all four of these characteristics support a firm's resource base (Riordan & Chris, 2006). But sustaining competitive advantage becomes a challenge in a networked environment where information is freely accessible and resources are shared. As a result, organizations pose a serious threat to their survival because any competitive advantage based on readily available, replicable resources would quickly become obsolete (Johnson et al., 2010). Creativity is a human talent that resides in the human body and develops with time through learning and experience. Innovation is the ability of the firm to operationalize the creative ideas of an employee for business purposes. In most cases, an ultimate artifact of innovation is a completely new, modified product/service/process or anything that strengthens the firm competitive base. The strategies that depend on these capabilities are worthwhile, and on the other hand it will be difficult for rivals to copy and duplicate (Riordan & Chris, 2006). Thus, as emphasized in RBV, creativity, and innovation are the strategic capabilities that embody all four characteristics and constitute an organization's competitive basis (Elidemir et al., 2020).

CREATIVITY AND INNOVATION

Creativity can be defined, in a broader sense, as a person's ability to develop and use naval ideas, concepts, and work methods as a solution to a current problem or one that arises in the future (Amabile, 1983; Elidemir et al., 2020; Srikalimah et al., 2020). This is an inner gifted skill of employees that enables them to think creatively to propose an inspired solution for a problem that everybody wants to address. Three key elements of creativity are included in Amabile's (1996) componential theory of individual creativity: expertise, creative thinking ability, and intrinsic task motivation. The theory states that people are most creative when their skills intersect with their deepest, most passionate intrinsic interests (T. M., Amabile, 1996). This heuristic process is difficult to observe and understand but can be practiced and developed in long run. The idea generation is the first step of the creative process which happens in all facets of life as well as in every level and dimension of a firm (Ferreira et al., 2020), therefore Gurteen, (1998) argues that creativity is the responsibility of every individual of the firm. However, Elidemir et al., (2020); Florida & Mellander, (2010) claims that the amount of creativity present in a person or firm is heterogeneous since it is not perfectly associated with formal education and is influenced by several factors like individual and organization. Individual factors that inspire creativity include personality, emotional intelligence, technical expertise, risk-taking ability, and knowledge (Amabile, 1996). In contrast, organizational factors include firm culture, climate for innovation, and team information sharing (Lenka & Gupta, 2020).

Innovation is introducing something new or converting creative ideas into a commercial product or service using the unique and core competencies of the firm (Inauen & Schenker-Wicki, 2011). It's about doing something new or discovering novel approaches to old problems. The evolutionist economic perspective holds that innovation does not come about by chance and that organizations do not spontaneously come up with ideas. They say that new knowledge is governed by prior knowledge, leading to innovation (Coombs & Hull, 1998). Another hand dynamic capability view of innovation states that a firm strategic capability generates new and combined competencies which in turn generate innovation (Saulais & Ermine, 2012). Considering all, innovation can be defined as a conscience process of redesigning, redeveloping existing, or completely new products, processes, services, or models that are commercially viable using creative ideas, within the firms to deliver greater value to the customer while protecting the existing competitive base of the firm. Accordingly, innovation is a process that often begins with the generation of ideas and concludes with their adoption or commercialization (Klein & Sorra, 1996; Oke et al., 2009). Idea generation starts with employee creativity (Lenka & Gupta, 2020; S. Zhao et al., 2020). Employee creativity is where fresh ideas first emerge because people are the ones who have them in their minds (Mumford & Gustafson, 1998). Therefore, many studies claimed that innovative business requires creative individuals (Roffe, 1999). Organizational traits such as firm knowledge management, absorptive capability, and information technology are found to be internal factors that influence an organization's performance in terms of innovation, whereas regional culture and government policies were discovered to be external exogenous factors of innovation (Ganguly et al., 2019; D. Liu & Zeinaly, 2020; S. Zhao et al., 2020). Many previous pieces of literature argue that knowledge is the most important resource for firm innovation, inseparable from effective knowledge management (S. Zhao et al., 2020).

KNOWLEDGE MANAGEMENT

According to the knowledge management theory, knowledge is a dynamic human activity of defending one's convictions on reality (Nonaka, 1994). It is a very personal and invisible asset that embodies the skills, competencies, intuition, commitment (Pathirage et al., 2007), and combined efforts of networks and partnerships (Smith, 2001). Knowledge links to humans and is obtained from formal education and personal experience in specific settings, therefore it may be unique to the individual and cannot reside outside the human brain (Harrington et al., 2019; López-Torres et al., 2019). This knowledge can traditionally be classified as general, domain-specific, and procedural knowledge (Yang & Rui, 2009), personal, shared, and the public; hard and soft; internal and external; foreground and background (Pathirage et al., 2007) tacit and explicit (Nonaka, 1994). The tacit and explicit remain the most common classification of knowledge (Gamble, 2020). The firm must develop the necessary knowledge internally or acquire it externally (Alavi & Leidner, 2001). This knowledge acquisition boosts the company's knowledge stock and gives a good basis for making decisions. Most researchers believe knowledge sharing is the most significant antecedent for continuous innovation and success (D. Liu & Zeinaly, 2020). Sharing of knowledge update the employee's current thinking and provide a new base for thinking and innovation. However many previous studies argued that knowledge is useless until applied properly, so they explained that firms should have room to practice and apply generated knowledge (Kim & Lee, 2010). The knowledge is reusable and replicated for similar problems, therefore knowledge sustainability is important for creativity and innovation. Considering all facets of knowledge, we defined knowledge management as an intentional and systematic process of creating, sharing, applying, and protecting knowledge (Batista et al., 2019; Harrington et al., 2019; López-Torres et al., 2019). Accordingly knowledge management has four main dimensions: knowledge creation, knowledge sharing, application, and protection.

Knowledge Management, Employee Creativity, and Firm Innovation

Concerning empirical studies, Yang & Rui, (2009) explored how knowledge acquisition, dissemination, and innovation affect new product creativity in China. They found a U relationship between knowledge acquisition and new product creativity whereas an inverted U shapes the relationship between knowledge dissemination and product creativity. The study also found that the creativity of new products is improving continuously with the increasing knowledge innovation. How innovation happens in pharmaceticular firms in India was investigated by Lenka & Gupta, (2020). The study found that employees' proactive personality, emotional intelligence, trust, and team knowledge sharing improve their learning which fosters corporate innovation. Further, it also discovered that innovation implementation in firms is improved by team creativity. The impact of knowledge-sharing direction on firm innovation in China was explored by S. Zhao et al., (2020), and the finding was interesting. According to the result, inbound knowledge sharing indirectly promotes firm innovation while outbound knowledge sharing does it directly. In addition, the study found that absorptive capacity and individual creativity have direct and significant impacts on organizational innovation performance. In particular, Spanish innovative companies, Muñoz-Pascual & Galende, (2017) found that knowledge and motivation management practices encourage creative employee behavior. The results further indicated that once employees have reached a medium-high level of extrinsic motivation, creativity will be affected solely by intrinsic motivation. Auernhammer & Hall, (2014) identified openness to change, encouraging new and/or unusual ideas, value-free communication, tolerating mistakes, intrinsically motivated staff, and leader support as necessary to nurture an environment conducive to knowledge creation, creativity, and innovation. In addition to that, the study found three main determinants that underpin knowledge creation and creativity: (1) structured space that creates expertise and experience for individuals while working in routine; (2) individuals' propensity to experiment with ideas, even at the risk of failure, (3) authorized and dedicated space designated specifically for individuals to explore new ideas. A systematic review conducted by (Castaneda & Cuellar, 2020) found dialogue as the main instrument that converts knowledge into innovation. Also, the review proved knowledge is exchanged to foster innovation. (Ganguly et al., 2019) found that both tacit knowledge sharing and the quality of knowledge are positively associated with innovation capability whereas (López-Cabarcos et al., 2020) found that both implicit and explicit knowledge transforms into profit directly through product innovation. Giustiniano et al., (2016) found in their study of knowledge collecting behavior on firm creativity that individuals' orientation toward learning from others significantly enhances organizational creativity. This relationship is negatively moderated by ICT usage.

HYPOTHESES DEVELOPMENT

Knowledge Creation and Employee Creativity and Innovation

Knowledge creation (KC) is the development and acquisition of necessary knowledge (Alavi & Leidner, 2001). Firm KC starts with the individual, and individual knowledge sharing provides the basis for KC (Chen, Xu, and Zhai, 2019). KC includes knowledge capturing and knowledge acquisition. Individuals acquire outside knowledge from external sources and capture inside knowledge through observation, training, teamwork, and interactions (Ting et al., 2021b). Extant studies state that KC provides a new baseline for firm creativity and innovation (Zhang & Zhang, 2018). The study believes that knowledge creation and employee creativity go together because both concepts intend to generate a novel knowledge/idea that has not been articulated earlier. The basement of innovation is new knowledge and idea generation, without this basement innovation is challenging. (Bergendahl & Magnusson, 2015) states that KC requires different types of collaboration and networking which expose employees to different experiences that lead to the generation of new ideas and provide the foundation for firm innovation. However Richtnér & Åhlström, (2010) states that top management control over explicit knowledge hampers KC and discourages innovation. Thus, the study believes that the continuous KC updates the existing stock of firm knowledge and employee current thinking necessary for creativity and innovation in a competitive business environment. Accordingly, study hypotheses that;

H1: Continuous knowledge creation stimulates employees' creative cells by encourading employee thinking patterns; then improves firm innovation.

Knowledge Sharing and Employee Creativity and Innovation

Knowledge sharing (KS) is social interaction (Fait et al. 2019), in which people exchange knowledge, skills, experiences, and practices. KS may be either between two humans or contribution to, extraction from a knowledge repository (Holsapple & Joshi, 2004). The objective of KS is to ensure the right knowledge is available to the right person at the right time to perform the right task. S. Zhao et al., (2020) claimed that KS facilitates employees to search for new and unknown knowledge, which avoids work duplication and reduces time, energy, and costs of employee innovation. D. Liu & Zeinaly, (2020) believes KS is a good basis for employees to obtain unique knowledge and insights which strengthen their creative mindest and innovative spirit. Many previous studies believe that inter-organizational KS helps firms capture strategic knowledge required to sharpen employee creativity and firm innovation (S. Zhao et al., 2020). According to the evolutionist view, innovation does not happen by accident and existing knowledge governs new knowledge, which encourages creativity and innovation. Accordingly, the study claims that KS lays foundation to the innovation exchanging new knowledge among its employees.

Further, the study believes that KS across firms enable them to develop competencies and generate new knowledge required for product, service, and process innovation. It enables firms to respond quickly to changes and develop innovative capabilities and thus provide a stage for continuous development and innovation. Accordingly, study hypotheses that;

H2: Continuous sharing of knowledge makes employees update and develops a strong platform required for firm innovation.

Knowledge Application and Employee Creativity and Innovation

Knowledge application (KA) is a process wherein knowledge is applied to solve problems, produce novel ideas, develop new products, and improve firm performance (Birasnav, 2014). According to Haamann & Basten, (2019), KA includes four steps: problem analysis, identification of source and search, appraisal, and decision and application. KA focus on enhancing company operations and bringing additional value to corporate activities. Knowledge is worth more when it is used to produce goods or provide services and a firm may challenge sustaining its advantage when new knowledge is not properly applied, thus firm performance frequently relies less on knowledge itself and more on the capacity to apply knowledge to practical application (Kim&Lee,2010). In light of this, the study assumes that creativity itself does not make any sense and innovation is required to make it valuable. Accordingly, KA provides a platform for innovation and makes it tested again and again, thus it encourages continuous creativity and innovation of employees. Based on the aforementioned theoretical underpinning, study hypotheses that;

H3: KA develops a strong platform for firm innovation

Knowledge Protection Employee Creativity and Innovation

Knowledge protection (KP) is the preservation of a firm operational knowledge for the future generation, and it can be done either formally or informally (Olander et al. 2014). The two most frequently employed formal KP mechanisms are intellectual property rights (IPRs) and contracts. IPRs include contracts, patents, trademarks, and copyright. Informal knowledge protection like secrecy takes place when IPR fails to protect knowledge. Firms tend to protect their oprational knowledge for two reasons: one, it contributes to maintaining the distinctiveness of the knowledge, and two, it enables the parties to transfer knowledge from one generation to the next (Olander et al., 2014). According to the evolutionist economic point of view, innovation is governed by new knowledge powered by existing knowledge. Based on that premise, we believe that safeguarding current operational knowledge encourages the creation of new knowledge, which fosters innovation. Thus, the study hypothesis that;

H4: Safeguarding current knowledge encourages new knowledge creation that leads to firm innovation

Creativity and Innovation

Creativity and innovation have a long-lasting unbreakable relationship it can easily be understood in the view of people about these concepts. Heap, (1989) defined creativity as "the synthesis of new ideas and concepts…where innovation is the implementation of creativity". Hence, many studies believed that these are two inseparable concepts and one does not exist without another (Chaubey & Sahoo, 2021). Recent studies by Ferreira et al., (2020); Lenka & Gupta, (2020) claimed that creativity facilitates firm innovation, (Lee et al., 2019; S. Zhao et al., 2020) and innovational and firm performance. Considering these theoretical and empirical insights the study assumes that employee creativity leads to making novel output that can be commercialized easily. Accordingly, the study hypothesis that;

H5: Employee creativity facilitates firm innovation

METHODOLOGY

Study Context Population and the Sample

The study is based on the banking industry because banks are knowledge-intensive firms, which offer an excellent environment for research on knowledge management. Knowledge-intensive means extend to which knowledge is a key factor in production (Coff, 2003). Knowledge-intensive businesses have significant R&D expenditures or a high reliance on educated or skilled labor (Yang & Rui, 2009). The Sri Lankan banking sector is one of the excellent examples where the majority of educated employees work and the minimum education level for state and private banks is Advanced Level qualification. Further, most banks either maintain their in-house R&D section or join university or external research institutes for product and service development. At present, the Sri Lankan banking industry in Sri Lanka comprises 26 Licensed Commercial Banks (13 domestic banks and 13 foreign banks) and 7 Licensed Specialized banks (1 saving bank, 2 housing financial institutions, a regional development bank, and 3 Licensed Specialized banks). All employees who currently work in the aforesaid category of the bank were included in the study population. The study mainly targeted (43414) staff who are employed at 10 licensed commercial banks (appendix: 01) due to the operation difficulty of reaching some commercial banks which operate in the capital city and licensed specialized banks that are dispersed across special regional areas of the country. The sample size was determined considering several factors. First, as per Morgan's table study should include 382+ responses to the samples as the target population exceeds forty thousand. Second, a 70-sample size was required based on the (PLS-SEM) sample size recommendation matrix (Sarstedt et al., 2017). The study distributed an online questionnaire among the respondent through the WhatsApp group of banking employees, with respondents expecting at least 386 completed responses. The questionnaire was distributed during 1st week of September. After a week, around 247 responses were received and the first reminder was given one week later, followed by a second reminder after two days.

Measurement of Variables

The study measured knowledge management through 16 items: 04 items each for KC, KS, KA, and KP. The scales produced by Kim & Lee, (2010); D. Liu & Zeinaly, (2020); Manhart & Thalmann, (2015); Olander et al., (2014); Ting et al., (2021a); Yang & Rui, (2009); S. Zhao et al., (2020) served as the basis for the development of these 16 items. Further, the study deployed scales created by Kim & Lee, (2010); Lee et al., (2019); Zhou & George, (2001); Chen et al. (2012), to create four questions to assess the creativity of employees. The final variable, innovation was measured through five items, and the scale was developed on scales of Koys and De Cotiis, (1991); Ritter et al, (2005); D. Liu & Zeinaly, (2020); Y. Zhao & Ko, (2020). All the items were rated on a seven-point scale. All predictor variables (KC, KS, KA, and KP) ranged from 1, "strongly disagree", to 7, "strongly agree" and criterion variables ranged from 1 'never' to 7, 'very often. The study developed the above scales considering Sri Lankan culture, the banking industry, and the target audience, which was carefully scrutinized by two expert academics. Upon their recommendation, the list of questions was finalized. The questionnaire consisted of 32 questions and the number was reasonable to avoid responses fatigue (Dassanayaka et al., 2022).

Control Variables

Employee creativity, innovation, and knowledge management practices are influenced by several factors (Cao et al., 2021; Giustiniano et al., 2016; Lee et al., 2019), so to rule out alternative explanations, the study-controlled employee gender (0=male, 1=female) years of experience, education level (1=A/L, 2= First degree, 3 = Higher), managerial role (1=no, 2=yes). The study additionally adjusted for employees' job autonomy (measured by two- items taken from Hackman and Oldham, 1974) as literature frequently emphasizes the role played by autonomy in fostering creativity (D. Liu et al., 2011).

Common Method Bias Treatment

The study minimized the common method bias problem in several ways. As per Podsakoff et al., (2003), the study first distinguished the measurement scale of predictor and criterion variables. Second, protected respondents' anonymity and reduced evaluation apprehension by removing questions that includes one correct answer. Third, improved the scales by (a) defining ambiguous or unfamiliar terms; (b) avoiding vague concepts (c) keeping questions simple, specific, and concise; (d) avoiding double-barreled questions; (e) avoiding complicated syntax.

DATA ANALYSIS

Data

The model estimation draws on data from banking employees. A total of 476 respondents rated their preferences on a 7 Likert scale. As indicated in figure 01, the sample size is technically large enough to estimate the PLS model with the complex PLS path model. The data set included 27 patterned questions and 12 incomplete questions. Incomplete and patterned questionnaires were excluded from the analysis, whereas questionnaires with few missing values were considered. Missing values were treated with the mean of responses (Weerasinghe & Dedunu, 2020b). Finally, the study ended up with 438 completed responses. The box plot diagnostics by means of IBM SPSS revealed no outlier observations. The skewness and the excess kurtosis values ranged between -1 and +1 with slight exceptions of KP_2 and F_2. This degree of non-normality of data in two indicators is not a critical issue (Sarstedt et al., 2017).

The essential information about the sample is shown in Table 1. The findings show that Bank of Ceylon (21.7%) and Peoples Bank (19.5%) obtained the greatest responses, respectively. HSBC Bank received the lowest response rates. Additionally, it was noticed that the majority of replies (66.1%) were between the ages of 26 and 35 and held a bachelor's degree (38.5%). 59 percent of the sample consisted of non-managerial workers, most of whom were male (57.9%).

Table 1. Sample profile

Description	Frequency	%	Description	Frequency	%
Bank			**Age**		
Bank of Ceylon	95	21.7	< 25	24	5.5
Peoples Bank	85	19.5	26-35	289	66.1
National Saving Bank	43	9.8	36-45	119	27.2
Sampath Bank	45	10.3	46-55	5	1.1
Commercial Bank	47	10.8	> 55	0	0
Hatton National Bank	49	11.2			
Seylan Bank	24	5.5	**Education Level**		
HSBC	7	1.6	Up to A/L	163	37.3
National Development Bank	24	5.5	Bachelor Degree	168	38.4
Pan Asia Bank	18	4.1	Masters or Higher	106	24.3
Gender			**Job Category**		
Male	253	57.9	Managerial	179	41
Female	184	42.1	Non-Managerial	258	59
A/L is the highest examination conducted by the Sri Lankan government to select candidates for university entrance					

Measurement Model Evaluation

PLS algorithm steps were deployed to evaluate the measurement model in stage one. All the constructs were measured reflectively. The initial run detected some potentially problematic measures having low item loadings below 0.7 [KC_1 (0.649), KP_4(0.669), I_1(0.539)], but item loading of (KC_1) and (KP_4) were more towards 0.7, therefore the study decided to remove item (I_1) which displayed item loading less than 0.6 from the analysis. Accordingly, all items exhibit a sufficient level of reliability. Cronbach's alpha values and composite reliability values were found within the threshold range of 0.7-0.95 (Table 2), and the AVE value was above the cut-off point (0.5), confirming the internal consistency, reliability, and convergent validity of the measurement model.

Table 2. Item loading, cross loading, convergent validity

Variable	Indicators	Descriptive		Convergent Validity		Internal Consistency	
		Mean	Overall Mean	Outer Loadings	AVE	Composite Reliability	Cronbach Alpha
	Range			>0.7	>0.5	>0.7	0.7 - 0.95
Knowledge Creation	KC_1	5.078	5.015	0.649	0.544	0.730	0.719
	KC_2	5.199		0.770			
	KC_3	4.725		0.734			
	KC_4	5.034		0.790			
Knowledge Sharing	KS_1	5.201	5.385	0.760	0.638	0.830	0.813
	KS_2	5.325		0.790			
	KS_3	5.291		0.820			
	KS_4	5.497		0.822			
Knowledge Application	KA_1	5.330	5.542	0.840	0.738	0.884	0.882
	KA_2	5.533		0.856			
	KA_3	5.556		0.866			
	KA_4	5.751		0.875			
Knowledge Protection	KP_1	5.842	5.551	0.737	0.572	0.771	0.753
	KP_2	5.693		0.807			
	KP_3	5.080		0.805			
	KP_4	5.590		0.669			
Creativity	C_1	5.384	5.378	0.737	0.578	0.779	0.845
	C_2	5.451		0.824			
	C_3	5.270		0.739			
	C_4	5.410		0.738			
Innovation	I_1		5.722	0.539**	0.582	0.760	0.758
	I_2	5.577		0.709			
	I_3	5.588		0.720			
	I_4	5.773		0.803			
	I_5	5.952		0.814			
Job Flexibility	F_1	5.499	5.573	0.949	0.912	0.914	0.904
	F_2	5.648		0.961			

**the item is more relevant to the measure creativity but the same item is can be best used for measuring innovation too. As the Item loading exceeds its cross loading, the item kept as it is.*
***Removed from the analysis*

Item cross-loadings, the confidence intervals of the HTMT, and the Fornell-Larcker criterion were used to assess the discriminant validity. As indicated in Table 3, the indicator's outer loadings on each construct are higher than its cross-loadings with other constructs except C_2. Table 4 indicated the Forner Larcker Criterion that demonstrates that the square root of each construct's AVE is greater than its highest correlation with any other construct. Accordingly, the discriminant validity of the measurement model was established with all the criteria satisfied.

Table 3. Item loading and cross loading

Variables	Knowledge Creation	Knowledge Sharing	Knowledge Application	Knowledge Protection	Creativity	Innovation	Job Flexibility
KC_1	**0.647**	0.392	0.278	0.257	0.473	0.470	0.249
KC_2	**0.771**	0.574	0.381	0.395	0.466	0.507	0.283
KC_3	**0.734**	0.436	0.391	0.336	0.483	0.491	0.437
KC_4	**0.791**	0.410	0.491	0.425	0.594	0.612	0.349
KS_1	0.586	**0.759**	0.332	0.351	0.538	0.486	0.311
KS_2	0.413	**0.797**	0.313	0.264	0.383	0.460	0.280
KS_3	0.503	**0.821**	0.390	0.309	0.464	0.583	0.292
KS_4	0.461	**0.818**	0.445	0.296	0.488	0.657	0.360
KA_1	0.414	0.415	**0.845**	0.318	0.477	0.571	0.361
KA_2	0.482	0.451	**0.852**	0.310	0.452	0.546	0.274
KA_3	0.460	0.376	**0.866**	0.297	0.365	0.496	0.346
KA_4	0.469	0.374	**0.873**	0.319	0.460	0.568	0.348
KP_1	0.198	0.161	0.165	**0.730**	0.296	0.258	0.304
KP_2	0.488	0.347	0.308	**0.812**	0.354	0.390	0.364
KP_3	0.368	0.352	0.373	**0.804**	0.275	0.382	0.397
KP_4	0.331	0.232	0.200	**0.668**	0.318	0.322	0.356
C_1	0.402	0.364	0.175	0.200	**0.738**	0.481	0.224
C_2	0.625	0.581	0.515	0.431	**0.822**	**0.728***	0.431
C_3	0.551	0.423	0.347	0.272	**0.741**	0.544	0.395
C_4	0.471	0.372	0.463	0.307	**0.738**	0.497	0.367
I_1	0.463	0.297	0.468	0.172	0.461	**0.539****	0.247
I_2	0.546	0.463	0.507	0.506	0.607	**0.708**	0.369
I_3	0.433	0.536	0.458	0.286	0.520	**0.706**	0.418
I_4	0.536	0.567	0.458	0.264	0.565	**0.785**	0.459
I_5	0.543	0.571	0.389	0.365	0.526	**0.784**	0.433
F_1	0.410	0.343	0.344	0.447	0.420	0.499	**0.949**
F_2	0.444	0.402	0.392	0.458	0.490	0.548	**0.960**

**the item is more relevant to the measure creativity but the same item is can be best used for measuring innovation too. As the Item loading exceeds its cross loading, the item kept as it is.*
***Removed from the analysis*

Table 4. Fornell larcker criterion

Variables	KC	KS	KA	KP	CR	IN	JF
KC	**0.738**						
KS	0.611	**0.799**					
KA	0.531	0.471	**0.859**				
KP	0.485	0.381	0.363	**0.756**			
CR	0.688	0.587	0.513	0.413	**0.760**		
IN	0.710	0.696	0.637	0.459	0.756	**0.710**	
JF	0.448	0.392	0.387	0.474	0.479	0.550	**0.955**
KC: Knowledge Creation, KS: Knowledge Sharing, KA: Knowledge Application; KP: Knowledge Protection, CR: Creativity, IN: Innovation, JF: Job Flexibility							

Structural Model: Stage Two

PLS runs the structural model with 5000 bootstrapping. The structural model (indicated in figure 02) was assessed for its predictive capabilities of the model through the coefficient of determination (R2), cross-validated redundancy (Q2), and path coefficients (Sarstedt et al., 2017). The first study checked the VIF values of the structural model to diagnose the collinearity problem, however, VIF values were well below the threshold value (5) and exhibited no collinearity problem in the model. We started the key target variable from the right-hand side of the model (innovation) in figure 2. The construct innovation has the strongest effect on KS (0.278), followed by CR (0.237), KA (0.164), and KP (0.090), while the effect of KC(0.057) is very close to zero. The bootstrapping result substantiates that the effect of KS, CR, KA, and KP is significant while KC does not have a significant effect at a 95% confidence level. Further, the study controls the effect of age, gender, educational level, experience, job category and flexibility, from which age, experience and flexibility have significant effects on employee innovation. The study also found that the model explains 75.2% of innovation's variance (i.e., $R^2 = 0.752$), which is relatively high.

Figure 2. Structural model

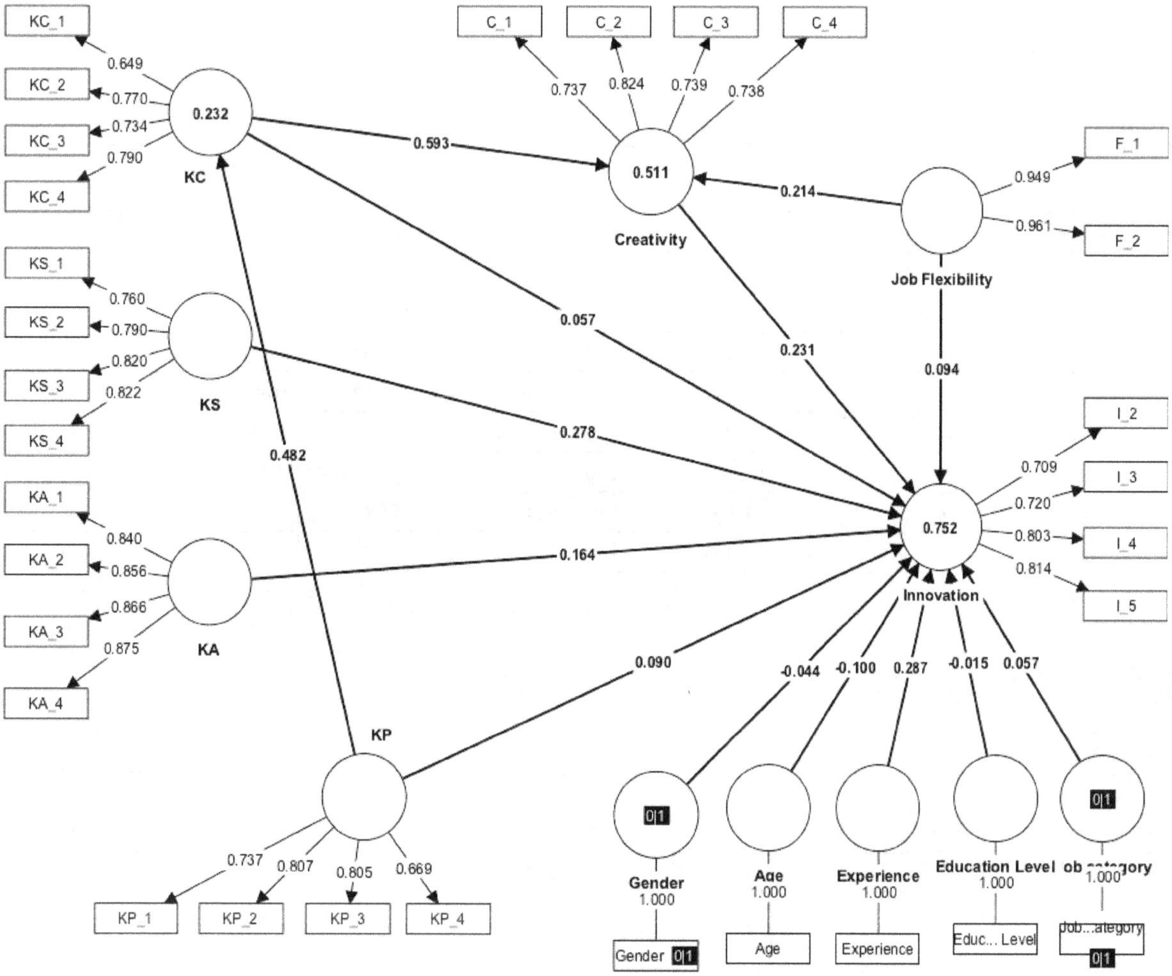

When analyzing the key predictor of creativity, which has a substantial R^2 of 0.511, the study finds that KS has the strongest significant effect (0.593) followed by the controlled variable JF (0.214), which is statistically significant at a 95% confidence level. KC has a value of 0.232, R^2 is clearly lower, but still satisfactory, considering that KP predicts the KC in the model. Analyzing the exogenous constructs' indirect effect on innovation, the study finds that KC (0.136), KP (0.093), and JF (0.049) have a significant indirect effect on innovation. Moreover, the study found specific indirect effects to the innovation along KP -> KC -> Creativity -> Innovation (0.065), KC -> Creativity -> Innovation (0.136), KP -> KC -> Creativity (0.286), JF -> Creativity -> Innovation (0.049). However, the indirect effect of KP -> KC -> Innovation (0.027) was not statistically significant.

The table 5 shows the f2 effect sizes. Relatively high effect sizes occur for the relationships KC -> Creativity (0.573), KP -> KC (0.308), KA -> Innovation (0.125), KS -> Innovation (123), KS->Innovation (0.123), Experience -> Innovation (0.163). These relationships have path coefficient of 0.20 or higher. Interestingly, the relationship between JF and creativity has 0.291 path coefficient but its effect size report 0.074, a relatively low effect. All other effect sizes in the structural model are week and perhaps insignificant.

Table 5. Path coefficient and effect size

Path	Path Coefficent	95% CI	*F2*	T statistics (|O/ STDEV|)	P values
Age -> Innovation	-0.102	(-0.165, -0.041)	0.058	3.230	0.001
Creativity -> Innovation	0.229	(0.160, 0.298)	0.123	6.507	0.000
Education Level -> Innovation	-0.014	(-0.065, 0.036)	0.002	0.545	0.586
Experience -> Innovation	0.291	(0.222, 0.359)	0.162	8.445	0.000
Gender -> Innovation	-0.043	(-0.135, 0.061)	0.015	0.856	0.392
Job Flexibility -> Creativity	0.213	(0.128, 0.294)	0.074	5.089	0.000
Job Flexibility -> Innovation	0.097	(0.037, 0.160)	0.024	3.122	0.002
Job category -> Innovation	0.059	(-0.046, 0.161)	0.001	1.060	0.289
KA -> Innovation	0.163	(0.094, 0.226)	0.125	4.911	0.000
KC -> Creativity	0.593	(0.528, 0.668)	0.573	17.196	0.000
KC -> Innovation	0.056	(-0.030, 0.148)	0.019	1.258	0.208
KP -> Innovation	0.084	(0.029, 0.141)	0.009	2.966	0.003
KP -> KC	0.482	(0.391, 0.568)	0.308	10.406	0.000
KS -> Innovation	0.280	(0.202, 0.358)	0.123	7.147	0.000
KP -> KC -> Creativity -> Innovation*	0.065	(0.042, 0.092)		5.075	0.000
KC -> Creativity -> Innovation*	0.136	(0.092, 0.181)		6.039	0.000
KP -> KC -> Creativity*	0.286	(0.220, 0.346)		9.095	0.000
KP -> KC -> Innovation*	0.027	(-0.014, 0.070)		1.259	0.208
JF -> Creativity -> Innovation*	0.049	(0.029, 0.075)		4.190	0.000

**specific indirect effects*
Note: The values in the brackets represent the lower and the upper bounds of the 95% confidence interval

DISCUSSION AND CONCLUSION

The study aimed to explore the impact of knowledge management on employee creativity and firm innovation considering the responses from the banking industry. First, the study hypothesis that knowledge creation stimulates creative cells of employees then improves firm innovation. The study found that knowledge creation is an alive, continuous process that happens through staff training, experiments, research & development, and networking with external institutes. The knowledge obtained through these sources encourages employees to look at problems from fresh perspectives and develop creative solutions for prolems. The test result confirms the hypothesis and indicated that KC significantly affects on f innovation through employee creativity. Surpricingly, the study failed to diagnose the direct effect of KC to innovation. This full mediation confirms that continuous creation of knowledge changes employee thinking patterns that stimulate creative cells of employees that lead firm innovation. The insight aligned with many previous findings (Giustiniano et al., 2016; Muñoz-Pascual & Galende, 2017; Saulais &

Ermine, 2012). (Yang & Rui, 2009) explains that product creativity is linked to knowledge acquisition and the firms that acquire more knowledge poster product creativity. Second, the study found that KS becomes a routine practice in the bank in which seniors frequently impart their insights to youngers. Cross-departmental training/workshops and seminars are frequently organized in banks to share knowledge among staff. This continuous sharing of knowledge makes employees update and develops a strong platform to embrace new technology and introduce new products and services. As many previous studies emphasized (Ganguly et al., 2019; D. Liu & Zeinaly, 2020; Wu & Lin, 2013; S. Zhao et al., 2020), this study also confirms the effect of KS on firm innovation.

Knowledge is useless unless it is applied (Kim & Lee, 2010), hence the study explores KA at banks in Sri Lanka. The findings reveal that banks competitively use their knowledge for improvement. Moreover, the study found that banks practice updating their SOPs/ work manual/working process regularly, replicate successful knowledge applications in their branches, use employee's knowledge and customer feedback for product and service development, and apply lessons learned from previous problems. Such KA makes a solid foundation for research experiments, creative employee ideas, and innovation. Hence, banks with such practices foster their innovation. The structural model conforms a statistically significant effect of KA on firm innovation, accordingly, hypothesis three is accepted. Our findings support the findings of (Choi et al., 2010; Haamann & Basten, 2019; Kim & Lee, 2010; Nesheim et al., 2011). KP has received yet insignificant attention from scholars, thus the study aimed to uncover its validity establishing a hypothesis that KP leads to innovation. The study found that banks use several mechanisms to safeguard operational knowledge for future application. Documenting SOPs/work manuals/special decisions and computer system applications are popular mechanisms to safeguard operational knowledge. Our structural model also conforms this relationship; accordingly, the study accepts hypothesis four. Further, the study confirms the evolutionary theory of innovation which states new knowledge is based on existing knowledge identifing a significant effect of KP on KC. Finally, study tests the effect of creativity on innovation. As others mentioned, the effect is significant and positive; accordingly, the study confirms hypothesis five. This finding further strengthens the previous findings (Chaubey & Sahoo, 2021; Ferreira et al., 2020; Lee et al., 2019; Y. Zhao & Ko, 2020).

IMPLICATION AND RECOMMENDATION

The study makes a valuable contribution to the literature in several ways. First, this study explores KM to make employee creativity and firm innovation prosper, especially in developing countries' banking industry. We contribute to the literature conceptualizing KM by adding KP largely unnoticed in KM literature, as an essential step of KM. Most existing studies conceptualized KM without a KP component, so the study filled that literature gap. Second, the study contributed to the literature by developing a scale to measure KM, creativity, and innovation considering the nature of the banking industry, especially in developing countries. There are many validated scales but all of them are based on developed societies, therefore application of such scales is problematic. Accordingly, propose scale will be a good platform for existing and future researchers who intend to explore KM in developing nations. Third, the study expands the empirical literature by adding how KM practices contribute to employee innovation and firm creativity, especially in the banking industry in Sri Lanka.

Furthermore, study findings provide valuable managerial implications to improve firm innovation through KM practices. The study discovered that KS, KA, and KP directly influence the firm innovation process, thus study advises firm management to encourage senior staff to share their knowledge with junior staff, and facilitates cross-departmental training/workshops/seminars as much as possible within the firm if they want to update their existing stock of knowledge in the firms. The company must establish a proper method to collect employee insights and customer feedback for the ongoing improvement of products, processes, and services to apply knowledge to business work. Operational knowledge can be protected by converting them into SOPs and work manuals through computer aid applications. Thus, business innovation is easy for firms only if they strategically manage their knowledge for business work. Further, managers can expedite the firm innovation process through employee creativity that is backed by KC, so that employees should be encouraged for academic and professional development, external collaboration, research, and experiments to create competitive knowledge that the firm requires. On another hand, the firm should facilitate employees to make use their creative inflows for business improvements. Here, experiments should be allowed, errors need to be accepted and performance should be admired so that employees feel free to apply creative ideas that increase firm innovation.

LIMITATIONS AND FUTURE RESEARCH AREAS

Several factors limited the study. First, the current study examines the impact of KM on employee creativity and firm innovation limiting to the banking industry. Future research designs can focus on another vibrating industry to explore how KM, creativity, and innovation interact in that context. Second, the study developed a KM model incorporating the KP as one of the main dimensions, however, KP has not received much attention in previous studies, therefore additional investigations are required to advance our understanding of the phenomenon. Third, the cross-sectional nature of the research enables the analysis of KM, creativity and innovation at only one specific point in time, not their overall behavior over a period of time. Future research should focus on a longitudinal study.

REFERENCES

Alavi, M., & Leidner, D. E. (2001). Review: Knowledge Management and Knowledge Management Systems: Conceptual Foundations and Research Issues. *Management Information Systems Quarterly, 25*(1), 107. doi:10.2307/3250961

Amabile, T. M. (1983). The social psychology of creativity: A componential conceptualization. *Journal of Personality and Social Psychology, 45*(2), 357–376. doi:10.1037/0022-3514.45.2.357

Amabile, T. M. (1996). *Creativity in Context*. Westview Press.

Astuti, E. S., Arifin, Z., Wilopo, W., & Iqbal, M. (2022). Effects of trading partner relationships and knowledge complementarity on innovation performance. *Journal of Asia Business Studies, 16*(1), 53–79. doi:10.1108/JABS-01-2019-0012

Auernhammer, J., & Hall, H. (2014). Organizational culture in knowledge creation, creativity and innovation: Towards the Freiraum model. *Journal of Information Science, 40*(2), 154–166. doi:10.1177/0165551513508356

Barney, J. (1991). Firm Resources and Sustained Competitive Advantage. *Journal of Management, 17*(1), 99–120. doi:10.1177/014920639101700108

Batista, L., Dora, M., Toth, J., Molnár, A., Malekpoor, H., & Kumari, S. (2019). Knowledge management for food supply chain synergies–a maturity level analysis of SME companies. *Production Planning and Control, 30*(10–12), 995–1004. doi:10.1080/09537287.2019.1582104

Bergendahl, M., & Magnusson, M. (2015). Creating Ideas for Innovation: Effects of Organizational Distance on Knowledge Creation Processes. *Creativity and Innovation Management, 24*(1), 87–101. doi:10.1111/caim.12097

Birasnav, M. (2014). Knowledge management and organizational performance in the service industry: The role of transformational leadership beyond the effects of transactional leadership. *Journal of Business Research, 67*(8), 1622–1629. doi:10.1016/j.jbusres.2013.09.006

Botega, L. F. de C., & da Silva, J. C. (2020). An artificial intelligence approach to support knowledge management on the selection of creativity and innovation techniques. *Journal of Knowledge Management, 24*(5), 1107–1130. doi:10.1108/JKM-10-2019-0559

Bulut, C., Kaya, T., Mehta, A. M., & Danish, R. Q. (2022). Linking incremental and radical creativity to product and process innovation with organisational knowledge. *Journal of Manufacturing Technology Management, 33*(4), 763–784. doi:10.1108/JMTM-01-2021-0037

Caiazza, R., Richardson, A., & Audretsch, D. (2015). Knowledge effects on competitiveness: From firms to regional advantage. *The Journal of Technology Transfer, 40*(6), 899–909. doi:10.100710961-015-9425-8

Cao, X., Ali, A., Pitafi, A. H., Khan, A. N., & Waqas, M. (2021). A socio-technical system approach to knowledge creation and team performance: Evidence from China. *Information Technology & People, 34*(7), 1976–1996. doi:10.1108/ITP-10-2019-0536

Castaneda, D. I., & Cuellar, S. (2020). Knowledge sharing and innovation: A systematic review. *Knowledge and Process Management, 27*(3), 159–173. doi:10.1002/kpm.1637

Central Bank of Sri Lanka. (2020). Economic and Social Statistics. Central Bank Annual Report.

Chaubey, A., & Sahoo, C. K. (2021). The drivers of employee creativity and organizational innovation: A dynamic capability view. *Benchmarking*. Advance online publication. doi:10.1108/BIJ-06-2021-0316

Chen, Y., Xu, Y., & Zhai, Q. (2019). The knowledge management functions of corporate university and their evolution: Case studies of two Chinese corporate universities. *Journal of Knowledge Management, 23*(10), 2086–2112. doi:10.1108/JKM-04-2018-0228

Choi, L., Lee, & Yoo. (2010). The Impact of Information Technology and Transactive Memory Systems on Knowledge Sharing, Application, and Team Performance: A Field Study. *Management Information Systems Quarterly, 34*(4), 855. doi:10.2307/25750708

Coff, R. (2003). Bidding Wars Over R&D intensive firms: Knowledge, opportunism and the market for corporate control. *Academy of Management Journal, 46*(1), 74–85. doi:10.2307/30040677

Coombs, R., & Hull, R. (1998). Knowledge management practices and path-dependency in innovation. *Research Policy, 27*(3), 237–253. doi:10.1016/S0048-7333(98)00036-5

Dassanayaka, D. M. C., Weerasinghe, I. M. S., Dahanayaka, S. N. S., Dedunu, H. H., Athurupana, K., & Muthuweera, N. K. G. (2022). Academics' attitudes towards online education amidst the Covid-19 outbreak. *International Journal of Educational Management, 36*(5), 661–677. Advance online publication. doi:10.1108/IJEM-10-2021-0414

Elidemir, S. N., Ozturen, A., & Bayighomog, S. W. (2020). Innovative behaviors, employee creativity, and sustainable competitive advantage: A moderated mediation. *Sustainability (Switzerland), 12*(8), 3295. Advance online publication. doi:10.3390u12083295

Ferreira, J., Coelho, A., & Moutinho, L. (2020). Dynamic capabilities, creativity and innovation capability and their impact on competitive advantage and firm performance: The moderating role of entrepreneurial orientation. *Technovation, 92–93*, 102061. Advance online publication. doi:10.1016/j.technovation.2018.11.004

Florida, R., & Mellander, C. (2010). There goes the metro: How and why bohemians, artists and gays affect regional housing values. *Journal of Economic Geography, 10*(2), 167–188. doi:10.1093/jeg/lbp022

Gamble, J. R. (2020). Tacit vs explicit knowledge as antecedents for organizational change. In Journal of Organizational Change Management (Vol. 33, Issue 6, pp. 1123–1141). Emerald Group Holdings Ltd. doi:10.1108/JOCM-04-2020-0121

Ganguly, A., Talukdar, A., & Chatterjee, D. (2019). Evaluating the role of social capital, tacit knowledge sharing, knowledge quality and reciprocity in determining innovation capability of an organization. *Journal of Knowledge Management, 23*(6), 1105–1135. doi:10.1108/JKM-03-2018-0190

Geisler, E., & Wickramasinghe, N. (2015). *Principles of Knowledge Management: Theory, Practice, and Cases.* Routledge. doi:10.4324/9781315686448

Giustiniano, L., Lombardi, S., & Cavaliere, V. (2016). How knowledge collecting fosters organizational creativity. *Management Decision, 54*(6), 1464–1496. doi:10.1108/MD-04-2015-0111

Grant, R. M. (1991). The Resource-Based Theory of Competitive Advantage: Implications for Strategy Formulation. *California Management Review, 33*(3), 114–135. doi:10.2307/41166664

Gurteen, D. (1998). Knowledge Creativity and Innovation. *Journal of Knowledge Management, 2*(1), 5–13. doi:10.1108/13673279810800744

Haamann, T., & Basten, D. (2019). The role of information technology in bridging the knowing-doing gap: An exploratory case study on knowledge application. *Journal of Knowledge Management, 23*(4), 705–741. doi:10.1108/JKM-01-2018-0030

Harrington, T. S., Srai, J. S., & Kumar, M. (2019). Knowledge management in SMEs and MNCs: Matching knowledge mobility mechanisms to supply network configuration profiles. *Production Planning and Control, 30*(10–12), 971–994. doi:10.1080/09537287.2019.1582103

Heap, J. (1989). *The Management of Innovation and Design.* Academic Press.

Helfat, C. E., & Peteraf, M. A. (2003). The dynamic resource-based view: Capability lifecycles. *Strategic Management Journal, 24*(10), 997–1010. doi:10.1002/smj.332

Holsapple, C. W., & Joshi, K. D. (2004). A formal knowledge management ontology: Conduct, activities, resources, and influences. *Journal of the American Society for Information Science and Technology*, *55*(7), 593–612. doi:10.1002/asi.20007

Inauen, M., & Schenker-Wicki, A. (2011). The impact of outside-in open innovation on innovation performance. *European Journal of Innovation Management*, *14*(4), 496–520. doi:10.1108/14601061111174934

Johnson, G., Whittington, R., Scholes, K., Angwin, D., & Regnér, P. (2010). *Exploring Strategy*. https://twitter.com/ExploreStrategy

Kim, S., & Lee, H. (2010). Factors affecting employee knowledge acquisition and application capabilities. *Asia-Pacific Journal of Business Administration*, *2*(2), 133–152. doi:10.1108/17574321011078184

Klein, K. J., & Sorra, J. S. (1996). The challenge of innovation implementation. *Academy of Management Review*, *21*(4), 1055–1080. doi:10.2307/259164

Lee, J., Kim, S., Lee, J., & Moon, S. (2019). Enhancing employee creativity for a sustainable competitive advantage through perceived human resource management practices and trust in management. *Sustainability (Switzerland)*, *11*(8), 2305. Advance online publication. doi:10.3390u11082305

Lenka, U., & Gupta, M. (2020). An empirical investigation of innovation process in Indian pharmaceutical companies. *European Journal of Innovation Management*, *23*(3), 500–523. doi:10.1108/EJIM-03-2019-0069

Liu, D., Chen, X.-P., & Yao, X. (2011). From autonomy to creativity: A multilevel investigation of the mediating role of harmonious passion. *The Journal of Applied Psychology*, *96*(2), 294–309. doi:10.1037/a0021294 PMID:21058804

Liu, D., & Zeinaly, S. (2020). A new model for investigating the role of IT-based innovation in the pharmaceutical knowledge-sharing attitude: A study of marketing biotechnology firms. *Kybernetes*. Advance online publication. doi:10.1108/K-07-2019-0505

Liu, Y., Chan, C., Zhao, C., & Liu, C. (2019). Unpacking knowledge management practices in China: Do institution, national and organizational culture matter? *Journal of Knowledge Management*, *23*(4), 619–643. doi:10.1108/JKM-07-2017-0260

López-Cabarcos, M. Á., Srinivasan, S., & Vázquez-Rodríguez, P. (2020). The role of product innovation and customer centricity in transforming tacit and explicit knowledge into profitability. *Journal of Knowledge Management*, *24*(5), 1037–1057. doi:10.1108/JKM-02-2020-0087

López-Torres, G. C., Garza-Reyes, J. A., Maldonado-Guzmán, G., Kumar, V., Rocha-Lona, L., & Cherrafi, A. (2019). Knowledge management for sustainability in operations. *Production Planning and Control*, *30*(10–12), 813–826. doi:10.1080/09537287.2019.1582091

Manhart, M., & Thalmann, S. (2015). Protecting organizational knowledge: A structured literature review. *Journal of Knowledge Management*, *19*(2), 190–211. doi:10.1108/JKM-05-2014-0198

Martins, E., Martins, N., & Terblanche, F. (2004). An organizational culture model to stimulate creativity and innovation in a university library. In *Advances in Library Administration and Organization* (Vol. 21, pp. 83–130). JAI Press., doi:10.1016/S0732-0671(04)21003-3

Melewar, T. C., & Navalekar, A. (2002). Leveraging corporate identity in the digital age. In Marketing Intelligence & Planning (Vol. 20, Issue 2, pp. 96–103). doi:10.1108/02634500210418518

Mumford, M. D., & Gustafson, S. B. (1998). Creativity syndrome: Integration, application, and innovation. *Psychological Bulletin, 103*(1), 27–43. doi:10.1037/0033-2909.103.1.27

Muñoz-Pascual, L., & Galende, J. (2017). The impact of knowledge and motivation management on creativity: Employees of innovative Spanish companies. *Employee Relations, 39*(5), 732–752. doi:10.1108/ER-05-2016-0096

Muthuveloo, R., Shanmugam, N., & Teoh, A. P. (2017). The impact of tacit knowledge management on organizational performance: Evidence from Malaysia. *Asia Pacific Management Review, 22*(4), 192–201. doi:10.1016/j.apmrv.2017.07.010

Nesheim, T., Olsen, K. M., & Tobiassen, A. E. (2011). Knowledge communities in matrix-like organizations: Managing knowledge towards application. *Journal of Knowledge Management, 15*(5), 836–850. doi:10.1108/13673271111174357

Nonaka, I. (1994). A Dynamic Theory of Organizational Knowledge Creation. *Organization Science, 5*(1), 14–37. doi:10.1287/orsc.5.1.14

Oke, A., Munashi, N., & Walumbwa, F. O. (2009). The Influence of Leadership on Innovation Processes and Activities. *Organizational Dynamics, 38*(1), 64–72. doi:10.1016/j.orgdyn.2008.10.005

Olander, H., Vanhala, M., & Hurmelinna-Laukkanen, P. (2014). Reasons for choosing mechanisms to protect knowledge and innovations. *Management Decision, 52*(2), 207–229. doi:10.1108/MD-11-2012-0791

Pathirage, C. P., Amaratunga, D. G., & Haigh, R. P. (2007). Tacit knowledge and organisational performance: Construction industry perspective. *Journal of Knowledge Management, 11*(1), 115–126. doi:10.1108/13673270710728277

Podsakoff, P. M., MacKenzie, S. B., Lee, J. Y., & Podsakoff, N. P. (2003). Common Method Biases in Behavioral Research: A Critical Review of the Literature and Recommended Remedies. In Journal of Applied Psychology (Vol. 88, Issue 5, pp. 879–903). doi:10.1037/0021-9010.88.5.879

Richtnér, A., & Åhlström, P. (2010). Top management control and knowledge creation in new product development. *International Journal of Operations & Production Management, 30*(10), 1006–1031. doi:10.1108/01443571011082508

Riordan, O. (2006). *Using the VRIO framework in practising firms taking the resource-based view (RBV).* Academic Press.

Roffe, I. (1999). Innovation and creativity in organisations: A review of the implications for training and development Competition and change. *Journal of European Industrial Training, 23*(4/5), 224–237. doi:10.1108/03090599910272103

Sarstedt, M., Ringle, C. M., & Hair, J. F. (2017). Partial Least Squares Structural Equation Modeling. In *Handbook of Market Research* (pp. 1–40). Springer International Publishing. doi:10.1007/978-3-319-05542-8_15-1

Saulais, P., & Ermine, J. L. (2012). Creativity and knowledge management. In VINE (Vol. 42, Issue 3, pp. 416–438). doi:10.1108/03055721211267521

Sharratt, M., & Usoro, A. (2003). Understanding Knowledge-Sharing in Online Communities of Practice. *Electronic Journal of Knowledge Management*, *1*(2), 187–196. www.ejkm.com

Smith, E. A. (2001). The role of tacit and explicit knowledge in the workplace. *Journal of Knowledge Management*, *5*(4), 311–321. doi:10.1108/13673270110411733

Srikalimah, S., Wardana, L. W., Ambarwati, D., Sholihin, U., Shobirin, R. A., Fajariah, N., & Wibowo, A. (2020). Do Creativity and Intellectual Capital Matter for SMEs Sustainability? The Role of Competitive Advantage. *Journal of Asian Finance. Economics and Business*, *7*(12), 397–408. doi:10.13106/jafeb.2020.vol7.no12.397

Ting, I. W. K., Sui, H. J., Kweh, Q. L., & Nawanir, G. (2021). Knowledge management and firm innovative performance with the moderating role of transformational leadership. *Journal of Knowledge Management*, *25*(8), 2115–2140. doi:10.1108/JKM-08-2020-0629

Weerasinghe, I. M. S., & Dedunu, H. H. (2020a). Contribution of academics to university–industry knowledge exchange: A study of open innovation in Sri Lankan universities. *Industry and Higher Education*. Advance online publication. doi:10.1177/0950422220964363

Weerasinghe, I. M. S., & Dedunu, H. H. (2020b). Do demographic factors matter in university-industry knowledge exchange? A study based on Sri Lankan university system. *Journal of Knowledge Management*, *25*(5), 973–988. doi:10.1108/JKM-02-2020-0092

Wernerfelt, B. (1984). *A Resource-based View of the Firm*. Academic Press.

Wu, L. W., & Lin, J. R. (2013). Knowledge sharing and knowledge effectiveness: Learning orientation and co-production in the contingency model of tacit knowledge. *Journal of Business and Industrial Marketing*, *28*(8), 672–686. doi:10.1108/JBIM-04-2011-0050

Yang, J., & Rui, M. (2009). Turning knowledge into new product creativity: An empirical study. *Industrial Management & Data Systems*, *109*(9), 1197–1210. doi:10.1108/02635570911002270

Zhang, W., & Zhang, W. (2018). Knowledge creation through industry chain in resource-based industry: Case study on phosphorus chemical industry chain in western Guizhou of China. *Journal of Knowledge Management*, *22*(5), 1037–1060. doi:10.1108/JKM-02-2017-0061

Zhao, S., Jiang, Y., Peng, X., & Hong, J. (2020). Knowledge sharing direction and innovation performance in organizations: Do absorptive capacity and individual creativity matter? *European Journal of Innovation Management*, *24*(2), 371–394. doi:10.1108/EJIM-09-2019-0244

Zhao, Y., & Ko, J. (2020). How do teaching quality and pedagogical practice enhance vocational student engagement? A mixed-method classroom observation approach. *International Journal of Educational Management*, *34*(6), 987–1000. doi:10.1108/IJEM-11-2019-0393

Zhou, J., & George, M. (2001). When job dissatisfaction lead to creativity. *Academy of Management Journal*, *44*(4), 682–696. doi:10.2307/3069410

Chapter 5
Fostering Creativity and Innovation:
Tourism and Hospitality Perspective

Amrik Singh
https://orcid.org/0000-0003-3598-8787
Lovely Professional University, India

Gaurav Bathla
Lovely Professional University, India

ABSTRACT

The tourism and hospitality sector fosters growth, prospers the hosts, and also offers immense potential for employment in various sections. Innovation is a decisive process for the well-being of an organization. With economic crises after COVID-19 and the slow recovery that continues, the authors believe that a solution can be improving the capacity to research and innovate to achieve sustainable development. The purpose of this chapter is to develop a meaningful debate on the creativity and innovations in the forms of new ideas, methods, and technology to better meet the evolving requirement of the organization and workforce sustainability. Further, exploring the future needs and circumstances rather than simply finding some responses to the situation, this chapter highlights challenges and prospects related to achieving creativity and innovation for business sustainability in tourism and hospitality.

INTRODUCTION

The tourism and hospitality industry is a vibrant industry that has seen tremendous growth in the last few years. The ever-changing economy and know-how will sway society, organizations, and managers according to Drucker (1992). In his view, the knowledge Society will require all its members to have basic computer skills as well as conventional literacy skills; political, social, and historical knowledge as well as the skills of learning-to-learn. In the present era, we can easily observe that most organizations have started their training center to improve the performance level of their employees. Eventually, this

DOI: 10.4018/978-1-6684-6732-9.ch005

Copyright © 2023, IGI Global. Copying or distributing in print or electronic forms without written permission of IGI Global is prohibited.

is because innovation and creativity are considered at the bottom of any tourism and hotel enterprise. Within the travel and tourism industry, a tourist product is typically made up of a variety of different elements. These components could either be material or immaterial in nature. For instance, in a particular location there may be a number of different suppliers that contribute to the creation of services. These may include hotels, restaurants, or travel guides. In addition, the provision of goods or services is not the only economic foundation upon which tourism is built. As a result, it is not possible to investigate the advancements made in the tourist sector within the confines of a single category of business. There has been a significant amount of research conducted on innovation due to its perceived importance as a driving force behind both economic expansion and gains in competitive advantage (Sipe & Testa, 2009). It has been determined that innovation is required for tourism businesses in order to maintain long-term stable production, growth, return, sustainable performance, and leadership (Yac, 2017). Because of the features of the customers that participate in tourism, the vast majority of tourists require unique and appealing ones. Because of this, the expectations of tourists and the trends that they follow are always shifting, and the demand structure that is true for one time may not be true for the one that comes after it. Whenever there is a shift in the demand from tourists, businesses are forced to come up with new approaches to their designs, procedures, methods, service contents, and distribution systems in order to keep up with the competition. In the context of businesses related to tourism, the preferences engendered by these shifts are regarded as falling within the ambit of innovation.

In the field of tourism, one of the subjects that is currently receiving the most attention from researchers in both the academic world and the professional world is the creation of innovative processes and products, as well as the marketing of innovative services and the development of new organisational structures and methodologies. In particular, destinations and businesses are compelled to innovate in response to the rising demand for tourist as well as the growing supply of tourism and the intensifying competition in the industry. Because innovation is a significant aspect that assists firms in achieving and maintaining a competitive advantage, particularly in environments that are subject to rapid change. The intensification of rivalry on both the national and international levels, as well as the saturation of existing markets, are the driving forces behind innovations. The current state of the market necessitates the ongoing development and distribution of novel goods and services, and the fact that this is the case is critical for all parties involved in tourism destinations. As a result, the development and implementation of an efficient innovation process in tourism destinations ought to be the primary focus of researchers and managers. The purpose of this paper is to define innovation, provide information about the concept of innovation and the diffusion of innovation, and discuss innovative approaches in the tourism sector. These innovative approaches include innovations in products and services, processes, organisational structures, and marketing strategies.

CONCEPT OF INNOVATION

The innovation concept includes a synopsis of the following topics: the definition of innovation, the significance of innovation, the factors that drive innovation, and the factors that contribute to the spread of innovation.

The Meaning of the Word "Innovation"

When used to the world of business, the term "innovation" can be understood in a variety of ways depending on the specific context. Numerous researchers have spent a great deal of time and effort over the course of many years analysing innovation in a variety of contexts. The word "innovation" derives from the Latin words "in" and "novare" (Bessant & Tidd, 2007) or "innovatio" (Peters & Pikkemaat, 2006) both of which imply "to make something new." The word "change" is what the dictionary means when it refers to "innovation." In 1934, Schumpeter was the first economist to introduce the concept of innovation to the economic realm (Carvalho & Costa, 2011).

According to Schumpeter, innovation is the creation of new goods, new processes, new markets, and new sources of raw materials; in other words, it is the process of giving a new form to an existing industrial system. Schumpeter was clear to point out that innovation and invention are not the same thing. Instead, he pointed out that inventions were associated with fundamental scientific or technological research, whereas innovations were subsequent refinements of these or the implementation of novel ideas (Hall & Williams, 2008). According to Weiermair (2006), Schumpeter identifies five distinct areas in which businesses have the potential to introduce innovation, and he views innovation as the driving force behind economic transformation. The development of a brand-new product or the enhancement of an existing one. The use of a brand-new production method. The expansion into new markets. The discovery of new locations where raw materials can be sourced. The reorganisation and/or restructuring of the business.

This classification differentiates innovation rather clearly from less significant shifts in the composition and delivery of products, such as the extension of product lines, the addition of service components, or product differentiation (Peters & Pikkemaat, 2006,). According to Rogers (1983) innovation can be defined as an idea, an application, or an object that is seen as novel by an individual or a community. In a similar vein, Kotler, Wong, Saunders, and Armstrong (2005) describe innovation as the development and marketing of concepts, goods, and technologies that are regarded by customers to be new. The development, progress, adoption, and commercialization of new processes, products, organisational structures, and methodologies are all examples of innovation, according to a different meaning of the term (Jorde & Teece, 1990; Thompson, 1965). According to Drucker (2014) innovation is the specific tool that entrepreneurs use to use change as an opportunity for a different business or a different service. This is the way by which entrepreneurs employ innovation. It's possible that innovation can be defined as the process of coming up with new ways of looking at problems or requirements, as well as the process of coming up with alternative solutions to problems in order to suit the demands of individuals or institutions (Demir, 2006) According to Kose (2012) innovation has both a direct and an indirect impact on the economies of countries and firms. Especially in the 21st century, innovation is of strategic importance in the creation of new products and services in order to meet the demands in current and previously unknown markets (Clair, 2008). Despite this, increased competition and a short product life force companies to continuously innovate (Akn, 2005). According to Demirsoy (2005) the definition of the marketing-oriented innovation idea may be investigated within the framework of four different approaches. These methods are consumer-oriented, company-oriented, product-oriented, and market-oriented. When taking a business-focused approach, one evaluates product innovation from the perspective of the company itself. This is known as the company-oriented method. The product-oriented strategy investigates how the introduction of a new item will affect the consumer's established patterns of behaviour. The fact that the product has been purchased by a tiny mass market is deemed to be the introduction of a new product. In the consumer-oriented strategy, a product is considered to be "new" in this strategy only if it is described as such by a potential customer.

The Significance of Creativity and Innovation

The economy as a whole, as well as individual companies and organisations, stand to benefit immensely from innovation. Every company has an ongoing goal of improving their performance in order to keep their current level of success. Numerous studies have found a correlation between effective growth and innovative practises. Bessant and Tidd (2011) state that economists have been debating for decades about the precise nature of the relationship between innovation and economic growth. Despite this, economists are in agreement that innovation is responsible for a considerable share of economic growth. Because of the market dynamics of the tourist industry, which include high levels of competition, businesses are required to innovate in order to remain competitive (Hall & Williams, 2008). Taking into consideration the meaning of the term "competitive advantage," productivity is connected to production and quality performance. Therefore, tourism businesses that invest in quality and product diversification tend to have a better chance of remaining competitive (Carvalho & Costa, 2011).

According to Yac (2017) innovation is viewed as obligatory for businesses in order to achieve goals such as long-term production stability, growth, yield, sustainable performance, and sector leadership. The fact that OECD countries spend $1.50 trillion each year on research and development, that more than 16,000 companies in the United States operate their own industrial research labs, that 17 percent of all firms' turnover in Germany was earned with newly introduced products, and that in the research-intensive sector, this figure was 38 percent, demonstrates the significance of innovation (Bessant & Tidd, 2011).

Factors Driving Innovation

The benefits of innovations can be interpreted in a variety of ways, including as an increase in adaptability, an improvement in the standard of goods and services offered, a reduction in the cost of labour, a decrease in overall costs, and a reduction in the amount of time required to fulfil the requirements of customers. There are significant gaps in innovation between different tourism subsectors due to the diverse nature of the tourism industry. There are a wide variety of opportunities for innovation within the tourist industry due to the diverse nature of the businesses that make up the sector, such as hotels, restaurants, and beach clubs. According to Hall and Williams (2008) the following factors can be considered to be drivers of tourist businesses: competition, economic performance, demand-led innovation, technology, firm-level strategy and resources, individual entrepreneurialism, and the involvement of the state. There are also certain drivers to consider when thinking about environmentally responsible innovation in its broader context. According to OECD (2013) the majority of business managers cited cost savings through process innovation as the primary reason. This was followed by obligation, as a result of scarce natural resources, and overall motivation and determination to go green on the part of the stakeholders. To summarise, the following are some of the reasons why tourism businesses should innovate: to increase market share; to improve product service quality; to improve product / service characteristics; to comply with regulations and standards; to ensure production flexibility; to reduce labour costs; to reduce material consumption; to save energy; to protect the environment; to meet shifting customer demands; to keep up with technological developments; and to respond to innovative endeavours by competitors.

Diffusion of Innovation

(Greenhalgh et al., 2008; Rogers, 1983; Tortella & Tirado, 2011) It is common knowledge that the research on the diffusion of innovation got its start with the studies of the French sociologist Gabriel Tarde, which were conducted in English and Germany-Austria schools in the early 1900s (Greenhalgh et al., 2008; Rogers, 1983; Tortella & Tirado, 2011). Everett Rogers is credited with contributing a fresh viewpoint to the field of study known as the theory of the dissemination of innovations by putting an emphasis on the significance of communication. Rogers compiled a total of 405 different case studies into his first book, which was titled "Diffusion of Innovations" and was published in 1962. In this book, Rogers created a hypothesis on how people and society as a whole embrace new ideas. Several distinct meanings of the term "innovation" have been discussed up until this point. As was said before, Rogers' innovation is described as an idea, application, or object that is viewed as new by adopters. This can be anything from a new object to a new software programme. The person's perception of the idea as being novel is what we mean when we talk about innovation. It is not necessary for the information to be recently acquired for an innovation to be regarded as truly novel. A person may have been aware of innovation for some time, but they may not have yet demonstrated any favourable or hostile behaviour toward it.

As a result, the concept of newness in innovation might be articulated through knowledge, the ability to persuade, or the choice to adopt (Rogers, 1983). According to Rogers (1983), the adoption rate of innovations can be affected by how such innovations are considered to have certain qualities. The term "perceived traits" refers to qualities that an individual identifies as contributing to the novelty's overall attractiveness or unattractiveness. According to Rogers (1983) the perceived innovative features that influence a decision to adopt an invention include relative benefit, compatibility, complexity, trialability, and observability.

Channels of Communication

According to Rogers (1983), communication is "the process through which persons create and share knowledge with each other in order to establish mutual understanding." Diffusion is a specialised form of communication in which information is exchanged for novel concepts. According to Rogers (1983), the essence of the diffusion process is the interchange of information that one individual communicates a new concept with a new person or with several others. This is true whether the individual shares the idea with one other person or with several others. The procedure can be broken down into its most elementary version as follows:

An Innovation

A person or organisation that is familiar with the invention or has previous experience utilising it, a second person or organisation that is not yet familiar with the innovation, and a communication route that links the two units together are the three components of an innovation ecosystem.

The medium through which information is transmitted from one individual to another is known as a communication channel.

According to Kose (2012) channels of mass media such as radio, television, and newspapers are frequently the quickest and most effective means for potential adopters to become aware of advances.

According to Rogers (1983) time is an essential component in the process of diffusion; nevertheless, this factor has been neglected in the majority of other research conducted in the field of behavioural science. There is no communication process that does not involve time in some way, although the vast majority of communication research that is not connected to diffusion is not interested in studying this component. The innovation-decision process, innovativeness and adopter categories, and the rate of adoption are the three components that make up the time dimension.

Rogers provides a definition of the innovation-decision process, which can be summarised as follows: an individual goes from having their first knowledge of an innovation to forming an attitude toward the innovation, to making a decision to adopt or reject the innovation, to putting the new idea into practise, and finally to confirming that this decision was the right one. There are five steps in total.

1. Knowledge,
2. Persuasion,
3. Choice,
4. Execution,
5. Confirmation

During the process referred to as "knowledge," the individual obtains information regarding innovation. When it comes to the stage of persuasion, the importance of individuals' favourable or negative attitudes toward innovation cannot be overstated. At this stage, the factors that most influence attitude are those that are seen to be associated with the innovation. The choice step involves deciding whether or not to adopt the innovation. Those individuals who are open to new ideas will start to put them into practise during the implementation stage. At last, in the phase of confirmation, the decision is assessed in order to determine whether or not the adoption, later adoption, abandonment, or rejection will continue. Another aspect of the temporal dimension that must be considered is the pace at which innovations are adopted. According to Günee (2010) the rate of adoption of innovation is a notion that is measured by how many members of the social system or what percentage of members of the social system accept the innovation within a certain time period of the innovation.

Rogers (1983) defines a social system as "a group of interrelated units that are engaged in cooperative problem solving to reach a common purpose." This definition describes a social system as "a set of interrelated units." It's possible for individuals, informal groups, organisations, and/or subsystems to make up a social system's components, often known as its members or units. In the process of spreading environmentally friendly innovations throughout an area, the social system can take the form of local restaurants or hotels, in addition to the people who use these types of businesses.

TOURISM PRODUCTS AND SERVICES

In the name of innovation, numerous adjustments can be made to the way an organisation functions, the method production factors are utilised, or the way the input and output process is carried out. It is feasible to observe that innovation is divided up into categories when viewed within the context of the developments that have taken place in the research that has been done on innovation. The literature contains a number of different classifications that various authors have created addressing the many sorts of innovation. The authors diversified these classifications by creating the dual classification (Anderson

& Tushman, 1990), the triple classification (Robertson, 1967), the quartet classification (OECD/EU, 2006), and the octal classification. For the purpose of this research, the most popular classification in the field of tourism studies (Palomares, 2008), known as the quartet (which consists of product innovation, process innovation, organisational innovation, and marketing innovation), was used to categorise the various types of innovations from the Oslo Guide.

Figure 1. Innovation in tourism products and services

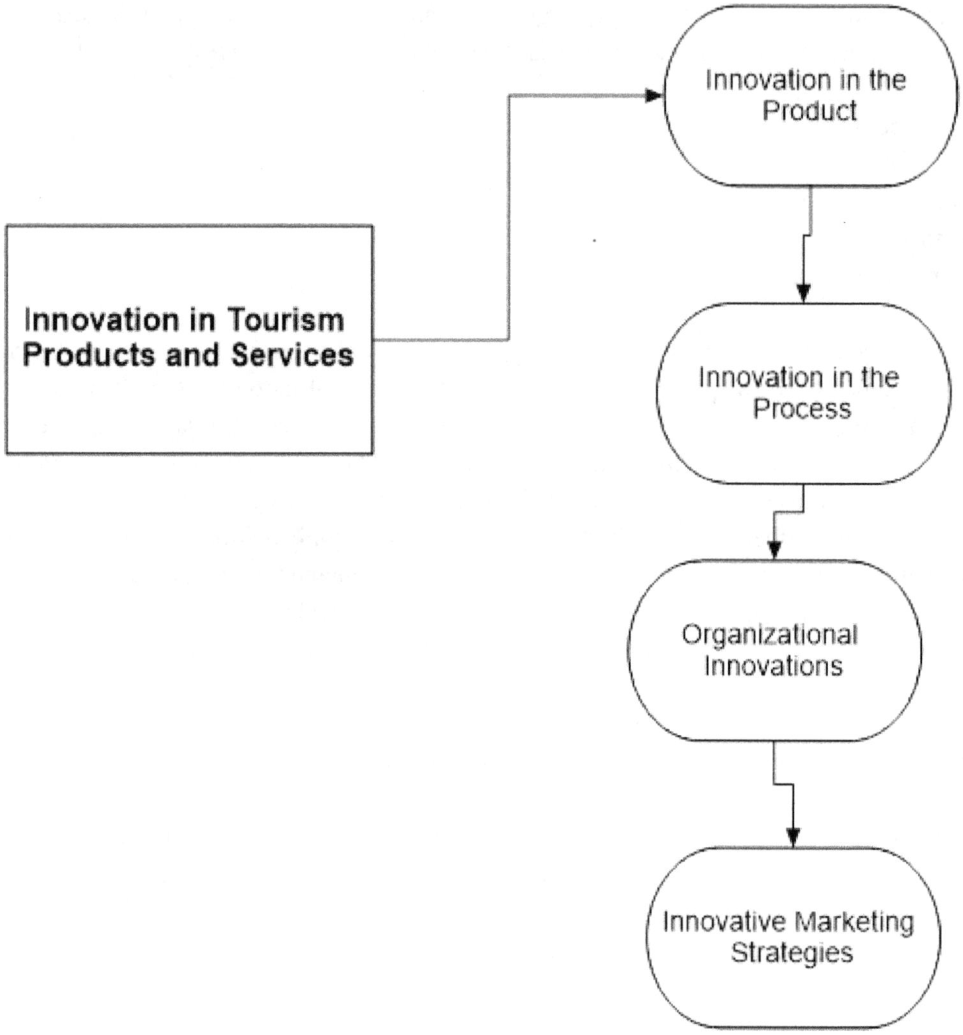

Innovation in the Product

Conforming to The Oslo Guide (OECD/EU, 2006), product innovation is defined as the introduction of a new or significantly better product according to the product's current features or planned applications. It is the invention and subsequent introduction of a good or service that is new, redesigned, or quite improved from earlier goods or services, as stated by Esemu and Wood (2013). The authors state that this is the definition of innovation. According to Danneels (2002), product innovation is acknowledged as the fundamental means of corporate renewal and the locomotive of a renaissance for firms. This is the case despite the fact that other methods of corporate renewal exist. According to Güle and Bülbül (2004), product innovation is the process by which values are supplied to consumers or innovations are developed that are directly tied to the requirements of consumers. According to Kose (2012) the introduction of new products into the market is a critical component of a successful revenue-boosting strategy for businesses. It is important to keep in mind that the primary commodity offered by the tourism industry is some form of service. As a result, product innovation is frequently used as a synonym for service innovation. Ottenbacher (2007, page 433) claims that the primary focus of research in today's world is on product innovation, despite the fact that the service sector accounts for more than 80 percent of the entire economy in the United States. The majority of tourism businesses' contributions to innovation come in the form of new services. According to Maráková and Medved'ová (2016) the types of innovations that occur most frequently in tourism destinations are product innovations and innovations related with the reorganisation of management. According to the findings of a literature review study (Ik et al., 2018) that was carried out in Turkey, the majority of tourism innovation research has been focused on service innovation. This finding was made in the context of tourist innovation research. According to Hjalager (2010) in the context of tourism, product innovations refer to changes that are directly perceived by customers and viewed as new; either in the sense of never experienced before or in the sense of being introduced for the very first time. To the extent that visitors are aware of recent developments in a product or service, those developments have a good chance of becoming a consideration in the subsequent decision to make a purchase. According to Palomares (2008) there is a lot of imitation in the tourism sector, even when it's not an exact copy. It can be challenging to maintain innovation in the tourism industry. When seen in this light, product innovations present a greater challenge to maintain than organisational innovations, marketing innovations, or process innovations. Innovations in tourism are difficult to patent because of the intangible nature of their products. According to Abdelillah and Esther (2001) the creation of technological innovations is more difficult than the creation of service innovations. This is because technological innovations are more about research and development, whereas service innovations are more about business and organisational skills. Additionally, according to Ottenbacher (2007), staff plays a significant role in service innovation because of the intangible nature of services, the simultaneousness of production and consumption, and the significance of human aspects in the delivery of services. In conclusion, as a result of the role that they play in the promotion of tourism in their respective governments, public institutions may also supplement the tourism product by providing a variety of services at the destination; more specifically, they invest in the development of innovative tourism products (Palomares, 2008). According to Hall and Williams (2008) the Canadian Tourism Commission, the primary national institution responsible for tourism, has one of its fundamental objectives defined in its strategic plan as being "product innovation and growth."

Innovation in the Process

According to Esemu and Wood (2013) a process innovation is a definition of a new or significantly improved production or distribution system application. According to Viederyte (2016) the activity of introducing new technology or approach to an existing process in order to assist an organisation in remaining competitive and meeting the requirements of consumers is considered to be process innovation. According to Hjalager (2010) the term "process innovations" refers to typically behind-the-scenes attempts that aim to increase efficiency, productivity, and flow. According to Razafindravelo (2017) the goals of process innovations can include reducing the costs of unit production and distribution, increasing value, or generating or delivering novel or significantly added-value products. According to Kose (2012), introducing new processes can be a useful tool for enhancing product quality, boosting production efficiencies, and lowering operating expenses. According to Carvalho and Costa (2011) process innovations "are the renovation of the prescriptive procedures for producing and delivering the service." Process innovations could be divided into two categories: innovation in production processes (back office) or innovation in the delivery process (front office). According to Downey (2007) process innovations have the potential to raise stockholder satisfaction by increasing efficiencies, whereas product innovations have the potential to increase customer satisfaction. According to the OECD (2013), the innovation of processes has not been a matter of routine for tourism businesses. However, as a result of increased competition in the global market place, process innovations are becoming ever more important. These innovations enable tourism operators, particularly those in developed economies, to lower the costs, driving to quality improvements, reduced prices, and enhanced profitability. Because it is totally within the profession of the employee and management to design, apply, and monitor the key changes without reference to external influences, process innovation is rather frequent in the majority of modern businesses (Kalivas et al., 2013). The tourist industry is one that sees a greater frequency of process innovations. For instance, Jacob, Tintoré, Aguiló, Bravo, and Mulet (2003) found that process innovations were nearly four times more common than product innovations at hotels located in the Balearic Islands. A similar finding was made by Peters and Pikkemaat (2006) in their research on the small and medium-sized hotel business. They discovered that process innovations are the most common type of innovation activities, but product innovations are hardly ever identified.

According to Buhalis and Law (2008), information and communication technologies are extremely important for a wide variety of process innovations, in addition to a variety of research topics. According to Maráková and Medved'ová (2016), on pages 34 and 35, the implementation of information and communication technologies can result in an increase in the productivity of businesses that are involved in the tourism industry. As a result of globalisation, process innovations in the tourism industry have become essential to the industry's continued existence. These innovations can help tourism businesses cut costs, which in turn can lead to improved quality, lower prices, and increased profitability. IT (internet, B2B information & reservation systems), a new controlling system, reorganisation of the company, further training of the workforce, and service optimization are some examples of process innovations in tourism businesses.

Organizational Innovations

The Oslo handbook defines organisational innovation as the implementation of a novel organisational approach within the business operations, organisational structure, or external relations of an enterprise. It is reasonable to anticipate that advances in organisational practises will increase business performance by reducing costs, enhancing employees' levels of happiness in their jobs, and obtaining access to non-commercial assets. According to Lynch (2007) organisational innovation refers to the modifications made to a company's organisational structure or management practises with the intention of enhancing the usability, quality of products and services, or the effectiveness of workflows. New methods of organisation or administration, such as the implementation of Total Quality Management (TQM) or self-steering groups, are examples of the types of innovations that fall under the umbrella term "organisational innovation" (Carvalho & Costa, 2011). In addition, organisational innovations are implemented with the goals of significantly enhancing the utilisation of the knowledge that employees already possess within the company, enhancing the quality of products and services, and standardising production.

The use of an organisational method (in business practises, working place organisation, or outer relations) that has not been employed previously by the enterprise and which results from strategic outcomes made by the management is what differentiates organisational innovation from other types of organisational change within an organisation. This is what makes organisational innovation distinct from other types of organisational change (Razafindravelo, 2017). Methods of organisational innovation have the potential to lead innovation processes in other parts of an organisation as well (Palomares, 2008). According to Drejer (2004) organisational innovations have a particularly significant impact on the efficiency of the entire organisation, despite the fact that the type of innovation being implemented has an effect on the degree to which innovation is performed in other domains. Additionally, according to Hall and Williams (2008) creative organisational strategies may potentially reduce costs or generate uniqueness, so making a firm more competitive. According to Sandybayev (2016) organisational innovation for individual tourist businesses leads to the improvement of working conditions, which is in addition to the positive influence it has on the economy. In addition, the outcomes of applying new organisational strategies, as stated by Palomares (2008) have the potential to have an effect not only on the company but also on the surrounding environment. Organizational innovations originating from public organisations have the potential to be beneficial to the structure of the tourism industry. These innovations can be based on destinations.

Innovative Marketing Strategies

(Downey, 2007; Dzhabdzhugazova, Blinova, & Orlova, 2016) Marketing innovation is the process of inventing new marketing approaches to bring improvements in price, position, packaging, product design, or promotion (Downey, 2007; Dzhabdzhugazova, Blinova, & Orlova, 2016). To be more specific, marketing innovations are the implementation of a new or progressively improved marketing strategy that helps develop the sales market (Carvalho & Costa, 2011; Palomares, 2008).

According to Eskiler, Ozmen, and Uzkurt (2011) "marketing innovation" is a notion that refers to more than just innovations in a product or service themselves. According to the authors, marketing innovation refers to the innovative practises that will take place inside the four components of the marketing mix known as the 4P.

According to Tüfekci and Tüfekci (2014) in order to evaluate the efficacy of innovation, it is necessary to measure it in relation to marketing performance. This is because marketing innovation encompasses the components of the marketing mix.

According to Axel (1999) the goal of marketing innovation is to locate better markets and to service the new market in a more effective manner. Employing a marketing system that the company has never utilised before is what distinguishes marketing innovation from other improvements that may be made to the company's marketing instruments (Razafindravelo, 2017). Specifically, the marketing innovations consist of the creation and implementation of new marketing approaches that have never been utilised by the company in the past. These methods have never been tried before. It is common knowledge that innovative marketing techniques are put to use frequently in the tourism industry and have an impact on businesses related to tourism. According to Hjalager (2010) for example, the development of the internet has led to a complete series of marketing innovations that effect on a large number of the tourism enterprises, and which have already led to an extensive reduction in traditional marketing and sales mediators such as travel agencies. These innovations have already led to an extensive reduction in the number of tourism businesses. In a positive development, the revival of innovation in one subsector may be enabled by the generation of sufficient demand from another subsector.

For instance, if a hotel implements a new marketing strategy that results in an increase in the number of tourists visiting the establishment, the restaurant next door may be inspired to implement a new strategy through which it extends the hours it is open (Hall & Williams, 2008). Co-production of the brand is one example of a marketing innovation that is included in innovative marketing practises. This practise can be seen, for instance, in the hospitality and tourism industries (Hjalager, 2010). Along with innovations in market study and data gathering methods, innovative means of promoting services and goods are also important among marketing innovations for tourism organisations (Razafindravelo, 2017; Sandybayev, 2016). Of particular significance among marketing innovations for tourism organisations are those connected with refining the quality and safety of tourist services (Razafindravelo, 2017; Sandybayev, 2016). When discussing environmentally friendly innovations, the term "marketing innovation" may refer to activities such as preliminary market research, market tests, and launch advertising. An eco-friendly strategy should be incorporated into the activities of market innovation. This approach should take into account eco-friendly components of the product 4P (promotion, packaging, placement, or pricing) (de Sancho, Dominguez, Macho, Alvarez, & Martire, 2013). One example of how hotels and other businesses in the food and beverage industry can innovate their marketing is by applying to environmentally friendly associations and working to fulfil the requirements of those associations.

CONCLUSION

These days, innovation is essentially a prerequisite for success. Businesses within the tourism industry that are looking to gain a competitive advantage in a setting that is both stable and long-lasting are attempting to develop their strategies in this general direction. Tourism businesses are encouraged to innovate in order to maintain long-term production consistency, growth and return on investment, as well as sustainable performance and leadership. The provision of quite comprehensive services is an expectation and requirement placed on tourism businesses by vacationers. In the tourism business, innovations are of great public value; in other words, they help to the realisation of the seasonality factor, the development of sustainable tourism, the enhancement of employment, and other related goals. (Sandybayev, 2016). According to Weiermair (2006), the most important innovations in the tourism industry are as follows: information technology, online travel services and tourism, new forms of business associations and cooperative marketing, quality assurance, marketing practises, customer and employee satisfaction, new forms of distribution (online booking), relationships with intermediaries, and reducing the costs of delivery of products. Within the context of an innovative organisational culture, in order for an organisation to endure for a significant amount of time, it requires creative goods in addition to an innovative organisational culture. Adopting innovation as "a culture of enterprise" is critical to ensuring the long-term viability of innovative practises inside an organisation. Consequently, beginning with the management of the company, each employee has important responsibilities in this regard. When determining the vision, mission, and goals of the company, managers shouldn't overlook the concept of innovation. They should also encourage the development of new ideas within the firm and facilitate their spread throughout the company. In addition, good innovation management requires the division and support of new ideas according to the available resources, as well as the recognition and remuneration of individuals who are innovative and adaptive.

REFERENCES

Abdelillah, H., & Esther, S. (2001). *The dynamic nature of innovation within mobile phone service providers in France.* doi:10.1108/EUM0000000005670

Akın, H. B. (2005). *Yeni ekonomi: strateji, rekabet, teknoloji yonetimi.* Çizgi Kitabevi.

Anderson, P., & Tushman, M. L. (1990). A cyclical model of how technological change occurs, with an emphasis on technological discontinuities and dominant designs. Administrative Science Quarterly.

Axel, J. (1999). Innovation on the market that is successful. *European Journal of Innovation Management, 2*(1), 6–11. doi:10.1108/14601069910248838

Carvalho, L., & Costa, T. (2011). A literature review accompanied by research on case studies focusing on innovations in the tourism industry. *Tourism & Management Studies*, 23–33.

Clair, D. S. (2008). *An investigation into new approaches to teaching business at the university level.* Pepperdine University.

Danneels, E. (2002). The dynamic relationship between product innovation and the competencies of a company. *Strategic Management Journal, 23*(12).

de Sancho, A. L., Dominguez, C., Macho, A. S. C., Alvarez, V. P., & Martire, F. (2013). Sustainable Innovation. Institute for Innovation and Technology.

Demir, K. (2006). Rogersın Yeniliğin Yayılması Teorisi ve Ġnternetten Ders Kaydı. *Kuram ve Uygulamada Egitim Yonetimi Dergisi, 12*(3), 367–392.

Demirsoy, C. (2005). *Yeniliğin Yayılması Modellerinin Yeniliği Benimseyen Kategorilerinin İnternet Bankacılığı Ürünü Üzerinde Bir İncelemesi.* Hacettepe Üniversitesi.

Downey, J. (2007). *Innovation management.* The Chartered Institute of Management Accountants.

Drejer, I. (2004). A Schumpeterian approach is taken to the problem of spotting innovative trends in service provider surveys. *Research Policy, 33*(3), 551–562.

Dzhabdzhugazova, E., Blinova, E., & Orlova, L. (2016). The hospitality industry's most cutting-edge developments. *International Journal of Environmental and Science Education.*

Esemu, T., & Wood, E. (2013). Innovation and the Creation of Value in Emerging Commercial Agricultural Sectors in Africa: Evidence From the Ugandan Flower Export Sector Quality Innovation: Knowledge, Theory, and Practices. IGI Global.

Eskiler, E., Ozmen, M., & Uzkurt, C. (2011). Bilgi Yonetimi Pazar Odaklılık ve Pazarlama Yeniliği ĠliÇkisi: Mobilya Sektoründe Bir AraÇtırma. *Eskişehir Osmangazi Üniversitesi İİBF Dergisi, 6*(1), 31–69.

Güle, Ç. H. K., & Bülbül, H. (2004). Yenilikcilik: İşletmeler İcin Stratejik Rekabet Aracı. Ankara: Nobel Yayıncılık.

Güne, Ç. S. (2010). *Yenilik Yayılımı: Bir Araştırma.* Ġstanbul Üniversitesi.

Hjalager, A.-M. (2010). An examination of the research done on innovative tourist practises. *Tourism Management, 31*(1), 1–12.

Iğık, C., Akoğul, E., TaÇ, S., Uyrun, A., Hajiyeva, T., Turan, B., & Dırbo, A. H. (2018). Turizm ve Ġnovasyon ĠliÇkisi: Literatür Taraması. *Journal of Tourism Intelligence and Smartness*, 34–74.

Jorde, T. M., & Teece, D. J. (1990). The implications of innovation and cooperation for both market competitiveness and antitrust laws. *The Journal of Economic Perspectives*, *4*(3), 75–96.

Köse, B. (2012). *Tüketici Yenilikçiliği ve Yeniliklerin Benimsenmesi: Bir Yenilik Olarak Mobil\sİnternet.* Afyon Kocatepe Üniversitesi.

Kotler, P., Wong, V., Saunders, J., & Armstrong, G. (2005). *Principles of Marketing* (4th ed.). Academic Press.

Lynch, L. M. (2007). The adoption and diffusion of organisational innovation: evidence for the United States economy. National Bureau of Economic Research.

OECD/EU. (2006). *Oslo Kılavuzu: Yenilik Verilerinin Toplanması ve Yorumlanması İcin İlkeler.* Ekonomik ĠÇbirliği ve Kalkınma Orgütü Avrupa Birliği Ġstatistiği Ofisi.

Ottenbacher, M. C. (2007). The management of innovation in the hospitality business, including the various approaches that can be taken to achieve success. *Journal of Hospitality & Tourism Research, 31*(4), 431–454.

Palomares, X. (2008). *Innovation Typology in the Tourism Industry* [Master's thesis]. Universitat de Girona.

Peters, M., & Pikkemaat, B. (2006). The application of innovation in tourism. *Journal of Quality Assurance in Hospitality and Tourism.*

Robertson, T. S. (1967). The actions that go into creating new things and the ways in which those new things spread. *Journal of Marketing, 31*(1), 14–19.

Rogers, E. M. (1983). *Spreading of new ideas and practises.* The Free Press.

Tortella, B. D., & Tirado, D. (2011). *The amount of water consumed by hotels in a seasonal destination with a large number of tourists.* Academic Press.

Tüfekci, N., & Tüfekci, O. K. (2014). *Pazarlama Yeniliği ile Pazarlama Performansı ĠliÇkisini Acıklamaya Yonelik Bir Vaka ÇalıÇması: Süleyman Demirel Üniversitesi Olimpik Yüzme Havuzu Orneği ve Bir Model Onerisi.* Academic Press.

Viederyte, R. (2016). The significance of organisational and operational innovations in international logistics organisations, as well as the anticipated advantages of these advancements. *Studies on Regional Formation and Development, 20*(3), 134-146.

Weiermair, K. (2006). *Product Improvement or Innovation: What is the key to success in tourism?* OECD Publishing.

Williams, A. (2008). *Innovation and tourism go hand in hand.* Routledge.

Yağcı, O. (2017). Turizm ĠÇletmelerinde Yenilik Yonetimi. In F. Okumuġ & U. Avcı (Eds.), Turizm İşletmelerinde Çağdaş Yonetim Teknikleri. Ankara: Detay Yayıncılık.

Chapter 6
Innovative Practices in Sustainable Ecotourism Promotion and Impacts:
Changes Through Dynamic Leadership

Shaheed Khan
https://orcid.org/0000-0002-5920-6703
Dharthi NGO, India

Freeda Maria Swarna M.
Dharthi NGO, India

Panch Ramalingam
Pondicherry University, India

ABSTRACT

Sustainable ecotourism, its promotion, and its impacts have a bearing on the world considering the fact that tourism, travel, and hospitality moved millions around the world and ensured a way of life for the local communities, governments, and businesses. But what drives sustainable ecotourism? Is it the destination, the product on offer, or anything else? It is the people, maybe the community, maybe one individual, who provides a phenomenal direction and ensures all others follow in the right spirit. The chapter is a tribute to four Indians who have contributed to sustainable ecotourism leadership and ensured various products that have helped ecotourism promotion and impacted the lives of the communities they have served. The work of these leaders has been mapped to two frameworks, which itself provide ample food for thought for the multitudes to adopt and move forward.

DOI: 10.4018/978-1-6684-6732-9.ch006

Copyright © 2023, IGI Global. Copying or distributing in print or electronic forms without written permission of IGI Global is prohibited.

INTRODUCTION

Sustainability thinkers agree that sustainable development requires a change in the way we think (Marshall et al. 2011). Mackey and Sisodia (2013) mention that 'Conscious leaders are usually strong individuals who possess exceptional moral courage and are able to withstand constant scrutiny and criticism from those who view business in a more traditional and narrow manner'. It is true that the Leaders who in India have focussed on Sustainable Ecotourism promotion in a direct or indirect sense have had difficulties, impediments which only shows the apathy that was exhibited towards the Leaders, whose only efforts have been to ensure sustainability and sustainability options. Today, when we look at the contributions, one clearly knows the efforts that were placed, and the 'circumspect suspicion' that the Management of these Leaders if they were in a formal environment of the Government or even the Private Sector would have had to go through. But come what may, these Leaders ensured for themselves, their conviction and their ability to stay ahead of the rest of us, move ahead, and contribute to the success in the domain of Sustainable Ecotourism, its promotion and the impacts that had larger ramifications on the community and the country.

ELEMENTS OF SUSTAINABLE LEADERSHIP

Tideman (et al., 2013) put forward a framework of Sustainable Leadership (SL) which implied the development of three new mind-sets (Context, Consciousness and Continuity) and three new skill sets (Connectedness, Creativity and Collectiveness); which became the elements of SL in their research paper.

Table 1. Sustainable leadership elements adopted from Tideman (et al., 2013) to the indian scenario (Column 3)

	SL Elements	Concepts (Economics and Business)	The Indian Context from a SL perspective
	1	2	3
	Mind-set		
1	Context	Recognising interdependence; complexity; ambiguity; interconnectedness; resource constraint; regulators; mega-trends	Regulations and complexity of law is multitude in India. How the Leaders are to figure out the nuances of managing change is a critical aspect.
2	Consciousness	Mind-sets; world-views; beliefs; mental models; attitudes	The *mores* and *folkways* contribute to much of the thought process and at times there is a fixation in the belief system, that will not move forward. How the Leaders make amends is critical to the scenario.
3	Continuity	Long-term horizon; courage; strength; common purpose; centredness; change processes	It is not about initiating a change or ushering in a thought process, it is how one can connect to the local scenario and move forward with strength on a continuous basis.
	Skill set		
4	Connectedness	Serving needs of all stakeholders; both long-term and short-term influencing; collaboration; trust; fairness; altruism; relatedness; needs instead of wants	With a myriad of stakeholders coming various economic, social and cultural background, the Leaders need to get to a better understanding which will ensure for themselves and the people with whom they are engaging.
5	Creativity	Innovation for sustainable shared value creation; sustainable business models; new value measurement models; flow	With multiple agencies and authorities, the Leaders in question need to ensure a creative connect with all stakeholders and business combinations for value creation on the short and long run.
6	Collectiveness	Scale up for collective impact; embedding sustainability in business structures; sustainable consumption	Considering the size of the nation, the Leaders need to ensure a community and societal connect which will ensure cumulative impacts of Economic, Environment, Socio-cultural, political as relevant to the geography and the community.

Roberts (2012) mentions, in order to be successful in the current context, transformational leaders typically exhibit the following five competencies:

1. **Holistic thinking.** They tend to see the 'whole' or big picture and avoid getting bogged down in siloed thinking
2. **Systems thinking.** They see relationships between parts of the organisation that others miss, fostering breakthrough innovation
3. **Humanistic thinking.** They are able to sense the emotions of others and connect on a 'heart' level when dealing with groups and teams
4. **Social optimism.** They can authentically envision today's big problems being solved, and use this vision to overcome cynicism
5. **Authentic filtering.** They quickly discern others' motives and react appropriately in complex social situations

The research team maps the five competencies to each of the individuals who have been considered for their Leadership Roles that have donned and still don, providing an opportunity for all us to have peek into their work, and unlearn/learn, how a Leader evolves in a difficult subject like Ecotourism, where everyone stands up and bats for the fact that with Ecotourism and its interventions, the earth, loses it pristine glory; but then these Leaders have stood against the odds and ensured a movement forward for others to emulate and take up the cudgels of a difficult subject to deal with and provide, strong, committed and vibrant Leadership, which will become a learning for all of us, as it is the legacy that we note and make an effort to understand.

Another Sustainable Leadership framework that the researchers would like to consider is the one put forward by Ferdig (2009); aptly titled the Sustainable Leadership Relational Model/framework, which will surely endear to the leaders that have been considered for the study.

Figure 1. Sustainable leadership relational model framework (Ferdig, 2009)

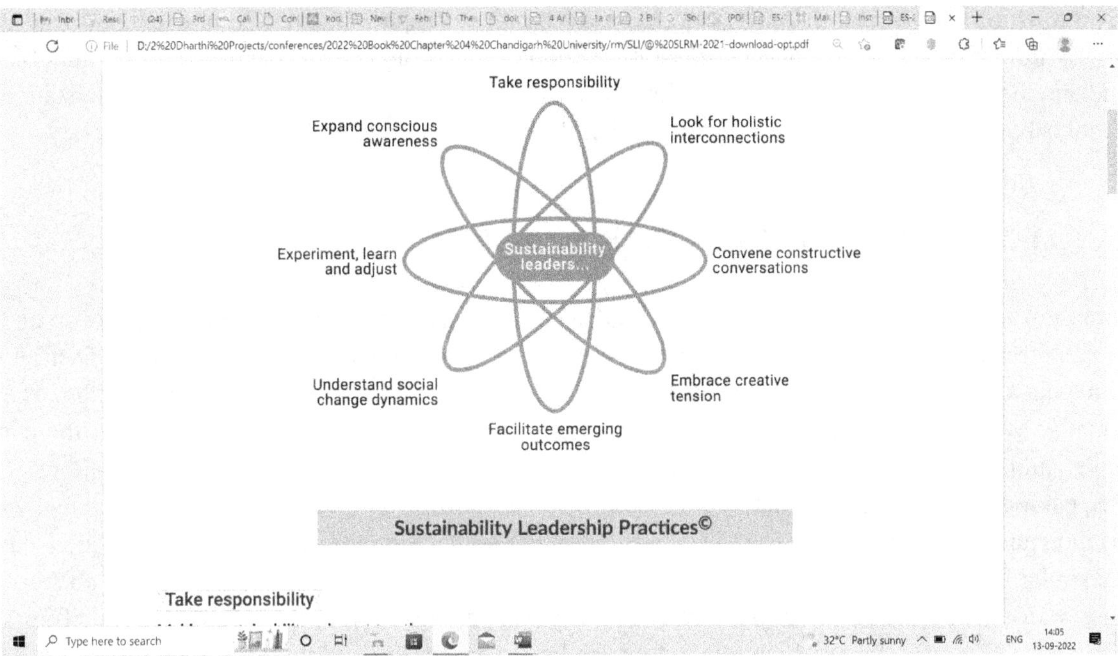

Ferdig (2007) further mentions that emerging discoveries in the complexity sciences viz., quantum physics, chemistry, biology, ecology, and social sciences point us toward a much different view of leadership that holds extraordinary potential for a powerful shift in our collective consciousness and actions. It ushers in a worldview that will challenge and lead towards to an alternative narrative. This view Ferdig (2007) further assumes that:

1. Anyone can choose to become 'a leader' and take responsibility for fostering sustainable conditions in workplaces, communities and even on a global scale; [the leaders portrayed in the chapter felt the need to usher in change in their workplaces and communities; true they had a worldview perspective; but they worked relentlessly from the local perspective. True in this genre, Legends like Jane

Goodall exist as global Leaders who give all of us the inspiration to create the small revolutions are a localized level];

2. The role of a Leader includes capabilities beyond those we currently attribute to Leaders, primarily, learning what it means to be a Leader 'with' other instead of Leader 'of' or 'over' others; [The traits the leaders have exhibited is not one to be recognized as a leader over many others; they just wanted to do the work on hand with complete commitment to the cause of the stakeholders and that inspiration lead the society, the community to recognize them as leaders. One can say that it was the love for the work that they professed, they contributed, leading one to refer to them and emulate their achievements]
3. A Leader cannot effectively operate outside of the holistic interconnections that exist among and between people and natural systems; [Well the question is where is the leader located? The Leader is with the people, the community, ensuring that they are in a position to provide for sustainable leadership which ensure a long-term factor for achievement and a way forward]

Clearly one can see that there is arbitrage or an argument to speak about sustainable leadership and the way it has helped in the ushering in sanity to a community, its people, the job at hand, the task at hand and the way we can move forward with elan and ensure a learning has happened by understanding the contributions of the four leaders we have identified as hero's who have contributed selflessly.

MANOJKUMAR IFS, AN INSTITUTION BUILDER

From the 1997 batch of Indian Forest Service Officers, Manojkumar, an individual who grew up under the mentorship of his mother Smt. Sarojini came from a quaint village, Tajlapur in Bidar District of Karnataka and came to learn of the hardships of the people and how to find solutions early on. These formative years of personal development ensured a qualitative understanding of the people, the community, and the administrative systems that he was part of.

Speaking with Narasimha Bhatt (Bhatt, 2022) an entrepreneur in the Joida area of Karnataka, who was motivated by Manojkumar as a Forest Officer in the area during his early career days, which led to Narasimha Bhatt creating a team of locals who would enact street plays (*Beedi Nataka*) to encourage conservation and preservation of the forests and also was instrumental in the creation of Kali Tourism Association (KTA) in Joida which focused on the local community and their involvement in tourism. Manojkumar, known to be an Institution builder provided the necessary encouragement, by providing inputs, training, network opportunities which has ensured a development and growth of the tourism system in the area as we see it today. Narasimha mentions, "the turning point came when Manojkumar conducted a workshop in the Kulgi Nature Camp which was the main source of inspiration and then on there was no looking back" Narasimha continues "he was with everyone, would sit with each one of us and ideate, it was the people connect that ensured the success of Manjokumar Sir in our area." One of the important aspects that Manojkumar helped build was to tell people about the wealth of the region and how to grow with it. Bhatt (2022a) recalling an episode as if it had happened yesterday, mentions, "Manoj Sir spoke of forest, and how visitors will come to see and enjoy the beauty, hence, we will have to develop Ecotourism, bring in sustainability, and thereby the forest itself will be saved…the way he focused on the Syntheri Rock, an important formation in the area of Dandeli, was phenomenal." Narasimha adds further, "Manoj Sir wanted a system in place, information to be provided to the visitors, which was a learning to the locals as well.....and he even got a Ecodevelopment Committee run by the Local community members, supported by the local Forest Staff created." This act of Manojkumar is a clear indication of his thought process that ensured the local community owns the institution and build upon on it in the future. Jagadeesh (2022) makes a mention of the fact that, the Kali Tiger Reserve (KTR) which is part of the Dandeli area, "had a logo, that was sees the creativity of Manojkumar...it was his involvement with the local community that ensured a connect and thereby the far reaching success."

Whilst discussing with the researchers, Manojkumar made a mention, "that he encouraged the local community members to come out with ideas, and helped to build upon them." Manojkumar mentions how when the Kali Tourism Association (KTA) conducted a workshop in a non-descript town called Hudsa in the Dandeli area, he invited Jungle Lodges and Resorts (JLR) (https://www.junglelodges.com) a leading provincial Government organization in Karnataka that promotes ecotourism and destinations, which are world renowned and engaged them with the local community, and encouraged how communication, information will support Community based ecotourism (CBE). Bhatt (2022) mentions, "this meeting ensured, the community stood together as one and joined in the movement to start the homestays in the area, homestays that are eco-friendly." "Today, the KTA has 25 permanent and 20 normal members in its group, and the meeting that were encourage from more than fifteen years, are conducted every month on the 25th without fail" mentions Narasimha.

SL Jagadeesh, a roommate of Manojkumar, and whom Manoj considers as a best friend; who currently works with the Provincial Horticulture University in the state of Karnataka as Associate Director of Research mentions, "Manojkumar would challenge himself not only academically and he has grown ensures that the work also challenges him and he stands up to the challenges and achieves the goal that is to be achieved" (Jagadeesh, 2022). An officer from the Indian Forest Service Santhosh Kumar, who worked as a team member with Manojkumar, confirms the same, "challenges, yes, he accepted them.....he has his own way of solving issues and problems." Kumar (2022) goes on to add, "it was his farsightedness that would ensure the challenges are solved...his focus on the 'process' than the 'person' would ensure success."

Going back to the challenges Manojkumar faced a Leader of a one of the oldest Zoo in India, the Mysore Zoo as its Executive Director (2004-06), Jagadessh mentions, "in my view it would have been one of the toughest times in his career...I saw him as a change-maker, when he took on the food contractors for feeding substandard food to the Zoo animals...he ushered in so many changes to ensure good feed reaches the animals in the Zoo, that the mafia with a strong underbelly in the system, even poisoned an elephant that was being gifted by the then President of India, Dr. Abdul Kalam to the Russia, one-day before it was to start its journey...this shook, Manojkumar...but he continued with the work... he worked with his inner strength...received necessary support from his superior officers and even the political elite." The researchers also gather from Jagadeesh that, "during these moments of his career Manojkumar even stopped reading newspapers, watching television, and despite all the pressure and tensions, carried on with his work, as a 'challenge' and ensured that communication which was the key to the success was done, and the Mysore Zoo became as we know of it today, one of the best in India and also financially sound."

Jagadeesh (2022) who has followed Manojkumar as his best friend, spoke of the fact that, "he never worked for his name, fame and success...he simply worked for society, the people, the community...in every post that he had adorned till date." "Though we have grown in age and experience and feel we are mature." Jagadeesh continues, Manoj is still the same as I saw him as a Forestry Student who moved ahead to pursue Master in Forestry in the Tamil Nadu Agriculture University, Coimbatore, Tamil Nadu...

where he majored on Teak Wood." Then one he was back as a Research Associate at the Agricultural University, Dharwad, Karnataka where he came under Prof. Nadagouder, who inspired him further and brought about the element of discipline. Jagadeesh mentions, "then on with his eyes set on Indian Forest Service Examination Manojkumar cleared the coveted examination with phenomenal scores in 1997 as a topper and moved to the Academy in Dehradun for the training and was later posted to Karnataka."

His work in the Research Wing of the Forest Department of Karnataka, his contributions as Chief Conservator of Forests (CCF) in Kodagu (Madikeri District) and Chamrajanagar have been exemplary. His work as CCF in Kodagu in managing the challenging Human Wildlife (Elephant) Conflict (HWC) that stands out. Getting the local community involved ensured that appreciation of the fact that, the issues need to be solved and not accentuated to unnecessary proportions. Considered as a HWC Zone of high intensity, Manojkumar was able to create community constructs, that helped manage the compensation based on the HWC and educate the difficult but unique scenario that the district in Karnataka faced. By creating the Kodagu Foundation to manage the issues, Manojkumar has ensured what many would not be able to do over years. To make a mention Kodagu/Coorg/Madikeri the land of the brave Kodavas and the land of Cauvery River, is home to Ecotourism that visitors not only flock from Karnataka but other parts of the India and the world.

Whether it was his work as the Head of Project Elephant or currently as Managing Director of Jungle Lodges and Resorts (JLR); Manojkumar has led from front in a silent way and ensured the necessary success that has to come in an organization. He always believes that people are important, but the process too has to be given equal importance; if not things fall apart. Jagadeesh (2022) mentioned about the most recent happenings when Manojkumar was on a field visit to Kabini an important destination of the JLR group; "he was able to solve minor and plaguing issues with an open hearted discussion with the employees…by asking for suggestions…and letting them to follow them with…which ensured success without any hindrance."

The researchers whilst engaged in a face-to-face discussion with Manojkumar brought out of the best of emotions in him, when he spoke about the strength his mother gave him as a child, which continues to stay with him as he performs his duties to the forest, the society, the people, the community. The researchers who have worked with Manojkumar and admired his acumen to solve issues amicably, without any distress or distraught speak about his simple ways of communication with people, here in case children of the Dandeli area; which led to the protection of the Hornbill, an endangered species by then on account of the fact that they were being killed for the meat by the locals. By targeting children who would visit the Dandeli area for sightseeing and camping; Manojkumar got an opportunity to interact and ensure a change in the minds of the children, whom he feels are the most important catalysts in ushering in change (NSJ, 2017). His story on the male Hornbill taking care of the female Hornbill who is the partner for life as they take care of the new born chicks in the cavity of a tree which is covered with mud and the female Hornbill would have shed its feathers to warm the chicks and is unable to fly. The Male Hornbill brings in food and the irony is that the locals kill the Hornbills for food, resulting in the family of Hornbills dying and yes, the Hornbills becoming extinct. The mere fact that the story told by Manojkumar is in a way is emotional and the children not only stopped eating the meat, but forced the adults in the house too; leading to the preservation and conservation of the Hornbill in the Dandeli area; leading to the area of 52.5 Sq. Km., becoming a Hornbill Conservation Reserve by a notification of the Government of Karnataka under the Wildlife Protection Act 1972 in 2011 (Chandra, 2011). This was the single most effort of Manojkumar which ensured the Hornbill received protection and the place was aimed at protecting, propagating, and developing the flora for the breeding and survival of the Hornbill; in fact, the Hornbill Conservation Reserve was the first of its type in the country (Chandra, 2011). Since the launch of the hornbill trail by the Tourism department of Karnataka, the wood depot located in Dandeli midtown attracts hundreds of tourists every day. This will now be a part of the conservation reserve to protect the rare birds characterised by their long, down-curved bill. Now a days Bird Festivals are being organized in the area leading to promotion of Sustainable Ecotourism and the destination has become a Birders paradise, all to the efforts of Manojkumar and the community that worked with him.

Currently as Managing Director of Jungle Lodges and Resorts, he mentions, that his task is to ensure the employees are empathized with, and managed well, who in turn will provide for a good experience to the visitors. He has ensured that changes are made in a subtle fashion that are acceptable to one and all, and they in turn ensure ownership and help the organization to be successful. Of course, being a core conservation and preservation of ecology, environment and forests officer, Manojkumar says, that we should move away from Tiger-centric tourism and ensure the visitors gets to enjoy every bit of the forest and its ecology, the flora, the fauna, the experiences that one can derive and ensure that they protect the environment and carry the message forward not only to the younger generation but the older ones as well.

Manojkumar marches on providing leadership to the conservation and preservation of the forests in Karnataka, creating benchmarks, for other to follow, and at best in a silent manner, and a silent person he is no noise, but work, the connect, the commitment, the communication, the people and to the process. People of Karnataka in a petition to retain Manojkumar had this to say, with more than two decades of service as an Indian Forest Service officer, he has had an unblemished record. Only a few IFS officers can place their hands on their heart and profess sincerity (Change.org n.d.). It is the ability of Manojkumar IFS to think from a holistic perspective, think humanely, and evolve social optimism, to usher in systems thinking, wherein institutions and processes will take precedence over people and plans and reacting appropriately to people and situations (Authentic Filtering) as mentioned by Roberts (2012) that ensures Manojkumar as a Dynamic Leader.

KIRAN CHAVAN, THE MAN WHO BROUGHT IN GREENERY

In the world of marketing, we always believe in Customer Delight and feedback. Reading one such feedback from a customer will help us to understand what a destination or a tourism product would look like.

"We went to Grape County for my birthday and I think this would be one of the most memorable birthdays I had. 250 acres of land with hills, 3 lakes, forest areas, natural flora and fauna, wild domestic animals and birds and so much more. We stayed in the lake view rooms which were so beautiful one of a kind. You can see the greens of the hills and lake on the foothills from the room and you can also enjoy boating and kayaking in the lake. Next day we went for Nature Trail and early morning walk in the greens and deeper areas. We also went around for property tour to take a look at their other properties like their forest stay rooms which are surrounded by lush trees and visited by certain wild animals as well, quite an adventure" (TripAdvisor, 2022). One read of the feedback would motivate more prospective visitors to travel to Nashik and sojourn at an Ecoresort called Grape County, which many consider to be one of the finest resorts in the state of Maharashtra.

Well Grape County was not all that is mentioned in the TripAdvisor feedback. To a perspective right, we have heard of areas that were green becoming deserts; we have heard about deforestation, concrete jungles coming up; but when we here of a place that was arid once upon a time and one individual on mission mode, ensured that, with his actions, support of a individuals, a buoyant community, turns an area into a green area; that in short is Kiran Chavan of Nashik, Maharashtra for you. Kiran not only planted saplings, but transplanted trees that were to be cut for road widening and brought them to the Grape County are which was part of 270 acres of barren land, adjacent to a Reserve Forest (As per Kiran more than 60,000 saplings were planted). Illustration 1 clearly demonstrates the way Grape County, famously known as GC has come about. Right to say, the vision of one man, Kiran Chavan, who wanted to blend the five elements of nature such that each and every ecotourist would get to connect with mother nature and learn as much.

Kiran was inspired by the fact that he wanted 'continuous growth' as a *mantra* that would ensure a success in his project. He just focused on the facet of the area being barren, it should have its Biodiversity and the elixir of life, water. Do whatever possible, that will ensure a change. Kiran also got an opportunity to travel to Mumbai and pursue a course through the Bombay Natural History Society (BNHS) (www.bnhs.org), which further inspired him to focus on bio-diversity and what it could do the environment. Besides, the peer interaction at BNHS, a book by Shiv Khera, 'You can win' inspired Kiran to move ahead, when everyone was pessimistic. Kiran simply believed in the facet of doing things differently and ensuring that it is done. Besides, he ploughed back to his network, that was to give Kiran his net worth over a period of time.

Figure 2. Satellite pictures of grape county (Chavan, 2022)

Luxpresso Magazine (2021), reported that visiting Grape County would be stepping into the wide-open luscious space and beautiful wooden landscapes. The stay at Grape County can help you reconnect with nature as well as yourself. Enjoying the sunrise over the mountains, simmering in the calming water, and indulging in different activities surely comes through as an exciting weekend getaway, where the only rule to follow is to take care of nature. The satellite images shown in illustrations (2 and 3), clearly provide an understanding as to what was done Kiran over a period of time.

Figure 3. Satellite picture of another space of GC (Chavan, 2022)

Figure 4. Tent accommodation closer to the Reserve Forest (Luxpresso Magazine, 2021)

As the area was being converted into a green zone and water harvesting measures were being taken, Kiran ensured that the construction of accommodation spaces gelled with the environment and ecology and would make it sustainable. Besides, creating tent accommodation (illustration 3), accommodation built on cantilevers, which did not interfere with the accommodation provided a phenomenal value add to the eco-tourist. iCraze (2021) reported that GC offers an unparalleled combination of a luxury resort and a first-class experience of nature. Any ecotourist would lap up the tourism product and get to understand nature better. Nidhi (2022) an eco-traveller had this to say in a review about GC. "....it is a home away from home, amidst the cradle of nature surrounded by well-maintained dense forest, three man-made lakes, which would collect the water during the rains..." The aim of Kiran was clear, ensure that the property takes care of itself without much of human intervention. The idea of bringing in a balance between humanity and nature by creating an ecosystem where all can co-exist is what Kiran and family thought of whilst establishing GC (Malhotra, 2021).

Looking at the sustainability initiatives of GC, it can be said it not only appears as a pledge, but as a prayer, "the core of GC functioning is centred around NATURE. Be it our eco living concept, the wellness retreats and our organic farm, GC believed that nature always takes care of us, so we need to take care of it. Our commitment to everything nature friendly can be seen in our ambition to always lookout for innovative and sustainable options. We take pride in our employees and all the members of our team in their enthusiasm towards sustainability."

With this bent of mind, Kiran has ensured that all attempts are made to put forward what Roberts (2012) mentions about the Holistic picture for GC, which would mean to ensure get to the bigger picture, working in a silo environment will not lead us anywhere; hence, a combination of facets that are put forward at GC has helped the ecotourist, to get to the best of nature. Kiran's' ability to think from a Systemic relationship of the organization, here in case GC and how to get to innovate ways of working around with existing resources has to be much appreciated. In GC one can see an emotion and each one of us get attracted to the emotion of preservation and conservation with a larger dimension of ensuring all the Eco visitors get to know new aspects and take it forward in their respective lives. Kiran, also mentioned in his discussions with the researchers, one of whom worked as his Sustainability Advisor for two quarters, that he was only surrounded by cynics, but it was his optimism that took him far and ensured what we see today. His whole idea was to ensure, ideation and a solution to every issue that came about whilst working on GC over the years. Kiran also feels that he has surprised everyone with his actions, and those believed that he will fail, have actually appreciated him for his vision, that had a right mission and an objective that was strong to achieve. So much so, Kiran Chavan will live as a phenomenal Leader who had a vision to move on and move fast, deliver the best possible Ecotourism product in a land that was barren and get people to think and apply his thought process to other places and ensure for the preservation and conservation of the environment and ecology, however, small it may be and contribute to the betterment of the Ecotourism.

RAKESH MATHUR, A RESPONSIBLE TRAVELLER

Rakesh Mathur, speaking at the Expo 2020 Dubai, India Pavilion, mainstreaming sustainability for future of tourism (India at Expo 2020, 2022), mentioned that "....70% of India Tourism is in the informal sector and bringing them under the umbrella of sustainability is important for all the stakeholders...." The aspects expressed by Mr. Mathur are real, and organizations like Responsible Tourism Society of

India (RTSOI) (https://rtsoi.org) (earlier known as Ecotourism Society of India-ESOI) which he helped found along with other doyens of Indian Tourism, Travel and Hospitality business, will play a dynamic role now and in the future to usher in the changes in Responsible Tourism in general, Ecotourism in particular and also bringing into the ambit certification and ecolabeling which will ever so important when it comes to standards which the world is adopting in a fast scale. RTSOIs game changer is the initiative of the 'responsible traveller,' will create a major buzz in the domain of sustainability, leading to the stakeholders to opt for ecolabeling and certifications. Rakesh led from the front to bring in a tripartite Memorandum of Understanding between RTSOI, Ministry of Tourism, Government of India (MoT, GoI) and the United Nations Environment Program (UNEP) which will ensure a 'Responsible Traveller' campaign to sensitize domestic travellers on the value of Responsible Travelling (Kumar, 2021). Rakesh has brought forth the finer aspects and mentions, "any Sustainability certification or eco-labelling should be 'practical' for the local environment; which will ensure for the stakeholders of tourism...in fact, it will become a collective responsibility to proceed towards sustainability with the Tourism and Hospitality service providers and most importantly the tourists playing a dynamic role in ushering in sustainability and Sustainable Ecotourism in particular."

For a person who practices what he preaches (Indian Express, 2011), Mr. Mathur sees sustainability in the eyes of the customer, who would like to focus on, "the positivity of Environment, the community, the weaker sections, women, the issues of waste and its management...thereby creating a responsible citizen and of course a Tourism organization that approaches Tourism and Hospitality with utmost sensitivity." Mr. Mathur is of the firm belief that Sustainability and its Certification in the Tourism system should not, "lead to 'whitewashing' by the tourism and hospitality stakeholders, but should be a movement towards a motivated business, an industry that will focus on the good of the world through Sustainable Tourism and Ecotourism."

Rakesh and his work have focused on ensuring that the carrying capacity of tourism at the destination is one that we all should take seriously. Rakesh adds, "there is no doubt a need for right auditing of the carrying capacity of the destinations, especially in the hill destinations in India which promote Ecotourism in a big way." Rakesh goes on further, "the Government at the Centre and States have to evolve and develop newer destinations to reduce traffic to the traditional destinations" Giving examples, Rakesh makes a mention of and comments, "how many of us have heard about Abbot Mount in Kumaon Hills...there are so many unexplored destinations in Pithoragarh, Almora, Kumaon Hills to mention a few which have to be developed and opened to promote quality Ecotourism and reduce the stress on the popular hills stations (Kumar, 2021a).

In order to promote Tourism in general and Ecotourism in particular which is a much more sensitive business proposition considering the fragility of the ecosystem, Rakesh believes that "we need to protect the places we love while receiving benefits that help us transform with our impact on the destination." Taking further inspiration and with a stoic determination, Rakesh exemplifies and elucidates that, "one needs various approaches to be taken, be it voluntary, statutory, or even punitive if necessary to ensure a motivation of the travellers and visitors to embrace the 'I am Responsible Traveller' initiative into a movement that will bring in the elements of responsibility to tourism and hospitality business" (RTSOI, 2021). Always available to speak to the concerned community or stakeholders of Ecotourism, Rakesh makes it a point to address them, whenever, wherever and, however. When he spoke to the remote communities and Forest Officers of Kanha Tiger Reserve (KTR) on the dynamics of Ecotourism promotion and the way it is to be done; the communities, the Village Heads (*Pradhan*), the Forest Officers, got a feel what is to be done to ensure quality in Ecotourism (RTSOI, 2022).

Rakesh was also instrumental in ensuring a thought process towards Sustainable Tourism in all its dimension when he was part of a team that helped in the creation of the Sustainable Tourism Criteria for India (STCI) (GK Today, 2014) based on the framework as established by the Global Sustainable Tourism Council (GSTC) (https://www.gstcouncil.org), a Global body with a footprint in most of the countries of the world. STCI were formulated by a committee constituted by the Ministry of Tourism of which Rakesh was a part of. STCI has been launched to develop tourism in India based on principles of sustainability and minimizing carbon footprints. While talking about sustainability, one should not only talk about conservation of resources but also our culture and heritage. All the stakeholders in the Tourism industry were to be made become eco-sensitive and implement the STCI (PIB, 2016). The principles of STCI included conservation of water, energy, culture, heritage, revival of ancient architecture, involvement of communities, protection of wildlife and non-exploitation of women, children and weaker sections (GK Today, 2014). Rakesh constantly makes a mention, the idea is not about creating a framework for implementation by others, it how we ensure that it is understood STCI and followed by each of the stakeholders to the last word possible. In his efforts to demystify the to the tourism and hospitality stakeholders especially in the Ecotourism Sector, Rakesh put forward these guidelines (RTSOI, 2018) for Natural and Wildlife Lodges which were well received.

1. Rainwater harvesting
2. Use of Renewable Energy
3. Local Food products
4. Engaging local community

Rakesh who ensures his thoughts are articulated with elan, says these are need of the hour and the requirement to ensure for the tourism and hospitality that is focussing on Ecotourism. Clearly the intent of Rakesh was to ensure a qualitative framework for the working of the Tourism and Hospitality domain, and a way forward to sustainable options for one and all.

Rakesh was part of the Chambal River Ecotourism Expedition, where the effort was to introduce nature-based tourism as an alternate income to the dacoit/bandit ridden area in central India. The Chambal Expedition was one of the practical initiatives that he undertook to create and ensure a tourism product that was sensitive, in a multitude of things that he has over the decades along with the Co-founder of RTSOI Mr. Mandip 'Mandy' Singh Soin, who was the founder of Ibex Expeditions. They floated the idea of Sustainable Tourism to the Madhya Pradesh Ecotourism Development Board (MPEDB), then led by Mr. AK Bhattacharya IFS as CEO and did the initial reconnaissance. Though the project has not seen the light of the day, if implemented, one of the major aspects of the proposal is employing former dacoits as tour guides, which would go a long way in making the region safe and rehabilitating dacoits with the promise of a stable, legitimate income. Tourism would also infuse much-needed money into the conservation of Chambal's heritage and biodiversity (Sood, 2019).

Figure 5. Rakesh Mathur (Center) along with Mandip 'Mandy' Singh Soin (Ibex Expeditions, n.d.)

The researchers have interacted with Rakesh Mathur Ji on multiple occasions and comes out to be a Leader who wears Sustainable Ecotourism on his sleeve and masquerades the same to ensure the best for the Tourism and Hospitality businesses. His approach to taking along people, from across the businesses is a learning by itself, and his ever-willing support, a that lit pep talk, will ensure even most pessimist of individuals, will stand motivated to move ahead and do good for self and the business one is holding on to.

Juxtaposing the five competencies of Roberts (2012) with Rakesh, one can see that he clearly understands the larger picture of the issue being addressed and ensures an understanding for the team and the way forward. Very innovative in approach, Rakesh ensures every issue is addressed by the concerned individual or stakeholders, which ushers in the facet of systemic thinking that ultimately brings in creativity to the project. All those who have interacted and got to work with Rakesh, consider him to be 'man of the heart' which clearly means, his approach is no doubt strict and straight forward, but when required, he ensures that the individuals and groups are taken into confidence as the groups move forward with the task at hand. His humane approach has endeared him to many in the tourism and hospitality business. It is the optimism in Rakesh that helps each one around him to move ahead and achieve the necessary success; it is the quick connect that he establishes, the leads one to accept the way of thinking, for the organization or the project concerned and move ahead. Facing complex situations on a day-to-day basis has ensured that Rakesh makes the best of difficult situations, being a phenomenal negotiator himself. In any complex situation, the right person to have as part of your team, is Rakesh Mathur, and he continues to contribute to the Tourism scenario in general and Ecotourism in particular as a Leader who is takes along a team of equals.

AKB, THE FOREST CRUSADER

Dedicating his life to Forestry, Environment, Ecotourism and Bamboo, Dr. Ajoy Kumar Bhattacharya, All India Topper (Concept, n.d.) of the 1983 batch of Indian Forest Service, who served in Madhya Pradesh and continues to work for the communities and the Foresters even to this day. Dr. Bhattacharya was a rare Civil Servant who had a Doctorate and a Post Doctorate (TERI, 2018) in the field of Ecology and Environment and used all his knowledge and experience to further the cause of Ecotourism more so based on the Community and the benefits they can accrue and the support they can provide to the forest department. He has been engaged as expert and consultant with many leading organisations and corporate including TERI, IIFM, Somaiya Group of Industries. He has wide range of overseas exposures, including University of Tasmania, UNFCC in New York, Universities of Syracuse and Vancouver, Universities of Yale and Washington, Marrakech (CoP 22) (TERI, 2018).

Though there have been many bureaucrats in the Forest Departments across India, but, AKB as he is popularly known as, is a unique blend of Research and Administration, something he did with elan, as observed by Mohamad Nahar a Ecotourism Consultant who was a student of AKB, when he taught at the famed Indian Institute of Forest Management (IIFM) (https://iifm.ac.in), Bhopal. Nahar (2022) was a student of AKB and learnt the nuances of Ecotourism, Community Development and Forest Conservation. Nahar mentions that, "AKB was a very polular Professor who carried with him, his students who respected him for his knowledge and ability to communicate in a succinct manner." "AKB introduced me to Ecotourism at IIFM and when he became the Founding Chief Executive Officer (CEO) of the First Ecotourism Development Board, that was set up in Madhya Pradesh, took me on rolls at the Madhya Pradesh Ecotourism Development Board (MPEDB) where my learning continued and continues till date." "He is a visionary in his own right and is a known Institution Builder with his out of the box thinking." Nahar categorically mentions, that whenever there was a difficulty in getting the support of the administrative machinery, he introduced the private public sector participation (PPP) which ensured continuity of the flow of thought and the administrative requirements for any project that was the need of the hour."

In the many discussions that AKB has had with the researchers of this article, he mentions, "throughout my career I have always tried to deliver. I believe in outcome and outputs with systems approach. I give my 100% to work in the existing situations, without blaming system, try to improve the system from within. For me, forestry has been a tool for sustainable development. I have successfully used Ecotourism and Bamboo as tools for sustainable development" and continues to do so even after retirement after he found the Integrated Development Organization (IDO) of which he is the Chairman. Shailendra Kumar, the CEO of IDO, who has seen and interacted AKB for more than two-decades mentions, "..... Bhattacharya Sir will study the finer aspects of the work that is being done, the impacts that it has on the community, how to bring in resources, however difficult, and once he has made up his mind, there is no looking back to any force on earth…he will ensure executing the job at hand, with multiple follow ups, with superiors, prodding the junior, talking to the forest staff, like a friend but at the end of the day ensuring that the work is done with elan" (Kumar, 2021).

It was his pioneering work in the domain of Ecotourism, that is remembered by one and all. His format years as a young forest administrator ensured the learnings and the interactions with the communities, administrators, non-governmental organizations (NGO) which ensured, he was able to implement the best of thoughts at MPEDB, that became a benchmark for other provinces in India to start specific operations on the front of Ecotourism by creating the Ecotourism Development Boards (EDB) on the lines that AKB had established in Madhya Pradesh. Acknowledging the contribution of AKB a forester in Karnataka, who wanted anonymity, mentions, "Bhattacharya really made use of the situation provided to him in MPEDB and created Standard Operating Procedures (SOP) which were to be implemented on the i) communities, who were part and parcel of any Ecotourism canvas, ii) the Resorts that were mushrooming in large numbers across Madhya Pradesh and the way to manage them, iii) the role of the Foresters, especially the 'cutting edge' staff, who only knew about preservation and conservation, and could not deal with the commercial activity of Tourism, iv) the Ecodevelopment Committees (EDC) that were formed to engage the communities, with the Foresters acting as Administrators…Bhattacharya had his hands full…but he managed to set a benchmark for many of us to follow across India, and we bettered the EDB set-up in Karnataka by creating a legal entity, which has augured well for the system at large." This really means much to the contribution of AKB, who always, mentions, that, "trials and tribulations of any job, is a challenge in itself, and MPEDB was a baby that I had to nourish and ensure it is cherished for posterity." Arun Rai, a contract employee of MPEDB, who was recruited by AKB during his tenure at MPEDB whilst discussing with one of the researchers at a program in Kanha mentions, "he was and is a task master; once if a decision is taken to implement an administrative decision… AKB will ensure…if we as executives in the MPEDB, were not able to understand some aspects of the work and interventions being done, he would step in, work with us, help us to understand and ensure, we carry on; though a task master, his humane approach is liked by one and all (Rai, 2022). The team at MPEDB, with whom the researchers have interacted, mention, that the main contribution of AKB to the field of eco-tourism includes organizing capacity building workshops and training courses for the local officers not only of the forest departments but other units of the Government as well. There was an instance of a training program, wherein the forests of Kanha and the Ecodevelopment Committee (EDC) members interacted and created artefacts to ensure quality ecotourism in the area. Based on the suggestions from one of the Range Forest Officers (RFO) who spoke of banks not providing loans and funds for the local communities to start enterprises in ecotourism and even agriculture related activities; AKB during the tea-break of the capacity building program, picks up his phone and calls the National Bank for Agriculture and Rural Development (NABARD) in the area, speaks with him and the next forty-five minutes the Manager is present addressing the gathering of Forest Officials and the Local Community, and believe it or not the NABARD officer was able to provide for loans for at least three individuals, based on which others would follow, and then there would be a movement. Those were the effective ways in which AKB ensured traction for the community and the Foresters and the forests.

AKB always believed in ensuring that documentation has to be done to ensure the future is aware of what was attempted and tried. The researcher in him ensured the writing continued, which led to much documentation throughout his career and still continues to do so. Some of the work that AKB published has been listed out for one to see the wide canvas he adopted and ensured people, bureaucrats, administrators, communities, activists got to know about the happenings.

Bhattacharya (2005) wrote a book, *Ecotourism and Livelihoods* which primarily were his experiences in the field, i.e., the forests of Madhya Pradesh. He wrote his book when he was on deputation as a Professor at the Indian Institute of Forest Management (IIFM) (https://iifm.ac.in) in Bhopal. The book focuses on capacity building For Local Authorities Tourism which is the most rapidly growing and biggest industry in the world and Ecotourism forms the largest proportion of the present tourism. His focus was on the fact that, since ecotourism involves maximum number of stakeholders, from local Communities to the Corporate world, proper capacity building of the major stakeholders for effective planning and management of ecotourism has become a prerequisite for the sustainable ecotourism development. This book attempts to fill in this gap. The book addresses the key issues concerning ecotourism management, with special focus on community participation. It deals with a range of Topics including the basic concept, forms, potential assessment, planning and case studies of ecotourism. At the same time, it discusses the New Concepts and techniques of ecotourism, viz. carrying capacity, community participation and auditing. The book has been a useful field guide for practitioners, researchers and other stakeholders in planning and implementation of ecotourism.

Bhattacharya (2001) worked on communities and how to ensure they get to activity that is sustainable in the forest. The book, *Community participation and Sustainable Forest Development, Global perspective* has been a sincere attempt to examine the phenomena of community participation, sustainable forest management, sustainable development with reference to the forest policies, forest acts and other relevant and necessary documents not only from India but from other countries. The focus of the book are the communities and how to engage them in a better for sustainable forest development.

Forests in India are under the exclusive control and management of the Federal/Central and State Governments. Speaking of public people private partnership in the forest management was something, that was dreaded by many for a long time, and some even dread it today. However, Bhattacharya (2007) edited a phenomenal work titled: *Public People Private Partnership for sustainable forest development* which the researcher would consider as a bible of sorts to managing the intricate forest ecosystems in India, despite all the difficulties and Laws that are at hand which will ensure stoppage of any work that one will envisage; as a path breaking contribution by Ajoy K. Bhattacharya, who people in the know fondly address as 'AKB.' The book is a compendium of research papers and articles that were presented at the IIFM workshop, and are of a great support to policy makers, conservationists, students and researchers of environment, ecotourism and ecology and even the environmental activists who can get a peep in the happenings on the front of the forest, ecology and environment. The compendium focuses on issues pertaining to participation of communities, individuals, and corporates in sustainable development of forests and wastelands. The authors of each chapter discuss at length the stakes of the i) Local communities, ii) leasing of forest land based on the Forest Conservation Law, iii) how to share the profits from the produce and iv) socio-economic and ecological implications. The work also identifies the issues, the problems, the constraints and makes an effort to suggest remedies and action that would have impact on the long run.

People, communities, *Gram Panchayats* through the Local Self-Government (LSG) mechanism play a pertinent role in Ecotourism and how it impacts not only the ecology and environment, but how does it impact the conservation and preservation methods. The Bio-diversity of an area or region has always been a question. Bhattarcharya (2005) through his field experiences brought out a book titled: *Training manual on People Bio-diversity Register*. Though a small book; it had all the documents and relevant action plans that the people at ground-zero had to make to ensure collation of data according to the Community Bio-diversity Register (CBR). The work actually encourages people at the village level to collect and collate data and ensure the way the impacts are recorded from across all angle, environmental, economic, social, cultural and even political. A contribution that has been considered as crème de la crème in Indian forestry is a work that he rendered by editing two volumes with a total of fifty-five papers, of which fifteen focused on Ecotourism. Bhattacharya (2007a) addresses the emerging issues in forestry, and focuses on five contemporary themes, viz., Ecotourism agroforestry, joint forest management, non-timber forest products and his favourite topic; public private partnership in forestry. So much was his vision, that the way he documented has ensured it becomes a primary read to anyone involved in Ecotourism in particular and forestry in general.

AKB always believed that, in accordance with the prime spirit of eco-tourism, the shape of tourism will have to be such as to make the forest-dependent communities' partner in the benefits of tourism, along with conservation of natural resources, environmental protection and social adaptability (MPEDB, 2005). This was many is a heady concoction, but if one were to gauge the impacts on the long run, on Ecotourism, it is a legacy that individuals like AKB leave behind for posterity. He looked beyond forests and ecotourism and collaborated with Mandip 'Mandy' Singh Soin FRGS, the legendary Adventurer from India, who was instrumental is establishing the Responsible Tourism Society of India (RTSOI) and made an effort to work out a Tourism Product in the River Chambal that was dreaded once upon a time on account of its dacoits; but today, the River with all its pristine beauty, the flora, the fauna and the yes, the various heritage sites that abound around the banks of the rivers and the ravines which still give an eerie feeling to at least one generation, and can evolved as a story line that falls into the cusp of the Wild West, but in an Indian parlance. But for various reasons the project never kicked off. Recently when the researchers were speaking to AKB he was recalling the splendid time, the ideation that was there, during the discussions on the river Chambal, spoke immensely about the flora and fauna and the intrigue that exists with the river and how we should promote the life-giving River as a tourism product and ensure the communities living on the banks of the river are taken care with quality employment and the visitors get an experience of a life-time.

Applying the framework of Roberts (2012) to the close to four decades of work done by AKB on the domain of Ecotourism one can mention that, the holistic thinking that AKB had in getting the larger picture and ensuring all elements of the Government machinery work in tandem along with other stakeholders, more importantly the Community, is something that he saw in the right spirit. His ability to work on the PPP initiative very early on in his career and at a time, when private sector participation in the Governmental works was seen as an impediment, AKB ensured phenomenal relationship that augured well for the system. Though AKB has been considered as strict in his approach towards administration; his ability to understand the emotion of the stakeholders has been seen in the way his associates vouch for him. He always approached pessimism, cynicism with strength, that ensured he was able to overcome the negative and work positively towards the cause of ensuring success for the project at hand. He never put down anyone or any organization. All were important in his view, and each had a role to play; the timing of his reactions in complex situations and scenarios ensured a forward movement in the projects undertaken. This makes AKB a Leader par excellence which each of us should adopt in our day-to-day life.

Figure 6. (Left to Right): Mr. Sujit Banerjee, Chairman of World Heritage Sites Committee, Mr. Mandip 'Mandy' Singh Soin, FRGS and AKB. Second Expedition in 2011 to propose Chambal as a World Heritage Site (Ibex Presentation, n.d.)

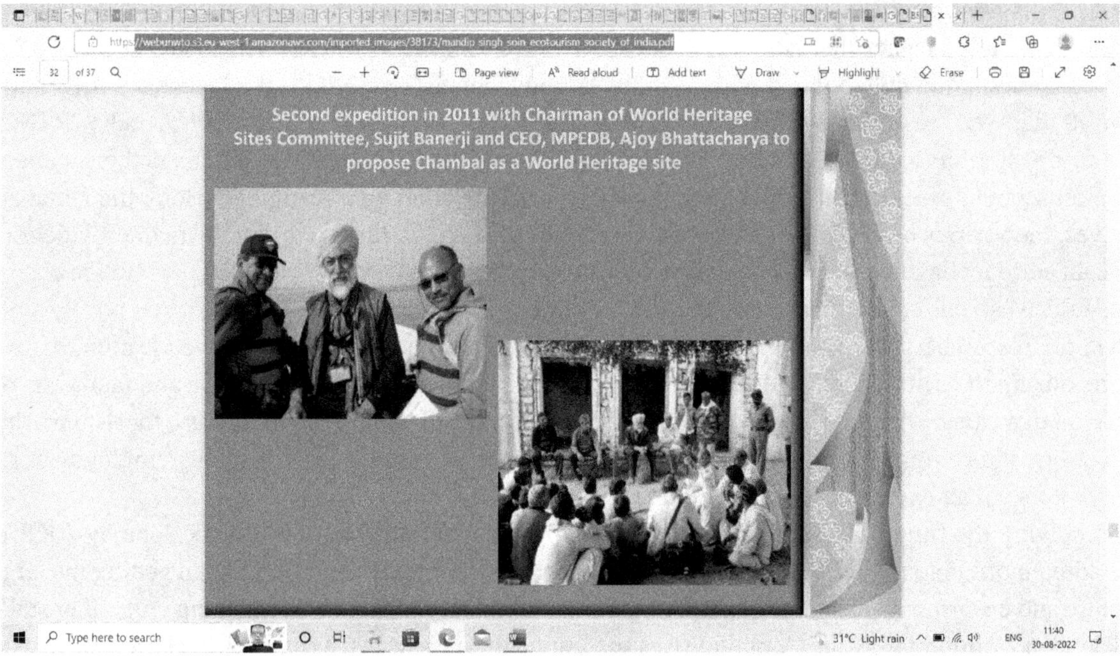

Table 2. Tideman (et al., 2013) framework of Sustainable leadership (SL) and its application on the four leaders

	Sustainable Leadership Elements	Concepts (Economics and Business)	The Indian Context from a SL perspective	Manojkumar	Kiran Chavan	Rakesh Mathur	AK Bhattacharya
	Mind-set						
1	Context	Recognising interdependence; complexity; ambiguity; interconnectedness; resource constraint; regulators; mega-trends	Regulations and complexity of law is multitude in India. How the Leaders are to figure out the nuances of managing change is a critical aspect.	Understand the set up well	Clear understanding	Quick to understand any issue at hand, dealing with the Government and Private Sector	Very well defined. No ambiguity
2	Consciousness	Mind-sets; world-views; beliefs; mental models; attitudes	The *mores* and *folkways* contribute to much of the thought process and at times there is a fixation in the belief system, that will not move forward. How the Leaders make amends is critical to the scenario.	Has a clear mind set which is to work with the people and put a process in place	Had a clear mind set and worked towards the goal	Plenty of clarity, mind maps what is to be done, short-term and long-term	Conscious of the fact what is to be done.
3	Continuity	Long-term horizon; courage; strength; common purpose; centredness; change processes	It is not about initiating a change or ushering in a thought process, it is how one can connect to the local scenario and move forward with strength on a continuous basis.	Work should go on even without my presence is the moto of Manojkumar	Work should go on. Educated the team of the requirements	Ensures follow-up for successful outreach that brings in success of the projects on hand	Follow-up was one of the successful postulates of his career
	Skill set						

Continued on following page

Table 2. Continued

	Sustainable Leadership Elements	Concepts (Economics and Business)	The Indian Context from a SL perspective	Manojkumar	Kiran Chavan	Rakesh Mathur	AK Bhattacharya
	Mind-set						
4	Connectedness	Serving needs of all stakeholders; both long-term and short-term influencing; collaboration; trust; fairness; altruism; relatedness; needs instead of wants	With a myriad of stakeholders coming various economic, social and cultural background, the Leaders need to get to a better understanding which will ensure for themselves and the people with whom they are engaging.	Always connected to the ground realities and the people	Knew what is to be done and by whom	Understand the needs of the stakeholders, and collaborates well by supporting the stakeholders	Connected to the ground realities and will to collaborate and ensure for the success of the project
5	Creativity	Innovation for sustainable shared value creation; sustainable business models; new value measurement models;	With multiple agencies and authorities, the Leaders in question need to ensure a creative connect with all stakeholders and business combinations for value creation on the short and long run.	Ability to solve issues in a creative way and ensure success for the system	Can be seen in bringing in people of all hues to ensure success	Believes in Value creation and works well with all stakeholders. Goal and the path to the goal is considered important	Always thought out of box and ensured brainstorming that led to success in every project undertaken
6	Collectiveness	Scale up for collective impact; embedding sustainability in business structures; sustainable consumption	Considering the size of the nation, the Leaders need to ensure a community and societal connect which will ensure cumulative impacts of Economic, Environment, Socio-cultural, political as relevant to the geography and the community.	Always with the community, a typical team player, never leaves anyone behind	Work together at all odds	Believes in the *mantra* of TEAM, together everyone achieves more	A true team player, knowing the strengths of each of his team members who come from diverse ways of life

REFERENCES

Bhattacharya, A. K. (2001). *Community participation and sustainable forest development, global perspective*. Concept Publishing.

Bhattacharya, A. K. (2005). *Ecotourism and Livelihoods*. Concept Publishing.

Bhattacharya, A. K. (2005). *Training Manual on People's Bio-diversity Register*. Concept Publishing.

Bhattacharya, A. K. (2007). *Public People Private Partnership for Sustainable Forest Development*. Concept Publishing.

Bhattacharya, A. K. (2007a). *Forestry for Next Decade: Managing Thrust Areas (Set of 2 Vols)*. Concept Publishing.

Chandra, N. S. (2011, September 2). *Reserve for Hornbills near Dandeli*. Retrieved from https://www.deccanherald.com/state/reserve-for-hornbills-near-dandeli-181997.html

Change.org. (n.d.). *Citizens: Retain IFS Officer Manojkumar #WeNeedManoj Back as Member Secretary KSPCB*. Retrieved from https://www.change.org/p/cm-of-karnataka-citizens-retain-ifs-officer-manoj-kumar-weneedmanoj-back-as-member-secretary-kspcb

Concept. (n.d.). *Book details, The Wildlife Memoirs, a forester recollects*. Retrieved from www.concept-pub.com/servlet/Detail?bookno=00001081

Expeditions, I. (n.d.). *Embracing the Sustainable Tourism Criteria of India for the Tour Operator Segment, Mandip Singh Soin, FRGS*. Retrieved from https://webunwto.s3.eu-west-1.amazonaws.com/imported_images/38173/mandip_singh_soin_ecotourism_society_of_india.pdf

Ferdig, A. (2007, March). Sustainability Leadership: Co-creating a Sustainable Future. *Journal of Change Management*, *7*(1), 25–35. doi:10.1080/14697010701233809

Ferdig, A. M. (2009). *Sustainability Leadership Relational Model and Practices*. Retrieved from https://www.sustainabilityleadershipinstitute.org/downloads/SLI_model_download.pdf

iCraze. (2021). *Grape County by Green Spaces. iCraze, January-February 2021*. Retrieved from https://www.magzter.com/stories/Lifestyle/iCraze/GRAPE-COUNTY-BY-GREEN-SPACES

India at Expo. (2022, January 9). *Expo 2020 Dubai, India Pavilion, Mainstreaming Sustainability for Future of Tourism*. YouTube. https://www.youtube.com/watch?v=Iq_z2Z2CzV4

Indian Express. (2011). The Boss of Heritage Holidays. *The New Indian Express*. Retrieved from. https://www.newindianexpress.com/lifestyle/2011/jul/31/the-boss-of-heritage-holidays-276867.html

Kumar, P. K. (2021, October 7). *We are a society of like-minded people working for a cause.* Retrieved from https://hospitality.economictimes.indiatimes.com/news/travel/we-are-a-society-of-like-minded-people-working-for-a-cause/86835984

Kumar, P. K. (2021a, October 7). *Industry should support RTSOI with CSR funds to spread the message of responsible tourism: Rakesh Mathur.* Retrieved from https://travel.economictimes.indiatimes.com/news/associations/industry-should-support-rtsoi-with-csr-funds-to-spread-the-message-of-responsible-tourism-rakesh-mathur/86834603

Mackey, J., & Sisodia, R. (2014). *Conscious Capitalism: Liberating the Heroic Spirit of Business.* Harvard Business School Press.

Magazine, L. (2021, July 1). *Grape County Eco Resort, Get one with Nature.* Retrieved from https://www.luxpressomagazine.com/post/grape-county-eco-resort-get-one-with-nature

Malhotra, P. (2021, January 19). *Create an ecosystem where we can all co-exist.* Retrieved from https://bwhotelier.businessworld.in/article/Create-an-ecosystem-where-we-can-all-co-exist-Chavan/19-01-2021-367116/

Marshall, J., Coleman, G., & Reason, P. (2011). Leadership for Sustainability: An Action Research Approach. Greenleaf Publishing. https://doi.org/10.4324/9781351278287.

MPEDB. (2005). *Madhya Pradesh State Forest Policy, 2005.* Retrieved from https://mpforest.gov.in/ecotourism/pdf/forestpolicy.pdf

Nidhi, B. (2022, July) *Heaven on Earth! 2nd home amidst nature. Place to be in your checklist.* Retrieved from https://www.tripadvisor.in/Hotel_Feature-g303883-d11880822-zft1-Grape_County_Resort.html

NSJ. (2017) *Chief Conservator of Forests Manojkumar (IFS), "Connect with Nature" and "The Role of Media in Conservation".* https://www.facebook.com/nsojbangalore/videos/chief-conservator-of-forests-manoj-kumar-ifs/1542730205785597/

PIB. (2016, March 14). *Sustainable Tourism Criteria for India.* Press Information Bureau, Government of India, Ministry of Tourism. Retrieved from https://pib.gov.in/newsite/PrintRelease.aspx?relid=137882#:~:text=The%20Ministry%20of%20Tourism%20has,been%20adopted%20by%20the%20stakeholders

Roberts, M. (2012). *Transformational Leadership.* www.world viewthinking.com

RTSOI. (2018). *Sustainable Tourism Criteria for India (STCI), Practicing Responsible Tourism.* Regional Workshop, Ahmedabad. Retrieved from https://www.rtsoi.org/wp-content/upoads/2019/11/Ahmedabad-Nov18-Report.pdf

RTSOI. (2021, August 20). *Rakesh Mathur, President, RTSOI talks about his approach of being a responsible traveller* [Video]. YouTube. https://www.youtube.com/watch?v=1c_RSPq0CpE 01:08

RTSOI. (2022). *Just another day in the office of Mr. Rakesh Mathur.* https://m.facebook.com/ResponsibleTourismSocietyOfIndia/videos/just-another-day-in-the-office-for-mr-rakesh-mathur-president-and-founding-membe/267810335525306/

Sood, S. (2009, March 1). *From bandits to birds like sonchiriya: The Story of Chambal.* Retrieved from https://www.cntraveller.in/story/bandits-birds-like-sonchiriya-real-story-chambal/

TERI. (2018). *AK Bhattacharya.* Retrieved from https://wsds.teriin.org/2018/bio/AK-Bhattacharya.pdf

Tideman, S. (2013). Sustainable Leadership: Towards a Workable Definition. *Journal of Corporate Citizenship, 49.* https://www.researchgate.net/publication/263604448_Sustainable_Leadership_Towards_a_Workable_Definition

Today, G. K. (2014, August 27). *Comprehensive Sustainable Tourism Criteria India (STCI) Launched.* Retrieved from https://www.gktoday.in/topic/comprehensive-sustainable-tourism-criteria-india-stci-launched/

TripAdvisor. (2022). *Grape County Resort Rooms: Pictures & Reviews* - Tripadvisor; www.tripadvisor.in

Chapter 7 Green Innovation in Tourism Businesses

Mehmet Tekeli
https://orcid.org/0000-0002-6069-4740
Karamanoğlu Mehmetbey University, Turkey

ABSTRACT

Today, while all countries worldwide emphasize the significance of environmental awareness, among the sector areas, the tourism sector is the one that should focus on this matter most. The current study aimed, with examples from the tourism industry, to reveal the perspective of tourism businesses on green innovation practices, their practices, and the results obtained. After giving information about the innovation concept, scope, and types in general, this study provided fundamental explanations about the green innovation concept, scope, and types and dealt with the concept of green innovation in tourism businesses. Finally, the current study that provided general information about tourism environmental awareness certificates assessed the tourism sector by presenting examples of green innovation applications.

INTRODUCTION

The ever-increasing industrial activities, technological developments, rapid population growth, and unconscious use of resources negatively affect the environment. Global corrective policies and discourses at various levels have become widespread to reduce these adverse, sometimes even irreversible, effects on the environment. International environmental regulations such as the Montreal Convention, the Kyoto Protocol, and rising public awareness have started a global struggle to prevent increasing environmental pollution. In this connection, organizations have beguen production, green management, and green marketing, to reduce or eliminate environmental pollution problems (Chen et al., 2006).

The importance of green innovation practices in the tourism industry, which interacts so much with the environment, is increasing. The close relationship between tourism and the environment leads businesses to work on environmental awareness (Işık et al., 2017; Rennings, 2000). In particular, increasing touristic movements, tourist concentrations, and touristic business enterprises worldwide can cause significant destruction to the environment. Destroyed natural resources take a long time to self-recover,

DOI: 10.4018/978-1-6684-6732-9.ch007

Copyright © 2023, IGI Global. Copying or distributing in print or electronic forms without written permission of IGI Global is prohibited.

and sometimes it may even become impossible. Therefore, businesses should adjust their competitive strategies according to current environmental conditions to respond to tourists' demands thoroughly (Porter & Linde, 1995).

Green innovation practices cover, concurrently with the technology development and sustainable development goals, the protection of nature in tourism, more efficient use of natural resources, prevention of damages to the environment, and reduction of waste (Carrillo-Hermosilla et al., 2010). Tourism businesses can create various adverse effects on the environment during their activities. Touristic activities such as bathing, cleaning, cooking, lighting, air-conditioning, golf course and garden irrigations, and swimming pools take the total energy consumption of hotels to high levels globally. For example, a visitor who settles in a touristic hotel meets 90% of his energy consumption from hotel resources and causes the use of more than 100 kg of fossil fuels in an average two-week vacation (Mastny, 2001). The tourism sector has a significant impact potential on the environment with its services such as accommodation, food and beverage, entertainment, transportation, etc. Therefore, adopting green innovations in the sector is of great significance.

The current study dealt with the green innovation concept within the tourism sector. In this context, after briefly touching on the innovation concept based on the literature studies, the current study discussed the green innovation approach and types, green innovation practices in tourism businesses, some international tourism labels and certificates, and examples of green innovation practices. Finally, it generally evaluated green innovation practices in the tourism sector.

THE CONCEPT AND SCOPE OF INNOVATION

In the business world, rapidly increasing globalization, knowledge, and competition, which affect technological developments, lead businesses to more innovation (Apanasovich et al., 2016: 30). In other words, today, commercial enterprises have to attach importance to innovation concept to survive into this tough rivalry of the market (Neff & Moss, 2011). Businesses have begun to attach great importance to innovation activities, especially since the 21st century. Although some think that the innovation concept attracts exaggerated attention in some areas, today, it attracts more attention from businesses due to market conditions (Demirci, 2012: 4).

The economist Joseph Schumpeter, known for his work on innovation, stated in his work titled The Theory of Economic Development that innovation is a directly influential factor in economic growth and competition. Schumpeter (1939) expressed that an invention or a discovery would have no financial value unless it contributed to a new product or production stage. In this framework, innovation, an economically important concept, connotes transforming discoveries or inventions into economically beneficial forms (Barutçugil, 1981; Rosegger, 1996). In this context, innovation is not just an invention or development; it also encompasses institutional, organizational, technical, and social applications (Larsen, 2005).

According to Freeman (1982), the innovation concept includes the first commercial use of a new process or tool and the design, method, production, and commercial activities carried out to market a new product. Drucker (1985) defines innovation as adopting and producing new products and services. The Oslo Manual prepared by OECD describes innovation as the realization of a new or significantly improved product or process, a new marketing method, or a new organizational method in internal business activities, organization, or external relations (Oslo Kılavuzu, 2005).

Businesses seek to gain a competitive advantage through innovation. In this respect, they approach innovation from a broad perspective and try to implement new technologies on the one hand and new ways of doing business on the other (Porter, 1990). As a result of the innovations implemented by the enterprises, a product, a service, or a more advanced method model may emerge (Vatan & Zengin, 2014). Different influential factors are available in the innovation work of enterprises. In general, the desire for growth, economic opportunities, willingness to try their abilities in new fields, financial situation, and competitiveness affect the innovation efforts of businesses (Afuah, 2009).

There are many classifications regarding the concept of innovation. According to the Oslo Manual, innovation is broadly classified into four categories: product, process, marketing, and organizational innovations. Product innovation is a commodity or service that has been significantly modified for the product's features or intended use. Such innovations include significant improvements in tools, components, software, technical specifications, or other functional aspects. Process innovation refers to new or significantly improved production or distribution methods or appropriate and new processes. Such innovations involve significantly improving techniques, equipment, and software. Marketing innovation improves product pricing, design, packaging, positioning, and promotion. In other words, it is the adoption of new marketing methods. Organizational innovation lays out machinery, equipment, external information, and training activities related to the organization (Oslo Kılavuzu, 2005).

THE CONCEPT AND SCOPE OF GREEN INNOVATION

After the industrial revolution, mass production quickly developed. With this development, the industry has started to consume natural resources intensively. The destruction of the environment and natural resources in such a manner has caused significant problems, such as high environmental pollution, increasing greenhouse gas emissions, thinning of the ozone layer, global warming, and climate change (Yin & Li, 2019). The growing environmental concerns in public, rising environmentally friendly consumer behaviors, domestic and international regulations, and sustainability policies have enabled the development and implementation of environmental policies and practices worldwide (Albort-Morant et al., 2017; Zailani et al., 2015). With these developments, the concept of sustainability has become more critical to eliminating adverse environmental effects, and the concepts of *environmental management*, induced by environmentally friendly approaches such as green innovation, green production, green management, and green marketing, have become widespread (Chen, 2008).

Green innovation, which aims to reduce environmental damage, appears as a sub-dimension of general innovations (Arfi et al., 2018; Song et al., 2019). In recent years, implementing various policies in many countries to eliminate or mitigate environmental damage has increased the interest in green innovation in the academic and political environment (Boons & Ludeke-Freund, 2013; Saunila et al., 2018). Defining the green innovation notion is problematic because of its similarity to many other concepts in the literature (Arundel et al., 2006). In the literature, various concepts such as "green innovation," "ecological innovation," "environmental innovation," and "sustainable innovation" are used interchangeably (Boons & Ludeke-Freund, 2013; Carrillo-Hermosilla et al., 2010; Hall, 2006).

Green innovation applications not only serve in green and clean sectors where renewable energy systems are available but also in various organizational, technical, and commercial sectors. Green innovation refers to product and process innovations that can apply in many industries and provide high environmental sustainability. Such innovations include green practices expressed in concepts such as environmental innovation, ecological innovation, sustainable innovation, innovation for sustainable development, clean technology, and sustainable production and marketing (Habash, 2018).

Chen et al. (2006) comprehensively describe green innovation as "hardware or software innovations related to green products and processes, including pollution prevention, energy conservation, waste recycling, green product designs and technological innovations within the corporate environmental management." In other words, green innovation is developing and implementing new attitudes, ideas, products, and processes to reduce negative environmental impacts and contribute to sustainable development goals (Rennings, 2000). In addition, green innovation includes efforts that can be developed and applied at every stage–from production to waste–to reduce environmental damage (Büyükkeklik et al., 2010).

Green innovation applications refer to the adoption of novel or developed products, processes, systems, applications, and techniques to minimize or prevent environmental damage. In this respect, green innovation practices cover all business activities within the framework of sustainability, such as ecological efficiency, ecological design, reduction of environmental footprints, waste management, recycling, reduction of emissions, and waste management (De Marchi, 2012). In addition, enterprises adopt green products, renewable energy, the reproduction of recycling agents, and green management approaches (Rennings, 2000). In this context, green innovation, which is effective in environmental protection, resource-saving, and long-term development (Yang et al., 2021), is vital for a sustainable economy and social development (Song et al., 2019).

Green innovation is the practice in which most businesses carry out innovation and sustainability studies simultaneously to increase economic gain and competitiveness. Organizations should consider environmental awareness activities as an opportunity to gain competitive advantage rather than as a cost-increasing factor or a threat (Lee et al., 2006). In today's conditions, businesses can gain competitive advantage when they meet environmentally sensitive consumer expectations and manage environmental problems systematically and strategically (Esty & Winston, 2007). In addition, businesses should produce innovative solutions against the changing conditions of products, processes, management systems, technologies, and consumer demands and expectations (Porter & Linde, 1995). Businesses head towards green innovation activities for reasons such as creating a good image in the eyes of consumers, using environmentally friendly production technologies, developing environmentally friendly marketing strategies, receiving government subsidies, and reducing the costs of recycling practices (Şenocak et al., 2018).

Green innovation is recommended as a strategic goal to ensure an environmentally, socially, and economically harmonious development (Zhou et al., 2021). The green innovation approach, which aims to reduce the environmental impact of the product in the design, production, use, and waste processes (Arfi et al., 2018), also contributes to the issues such as meeting new consumer demands, creating value and increasing productivity (Albort-Morant et al., 2017). Green innovation, an efficient approach to social development and the development of the urban environment, aims to increase energy efficiency and reduce consumption (Fei et al., 2016). Since green innovation practices positively affect environmental, social, and economic results, they also significantly contribute to business sustainability (Aguilera-Caracuel & Ortiz-de-Mandojana, 2013; Zhang et al., 2019). On the other hand, the significance businesses attach to sustainability in terms of social, institutional, and economic aspects increases their tendency to invest in green innovations (Saunila et al., 2018).

Green innovation is an influential force for businesses to compete in the world market, considering the environmental dimension of global competition. In addition, green innovation practices are accepted as an effective tool to reduce or prevent environmental damage caused by business activities to ensure sustainable development (Göral et al., 2013).

CLASSIFICATION OF GREEN INNOVATION

Researchers have classified green innovation in different ways: Chen et al. (2006) and Tang et al. (2018) sorted green innovation as *Green Product Innovation* and *Green Process Innovation*, while some researchers categorized green innovation practices in three ways: *Green Product Innovation, Green Process Innovation, and Green Organizational Innovation* according to the innovation field or subject (Cheng et al., 2014; Chiou et al., 2011; Kammarer, 2008; Rennings et al., 2006).

Green Product Innovation

Green product innovation, which is increasingly strategically significant in theory and practice, occurs from the interaction between innovation and sustainability (Dangelico & Pujari, 2010). Green product innovations implemented by businesses emerge as a crucial factor in achieving goals in issues such as economic development, competition, a better quality of life, and environmental sustainability (Dangelico & Pujari, 2010; Carrillo-Hermosilla et al., 2010). The concept of green product innovation, defined as the production of new products that cause less harm to the environment (Tang et al., 2018: 40), pertains to the innovation of products that include environmentally friendly packaging, environmentally friendly materials, ecological labeling and recycling (Chen et al., 2006; Chen, 2008). Because of its scope, green product innovation provides simultaneous benefits to producers, consumers, and the environment. In this respect, green product innovation has a triple effect (Kammarer, 2008).

Green product innovation is a multifaceted process that draws attention to three critical environmental focal points–*material, energy, and pollution*–based on the impacts of different stages of a product's physical life cycle–*production, utilization, and disposal*–on the natural environment. Green product innovation practices focus on critical environmental aspects such as pollution, materials, and energy. In other words, initiating green product innovation at any stage of the product life cycle can provide businesses with a competitive advantage and product differentiation (Dangelico & Pujari, 2010). Green product practices generally include improving materials or technical product components, launching new or improved products, reducing the negative impact of products on the environment throughout their lifecycle, and developing new products to meet consumer demands and expectations (Xie et al., 2019).

Green Process Innovation

Green process innovation covers clean technology and eco-saving equipment utilizations to increase energy efficiency, reduce greenhouse gas emissions and optimize resource use (Khan & Johl, 2019). Such innovations refer to the ability of enterprises to improve their production processes, save money and develop new approaches to prevent pollution (Chen et al., 2006; Cheng et al., 2014). Green process innovation is essentially about waste recycling, pollution prevention, energy saving, and preventing environmental damage (Yücel, 2021).

It is possible to divide green process innovations into two "clean technologies" and "end-of-pipe technologies" (Rennings et al., 2006). End-of-pipe technologies include tools such as wastewater treatment systems, exhaust cleaning equipment, sound absorbers, incinerators, etc., which are not directly part of the production process but ensure compliance with environmental protection. Clean technologies, on the other hand, include innovations related to less use of resources, energy, or by-products while trying to reduce the situations that may harm the environment during production activities. Using organic solvents and integrating the combustion chamber into the green innovation process are among the sample innovations in this regard (Rennings et al., 2006).

End-of-pipe technologies have been developed to comply with environmental regulations such as water conservation, waste disposal, air quality control, and noise reduction technologies. Clean technologies, on the other hand, provide continuous improvement and cost advantage for the production process in business activities (Chiou et al., 2011). Such green process innovations reduce the production cost of enterprises and increase resource efficiency. Thus, green process innovations significantly reduce the overall costs of the enterprise and provide a sustainable competitive advantage (Chang, 2011; Chen, 2008). In the green process innovations, enterprises need to meet some criteria related to the production process (Chen et al., 2006):

- Ensuring waste emission and effectively reducing hazardous materials
- Reuse of waste and emissions through recycling processes
- Less consumption of substances such as water, oil, electricity, and coal
- Reducing raw material consumption

In general, the technologies which cover green process innovations focus on a sustainable environment and business-beneficial matters such as waste management, reducing pollution, protecting water and raw materials, saving energy, and increasing productivity (Chen et al., 2006). In addition, a business can fully implement green innovation with an integrated innovation approach at both the product and process levels (Li et al., 2019), and thus, the business might impact the environment positively. On the other hand, integrating green products and green process innovations impacts business performance positively (Tang et al., 2018).

Green Organizational Innovation

Green organizational innovations involve reorganizing processes and responsibilities in the business to reduce environmental impacts. Environmental management systems can be cited as a typical example of Green organizational innovation (Rennings et al., 2006). In other words, green organizational innovation covers innovations that affect the activities and processes of the enterprise. Besides, adopting environmental management systems and acting in accordance with these systems is within the framework of green organizational innovations (Göral et al., 2013). Such innovations include new ways of organizing business processes, new business forms, and new relationships with other businesses and public enterprises (Horbach et al., 2012). Enterprise objectives, strategies, management attitudes, and organizational structures fully affect the implementation of green organizational innovations. Such innovations have a process that widely impacts the current ways of doing business (Küçükoğlu, 2014).

Environmental management and control systems in businesses, pollution prevention schemes, and defining and reporting responsibilities related to materials, energy, waste, and water use can be examples of green organizational innovations (Triguero et al., 2013). Green organizational innovations are a supporting factor for other green innovations (Rennings et al., 2006) and contribute to the enterprise's environmental compatibility by helping the green product and process innovation implementations (Cheng et al., 2014). Usually, green organizational innovations provide a suitable basis for developing and simply implementing other innovation types.

GREEN INNOVATION IN TOURISM BUSINESSES

Since environmental factors make up the most important source of tourism, there is a close interaction between tourism and the environment. Therefore, tourism businesses benefiting from the natural environment must demonstrate an environmentalist approach by considering sustainability. In this respect, the importance of green innovation practices for the tourism industry is increasing. Environmental values should be emphasized for the improvement of tourism at a destination. Uncontrolled and unconscious expansions in accommodation, food and beverage, entertainment, transportation, and souvenir areas in a tourism business can harm the environment. This kind of expansion might cause damage to the natural resources of the region and its attractiveness. Therefore, essential to the existence of tourism is a sustainable environment (Işık & Barlak, 2018).

Green innovation in tourism refers to protecting nature, more efficiently using natural resources, preventing environmental damage, and reducing waste simultaneously with developing technology and within sustainable development goals. In the tourism sector, green innovation practices are mainly concerned with reducing environmental pollution, providing cost advantage, and gaining competitiveness and sustainability. In this respect, green innovation practices, a common approach in business and environmental policies, focus on economic development and competition (Carrillo-Hermosilla et al., 2010).

Tourism businesses can create various unfavorable effects on the environment during their activities. Research on this subject reports that the tourism sector causes 4.6% of global warming (İpar & Aksu, 2022). In addition, according to the data prepared by UNWTO in 2007, the accommodation sector is responsible for 21% of the world's carbon dioxide emissions (Lo et al., 2014). For this reason, tourism, which has many social, cultural, and economic benefits for individuals, also poses a significant threat to the natural environment (Korkmaz & Atay, 2019). Developing green innovation and environmental awareness will be influential in reducing environmental damage. In this direction, concepts such as "environmentally friendly hotel," "green hotel," or "green management" are gaining importance in tourism. Green hotels are touristic businesses that have solid and liquid waste management systems, prioritize recycling and reusing activities, save water and energy, and give importance to protecting biological diversity (Güneş, 2011).

The concept of green hotel, which is becoming increasingly widespread, causes changes in hotel design and operation in many classifications, from boutique hotels to world-renowned hotel chains. While some of the ever-increasing number of green hotels do not have any electronic equipment, some simply try to save money by changing towels and sheets whenever customers want. However, the best solution for touristic facilities in the globalizing world should be to reduce the total carbon footprint and water consumption by using all new technologies (Hotel Restaurant Magazine, 2022a). In other words, tourism businesses should make product, process and organizational innovations in order to meet the changing touristic demand, while minimizing the negative effects of these innovations on the environment. Thus, both the expectations of tourists can be met and important responsibilities can be fulfilled for the sustainability of tourism.

Studies on environmental awareness in the tourism sector started in the early 1980s. During these periods, ecological efficiency gained importance, and solutions for environmental pollution began to be emphasized. At the beginning of the 1990s, various award and certificate programs became widespread for tourism enterprises, especially for accommodation businesses and travel agencies. Today, many touristic enterprises, especially international chain hotels, focus on environmental approaches and follow different policies in this field (Korkmaz & Atay, 2019).

ENVIRONMENTAL AWARENESS CERTIFICATES AND GREEN INNOVATION EXAMPLES IN TOURISM

Tourism enterprises have turned to environmentalist approaches to prevent environmental damage resulting from tourism activities. In this direction, tourism businesses have started to adopt some titles such as "Environmentally friendly hotels," "Green hotels," etc. However, to obtain these titles, tourism businesses need to meet some criteria and have particular certificates such as eco-labels and eco-certificates.

Ecological labeling is the sign that shows the effect of the product on the environment at every stage and aims to inform the consumers. The products or processes of the tourism business obtain an eco-label if they meet the "ecologically reliable" criteria of the organization that issues the eco-label (Korkmaz & Atay, 2019). About 60 "green hotel" labels are available worldwide, and they differ according to geographical scale, tourism sub-sectors, focal points, and certification method (Lo et al., 2014). The labels showing environmental awareness, such as Green Globe, Green Key, Green Seal, Green Leaf, Ecotel, and Blue Flag, are among the most well-known ones (Buckley, 2013; Korkmaz & Atay, 2019; Tan & Wright, 2022; Yılmaz & Atik, 2022). Apart from these labels, hotel businesses can also obtain certificates such as EU Label, EU Ecolabel, LEED, BREEAM, EMAS, CASBEE, Green Star, and ISO 14001 for their facilities, just like businesses in other sectors (Korkmaz & Atay, 2019; Yılmaz & Atik, 2022). In general, the requirements tourism enterprises should fulfill to obtain eco-labels can be classified as follows (Giritlioğlu & Güzel, 2015: 891):

- Water saving and energy efficiency
- Recycling waste and reducing the use of harmful substances
- Use of renewable energy sources
- Environmentally friendly planning of tourism businesses
- The compatibility of tourism businesses with the environment. Their practices regarding environmental regulations and activities
- Practices of tourism enterprises regarding environmental awareness, personnel training, and cooperation with institutions and organizations

Green-friendly hotels widely attach importance to energy and water saving, recycling, reuse of towels, environmental cleaning, organic foods, durable service items, well-trained personnel in green practices, donations to environmental foundations, etc. (Han & Kim, 2010; Lee et al., 2010). Non-durable consumer goods that cause air, water, and soil pollution and waste energy and water are the most significant factors that cause environmental damage in tourism (İpar & Aksu, 2022).

Mensah (2004) states that some environmental practices reduce the operational costs of hotels. Energy-saving light bulbs, using washing machines' discharge water in toilet flushes, irrigating golf courses and gardens using treated wastewater, implementing comprehensive environmental protection and waste recycling programs, employing power tracking systems, raw material conversion, using energy efficiency programs, double glazing applications are efficient processes lowering the corporational costs in hotel businesses (Mensah, 2004).

Green hotels perform some saving-based green innovation practices for cost advantages and environmental awareness. For example, Hilton group hotels, employing the LightStay system for systematic energy and water consumption management from a single center has reduced water consumption by 7.5%, carbon dioxide emissions by a 10.9%, and energy consumption by 9.7%, and saved over 174 million dollars in total. The Rotorua Hotel has achieved significant savings thanks to the sensor application in the toilets and low-pressure shower heads. The Westin San Francisco Hotel, which has implemented a waste recycling program, profited $6000 annually from waste, such as 22000 tons of paper, aluminum, food, and beverage (Aydin & Aydın, 2016). Similarly, the Westin Bayshore Hotel has saved approximately $100,000 by reducing its annual electricity consumption by replacing the light bulbs used in the hotel with energy-saving ones and using smart monitors to reduce the climatization in empty spaces. (Walsh & Dodds, 2017).

Regnum Carya Golf & Spa Resort, which obtained the first LEED Gold certificate in Turkiye, returns rain and shower water to nature with its gray pipe system. In addition, its architectural structure, which benefits from sunlight with its large windows, is among the best examples of green hotels (Özar Berksü, 2020). Saçılık and Çevik (2014) have stated that Güngör Ottoman Palace Hotel–which has ISO 14001 environmental management system–sends all environmentally-threatening waste oils, personal care product residues, and bathroom garbage to recycling companies. Besides, the hotel uses energy-saving faucets in all rooms and solar energy for power requirements. Reportedly, these practices reduced energy consumption by 40-50% and water consumption by 20-30%.

The wastes generated during the construction of the LEED Gold-certified Mandarin Oriental Bodrum Hotel were used in recycling and reusing areas. Their landscape planning included less water-requiring plants suitable for the region's climate. A sea-water treatment system serves for garden irrigation. In addition, energy-saving glasses chosen by the hotel provide energy savings of 34%. The hotel's interior chemicals–such as pastes, adhesives, and paints–were selected with low VOC ratios (Özar Berksü, 2020).

The LEED Silver-certified Clarion Hotel Golden Horn has energy-saving faucets and mechanical equipment in line with international standards to ensure water and energy efficiency. In addition, the hotel has electric vehicle charging stations and bicycle parking areas to support alternative transportation options and tools and reduce carbon dioxide emissions from motor vehicles (Özar Berksü, 2020).

The LEED Gold certified Renaissance Istanbul Bosphorus hotel seeks to reduce its carbon footprint with green practices such as efficient climatization, maximum use of sunlight, increased indoor quality, using local and recycled materials, using environmentally friendly materials, and generating its own electricity. The hotel preferred energy-saving LED bulbs with 60-70% electricity savings. With the Grey Water System, the wastewater in sinks and showers is filtered and used in WCs, thus saving 30-40% of water. In addition, they educate the hotel employees on environmental awareness within brand reputation (Hotel Restaurant Magazine, 2022b).

As in every field, the tourism sector has to follow and implement green innovations. Because today, people who want to travel, stay and vacation not only look at the stars of the hotels, but also take into account the symbols and certificates that show the environmental sensitivity of the business. Accordingly, the number of hotels that define themselves as environmentally friendly is also increasing. Thus, thanks to the green innovations applied in tourism businesses, awareness is created on issues such as the necessity of sustainable travel and tourism, the importance of environmentally friendly hotels and eco-labels. Some of the points to be considered by environmentally friendly hotels in order to create these awareness are as follows (Güneş, 2011):

- Utilizing alternative energy sources
- Avoiding the use of harmful chemicals and cleaning agents as much as possible in housekeeping and laundry

- Making use of alternative options (such as using treated wastewater for toilet expenses or garden irrigation) to protect natural resources
- Taking care to offer locally grown products and organic foods to tourists
- To save energy and water
- To ensure that conference and meeting rooms are arranged with an environmentalist approach
- Choosing cotton or organic cotton products for towels, covers and sheets, in terms of being healthier
- To raise awareness of both tourists and personnel about environmental approaches
- Creating public awareness on this issue by including environmentalist approaches on the hotel's website
- Ensuring participation in environmentally sensitive activities
- Products such as towels, sheets and pillowcases in the rooms are not changed too often, unless necessary, during the use of the same guest
- Having non-smoking rooms and health clubs in hotels
- Making extra efforts on environmental issues

Environmentally friendly activities implemented by hotel businesses mainly focus on reducing environmental damage. On the other hand, these applications are used as an important strategy to influence the preferences of tourists who want to buy environmentally friendly goods and services. In this context, hotel businesses that focus on the environment and seek innovative solutions to ensure sustainable competition can improve environmental performance. In addition, hotel businesses can launch new green products and create new markets in this way (Leenders and Chandra, 2013).

In general, green hotel practices include the adoption of environmentalist approaches such as saving water and energy, reducing environmentally harmful uses, recycling, encouraging recycled material utilization, using renewable energy resources, lowering costs, ensuring optimal use of labor, environmentally friendly investing, etc. (Süklüm, 2018). In addition, green hotels gain significant advantages in terms of competition, ecological responsibility, risk minimization, media recognition, employees' loyalty, social assistance, productivity, local communities' support, and improving investor relations (Akandere & Zerenler, 2017).

CONCLUSION

Since the tourism industry has many relationships with the environment, environmental awareness in this sector is more significant than in others. In particular, globally increasing touristic movements, tourist concentrations, and touristic enterprises severely threaten the environment. Therefore, while making innovations in accordance with the changing demand, tourism enterprises should also consider the adverse effects of the enterprise on the environment. In addition, changing preferences and increasing environmentalism lead tourism enterprises to adopt environmentally friendly approaches.

Tourism enterprises, which adopt environmental approaches, gain competitive advantages in the market and become sustainable. Tourism businesses, which are aware of this situation, are more willing to implement green innovation. The priorities of tourism businesses, using green products, processes, and organizational innovations, are the issues such as reducing environmental pollution and destruction, reducing costs, and increasing competitiveness and sustainability.

Green innovation applications carried out in tourism enterprises may require huge investments, and compensating for these investments may take a long time (Ipar & Aksu, 2022). However, over time, tourism businesses can gain a significant competitive advantage by being the first choice of environmentalist tourists. In addition, tourism businesses, which contribute significantly to their environment's sustainability, can reduce their costs by saving water and energy with their green innovations.

For tourism businesses to continue their activities in the long term, they need to consider the balance between conservation and utilization within a sustainability framework and use environmental values without overexploiting them (Tekeli & Kırıcı, 2020). In addition, tourism enterprises' environmentalist production and marketing innovations reduce the unfavorable effects on the environment significantly. As a result, green innovations, the common point of economic development, business policies, and environmental policies, are a strong focal point in reducing the rising environmental issues.

FUTURE RESEARCH DIRECTIONS

Within the scope of green innovation, there are many applications that tourism businesses and stakeholders can do to protect the environment. Considering the environmentally sensitive attitudes of individuals, it becomes clear that businesses need to constantly renew themselves. On the other hand, environmental factors constitute the main source of tourism activities. These basic elements should be used in a sustainable way by tourism businesses. Within the scope of sustainability, tourism businesses need to implement green innovations, both inside and outside the building, in a way that best meets the expectations of individuals. At this point, businesses should lead other stakeholders. In addition, tourism businesses, managers and all stakeholders should be willing to determine and implement strategies by prioritizing environmental awareness. On the other hand, the green innovation policies of tourism businesses should be compatible with national and international policies. At this point, the evaluation of the appropriateness and effectiveness of national and international policies and the practices of businesses is an important issue for both managers and researchers. Especially researchers have important duties in revealing the effects of green innovation practices on the environment in a systematic way.

REFERENCES

Afuah, A. (2009). *Strategic innovation*. Routledge. doi:10.4324/9780203883242

Aguilera-Caracuel, J., & Ortiz-de-Mandojana, N. (2013). Green innovation and financial performance: An institutional approach. *Organization & Environment*, *26*(4), 365–385. doi:10.1177/1086026613507931

Akandere, G., & Zerenler, M. (2017). Yeşil otellerde yeşil tedarik zinciri yönetimi ve işletme performansına etkisi. *Uluslararası Turizm ve Sosyal Araştırmalar Dergisi*, *2*, 77–98.

Albort-Morant, G., Henseler, J., Leal-Millán, A., & Cepeda-Carrión, G. (2017). Mapping the field: A bibliometric analysis of green innovation. *Sustainability*, *9*(6), 1011. doi:10.3390u9061011

Apanasovich, N., Heras, H. A., & Parrilli, M. D. (2016). The impact of business innovation modes on SME innovation performance in post-Soviet transition economies: The case of Belarus. *Technovation*, *57*, 30–40. doi:10.1016/j.technovation.2016.05.001

Arfi, W. B., Hikkerova, L., & Sahut, J. M. (2018). External knowledge sources, green innovation and performance. *Technological Forecasting and Social Change, 129*, 210–220. doi:10.1016/j.techfore.2017.09.017

Arundel, A., Lorenz, E., Lundvall, B. A., & Valeyre, A. (2006). The Organization of Work and Innovative Performance: A comparison of the EU-15. In *Druid Working Papers* (pp. 12-48). Aalborg University.

Aydın, Ç., & Aydın, C. (2016). Konaklama sektöründe enerji kullanımı ve sıfır enerjili binalar kavramı. In 8. lisansüstü turizm öğrencileri araştırma kongresi bildiri kitabı (pp. 34-47). Bizim Büro Matbaacılık ve Basımevi.

Barutçugil, İ. (1981). *Teknolojik yenilik ve araştırma geliştirme yönetimi*. Bursa Üniversitesi Yayınları.

Boons, F., & Lüdeke-Freund, F. (2013). Business models for sustainable innovation: State-of-the-art and steps towards a research agenda. *Journal of Cleaner Production, 45*, 9–19. doi:10.1016/j.jclepro.2012.07.007

Buckley, R. (2013). Social-benefit certification as a game. *Tourism Management, 37*, 203–209. doi:10.1016/j.tourman.2013.01.004

Büyükkeklik, A., Toksarı, M., & Bülbül, H. (2010). Çevresel duyarlılık ve yenilikçilik üzerine bir araştırma. *Süleyman Demirel Üniversitesi İktisadi ve İdari Bilimler Fakültesi Dergisi, 15*(3), 373–393.

Carrillo-Hermosilla, J., Del Río, P., & Könnölä, T. (2010). Diversity of eco-innovations: Reflections from selected case studies. *Journal of Cleaner Production, 18*(10-11), 1073–1083. doi:10.1016/j.jclepro.2010.02.014

Chang, C. H. (2011). The influence of corporate environmental ethics on competitive advantage: The mediation role of green innovation. *Journal of Business Ethics, 104*(3), 361–370. doi:10.100710551-011-0914-x

Chen, Y. S. (2008). The driver of green innovation and green image–green core competence. *Journal of Business Ethics, 81*(3), 531–543. doi:10.100710551-007-9522-1

Chen, Y. S., Lai, S. B., & Wen, C. T. (2006). The influence of green innovation performance on corporate advantage in Taiwan. *Journal of Business Ethics, 67*(4), 331–339. doi:10.100710551-006-9025-5

Cheng, C. C., Yang, C. L., & Sheu, C. (2014). The link between eco-innovation and business performance: A Taiwanese industry context. *Journal of Cleaner Production, 64*, 81–90. doi:10.1016/j.jclepro.2013.09.050

Chiou, T. Y., Chan, H. K., Lettice, F., & Chung, S. H. (2011). The influence of greening the suppliers and green innovation on environmental performance and competitive advantage in Taiwan. *Transportation Research Part E, Logistics and Transportation Review, 47*(6), 822–836. doi:10.1016/j.tre.2011.05.016

Dangelico, R. M., & Pujari, D. (2010). Mainstreaming green product innovation: Why and how companies integrate environmental sustainability. *Journal of Business Ethics, 95*(3), 471–486. doi:10.100710551-010-0434-0

De Marchi, V. (2012). Environmental innovation and R&D cooperation: Empirical evidence from Spanish manufacturing firms. *Research Policy, 41*(3), 614–623. doi:10.1016/j.respol.2011.10.002

Demirci, A. E. (2012). Yenilik yönetimi. In Temel kavramlar (pp. 2-15). Açıköğretim Fakültesi Yayınları.

Drucker, F. P. (1985). *Innovation and entrepreneurship, practice and principles*. Perfect Bound.

Esty, D. C., & Winston, A. S. (2007). *Yeşilden altına akıllı şirketler çevreci stratejiler ile nasıl avantaj yaratır?* Mediacat.

Fei, J., Wang, Y., Yang, Y., Chen, S., & Zhi, Q. (2016). Towards eco-city: The role of green innovation. *Energy Procedia, 104*, 165–170. doi:10.1016/j.egypro.2016.12.029

Freeman, C. (1982). *Innovation and long cycles of economic development. Seminário Internacional*. Universidade Estadual de Campinas.

Giritlioğlu, İ., & Güzel, M. O. (2015). Otel işletmelerinde yeşil yıldız uygulamaları: Gaziantep ve Hatay bölgesinde bir araştırma. *Journal of International Social Research, 8*(40), 889–904. doi:10.17719/jisr.20154013968

Göral, R., Akgöz, E., & Topuz, Ç. (2014). *Turizm işletmelerinde yeşil iş modeli inovasyonu yönetim aracı olarak yeşil inovasyon radarı. In Ulusal Turizm Kongresi Bildiriler Kitabı*. Detay Yayıncılık.

Güneş, G. (2011). Konaklama sektöründe çevre dostu yönetimin önemi. *Karamanoğlu Mehmetbey Üniversitesi Sosyal ve Ekonomik Araştırmalar Dergisi, 13*(20), 45–51.

Habash, R. (2017). *Green Engineering: Innovation, Entrepreneurship and Design*. CRC Press. doi:10.4324/9781315116389

Hall, J. (2006). Environmental supply chain innovation. In *Greening the supply chain* (pp. 233–249). Springer. doi:10.1007/1-84628-299-3_13

Han, H., & Kim, Y. (2010). An investigation of green hotel customers' decision formation: Developing an extended model of the theory of planned behavior. *International Journal of Hospitality Management, 29*(4), 659–668. doi:10.1016/j.ijhm.2010.01.001

Horbach, J., Rammer, C., & Rennings, K. (2012). Determinants of eco-innovations by type of environmental impact-The role of regulatory push/pull, technology push and market pull. *Ecological Economics, 78*, 112–122. doi:10.1016/j.ecolecon.2012.04.005

Hotel Restaurant Magazine. (2022a). *Turizm sektöründe yükselen trend yeşil oteller*. https://www.hotelrestaurantmagazine.com/turizm-sektorunde-yukselen-trend-yesil-oteller/

Hotel Restaurant Magazine. (2022b). *Türkiye'nin en çevreci beş yıldızlı oteli Renaissance İstanbul Bosphorus Hotel*. https://www.hotelrestaurantmagazine.com/turkiyenin-en-cevreci-bes-yildizli-oteli-renaissance-istanbul-bosphorus-hotel/

İpar, M. S., & Aksu, M. (2022). Turistlerin yeşil otel tercihlerine yönelik algıları, çevreci davranış eğilimleri ve davranışsal niyetlerle ilişkisi. *Journal of Gastronomy, Hospitality and Travel, 5*(1), 440–463.

Işık, C., & Barlak, S. (2018). Otel yöneticilerinin yeşil inovasyon algıları: İstanbul ili örneği. *Journal of Tourism Intelligence and Smartness, 1*(1), 14–26.

Işik, C., Kasımatı, E., & Ongan, S. (2017). Analyzing the causalities between economic growth, financial development, international trade, tourism expenditure and/on the CO2 emissions in Greece. *Energy Sources. Part B, Economics, Planning, and Policy, 12*(7), 665–673. doi:10.1080/15567249.2016.1263251

Kammarer, D. (2008) *Determinants of environmental product ınnovation a comparative study on manufacturers of electrical and electronic appliances in Germany and California.* (Publication No. 18057) [Doctoral dissertation, ETH Zurich]. ETH Zurich Research Collection.

Khan, P. A., & Johl, S. K. (2019). Nexus of comprehensive green innovation, environmental management system-14001-2015 and firm performance. *Cogent Business & Management, 6*(1), 1–12. doi:10.1080/23311975.2019.1691833

Korkmaz, H., & Atay, L. (2017). Otel işletmelerinde yeşil pazarlama ve çevre sertifikalarının değerlendirilmesi. *Aksaray Üniversitesi İktisadi ve İdari Bilimler Fakültesi Dergisi, 9*(4), 113–126.

Küçükoğlu, M. T. (2014). *Sürdürülebilirlik ve yeşil yenilik perspektifinde Türk işletmelerin incelenmesi* [Yayınlanmamış Doktora Tezi]. İstanbul Üniversitesi.

Larsen, O. M. (2005). *Governing innovation for sustainable development: integration of environmental and innovation policies in Norway* [Unpublished Master's Thesis]. University of Oslo.

Lee, J. J., Gemba, K., & Kodama, F. (2006). Analyzing the innovation process for environmental performance improvement. *Technological Forecasting and Social Change, 73*(3), 290–301. doi:10.1016/j.techfore.2004.03.008

Lee, J. S., Hsu, L. T., Han, H., & Kim, Y. (2010). Understanding how consumers view green hotels: How a hotel's green image can influence behavioural intentions. *Journal of Sustainable Tourism, 18*(7), 901–914. doi:10.1080/09669581003777747

Leenders, M. A., & Chandra, Y. (2013). Antecedents and consequences of green innovation in the wine industry: The role of channel structure. *Technology Analysis and Strategic Management, 25*(2), 203–218. doi:10.1080/09537325.2012.759203

Li, P., Menon, M., & Liu, Z. (2019). Green innovation under uncertainty-a dynamic perspective. *International Journal of Services. Economics and Management, 10*(1), 68–88.

Lo, J. Y., Chan, W., & Zhang, C. X. (2014). Tools for benchmarking and recognizing hotels' green effort—Environmental assessment methods and eco-labels. *Journal of China Tourism Research, 10*(2), 165–185. doi:10.1080/19388160.2013.857626

Mastny, L. (2001). *Traveling ligh new paths for international tourism.* Worldwatch Paper.

Mensah, I. (2004, May). *Environmental management practices in US hotels.* Hotel Online. https://www.hotel-online.com/News/PR2004_2nd/May04_EnvironmentalPractices.html

Neff, D. J., & Moss, R. C. (2011). *The future of nonprofits: Innovate and thrive in the digital age.* John Wiley & Sons. doi:10.1002/9781118386781

Oslo Kılavuzu. (2005). *Yenilik verilerinin toplanması ve yorumlanması için ilkeler.* OECD/Eurostat Ortak Yayımı.

Özar Berksü, Z. (2020, June 2). *Türkiye'nin en iyi çevre dostu otelleri.* Oggusto. https://www.oggusto.com/surdurulebilir-yasam/turkiyenin-en-iyi-cevre-dostu-otelleri

Porter, M. E. (1990). The competitive advonioge of notions. *Harvard Business Review*, 73–93.

Porter, M. E., & Linde, C. V. D. (1995). Green and competitive: Ending the stalemate. *Harvard Business Review*, 120–134.

Rennings, K. (2000). Redefining innovation-eco-innovation research and the contribution from ecological economics. *Ecological Economics, 32*(2), 319–332. doi:10.1016/S0921-8009(99)00112-3

Rennings, K., Ziegler, A., Ankele, K., & Hoffmann, E. (2006). The influence of different characteristics of the EU environmental management and auditing scheme on technical environmental innovations and economic performance. *Ecological Economics, 57*(1), 45–59. doi:10.1016/j.ecolecon.2005.03.013

Rosegger, G. (1996). *The economics of production and innovation.* Butterworth-Heinemann Inc.

Saçılık, M. Y., & Çevik, S. (2014). Çevreye duyarlı otelcilik kapsamında yeşil yıldız uygulaması: Antakya Güngör Palace örneği. In E. Koç, H. Abdioğlu, & R. Kılıç (Eds.), *The 9th international conference: New perspectives in tourism and hospitality* (pp. 404-414). Academic Press.

Saunila, M., Ukko, J., & Rantala, T. (2018). Sustainability as a driver of green innovation investment and exploitation. *Journal of Cleaner Production, 179*, 631–641. doi:10.1016/j.jclepro.2017.11.211

Schumpeter, J. (1939). *Business cycles: A theoretical, historical, and statistical analysis of the capitalist process.* McGraw-Hill Book Company.

Şenocak, B., & Mohan, Y. B. (2018). İşletmelerde çevresel sürdürülebilirlik bilinci ve yeşil işletmecilik uygulamaları ile işletme başarısı arasındaki ilişki. *Süleyman Demirel Üniversitesi İktisadi ve İdari Bilimler Fakültesi Dergisi, 23*(1), 161–183.

Song, M., Fisher, R., & Kwoh, Y. (2019). Technological challenges of green innovation and sustainable resource management with large scale data. *Technological Forecasting and Social Change, 144*, 361–368. doi:10.1016/j.techfore.2018.07.055

Süklüm, N. (2018). Yeşil otellerin maliyetler açısından değerlendirilmesi. *Hitit Üniversitesi Sosyal Bilimler Enstitüsü Dergisi, 11*(1), 375–394.

Tan, Y. S., & Wright, A. S. (2022). Exploring "smart and green" concepts: A new synergy for Irish hospitality. *Tourism and Hospitality, 3*(1), 276–296. doi:10.3390/tourhosp3010019

Tang, M., Walsh, G., Lerner, D., Fitza, M. A., & Li, Q. (2018). Green innovation, managerial concern and firm performance: An empirical study. *Business Strategy and the Environment, 27*(1), 39–51. doi:10.1002/bse.1981

Tekeli, M., & Kırıcı Tekeli, E. (2020). Sustainable gastronomic tourism. In F. Türkmen (Ed.), *Selected academic studies from Turkish tourism sector* (pp. 113–133). Peter Lang.

Triguero, A., Moreno-Mondéjar, L., & Davia, M. A. (2013). Drivers of different types of eco-innovation in European SMEs. *Ecological Economics*, *92*, 25–33. doi:10.1016/j.ecolecon.2013.04.009

Vatan, A., & Zengin, B. (2014). Çevresel inovasyon ve konaklama işletmelerindeki uygulamalar üzerine bir araştırma. *The Journal of Academic Social Science*, *2*(8), 511–530. doi:10.16992/ASOS.458

Walsh, P. R., & Dodds, R. (2017). Measuring the choice of environmental sustainability strategies in creating a competitive advantage. *Business Strategy and the Environment*, *26*(5), 672–687. doi:10.1002/bse.1949

Xie, X., Huo, J., & Zou, H. (2019). Green process innovation, green product innovation, and corporate financial performance: A content analysis method. *Journal of Business Research*, *101*, 697–706. doi:10.1016/j.jbusres.2019.01.010

Yang, Z., Chen, H., Du, L., Lin, C., & Lu, W. (2021). How does alliance-based government-university-industry foster cleantech innovation in a green innovation ecosystem? *Journal of Cleaner Production*, *283*, 1–17. doi:10.1016/j.jclepro.2020.124559

Yılmaz, O., & Atik, K. (2022). Çanakkale kent merkezindeki leed sertifikalı yeşil binalar üzerine araştırmalar: Çanakkale Esas 17 Burda Avm örneği. *Kırklareli Üniversitesi Mühendislik ve Fen Bilimleri Dergisi*, *8*(1), 88–108.

Yin, S., & Li, B. (2019). Academic research institutes-construction enterprises linkages for the development of urban green building: Selecting management of green building technologies innovation partner. *Sustainable Cities and Society*, *48*, 1–23. doi:10.1016/j.scs.2019.101555

Yücel, D. (2021). İnovasyonun yeni yüzü: Açık yeşil inovasyon. *Ekonomik ve Sosyal Araştırmalar Dergisi*, *17*(2), 419–441.

Zailani, S., Govindan, K., Iranmanesh, M., Shaharudin, M. R., & Sia Chong, Y. (2015). Green innovation adoption in automotive supply chain: The Malaysian case. *Journal of Cleaner Production*, *108*, 1115–1122. doi:10.1016/j.jclepro.2015.06.039

Zhang, D., Rong, Z., & Ji, Q. (2019). Green innovation and firm performance: Evidence from listed companies in China. *Resources, Conservation and Recycling*, *144*, 48–55. doi:10.1016/j.resconrec.2019.01.023

Zhou, X., Yu, Y., Yang, F., & Shi, Q. (2021). Spatial-temporal heterogeneity of green innovation in China. *Journal of Cleaner Production*, *282*, 1–10. doi:10.1016/j.jclepro.2020.124464

KEY TERMS AND DEFINITIONS

Carbon Footprint: It is the sum of the cumulative greenhouse gas emissions directly or indirectly caused by human activities.

Clean Technology: Clean technologies include innovations related to less use of resources, energy, or by-products while trying to reduce the situations that may harm the environment during production activities.

Ecological Labeling: These signs show the products' environmental impacts at every stage and aim to inform the consumers.

End-of-Pipe Technologies: End-of-pipe technologies include tools such as wastewater treatment systems, exhaust cleaning equipment, sound absorbers, incinerators, etc., which are not directly part of the production process but ensure compliance with environmental protection.

Green Hotel: Touristic enterprises, having solid and liquid waste management systems, emphasizing recycling and reuse, water and energy savings, and biological diversity protection.

Green Innovation: Improving and implementing new attitudes, ideas, products, and processes in a way that reduces negative environmental impacts and supports sustainable development goals.

Green Organizational Innovation: These innovations include reorganizing processes and responsibilities in the business to reduce environmental impacts.

Green Process Innovation: It applies to using clean technology and eco-saving equipment to increase energy efficiency, reduce greenhouse gas emissions and optimize resource use.

Green Product Innovation: A multifaceted process that draws attention to three chief environmental focal points (material, energy, and pollution) based on the impacts of the different stages of a product's physical life cycle (production process, product use, and disposal) on the natural environment.

Innovation: The first commercial use of a new process or tool; or the design, method, production, and commercial activities carried out to market a new product.

Sustainability: Meeting the needs of the present generation without overexploiting resources and destroying the ability of future generations to meet their needs.

Sustainable Tourism: An approach that aims to meet the needs of tourists, the tourism industry and local communities without compromising the ability of future generations to meet their needs.

Chapter 8
Application of Artificial Intelligence and Robotics in Tourism and Hospitality Marketing

Ebru Kemer
Nigde Omar Halisdemir University, Turkey

Pankaj Kumar Tyagi
https://orcid.org/0000-0001-9504-541X
Chandigarh University, India

ABSTRACT

Rapid technological developments have affected business areas and caused differences in products and services. The tourism and hospitality industry has also been affected by these rapid developments, and the use and importance of new technologies have increased. In this context, this research aims to evaluate the use of artificial intelligence and robotic technologies in the field of tourism marketing with data obtained from secondary data. As a result of the research, it has been determined that artificial intelligence and robotic technology applications in the tourism sector offer personalized and new opportunities for tourists in their travel decisions. Within the scope of the research, it has been suggested that these opportunities offered through big data are important in reducing operating costs and ensuring personnel productivity and competitive advantage. Therefore, using artificial intelligence in tourism marketing positively contributes to the systematic analysis of customer information.

INTRODUCTION

With the rapid development of technology, low cost, high efficiency, and high speed have gained importance in industries. Industries that follow technological developments have started to give importance to artificial intelligence and automation systems by following digital developments (Gürdin, 2020). Digital

DOI: 10.4018/978-1-6684-6732-9.ch008

Copyright © 2023, IGI Global. Copying or distributing in print or electronic forms without written permission of IGI Global is prohibited.

technologies are seen as the primary source of innovation in the world (Petković, Pindţo & Molnar Agic, 2018). The tourism and hospitality industry has also adapted to digital transformation depending on these developments (Topsakal, Yüzbaşıoğlu & Bahar, 2018, p. 253). The advantages of the tourism and hospitality industry in terms of the economy of countries, the size of the sector, and the high employment rate reflect the need to adapt to this transformation (Erkmen & Gönenç Güler, 2020). It is also stated that the tourism and hospitality industry is an industry that attracts attention to artificial intelligence and robotic applications (Rosete, Soares, Salvadorinho, Reis & Amorim, 2020).

In the tourism and hospitality industry, artificial intelligence and robotic technologies are used in the front office, cooking, baggage services, guiding customers, and welcoming customers (Seo & Lee, 2021; Belanche, Casola, Flavian & Schepers, 2020: 204). In addition, providing guidance services in the tourism and hospitality industry; There are "mobile guide, audio guide, guide player, interactive multimedia tour guide" GPS supported map and location applications, guide player, audio guide application, interactive multimedia tour guide, a mobile guide, guide port" systems that can be called Technological Guide (TR). Yıldız, 2018, p. 4686). In addition to this, service robots are also used in the tourism and hospitality industry. It is stated that the market value of service robots is estimated at "$55.72 billion by 2026 with an annual growth rate of 30 percent" (Seo & Lee, 2021, p. 2). Robotization of the tourism and hospitality industry; increases the opportunity to improve operational processes and provide personalized service to the guest. In this case, competitiveness increases as innovative and creative (Ivkov, Bleši´c, Dudi´c, Pajtinková Bartáková and Dudi´c, 2020).

When the relevant literature is examined, the use of artificial intelligence and robotic technologies in the tourism industry (Devitt, 2019; İbiş, 2019; Osawa, Akiya, Koyama, Ema, Kanzaki, Ichise & Kubo, 2017; Ohlan, 2018; Trejos, 2016; Ivanov & Webster, 2017; Yalçın Kayıkçı & Kutluk Bozkurt, 2018; Zlatanov & Popesku, 2019; Çetinkaya, 2019; Bozkurt Uzan & Cute, 2020; Lu, Zhang & Zhang, 2021; Vatan & Doğan, 2021). The limited number of studies on the use of artificial intelligence and robotic technologies in tourism marketing and the increase in the use and importance of new technologies in the tourism and hospitality industry necessitated this study. In this context, this research aims to evaluate the use of artificial intelligence and robotic technologies in the field of tourism marketing with data obtained from secondary data. Due to the limited number of studies on the use of artificial intelligence in tourism marketing, it is thought that this study will make significant theoretical contributions to the relevant literature. In addition, the study; Depending on the technological developments experienced, it is thought that current developments and artificial intelligence and robot technologies in the literature will contribute to sector practitioners and researchers for the use of tourism marketing. First of all, the concept of artificial intelligence and its applications will be discussed in this context. Then, the importance of artificial intelligence and robotic technologies in the tourism and hospitality industry, and finally, the application examples of artificial intelligence and robotic technologies in tourism marketing will be given.

BACKGROUND

Artificial Intelligence and Robotic Technologies

Society's distinction between subject and object reveals modern man not only the relationship of man with a man but also the relation of man with technology. The whole world consists of human and non-human actions (Latour, 2010). Technology is central to defining modern society. In the ideology of industrialization, technology is at the forefront, albeit implicitly. This industrial class is considered the dominant class, emphasizing scientists and engineers. The natural rulers of this class, which includes all groups that are productive in society, are the classes that dominate the industry with scientists. Science and technology require restructuring in an ideal society as society and technology are intertwined (Saint Simon, 1964; Saint Simon, 1975). Weber determined that with the development of modern society, rationalization developed in the west. Rationalization, in a sense, is considered a set of systematic and routine actions. Weber bases technology on this idea and states that technology is rationalization and compliance with the technique of science (Weber, 1975).

If science is considered as a social construction, its technology should be seen as a social construction. However, considering science as it directs technology shows that technology and social construction processes of science are not considered. There is a reciprocal relationship between science and technology. This way of thinking can be thought of as the construction of technology and social life (Sismondo, 2010). Technology has entered our lives so much that technological tools have become a whole of our bodies. Our relationship with the world becomes a relationship with the development of technology. Technology manipulates the relationship between people and the world (Ihde, 2010). These changes experienced with modernization have been handled differently in technology studies.

When the place of technology in social society is questioned, it has been determined that research and knowledge are the most important effects (Lyotard, 1984). The nature and technological developments created by technology are about technology and human effects. In this context, technology is a form of interpretation and understanding of the real thing. Therefore, technology is considered a force in our daily lives (Feenberg, 2010; Feenberg, 2017). Modern technology is seen as both a resource and an area where these resources are stored (Heidegger, 1977). These economic, social, and cultural changes and the process of making sense show that science and technology are on the way to new social concepts (Heise, 2004).

The effect of technological development on the social sphere depends on humanity's adoption of existing technologies rather than the nature of technology. Technology does not develop independently of the society in which it lives and develops. There is a relationship between social institutions and the effect of technology on the internal dynamics of technology. The effect of technology on social, political, and economic relations is an essential factor in the development of the social structure. The existence of specific technologies in any culture and the continuation of this culture occur under the influence of socially based forces such as gender, political power, and social classes (Mesthene, 1971). Social groups that direct technological products are heterogeneous groups depending on the purpose of using technology. These groups can be classified according to the problems that arise depending on "age, gender or purpose of use" and the solutions brought to them (Sismondo, 1993, p. 140).

In this research, the use of robotic technologies and artificial intelligence in tourism marketing is based on the social construction theory of technology. The theory of social construction of technology was expressed by Berger and Luckmann (1966) as "reality is socially constructed and the construction process is the subject of the sociology of science". According to Berger and Luckmann, social institutions exist because a significant part of society is aware of them, acts accordingly, and reinforces the legitimacy of these institutions in the process (Berger & Luckman, 2008). Social construction theory evolves as a result of technological developments and accumulations. Social change is a "transition from one social structure to another" (Burke, 2014, p. 145-158). Various theories explain changes in social relations, social institutions, and strata. While social change sometimes describes the internal changes in the internal structure of the society, it sometimes deals with major and comprehensive changes such as political and cultural structuring. Depending on this differentiation, the effort to understand the change in social life and the understanding of concepts such as "growth and evolution" by the internal dynamics of the society reveal the model of society (Burke, 2014, p. 145-158).

The increase in communication between individuals has affected communication and the disciplines affected by communication, using the internet to communicate with each other. In addition, the fact that institutions started to use the internet in business life has led to a complete change in corporate life. Therefore, businesses that resisted the system and failed to realize the change became unable to compete and had to terminate their activities. Being able to perceive the recycling of consumers and constantly updating and understanding the wishes and needs of the consumer is essential in terms of marketing strategy (Bulunmaz, 2016).

Technology is constantly being renewed and developed. Every day a new device comes out, and innovations are added to these devices. These changes in technology and the factors affecting the growth and development of the industry are listed below (Kiper, 2014, p. 59-122).

- Development and improvement of technological services, finding new services
- Improvement of technological devices, the emergence of new devices
- Technology becoming a global market
- Coming to more affordable prices for technological services and devices
- Increasing access to technology
- Increasing education on technology
- Increase and development of vocational education in the field of technology
- Development and proliferation of technological organizations and fairs
- Revenue growth in the tech industry
- Competition between companies providing technology services/devices

With the developments in the field of information and communication and the change in phones and communication systems, businesses have started to become a part of the increasingly digitalized life (Bağcı & İçöz, 2019). The concept of technology is expressed as "a process that is constantly developing and has an impact on the behaviors and living spaces in which it is reproduced in our daily life, which is open to development, and which is based on the ability to think, realize and produce information" (Topsakal, Yüzbaşıoğlu & Bahar, 2018). The fact that digitalized systems lead to innovations and differences has revealed new technological infrastructures and systems in the field of technology (Yelkikalan, Özcan, S., & Temel 2019). One of these changes has the economic value that emerged in the Industry 4.0 era; artificial intelligence, 3D (three-dimensional) printers, robotics and bio, nano and space technology is the intelligent production period in which every living-inanimate object can communicate and interact with other objects through internet connections (Bulut & Akçacı, 2017). The concept of Industry 4.0 is stated as "the integration of complex physical machines and devices with networked sensors and software used to predict better, control and plan business and societal outcomes" or "a new level of value chain organization and management throughout the product lifecycle". Mrugalska and Wyrwicka (2017). In the era of Industry 4.0, devices and devices have been made smart, and by connecting objects to each other, artificial intelligence applications have started to take their place in the business world (Bulut & Akçacı, 2017). With technological developments, new production systems such as controllable digital environments, autonomous machines, and artificial intelligence have emerged in the application of human elements in production processes that will create a connection between digital and physical systems

(Kagermann, Wahlsterand & Helbig, 2013). In artificial intelligence systems, the focus is on making machines think in a way similar to human thinking. In addition, it is designed with the ability to solve complex problems and perform the tasks undertaken by thinking like humans. For this reason, artificial intelligence programs need human knowledge and experience to analyze complex data. Implementing the decisions taken by humans is possible with artificial intelligence Technologies (Nabiyev, 2012; Adalı, 2017, Tsaih & Hsu, 2018).

Artificial intelligence systems examine anything and can apply the parameters determined from this examination. For this reason, artificial intelligence tries to solve problems according to determined situations (Yeğin, 2020). A sub-category of artificial intelligence; The concepts of machine learning, machine intelligence, and intelligent machine development are among the definitions of artificial intelligence. It is stated that the concept of artificial intelligence emerged between 1950-1980, machine learning between 1980-2006, and deep learning between 2006-2017. Artificial intelligence applications are stated as the most important technological innovation that came with the Industry 4.0 revolution (Bayuk & Demir, 2019). Artificial intelligence; is a technology that has started to be used in business administration, medicine, automotive, and education. Artificial intelligence, which is the focus of attention of professional groups such as engineers, information technology experts, and analysts, has also started to be used in social sciences (Jarek & Mazurek, 2019). According to another definition, it is stated as "having the ability to perform tasks given for enhanced mental phenomena such as reasoning, understanding, learning from previous experiences, which are realized by a computer or a machine under the supervision of a computer, which mostly has human-specific qualities" (Nabiyev, 2012, p. 25).

Usage areas of artificial intelligence technologies; It is possible to summarize it as systems that think and act like humans, expert systems, natural language processing, robots, image processing, and machine learning (Adalı, 2017). Artificial intelligence is "human intelligence technology created with the help of computer programs" (Tsaih & Hsu, 2018, p. 127). Using artificial intelligence systems to solve large and complex problems of enterprises is one of the most significant advantages of analyzing data with the help of artificial intelligence and doing more work with less effort. Using this data, it is possible to offer appropriate products and services at the right time and place. Such services will be effective in customers' choosing the business and purchasing. Businesses that want to take advantage of these opportunities should use artificial intelligence technologies (Yeğin, 2020). In addition, these concepts developed with artificial intelligence are used in applications such as search suggestions, voice recognition, virtual assistants, and image recognition (Shahid & Li, 2019). Digital technologies are seen as the primary source of innovation and labour savings to become the industry leader in the world. Digital transformation rewards those who adapt and those who do not, causing them not to exist in the sector (Petković, Pindţo & Molnar Agić, 2018). Artificial intelligence is studied based on four essential bits of intelligence. (Huang & Rust, 2018, p. 156-160).

- Mechanical intelligence (simple and repetitive tasks): Use of service robots in hotels and tourism, use of chatbots in customer service, search engines, etc.
- Analytical intelligence (thinking and information processing): Machine learning, Big Data analysis and their use in detecting system problems, paying taxes, etc. applications.
- Intuitive intelligence (complex information processing, intuitive thinking, and interaction): Intelligent operating systems for businesses, reporting with artificial intelligence methods, writing text, interpreting psychoanalytic data, etc.

- Empathic intelligence (emotional interaction): Personal robots for the mental comfort of patients, emotional perception, and effective communication of customers with analysis of customer behavior and movements.

As an important form of artificial intelligence application, service robots are not specific to a single sector, but it can be stated that they are used in many activities, as well as attracting more attention in a single sector of hospitality and tourism (Rosete, Soares, Salvadorinho, Reis & Amorim, 2020). According to the ISO 8373: 2012 standard of the International Organization for Standardization, service robots are defined as "a robot that performs useful tasks for people or equipment outside of industrial automation applications" (International Organization for Standardization, 2012). Service robots are focused on improving customer experiences by providing human-like services and interactions. This way, an excellent competitive strategy can be created by making a difference with an innovative service approach (Kuo, Li-Cheng & Tseng, 2017. Artificial intelligence provides "human-like" features such as dexterity, memory adaptability, and physical strength by providing autonomy to machines. They are thought to gain new human-like abilities by interacting with humans and other robots (Arduengo & Sentis, 2019, p. 1). Developments in robot technologies have ranged from traditional industrial robots to service robots (Özgürel & Kılınç Şahin, 2021: 1851). t robots can be defined as "system-based autonomous, adaptive interfaces that serve, communicate and interact with the customers of a tourism business" (Wirtz, Patterson, Kunz, Gruber, Lu, Paluch & Martins, 2018, p. 909). Robots are used today in labour and services, military and security, research and education, entertainment, medicine and health services, personal care and companions, and environmental cleaning (Lin, Pearson, & Liping, (2011, p. 944-945). Robotization of the tourism sector and provision of services. It offers opportunities such as improving the operation processes, increasing the service quality, and customizing the services offered to the guests. These applications increase the competitiveness of tourism enterprises as innovative and creative (Ivkov, Bleši´c, Dudi´c, Pajtinková Bartáková & Dudi´c, 2020, p. 1).In the future, it is thought that the interactions between robots and human relations will be similar to human-human interactions. It is thought that the understanding of human emotions by robots will have positive effects, especially in the tourism sector, especially tourists (Fondevila Gascón, Marqués-Pascual, Muñoz González, & Polo López, 2019).

Artificial Intelligence and Robotic Technologies in Tourism Marketing

Adapting businesses and consumers to changing living conditions has led to market changes. Now, in today's markets, the information in the product community, not the product, has become more important. And it is seen that computers are replaced in an electronic environment and geographical location and space (Rayport & Sviokla, 1994). Thanks to digital marketing and digital channels, businesses can reach larger customer groups and provide speed and convenience in after-sales service by providing a better understanding of the service (Ryan, 2016). Aksoy (2009, p. 52-54) examined the marketing activities businesses and customers participate in through technology under ten titles.

- Production on the Internet is information-oriented rather than physical products.
- Unlike traditional markets, digitising information and reproducing it in large quantities is possible.
- Distance is losing its importance.
  •Fast and instant access can be provided.

- People constitute the basic assets of internet marketing.
- Networks reduce costs and increase efficiency, creating a rapidly growing structure.
- The power in the electronic market is proportional to how efficiently information is managed.
- Bargaining power is transferred from businesses to consumers.
- Network value increases in proportion to the market share.
- Businesses can communicate directly with the consumer.
- Elimination of time and space constraints offers global alternatives.

Marketing through technology can easily communicate between the customer and the business through different networks "website, social media platforms, blogs or the internet" (Özmen, 2013). The adaptation of consumers to these developments increases the use of marketing through technology. (Alan, Kabadayı & Erişke, 2018).

Artificial intelligence in marketing; affects many situations such as time, cost, and competitiveness. With the opportunities it provides and advanced machine algorithms, artificial intelligence undertakes excellent tasks in the issues that marketers have difficulty in using big data. With the big data provided by these algorithms, predictive comments about consumers can be made. Forecasts about which customers may turn to which product, which product they will be satisfied with, and which product they need can be given as examples. In this case, businesses can work to ensure consumer satisfaction with the estimates they provide (Jänisch, 2018). Machine learning in artificial intelligence systems also includes communication between consumers and businesses by predicting the next step of customers. In the field of marketing, effective results are obtained with these three concepts, namely "big data, machine learning, effective solutions" (Tjepkema, 2019). In different AI concepts in marketing, "artificial intelligence generated content, intelligent content creation, voice search, programmatic media acquisition, trend modeling, forecast analysis, scoring guidance, ad targeting, dynamic pricing, web and app personalization, chatbots, retargeting, predictive customer service, marketing automation, dynamic Emails concepts are included (Smartinsight, 2022).

Artificial intelligence can analyze the data for consumers and benefit from these data without the need for human intervention. The intelligent system they propose is listed below. (Perakakis, Mastorakis, & Kopanakis, 2019, p. 1-12).

1. Data collection: It is a data collection application from web and social media platforms. Data is usually anonymized.
2. AI micro-analysis of collected data (Sentiment analysis, text analysis, image recognition, etc.): In this step, each collected post is analyzed separately with smart algorithms to enrich it with semantic information (language in which it is written, gender of the author, location, etc.).
3. Social intelligence analysis/ Social AI Analysis: Data is treated as a cluster rather than individual posts in this step. This way, patterns are discovered and useful information can be drawn automatically.
4. Expert advice: In addition, the results from step 3 are displayed to users, and personalized advice sets can be created for different situations. These recommendations are intended to help improve marketing actions.
5. Re-evaluation: Since the purpose of the system is to improve a brand's online marketing efforts on social media, it is essential to monitor and repeat the measurement regularly. A comparison can be made between the new and old values to assess whether the metrics are improving.

According to traditional marketing, using artificial intelligence increases the campaign and efficiency by segmenting the market. These advantages are mentioned below: (Brenner, 2019):

- Ability to find hidden patterns in data that humans cannot detect.
- Automatic update of segmentation in a rapidly changing market.
- Unlimited number and size of partitions can be created.
- Higher levels of customization.
- Requires very little maintenance and or human intervention.
- Scalable

With technological developments, the marketing field provides the consumers and market segments with the effective use of information about their characteristics through the database and making use of these databases. With this method, it has become easier to evaluate whether the goals intended to be achieved by the consumers have been achieved. Making strategic decisions and reaching targets, acting customer-oriented, and effective communication is realized. These effects are provided by integrating technological methods and tactics used in marketing, marketing communication tools, and marketing mix elements (Erdoğan, 2013). There are two important factors affecting marketing today. Technological developments and integrated marketing constitute these actors. In addition, "structural changes in advertising agencies, structural changes in advertisers and distribution channels, increasing costs of traditional advertising media, globalization, changing expectations of advertisers, the decreasing effect of traditional advertising environments and zapping phenomenon, technological developments and data-based systems, change in consumer trends. " is among the important issues (Odabaşı & Oyman, 2005, p. 65-69).

Artificial intelligence is on the rise in the field of marketing, and it appears in many areas of marketing. (Pehlivan, 2018). Internet and information technologies in the tourism and hospitality industry: provide convenience in office automation, travel agencies, and reservations management, and are important for product diversification and the continuity of tourism businesses in the field of personal service (Ay, 2009). Artificial intelligence and robotic technology applications have started to be used in the tourism and hospitality industry; It is used to provide new opportunities for customers in travel decision-making, purchasing decisions, payment systems, and travel consultancy (Zlatanov & Popesku, 2019). Artificial intelligence performs tasks requiring human intelligence has made this technology attractive for the tourism sector (Revfine, 2020). According to İbiş (2019, p. 409), artificial intelligence in the tourism sector; Receptionists, luggage carriers, luggage storage robots, and vacuum cleaners are used as service robots in various ways. It is stated that it is possible to provide uninterrupted instant services in tourism 24 hours a day, 7 days a week, using the natural language processing and feature identification functions of artificial intelligence. (Tsaih & Hsu, 2018).

It is thought that as the use of service robots becomes widespread, they will play an important role in creating customer experience. It is emphasized that human-robot interactions may affect customer experience creation and marketing activities in the tourism and hospitality industry in the future. In addition, it is emphasized that the opportunities it provides such as "managing customer relationship management databases and establishing customer employee relations" will return to the business as an element that increases customer loyalty (Murphy, Gretzel & Pesonen, 2019: 4-6). Artificial intelligence and robotic applications in the tourism and hospitality sector; It is used in hotels, restaurants, and airports for cleaning rooms, delivering goods, carrying luggage, cooking, and cleaning (Trejos, 2016; Ivanov,

Webster, & Berezina, 2017; Ivanov & Webster, 2017; Osawa, Akiya, Koyama, Ema, Kanzaki, Ichise & Kubo, 2017; Yalçın Kayıkçı & Kutluk Bozkurt, 2018; Ohlan, 2018; Ibiş, 2019; Devitt, 2019; Zlatanov & Popesku, 2019; Çetinkaya, 2019; Bozkurt Uzan & Cute, 2020; Vatan & Doğan, 2021; Lu, Zhang & Zhang, 2021) is used.

Customer service and customer retention will be among the most important applications that present the importance of artificial intelligence in the future (Tjepkema, 2019). Customer-oriented messages can be targeted and applied with artificial intelligence in the marketing activities of businesses. Messages are created depending on people's individual behaviors, and customer-oriented message contents are seen as an element that encourages the customer (Pels, 2018). Artificial intelligence in the tourism and hospitality industry; creates positive contributions in terms of tourism marketing in analysing customer information and taking effective marketing decisions (Li, 2019). Artificial intelligence provides personal products and services by addressing the wishes and needs of people and obtaining information about their behaviors and preferences (Jarek & Mazurek, 2019: 46). In the tourism and hospitality industry, services are provided by providing innovations in the field of automation instead of direct interpersonal communication and interaction (Tussyadiah, 2020).

Artificial intelligence and robotic applications in the tourism and hospitality industry benefit from detecting possible customer behaviors by using customer data (Bayuk & Demir, 2019; Shahid & Li, 2019). Big data is used through artificial intelligence and this data is used for customer profile analysis and effective market (Zsarnoczky, 2017). Wang (2018, p. 374) reduced the costs of businesses, They stated that they benefited from smart systems for personnel productivity, increasing customer satisfaction, and brand image. An example of artificial intelligence for tourism marketing is the "Meet Sam application" used by FCM Travel Asia. With this application, tourists can provide support from the beginning to the end of the trip. Personal experiences offered to guests come It is less costly than traditional marketing. Therefore, it is among the great opportunities offered to marketers (Arsenijevic & Jovic, 2019, p. 19). Chatbots used in the tourism sector are also an important tool in terms of marketing. Travel robots provide personalized service for consumers to create their journeys (Zlatanov & Popescu, 2019). In addition, artificial intelligence-supported applications provide a transparent and open service by reducing customers' bad purchasing experiences (Zhang & Sun, 2019). Therefore, the competitive advantage that artificial intelligence provides for customer relationship management, customer and employee relations through big data and the competitive advantage it provides to the business reveals the importance of using artificial intelligence in tourism marketing.

CONCLUSION

The development of science and technology has affected many industries. The service sector is also among the sectors affected by these developments. Changes in technological developments also affect the tourism sector, which is a part of the service sector, in many ways. In this context, this research aims to evaluate the use of artificial intelligence and robotic technologies in the field of tourism marketing with data obtained from secondary data. Customer satisfaction is considered the most important success of businesses. Ensuring customer satisfaction is related to the satisfaction of customers with the goods and services they receive. For this reason, businesses must organize their services effectively and increase their service quality (Şahin & Şen, 2017, p. 1176).

Considering the effect created by artificial intelligence today, it is thought that it will change all the processes before it, such as the internet and electricity. People are expected to replace people in repetitive jobs that can be effective, especially in decision-making processes in areas such as marketing and management, where people's expertise is utilized. Therefore, artificial intelligence technology is expected to differentiate people in the future (Arıkuşu, 2017, p. 67). Using big data, artificial intelligence is used in terms of customer profile analysis and effective marketing. The use of big data provided by artificial intelligence is essential in terms of reducing costs by reaching information about customers, increasing customer satisfaction, and providing personnel efficiency and image (Zsarnoczky, 2017; Wang, 2018). In addition, in the decision-making process related to travel, smart systems complement each other in terms of removing complexity (Zlatanov & Popesku, 2019). As a result of the research, it has been determined that artificial intelligence and robotic technology applications in the tourism sector offer personalized and new opportunities for tourists in their travel decisions. These opportunities offered through big data are important in terms of reducing operating costs and ensuring personnel efficiency and competitive advantage. Therefore, the use of artificial intelligence in tourism marketing contributes positively to the systematic analysis of customer information.

Suggestions for using artificial intelligence and robotic technologies in the tourism sector are given below. If these suggestions are taken into account, it is thought that the use of artificial intelligence applications as a marketing tool will create opportunities for sector practitioners such as reducing costs, increasing profits, and gaining a competitive advantage.

In the tourism sector, promotion can be made by raising awareness of consumers for artificial intelligence and robotic technologies.

Artificial intelligence-supported automation can be used in communication with the customer.

The service provided to customers can be customized.

With the big data processing method provided by artificial intelligence automation, potential customers can be identified and support can be provided.

Guide robots can be used in areas such as airports and terminals where customers are busy and need help the most.

This situation can be used as a marketing tool by providing support services with artificial intelligence systems for elderly and disabled customers.

The popularity of artificial intelligence-supported businesses can be increased in the marketing of tourism businesses where artificial intelligence and robotic technologies are used.

This research evaluated the developments of artificial intelligence and robotic technologies for marketing applications by examining secondary data. Examining secondary data about the use of artificial intelligence and robotic technologies in the research is among the limitations of the research. In addition, considering the tourism sector in the research, evaluating the tourism and hospitality industry is another limitation of the research. Detailed information on the use of artificial intelligence and robotic technologies in marketing in different sectors can be obtained in future research. In this way, each sector can be examined in detail and compared. In addition, the opinions of stakeholders in the tourism and hospitality industry can be taken and comparisons can be made with these evaluations. Based on the data obtained, suggestions are given for the use of artificial intelligence and robotic technologies in the field of marketing.

REFERENCES

Adalı, E. (2017). Yapay zeka. *İTÜ Vakfı Dergisi*, *75*, 8-13.

Aksoy, R. (2009). *İnternet Ortamında Pazarlama*. SeçkinYayıncılık.

Alan, A. K., Kabadayı, E. T., & Erişke, T. (2018). İletişimin yeniyüzü: Dijital pazarlama ve sosyal medya pazarlamasi. *Electronic Journal of Social Sciences*, *17*(66), 123–134.

Arduengo, M., & Sentis, L. (2019). Robot economy: ready or not, here it comes. Retrieved from: https://arxiv.org/abs/1812.01755

Arıkuşu, S. (2017). Yapay Zeka İle Neler Yapabilirsiniz? *Techstar*, *3*(18), 67.

Arsenijevic, U., & Jovic, M. (2019). Artificial ıntelligence marketing: chatbots. *International Conference on Artificial Intelligence: Applications and Innovations*, 19-22.

Ay, L. (2009). Bilgi Teknolojisindeki Gelişmelerin Seyahat Acentalarına Yansımaları; Onlıne Seyahat Acentacılığı. *Sosyal Ekonomik Araştırmalar Dergisi*, *9*(17), 117–136.

Bağcı, E., & İçöz, O. (2019). Z ve alfa kuşağı ile dijitalleşen turizm. *Güncel Turizm Araştırmaları Dergisi*, *3*(2), 232–256. doi:10.32572/guntad.578926

Bayuk, M. N., & Demir, B. N. (2019). Endüstri 4.0 kapsamında yapay zeka ve pazarlamanın geleceği. *Journal Of Social. Humanities and Administrative Sciences*, *5*(19), 781–799. doi:10.31589/JOSHAS.163

Belanche, D., Casalo, L. V., Flavian, C., & Schpers, J. (2020). Service robot implementation: A theoretical framework and research agenda. *Service Industries Journal*, *40*(3-4), 203–225. doi:10.1080/02642069.2019.1672666

Berger, P. L., & Luckmann, T. (2008). *Gerçekliğin Sosyal İnşâsı* (çev. Vefa Saygın Öğütle), İstanbul. *Paradigma (Maracay)*.

Bozkurt Uzan, Ş., & Sevimli, Y. (2020). Gastronomideki robotik uygulamalar ve yapay zekâ. *Tourism and Recreation*, *2*(2), 46–58.

Brenner, M. (2019). *How to ımprove customer segmentation with AI*. Retrieved from: https://marketinginsidergroup.com/artificial-intelligence/how-to-improve-customer-segmentationwith-ai/

Bulunmaz, B. (2016). Gelişen teknolojiyle birlikte değişen pazarlama yöntemleri ve dijital pazarlama. *TRT Akademi*, *1*(2), 348–365.

Bulut, E., & Akçacı, T. (2017). Endüstri 4.0 ve İnovasyon Göstergeleri Kapsamında Türkiye Analizi. *ASSAM Uluslararası Hakemli Dergi*, *4*(7), 55–77.

Burke, P. (2014). Tarih ve Toplumsal Kuram. Tarih Vakfı Yurt Yayınları.

Çetinkaya, F. Ö. (2019). *Sosyal medya ve Turizm 4.0*. Detay Yayıncılık.

Erkmen, B., & Gönenç Güler, E. (2020). Turizm ve dijitalleşme: 'Haskovo-Edirne Kültürel ve TarihiDestinasyonlar Projesi' örneği. *Tourism and Recreation*, 111-118.

Devitt, M. (2019). *How can I help you? The emergence of robots in hotels and restaurants*. Retrieved from: https://www.robotshop.com/community/blog/show/how-can-i-help you-the-emergence-of-robots-in-hotels-and-restaurants/

Erdoğan, B. Z. (2013). Pazarlama İletişimi Kavramı ve Öğeleri. Anadolu Üniversitesi Yayınları.

Fondevila Gascón, J. F., Marqués-Pascual, J., Muñoz González, M., & Polo López, M. (2019). The impact of robotics on the tourism sector: The case of Barcelona. *Harvard Deusto Business Research, VIII*(1), 49–61. doi:10.3926/hdbr.225

Feenberg, A. (2017). Critical theory of technology and STS. *Thesis Eleven, 138*(1). 3-12.

Feenberg, A. (2010). Eleştirel Teknoloji Teorisi: Genel Bir Bakış. In Teknoloji ve toplum: Yıkıcı bir direniş ve yeniden yapılanma. Kalkedon Yayınları.

Gürdin, B. (2020). Robonomi ve müşteri memnuniyeti: Hizmet robotlarına ilişkin literatür taraması. *Ekonomi Maliye İşletme Dergisi, 3*(1), 85–100. doi:10.46737/emid.732024

Heidegger, M. (1977). *The Question Concerning Technology And Other Essays*. Garland Publishing.

Heise, U. K. (2004). Science, Technology And Postmodernism. In The Cambridge companion to postmodernism içinde (pp. 136-167). Cambridge University Press. doi:10.1017/CCOL0521640520.008

Ihde, D. (2010). Heidegger on technology: One size fits all. *Philosophy Today, 54*(Supplement), 101–105. doi:10.5840/philtoday201054Supplement53

Huang, M.-H., & Rust, R. (2018). Artificial Intelligence in Service. *Journal of Service Research, 21*(2), 155–172. doi:10.1177/1094670517752459

International Organization for Standardization. (2012). Retrieved from: https://www.iso.org/obp/ui/#iso:std:iso:8373:ed-2:v1:e

Ivanov, S., Webster, C., & Garenko, A. (2018). Young Russian adults' attitudes towards the potential use of robots in hotels. *Technology in Society, 55*, 24–32. doi:10.1016/j.techsoc.2018.06.004

Ivkov, M., Bleši´c, I., Dudi´c, B., Pajtinková Bartáková, G., & Dudi´c, Z. (2020). Are future professionals willing to implement service robots? Attitudes of hospitality and tourism students towards service robotization. *Electronics, 9*(1942), 1-16.

İbiş, S. (2019). Turizm endüstrisinde robotlaşma. *Türk Turizm Araştırmaları Dergisi, 3*(3), 403–420. doi:10.26677/TR1010.2019.169

Jarek, K., & Mazurek, G. (2019). Marketing and artificial ıntelligence. *Central European Business Review, 8*(2), 46–55. doi:10.18267/j.cebr.213

Jänisch, R. (2018). *Künstliche Intelligenz Revolutioniert Das Marketing*. Retrieved from: https://www.iox.bot/kunstliche-intelligenz-im-marketing

Kagermann, H., Wahlsterand, W., & Helbig, J. (2013). Recommendations for implementing the strategicinitiative industrie 4.0: Final report of the ındustrie 4.0 working group. *Securing the Future of GermanManufacturing Industry*. Retrieved from: https://www.researchgate.net/publication/357467063_Turizmde_Dijitallesme_Akilli_Turizm_Uygulamalari_Dijital_Turizm_ve_Turizm_40_Digitalization_in_Tourism_Smart_Tourism_Applications_Digital_Tourism_and_Tourism_40

Kiper, M. (2004). Teknoloji transfer mekanizmalari ve bu kapsamda üniversite– sanayi işbirliği. *Teknoloji, Türk Mühendis ve Mimar Odaları Birliği,* 59-122.

Kuo, C. M., Chen, L. C., & Tseng, C. Y. (2017). Investigating an innovative service with hospitality robots. *International Journal of Contemporary Hospitality Management, 29*(5), 1305–1321. doi:10.1108/IJCHM-08-2015-0414

Latour, B. (2010). *The pasteurization of france*. Harvard University Press.

Li, J. J., Bonn, M. A., & Ye, B. H. (2019). Hotel employee's artificial intelligence and roboticsawareness and its impact on turnover intention: The moderating roles of perceivedorganizational support and competitive psychological climate. *Tourism Management, 73*(1), 172–181. doi:10.1016/j.tourman.2019.02.006

Lin, Y. C., Pearson, E. T., & Cai, L. A. (2011). Food as a form of destination identitiy: A tourism destination brand perspective. *Tourism and Hospitality Research, 11*(1), 30–48. doi:10.1057/thr.2010.22

Lu, L., Zhang, P., & Zhang, T. (2021). Leveraging "human-likeness" of robotic service at restaurants. *International Journal of Hospitality Management, 94*, 1–9. doi:10.1016/j.ijhm.2020.102823

Lyotard, J. F. (1984). *The Postmodern Condition: A Report On Knowledge*. University of Minnesota Press.

Mesthene, E. G. (1971). *Technological Change-Its Impact on Man and Society*. Harvard University Press.

Mrugalska, B., & Wyrwicka, M. K. (2017). Towards Lean Production In Industry 4.0. 7th International Conference on Engineering, Project, and Production Management. *Procedia Engineering, 182*, 466–473. doi:10.1016/j.proeng.2017.03.135

Murphy, J., Gretzel, U., & Pesonen, J. (2019). Marketing robot services in hospitality and tourism: The role of anthropomorphism. *Journal of Travel & Tourism Marketing, 36*(7), 784–795. doi:10.1080/10548408.2019.1571983

Nabiyev, V. V. (2012). *Yapay Zekâ: İnsan-Bilgisayar Etkileşimi*. Seçkin Yayıncılık.

Odabaşı, Y., & Oyman, M. (2005). Pazarlama İletişimi Yönetimi. MediaCat Kitapları.

Ohlan, R. (2018). Role of information technology in hotel industry. *International Journal of Scientific Research in Computer Science, Engineering, and Information Technology, 3*(2), 277–281.

Osawa, H., Akiya, N., Koyama, T., Ema, A., Kanzaki, N., Ichise, R., & Kubo, A. (2017). What is real risk and benefit on work with robots? From the analysis of a robot hotel. *Proceedings of HRI2017 Companion of the 2017 ACM/IEEE International Conference on Human-Robot Interaction*. 10.1145/3029798.3038312

Özgürel, G., & Kılınç-Şahin, S. (2021). Turizmde robotlaşma: Yiyecek-içecek sektöründe robot şefler ve robot garsonlar. *OPUS–Uluslararası Toplum Araştırmaları Dergisi, 18*, 1849–1882.

Özmen, Ş. (2013). *Ağ Ekonomisinde Yeni Ticaret Yolu: E-Ticaret.* İstanbul Bilgi Üniversitesi Yayınları.

Pehlivan, B. (2018). *Yapay Zeka ile Dijital Pazarlama Dönüşümü.* Retrieved 08/10/22 from: Marketing Türkiye, Retrieved from: https://www.marketingtr.net/tr/blog/detay/Yapay-Zeka-ile-Dijital-PazarlamaDonusumu/6/160/0

Pels, H. (2018). *The Complete Guide to AI Marketing in 2018.* Retrieved from: Emarsy:https://www.emarsys.com/resources/blog/complete-guide-to-ai-marketing/

Perakakis, E., Mastorakis, G., & Kopanakis, I. (2019). Social Media Monitoring: An InnovativeIntelligent Approach. *Designs, 3*(24), 1–12.

Petković, G., Pindţo, R., & Molnar Agić, M. (2018). Digital Economy and (non) IncrementalChanges in Tourism and Retail Business Model. *Ekonomika Preduzeća, 1*(2), 151–165. doi:10.5937/EKOPRE1802151P

Rayport, J. F., & Sviokla, J. (1995). Exploiting the Virtual Value Chain. *Harvard Business Review, 73*(6), 75–85.

Revfine. (2020). *How Artificial Intelligence is Changing the Travel Industry.* Retrieved from: https://www.revfine.com/artificial-intelligence-travel-industry/

Rosete, A., Soares, B., Salvadorınho, J., Reis, J., & Amorım, M. (2020). service robots in the hospitality ındustry: an exploratory literature review. Lecture Notes in Business Information Processing, 377.

Ryan, D. (2016). *Understanding digital marketing: marketingstrategies for engaging the digital generation.* Kogan Page Publishers.

Saint Simon, H. (1964). *Social organization, the science of man, and other writings.* Harper & Row.

Saint Simon, H. (1975). *Henri de Saint Simon, 1760-1825: Selected writings on science, industry and social organization.* Holmes and Meier Publishers.

Seo, K. H., & Lee, J. H. (2021). The Emergence of Service Robots at Restaurants: Integrating Trust. *Perceived Risk, and Satisfaction, 13*(8), 1-16.

Shahid, M. Z., & Li, G. (2019). Impact of artificial intelligence in marketing: a perspective of marketing professionals of pakistan. *Global Journal of Management and Business Research: E Marketing, 19*(2), 26-33.

Sismondo, S. (2010). *An introduction to science and technology studies.* Blackwell Publishing.

Sismondo, S. (1993). Some Social Constructions, Social Studies of Science. *Sage Publication, 23*(3), 515–553.

Şahin, A., & Şen, S. (2017). Hizmet kalitesinin müşteri memnuniyeti üzerine etkisi. *Uluslararası Sosyal Araştırmalar Dergisi, 10*(52), 1176–1184.

Tjepkema, L. (2019). *What Is Artificial Intelligence Marketing & Why Is It So Powerful?* Retrieved 08/10/22 from: Emarsys:https://www.emarsys.com/resources/blog/artificial-intelligence-marketing-solutions/

Topsakal, Y., Yüzbaşıoğlı, N., & Bahar, M. (2018). Endüstri 4.0 çağında 'akıllı' olma yolunda oteller için öneriler, 2. In Uluslararası Turizmin Geleceği; İnovasyon, Girişimcilik ve Sürdürebilirlik Konferansı (pp. 252-256). Mersin.

Trejos, N. (2016). *Introducing Connie, Hilton's new robot concierge.* Retrieved from: https://www.usatoday.com/story/travel/roadwarriorvoices/2016/03/09/introducing-connie-hiltons-new-robot-concierge/81525924/

Tsaih, R.-H., & Hsu, C. C. (2018). *Artificial intelligence in smart tourism: A conceptual framework.* The 18th International Conference on Electronic Business, Guilin, China.

Tussyadiah, I. (2020). A review of research into automation in tourism: Launching the annals of tourism research curated collection on artificial intelligence and robotics in tourism. *Annals of Tourism Research, 81*(3), 1–13. doi:10.1016/j.annals.2020.102883

Smartinsight. (2022). *Artificial Intelligence.* Retrieved from: https://www.smartinsights.com/tag/artificial-intelligence-ai-for-marketing/

Vatan, A., & Doğan, S. (2021). What do hotel employees think about service robots? A qualitative study in Turkey. *Tourism Management Perspectives, 37*, 1–10. doi:10.1016/j.tmp.2020.100775

Wang, Y. (2018). Intelligent customer service system design based on natural language processing. In *5th International Conference On Electrical & Electronics Engineering And Computer Science (ICEEECS)* (pp. 374-379). Francis Acad Press.

Weber, M. (1975). Science as a vocation. In From Max Weber: Essays in sociology (pp. 129-159). Oxford University Press.

Wirtz, J., Patterson, P. G., Kunz, W. H., Gruber, T., Lu, W. N., Paluch, S., & Martins, A. (2018). Brave new world: Service robots in the frontline. *Journal of Service Management, 29*(5), 907–931. doi:10.1108/JOSM-04-2018-0119

Yalçın Kayıkçı, M., & Kutluk Bozkurt, A. (2018). Dijital çağda Z ve Alpha kuşağı, yapay zeka uygulamaları ve turizme yansımaları. *Sosyal Bilimler Metinleri, 1*, 54–64.

Yeğin, T. (2020). The place and future of artificial intelligence in marketing strategies. *Ekev Akademi Dergisi, 24*(81), 489–506.

Yelkikalkan, N., Özcan, S., & Temel, K. (2019). Endüstri 4.0 Farkındalığının Belirlenmesi: Çanakkale Onsekiz Mart Üniversitesi Örneği. *Journal of Entrepreneurship and Development, 14*(1), 31–44.

Yıldız, S. (2018). Profesyonel turist rehberlerinin teknolojik rehber algısını belirlemeye yönelik bir araştırma: İstanbul örneği. *Journal of Social and Humanities Sciences Research, 5*(31), 4686–4697.

Zhang, L., & Sun, Z. (2019). The application of artificial intelligence technology in the tourism industry of Jinan. *Journal of Physics: Conference Series, 1302*(3), 032005. doi:10.1088/1742-6596/1302/3/032005

Zlatanov, S., & Popesku, J. (2019). *Current applications of artificial intelligence in tourism and hospitality*. International Scientific Conference on Information Technology and Data Related Research, Belgrade, Serbia. 10.15308/Sinteza-2019-84-90

Zsarnoczky, M. (2017). How does artificial intelligence affect the tourism ındustry? *Vadyba Journal of Management*, 2(31), 85–90.

Chapter 9
Technological Innovations in Tourism Businesses: A Study on Contemporary Trends

Pramendra Singh
Amity University, Noida, India

Disha Sharma
https://orcid.org/0000-0003-2124-0970
Amity University, Raipur, India

ABSTRACT

Technological innovations are bringing major breakthroughs and radical changes in the way businesses function. These technological innovations are helping all the industries to smooth their functions and provide better experiences to the customers. The tourism industry is also witnessing tremendous improvements in technological innovations. The chapter aims to study the different types of technologies that have emerged in recent times in tourism businesses. This study is conceptual in nature and uses various secondary sources for data collection along with the study of various cases to comprehend the usage of technology. The study concludes in supporting the statement made by world's largest and nodal tourism organization, United Nations World Tourism Organization, that technology and digitization are emerging, disrupting, and affecting our lives in such a way that augurs the begging of the next generation industrial revolution.

INTRODUCTION

As per the accepted definitions worldwide, development has many elements. Economic development occupies the centre stage of nations aspirations. And for economic development, the nations have to encourage the businesses through policies, practices and participation. Tourism is one of the major industries in the world which has the capacity of generating multiplier effect which helps in creating employment and generating revenue on a large scale. Tourism businesses operate in highly competitive

DOI: 10.4018/978-1-6684-6732-9.ch009

Copyright © 2023, IGI Global. Copying or distributing in print or electronic forms without written permission of IGI Global is prohibited.

and fragile environment and gets affected by different forces. Therefore, the tourism businesses have to adopt best practices to remain in the competition and grow sustaining various forces.

The businesses look to smoothen their operations, enhance collaboration, offer novelty, solve problems, promote sustainability etc. Business organizations try hard to achieve these objectives with minimal time effort and endeavours using modern technology. Technology has advanced leaps and bounds in today's era. Various aspects of modern technological innovations are related but not limited to Artificial Intelligence (AI), Virtual Reality (VR), Augmented Reality (AR), Internet of Things (IoT), Big Data, Robots, Chatbots, mobile applications etc. These technological tools are helping all the industries to smoothen their functions and provide better experiences to the customers.

All the sectors within tourism industry have been gradually adopting these technologies since their necessities were felt to enhance performance. Hotels, restaurants, airlines, travel agencies, transport operators are now aligning their businesses keep in mind utmost utility of the modern technological innovations and tools. In last few years the tourism industry had to suffer much because of COVID outbreak which prompted the industry to look into and devise plans for revival. And in this endeavour, technology proved to be playing a significant role. Many technologies were used by tourism businesses during COVID outbreak also to remain afloat in the industry.

Technology is used in tourism industry for information search, getting updates, product development, interpreting the destinations and their attractions, make bookings, during tour services, travel convenience, customer interaction, service delivery, personalization and customization, enhancing experiences, navigation, marketing, data security, connectivity, performance enhancement, inventory management, financial resource management etc. Tourism industry must continuously innovate and generate better business opportunities for ensuring competitiveness, growth and sustainable development of the industry. This article will help the readers and researchers in understanding the applicability of technology in tourism industry. It will also help in augmenting the knowledge about the crucial role technological innovations play for the growth and development of the tourism businesses and tourism industry in general. The study will contribute to the field of knowledge regarding tourism and technology.

TOURISM: THE GLOBAL PHENOMENA

During the pandemic period the hospitality tourism industry has taken a major beating, we found airlines grounded, train wheels stopping, and empty hotels with a lot of people being laid off during the pandemic (Lai & Nepal, 2006). We have our spate of lockdowns though some countries are somehow still under its shadow, brought to us the technological innovation. Thus, the focus of technological innovation is to count on capitalizing on new opportunities in the market. Technological innovations are always looking at new horizons and what's coming next (Buckley, 2006).

As the number of who travel increases, previously unexplored tourist attractions become more popular. Between 1995 and 2015, the number of tourists increased almost 15 times on average. The trend in global tourism is based on the working of tourism machinery working to travel more, visit more, and spend a bit more (Najda-Janoszka & Kopera, 2014). Tourism has literally exploded the regions and countries all around the world had identified tourism as a driver of employment and of economic growth. This simply means that the number of visitors at any given point in time is directly proportional to the flow of money into the destination resulting in better-off the citizen and economic growth. This simplifies the equation that the more visitors will come the more money the destination will generate and by that logic the destinations that attracted the most visitors were the most successful destinations. These destinations are the real winners and are often called bucket list destinations (Labanauskaitė, Fiore, & Stašys, 2020).

In the course of time, these destinations get evolved with the new term called over-tourism. Over tourism is the phenomenon where the destinations are visited by excessive visitors causing adverse effects for the destination places (Abdallah, 2022). The host communities started to find their voice, for fly shame, to protect the environment, labelling the industry as extractive, and sometimes it is not welcoming. There was a growing feeling that the industry is mining the places, culture, and heritage for mere profit and without undue consideration. Surprisingly, all the while the number kept growing say up to 1.4 billion by 2019 and predicted to double to 3 billion by 2030, and in fact, the industry proclaimed that the growth in the tourism industry was actually unstoppable (Irfan et al., 2022).

Until the pandemic has devastated the global travel and tourism industry like none another sector. In Europe, the revenues were down almost 50 percent by 2020. The destinations are trying to win back the tourist again but facing many challenges, new stiff competition from the outdoors, ongoing international restrictions on travel, COVID protocol, etc (Khanal & Shimizu, 2019). Thus the post-COVID revival of the industry is based on the working patterns (that is the remote workers) and technological intervention. Pre-pandemic tourism was big business accounting for more than 10 percent of total GDP, it is much more in the case of tourism-dependent countries (Ivanović, Milojica, & Roblek, 2016).

The prime role in post-COVID tourism recovery is played by the vaccination, followed by the financial support provided by the government by granting soft loans, offering grants to small and medium enterprises, and remodelling the business (Lai & Nepal, 2006; Najda-Janoszka & Kopera, 2014). Also, a continuing shift towards ecotourism can be seen post-COVID, this will help in local job creation and focus on conservation. Adding up adventure travel and wellness and health tours can help the countries entering the niche markets.

Surreal Tourism Businesses: The Backbone of The Industry

The slowing down of the economy, the decline in the GDP, the decreased travel has induced the dire situation in order to cope up with the statistics of pre COVID phase. Many forms of tourism businesses have been geared up by the tourist destinations to find their revival.

Adventure Tourism

Imagine hiking past endless waterfalls, through glaciers, and volcanoes that erupted a decade ago is difficult and dramatic (Ivanović et al., 2016). As for the thrill part, people consider discomfort as the key, for some people the vacations can be to sit on the beach side or visit a temple, but on the other side the people nowadays like adventure activities that test their endurance and strength (Beedie & Hudson, 2003). In research, the traveller expected the adventure as an opportunity and they have a belief that the risk and the discomfort are able to give them new perspectives that can be taken back and applied in daily life (Buckley, 2006). Adventure tourism is a new and trending concept that takes place in thrilling places (Rantala, Rokenes, & Valkonen, 2018).

Ayurveda Tourism

The legendary ancient medical practitioner of India *Charak* says that ***'the body when combine with the sense organs, mind and soul becomes life'***. In India, Ayurveda is the emerging wellness tourism market that performs ancient healing practices, naturopathy, yoga, and other Ayurveda treatments to mostly foreign visitors seeking wellness vacation (Khanal & Shimizu, 2019). As per Vedic literature, Ayurveda offers holistic wellness providing great medicinal value with the natural herbs and the oil used during the therapy (Hübscher, 2021). This novel business idea and the response from the tourists is a reflection of the trending travel-related business (Hjalager, 2002).

Corporate Hospitality Event Planning

In the process of entertainment corporate hospitality event planning business is giving services to the corporate for their staff, clients, or stakeholders (Beedie & Hudson, 2003). The basic agenda behind this category is to keep your clients happy in the terms of business entertainment. These business practices can be adopted for the purpose of novel business ideas. Corporate events have changed in part and it never goes unrecognized to treat your guests with politeness, courtesy, and respect (Hjalager, 2010).

Double-Decker Bus Tours and Cruise Tours

The opportunity to see the destination along with enjoying the way to it. Be it enjoying a ride on the double-decker bus or enjoying the stay on the cruise along with all the amenities available (Kurtzman & Zauhar, 2003). The tour of the busses and cruise delineate as they move through the routes and stops. This involves experience-enabled sightseeing through bus tours and cruise ships ride. This business involves crafting a proper marketing strategy and appropriate sales promotion to fetch the tourists (Ratten, 2020).

Ecotourism

Ecotourism is a form of tourism involving tourism in a responsible way toward natural areas. Which involves conversing with the environment and improving the well-being of the local people (Lai & Nepal, 2006). This evolved with the concept of over-tourism which requires action to fix the unbalanced tourism. Ecotourism is concerned with educating travellers on the local environment and based on the agenda that if you want to grow the destination it has to grow organically by ecological conservation (Buckley, 2006).

Travel Photography, Agency and Blog

The documentation of an area's landscape, culture, people, custom, and the history is called travel photography a genre of photography. An art and passion of capturing the moment that enhances the beauty of that place (Kurtzman & Zauhar, 2003). Whereas the agency can provide service which is most common popular among all the travel business ideas. Travel agency work is all about making travel arrangements for the travellers and their trips. And being a passionate traveller any one can go for blogging. Blog is all about sharing your traveling experiences and making money out of it (Dodds & Butler, 2019).

Sustainable Tourism

Sustainability has become a day to day talk these days. Right from the international platform like United Nations & its organizations to different stakeholders across the world have been talking about and trying to implement it core principles. The world cannot bear the overburden being rendered by the human beings in different form for so long. Therefore, maintaining the environmental, economic and social sustainability is much needed. Tourism and hospitality industry too have the responsibility of providing all resources and activities in sustainable manner. The aspect of sustainability is applied to all forms of tourism irrespective of place, people, and parties.

Other Forms of Tourism

Tourism has multi faces and forms which caters to all kinds of demands and services. It also provides opportunities to people from all walks of life to participate and practice. These different forms of tourism activities are being popularized and promoted with the help of technology which have even created distinctive identity for the destinations.

Technological Innovations: Evolution & Diversification

There is a real need to partner with others, to work closely as well as influence more technology solutions so that it can drive more impact for a unit of efforts this could be a stepping stone for making travel and tourism more sustainable (Hübscher, 2021; Tejada & Moreno, 2013). This also means having zero impact travel, zero footprints, and zero carbon travel in the destination place. Concern to AI is being extensively used in traveling, helps to make sure what we are bringing, are the travellers getting what they what, and making things accessible for the consumers in an economical and efficient way (Ivanović et al., 2016; Jurevičienė & Ivanova, 2013).

The tourism community must work together to reduce the complexity by using AI, which is extensively using a lot of AI. It starts with the conversion of textual content of the traveller with the help of AI (Gretzel, Werthner, Koo, & Lamsfus, 2015). This will help the travel agency to provide better assistance, create more economical trips, and better experience for the travellers. The latest addition in artificial intelligence is about mobile which is a primary source of interaction, micro services that open doors for industry intervention, the cloud that has enabled the travel company to have beyond legacy, block chain mediation (Zsarnoczky, 2017).

The hyper connection between people now a day's tourists who are consumers and the places we are missing, the products we are consuming, we are not just to consume but we could make a positive impact and it can be done equitably effortlessly (Ratten, 2020). Though, in the present scenario tourism business are also looking in the scenario to smoothen the operations, improve collaboration, stimulate sustainability, and introducing novelty.

TECHNOLOGY IN TOURISM INDUSTRY: UNWTO'S PERSPECTIVE

Many international organizations have recognized the role of technology in today's world as the beginning of fourth industrial revolution because the way technology is emerging, disrupting, and affecting our lives is phenomenal. Tourism industry was one of the earliest industries which adopted the digitization of business processes be it online flight booking, hotel booking or any other business operations. The digitization seems to be contributing for enhancing experiences to become more seamless, upward, frictionless and of high quality to achieve the United Nation's sustainable development goals.

United Nations World Tourism Organization has rightly elaborated the importance of technology in tourism industry as –

"The use of technologies including the 'Internet of Things', location-based services, artificial intelligence, augmented and virtual reality, and blockchain technology (see definitions below) has resulted in a tourism offer that is more attractive, efficient, inclusive, and economically, socially and environmentally sustainable than its predecessor. It has also facilitated innovation and rethinking of processes, with a view to tackling challenges such as seasonality and overcrowding and developing smarter destinations".

TECHNOLOGY & TOURISM BUSINESSES

Adoption of innovative ideas and new technology is not a new phenomenon for any businesses. All businesses strive to get competitive advantage, retain employees, and satisfy the needs of the customers which changing paradigm. Technology has brought in many changes in the operations and functionality of the businesses be it production, marketing, delivery, or consumption. As tourism industry is one of the largest service industries in the world, also get influenced from many factors including technological factors. Out of many other factors, technological factor has contributed significantly to the evolution of the tourism industry and also played pivotal role in shifting the tourism business operations from offline to online mode drastically (Firoiu & Croitoru, 2013).

Tourism businesses be they are small or large have now adopted the technological trends to remain significant in the industry. Adoption of new technology increases the productivity by enhancing the business efficiency, effectiveness, and capacity (Neuhofer et al., 2014). Therefore, offline tourism businesses in line with online businesses are also now keen to partially or fully adopt new technology for simplification of their businesses.

With the growing trend of technology adoption among businesses, it is inferred that new technology creates opportunities, simplify processes and enable the automation functions within the business organizations. Even in this new digital era, businesses heavily rely on technology and internet to market themselves. The technology supported marketing strategies and policies have more impact on the tourism industry (Liberato et al., 2018). The only requisite is that the business planners and strategists need to understand the importance of changing technological trends and accordingly strive to get incorporated them into their business modules.

Picking up the Tour: ICT Based Searching & Booking

'No visibility no sales. The famous quote represents the harsh reality of today's cutthroat competition where numerous service providers struggle to remain in the competition and get competitive advantage over others. As tourism is a service-based industry, it depends on leads (queries) which could be converted into bookings and business put all efforts to generate these leads. Therefore, it becomes very important to get noticed and provide right information at right time to the prospective customers. Internet and modern technological gazettes have made this process easy and accessible for all. Tourists in modern time have access to all information through internet and tend to book tourism services online which provides them convenience, saves time and gives better offers.

Information and communication technology (ICT) in modern times is the boon for tourism industry through which it fetches a lot of information regarding tourism destinations, service providers therein, attractions and other information necessitated to better serve the tourists (Maloney Tichaawa et al., 2017). This new era of digital outreach has given power to all tourists to have access to all kind of information by sitting in their home. Tourists can get information about the destination, attractions, availability of accommodation & accessibility, activities, guiding services, weather conditions, demand etc. "Augmented reality is believed to be helping individuals or consumers to enjoy more freedom in searching, viewing, selecting and purchasing products or services" ((Dadwal & Hassan, 2015, p.80).

Technology has expanded exponentially in all domains of the tourism industry. But the use and management of technology in tourism businesses significantly differ depending upon their size, human resources, location and financial capacity (Roult et al., 2016). ICT being one of the elements of technology has a pivotal role in fetching a large amount of data with a short span of time. ICT has also provided wide range of opportunities for all in tourism supply chain and the major investments has been made in re-engineering information transactions (Stamboulis & Skayannis, 2003). Tourism businesses are investing humongous amount in updating their technologies and processes to save time and efforts.

Mobile technology along with ICT becomes very important and effective tool in searching for the tourism related content and making the bookings. Using mobile technology, not only business but also the online tourism communities provide a wide range of facilities to the users by assisting them in pre-travel phase and on-trip assistance (Dippelreiter et al., 2009). The tourism online communities have become very active with the expansion of internet across the world. Taking this advantage, online tourism communities assist tourists in unknown environments regarding all their travel related needs. So, technology assists all including the tourists.

Technological Assistance: Product Development & Travelling Convenience

The most important thing for any business is its product which defines the probability of its success in the market place. Quality, quantity, design, packaging, offering, price, marketing everything is related to and defined on the basis of products. All the strategies of the business organizations revolve around the products. Tourism businesses are also conscious about this fact. As a result, the tourism business have product development department in their organizations which deals with every aspect of research and development of the products. Tourism businesses to an extent very much supported and assisted by technology in product development and its marketing. Technology supports the interactivity between tourism businesses and tourists and as a result it re-engineers the entire process of tourism product development, management and marketing (Buhalis & O'connor, 2005).

Technology in its different form is useful in product development for the tourism businesses. With the advent of 5th generation (5G) mobile technology, it will bring momentum into new and emerging concepts like e-tourism, mobile tourism, smart tourism which will empower Augmented Reality (AR), Virtual Reality (VR) etc. which ultimately help the businesses in coming out with innovative products and creating unique experiences (Chen et al., 2020). Technology also contributes in bringing different stakeholders and ideas at one forum to contribute in pondering over the changes in market needs. Tourism stakeholders create a collaborative environment in which they could contribute to ideas for an integrated tourism service and product development which will be useful in overcoming knowledge barriers surrounding digital technology (McCabe et al., 2012). A good product will serve good cause and will create good will.

Technology has been instrumental in proving to be the catalyst in facilitating the tourist accessibility to different destinations worldwide, streamlining the tourism activities and increasing the popularity of online travel services (Firoiu & Croitoru, 2013). Technology in its different forms helps tourists for travelling to far flung areas in minimal time with ease and affordability. One of the emerging technologies blockchain has been adopted by all industries including tourism which is simplifying and speeding up the system of checking in of the travelers at the ports & airports, etc. and it will significantly impact on tourism businesses and how their processes are handled (Erceg et al., 2020). Be it any mode of transport, technology has spread horizontally & vertically in all sectors to smoothen the processes and accessibility.

Interpreting the Destination: Enhancing Experience-Based Tourism Through Technology

It is a common saying in tourism industry that 'tourism products are first sold and then manufactured' attributing towards their intangible characteristic. As the destination is marketed, services are created and things are anticipated for tourists, so the expectations for the destinations are generated in the minds of tourists. Tourists pay money to get the experiences for which the expectations have been created in their mind. Hence experiences of tourists matter in tourism industry which ultimately decides the success of the businesses. Experience emerges as a result of interaction between tourists and the destination, so continuous creation of new experiences for the tourists is key to experience-based tourism (Stamboulis & Skayannis, 2003). In creating value experience for the tourists, technology has emerged as novel modern tool. Tourists' demand and needs getting phenomenal shift from the traditional stereotype to more experience-based outcome. Technology is significantly changing the tourism experiences and technology along with co-creation of experiences have become the parameters to visitor satisfaction ((Neuhofer et al., 2014). Tourist experience at the destination is further enhanced by the use of internet and associated technological products & digital media (Liberato et al., 2018).

Internet truly has paved way for understanding the destination and its different elements. The history of the place associated events, legends, culture and festivals can really be understood with the help of modern technological gazettes. The interpretation of the attractions now does not rely on physical existence of the guides rather it can be done through the use of technology. Technology has eased many barriers like language barrier, cultural barrier, regionality barrier, connectivity barriers etc. by interpreting the destination and its attractions through audio-video devices, virtual tour gadgets, experience driven content and other recommendations of to do lists at the destination (Jadhav & Mundhe, 2011).

Performance Enhancement Through Technology: Business Intelligence and Marketing Practices

Marketing is a phenomenon represents the customer-oriented approach of the business organizations. Marketing is considered as a function of the management to identify customer needs and come up with the requisite product in affordable price at right time. In last few decades, new elements in marketing have evolved like service marketing, relationship marketing, network-based marketing, business-to-business marketing along with customer centric marketing approaches.

With the advent of new technology and advancement of internet base, the world has also witnessed new marketing approaches and processes which are known as electronic marketing (e-marketing), digital marketing, online marketing and social media marketing (Grönroos, 2006). Traditional marketing had its own benefits, but the online marketing approach gives you more liberty in sense that it serves 24*7 availability to customers who search, research, purchase and intend to buy the product or service (Taherdoost & Jalaliyoon, 2014). E-marketing provides extensive information to the customers without and human intervention, reduces the cost for the businesses and enhance the reach among masses (Sheth & Sharma, 2005). This concept also applies in tourism industry. A relationship between the conventional marketing and digital marketing can be established using technology to be innovative and interactive in a highly competitive market characterized by the preferential changes of the tourists' demand in tourism industry (Liberato et al., 2018). Like other industries, tourism industry has also adopted new ways of marketing their businesses and products through technology popularly known as digital marketing which includes online advertising, websites, search engine optimization, social media handles etc. (Jadhav & Mundhe, 2011).

Using the digital technology and internet, social media is now within reach for people from all walks of life. Tourism businesses have now started investing into social media marketing because of internal and external factors like pressure from the competitors and also because of its easy and fast reach among the masses (Matikiti et al., 2018). Technology has also contributed in marketing of the products & services through different ways. "Augmented reality marketing (ARM) is in practice and a new rising trend. This is growing due to various factors that are related to technology adoption, consumer buying intentions and loyalty; social norms, personalisation, novelty, socialisation, accessibility, easiness, fun and so on" (Dadwal & Hassan, 2015, p.90). Technology has given great leverage to the tourism businesses to find suitable market and make strategies accordingly for increasing their efficacy and effectiveness.

VARIOUS ASPECTS OF TECHNOLOGY & ITS ADOPTION IN TOURISM INDUSTRY

The technology has grown much with the expansion of internet around the world throughout all the industries including tourism. The technology has various aspects, and its utility goes beyond boundaries. Some of the modern technological tools and their applicability in tourism industry is mentioned below: -

Table 1. Technology and its use in the tourism industry

Technology	Use in tourism industry
Voice search & voice control	- Search for airline tickets, hotel rooms & other travel experiences with the help of smartphone, speaker, artificial intelligence assistant - Voice control hotel room lights, heating, amenities etc.
Robots	- To greet customers, cleaning, luggage handling, taking restaurant orders, serving food, screening etc.
Contactless payment	- Reduces the need to carry cash
Virtual Reality (VR)	- Virtual tours, 360^0 tours, virtual travel service experience, virtual monument or museum visit etc.
Artificial Intelligence (AI)	- Track customer review & comments on social media, improve personalization, fast response, manage inventories etc.
Chatbots	- Swift response on 24/7 basis, answer common questions, enhance customer interaction
Cyber security	- Protects data, prevent cyber attacks
Internet of Things (IoT)	- Provides interconnectivity among devices & data transfer, control devices
Recognition technology	- Finger print or facial or retina recognition for smooth mobility and transfer
Augmented Reality (AR)	- Augments surrounding & experiences, provides information & entertainment
Big Data	- For customization, manage business performance, revenue management, anticipate demand, promotional strategies etc.
Mobile applications	- For everything starting from searching travel information, updates, customization, comparing, booking, payment, feedback etc.
Smart navigation	- To search places, seamless travel, finding restaurants & other places of interest etc.
Digital marketing	- Online, digital or social media marketing for tourism products & services

CONCLUSION

Like any other industry, tourism has also become highly competitive which has many service providers and employs millions of people. To remain competitive and survive, the tourism businesses need to remain vigilant about the technological developments and adopt them for improving their performance. Tourism service providers at the destinations also need to collaborate with other stakeholders at the destination in order to provide technology enabled real time services to remain competitive and take the advantages (McCabe et al., 2012). Tourists have become more sophisticated and experienced; therefore, it has become difficult to easily please them (Buhalis & O'Connor, 2005). The businesses need to be smart to use smart technology. Smart tourism technology contributes to tourists' overall level of satisfaction and consists of some elements including informativeness, accessibility, interactivity, personalization & security.

"Tourism enterprises need to understand, incorporate and utilise ICT systems strategically in order to: serve their target markets; improve their efficiency; maximise their profitability; enhance their services; and maintain their long-term profitability" (Maloney Tichaawa et al., 2017, p.26).

Tourism businesses not only themselves adapt the modern technological innovations but also ensure technical adoptability in their human resources. The tourism businesses must strive to innovate and train their human resources for technological adoption because the industry now has become highly economically competitive (Roult et al., 2016). The more tourism businesses are tech friendly, there is a more probability of their success.

LIMITATIONS

The study is purely based on secondary data and focused on the adoption, utility, and applicability of technological trends in tourism businesses. This study is conceptual in nature and sheds light on recent technological trends in tourism businesses. It has got limitation in terms of being industry specific and covering to some extent the contemporary trends in terms of technological innovation in tourism businesses. Further research can be carried out with regard to use of technology in other industries and covering related aspects of technology and businesses.

REFERENCES

Abdallah, A. (2022, April). Reviving a Collapsing Country's Economy Through Cultural Heritage: A Case Study of Tourism in Lebanon. *Journal of Hospitality and Tourism Management*, *6*(1), 1–7. doi:10.11648/j.ijhtm.20220601.11

Beedie, P., & Hudson, S. (2003). Emergence of mountain-based adventure tourism. *Annals of Tourism Research*, *30*(3), 625–643. doi:10.1016/S0160-7383(03)00043-4

Buckley, R. (2006). Adventure tourism research: A guide to the literature. *Tourism Recreation Research*, *31*(2), 75–83. doi:10.1080/02508281.2006.11081265

Buhalis, D., & O'connor, P. (2005). *Information Communication Technology Revolutionizing Tourism*. Academic Press.

Chen, S., Law, R., Xu, S., & Zhang, M. (2020). Bibliometric and visualized analysis of mobile technology in tourism. In Sustainability (Switzerland) (Vol. 12, Issue 19, pp. 1–16). MDPI. doi:10.3390u12197975

Dadwal, S. S., & Hassan, A. (2015). The augmented reality marketing: A merger of marketing and technology in tourism. In Mobile Computing and Wireless Networks: Concepts, Methodologies, Tools, and Applications (Vols. 1–4, pp. 63–80). IGI Global. doi:10.4018/978-1-4666-8699-1.ch005

Dippelreiter, B., Grün, C., Pöttler, M., Seidel, I., Berger, H., Dittenbach, M., & Pesenhofer, A. (2009). Online Tourism Communities on the Path to Web 2.0: An Evaluation. *Information Technology & Tourism*, *10*(4), 329–353. doi:10.3727/109830508788403132

Dodds, R., & Butler, R. (2019). The phenomena of overtourism: A review. *International Journal of Tourism Cities*, *5*(4), 519–528. doi:10.1108/IJTC-06-2019-0090

Erceg, A., Sekuloska, J. D., & Kelic, I. (2020). Blockchain in the tourism industry - A review of the situation in Croatia and Macedonia. In Informatics (Vol. 7, Issue 1). MDPI Multidisciplinary Digital Publishing Institute. doi:10.3390/informatics7010005

Firoiu, D., & Croitoru, A. G. (2013). Tourism and tourism infrastructure from the perspective of technological changes. *Romanian Economic & Business Review, 8*(2), 93-103.

Gretzel, U., Werthner, H., Koo, C., & Lamsfus, C. (2015). Conceptual foundations for understanding smart tourism ecosystems. *Computers in Human Behavior, 50*(1), 558–563. doi:10.1016/j.chb.2015.03.043

Grönroos, C. (2006). On defining marketing: Finding a new roadmap for marketing. *Marketing Theory, 6*(4), 395–417. doi:10.1177/1470593106069930

Hjalager, A. M. (2002). Repairing innovation defectiveness in tourism. *Tourism Management, 23*(5), 465–474. doi:10.1016/S0261-5177(02)00013-4

Hjalager, A. M. (2010). A review of innovation research in tourism. *Tourism Management, 31*(1), 1–12. doi:10.1016/j.tourman.2009.08.012

Hübscher, M. (2021). Megaprojects, gentrification, and tourism. A systematic review on intertwined phenomena. *Sustainability (Switzerland), 13*(22), 12827. Advance online publication. doi:10.3390u132212827

Irfan, M., Ahmad, M., Fareed, Z., Iqbal, N., Sharif, A., & Wu, H. (2022). On the indirect environmental outcomes of COVID-19: Short-term revival with futuristic long-term implications. *International Journal of Environmental Health Research, 32*(6), 1271–1281. doi:10.1080/09603123.2021.1874888 PMID:33448868

Ivanović, S., Milojica, V., & Roblek, V. (2016). A Holistic Approach to Innovations in Tourism. *International Conference on Economic and Social Studies (ICESoS'16)*, 367–380. Retrieved from https://www.researchgate.net/publication/301295108

Jadhav, V. S., & Mundhe, S. D. (2011). Information technology in Tourism. *International Journal of Computer Science and Information Technologies, 2*(6), 2822–2825. http://www.maharashtratourism.gov.in

Jalaliyoon, N., Hamed Taherdoost, A., Lumpur, K., & Neda Jalaliyoon, M. (2014). Marketing vs E-Marketing Steganography View project E-Commerce Quality Assessment; Evaluation of the Quality of E-Service View project. *International Journal of Academic Research in Management, 3*(4). https://www.researchgate.net/publication/282654148

Jurevičienė, D., & Ivanova, O. (2013). Behavioural Finance: Theory and Survey [Finansinė Elgsena: Teorija Ir Tyrimas]. *Mokslas - Lietuvos Ateitis, 5*(1), 53–58. doi:10.3846/mla.2013.08

Khanal, B. P., & Shimizu, T. (2019). Strategies for Development of Yoga, Ayurveda, and Meditation-based Health Tourism in Nepal: Using SWOT Analysis. *Journal of Tourism & Adventure, 2*(1), 85–107. doi:10.3126/jota.v2i1.25934

Kurtzman, J., & Zauhar, J. (2003). A Wave in Time – The Sports. *Journal of Sport Tourism, 8*(1), 35–47. doi:10.1080/1477508032000093443

Labanauskaitė, D., Fiore, M., & Stašys, R. (2020). Use of E-marketing tools as communication management in the tourism industry. *Tourism Management Perspectives, 34*, 1–8. doi:10.1016/j.tmp.2020.100652

Lai, P. H., & Nepal, S. K. (2006). Local perspectives of ecotourism development in Tawushan Nature Reserve, Taiwan. *Tourism Management, 27*(6), 1117–1129. doi:10.1016/j.tourman.2005.11.010 PMID:32287717

Liberato, P., Liberato, D., Abreu, A., Alén-González, E., & Rocha, Á. (2018). Generation Y: The Competitiveness of the Tourism Sector Based on Digital Technology. *Advances in Intelligent Systems and Computing, 724*, 227–240. doi:10.1007/978-3-319-74980-8_21

Maloney Tichaawa, T., Mhlanga, O., & Sicwebu, S. (2017). The Impact of Information Communication Technologies (ICTs) on Tourism Businesses in East London, South Africa. In ACTA Universitatis Danubius (Vol. 13). Academic Press.

Matikiti, R., Mpinganjira, M., & Roberts-Lombard, M. (2018). Application of the Technology Acceptance Model and the Technology–Organisation–Environment Model to examine social media marketing use in the South African tourism industry. *South African Journal of Information Management, 20*(1). Advance online publication. doi:10.4102ajim.v20i1.790

McCabe, S., Sharples, M., & Foster, C. (2012). Stakeholder engagement in the design of scenarios of technology-enhanced tourism services. *Tourism Management Perspectives, 4*, 36–44. doi:10.1016/j.tmp.2012.04.007

Najda-Janoszka, M., & Kopera, S. (2014). Exploring Barriers to Innovation in Tourism Industry – The Case of Southern Region of Poland. *Procedia: Social and Behavioral Sciences, 110*, 190–201. doi:10.1016/j.sbspro.2013.12.862

Neuhofer, B., Buhalis, D., & Ladkin, A. (2014). A Typology of Technology-Enhanced Tourism Experiences. *International Journal of Tourism Research, 16*(4), 340–350. doi:10.1002/jtr.1958

Pai, C. K., Liu, Y., Kang, S., & Dai, A. (2020). The role of perceived smart tourism technology experience for tourist satisfaction, happiness, and revisit intention. *Sustainability (Switzerland), 12*(16), 6592. Advance online publication. doi:10.3390u12166592

Rantala, O., Rokenes, A., & Valkonen, J. (2018). Is adventure tourism a coherent concept? A review of research approaches on adventure tourism. *Annals of Leisure Research, 21*(5), 539–552. doi:10.1080/11745398.2016.1250647

Ratten, V. (2020). Tourism entrepreneurship research: A perspective article. *Tourism Review, 75*(1), 122–125. doi:10.1108/TR-06-2019-0204

Roult, R., Gaudette, M., Auger, D., & Adjizian, J.-M. (2016). Site Management and Use of social media by Tourism Businesses: The Case of Quebec. *Czech Journal of Tourism, 5*(1), 21–34. doi:10.1515/cjot-2016-0002

Sheth, J. N., & Sharma, A. (2005). International e-marketing: Opportunities and issues. *International Marketing Review, 22*(6), 611–622. doi:10.1108/02651330510630249

Stamboulis, Y., & Skayannis, P. (2003). Innovation strategies and technology for experience-based tourism. In Tourism Management (Vol. 24). doi:10.1016/S0261-5177(02)00047-X

Tejada, P., & Moreno, P. (2013). Patterns of innovation in tourism "Small and Medium-size Enterprises.". *Service Industries Journal, 33*(7–8), 749–758. doi:10.1080/02642069.2013.740469

Zsarnoczky, M. (2017). Social sciences How Does Artificial Intelligence Affect The Tourism Industry? *Journal of Management, 31*(2), 84–90.

Chapter 10
Management of Innovation:
Theories and Practice

Afzal Sayed Munna
https://orcid.org/0000-0001-7302-8037
University of Sunderland in London, UK

Md Sadeque Imam Shaikh
University of Wales Trinity Saint David, London, UK

Anupam Mazumdar
University of Wales Trinity Saint David, London, UK

ABSTRACT

Innovation management is a prime concept of making changes and innovations in the business to make the business globally famous. The conceptual understanding of the innovative strategies has been covered in this book. Besides this, the discussion of key elements and the challenges a company might face to implement innovation has been discussed here. Identification and discussion, including the application of the innovation, have been covered here. The impact of the implementation of innovation-based managerial theories as well as practices have also been evaluated within the study to develop a critical understanding of business proceedings.

INTRODUCTION

Innovation is a leading-edge weapon of modern science based on which technological advancement and transverse business growth can be incorporated within organisations. As per the ideas of Almehdia *et al.* (2019), innovation can be defined as a sequential combination of activities such as product development, decision making and infrastructure transformation. Thus, innovation result came out positively and motivated the company. Innovation in management aims to generate a sustainable alteration culture within the management system of an organisation. In order to transform a business, the impact of innovation management is massive. Every organisation needs innovation in order to make the business successfully

DOI: 10.4018/978-1-6684-6732-9.ch010

Copyright © 2023, IGI Global. Copying or distributing in print or electronic forms without written permission of IGI Global is prohibited.

grow based on which they can anticipate its competitors. However, management faces key factors and challenges to uplift the innovation, which further assists the business successfully in the global market. According to business owners, innovation escalates the success rate of a business or organisation by making the customer satisfied and the employee valuable. This practice is a part of the routine innovation method. Furthermore, positive feedback will help to give employees self-esteem and confidence so they can be more efficient and productive about their work. In this book, the further scope of business evaluation has been evaluated to manage the innovation in the business process effectively.

CONCEPTUAL UNDERSTANDING OF INNOVATION IN MANAGEMENT

The approach to innovation is improved in order to enhance the quality of existing products or services. In the context of discussing innovation in management, there are four types of innovation management such as ***"Incremental innovation ", "Sustaining innovation" "Disruptive innovation" and "breakthrough innovation"*** which will be discussed further.

"Incremental Innovation"

Incremental Innovation lies in the era of business management, where the business requires reinventing itself in order to make business successful. In this plan, the ideas of implementation have to be unique so that the company can thrive among the clients as well as the employees. This is a particularly smaller series of improvements in order to make the existing products or services more attractive and effective. This innovative program is generally a low-cost program in order to generate low-margin profits. Companies added different features or upgrades to a particular product or service in contemplation of adding new customers. As per the view of O'Reilly and Binns (2019), the importance of incremental innovation is that this method allows the company or the organisation to grow the business by getting feedback from their customer base and which will further change the landscape of marketing. Therefore, to mitigate this problem, companies should use a different campaigning program so that they can use that campaign as a promotional method which saves time and cost.

"Sustaining Innovation"

Sustainable innovation is mainly involved in bringing the habitual usage of the "idea", "concept", "practice", and "Products". The contributions of these attributes to the "ecological environment", "social cohesion", and "economic viability" are primarily based on the sustainable innovation of management. This is an intentional way for companies to make the change by initiating long-term social and environmental benefits. This method also includes the economic benefits of the company so that the organisation can further assist significant changes in society. Taking the idea of Stubbs (2019) into consideration, it can be stated that with sustainable innovation, the company tries to increase customer strength by giving a minimal price range while concentrating on the environment by reducing effective products such as plastic. However, on the other hand, it is a costly method, and sometimes companies do not have supplements for doing this. Thus, to mitigate this company is valuing society as well as the well-being of their customers by generating sustainable innovation in their organisation.

Figure 1. Types of innovation within different industry settings

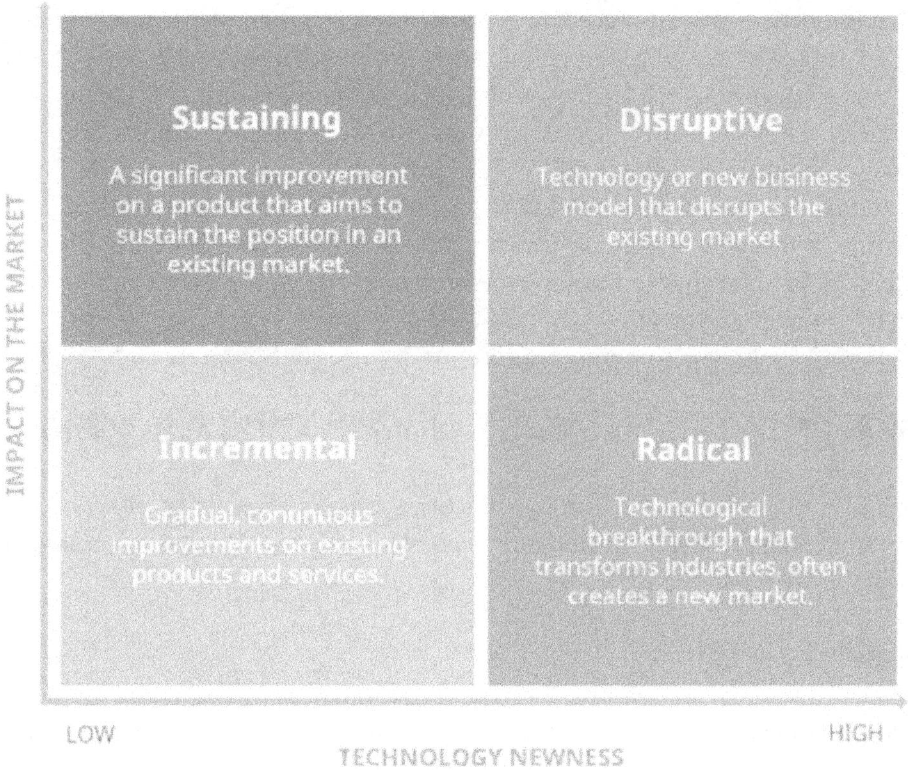

The above figure showcases the influence of different types of market settings within the process of obtaining innovation within firms. Disruptive and radical settings have the potential to incorporate technological advancements easily, whereas sustaining and incremental innovation can be incorporated gradually.

"Breakthrough innovation"

Breakthrough innovation priory comes from the inside of the company or organisation, which will further push the management to do something innovatively at the next level. Followed to the review of Almehdia *et al.* (2020), this method is basically investing in new technologies and ideas according to the current market demand the company fundamentally changes the product or service. This innovation procedure tries to establish an utterly unique and innovative product or service in order to pass the competitive advantage and make a custom preferable business module. Besides this, this particular innovation has a huge risk factor as it is breaking the marketing pattern. In order to avoid this problem, companies should be conscientious about their investment method so that they can overcome the loss. This Breakthrough innovation can enjoy the "first mover" establishment as this method can have early access to the local as and global market.

"Disruptive Innovation"

Disruptive innovation is a general procedure of using technology in order to create a new and unique market value in parallel to the old and existing market value. Small enterprises generate this method to do their business by displacing the leading firms so that the small company could take the lead in the market. Taking the ideas of Ghasmeghases and Callic (2020) into consideration, it can be stated that Disruptive innovation mainly implies exploring the customer choices, and companies implement ideas accordingly so that they can gather a variety of customers. The firms are trying to maintain a lower margin to disrupt the existing market and initiate some argumentative sales in the context of catching customer attention. In order to avoid loss, the company should focus on the quality of the product so that they can attract more customers.

DISCUSSION OF THE KEY ELEMENTS OF INNOVATION MANAGEMENT

In order to generate innovation in management, there are some key elements that need to be elaborated. The elements are ***"collaboration", "ideation", "implementation" and "value creation"*** thus these elements will be discussed further.

"Collaboration"

Collaboration can be defined as joint initiatives between two or more organisations to fulfil mutual business objectives through utilising diverse resources. Based on the views of Morrison *et al.* (2020), the organisation obtains derivational strategies and innovation such as data-driven marketing and product development within collaborative initiatives in the present situation of the business. Teamwork is the most essential aspect nowadays as this global and digital technology is getting more challenging and complicated. Therefore, the company uses collaborative programs in order to generate new strategies and approaches. This type of group work encourages companies to work harder and develop innovative ideas to expand their business globally. As per the ideas of Morrison *et al.* (2020), good communication with different companies can make this collaboration program much easier. However, on the other hand, the collaboration method could not be a successful program if both the companies do not have a cooperative ideology. In order to mitigate this, the basic aim of this program should be concentrating on personal upliftment, which will further assist in cutting the extra cost price as the promotional method is organised by both companies. Besides this, both companies can have each other's customer base to target more customers, which will further help them generate huge revenue. Hence, the primary goal of the collaboration program is to build affordable business planning in order to approach different sectors of business management.

"Ideation"

Ideation can be elaborated by stating that it is a unique idea in order to make the business successful in this competitive business environment. For the economic development of a country, the acceleration of entrepreneurship is much needed. It can be generated that ideation is the most crucial factor in order to make gross domestic rates high. Local business owners have a grasp over society rather than big companies as the price margin of these products is very cheap and affordable. Some big companies need to input ideation methods in order to create something extraordinary so that they can attract local customers. Followed to the review of Fenwick et al. (2020), the "second stage business" plays a critical role in growing and nurturing the innovative business plan more effectively. However, on the other hand, implementing the ideation method could be a highly complex method as this method involves lots of dedication and raw material. Ideation includes the enhancement of the business with the help of different innovation plans and strategies; thus, it could develop a business-friendly environment for the company.

"Implementation"

Implementation is generally explained by stating the practical usage of a certain idea or plan. Nowadays, technology is changing the daily lifestyle of customers as well as it is generating a revolution in the context of business management. Taking the ideas of Plowman (2019) into consideration, it can be stated that when technology meets innovation, it creates something extraordinary and unreal. Thus, the companies are trying to implement both of them together. In order to implement the ideas, the business owner needs to identify the local business enterprises which will further help them to gather the knowledge of local marketing factors. Besides this, communication with the local personnel can help the company understand the place's investment opportunities. Implementation methods also include the banking factors like the loan-taking method and tax returns method that will help the company to evaluate the expected revenue. However, on the other hand, sometimes an economic crisis hits the company as well as the business market, so the company needs to focus on the innovative method and implement them in a very exquisite way. From the technological aspect, implementing new technologies or hi-tech software in the process of escalating a business might be a hazard for a company because the management needs to train their employees in order to access that software.

"Value Creation"

Every innovation needs to generate some value in the context of generating revenue. As per the ideas of (Ismael *et al.* 2019), value creation is associated with eradicating competition and securing long-term customers for the product and services of an individual business. In addition, irrelevant and irrational business ideas can reduce their potential for market penetration due to a lack of innovation. Value can be determined in various ways from a business perspective, such as "existing products", "new products", and "cost reduction". Thus, from that, the company can generate its yearly turnover. As per Ismael *et al.* (2019), Present-day businesses seek creativity and innovation to uplift the value of the business because this is the only way to survive and generate growth in this overly competitive, rapidly changing market. However, on the other hand, many companies develop some experimental products or services to evaluate the feedback from their client base and make the improvisation accordingly for the final project; thus, the procedure is very time-consuming. To mitigate the problem with this, the everlasting need for finding new ideas and innovations with the help of technologies and feedback from customers can assist a company in generating value for a product or a project to gather a vast profit.

Figure 2. Value creation strategies within businesses

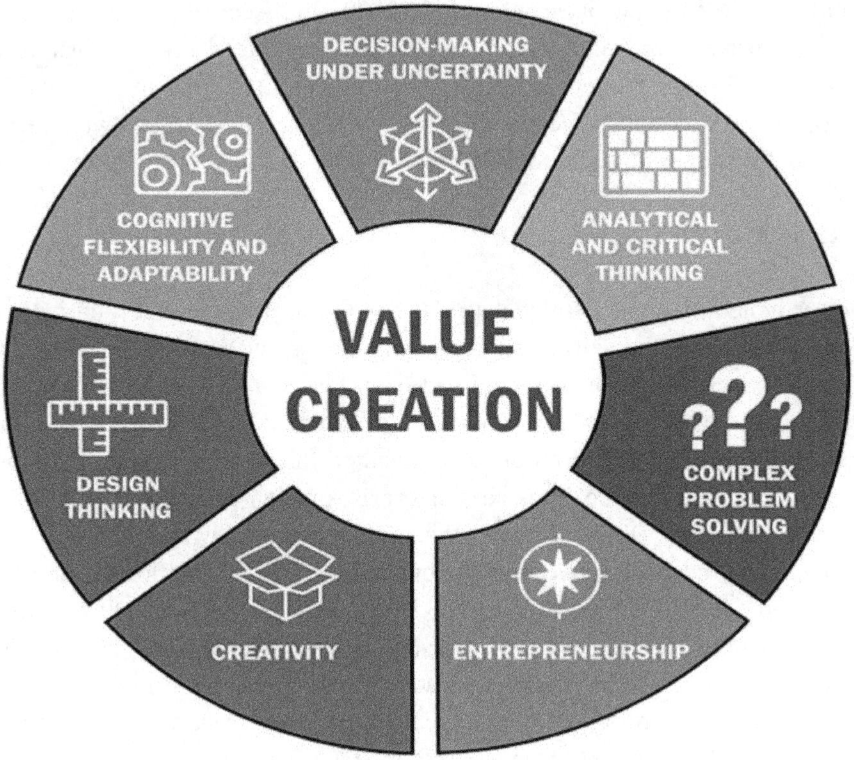

The above figure has showcased different strategies for creating value within organisations through innovation, such as providing cognitive flexibility and adaptability features to the employees. In addition, skills such as decision making and complex problem solving can also be acquired by organisational leaders in order to bring value to the business through optimising innovation.

CHALLENGES OF INNOVATION MANAGEMENT

Ineffective Empowerment of Employees

Employee empowerment is one of the key attributes of innovation in management, through which organisational change can be obtained. As per the views of Frishammar *et al.* (2019), managers of different organisations often become perplexed in making decisions regarding obtaining innovation due to emerging rates of distractions to innovation. On the other hand, the lack of development of new ideas and risk-taking capabilities has also become a major challenge for organisations to obtain innovation. In a survey by the labour commission of the UK, It has been found that 37% of employees do not feel empowered due to a lack of leadership support and individual fear of taking risks (Hbr.org, 2018). The less empowered employees can be subjected towards adequate motivation through arranging reward initiatives, based on which congregational impacts on employee behaviour can be obtained. As opined by Frishammar *et al.* (2019), it is also important to provide flexibility as well as decision-making scenarios to the employees in order to ring motivation and self-confidence within the workforce. However, managers can engage employees within decision-making and open communication scenarios to empower the workforce to obtain innovation within business operations.

Centralised Approach Towards Innovation

Innovation is a set of functional attributes that require teamwork, based on which product workforces can perform effective R&D initiatives. Based on the views of Tidd and Bessant (2018), innovation has become the responsibility of a particular functional group, such as R&D and product or service development, which has centralised the initiative. On the other hand, myths regarding the effectiveness of centralising innovation can also cause severe hindrances to the pace of innovation. As opined by Maier *et al.* (2019), individual departments can also provide unique perspectives for solving the problems regarding innovation implementation, based on which a decentralised approach can be developed. However, managers can create a team-based approach of dividing the workloads of innovation management, such as planning and decision-making among respective employees, to overcome the challenge of centralisation.

Lack of Motivation Towards Adopting Innovation

Motivation is one of the key attributes within organisations to obtain technological advancements due to its capability to maintain high-quality workforce performance. However, as per the ideas of Niewöhner*et al.* (2019), increased responsibility, workloads and organisational conflicts can deteriorate the level of motivation within employees. On the contrary, lack of job flexibility and inadequate technological implementation and utilisation training can also be a significant challenge in deriving employee motivation. However, managers can initiate motivational programs such as inventing gestures, skill development training and monthly contests to encourage employees to indulge themselves within the process of innovation management.

Technical Feasibility

Technical feasibility, including expenditures on purchasing advanced gadgets, subscription charges for leading-edge software and maintenance costs, has become one of the major challenges of obtaining innovation within organisations. According to Maier *et al.* (2019), a lack of financial and human resources has impacted the process of innovating workplaces with advanced mechanisms and gadgets. On the other hand, inappropriate incorporation of technical support systems can also increase organisations' expenditures, which can also derive financial risk (Frishammar*et al.* 2019). However, organisations can incorporate joint marketing and product development strategies to utilise equivocal resources within business measures, based on which exponential business growth can be seen.

IDENTIFICATION AND DISCUSSION OF THE THEORIES RELATED TO INNOVATION MANAGEMENT

Innovation-Diffusion theory

Diffusions of innovation can be defined as the process of communicating through certain channels to develop an infuriated social system for incorporating innovation. As per the ideas of Al-Rahmi *et al.* (2019), these interpersonal communication channels attempt to identify certain aspects that influence the rate of adoption of specific innovation within workplaces. On the other hand, organisations, individuals, and large clusters adopt several adopter categories on the basis of their innovativeness, such as innovators, early and late majority, early adopters and laggards. As opined by Pinho *et al.* (2021), it has been found that these adopter categories help organisations to choose specific innovations such as HRM, productivity or CSR approaches, based on which effective deliverables of innovation can be fulfilled. However, respective managers can incorporate diffusion-based innovation through developing risk-taking measures, competitive advantage, and curiosity within employees, which can foster exponential growth.

Figure 3. Model of diffusion-based innovation

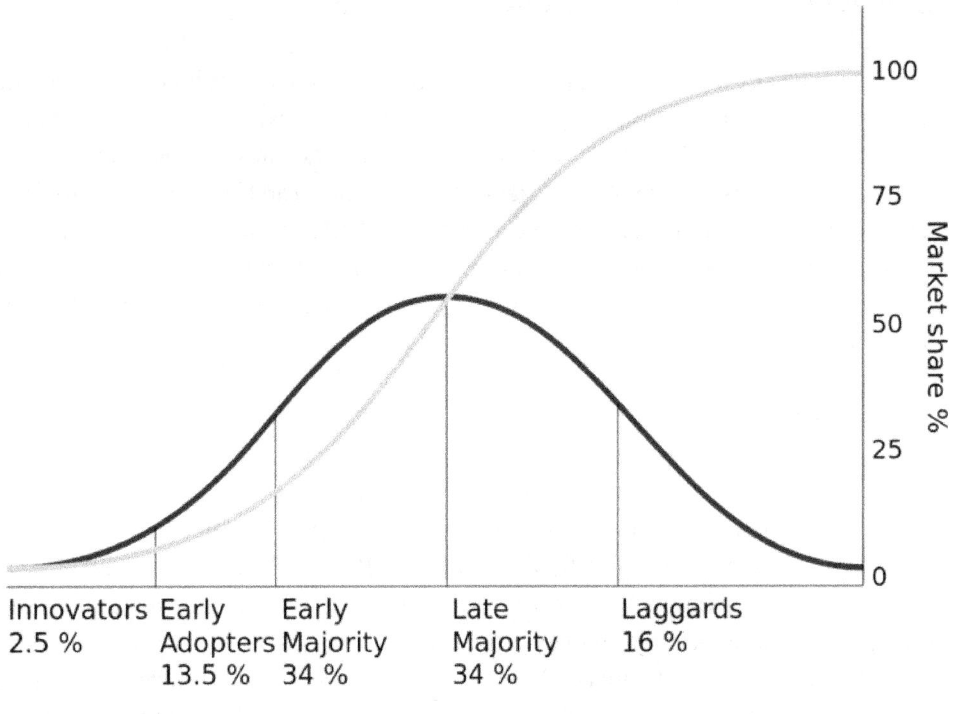

Several factors can affect the adoption rate of innovation within organisations, such as compatibility, complexity, trial ability, observe ability and relative advantage. Based on the ideas of Marak *et al.* (2019), requirements of consistency in technological adoption can generate ineffective compatibility and disadvantage of outperforming, which can cause diffusion. On the contrary, the lack of experimental measures or trials can also impact the process of identifying suitable innovations for organisations, based on which complex financial and decision-making scenarios can be seen (Al-Rahmi *et al.* 2019). However, managers can utilise diffusions of innovation patterns to identify new and innovative ideas within employees through conducting brainstorming and decision-making programs within the workplace, based on which effective organisational change can be obtained efficiently.

Concerns-Based Adoption Model

Successful implementation of a new program is associated with providing staff with adequate resources, materials, and training. As per the views of Kim and Lee (2020), three diagnostic dimensions of the Concerns-based adoption model such as innovation configuration, stages of concern and levels of utilisation, plays an important role towards the adoption of innovation. On the contrary, inexplicable, and impractical hopes can impact the process of assessing the concerns of the employees in an adverse manner due to which job dissatisfaction and hindrance can be seen (Trapani and Annunziato, 2019). Hence, managers can utilise innovative configurations as the roadmap for implementing high-quality innovation within workplaces, based on which exponential growth can be incorporated.

Figure 4. Concerns based adoption model

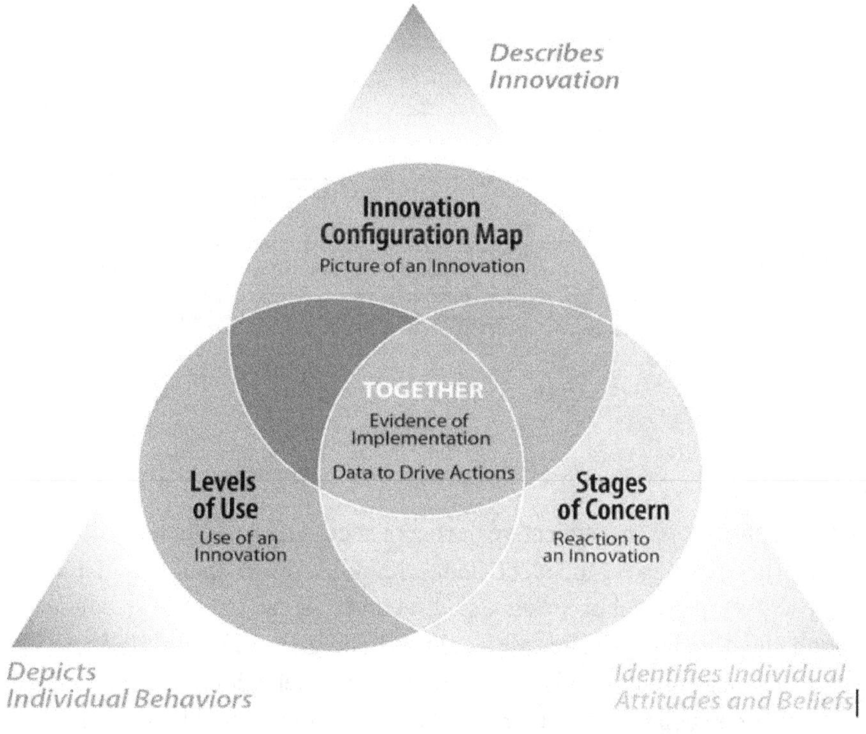

The stages of the concern process include questionnaires, semi-structured interviews, and open-ended statements, which enable leaders to assess the attitudes as well as beliefs of individual employees. Based on Mize *et al.* (2020), these attributes help managers to take action to address specific concerns related to implementing technological advancements within organisations. Contrarily, ineffective progression towards measuring "Level of Utilisation" can degrade the process of determining the performance of employees and their ability to handle technological equipment. As opined by Trapani and Annunziato (2019), it has been found that first-hand observations after implementing a new program such as machine learning-driven analytics can help managers make decisions regarding specific workforce requirements. However, effective training conjectures regarding new program implementation can enhance managers' capability to assess the workforce's needs.

Technology Acceptance Model

The technology acceptance model is a theory of IT system incorporation within organisations. Those models foster the users to accept and utilise specific technologies. However, per Rafique *et al.* (2020) views, many factors influence users' decision towards accepting and utilising particular technologies, such as perceived usefulness and perceived ease of use. On the contrary, external variables such as social influence can also determine prudential behaviour change within specific employee groups, generating job dissatisfaction. However, validity and reliability checking of specific technological trends within individual organisations can be performed by managers by adopting the parameters of the technology acceptance model, which can enhance the provision of technology utilisation.

Figure 5. Technology acceptance model

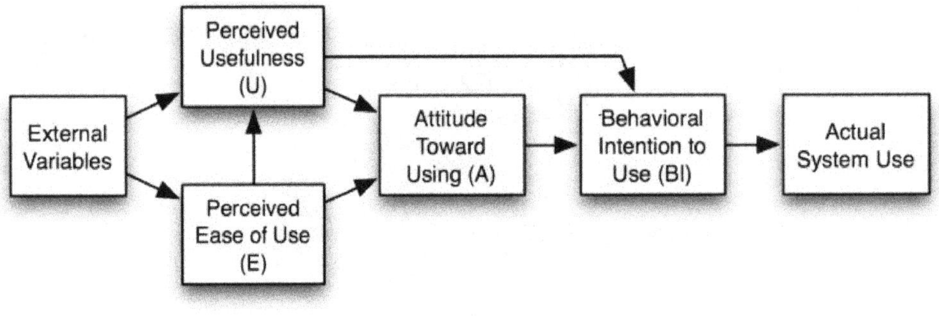

The above figure showcases the subjective norms of accepting specific technologies within organisations, such as performance image of the identified technology, output quality and demonstrability. Based on Salloum *et al.* (2019), practical experience and satisfaction can change the behaviours of employees towards accepting and utilising specific technical tools and gadgets within business operations. On the contrary, the model's major limitation is pertaining to users' behaviour that can be inevitably evaluated through subjective norms such as interpersonal influence and behavioural intention (Rafique *et al.* 2020). Hence, these limitations can be overcome by underpinning surveys of technological acceptance within workforces, based on which effective hindrance measuring capability can be generated within workforces.

Model of Three Horizons of Growth

The model of three horizons of growth is essential for structuring the initiatives and findings of business operations and developing a balance between short and long-term innovation attributes. As opined by Markopoulos *et al.* (2019), the three horizons model can maximise the potential of adopting innovation within organisations through deriving regulatory measures such as social compliance and perceived learning. The first horizon is the initiatives of core business such as decision making and HR planning, whereas the second horizon is associated with the development of new opportunities within emerging businesses. On the other hand, the third horizon is associated with new ideologies and innovative thinking, which can impact the financial as well as a reputational image of organisations due to lack of supervision (Travassos *et al.* 2018). Hence, managers can make incremental improvements rather than subjective purchasing, which can reduce the risk of financial losses within business operations.

Figure 6. Model of three horizons of growth

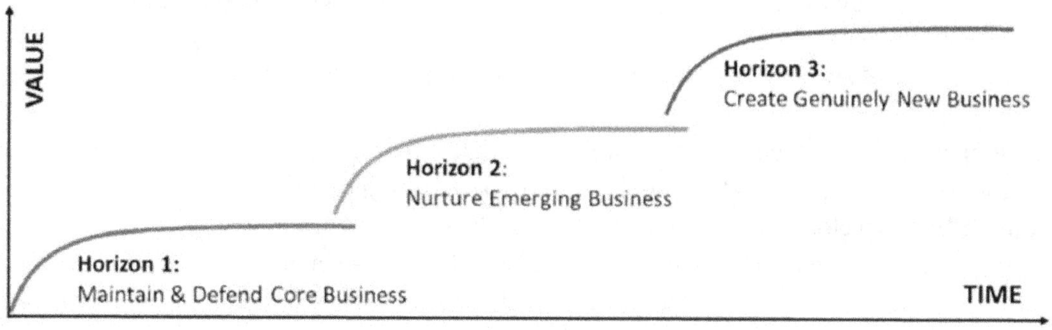

Developing balance between the three horizons is one of the foremost priorities within organisations having technical transformation for eradicating the financial as well as reputational risk measures. Based on the views of Travasso s*et al.* (2018), the strategic framework can state transformational capacities of organisations through measuring the horizons of innovation. Contrarily, different interpretations of the horizons within specific workforces can develop inappropriate corporate context, based on which derivational outputs might be obtained (Markopoulos *et al.* 2019). However, managers can differentiate focus, goals and competitive advantage within workforces through depicting the horizons of growth to enhance the future performance of business conjectures.

APPLICATION OF THE IDENTIFIED THEORIES

Application of Innovation-Diffusion Theory

Developing Risk Measures

Risk regarding heavy investments in technological advancements can be handled through the development of contingency planning based on the attributing factors of the diffusion patterns of business. As per the views of Al-Rahmi *et al.* (2019), increasing adoption rates of innovation such as HR policies and IT infrastructures have become emerging trends within industries, which can be clustered as well as monitored through incorporating the diffusion model of innovation. For instance, Facebook has utilised the diffusion model to enlarge the market from students and professionals to society (Von Nordheim *et al.* 2018). Furthermore, in the higher education industry, technological incorporation has become a revolutionary aspect due to the increased number of students within business innovation practising organisations. Hence, incorporating experimented innovations can mitigate the issues of risk derivation, based on which capability of adopting innovations can be increased within organisations.

Understanding the Acceptance of Promotional Gestures in Marketing

Classification of adopter categories helps managers to assess the trajectory towards promotional acceptance within the targeted audience of a marketing approach. Based on the ideas of Von Nordheim *et al.* (2021), marketing trajectories can be streamlined with innovations such as specific types of advertisements and promotional events. On the other hand, a lack of expertise in understanding the business and audience requirements can bring challenges to market segmentation, which can generate uncertainties towards practising the attributes of diffusions. Moreover, managers can incorporate young and creative individuals who can develop innovative marketing trajectories for invading new markets and gain a critical understanding of the performance parameters of specified marketing initiatives.

Identifying and Recruiting Early Adopters for Accelerating Consumer Acceptance

Early adopters have the potential to try new technologies within business operations and establish a clarified utility of the identified technology in society. As opined by Lazim *et al.* (2021), radical utilisation of innovation can help managers to derive consumer acceptance through obtaining feedback. On the other hand, improper articulation of subjective early adopters can cause social and personal derivation, based on which consumer dissatisfaction and turnover can be seen within organisations. Based on the views of Marak *et al.* (2019), it is important to set priorities on risk-averse measures that can develop an automated sweeping framework of unpleasant innovation. However, managers can provide sustainable education regarding technology handling to the employees, which can foster personal growth of the workforce as well.

Utilisation of Concerns-Based Adoption Model

Deriving Evidence and Quality of Innovation Implementation

The concerns-based adoption model framework can provide evidence-based information regarding the quality of implementation of specific technologies within organisations. Per the views of Nair and Rajappan (2021), managers can use the dimensions developed within the Concerns-based adoption framework to drive decisions and actions regarding uncertain and transitional changes during the process of incorporating innovation. In addition, the concerns-based adoption framework provides legal viability for businesses to identify organisational and regulatory outcomes based on evidence-based trajectories. For instance, marketing analysts of "Tesla", an automotive and clean energy manufacturing company, have utilised the concerns-based adoption model's dimensions to analyse innovation implementation within the manufactured vehicles (Ir.tesla.com, 2020). However, managers can also develop open-ended questionnaires to acknowledge new ideologies of employees that can effectively foster innovation.

Articulating Preparations of Organisations Towards Obtaining Innovation

Specific goals and circumstances of organisations can be considered under the dimensions of CBDM, based on which a linear trajectory can be developed towards incorporating innovation. Based on the ideas of Mize *et al.* (2020), dimensions of innovation configurations can be utilised along with states of concern to articulate organisational concerns such as conflicts, job dissatisfaction and communication error. Hence, levels of non-utilisation and advance utilisation can be pearly reviewed by the managers of organisations in order to articulate the preoperational trajectories of the workforce towards obtaining innovation.

Providing Support Towards Assessing the Performance of Newly Adopted Innovations

Newly adopted innovations such as HR policies and technological advancements require transgenic up-gradation at regular intervals. As per the ideas of Kim and Lee (2020), the dimension of "Levels of utilisation" can be utilised to provide support for the process of upgrading the manual changes of a particular innovation system due to changing patterns of workforce requirements. On the other hand, ineffective monitoring of systematic utilisation of a newly implemented technology can degrade the quality of organisational output due to lack of maintenance. However, managers of individual educational authorities can develop a workspace-based setting, which can be utilised to provide indoor vocational facilities for students, based on which skills of individual students can be increased in an effective manner.

Application of Technology Acceptance Model

Measuring the Performance of Organisation After Adopting New Technologies

Attributes of the technology acceptance model such as compatibility, mobility and upgradability are mostly used within IT companies to develop customised technologies for the respective consumer bases. Based on the views of Salloum *et al.* (2019), cognitive and emotional; aspects of employees can be accessed through the attributes of the technology acceptance model, which can verify the level of acceptance of newly adopted innovation within the workforce. On the other hand, factors such as changing patterns of utilising customised innovations can impact the process of measuring the performance of organisations due to unnoticed binary regulations. Hence, managers can acknowledge the change made within innovation implementation in order to add the binary function to the derivational performance measurement process.

Determining the Technology Utilisation Abilities of Organisations

The ability to utilise technology depends on several factors such as financial capability, exponential growth, and innovative working infrastructure. As opined by Rafique *et al.* (2020), perceived usefulness and ease of use can be utilised by the business analysts of organisations to articulate the demand of particular innovation systems within workplaces, based on which indigenous capability can be assessed. For instance, Aston Martin, which is a UK-based car manufacturer, has incorporated the attributes of perceived usefulness to determine the capability of adhering to the emerging technologies across the globe (Astonmartinlagonda.com, 2021). However, managers of automobile industries can also utilise the attribute of perceived usefulness to obtain classified feedback from regular clients, which can be helpful in determining the ability of adhere to technological advancements.

Providing Online Entrepreneurship Education to Novice Entrepreneurs

The technology acceptance model can also be utilised within education trajectories to provide novice entrepreneurs with knowledge. Based on Markopoulos *et al.* (2019), the integration of network technologies can be useful for the development of rigid teaching channels that have accessibility to a range of topics, including entrepreneurship. On the other hand, a lack of evidence-based practices and inadequate channels can deteriorate the conjecture of providing lessons to the new entrepreneurs. Moreover, incorporating diversified and connected entrepreneurial groups can enhance the process of providing online entrepreneurship education to novice entrepreneurs in an effective manner.

UTILISATION OF THE FRAMEWORK OF THREE HORIZONS OF GROWTH MODEL

Deriving Present Values of Organisations in Terms of Innovation

The first horizon of core values of a particular business can derive the present value of specific organisations through aligning the performance with technological drawbacks. For instance, McLaren, which is a UK-based automobile company has utilised the three horizons of growth model to streamline the drawbacks with present performance (Mclaren.com, 2021). On the other hand, ineffective technological drawback analysis can be resulted in wrong value prediction, which can deteriorate the performance in an adverse manner. Hence, a regulative timeline for measuring performance of a particular company can be helpful, which can enhance the technical value of organisations.

Segmenting the Market for Future Growth

Market segmentation is one of the leading-edge innovation analogies which can bring exponential growth within organisations. As per the views of Rafique *et al.* (2020), the second horizon of the growth model which is associated with segmenting the market can be utilised by the managers through data driven analytics to assess the best suited market for a particular organisation. On the other hand, opportunities of reaching new customers, markets or goals can also be assessed by the second horizon of the growth model, based on which innovative marketing conjectures can be performed. However, managers can also develop customised service analogies to reduce the initial cost of technology investments and market segmentation.

Diversifying Business

Businesses can be diversified through regulative monitoring and incorporating collaborative initiatives. Based on the ideas of Travassos *et al.* (2018), the third horizon can be utilised to develop a clear set of innovative trajectories within workforces to develop collaborations with IT organisations. On the other hand, lack of financial and resource related measures during collaborative initiatives can increase financial risks, based on which heavy losses can be seen. As opined by Lazim *et al.* (2021), measures of penetrative collaboration as well as considerable investments on monitoring the performance of individual markets can enhance the potentiality of organisations towards incorporating innovation within business operations. Moreover, this particular framework of business growth can direct the overall workforce towards technological advancements. Based on which sustainable innovation can be obtained within organisations.

BEST PRACTICES OF UTILISING INNOVATION WITHIN MANAGERIAL ASPECTS

Innovation is associated with managerial aspects within organisations, based on which effective change can be oriented within business settings. As per the views of Lo and Campuus (2018), continuous improvement and customer friendly innovation can bring social sustainability within business proceeding. In order to enhance innovation, there are some specific methods that are considerably better in the context of managerial aspects.

"Emphasising on Continuous Improvement"

Innovation needs improvement and improvisation in order to carry forward its true essence. As per the ideas of Tien *et al.* (2019), an organisation should always look after the improvement of any plan or strategies for the purpose of targeting new customers. However, on the other hand, this continuous improvement needs a long-term money backup as it is an expensive procedure. Therefore, to mitigate this problem, companies should focus on the basics and needed importance. Thus, it will give some time to the organisation to collect the expenditures.

"Understanding Customers Need"

While making a strategic way to develop a product or a service companies and organisations need to follow the customer choices and their target audience. However, on the other hand, sometimes companies face difficulties in the time of launching a new product as people could not trust the new product. Following the review by Lo and Campuus (2018), to mitigate this problem, companies need to earn the trust of their customers by doing innovative promotional methods so that they attract the customers.

"Fostering the Innovative Culture"

Companies should always be open-minded enough so that they can accept the changes with a positive outlook. Taking the ideas of Aprian a*et al.* (2019) into consideration it can be stated that, This Fostering method is very helpful in order to catch any new ideas and plans in order to make the business successful. Therefore, to mitigate these problems companies need to adopt this foster culture so that they can further participate in this business environment and make unique and innovative products.

"Set and Track Goals Regularly"

Every small or big plan needs a perfect execution process thus this innovative business strategy also needs a good systematic process in order to execute the goal. Planning a dedicated goal for a dedicated project then the managerial department should track it on a regular basis if there's any kind of backlog. However, on the other hand, companies set some absurd goals which could not be fulfilled thus it slows the innovative implementation. In order to mitigate this problem, companies should follow some strategies and need to make some realistic goals in order to make the goals relevant to the business.

FURTHER SCOPE OF IMPROVING INNOVATION MANAGEMENT WITHIN ORGANISATIONS

Improvement in innovation management can help the organisation in different aspects, which will be discussed further shortly.

"Commitment to Innovation"

Commitment to innovation and uniqueness in the context of managerial aspects will further help the company to support expanding the business in a very day-to-day manner. As per the ideas of Chanana (2021), management will help the employees to become motivated and do them efficiently. However, on the other hand, it makes the employees dependent on the management. In order to mitigate this, companies should divide the job accordingly so that no one can face any problems.

"Strategic Orientation"

Strategic Orientation is an adaptation of a planned routine in order to fulfil a bigger goal. Taking the ideas of Hayat *et al.* (2021) into consideration, it can be stated that, by prioritising the goals, every employee should do the work dedicatedly to succeed as a team. However, on the contrary, if one employee is not severe enough to maintain this strategy, thus the whole team has to suffer. Therefore, companies need to work on employee performance very minutely to solve this problem.

"Clear Responsibilities"

The idea of the innovation procedure is very organised and disciplined so that the company can meet every attribute of the innovation. Followed by the review of Zang *et al.* (2021), the roles for a particular project should be divided according to the knowledge and the efficiency of the employees. However, on the other hand, sometimes management chooses the wrong employees for the wrong role and that company can suffer a huge loss. To avoid this problem, companies need to evaluate the basic areas of knowledge of their employees so that they initiate the project accordingly.

"Innovation Culture"

Innovation culture requires some unique strategy to comprehend the business market's operational work. Therefore, the management is focusing on different attributes and values in the context of taking a more considerable risk and willingly taking new ideas to promote the business globally with colossal revenue. However, on the other hand, this innovative culture involves some significant risks as the company evaluates some unique plans or products in the market. Hence, managers of different higher educational organisations can believe that innovation can bring leadership qualities to students through reciprocal learning initiatives.

CONCLUSION

Henceforth, it can be concluded that the management of innovation is one of the much-needed discussions in the context of business escalation. The primary ideas of innovation and the impact of innovation in business have been covered in this chapter. Besides this, the conceptual understanding with the help of some attributes such as ***"Incremental innovation ", "Sustaining innovation" "Disruptive innovation" and "Breakthrough innovation" has*** also been evaluated in this chapter for the purpose of having a thorough understanding and idea about innovation in management. However, the key elements of management are ***"collaboration", "ideation", "implementation" and "value creation"***, which have been discussed in order to evaluate the basic factors of management in contemplation of innovation and uniqueness. On the other hand, the challenges like technical feasibility, lack of motivation, centralised approach, and inefficient employees that a company faces in order to implement those innovative plans have also been discussed in this chapter. Theories related to the identification and discussion of innovation have also been evaluated vastly in this chapter. Application with the identified theories including the best practices of the utilisation in the context of managerial authority has also been considered in this chapter. Besides this, the future scope is related to improving innovation management in order to generate profits.

REFERENCES

Al-Rahmi, W. M., Yahaya, N., Aldraiweesh, A. A., Alamri, M. M., Aljarboa, N. A., Alturki, U., & Aljeraiwi, A. A. (2019). Integrating technology acceptance model with innovation diffusion theory: An empirical investigation on students' intention to use E-learning systems. *IEEE Access: Practical Innovations, Open Solutions*, *7*, 26797–26809. doi:10.1109/ACCESS.2019.2899368

Almehida, F., Santos, J. D., & Monteiro, J. A. (2020). The challenges and opportunities in the digitalization of companies in a post-COVID-19 World. *IEEE Engineering Management Review*, *48*(3), 97–103. doi:10.1109/EMR.2020.3013206

Apriana, D., Kristiawan, M., & Wardiah, D. (2019). Headmaster's competency in preparing vocational school students for entrepreneurship. *International Journal of Scientific & Technology Research*, *8*(8), 1316–1330.

Astonmartinlagonda.com. (2021). *Aston Martin Lagonda Annual Report.* Available at: https://www.astonmartinlagonda.com/investors/annual-report

Chanana, N., & Sangeeta. (2021). Employee engagement practices during COVID-19 lockdown. *Journal of Public Affairs*, *21*(4), e2508. doi:10.1002/pa.2508 PMID:33041656

Fenwick, M., & Vermeulen, E.P. (2020). Banking and regulatory responses to FinTech revisited-building the sustainable financial service 'ecosystems' of tomorrow. *Singapore Journal of Legal Studies*, 165-189.

Frishammar, J., Richtnér, A., Brattström, A., Magnusson, M., & Björk, J. (2019). Opportunities and challenges in the new innovation landscape: Implications for innovation auditing and innovation management. *European Management Journal*, *37*(2), 151–164. doi:10.1016/j.emj.2018.05.002

Ghasemaghases, M., & Callic, G. (2020). Assessing the impact of big data on firm innovation performance: Big data is not always better data. *Journal of Business Research*, *108*, 147–162. doi:10.1016/j.jbusres.2019.09.062

Hayat, M., Shakeel, M., & Chen, B. (2021). Impact of work ethics and work environment on project success with the moderating role of job engagement. *Science Journal of Business and Management*, *9*(1), 15. doi:10.11648/j.sjbm.20210901.12

Hbr.org. (2018). *When Empowering Employees Works.* Available at: https://hbr.org/2018/03/when-empowering-employees-works-and-when-it-doesnt

Ir.tesla.com. (2020). *Tesla Investor Relations.* Available at: https://ir.tesla.com/

Ismail, N. N. H. M., Nasir, M. K. M., & Rahman, R. S. A. R. A. (2021). Factors that influence women to be involved in entrepreneurship: A case study in Malaysia. *Creative Education*, *12*(04), 837–847. doi:10.4236/ce.2021.124060

Kim, J., & Lee, J. (2020). An Investigation of Teachers' Stages of Concern and Levels of Use about SW Education Based on Concerns-Based Adoption Model. *The Journal of the Korea Contents Association*, *20*(8), 75–87.

Lazim, C. S. L. M., Ismail, N. D. B., & Tazilah, M. D. A. K. (2021). Application of technology acceptance model (TAM) towards online learning during covid-19 pandemic: Accounting students perspective. *Int. J. Bus. Econ. Law*, *24*(1), 13–20.

Lo, F. Y., & Campos, N. (2018). Blending Internet-of-Things (IoT) solutions into relationship marketing strategies. *Technological Forecasting and Social Change*, *137*, 10–18. doi:10.1016/j.techfore.2018.09.029

Maier, D., Maftei, M., Maier, A., & Biţan, G. E. (2019). A review of product innovation management literature in the context of organization sustainable development. *Amfiteatru Economic*, *21*(13), 816–829. doi:10.24818/EA/2019/S13/816

Marak, Z. R., Tiwari, A., & Tiwari, S. (2019). Adoption of 3D printing technology: An innovation diffusion theory perspective. *International Journal of Innovation*, *7*(1), 87–103. doi:10.5585/iji.v7i1.393

Markopoulos, E., Aggarwal, V., & Vanharanta, H. (2019), September. Democratization of intrapreneurship and corporate entrepreneurship within the mckinsey's three horizons innovation space. In *International Conference on Human Systems Engineering and Design: Future Trends and Applications* (pp. 1007-1017). Springer.

Mclaren.com. (2021). *Annual Results - McLaren Investors*. Available at: https://investors.mclaren.com/sites/mclaren-ir/files/report-document/mclaren-group-limited-2020-annual-report.pdf

Mize, M., Trexler, C. J., Crump, A., Young, G. M., Buntong, B., & LeGrand, K. (2020). Piloting of the concerns-based adoption model: Farmer concerns about the participatory guaranteed system in Cambodia. *Journal of International Agricultural and Extension Education*, *27*(3), 75–87.

Morrison-Smith, S., & Ruiz, J. (2020). Challenges and barriers in virtual teams: A literature review. *SN Applied Sciences*, *2*(6), 1–33. doi:10.100742452-020-2801-5

Nair, R. S., & Rajappan, S. (2021). The New-Normal in Education: Comprehending the Stages of Concern through the Concerns-based Adoption Model (CBAM). *Human Resource Management Practices for Industry*, *4*(0), 209.

Niewöhner, N., Asmar, L., Wortmann, F., Röltgen, D., Kühn, A., & Dumitrescu, R. (2019). Design fields of agile innovation management in small and medium sized enterprises. *Procedia CIRP*, *84*, 826–831. doi:10.1016/j.procir.2019.04.295

O'Reilly, C., & Binns, A. J. (2019). The three stages of disruptive innovation: Idea generation, incubation, and scaling. *California Management Review*, *61*(3), 49–71. doi:10.1177/0008125619841878

Pinho, C., Franco, M., & Mendes, L. (2021). Application of innovation diffusion theory to the E-learning process: Higher education context. *Education and Information Technologies*, *26*(1), 421–440. doi:10.100710639-020-10269-2

Plowman, J. (2019). *Unreal Engine Virtual Reality Quick Start Guide: Design and Develop Immersive Virtual Reality Experiences with Unreal Engine 4*. Packt Publishing Ltd.

Rafique, H., Almagrabi, A. O., Shamim, A., Anwar, F., & Bashir, A. K. (2020). Investigating the acceptance of mobile library applications with an extended technology acceptance model (TAM). *Computers & Education, 145*, 103732. doi:10.1016/j.compedu.2019.103732

Salloum, S. A., Alhamad, A. Q. M., Al-Emran, M., Monem, A. A., & Shaalan, K. (2019). Exploring students' acceptance of e-learning through the development of a comprehensive technology acceptance model. *IEEE Access: Practical Innovations, Open Solutions*, *7*, 128445–128462. doi:10.1109/ACCESS.2019.2939467

Stubbs, W. (2019). Strategies, practices, and tensions in managing business model innovation for sustainability: The case of an Australian BCorp. *Corporate Social Responsibility and Environmental Management*, *26*(5), 1063–1072. doi:10.1002/csr.1786

Tidd, J., & Bessant, J. (2018). Innovation management challenges: From fads to fundamentals. *International Journal of Innovation Management*, *22*(05), 1840007. doi:10.1142/S1363919618400078

Tien, N.H., Phu, P.P., & Chi, D.T.P. (2019). The role of international marketing in international business strategy. *International Journal of Research in Marketing Management and Sales, 1*(2), 134-138.

Trapani, B., & Annunziato, A. (2019). Crossing the Bridge of Change: Measuring Instructional Change Using the Concerns Based Adoption Model. *Journal for Leadership and Instruction*, *18*(1), 12–16.

Travassos, J. M., Martins, S. S., Simões, J. C., & Mansur, W. J. (2018). Radar diffraction horizons in snow and firn due to a surficial vertical transfer of mass. *Brazilian Journal of Geophysics*, *36*(4), 507–518. doi:10.22564/rbgf.v36i4.1978

Von Nordheim, G., Boczek, K., & Koppers, L. (2018). Sourcing the Sources: An analysis of the use of Twitter and Facebook as a journalistic source over 10 years in The New York Times, The Guardian, and SüddeutscheZeitung. *Digital Journalism*, *6*(7), 807-828.

Zhang, Y., Liu, S., Tan, J., Jiang, G., & Zhu, Q. (2018). Effects of risks on the performance of business process outsourcing projects: The moderating roles of knowledge management capabilities. *International Journal of Project Management*, *36*(4), 627–639. doi:10.1016/j.ijproman.2018.02.002

Chapter 11
Central Bank Digital Currency, Poverty Reduction and the United Nations Sustainable Development Goals

Peterson K. Ozili
https://orcid.org/0000-0001-6292-1161
Central Bank of Nigeria, Abuja, Nigeria

ABSTRACT

This chapter examines the role of central bank digital currency for poverty reduction and sustainable development. In the chapter, the author argues that a CBDC can eliminate poverty by first increasing financial inclusion which then gives poor people access to affordable credit and other basic financial services which they can use to improve their welfare, thereby enabling them to rise above poverty. This argument is valid only if a central bank digital currency is specially designed to incorporate features that increase financial inclusion for poor banked and unbanked adults. The argument may not apply to cases where a CBDC is not designed to increase financial inclusion as is the case in developed countries.

INTRODUCTION

The objective of this paper is to discuss how central bank digital currency (CBDC) can help to reduce the level of poverty towards the attainment of the United Nations sustainable development goals (SDGs). This topic is important to policymakers who are interested in poverty reduction mechanisms. This study is also relevant to researchers conducting research on how to reduce the level of poverty towards the realization of the sustainable development goals.

CBDC is a recent financial innovation in the payment system. Prior to the introduction of CBDCs, several studies in the financial innovation literature show that financial innovations such as Fintech can contribute to poverty reduction in many societies (Ajide, 2016; Hulme et al 1997; Michael et al, 2022). Other studies emphasize the risk of financial innovation and its implications for development (e.g. Al-

DOI: 10.4018/978-1-6684-6732-9.ch011

Copyright © 2023, IGI Global. Copying or distributing in print or electronic forms without written permission of IGI Global is prohibited.

len and Gale, 1994; Ozili, 2022e). Although existing studies show that financial innovation plays an important role for poverty reduction, the literature has not examined the relationship between CBDC, poverty reduction and sustainable development. This relationship is important because it can provide new insights about how digital innovations can support the realization of the United Nations sustainable development goals (SDGs). In this paper, it was argued that CBDC may be linked to poverty reduction towards greater sustainable development.

Poverty reduction or poverty elimination is the first goal among the 17 UN SDGs. Poverty is commonly defined as the number of people living below the poverty line (see, for example, Wratten, 1995; Tilak, 2002). Poverty is multidimensional; in the sense that, insufficient income or lack of any income can lead to deterioration in health, education and welfare of poor people. For this reason, the United Nations is spearheading efforts to reduce poverty in countries in the global south particularly in developing countries.

Several innovations are emerging that contribute to efforts aimed at reducing the level of poverty. Some of these innovations include digital financial services, the microfinance agenda, blended poverty financing, aid allocation among others. In the academic literature, a number of studies have examined how innovations can help to reduce the level of poverty (e.g. Johnson and Rogaly, 1997; Kelikume, 2021; Yonah and Salim, 2008; Collier and Dollar, 2002). These studies show that, with the right pre-conditions in place, digital financial services and microfinance schemes can reduce poverty to some extent. Another emerging innovation in the economic system is central bank digital currency.

A central bank digital currency is money or currency in digital form (Ekong and Ekong, 2022). Interest in CBDC is growing rapidly among policy makers and central banks around the world. The economic benefits of a central bank digital currency are enormous. They include the effective conduct of monetary policy, the reduction in cash management cost, increase in foreign remittance, low-cost transactions, increase in the level of financial inclusion, improved payment efficiency, increase in tax revenue from the digital economy, and facilitating the growth of the digital economy. (see, for example, Bordo and Levin, 2017; Ozili, 2022a; Engert and Fung, 2017; Ozili, 2022b).

As a result of these benefits, many emerging and developing countries are planning to adopt a central bank digital currency such as Brazil, Peru, Nigeria, Ghana and India. They plan to adopt a central bank digital currency as an alternative payment solution. However, despite the potential benefits of central bank digital currency, some developed countries, such as the United States and Australia, are not convinced that they need a central bank digital currency because they believe they already have a very robust payments system while other developed countries, such as Canada and the UK, are conducting intensive research into central bank digital currency before formally adopting it. This shows that central bank digital currency is gaining widespread attention among central banks. Some central banks are exercising caution before adopting a central bank digital currency while others have already adopted a central bank digital currency such as Nigeria (Ozili, 2022a).

Despite the growing interest in central bank digital currency in the world, there has been no attempt to assess how a central bank digital currency can contribute to poverty reduction towards the attainment of the United Nations sustainable development goals. To date, the literature has not examined the opportunities that central bank digital currency present for poverty reduction towards the attainment of the sustainable development goals. Therefore, this paper discusses how central bank digital currency can help to reduce the level of poverty towards the attainment of the sustainable development goals.

This study contributes to the literature in the following ways. First, this paper contributes to studies in the literature that assess the drivers of sustainable development. Studies in this literature include Sachs et al (2019), Vinuesa et al (2020) and Esquivel and Sweetman (2016). The present study shows that central bank digital currency can be used to expand financial services and offer more opportunities to poor people, allowing them to use available digital financial services to improve their welfare. Second, this paper contributes to the emerging central bank digital currency literature. Studies in this literature include Davoodalhosseini (2021), Ozili (2022c), Selgin (2021) and Ozili (2022d). The paper contributes to this literature by showing that CBDC is a potential factor that could help to reduce the level of poverty.

The paper also contributes to the theoretical literature. It contributes to the diffusion innovation theory by showing that innovation adoption (e.g. CBDC adoption) for poverty reduction might take some time due to the innovation diffusion process that create early adopters and late adopters (Lee et al, 2011). This study also contributes to studies that use the technology acceptance model to explain new innovation. The technology acceptance model states that perceived ease of use and usefulness of a technological tool determines the extent of consumer acceptance (Charness and Boot, 2016).

The rest of the paper is structured in the following way. Section 2 presents the literature review. Section 3 presents the discussion on how CBDC reduces the level of poverty. Section 4 presents the policy implications for sustainable development. Section 5 concludes.

LITERATURE REVIEW

Poverty and Sustainable Development

An extensive literature examines the link between poverty and sustainable development. Anyanwu and Anyanwu (2017) show that the key factors that increase the level of poverty in sub-Saharan Africa are high income inequality, oil-dependence, institutionalized democracy, high prevalence of HIV among the female youth and increased civil war episodes while the key factors that reduces the level of poverty in sub-Saharan Africa are high levels of economic development (income per capita), high general government final consumption expenditure, high official development assistance and aid received, urbanization and access to improved water source. Das Gupta et al (2011), in a survey of literature, show that rapid population growth can constrain economic growth in low-income countries that have a poor policy environment. Population growth also exacerbates pressure on environmental common property resources (Das Gupta et al, 2011). Schleicher et al (2018) argue that the SDGs can provide an opportunity for better environment–poverty integration. Schleicher et al (2018) further argue that, in order to realize this goal, SDG-related activities will need to challenge the institutional status quo; transform how we measure, understand and implement development. There is also a need to design interventions that reflect local visions of development; and address ultimate drivers of environmental degradation and poverty (Schleicher et al, 2018).

Manaf and Ibrahim (2017) show that Malaysia's poverty eradication and development programs are underpinned by political stability, inclusiveness, strong political will and the overall importance it attaches to ethnic tolerance and national unity. Reed (2002) examines the factors responsible for promoting poverty alleviation and protecting environmental assets in rural areas of developing countries. Reed (2002) concludes that policy makers face difficult trade-offs that must balance the pursuit of short-term economic gains of export–led growth against long-term benefits of social cohesion, environmental stability and steady productivity gains associated with sustainable development. Reed (2002) concludes by affirming that civil society must play an expanded role in reshaping current policies and practices to support sustainable development. Kao et al (2016) show that corporations can enhance the working abilities of the poor by sharing technologies and resources and providing skills training and education to empower them to rise above poverty. Kao et al (2016) also argue that corporations can establish poverty reduction businesses to provide poor people with job opportunities, or introduce social network resources to assist poor people in starting a business.

Bahmani-Oskooee and Oyolola (2009) examine the impact of foreign aid on poverty reduction using pooled time-series and cross sectional data from 49 developing countries. They find that foreign aid is effective in reducing poverty. Chowdhury (2009) argues that although microfinance has developed some innovative management and business strategies, its impact on poverty reduction remains in doubt. Harber (2002) examines the political relationship between education and poverty reduction. Harber (2002) argues that authoritarian rule in Africa has exacerbated levels of poverty. However, the achievement of greater levels of democracy will not be possible unless political culture and civil society in Africa become more democratic but this will depend on the spread of more democratic values and behaviors. Harber (2002) also emphasize that education must play a part in fostering greater democracy. Ogun (2010) investigates the impact of infrastructural development on poverty reduction in Nigeria. Ogun (2010) finds that infrastructural development leads to poverty reduction, and social infrastructure explains a higher proportion of the forecast error in poverty indicators relative to physical infrastructure. This suggests that massive investment in social infrastructure in cities would drastically reduce poverty in the urban areas (Ogun, 2010).

Chibba (2008) argues that evidence-based policy, sound institutions and sensible macroeconomic policies are required in developing countries, but they are not sufficient to tackle poverty and promote pro-poor economic growth. Chibba (2008) argues that solutions to address global and national poverty reduction goals require paying attention to the potential and positive impact of political economy, technology-based solutions, market-based approaches, private sector development and related interventions that are linked to inclusive development and financial inclusion. Chibba (2008) further points out that while there is no consensus among policymakers, businessmen, academics and practitioners on how best to address poverty reduction in developing countries (Chibba, 2008), there are plenty of creative and path-breaking approaches that are proving to be successful. Veen and Preece (2005) argue that adult education can and should contribute significantly to poverty reduction. Veen and Preece (2005) argue that successful contribution of adult education to poverty reduction programs includes agricultural extension, vocational education, community development and training for active citizenship.

CBDC and Development

Few studies attempt to link CBDC to some development outcomes. But these studies did not link CBDC to poverty reduction for sustainable development. For instance, Cukierman (2020) argues that a CBDC opens up welfare-enhancing opportunities for users due to its ability to reduce transaction costs. Cukierman (2020) further argues that governments and central banks can use CBDC to maximize national social welfare. Ozili (2022f) argues that CBDC can be used to support the transition to a circular economy by making central bank digital currency accessible to circular businesses and other players in the circular economy sector, and second, by designing the CBDC in a way that allows it to support circular economy goals. Ozili (2022f) further argues that CBDC creates a gateway that allows a central bank to offer financial assistance to distressed circular businesses. Other studies link CBDC to financial inclusion which is an important development outcome. Murakami et al (2022) show that CBDC can increase financial inclusion by providing a savings vehicle that allow households to smooth consumption. They also argue that CBDC adoption is more important for developing countries that have a lower degree of financial inclusion. Ozili (2022d) suggest that CBDC can increase financial inclusion by improving access to digital financial services and increasing the efficiency of digital payments. Banet and Lebeau (2022) analyze the impact of a CBDC on financial inclusion, and find that a CBDC that has low transaction cost and has high interest rate on CBDC deposits increases financial inclusion. Didenko and Buckley (2021) show that if a CBDC is well-designed and well-implemented, it can increase financial inclusion by bringing more people into the financial system so that they can access low-cost financial services.

DISCUSSION

How CBDC Reduces the Level of Poverty

Recall that the first sustainable development goal is to eliminate poverty or reduce poverty significantly. CBDC can help to attain this goal through greater financial inclusion. Financial inclusion generally involves providing access to basic and affordable formal financial services to unbanked adults (Ozili, 2018). This is how it works. The first step is to ensure that the CBDC is designed to promote financial inclusion. This can be done by ensuring that the CBDC has a feature for offline usage and by ensuring that people who do not have a formal bank account can hold and use CBDC retail payments. A CBDC that have these two features can increase financial inclusion by ensuring that (i) poor people that do not have a bank account are able to use CBDC and make payment up to a significant threshold, (ii) poor people are able to bypass the burdensome documentation required to open a bank account, (iii) providing an option to take loans in the form of CBDC, and (iii) by ensuring that people who do not have internet connectivity can use CBDC for payments.

A CBDC opens up a lot of opportunities for poor people. It offers low transaction cost, and gives poor people access to available credit, savings and investment products that are provided by formal financial institutions. Poor people can then choose from a range of formal financial services the one that meets their needs which they can reasonably afford. They can take advantage of available loan products and the loan can be paid into their CBDC accounts or wallets and they can use the loan to improve their welfare by spending on basic consumption, education, healthcare and by saving some funds for emergency purposes, thereby helping them to rise above the poverty line. This shows that CBDC can reduce poverty by increasing financial inclusion which in turn gives poor people more opportunities to improve their welfare using CBDC-based financial services such as loans, savings and investment products, thereby contributing to the attainment of the United Nations sustainable development goal to eliminate extreme poverty.

CBDC and the Role of Financial Institutions for Poverty Reduction

Once a CBDC has been issued by the central bank, the central bank can distribute CBDC to citizens through regulated financial institutions. Financial institutions can assist poor people in registering and opening a CBDC account and can provide essential customer support services to poor people during the CBDC on-boarding process. Financial institutions can use their apps and platforms to promote CBDC to retail customers. Financial institutions can use advertising materials to encourage low income and poor customers to use CBDC-based financial services such as retail loans, insurance and deposits. CBDC-based financial services can also be tailored to meet the needs of people with low income. Also, the benefit of using CBDC for payments should always exceed the cost of using CBDC at all times. The associated cost should be sufficiently low to encourage poor people to use CBDC. Finally, the cost of converting paper money to CBDC and converting CBDC holdings back to paper money should be cost-free to encourage poor people to voluntarily use CBDC for payments when they feel like doing so.

CBDC and the Role of Digital Technology Providers for Poverty Reduction

Digital technology providers can play a role in promoting central bank digital currency for poverty reduction. First of all, the digital technology partners involved in the creation of a CBDC should liaise with the central bank and suggest ways to eliminate cost structures in CBDC design that increase transaction cost which may be expensive for poor people. Digital technology providers should develop low-cost mobile phones and digital devices that are affordable to poor people. When mobile phones are too expensive for poor people to buy, it will be difficult for poor people to buy the mobile phones they need to transact with a central bank digital currency. It is essential for digital technology providers to produce cheap mobile phones as it is a major tool that poor customers need to use to transact with a central bank digital currency. Also, it is important for digital technology providers to reduce the cost of internet connectivity so that it is affordable for poor people.

POLICY IMPLICATION FOR SUSTAINABLE DEVELOPMENT

First, policy makers should ensure that CBDC is easily affordable and accessible to poor people. Poor people should have access to affordable mobile phones or digital devices that can be used manage their CBDC holdings. Such mobile phones or digital devices should be affordable to encourage poor people to own a mobile phone which they can use to hold and manage their CBDC. Policy makers should ensure that mobile phones and digital devices are abundant in supply and at low-cost. This will increase the demand for CBDC among poor people and increase financial inclusion when poor people begin to use CBDC for retail transactions. It will give them an opportunity to use available financial services to rise above poverty. Second, policymakers need to introduce digital literacy programs to educate poor people on what a CBDC is, what it can accomplish for them and how to use it. Policymakers will also need to introduce online digital security programs to teach poor people how to protect their CBDC wallets or token-based CBDC from been hacked by hackers who want to steal people's CBDC holdings. Third, policy makers should ensure that CBDC is embraced by everyone in society especially by retailers and poor consumers. Poor people mostly patronize retail agents especially road-side retail agents but these agents may refuse to accept CBDC payments for many reasons. Policymakers should provide incentives and rewards to retail merchants that embrace and use CBDC. Such incentives or rewards are important because it may be nearly impossible for poor people to use CBDC when the retail merchants in their community do not embrace or accept CBDC payments. So, there is a need to ensure that retail business agents embrace CBDC. Finally, policymaker should continuously improve the CBDC design to reflect new changes, developments and innovations that lead to greater access to finance in a sustainable way.

CONCLUSION

This paper examined the role of central bank digital currency for poverty reduction and sustainable development. It argued that a CBDC can eliminate poverty by first increasing financial inclusion which then gives poor people access to affordable credit and other basic financial services which they can use to improve their welfare, thereby enabling them to rise above poverty.

The implication of the study is that a CBDC can lead to poverty reduction only when CBDC design has features that increase financial inclusion for poor people. Policy makers can ensure that the CBDC used in their respective countries is designed to incorporate features that enhance financial inclusion which is vital for poverty reduction and for the attainment of the United Nations sustainable development goals.

Future studies should assess how CBDC can aid the attainment of the other sustainable development goals. Such studies should assess how retail CBDC can be used to achieve other sustainable development goals such as climate action, quality education and good health and wellbeing. Future studies can also assess how CBDC can be used to achieve economic development objectives.

REFERENCE

Ajide, F. (2016). Financial innovation and sustainable development in selected countries in West Africa. *Journal of Entrepreneurship, Management, and Innovation*, *12*(3), 85–112. doi:10.7341/20161234

Allen, F., & Gale, D. (1994). *Financial innovation and risk sharing*. MIT Press.

Anyanwu, J. C., & Anyanwu, J. C. (2017). The key drivers of poverty in Sub-Saharan Africa and what can be done about it to achieve the poverty sustainable development goal. *Asian Journal of Economic Modelling*, *5*(3), 297–317. doi:10.18488/journal.8.2017.53.297.317

Bahmani-Oskooee, M., & Oyolola, M. (2009). Poverty reduction and aid: Cross-country evidence. *The International Journal of Sociology and Social Policy*, *29*(5-6), 264–273. doi:10.1108/01443330910965796

Banet, J., & Lebeau, L. (2022). *Central Bank Digital Currency: Financial Inclusion vs. Disintermediation.* Working Paper 2218.

Bordo, M. D., & Levin, A. T. (2017). Central bank digital currency and the future of monetary policy (No. w23711). National Bureau of Economic Research.

Charness, N., & Boot, W. R. (2016). Technology, gaming, and social networking. In *Handbook of the Psychology of Aging* (pp. 389–407). Academic Press. doi:10.1016/B978-0-12-411469-2.00020-0

Chibba, M. (2008). Poverty reduction in Developing countries. *World Economy*, *9*(1), 197–200.

Chowdhury, A. (2009). *Microfinance as a poverty reduction tool: a critical assessment.* DESA Working Paper No. 89.

Collier, P., & Dollar, D. (2002). Aid allocation and poverty reduction. *European Economic Review*, *46*(8), 1475–1500. doi:10.1016/S0014-2921(01)00187-8

Cukierman, A. (2020). Reflections on welfare and political economy aspects of a central bank digital currency. *Manchester School*, *88*(S1), 114–125. doi:10.1111/manc.12333

Das Gupta, M., Bongaarts, J., & Cleland, J. (2011). *Population, poverty, and sustainable development: A review of the evidence.* World Bank Policy Research Working Paper, (5719).

Davoodalhosseini, S. M. (2021). Central bank digital currency and monetary policy. *Journal of Economic Dynamics & Control*, 104150.

Didenko, A. N., & Buckley, R. P. (2021). *Central Bank Digital Currencies: A Potential Response to the Financial Inclusion Challenges of the Pacific.* UNSW Law Research Paper, No- 63.

Ekong, U. M., & Ekong, C. N. (2022). Digital currency and financial inclusion in Nigeria: Lessons for development. *Journal of Internet and Digital Economics*, *2*(1), 46–67. doi:10.1108/JIDE-11-2021-0018

Engert, W., & Fung, B. S. C. (2017). *Central bank digital currency: Motivations and implications.* Bank of Canada Staff Discussion Paper No 16.

Esquivel, V., & Sweetman, C. (2016). Gender and the sustainable development goals. *Gender and Development*, *24*(1), 1–8. doi:10.1080/13552074.2016.1153318

Harber, C. (2002). Education, democracy, and poverty reduction in Africa. *Comparative Education*, *38*(3), 267–276. doi:10.1080/0305006022000014133

Hulme, D., Mosley, P., Wood, G. D., & Sharif, I. A. (1997). Finance for the poor or poorest? Financial innovation, poverty, and vulnerability. In *Who needs credit? Poverty and finance in Bangladesh.* Zed Books.

Johnson, S., & Rogaly, B. (1997). *Microfinance and poverty reduction.* Oxfam. doi:10.3362/9780855988005

Kao, T. Y., Chen, J. C., Wu, J. T. B., & Yang, M. H. (2016). Poverty reduction through empowerment for sustainable development: A proactive strategy of corporate social responsibility. *Corporate Social Responsibility and Environmental Management*, *23*(3), 140–149. doi:10.1002/csr.1365

Kelikume, I. (2021). Digital financial inclusion, informal economy, and poverty reduction in Africa. *Journal of Enterprising Communities: People and Places in the Global Economy*, *15*(4), 626–640. doi:10.1108/JEC-06-2020-0124

Lee, Y. H., Hsieh, Y. C., & Hsu, C. N. (2011). Adding innovation diffusion theory to the technology acceptance model: Supporting employees' intentions to use e-learning systems. *Journal of Educational Technology & Society*, *14*(4), 124–137.

Manaf, N. A., & Ibrahim, K. (2017). Poverty reduction for sustainable development: Malaysia's evidence-based solutions. *Global Journal of Social Sciences Studies*, *3*(1), 29–42. doi:10.20448/807.3.1.29.42

Michael, B., Koroleska, N., Tai, A., & Wong, D. W. H. (2022). A critical look at using financial technology policy to promote the sustainable development goals. *Sustainable Development*, *30*(6), 1911–1920. doi:10.1002d.2358

MurakamiD.ShchapovI.Viswanath-NatrajG. (2022). CBDCs, Financial Inclusion, and Monetary Policy. *Available at* SSRN 4102397.

Ogun, T. P. (2010, August). Infrastructure and poverty reduction: Implications for urban development in Nigeria. In *Urban Forum* (Vol. 21, No. 3, pp. 249-266). Springer Netherlands.

Ozili, P. K. (2018). Impact of digital finance on financial inclusion and stability. *Borsa Istanbul Review, 18*(4), 329–340. doi:10.1016/j.bir.2017.12.003

Ozili, P.K. (2022a). Central bank digital currency research around the world: a review of literature. *Journal of Money Laundering Control.*

Ozili, P. K. (2022b). Central bank digital currency in Nigeria: opportunities and risks. In The New Digital Era: Digitalisation, Emerging Risks and Opportunities (Vol. 109, pp. 125-133). Emerald Publishing Limited. doi:10.1108/S1569-37592022000109A008

OziliP. K. (2022c). Central bank digital currency can lead to the collapse of cryptocurrency. *Available at* SSRN 3850826.

Ozili, P. K. (2022d), Can Central Bank Digital Currency Increase Financial Inclusion? Arguments for and Against. In Big Data Analytics in the Insurance Market (Emerald Studies in Finance, Insurance, and Risk Management). Emerald Publishing Limited. doi:10.1108/978-1-80262-637-720221013

Ozili, P. K. (2022e). Embedded finance: assessing the benefits, use case, challenges and interest over time. *Journal of Internet and Digital Economics.*

Ozili, P. K. (2022f). Circular Economy and Central Bank Digital Currency. *Circular Economy and Sustainability*, 1-16.

Reed, D. (2002). Poverty and the environment: Can sustainable development survive globalization? *Natural Resources Forum, 26*(3), 176–184. doi:10.1111/0165-0203.00019

Sachs, J. D., Schmidt-Traub, G., Mazzucato, M., Messner, D., Nakicenovic, N., & Rockström, J. (2019). Six transformations to achieve the sustainable development goals. *Nature Sustainability, 2*(9), 805–814. doi:10.103841893-019-0352-9

Schleicher, J., Schaafsma, M., & Vira, B. (2018). Will the Sustainable Development Goals address the links between poverty and the natural environment? *Current Opinion in Environmental Sustainability, 34*, 43–47. doi:10.1016/j.cosust.2018.09.004

Selgin, G. (2021). Central Bank Digital Currency as a Potential Source of Financial Instability. *The Cato Journal, 41*, 333.

Tilak, J. B. (2002). Education and poverty. *Journal of Human Development, 3*(2), 191–207. doi:10.1080/14649880220147301

Veen, R. V. D., & Preece, J. (2005). Poverty reduction and adult education: Beyond basic education. *International Journal of Lifelong Education, 24*(5), 381–391. doi:10.1080/02601370500169723

Vinuesa, R., Azizpour, H., Leite, I., Balaam, M., Dignum, V., Domisch, S., Felländer, A., Langhans, S. D., Tegmark, M., & Nerini, F. F. (2020). The role of artificial intelligence in achieving the Sustainable Development Goals. *Nature Communications, 11*(1), 1–10. doi:10.103841467-019-14108-y PMID:31932590

Wratten, E. (1995). Conceptualizing urban poverty. *Environment and Urbanization, 7*(1), 11–38. doi:10.1177/095624789500700118

Yonah, Z. O., & Salim, B. A. (2008). *ICTs as tools for poverty reduction.* Academic Press.

Chapter 12
Embracing Business Sustainability Through Innovation and Productivity in the Automotive Sector:
Creativity, Collaboration, and Generating Savings

Anthony D. Bolton
https://orcid.org/0000-0002-1259-7479
University of South Africa, South Africa

Leila Goosen
https://orcid.org/0000-0003-4948-2699
University of South Africa, South Africa

Elmarie Kritzinger
https://orcid.org/0000-0002-5141-4348
University of South Africa, South Africa

ABSTRACT

The purpose of the study reported on in this chapter was to explore and attempt to answer the primary research question: To what extent can embracing business sustainability through digital transformation, implemented via unified communication and collaboration (UC&C) technologies, impact innovation and productivity in the global automotive sector? This will be presented against the background of embracing business sustainability through innovation and creativity in the service sector. Apart from creativity, collaboration, and generating savings featured in the subtitle of the chapter, changing work practices were also identified as a factor impacting innovation.

DOI: 10.4018/978-1-6684-6732-9.ch012

Copyright © 2023, IGI Global. Copying or distributing in print or electronic forms without written permission of IGI Global is prohibited.

INTRODUCTION

This section will introduce the general perspectives of the chapter and end by specifically stating the objectives. In the proceedings of the annual conference of the South African Institute of Computer Scientists and Information Technologists (SAICSIT), Bolton, Goosen and Kritzinger (2016) introduced enterprise digitization enablement through Unified Communication and *Collaboration* (UC&C) technologies.

As part of this book, the chapter intends to provide comprehensive research about embracing business sustainability through innovation and productivity, as well as creativity, in the service and automotive sectors.

According to Tyagi, Singh, Tyagi and Singh (2021, p. 1), the survival of businesses no longer only "depends on meeting demand but" on meeting the demand by ensuring that customers' needs are met in terms of *convenience and speed.*

With ever-*increasing* pressure and competition towards *organizational efficiency* in the global automotive sector, like this book, the chapter aims to contribute to knowledge of various *changing work practices.* As a contributing chapter, this one will explore recommended topics and objectives selected from those suggested for the book and the target audience as indicated.

The contribution of the authors is expected to describe a case study and case examples about embracing business sustainability through innovation and productivity, as well as creativity. The findings discussed in a chapter on results and interpretation (Bolton, Goosen, & Kritzinger, 2022c) suggested that in the context of the global automotive sector case study subject, General Motors (GM), the digital transformation delivered through a combination of UC&C technologies promoted communication and *collaboration* between employees. A review of the digital transformation showed evidence of a significant shift in system and technology capabilities, underpinning upper-level employee communication and *collaboration changing work practices.*

Bolton, Goosen and Kritzinger (2022b, p. 71) indicated that General Motors as organization "represents an extensive global enterprise with many business functions that are common across" the automotive sector (finance, marketing, Information Technology (IT), "legal, Human Resources (HR), sales, manufacturing and product design)."

In line with the theme of the book, on Embracing Business Sustainability through Innovation and Creativity in Service Sector, this chapter will also report on developments related to e.g., *tourism, hospitality*, finance, IT, *education*, health and social care, online business and other service sectors.

From the recommended topics suggested for the book, this chapter will especially address the following:

- The age of creativity - people and organizations in the service sector
- Entrepreneurial nomads and *changing work practices* in the service sector
- Management of innovation in the service sector
- Disruptive innovation and contingency theory in the service sector
- The search for sustainable business excellence in the service sector
- The role of knowledge in creativity and innovation in the service sector, as well as
- Practicing creativity and innovation through charismatic/visionary leadership in the service sector

OBJECTIVES

The purpose of the study reported on in this chapter was to explore and attempt to answer the primary research question: *To what extent can embracing business sustainability through digital transformation, implemented via unified communication and collaboration technologies, impact innovation and productivity in the global automotive sector?* The theoretical design of the study generated four research questions that were used to guide the research processes of observation, analysis and evaluation of the research data.

As part of the proposed book, this chapter is expected to provide an in-depth understanding of various dimensions of embracing business sustainability through innovation, productivity and creativity by additionally recognizing aspects related to:

- Sustainability, Innovation and Gap Forecasting,
- Understanding of the need for, and employability of, creative models for sustainable *changing work practices*,
- The Scope of Disruptive Business Innovation,
- Necessity for, and Emerging Trends related to, Dynamic Leadership and Entrepreneurial Thinking,
- Strategic Involvement of Predictive Analytics, and
- Tactical Involvement and Applications of Machine Intelligence.

The next BACKGROUND section of the chapter will provide broad definitions and discussion of the topic, on Embracing Business Sustainability Through Innovation and Productivity in the Automotive Sector, and incorporate the views of others (in the form of a *literature review*) into the discussion to support, refute, or demonstrate the authors' position on the topic.

The MAIN FOCUS OF THE CHAPTER will be presenting the authors' perspective on the issues, challenges, problems, etc., as these relate to the main theme of the book, on Embracing Business Sustainability Through Innovation and Creativity in Service Sector, and arguments supporting the authors' position. It will also compare and contrast with what had been, or is currently being, done as these relate to the specific topic of the chapter, on Embracing Business Sustainability Through Innovation and Productivity in the Automotive Sector.

The following section of the chapter will discuss SOLUTIONS AND RECOMMENDATIONS in dealing with the issues, challenges, problems, etc. presented in the preceding section.

Thereafter, future and emerging trends will be discussed, as well as providing insight about the future of the theme of the book, on Embracing Business Sustainability Through Innovation and Creativity in Service Sector, from the perspective of the chapter focus. The viability of a paradigm, model, implementation issues of proposed programs, etc., may also be included in this section. FUTURE RESEARCH DIRECTIONS within the domain of the topic, on Embracing Business Sustainability Through Innovation and Productivity in the Automotive Sector, will finally be suggested.

Finally, the CONCLUSION will provide a discussion of the overall coverage of the chapter and concluding remarks.

BACKGROUND

The Requirement for Broad Information and Communication Technology Investment and Transformation

In the automotive sector, the underlying service architecture of Information and Communication Technology (ICT) systems and UC&C technologies needed to support broad and pervasive delivery of the digital transformation of such technologies required substantial investment. Contrasting a review of ICT systems and end user communication and *collaboration* outcomes suggested that to achieve pervasive end user *ease of use and adoption*, planning and investment needed to encompass and consider elements of technology architecture that extended beyond core UC&C elements, such as the software client, as well as video and voice functions. For example, to ensure that users maintained a consistently positive perception of value in the new digital toolset, reliability and service quality needed to be assured. In order to provide such assurance, the technology landscape extended into multiple layers of the communication and *collaboration* architecture, such as the Local Area Network (LAN), Wide Area Network (WAN) and carrier, as well as Class of Service (CoS) and Quality of Service (QoS), were required.

The Age of Creativity - People and Organizations in the Service Sector

In an encyclopedia of organizational knowledge, administration, and technologies, Bolton, Goosen and Kritzinger (2021a) showed how a global automotive organization was using unified communication and collaboration technologies.

The purpose of the study reported on by Kemer (2022, p. 164) was to determine the *relationships* between the "organizational innovation capabilities of hotel businesses" and "mobile applications. In line with this purpose, data were collected".

The Scandinavian journal article on management by Sørensen (2008, p. 86) expressed "the hope that culture and its productive principle, 'creativity'," was able to support the entrepreneur as 'savior' in the age of creativity through the movement described as "a global wave of change".

In the age of technology, measuring the digital creativity of millennials without including "digital creative outlets may miss out on learning about many of the ways in which adolescents show their creativity" (Hoffmann, Ivcevic, & Brackett, 2016, p. 153).

Practicing Creativity and Innovation Through Leadership in the Service Sector

In stories from the field about practicing structural social work based on practitioners' use of creativity, the term creativity in the paper by George, Coleman and Barnoff (2010, p. 13) referred "to the intentional ways in which practitioners" blended "the structural social work approach" at the time. The latter authors explained how one could "do so through the use of" 'creativity', where practice infused with 'creativity' involved practitioners' conscious blending of the said structural approach.

The empirical study reported on in the international journal article on academic research in business and social sciences by Haque, et al. (2015, p. 281) explored "different leadership styles' dimensions influencing" *indicators of cultural change in communication and collaboration* related to female employees' motivation in the rapidly improving IT sector of a developing country, with responses from Pakistan.

"Exile proved potentially easier for women whose creativity was not essentially based on the German language" (Finnan, 2006). As an example, two "photographers who were able to continue their careers successfully" were practicing modernity in an instance of female creativity in the Weimar republic.

The Scope of Disruptive Business Innovation, Contingency Theory and the Search for Sustainable Business Excellence in the Service Sector

In line with the recommended topics on Disruptive Innovation and Contingency Theory in the Service Sector and the Search for Sustainable Business Excellence in the Service Sector provided for this book, the book on Disruptive Innovation for Business Excellence in the Service Sector contained a chapter by Tyagi and Tyagi (2022, p. 41) on customer perception and brand image through sensory marketing, which indicated that firms "can be seen as value facilitators, offering various types of services for consumer consumption, as well as value-generating methods, while following a service viewpoint."

The book by Donaldson (2001, p. xvi) was a more comprehensive treatment of the contingency theory of organizations and its research, as it was "broader in the range of theories considered under the contingency umbrella."

In their journal article on *educational* administration, Tarter and Hoy (1998) indicated that moving toward a "proposed contingency theory of decision making" had practical utility and significance. The latter authors therefore asked: "What else does this contingency approach suggest to administrators?"

The management review article by Luthans and Stewart (1977, p. 182) proposed "that a General Contingency Theory (GCT) can best meet" important goals in the field of management, as it included constructs relevant to the "development of a comprehensive contingency theory of management."

The management accounting research article by Otley (2016, p. 42) *reviewed "literature* on the contingency theory of management accounting" and control for 1980–2014. It was "suggested that the narrow view of contingency that relies on responses to generally applicable questionnaires needs to be replaced by a more tailored approach that takes into account the context of specific organizations" {33}.

Another *review of literature* on "contingency theory in management accounting research in a chronological order" was presented by Islam and Hu (2012, p. 5159). Based on the African journal article on business management, the latter authors indicated that commonly, "contingency theory studies postulate that organizational outcomes are the consequences of a *fit* or match between two or more contingent factors."

The purpose of the paper by Bolboli and Reiche (2013, p. 331) in the total quality management (TQM) journal was "to develop a holistic model for reviewing" sustainable "business excellence (BE) concepts from a systemic perspective and to propose an implementation guideline" and roadmap.

Strategic Involvement of Predictive Analytics

The strategic role of institutionalization for accommodation enterprises in terms of organizational innovation was discussed in the Gaziantep University journal article on social sciences by Özkoç and Kemer (2017).

The research by Kemer (2021a, p. 99) aimed to determine the impact of the innovation capabilities of hotel business managers on their "Industry 4.0 perceptions. In line with this purpose, data were collected with a survey".

Against the background of research on innovations in technology and marketing for the connected consumer, the chapter by Nadda and Arnott (2020, p. 401) indicated that *tourism* businesses had become virtual organizations linked to information technologies available for marketing innovation in tourism, "as well as using other platforms" on social media.

The journal article on applied sciences by Buyukkeklik, Ozoglu and Kemer (2014) presented research in the Cappadocia region in Türkiye with regard to buyer-supplier *relationships* in *tourism* supply chains.

The aim of the study reported on by Eriş and Kemer (2020, p. 7884) in the Indian journal article on forensic medicine and toxicology was "to determine the medical *tourism* awareness of health workers in public hospitals in (the) South Eastern Anatolian Region."

An evaluation study by Tyagi and Gupta (2019, p. 787) "was conducted to understand sources of recruitment and selection" processes "in the *travel* trade business" organizations of "Chandigarh. Many sources of recruitment such as internal and external" ones were used "for the selection of employees."

The revolution of the social web and mobile technologies had "a tremendous impact on the world". Noticeably, this revolutionary phenomenon had brought opportunities for computer-mediated marketing strategies, social media and online brand communities. Hui and Nadda (2015, p. 157) therefore explored the concept of interactivity and its dimensions.

In the context of *tourism and hospitality* management, Rahimi, Nadda, Hyseni and Mulindwa (2016, p. 223) indicated that the "economic ramifications of tourism and hospitality have led to the considerable growth of global *education* in this industry. The ever-changing needs of this industry for appropriate skills and expertise have made it more competitive in nature, which has led to the increase in studies exploring the motivations" of South Asian students to study tourism and hospitality in the United Kingdom.

Various proceedings from the South Africa International Conference on *Educational Technologies* (SAICET) showed how the latter can be used for an Information and Communication Technologies for Development (ICT4D) Massive Open Online Course (MOOC) and/or for growing innovative e-schools in the 21st century, through a community engagement project (Goosen, 2015). Such *educational technologies* can further be used in distance education, when taken beyond the horizon with qualitative perspectives (Goosen & Mukasa-Lwanga, 2017).

MAIN FOCUS OF THE CHAPTER

Issues, Challenges, Problems

Globalization "and the resulting increase in competition" had forced organizations "to seek unique ways to gain a competitive advantage" (Ali, Upadhyay, & Kumar, 2017, p. 130). One of the promotional strategies and new service opportunities in emerging economies is related to issues in service marketing.

The study by Nadda, Rafiq and Tyagi (2017, p. 1) tried to evaluate the effectiveness of "and challenges faced by adopting" Recruitment Process Outsourcing (RPO) *practices* in the Indian hotel sector. The research objectives were driven by "the purpose of the research", which dealt "with distinct issues related to RPO and various perspectives" on utilizing RPO.

Challenges for the global automotive sector towards a post COVID-19 era in terms of the impact of digital transformation were presented in the chapter by Bolton, et al. (2022c).

Seemingly every day, there is another innovation, gadget and/or technique, which offer access "to the fast development of information" (Kaur & Bharti, 2019, p. 1). These days, information is expanding immensely, and the latter authors therefore felt the need to conduct a survey on the challenges related to big data.

Schoonhoven (1981, p. 349) indicated that a contingency process was "believed to be operating. The five problems" with contingency theory were illustrated by testing hypotheses and assumptions hidden within the language of contingency 'theory'.

An empirical study and analysis of blockchain technology by Bharti and Anand (2021, p. 728) presented at the third International Conference on Inventive Research in Computing Applications (ICIRCA) endeavored to investigate e.g., the difficulties "for the momentum or future uses of" blockchain technology.

"In the virtual world, most" cyber-attacks are carried out by a botnet. Botnets are "one of the most versatile threats because" these are controlled remotely. In an international journal article on computing and digital systems, Joshi, Ranjan and Bharti (2021, p. 1319) therefore presented an Artificial Neural Network (ANN)-based multi-class classification of Peer-to-Peer (P2P) botnets.

In the proceedings of the 43rd conference of the Southern African Computer Lecturers Association (SACLA), Goosen and Naidoo (2014) showed how computer lecturers were using their institutional Learning Management System (LMS) for ICT *education* in the cyber world – this is needed, as Goosen (2016) indicated that both learners at basic *education* (school) and students at higher *education* (e.g., universities) levels need access to e-learning.

The paper by Sharma, Ranjan and Bharti (2021, p. 1) presented at the 12th International Conference on Computing Communication and Networking Technologies (ICCCNT) proposed "a new Image Encryption Algorithm (IEA) using a new bit shifted logistic map. The Bit Shifted Logistic Map (BSLM) is used for the generation of pseudo-random numbers for the further encryption/decryption process. … The IEA is ensured to … achieve two basic cryptographic properties": confusion and diffusion.

Practicing Creativity and Innovation Through Leadership in the Service Sector

A profiling of scholars of creativity in terms of practicing the process "ranged over a number of topics related to" practicing creativity. Some of the key themes emphasized by Root-Bernstein in a discussion with Keenan and Mishra (2016, p. 201) included "creativity, its challenges, how it can be developed, and the implications that technology can have on that process."

In a journal article in the Physics conference series, Suyidno, et al. (2020, p. 2) found that "teachers' negative beliefs in science, technology, engineering, and mathematics along with their learning are believe to be the main factors" related to the barriers to scientific creativity of physics teachers in practicing scientific creativity, especially when designing creative products.

The Search for Sustainable Business Excellence in the Service Sector

In the journal article by Khoo and Tan (2002, p. 204), "the Australian Business Excellence Framework was used to help implement" and achieve sustainable business excellence "objectives in an organization. The challenges" evident in corporate social responsibility, environmental management "and sustainable business practices were identified."

In the context of total quality management and business excellence, Kristensen and Westlund (2004, p. 629) discussed accountable business performance measurement for sustainable business excellence. Sustainable business excellence, "in the sense of achieving long-term, stable, and excellent financial and non-financial performance, is still rather an exception than a rule in the business community." In the same context, the purpose of the paper by Gan, Chong, Yuen, Yen Teoh and Rahman (2021, p. 1405) was "to explore the complexity of executive coaching by proposing a comprehensive executive coaching framework that examines the important constructs and the entire impact of executive coaching effectiveness in Malaysia" in "order to bridge the gap and provide" organizations "with practical assistance in dealing with the effectiveness of executive coaching" towards sustainable business excellence.

Sustainability, Innovation and Gap Forecasting

"Businesses tend to operate under the influence of their internal and external" environments for favorable outcomes "and competitive sustainability. Under such circumstances," customer relationship management (CRM) in *tourism* becomes important. Rahimi, Nadda and Wang (2018, p. 16) therefore provided concepts, methodologies, tools, and applications related to digital marketing and consumer engagement.

"The impact of *tourism* on the local community and environment" had raised concerns related to "the sustainability of tourist destinations. Therefore, in" the Environment, Energy and Earth Sciences (E3S) Web of Conferences paper by Singh, Tyagi and Tyagi (2021, p. 1), an evaluation of sustainable tourism *practices* in the state of Bihar, India was presented.

Sustainable and inclusive quality *education* can be promoted through research-informed practice on information and communication technologies (Goosen, 2018a).

Tactical Involvement and Applications of Machine Intelligence

Intrusion detection systems (IDSs) help to monitor a network and identify "malicious activities that occur on" a network. IDSs also "help to secure the network by analyzing … network traffic information. These days various machine learning algorithms are used to detect network attacks. In" their paper presented at the third 3rd International Conference on Advances in Computing, Communication Control and Networking (ICAC3N), Devi and Bharti (2021, p. 1357) analyzed "network traffic using machine learning approaches." Some of the classifications included detection rate, "false-positive rate, and the average cost for misclassification. The main purpose of" the paper was to detect attacks on the network and develop a data analysis tool with Python that helped to detect and prevent access to the network by various malicious intruders.

Entrepreneurial Nomads and Changing Work Practices in the Service Sector

The chapter by Bolton, Goosen and Kritzinger (2021b), describing an empirical study into the impact on innovation and productivity towards *the post-COVID-19 era* in terms of the digital transformation of an automotive enterprise, appeared in a handbook of research not only addressing sustainability, innovation and ICTs, but also entrepreneurship.

The Role of Knowledge in Creativity and Innovation in the Service Sector

"Social networks and online communities are increasingly becoming" big players "in the field of *tourism* marketing. Consumer behavior is increasingly more influenced by the information exchanged" amongst these communities. The Turkish journal article on contemporary issues in business and government by Tyagi, Singh, Singh and Tyagi (2021, p. 149) thus investigated the role of social crowdsourcing in mobile tourism.

Revolutionary developments in the fields of information and communication technologies had opened up new global avenues for "marketing *tourism and hospitality* products." Against the background of research on global hospitality and tourism management, Nadda, Dadwal, Mulindwa and Vieira (2015, p. 142) discussed the role of social media in tourism.

The purpose of the research by Kemer (2021b, p. 226) was "to determine the role of agricultural products in creating" and establishing "gastronomic identity. For this purpose, the agricultural product potato, which is mostly grown in Niğde province in" Türkiye "and given importance to its production and development, has been evaluated in terms of gastronomic identity.

The research by Kemer (2021c, p. 1877) aimed to determine the moderating role of professional occupational commitment and "the effect of the income level of accommodation business *managers* on job satisfaction", while Goosen and Van der Merwe (2015) discussed e-learners, teachers and *managers* at e-schools in South Africa.

Strategic Involvement of Predictive Analytics

"The hope of livelihood enhancement for the mountain dwellers" of the Chakrata region of Uttarakhand had "been a climacteric and novel effort by many international and national organizations" (Gupta, Rout, & Tyagi, 2019, p. 47). A strategic analysis of community-based tourism development amid complex mountain issues was therefore provided in an international journal article on *hospitality and tourism* systems.

SOLUTIONS AND RECOMMENDATIONS

Solutions

Kaur and Bharti (2019) presented a chapter on Big Data processing using Spark in the *cloud*, as well as solutions from vendors.

In a book on the integration and implementation of the *Internet of Things* (IoT) through *cloud computing,* Bolton, Goosen and Kritzinger (2021c) reported on solutions obtained with regard to the integration and implementation of the Internet of Things through digital transformation in terms of impact on productivity and innovation. "With rapid growth and development in" technologies, *cloud computing* had "become a dominant platform for small businesses as well as major enterprises. Cloud computing" in *tourism* streamlined digital marketing strategies for the tourism, *hospitality*, and airline industries (Nadda, Chaudhary, & Arnott, 2020, p. 141).

A systematic *review* of smart energy transmission through 'SMART GRID' as an application of the *IoT* by Anand, Bharti and Singh (2021, p. 563) presented at ICAC3N indicated that electricity transmission is a necessity for any civilization these days, as this "is the major energy source for households, businesses, and other organizations and groups", especially if such groups are working in the Information Technology class (Mentz & Goosen, 2007).

Ensuring ethical data management and research integrity in the context of engagement with the research community indicated (Goosen, 2018c), as well as ethical decisions with regard to the information and communication technologies used for the development of solutions in this research (Goosen, 2018d), were priorities.

Discussion of Solutions Relating to the Research Hypotheses

Digital Transformation of Communication and Collaboration Technologies

H1: The digital transformation of communication and collaboration achieved through UC&C technologies resulted in increased inclusion and engagement of people and teams across the global automotive sector.

Wireless network design and consideration of factors, such wireless spectrum, radio and network contention for elements, such as video, needed to be purposefully designed in order to assure a high-quality experience, support end user perception of reliability and perceived benefit. As discussed in the review of relevant scholary literature and supported through the findings of the end user survey and interview results (see Bolton, et al., 2022c), perceived positive benefits through *ease of use* of a system are influencers in the *adoption* of new technologies. Pervasive end user adoption is arguably a precursor to achieving pervasive impact in relation to UC&C *changing work practices* and *indicators of cultural change in communication and collaboration* within the enterprise user population.

In the context of digital transformation, the findings of the study suggested that the Enhanced UC&C (E-UC&C) framework presented and applied within the research case study provided a broad frame of reference that delivered digital transformation at the required scale, inclusive of supporting governance processes. End user *adoption* metrics within the GM case study supported a view of rapid and pervasive technologies *adoption*. The metrics additionally showed prolific use of the broader range of sub-features delivered within the E-UC&C framework, supported by the new tools and technical architecture. The parallel tracking of financial benefit, in addition to the qualitative data acquisition relating to end user experience, provided evidence of significant *savings generated* through digital transformation.

Ease of use and adoption was not only identified as a factor from *survey* results, but also as a *transformation* factor.

Indicators of cultural change in communication and collaboration and *legacy reduction and elimination* were also identified as *transformation* factors.

Digital Persona

H2: Digitally transformed social presence and real-time status indicators positively influence the perception of increased productivity in people and team performance.

Perceived Productivity

H3: Digitally transformed multi-channel persona capabilities facilitated through a consolidated software client influence the perception of increased productivity in people.

"Factors relating to productivity identified from the interview data in the study related to *increased* enterprise *efficiency*, *convenience and speed*, *relationships* and *satisfaction*" (Bolton, Goosen, & Kritzinger, 2020b, p. 60). The latter chapter discussed the impact of unified communication and *collaboration* technologies on productivity and innovation towards promoting inclusive growth in the Fourth Industrial *Revolution* (4IR). A study of *tourist* perception towards usage of a mobile wallet by Tyagi, Singh, Tyagi and Singh (2021, p. 1) in a Turkish journal article on computer and mathematics *education* indicated that the "digital *revolution* changed the way" the world functioned "in more ways that anyone could imagine. From being able to buy a small chocolate to paying for cars, almost anything can be bought using a mobile phone".

Increased organizational efficiency was not only identified as a *productivity* factor, but also from *survey* results, as well as a *transformation* factor.

The issue of *convenience and speed* referred to in the introduction of this chapter was identified in this study as one of the factors that impacted *productivity* (see e.g., Bolton, et al. 2022c).

Another one of the factors found to impact *productivity* was *relationships.*

Enhancing Innovation

H4: Enterprise-wide engagement through digitally transformed UC&C technologies can increase innovation generating activities across the global automotive sector value chain.

Understanding of the Need for, and Employability of, Creative Models for Sustainable Changing Work Practices

Creativity, collaboration and *changing work practices* were identified as *innovation* factors, while *generating savings* was not only identified as an *innovation* factor, but also as a *transformation* factor.

In a handbook on the development of new business models and consumer experience, Bolton, Goosen and Kritzinger (2022a) discussed the impact of digital transformation via unified communication and *collaboration* technologies on *productivity* and *innovation* at a global enterprise.

RECOMMENDATIONS

Different criteria and guidelines for selection and implementation (Goosen, 2004) can lead to a community of individuals being linked together, "such as geographic positioning, centers of interest and needs that may be close or similar" (Tyagi, et al., 2021, p. 149). Such "social media users can exchange views, opinions, experiences," recommendations and/or disclaimers.

FUTURE RESEARCH DIRECTIONS

Necessity for, and Emerging Trends related to, Dynamic Leadership and Entrepreneurial Thinking

The chapter in the handbook of research on integrating social media into strategic marketing by Nadda, Dadwal and Firdous (2015, p. 359) provided insight into "contemporary developments in social media marketing with special reference to" emerging trends related to online technologies and the influence of these on various marketing operations.

When the phrase 'theory of business (corporate) strategy' was used in the strategic business planning paper by Hofer (1990, p. 152), it was to be "understood to mean a contingency theory of business (corporate) strategy." The purpose was "to take the first steps in the" direction toward a contingency theory of business strategy.

Continuous improvements in terms of emerging trends related to economies had "created more opportunities for industrialization and rapid growth. This not only leads to higher standards in accounting", but also promotional strategies and new service opportunities (Nadda, Dadwal, & Rahimi, 2017).

A critical review of finger vein recognition by Kumar and Bharti (2021, p. 1) presented at ICIRCA indicated that the specific parts of the "human body used for vein recognition are (the) finger, palm, hand dorsal and wrist. The merit of the popularity of" finger vein recognition techniques for human identification "depends upon key techniques, evaluation" methods, "application in mobile and portable devices", *ease of use and adoption*, future emerging trends, etc.

Management of Innovation in the Service Sector

Emerging trends with regard to technologies for the management of innovation and productivity in the automotive and *software* sectors in terms of impact of digital transformation on communication were discussed in the book in which the chapter by Bolton, et al. (2022b) was published, while emerging trends and strategies for a global automotive enterprise towards a post COVID-19 era in terms of the impact of digital transformation were the topics in the authors' most recent chapter (Bolton, et al., 2022c).

Future research directions applicable to the study discussed in this chapter were detailed in especially the chapter by Bolton, et al. (2021a).

Sustainability, Innovation and Gap Forecasting

"Overconsumption is fueled by the idea that the more people buy, the happier they become; however, this is not compatible with sustainability and the future of the planet." In a case study of Türkiye, Atrek and İlter (2017, p. 32) therefore interrogated social innovation *practices* in services for sustainable consumption.

Space *tourism* is considered to be "becoming increasingly significant and is expected to be in greater demand in the future. Therefore, the aim" of the journal article on *travel and hospitality* management by Kirici Tekeli, Kemer and Kasap (2022, p. 81) was to engage in a process of meaning creation through an analysis of space tourism posters via semiotic analysis.

Tactical Involvement and Applications of Machine Intelligence

In a *review* towards a machine learning spectrum for Bioinformatics presented at ICAC3N, Sharma and Bharti (2021, p. 199) indicated that machine learning "is a science developed as a subfield of Artificial Intelligence" (AI) in the late 1990's "that will improve in the future." This research included "information about machine learning, its approaches and how machine Learning is being used in Bioinformatics."

While the paper presented at the International Conference on Electronics and Renewable Systems (ICEARS) by Singh, et al. (2022) provided a descriptive bibliometric analysis and future research directions with regard to robotics and artificial intelligence in the *hospitality* sector, the paper by Tyagi, Tyagi, Singh, Jain and Singh (2022) presented at the same conference looked at *tourist* experiences through mobile augmented reality and the chapter by Goosen (2022) at augmented/virtual reality technologies and assistive/humanoid robots in the context of students with autism spectrum disorders.

Providing insight about the future of the theme of the book, on Embracing Business Sustainability Through Innovation and Creativity in Service Sector, and in line with the recommended topics on

Disruptive Innovation and Contingency Theory in the Service Sector and the Search for Sustainable Business Excellence in the Service Sector suggested for this book, the book on disruptive innovation and emerging trends with regard to technologies for business excellence in the service sector contained a chapter by Tyagi and Tyagi (2022).

Steps had been taken by the Minnesota University Minneapolis strategic management research center "to examine contingency theory. Morever," Van de Ven and Drazin (1984) considered contingency theory *literature* and provided "a repertoire of alternative directions to further the development of" the concept of *fit* in contingency theory. In their journal article, it was "unclear whether to conclude that" the research by Drazin and Van de Ven (1985) "did not address contingency theory or to conclude that contingency theory operated as an untested assumption underlying" alternative forms of *fit* in contingency theory.

The journal article on management by Tosi and Slocum (1984, p. 9) put forward "the proposition that performance is a consequence of the *fit* between several factors", including "structure, people, technology, strategy, and" *indicators of cultural change in communication and collaboration*, which was common to all contingency approaches, as well as some suggested future research directions.

Study Limitations

The limitations of this study included the fact that the research design and case study focused on a global enterprise within the automotive sector. The research required observation and study of the digital transformation process and analysis of the pre- and post-transformation states in order to evaluate the established research hypotheses and questions. To achieve this objective, a global enterprise was leveraged as a case study subject and the General Motors corporation selected. Opportunities for the researcher to engage with an enterprise at a global scale and influence the investment and transformation within such a company was limited. As an executive within General Motors, the first author was hired to transform the global telecommunication landscape of systems and services, and this opportunity was aligned with the academic pursuit resulting in the thesis discussed in this chapter.

In this way, the unprecedented access gained from the role of the first author, in terms of knowledge of innovation in the automotive sector, within GM and the opportunity associated with guiding their transformation, while limited to a particular global automotive enterprise, represented a unique research opportunity.

The study was also limited in terms of the timeframe provided for observation post-transformation. Due to the lengthy planning, investment and execution of such a broad transformation, the post-transformation observation period was limited to approximately eight months of deployment of the UC&C technologies to the general user population of GM.

As indicated within the population of the user survey (see e.g., Table 2 in Bolton, Goosen, & Kritzinger, 2020a, p. 104), just under half of the respondents had IT experience and technical skills at varying levels. The process for deployment of the technologies was structured with a focus on delivery to a pre-production cohort of users consisting of IT employees and business users. This pre-pilot was required to validate the production readiness of the new systems, tools and associated training and end user C&C materials.

Some bias in responses relating to *ease of use and adoption*, for example, could have been introduced into the survey response data, due to the more extensive than normal distribution of IT-associated staff. It is reasonable to suggest that with 56% of respondents coming from non-IT functions within GM and little to no prior background in digital and virtual *collaboration*, that any bias introduced by the IT-skilled staff was offset. The detailed interviews were not limited in this way, as individual employees were specifically selected to ensure a broad and diverse inclusion of skills, experience and business functional knowledge. General Motors represents many global enterprises from the standpoint of scale, business functions and manufacturing.

It is not assumed that the pre-transformed technical environment within GM parallels that of other large enterprises, as each business is unique in its history of technical development and maturity. GM does represent large enterprises that engage in cross-, multi- and trans-disciplinary approaches to (Goosen, 2018b) industrial business processes at a *global* scale, who are transforming from a mostly non-digital environment with low levels of digital and virtual communication and *collaboration* between functions.

CONCLUSION

The study reported on in this chapter proposed that the digital transformation of end user communication and *collaboration* tools and processes through technologies, such as UC&C, can enhance employee communication and *collaboration* within a large-scale global enterprise. Through a focus on a global automotive enterprise, the study had shown that positive results can be achieved regarding *increased* end user perceived productivity and *organizational efficiency* associated with innovative creativity communication and *collaboration* activities. Additionally, results showed that the digital transformation can *generate* significant direct *savings*. The *savings generated* were derived from a combination of the digital transformation in the cost of communication and *collaboration* technologies, resulting in improved employee productivity, for example, the *reduction and elimination* of time-wasting travel and strict meeting schedules related to *legacy* issues.

This theory extended to suggest that feature-rich ad-hoc communication and *collaboration* technologies can shift towards *indicators of cultural change in communication and collaboration* within the sector and between its users. The study had shown that such *indicators of cultural change in communication and collaboration* were evident, with end users *changing* traditional communication-related *work practices* and customizing these to better leverage the benefits that the new UC&C toolset had to offer. The study also showed, however, that to achieve pervasive *ease of use and adoption*, together with full benefits, from the digital transformation, the framework for transformation needs to be horizontally broad, from the standpoint of feature delivery, as well as deep, from a system and architecture perspective. In order to assure quality and consistent post-transformation experiences, consideration is required of systems adjunct to the end user experience associated with the UC&C features.

The study proposed a framework called E-UC&C that was proven to be successful in deployment within General Motors as a guide to the digital transformation of communication and *collaboration* technologies. The framework proposed a novel configuration of structured modules and an associated relationship/dependency matrix. The E-UC&C framework assisted in ensuring that all dependent adjunct systems associated with the effective operation of UC&C features at a user level were integrated, transformed and aligned with the end user experience expectations. The focus within the framework was also placed on effective transition management to ensure as seamless a transition to the digital toolset for the end user as possible.

REFERENCES

Ali, M., Upadhyay, A., & Kumar, V. (2017). Issues in Service Marketing in Emerging Economies. In V. Nadda, S. Dadwal, & R. Rahimi (Eds.), *Promotional Strategies and New Service Opportunities in Emerging Economies* (pp. 130–143). IGI Global. doi:10.4018/978-1-5225-2206-5.ch006

Anand, D., Bharti, V., & Singh, S. (2021, December). Systematic review on the smart energy transmission through "SMART GRID" - An application of IoT. In *3rd International Conference on Advances in Computing, Communication Control and Networking (ICAC3N)* (pp. 563-568). IEEE. 10.1109/ICAC3N53548.2021.9725663

Atrek, B., & İlter, B. (2017). Social Innovation Practices in Services for Sustainable Consumption: The Case of Turkey. In V. Nadda, S. Dadwal, & R. Rahimi (Eds.), *Promotional Strategies and New Service Opportunities in Emerging Economies* (pp. 32–65). IGI Global. doi:10.4018/978-1-5225-2206-5.ch002

Bharti, V., & Anand, D. (2021, September). The Empirical study and analysis of the Blockchain Technology. In *Third International Conference on Inventive Research in Computing Applications (ICIRCA)* (pp. 728-734). IEEE. 10.1109/ICIRCA51532.2021.9544657

Bolboli, S. A., & Reiche, M. (2013). A model for sustainable business excellence: Implementation and the roadmap. *The TQM Journal, 25*(4), 331–346. doi:10.1108/17542731311314845

Bolton, A., Goosen, L., & Kritzinger, E. (2016). Enterprise Digitization Enablement Through Unified Communication and Collaboration. *Proceedings of the Annual Conference of the South African Institute of Computer Scientists and Information Technologists*. Johannesburg: ACM. 10.1145/2987491.2987516

Bolton, A., Goosen, L., & Kritzinger, E. (2020b). The Impact of Unified Communication and Collaboration Technologies on Productivity and Innovation: Promotion for the Fourth Industrial Revolution. In S. B. Buckley (Ed.), *Promoting Inclusive Growth in the Fourth Industrial Revolution* (pp. 44–73). IGI Global. doi:10.4018/978-1-7998-4882-0.ch002

Bolton, A., Goosen, L., & Kritzinger, E. (2021b). An Empirical Study into the Impact on Innovation and Productivity Towards the Post-COVID-19 Era: Digital Transformation of an Automotive Enterprise. In L. C. Carvalho, L. Reis, & C. Silveira (Eds.), *Handbook of Research on Entrepreneurship, Innovation, Sustainability, and ICTs in the Post-COVID-19 Era* (pp. 133–159). IGI Global. doi:10.4018/978-1-7998-6776-0.ch007

Bolton, A., Goosen, L., & Kritzinger, E. (2021c). The Integration and Implementation of the Internet of Things Through Digital Transformation: Impact on Productivity and Innovation. In P. Tomar (Ed.), Integration and Implementation of the Internet of Things Through Cloud Computing (pp. 85-112). IGI Global. doi:10.4018/978-1-7998-6981-8.ch005

Bolton, A. D., Goosen, L., & Kritzinger, E. (2021a). Unified Communication Technologies at a Global Automotive Organization. In M. Khosrow-Pour (Ed.), *Encyclopedia of Organizational Knowledge, Administration, and Technologies* (pp. 2592–2608). IGI Global. doi:10.4018/978-1-7998-3473-1.ch179

Bolton, A. D., Goosen, L., & Kritzinger, E. (2022a). Impact of Digital Transformation via Unified Communication and Collaboration Technologies: Productivity and Innovation at a Global Enterprise. In M. Rodrigues & J. Proença (Eds.), *Impact of Digital Transformation on the Development of New Business Models and Consumer Experience* (pp. 271–298). IGI Global. doi:10.4018/978-1-7998-9179-6.ch014

Bolton, A. D., Goosen, L., & Kritzinger, E. (2022b). Emerging Technologies for Innovation and Productivity Management in the Automotive Industry: Impact of Digital Transformation on Communication. In Emerging Technologies for Innovation Management in the Software Industry (pp. 60-85). IGI Global. doi:10.4018/978-1-7998-9059-1.ch003

Bolton, A. D., Goosen, L., & Kritzinger, E. (2022c). Challenges and Emerging Strategies for a Global Automotive Enterprise Towards a Post-COVID-19 Era: The Impact of Digital Transformation. In A. Pego (Ed.), *Handbook of Research on Global Networking Post COVID-19* (pp. 76–109). IGI Global. doi:10.4018/978-1-7998-8856-7.ch005

Bolton, T., Goosen, L., & Kritzinger, E. (2020a). Security Aspects of an Empirical Study into the Impact of Digital Transformation via Unified Communication and Collaboration Technologies on the Productivity and Innovation of a Global Automotive Enterprise. Communications in Computer and Information Science, 1166, 99-113. doi:10.1007/978-3-030-43276-8_8

Buyukkeklik, A., Ozoglu, B., & Kemer, E. (2014). Buyer-supplier relationship in tourism supply chains: A research in Cappadocia Region in Turkey. *Journal of Applied Sciences*, *14*(7), 660–668. doi:10.3923/jas.2014.660.668

Devi, R., & Bharti, V. (2021, December). Analysis of Network IDS using Data Analysis tool With Python. In *3rd International Conference on Advances in Computing, Communication Control and Networking (ICAC3N)* (pp. 1357-1360). IEEE. 10.1109/ICAC3N53548.2021.9725784

Donaldson, L. (2001). The contingency theory of organizations. *Sage (Atlanta, Ga.)*.

Drazin, R., & Van de Ven, A. H. (1985). Alternative forms of fit in contingency theory. *Administrative Science Quarterly*, *30*(4), 514–539. doi:10.2307/2392695

Eriş, H., & Kemer, E. (2020). Medical Tourism Awareness of Health Workers. *Indian Journal of Forensic Medicine & Toxicology*, *14*(4), 7884–7889.

Finnan, C. (2006). *Practicing Modernity: Female Creativity in the Weimar Republic*. Königshausen & Neumann.

Gan, G. C., Chong, C. W., Yuen, Y. Y., Yen Teoh, W. M., & Rahman, M. S. (2021). Executive coaching effectiveness: Towards sustainable business excellence. *Total Quality Management & Business Excellence*, *32*(13-14), 1405–1423. doi:10.1080/14783363.2020.1724507

George, P., Coleman, B., & Barnoff, L. (2010). Stories from the field: Practicing structural social work in current times: Practitioners' use of creativity. *Critical Social Work*, *11*(2), 13–27.

Goosen, L. (2004). *Criteria and Guidelines for the Selection and Implementation of a First Programming Language in High Schools*. Potchefstroom Campus: North West University. Retrieved from http://hdl.handle.net/10394/226

Goosen, L. (2015). Educational Technologies for Growing Innovative e-Schools in the 21st Century: A Community Engagement Project. In D. Nwaozuzu, & S. Mnisi (Ed.), *Proceedings of the South Africa International Conference on Educational Technologies* (pp. 49 - 61). Pretoria: African Academic Research Forum.

Goosen, L. (2016, February 18). *"We don't need no education"? Yes, they DO want e-learning in Basic and Higher Education!* Retrieved from https://uir.unisa.ac.za/handle/10500/20999

Goosen, L. (2018a). Sustainable and Inclusive Quality Education Through Research Informed Practice on Information and Communication Technologies in Education. In L. Webb (Ed.), *Proceedings of the 26th Conference of the Southern African Association for Research in Mathematics, Science and Technology Education (SAARMSTE)* (pp. 215 - 228). University of Botswana.

Goosen, L. (2018b). Trans-Disciplinary Approaches to Action Research for e-Schools, Community Engagement, and ICT4D. In T. A. Mapotse (Ed.), *Cross-Disciplinary Approaches to Action Research and Action Learning* (pp. 97–110). IGI Global. doi:10.4018/978-1-5225-2642-1.ch006

Goosen, L. (2018c). Ethical Data Management and Research Integrity in the Context of e-Schools and Community Engagement. In C. Sibinga (Ed.), *Ensuring Research Integrity and the Ethical Management of Data* (pp. 14–45). IGI Global. doi:10.4018/978-1-5225-2730-5.ch002

Goosen, L. (2018d). Ethical Information and Communication Technologies for Development Solutions: Research Integrity for Massive Open Online Courses. In C. Sibinga (Ed.), *Ensuring Research Integrity and the Ethical Management of Data* (pp. 155–173). IGI Global. doi:10.4018/978-1-5225-2730-5.ch009

Goosen, L. (2022). Augmented/Virtual Reality Technologies and Assistive/Humanoid Robots: Students With Autism Spectrum Disorders. In S. Dhamdhere & F. Andres (Eds.), *Assistive Technologies for Differently Abled Students* (pp. 239–267). IGI Global. doi:10.4018/978-1-7998-4736-6.ch012

Goosen, L., & Mukasa-Lwanga, T. (2017). Educational Technologies in Distance Education: Beyond the Horizon with Qualitative Perspectives. In U. I. Ogbonnaya, & S. Simelane-Mnisi (Ed.), *Proceedings of the South Africa International Conference on Educational Technologies* (pp. 41 - 54). Pretoria: African Academic Research Forum.

Goosen, L., & Naidoo, L. (2014). Computer Lecturers Using Their Institutional LMS for ICT Education in the Cyber World. In C. Burger, & K. Naudé (Ed.), *Proceedings of the 43rd Conference of the Southern African Computer Lecturers' Association (SACLA)* (pp. 99-108). Nelson Mandela Metropolitan University.

Goosen, L., & Van der Merwe, R. (2015). e-Learners, Teachers and Managers at e-Schools in South Africa. In C. Watson (Ed.), *Proceedings of the 10th International Conference on e-Learning (ICEL)* (pp. 127 - 134). Nassau: Academic Conferences and Publishing International.

Gupta, S. K., Rout, P. C., & Tyagi, P. (2019). Community Based Tourism Development Amid Complex Mountain Issues: A Strategic Analysis of Chakrata Region of Uttarakhand. *International Journal of Hospitality and Tourism Systems*, *12*(1), 47–55.

Haque, A. U., Faizan, R., Zehra, N., Baloch, A., Nadda, V., & Riaz, F. (2015). Leading Leadership Style to Motivate Cultural-Oriented Female Employees in IT Sector of Developing Country: IT Sectors' Responses from Pakistan. *International Journal of Academic Research in Business & Social Sciences, 5*(9), 280–302. doi:10.6007/IJARBSS/v5-i9/1836

Hofer, C. W. (1990). Toward a contingency theory of business strategy. In *Strategische Unternehmungsplanung/Strategische Unternehmungsführung* (pp. 151–175). Physica. doi:10.1007/978-3-662-41484-2_7

Hoffmann, J., Ivcevic, Z., & Brackett, M. (2016). Creativity in the age of technology: Measuring the digital creativity of millennials. *Creativity Research Journal, 28*(2), 149–153. doi:10.1080/10400419.2016.1162515

Hui, W., & Nadda, V. (2015). Interactivity: The concept and its dimensions. In Computer-mediated marketing strategies: Social media and online brand communities (pp. 157-184). IGI Global.

Islam, J., & Hu, H. (2012). A review of literature on contingency theory in managerial accounting. *African Journal of Business Management, 6*(15), 5159–5164.

Joshi, C., Ranjan, R. K., & Bharti, V. (2021, April). ANN based Multi-Class classification of P2P Botnet. *International Journal Of Computing and Digital Systems, 11*(1), 1319–1325. doi:10.12785/ijcds/1101107

Kaur, K., & Bharti, V. (2019). A Survey on Big Data—Its Challenges and Solution from Vendors. In *Big Data Processing Using Spark in Cloud* (pp. 1–22). Springer. doi:10.1007/978-981-13-0550-4_1

Keenan, S. F., & Mishra, P. (2016). Profiling scholars of creativity: Practicing the process with Dr. Michele Root-Bernstein. *TechTrends, 60*(3), 200–203. doi:10.100711528-016-0055-2

Kemer, E. (2021a, April). The Impact of Hotel Business Managers' Innovation Abilities on Perceptions of Industry 4.0. In *Proceedings of the Conference on Managing Tourism Across Continents* (p. 99). University of South Florida M3 Center Publishing. 10.5038/9781955833011

Kemer, E. (2021b). The Role of Agricultural Products in Establishing Gastronomic Identity. *Journal of Gastronomy. Hospitality and Travel, 4*(2), 226–232.

Kemer, E. (2021c, December). The Moderating Role of Occupational Commitment in the Effect of Income Level on Job Satisfaction. *Journal of Social Sciences of Mus Alparslan University, 9*(6), 1877–1890. doi:10.18506/anemon.1003065

Kemer, E. (2022). The Relationship Between Organizational Innovation and Mobile Applications in Hotel Businesses. In *Disruptive Innovation and Emerging Technologies for Business Excellence in the Service Sector* (pp. 164–185). IGI Global. doi:10.4018/978-1-7998-9194-9.ch008

Khoo, H. H., & Tan, K. C. (2002). Using the Australian business excellence framework to achieve sustainable business excellence. *Corporate Social Responsibility and Environmental Management, 9*(4), 196–205. doi:10.1002/csr.28

Kirici Tekeli, Ü. E., Kemer, Ü. E., & Kasap, G. (2022). A Process of Meaning Creation: An Analysis of Space Tourism Posters via Semiotic Analysis. *Journal of Travel & Hospitality Management/Seyahat ve Otel Isletmeciligi Dergisi, 19*(1), 81-98.

Kristensen, K., & Westlund, A. H. (2004). Accountable business performance measurement for sustainable business excellence. *Total Quality Management & Business Excellence*, *15*(5-6), 629–643. doi:10.1080/1478336041000168011б

Kumar, R., & Bharti, V. (2021, September). A Critical Review of Finger Vein Recognition Techniques for Human Identification. In *Third International Conference on Inventive Research in Computing Applications (ICIRCA)* (pp. 1-9). IEEE. 10.1109/ICIRCA51532.2021.9544906

Luthans, F., & Stewart, T. I. (1977). A general contingency theory of management. *Academy of Management Review*, *2*(2), 181–195. doi:10.2307/257902

Mentz, E., & Goosen, L. (2007). Are groups working in the Information Technology class? *South African Journal of Education*, *27*(2), 329–343.

Nadda, V., & Arnott, I. (2020). Marketing Innovation in Tourism. In *Handbook of Research on Innovations in Technology and Marketing for the Connected Consumer* (pp. 401–415). IGI Global. doi:10.4018/978-1-7998-0131-3.ch019

Nadda, V., Chaudhary, H. S., & Arnott, I. (2020). Cloud computing in tourism. In Digital Marketing Strategies for Tourism, Hospitality, and Airline Industries (pp. 141-155). IGI Global. doi:10.4018/978-1-5225-9783-4.ch007

Nadda, V., Dadwal, S., & Rahimi, R. (Eds.). (2017). *Promotional Strategies and New Service Opportunities in Emerging Economies*. IGI Global. doi:10.4018/978-1-5225-2206-5

Nadda, V., Rafiq, Z., & Tyagi, P. (2017, Mar 3). *Effectiveness and Challenges of Recruitment process outsourcing (RPO) in the Indian Hotel Sector.* Retrieved from Munich Personal RePEc Archive: https://mpra.ub.uni-muenchen.de/77164/

Nadda, V. K., Dadwal, S. S., & Firdous, A. (2015). Social media marketing. In *Handbook of Research on Integrating Social Media into Strategic Marketing* (pp. 359–379). IGI Global. doi:10.4018/978-1-4666-8353-2.ch021

Nadda, V. K., Dadwal, S. S., Mulindwa, D., & Vieira, R. (2015). Role of social media in tourism. In *Handbook of Research on Global Hospitality and Tourism Management* (pp. 142–162). IGI Global. doi:10.4018/978-1-4666-8606-9.ch009

Otley, D. (2016). The contingency theory of management accounting and control: 1980–2014. *Management Accounting Research*, *31*, 45–62. doi:10.1016/j.mar.2016.02.001

Özkoç, A. G., & Kemer, E. (2017). The Strategic Role of Institutionalization for Accommodation Enterprises in Terms of Organizatıonal Innovation. *Gaziantep University Journal of Social Sciences*, *16*(2), 568–578.

Rahimi, R., Nadda, V., Hyseni, B., & Mulindwa, D. (2016). Motivations of South Asian students to study tourism and hospitality in the United Kingdom. *Tourism and Hospitality Management*, *12*, 223–234.

Rahimi, R., Nadda, V. K., & Wang, H. (2018). CRM in tourism: Customer relationship management (CRM). In Digital Marketing and Consumer Engagement: Concepts, Methodologies, Tools, and Applications (pp. 928-955). IGI Global.

Schoonhoven, C. B. (1981, September). Problems with contingency theory: Testing assumptions hidden within the language of contingency "theory". *Administrative Science Quarterly, 26*(3), 349–377. doi:10.2307/2392512 PMID:10252610

Sharma, M., Ranjan, R. K., & Bharti, V. (2021, July). A new image encryption algorithm using a bit shifted logistic map. In *12th International Conference on Computing Communication and Networking Technologies (ICCCNT)* (pp. 1-5). IEEE. 10.1109/ICCCNT51525.2021.9580146

Sharma, R., & Bharti, V. (2021, December). A Review Towards Machine Learning Spectrum for Bioinformatics. In *3rd International Conference on Advances in Computing, Communication Control and Networking (ICAC3N)* (pp. 199-202). IEEE. 10.1109/ICAC3N53548.2021.9725652

Singh, A. K., Tyagi, P. K., Jain, E., Tyagi, P., Singh, A. K., & Sharma, N. (2022, March). Robotics and Artificial Intelligence in Hospitality Sector: A Descriptive Bibliometric Analysis and Future Research Directions. In *International Conference on Electronics and Renewable Systems (ICEARS)* (pp. 1484-1491). IEEE. 10.1109/ICEARS53579.2022.9752272

Singh, A. K., Tyagi, P. K., & Tyagi, P. (2021). Evaluation of sustainable tourism practices in the state of Bihar, India. *E3S Web of Conferences. 296.* doi:10.1051/e3sconf/202129605013

Sørensen, B. M. (2008). 'Behold, I am making all things new': The entrepreneur as savior in the age of creativity. *Scandinavian Journal of Management, 24*(2), 85–93. doi:10.1016/j.scaman.2008.03.002

Suyidno, S., Susilowati, E., Arifuddin, M., Sunarti, T., Siswanto, J., & Rohman, A. (2020, March). Barriers to scientific creativity of physics teacher in practicing creative product design. *Journal of Physics: Conference Series, 1491*(1), 012048. Advance online publication. doi:10.1088/1742-6596/1491/1/012048

Tarter, C. J., & Hoy, W. K. (1998). Toward a contingency theory of decision making. *Journal of Educational Administration, 36*(3), 212–228. doi:10.1108/09578239810214687

Tosi, H. L. Jr, & Slocum, J. W. Jr. (1984). Contingency theory: Some suggested directions. *Journal of Management, 10*(1), 9–26. doi:10.1177/014920638401000103

Tyagi, P., Tyagi, P. K., Singh, A. K., Jain, E., & Singh, A. K. (2022, March). Tourist Experiences Through Mobile Augmented Reality. In *International Conference on Electronics and Renewable Systems (ICEARS)* (pp. 1605-1610). IEEE. 10.1109/ICEARS53579.2022.9752325

Tyagi, P. K., & Gupta, S. K. (2019, March). Recruitment and Selection Process in Travel Trade Organisations of Chandigarh: An Evaluation. *Journal of Emerging Technologies and Innovative Research, 6*(3), 787–794.

Tyagi, P. K., Singh, A. K., Singh, D. V., & Tyagi, P. (2021). The Role of Social Crowdsourcing in Mobile Tourism. *Journal of Contemporary Issues in Business and Government, 27*(3), 149–161.

Tyagi, P. K., Singh, A. K., Tyagi, P., & Singh, V. (2021). A Study on Tourist Perception Towards Usage of Mobile Wallet. *Turkish Journal of Computer and Mathematics Education, 12*(13), 1–8.

Tyagi, P. K., & Tyagi, P. (2022). Customer Perception and Brand Image Through Sensory Marketing. In *Disruptive Innovation and Emerging Technologies for Business Excellence in the Service Sector* (pp. 41–68). IGI Global. doi:10.4018/978-1-7998-9194-9.ch003

Van de Ven, A. H., & Drazin, R. (1984). *The concept of fit in contingency theory.* Retrieved from Minnesota University Minneapolis strategic management research center: https://apps.dtic.mil/sti/pdfs/ADA152603.pdf

Chapter 13
Cybersecurity Strategy, Formulation, Management, and Sustainability Issues in Digital Transformation and Sustainability

Gurinder Pal Singh
https://orcid.org/0000-0003-2820-8498
Chandigarh University, India

Vishal Bharti
Chandigarh University, India

Manish Kumar Hooda
Semiconductor Laboratory, India

ABSTRACT

Digitalization of financial services has stimulated regulatory and regulatory concerns, technological progress, new capacities and client expectations, and has exposed the sector to competition. A dramatic, expensive, and risky turning moment challenged the conventional banking industry's viability. However, some safety and ethical difficulties still exist when it comes to the adaptation of business sustainability. Global transformation, harmonization, and convergence will be expanded, turning financial services into intelligent services in the services sector. The editorial argues that for digital transformation, we must first expand our understanding of the interactions and interrelationships that contribute to knowledge, creativity, and value creation among society's participants. Cybersecurity is a modern topic that is becoming a major concern owing to the epidemic in the industrial and service sectors. This research exposes cybersecurity strategy, formulation, management, sustainability issues, and organizational and corporate culture management in digital transformation.

DOI: 10.4018/978-1-6684-6732-9.ch013

Copyright © 2023, IGI Global. Copying or distributing in print or electronic forms without written permission of IGI Global is prohibited.

INTRODUCTION

Crimes committed online and online attacks are among the most pressing and significant challenges facing our modern digital world (Akhgar, 2014). The unprecedented circumstances resulting from COVID-19 and the pandemic have brought the state of the global economy to the forefront of the operational procedures carried out by businesses. Through digital transformation, digital aspects, which are becoming ever more significant, will continue to be represented in everyday corporate life. An increase in the number of cyber assaults has occurred as a direct result of the growing influence that digital technologies have on businesses' managerial and strategic practices. According to (Ismail et al., 2020), malicious assaults and cyber criminals negatively impact the economy of the entire world by stealing secret and valuable information from organizations. According to (Hellström, 2007), the problems that are caused by cyber-attacks and the systemic vulnerabilities of enterprises call for the creation, harmonization, and enhancement of management and strategy. Taking precautions in the realm of cybersecurity in the context of human resources, operations, sales, after-sales services, promotion, and the provision of competitive advantage has emerged as an important requirement for management and strategy in modern enterprises

This chapter contributes to the corpus of knowledge by bringing to light the necessities of today's digital world. These criteria include increasing management and strategy, establishing digital and cyber protection strategies, and correcting digital transformation gaps. The eradication of cyberattacks, which now harm today's global economy and organizations, as well as the weaknesses caused by digital transformation, is a topical concern, and the chapter concentrates on this subject explicitly. Along these lines, points like computerized change, the impacts of online protection on organizations, information and data security, application and programming security, organization and correspondence security, functional security, digital methodology advancement, feasible preparation and transformation, network safety dangers, cybercrime, cyber terrorism, digital administration, and system issues are talked about in this part.

RESEARCH METHODOLOGY

A process called systematic review was used to put up this study. The steps involved in conducting a systematic review are as follows: preparation for the study; data collection; analysis of data; assessment of data; implications; and reporting ('Book Review', 2006). The consequences of cybercrime on management and strategy served as a major source of motivation for the writing of this chapter. Cyberattacks pose a danger to both the global economy and enterprises throughout the world. The issue of cybersecurity is currently prevalent and is evolving into a significant risk. The problem is getting worse as a result of the pandemic that has swept across the industrial and service industries. Given this background, the following research topics were selected for the investigation:

- R1. What kinds of consequences can poor cybersecurity have for businesses?
- R2. What are the components that go into the creation of a cyber-strategy for businesses?
- R3. What are some ways in which organizations could improve their cyber management and strategy?

After the examination questions were laid out, the accompanying terms were picked as the catchphrases for the writing audit led in scholastic data sets (Google researcher, Web of Science, Emerald

Insight, and Taylor and Francis): the executives, system, the board and procedure, digital, digital assault, cybercrime, network safety, computerized change, advanced administration, and computerized methodology. During the quest for watchwords, a sum of 214 articles that were straightforwardly pertinent to the subject was gotten to. It required close to about fourteen days to finish the exploration, examination, and report composing.

Following the completion of the literature review, the following procedures for the information gathered from academic databases were carried out in the study: summarising, classifying, extracting data, discussing, categorizing, and presenting the findings (Briner et al., 2009). Following these processes, the names of the articles and the material that were found to be relevant to the investigated issue were determined and reported.

CYBER-MANAGEMENT AND STRATEGY

It is vital to take steps in this direction as a result of the fact that cyber assaults and threats are increasingly hurting the businesses and organizations of today. The adoption of a cyber-management and strategy approach provides crucial safety precautions that are necessary to fulfil the requirements of digital transformation and innovation (Boeke, 2018). Digital administration and procedure approaches offer extra benefits in a wide range of spaces, including the administration of HR, computerized client bookkeeping, virtual showcasing, virtual advancement, web-based preparing and correspondence, internet buying and instalment, advanced functional exchanges, computerized obtainment and coordinated factors the board, and advanced after-deals administration arrangement.

The cyber approach is beneficial to management and strategy in that it generates substantial momentum in the areas of human resources and operational management. In terms of performance in terms of human resources policy, it is crucial to ensure that all of the devices and systems that have been introduced into the organization as part of the digital transformation are running efficiently. The protection of workers' and candidates' personal information is contingent on the state of cybersecurity (L. A. Gordon et al., 2016). On the other hand, to maintain a competitive edge and ensure the company's long-term viability, it is vital to ensure the safety of sensitive information, such as that about the company's environment, culture, organizational structure, and research and development initiatives. (Hines, 1993) (Obermayer et al., 2022) It is important to coordinate network safety into the administration and methodology of the endeavour in the execution of essential (inbound and outbound strategies, tasks, advertising and deals, administration) and backing (firm foundation, HR the board, innovation, acquisition) exercises. The making of the organization's technique because of the continually moving developments and perils presented by advanced innovation assists with upgrading the worth chain.

Cybersecurity Threats

Apps designed to safeguard users against the potentially destructive consequences of malicious software running on smart and digital devices, computers and servers, electronic systems, and networks are known as cybersecurity applications. Because they pose a risk to information security throughout the internet and the electronic network, these applications might result in significant monetary and physical losses. The security of an organization's operations, networks, applications, information, long-term viability, and long-term strategy are all dependent on cybersecurity.

As per (Ben-Asher & Gonzalez, 2015), firms that succumb to malevolent assaults that jeopardize their online protection, like social designing, ransomware, refusal of administration assaults, and distributed computing weakness attacks, experience money-related misfortunes. These attacks, which are taking place in a worldwide environment, generate severe restrictions and vulnerabilities in the commercial world of today, which is becoming increasingly reliant on digital gadgets. In the context of management strategy, the vulnerabilities of firms are frequently found to be their exposure to cybersecurity risks (Razzaq et al., 2013). Techniques such as phishing and scareware are used in social engineering to gain control of the digital connection points that constitute social media accounts, e-blogs, and emails. These digital connection points create the communication link that businesses have with their consumers (Krombholz et al., 2015).

These attacks, which are designed to exploit vulnerabilities in human psychology, have a deleterious impact on the management and operational activities of enterprises. Encrypting software is what we refer to as ransomware (Brewer, 2016). The release of tainted data is contingent on satisfying the hackers' demand for money. These hackers have their sights set on a variety of establishments, including hospitals, governmental institutions, organizations, and corporations. An assault known as a denial-of-service is carried out when a host's network service is either momentarily or indefinitely disrupted by the transmission of unnecessary requests to the host's computers (Carl et al., 2006). These kinds of assaults are directed at payment gateways, banks, applications for processing credit card payments, and web servers that host payment application websites (Fu et al., 2016). The following is a list of the most often found cloud computing vulnerabilities and attacks: Breach of contract issues about the company network, lock-in with cloud service providers, and control issues relating to this matter.

When it comes to major corporations, cybersecurity risks can arise from a variety of sources: supply chain participants, halt and catch-fire scenarios; illegal takeover; weak passwords; worm and virus infections; crypto-ransomware attacks; employee mistakes; industrial software errors; sabotage; and insufficient cyber security policies. Some of these risks are listed below. Malicious attacks have the most significant impact on small and medium-sized businesses (Hutchinson & Warren, 2003). Mainly due to the extremely restricted financing source that these firms devote to their cybersecurity efforts. On the other side, one of the key focuses of the assault is on huge corporations and holdings in particular. One of the primary targets of the assault is the financial sector, specifically banks, financial institutions, intelligence agencies, and telecommunications corporations (Bendovschi, 2015) (Lanier Watkins, 2016).

Cybercrime

Assaults that include unapproved admittance to data frameworks through PC and web organizations, like surveillance, monetary robbery, catching information, burglary of monetary information and passwords, obstructing the utilization of the framework and signing in, hindering or postponing correspondence, and unapproved recording of correspondence are instances of exercises that fall under the classification of cybercrime (Ross Anderson, Chris Barton, et al., 2013). These kinds of assaults entail infringing on a person's personal and financial rights by invading their right to privacy in their private and professional lives within the framework of international and regional law (McQuade, 2006). On the other hand, it's possible that these offenses were committed by members of the company's staff. Information forgery that leads to unfair competition is included in the category of cybercrime. These kinds of assaults allow third parties to get access to a company's confidential business information, as well as details about a project or proposals that will be put out in competitive bids.

Phishing, hate speech, hacking, and digital pornography are all forms of cybercrime that are increasingly being committed against organizations. These are carried out to cause harm to the reputation of organizations, of obtaining sensitive information, and of disclosing the financial information of the firm. In some forms of cybercrime, such as typologies, an attempt is made to illegally obtain secret information by going through a company's corporate website and various computer networks.

Cyberterrorism

The term "cyber terrorism" refers to assaults on computer networks and the internet that are carried out to wreak severe havoc on the moral fabric of communities, nations, and mankind as a whole (S. Gordon & Ford, 2006). These assaults are being carried out to inflict harm on the targets that have been selected by activating the action plans of terrorist groups (Weimann, 2005). Cyberterrorism in general does not target people. However, in the pursuit of their goals, terrorist organizations may aim their attention toward the leaders of nations or communities (B. Collin, 1997). It's possible that a nation's oil or chemical sector was the target of a cyberattack launched against the production capacity of a firm or holding company. This objective is especially clear in the case of cyberattacks directed at certain businesses that play a significant part in the export capability of the country. Digital psychological oppression can have serious repercussions, including insurgency, savagery, social distress, financial and political precariousness, and even a death toll (Chen et al., 2020). It is urgent for organizations who work with public foundations or proposition their administrations to people in general through offers to make the fitting moves in this regard (Dorothy E. Denning, 2001).

Digital Transformation

The construction of solutions by using digital components in the context of addressing societal, organizational, sectoral, workplace, and corporate demands is what we mean when we talk about digital transformation (Matt et al., 2015). These attributes are orchestrated with the advanced parts of hierarchical organizing, functional cycles, data organizations, correspondence, authoritative culture, business culture, hierarchical environment, schooling, flexibility, and numerous different difficulties. W Regarding usefulness, synchronizing the advanced angles with the association and the parts of the business is fundamental. The change to computerized makes significant commitments to the association's design as well as the organizations' associations with the outer climate and their inward working (Vial, 2019).

In light of advanced change, representative preparation in human assets the board, the executives of the enrolment cycle, assurance of qualified worker rules, online tests, data set administration connected with educational program vitae, work commitment and necessities review applications, and utilization of virtual entertainment have all been affected (Vardarlier, 2020). This impact is huge as far as the representatives' capacity to change by the gig and the workspace, as well as their capacity to exploit professional possibilities. Workers can work somewhat in pandemics and strange circumstances on account of computerized change, which likewise works with the transmission of data in representative pioneer correspondence and commitment. While an arising innovation is coordinated into the current mechanical framework of an organization or association, it empowers data and criticism to be communicated and gathered speedily and powerfully. Along these lines, the progress of computerized components into parts of HR the board well affects the adequacy of organizations.

In the present climate, the stock of unrefined substances, assembling, and coordinated operations all benefit from the utilization of advanced assets. Among the perceived utilizations of the Industrial Internet of Things (IIoT) are producing advances. These assembling advances incorporate shrewd robots, modern savvy glasses, expanded reality, miniature framework development, wearable innovation, brilliant oil field trailblazer, and Wi-Fi network organization (O'Neill, 2014). These applications offer various advantages, some of which remember expanded efficiency and execution for assembling; further developed quality in correspondence organizations; a decrease in reliance on labor supply; development; time reserve funds; counteraction of work squander; and worked on word-related well-being and security. IIoT industry 4.0 is otherwise called the advanced plant and shrewd assembling (Bradac et al., 2019). These are both names for the same concept. Solutions that have been developed specifically for the operational use of data can be used to do real-time analytics. When many tasks are combined into one, complicated functions can be simplified to a more manageable form. These innovations produce significant results that are relevant to management and strategy. As a result, expenses are cut and the amount of time it takes to get items to market is cut down. Improvements in terms of safety, efficiency, and performance may be made in the production system as a result of the implementation of IIoT and digital transformation.

As per (Michael Schneier, Michael Schneier, Roger Bostelman, 2015), robot gadgets and computerization give critical data to the creation and arranging group with regards to shortcomings underway, botch estimates, and cause-impact surmising. This technical and digital revolution allows for improvements to be made to the product's quality, as well as error-free manufacturing in the areas of measurement and molds, as well as assembly, and more sustainable production. The intricacy of the information and the examination of a wide variety of criteria both contribute to the major challenges that are presented in terms of management. A huge number of assets that are a part of the manufacturing process may now be controlled in a manner that is both professional and strategic thanks to the IIoT's complexity. The Industrial Internet of Things allows for improvements in turnover, efficiency, and constraint management (Boyes et al., 2018).

Cybersecurity's Effects on Business

The protection of data, servers, mobile devices, electronic systems, computers, and networks against unauthorized access or use is referred to as cybersecurity (Kemmerer, 2003). Applications and software are responsible for providing this level of defence. These programs and software guarantee the protection of information technology and the eradication of security dangers that have emerged as a result of the technological revolution. In addition to this, it offers specific information on potential dangers, the intensity, and breadth of the attack, the type of software used, and the level of encryption used during the assault (Lezzi et al., 2018). In light of this, tactical countermeasures can be implemented to defend the company's network from harmful assaults that are being planned. Cybersecurity ensures the safety of software that allows for remote control through mobile computing (Ten et al., 2010). Information and data security, application and programming security, organization and correspondence security, functional security, digital technique creation, and economical preparation and transformation are the six essential foci of network protection (Management Association, 2018) (See Figure 1).

Data and Information Security

Data and information guarantee the maintainability of the business and its inward working, stream in the execution of the procedure, correspondence between units, congruity of relations with the outside climate, execution underway and arranging, correspondence in obtainment and operations, quality in absolute proficiency and execution, corporate cooperative energy, and the improvement of proactive ways of behaving (Bojanc & Jerman-Blažič, 2008). Within the framework of the operational operations of the company, maintaining the data's integrity as accurately as possible is an essential aspect that must be guarded. Cybersecurity safeguards the data that is necessary for making decisions that are both time-sensitive and directed toward the future, including those about performance, efficiency, production, marketing, sales, customer volume, and future customers. Facts that a company has learned about either from the outside or the inside of the company are examples of information. It is essential to have access to relevant information when working in a learning organization (Chatterjee, 1995). Through the use of information, decisions are made on the long-term and short-term implementation of things like strategy development, planning, and tactics. Because of this, ensuring the safety of sensitive company information is vitally crucial while making choices in the workplace. There is a strong connection between the data, which is successful in the operational administration of the organization, and the information, which is effective in the making of strategic choices. Therefore, threats, dangers, and security vulnerabilities that arise in the data and information security of a business can create severe damage in the settings of financial management, strategic planning, and managerial oversight.

Data and information guarantee the manageability of the business and its inward working, progression of relations with the outside climate, execution underway and arranging, correspondence in obtainment and strategies, quality in all-out proficiency and execution, corporate cooperative energy, and the advancement of proactive ways of behaving. Information uprightness is a fundamental perspective that should be shielded about functional business processes. Network safety safeguards the information that is valuable for settling on constant and future-arranged choices, like execution, effectiveness, creation, showcasing, deals, client volume, and future clients.

Data comprises outside or inward business climate-determined realities. Significant data can be gotten through learning associations. Data is utilized to go with choices in regards to long-and momentary execution, including methodology configuration, arranging, and strategies. Therefore data security is fundamental for business independent direction. Viable information for the functional organization of a business is straightforwardly attached to compelling data for settling on essential choices. Subsequently, dangers, risks, and security weaknesses that emerge in the information and data security of a business can result in huge monetary, vital, and executive misfortunes.

Figure 1. Functions of cybersecurity
Source: (Management Association, 2018)

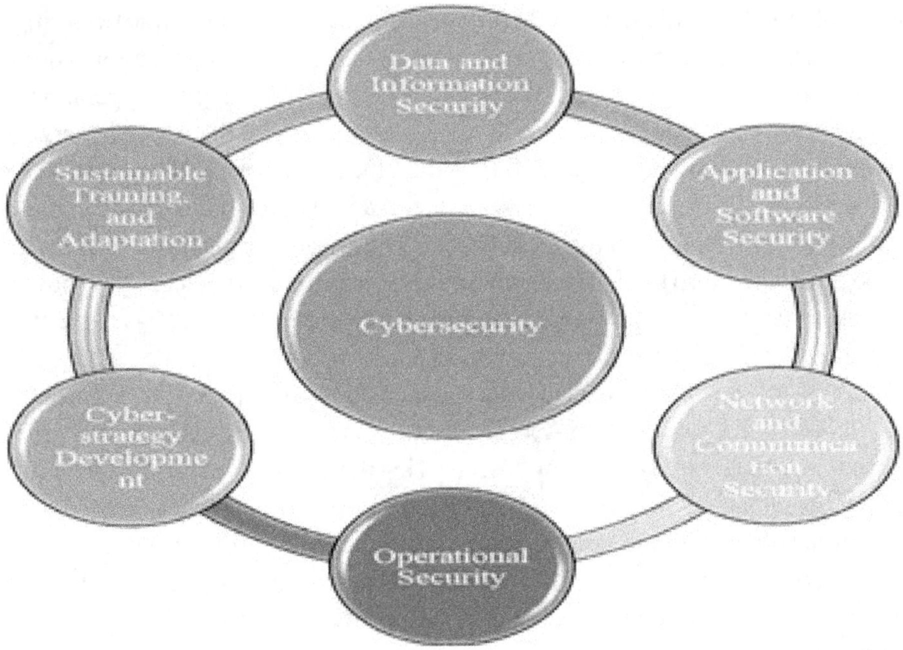

Application and Software Security

Applications and programming that have been compromised risk the usefulness of advanced components. This danger can bring about the noteworthy of proprietary innovations, the capture of staff and administration data, and harm to creation and administration capacities brought about by IoT and IIoT. In the creation, refreshing, and the executives of programming and applications, it is important to take security against digital dangers. Considering present-day PC infections and cyberattacks, organizations must do redesigns and reviews to guarantee their security (Cass, 2001).

The assembling, arranging, and strategies exercises of organizations depend intensely on applications and programming. Safeguarding these components against digital dangers is pivotal and fundamental for on-time item conveyance to clients, subsequently guaranteeing execution and effectiveness. These innovative applications and programming are as of now used in modern robots.

Cobots (Cooperative Robots) created for human-robot collaboration are used in mechanical computerization. These mechanically pertinent innovations include joint effort, reasonableness for risk investigation, light and minimal development, a little impression, adaptability, low energy utilization, an incorporated power and force sensor, and straightforward combination into independent vehicles (Automated Guided Vehicles). Cooperative robots (CoBots) can turn on all tomahawks at 360 degrees and don't need routine support (UR3 and UR3e-6th hub). These robots are furnished with transport following, force control, palletizing, catapulting, g-code programming connection points, and internet preparation. Despite these highlights, seventeen strong, adjustable inbuilt safety efforts stay lacking to safeguard against cyber threats (Cherubini et al., 2016). Because of their advantageous results, especially in the assembling area, and network protection dangers, robots and programming should be ceaselessly refreshed and outfitted with specific security safeguards. Conceivable digital attacks on the product and data frameworks of cobots and modern robots might disturb creation by imperilling representative security. Explicitly in the controller and the board through the Internet organization, this present circumstance might emerge. Programming weaknesses in robot refresh present grave risks. Thus, it is fundamental to analyze the linkages between the tasks of cobots ahead of time, distinguish security blemishes, and take the required digital precautionary measures.

Numerous ventures, including food, rural, metal, car, power, gadgets, innovation, plastic, polymer, furniture, medication, science, lab, cooking, and coordinated factors, are altogether affected by IIoT and cobots programming weaknesses. This situation influences an assortment of capacities, including supply, coordinated operations, administration, and assembling. In this situation, client satisfaction and interest in items and administrations both downfall. On the opposite side, these applications and organizations that keep representatives from performing dangerous exercises increment the danger to employer stability. Word-related mishaps might result from expected mechanical robotization and IIoT security chances. (Bayram, Ünan, and Ardc, 2017) found that these applications, which furnish representatives with a protected working environment, can diminish worker bliss inferable from potential digital risks.

Network and Communication Security

A standard collection of communication protocols is utilized by a computer network. According to (Nguyen et al., 2015), the tool that facilitates the connecting of computers to one another also facilitates the flow of information through digital interconnections and network nodes. Therefore, it is possible to keep communication flowing between the headquarters and the branches. Technology advancements in the form of wired and wireless networking provide a major advance for this communication (Flammini et al., 2009). Even though these networks make it possible for devices to communicate with one another, they are also vulnerable to serious cyberattacks. According to Stallings's research from 1996, Internet protocol (IP) plays a significant role in the process of transferring packets to their respective destination IP addresses. During the process of routing datagrams and encapsulating data into datagrams, these functions may expose themselves to vulnerabilities. The deployment of protocols and the development of security measures against cyber threats are required for the transfer of the IP header and IP data to the transport stage. This transition depends on IoT playing an active part in the process. These dangers may manifest themselves in the protocols used for communication during the control of network traffic.

Operational Security

To get data packets to their intended IP addresses, the Internet Protocol (IP) is required. These routines may be exposed to vulnerabilities during the routing and encapsulation of datagrams (Jaiswal et al., 2021). As a prerequisite for the Internet of Things (IoT) to play an active role in transmitting headers and data to the transport stage, cyber security measures must be taken and protocols must be implemented. Protocols used to communicate during network traffic control may introduce these concerns. Synced devices, such as printers, fax machines, digital cameras, and other smart gadgets, inherit the computer network's security flaws. It is necessary to protect the storage servers of the devices from security breaches induced by the hazards and threats outlined above. It is crucial to secure network-connected devices from cybercriminals in the context of information security, the preservation of trade secrets, and the long-term viability of organizations. Interaction between machines and the Internet of Things

(IoT) are critical components of smart manufacturing systems' production processes. Digital communication technology, cloud computing, and artificial intelligence are all examples of these technologies. In contrast, harmful malware and ransomware are vying for the attention of users of these technologies. Hence, innovation and security strategies must be realized to prevent any dangers and hazards that may arise as a result of an absence of security.

Cyber-Strategy Development

Innovations in the field of production technology have led to the development of new methods for increasing production capacity, better using corporate resources, and using the cloud to manufacture products rather than constructing them from scratch (Chaudhuri et al., 2021). The traditional creation assets engaged with the production, improvement, and plan of the item might be changed into an ongoing creation configuration utilizing this innovation. Exercises like preparation, directing, detailing, and controlling creation limits and orders are helped out through the utilization of cloud fabricating. Notwithstanding, these improvements accompany a serious level of hazard as far as cyber criminals. Digital transformation, software and update issues, as well as corporate software integration all represent significant threats to the security of computer networks and information systems.

Organizations may suffer severe costs if design models are stolen by cybercriminals. Cyberattacks can expose critical information about the organization, such as customer data, financial data, suppliers, and distribution routes, which can hurt the company's long-term success. Data on client portfolios, company secrets, profitability, and efficiency, as well as financial information and distribution channels, are some of the elements that go into this analysis. If the company is unable to retain its position in the market as a consequence of this, it will lose its competitive advantage. As a result, the business must devise proactive defences against potential cyber-attacks. In the end, the company's total cyber strategy may be summarised by the proactive defence tactics described above. Each of these has been described in detail below: It is imperative that you: 1) Keep tabs on the situation, 2) Pay attention to your senses, 3) Develop countermeasures, 4) Prepare for potential threats, and 5) Improve your system to withstand future attacks (Özsungur, 2021) (Figure 2).

Figure 2. Businesses' cyber-strategy factors
Source: (Özsungur, 2021)

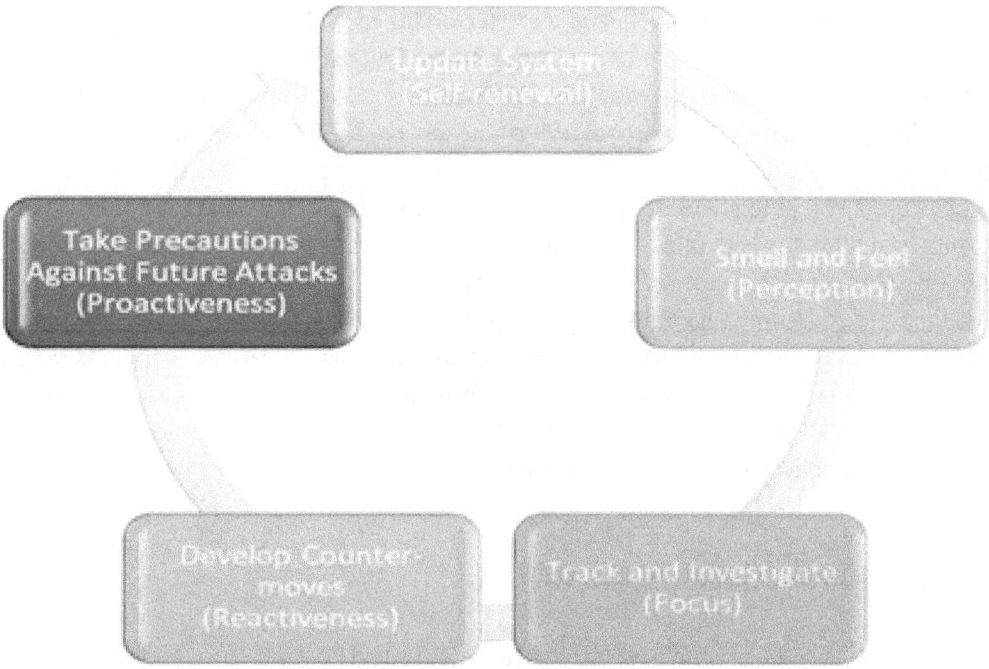

Sustainable Training, and Adaptation

Employees, executives, stakeholders, customers, consumers, suppliers, and sector representatives are all examples of those who get strategic knowledge in the context of management and strategy through the process of training. Topics like corporate cause-effect interactions, innovation, environmental analysis (OBRRTA), entrepreneurship, technology, and digital transformation are all examples of this type of knowledge transfer taking place in the context of connections between individuals and corporations. In today's increasingly digital environment, a company's strategic management must include education on the threats posed by cyberattacks.

The procedures and principles associated with growing technology and digital transformation must be taken into account by the managerial strategies that are implemented. Even though the strategies are a collection of long-term goals, they nevertheless need to be adapted to the circumstances of the emerging world. The process of adaptation that is necessitated by digital transformation calls for the use of software and innovative thinking. Specifically, the digital demands that surfaced during the pandemic time illustrate this necessity in a very obvious way. When dealing with extreme situations like pandemics, virtual applications and online education become increasingly important. Education on compliance in digital transformation and cyber threats is necessary for ensuring employee-leader interaction, developing customer-business relations, maintaining a competitive advantage, the business's ability to sustain its competitive advantage, promotion strategies, sustainability in strategic management, strategic human resources management, the development of customer-business relations, and the business's ability to maintain its competitive advantage.

It is essential, about the protection of sensitive information, to educate workers on the potential dangers posed by the use of digital devices and online threats. Employees should get ongoing instruction on such issues as cybercrime, cyberattack, and cyberterrorism, as well as cybersecurity safeguards and emergency response plans. Topics such as password protection, avoiding clicking on links in e-mails that contain suspicious and harmful software, and information security should be included in the training material. 2011-2016 eLearning Industry.com. All rights reserved. Employees should be kept informed at all times about the procedures that should be carried out and the precautions that should be taken to secure the business's computers and personal accounts from acts of espionage and theft of corporate funds. It is important that some of this training be done in a practical setting. On the other hand, people who work in the information technology department have to be put through training that is distinct from that of other employees. During this training, participants should be instructed on the best practices for safeguarding sensitive and essential business data, such as a company's servers, software, confidential business information, data, customer and employee information, and supplier details. Through the protection of the company's databases and trade secrets, sustainable training ensures that the company will continue to be profitable in the face of any potential cyber assaults.

SOLUTIONS AND RECOMMENDATIONS

Attacks on computers over the internet and criminal activity online pose a risk to modern enterprises and the economy as a whole. Even though these dangers represent the shortcomings of organizations, they are crucial risk factors in the context of operations and management. As a result, it is essential to fortify the company's infrastructure for the protection of information and data. Because of the security openings that are presented by computerized change, the authoritative setting of network protection requires coordination and cooperation in the association between the divisions of the association. The security of PCs and organizations ought to be gotten all through the formation of cooperative activities, as well as during inside correspondence and correspondence. Then again, with regards to business foundation, both programming overhauls and new programming ought to be viewed as to build up the framework.

Programmed bundling frameworks, Gircontrol in addition to bundling, new CA-9S, RS 485, HUB Box, Modbus (RTU, TCP), and Industry 4.0 ought to all incorporate programming that shields them from digital assaults (Fovino et al., 2009); (Huitsing et al., 2008). With regards to data security, the insurance of proprietary innovations, and the functional manageability of organizations, fundamental to safeguard gadgets that have a correspondence interface through the network from being undermined by cyber criminals. Avoiding potential risk ought to be finished in an essential way given that the progress of the IP header and IP information, in which IoT assumes a functioning part, to the vehicle stage relies upon going to security lengths against digital dangers and carrying out conventions.

Since spam posts and connections partook in remarks might contain malware, workers ought to get continuous preparation on the potential dangers presented by these sorts of content, as well as security conventions, recent concerns, the venture's framework foundation, IIoT, and network frameworks, the end of safety weaknesses, new age digital assault types, and pernicious programming. If a cyberattack happens, it means quite a bit to save, back up, and secure managerial records, papers containing proprietary innovations, information connecting with creation and arranging, as well as data on clients and partners.

The stockpiling upholding of information must be finished on servers furnished with trustworthy programming. Section/Cell-Level Encryption, which gives encryption in the data set, Transparent Data

Encryption (TDE), which assumes a basic part in the encryption of circles, and reinforcement Encryption, which encodes SQL reinforcements, are basic SQL Server capabilities in network safety, and they should be safeguarded by online protection programming. Straightforward Data Encryption (TDE) assumes a basic part in the encryption of plates (Coles & Landrum, 2009); (Wiese et al., 2020). The level of information that workers have concerning surveillance and monetary burglary ought to be raised, and PCs and individual records that should have a place with the association be sufficiently safeguarded against both of these dangers. Then again, workers of the data innovation division ought to get particular expert preparation that is unmistakable from that which is given to different representatives, and the privacy of delicate information, for example, encryption connected with the organization's network safety, ought to be secured.

Game plans for managing crises, for example, cyberattacks, ought to be created by firms' HR executives and other vital divisions. It is prompted that a few divisions, for example, creation arranging, advertising, acquirement, and operations cooperate to deliver these activity plans. In crisis activity plans, thought ought to be given to various worries, including the chance of digital assaults, the presence of mechanical weaknesses, and the need of protecting and backing up data sets containing clients' secret data.

CONCLUSION

An important goal of this chapter was to inspire corporate leaders to think creatively about how they may protect themselves against the onslaught of new forms of cybercrime and cyberattacks that are on the rise. With this chapter's conclusions, we learn how to reduce the dangers, risks, and vulnerabilities that come with the digital transformation of firms, which is a critical component of global economic and free market dynamics. These crucial ideas are exposed even though this is not an empirical study. According to the conclusions of this study, six unique functions are the major focus of cybersecurity. Additionally, they are responsible for data and information protection as well as the establishment of cyber strategies as well as the development of sustainable training and adaptation. Other parts of cyber-strategy that should be taken into account, according to the findings, include things like the ability to "perceive" (smell and feel), "track" (examine), "make counter-moves," and "take measures against future assaults."

REFERENCES

Akhgar, B. (2014). *Cyber crime and cyber terrorism investigator's handbook.* Elsevier.

Anderson, R. (2013). *Chris Barton, et al.* Measuring the Cost of Cybercrime. doi:10.1007/978-3-642-39498-0__12

Ben-Asher, N., & Gonzalez, C. (2015). Effects of cyber security knowledge on attack detection. *Computers in Human Behavior*, *48*, 51–61. doi:10.1016/j.chb.2015.01.039

Bendovschi, A. (2015). Cyber-Attacks – Trends, Patterns and Security Countermeasures. *Procedia Economics and Finance*, *28*, 24–31. doi:10.1016/S2212-5671(15)01077-1

Boeke, S. (2018). National cyber crisis management: Different European approaches. *Governance: An International Journal of Policy, Administration and Institutions*, *31*(3), 449–464. doi:10.1111/gove.12309

Bojanc, R., & Jerman-Blažič, B. (2008). An economic modelling approach to information security risk management. *International Journal of Information Management*, *28*(5), 413–422. doi:10.1016/j.ijinfomgt.2008.02.002

Boyes, H., Hallaq, B., Cunningham, J., & Watson, T. (2018). The industrial internet of things (IIoT): An analysis framework. *Computers in Industry*, *101*, 1–12. doi:10.1016/j.compind.2018.04.015

Bradac, Z., Marcon, P., Zezulka, F., Arm, J., & Benesl, T. (2019). Digital Twin and AAS in the Industry 4.0 Framework. *IOP Conference Series. Materials Science and Engineering*, *618*(1), 012001. doi:10.1088/1757-899X/618/1/012001

Brewer, R. (2016). Ransomware attacks: Detection, prevention and cure. *Network Security*, *2016*(9), 5–9. doi:10.1016/S1353-4858(16)30086-1

Briner, R. B., Denyer, D., & Rousseau, D. M. (2009). Evidence-Based Management: Concept Cleanup Time? *The Academy of Management Perspectives*, *23*(4), 19–32. doi:10.5465/AMP.2009.45590138

Carl, G., Kesidis, G., Brooks, R. R., & Suresh Rai. (2006). Denial-of-service attack-detection techniques. *IEEE Internet Computing*, *10*(1), 82–89. doi:10.1109/MIC.2006.5

Cass, S. (2001). Anatomy of malice [computer viruses]. *IEEE Spectrum*, *38*(11), 56–60. doi:10.1109/6.963235

Chatterjee, D. (1995). Book Reviews: Peter M. Senge, The Fifth Discipline: The Art and Practice of the Learning Organ ization. New York: Doubleday, 1990, pp. viii + 424, Rs 415. *Journal of Human Values*, *1*(1), 146–149. doi:10.1177/097168589500100115

Chaudhuri, A., Datta, P. P., Fernandes, K. J., & Xiong, Y. (2021). Optimal pricing strategies for manufacturing-as-a service platforms to ensure business sustainability. *International Journal of Production Economics*, *234*, 108065. doi:10.1016/j.ijpe.2021.108065

Chen, L., Yue, D., Dou, C., Chen, J., & Cheng, Z. (2020). Study on attack paths of cyber attack in cyber-physical power systems. *IET Generation, Transmission & Distribution*, *14*(12), 2352–2360. doi:10.1049/iet-gtd.2019.1330

Cherubini, A., Passama, R., Crosnier, A., Lasnier, A., & Fraisse, P. (2016). Collaborative manufacturing with physical human–robot interaction. *Robotics and Computer-integrated Manufacturing*, *40*, 1–13. doi:10.1016/j.rcim.2015.12.007

Coles, M., & Landrum, R. (2009). Asymmetric Encryption. In Expert SQL Server 2008 Encryption (pp. 73–110). Apress. doi:10.1007/978-1-4302-3365-7_4

Collin, B. (1997, March). Future of Cyberterrorism. *The Physical and Virtual Worlds Converge.*, *13*(2), 15–18.

Denning. (2001). Activism, Hacktivism, and Cyberterrorism: The Internet as a Tool for Influencing Foreign Policy. In *Networks and Netwars The Future of Terror, Crime, and Militancy* (pp. 239–288). RAND Corporation. https://www.rand.org/pubs/monograph_reports/MR1382.html

Flammini, A., Ferrari, P., Marioli, D., Sisinni, E., & Taroni, A. (2009). Wired and wireless sensor networks for industrial applications. *Microelectronics Journal*, *40*(9), 1322–1336. doi:10.1016/j.mejo.2008.08.012

Fovino, I. N., Carcano, A., Masera, M., & Trombetta, A. (2009). Design and Implementation of a Secure Modbus Protocol. In C. Palmer & S. Shenoi (Eds.), *Critical Infrastructure Protection III* (Vol. 311, pp. 83–96). Springer Berlin Heidelberg. doi:10.1007/978-3-642-04798-5_6

Fu, K., Cheng, D., Tu, Y., & Zhang, L. (2016). Credit Card Fraud Detection Using Convolutional Neural Networks. In A. Hirose, S. Ozawa, K. Doya, K. Ikeda, M. Lee, & D. Liu (Eds.), *Neural Information Processing* (Vol. 9949, pp. 483–490). Springer International Publishing. doi:10.1007/978-3-319-46675-0_53

Gordon, L. A., Loeb, M. P., & Zhou, L. (2016). Investing in Cybersecurity: Insights from the Gordon-Loeb Model. *Journal of Information Security*, *07*(02), 49–59. doi:10.4236/jis.2016.72004

Gordon, S., & Ford, R. (2006). On the definition and classification of cybercrime. *Journal in Computer Virology*, *2*(1), 13–20. doi:10.100711416-006-0015-z

Hellström, T. (2007). Critical infrastructure and systemic vulnerability: Towards a planning framework. *Safety Science*, *45*(3), 415–430. doi:10.1016/j.ssci.2006.07.007

Hines, P. (1993). Integrated Materials Management: The Value Chain Redefined. *International Journal of Logistics Management*, *4*(1), 13–22. doi:10.1108/09574099310804920

Huitsing, P., Chandia, R., Papa, M., & Shenoi, S. (2008). Attack taxonomies for the Modbus protocols. *International Journal of Critical Infrastructure Protection*, *1*, 37–44. doi:10.1016/j.ijcip.2008.08.003

Hutchinson, D., & Warren, M. (2003). Security for Internet banking: A framework. *Logistics Information Management*, *16*(1), 64–73. doi:10.1108/09576050310453750

Ismail, M., Shaaban, M. F., Naidu, M., & Serpedin, E. (2020). Deep Learning Detection of Electricity Theft Cyber-Attacks in Renewable Distributed Generation. *IEEE Transactions on Smart Grid*, *11*(4), 3428–3437. doi:10.1109/TSG.2020.2973681

Jaiswal, A., Kumar, S., Kaiwartya, O., Kumar, N., Song, H., & Lloret, J. (2021). Secrecy Rate Maximization in Virtual-MIMO Enabled SWIPT for 5G Centric IoT Applications. *IEEE Systems Journal*, *15*(2), 2810–2821. doi:10.1109/JSYST.2020.3036417

Kemmerer, R. A. (2003). Cybersecurity. *25th International Conference on Software Engineering, 2003. Proceedings*, 705–715. 10.1109/ICSE.2003.1201257

Krombholz, K., Hobel, H., Huber, M., & Weippl, E. (2015). Advanced social engineering attacks. *Journal of Information Security and Applications*, *22*, 113–122. doi:10.1016/j.jisa.2014.09.005

Lezzi, M., Lazoi, M., & Corallo, A. (2018). Cybersecurity for Industry 4.0 in the current literature: A reference framework. *Computers in Industry*, *103*, 97–110. doi:10.1016/j.compind.2018.09.004

Management Association. (Ed.). (2018). Cyber Security and Threats: Concepts, Methodologies, Tools, and Applications. IGI Global. doi:10.4018/978-1-5225-5634-3

Matt, C., Hess, T., & Benlian, A. (2015). Digital Transformation Strategies. *Business & Information Systems Engineering*, *57*(5), 339–343. doi:10.100712599-015-0401-5

McQuade, S. (2006). Technology-enabled Crime, Policing and Security. *The Journal of Technology Studies*, *32*(1). Advance online publication. doi:10.21061/jots.v32i1.a.5

Nguyen, K. T., Laurent, M., & Oualha, N. (2015). Survey on secure communication protocols for the Internet of Things. *Ad Hoc Networks*, *32*, 17–31. doi:10.1016/j.adhoc.2015.01.006

O'Neill, M. (2014). The Internet of Things: Do more devices mean more risks? *Computer Fraud & Security*, *2014*(1), 16–17. doi:10.1016/S1361-3723(14)70008-9

Obermayer, N., Csizmadia, T., & Hargitai, D. M. (2022). Influence of Industry 4.0 technologies on corporate operation and performance management from human aspects. *Meditari Accountancy Research*, *30*(4), 1027–1049. doi:10.1108/MEDAR-02-2021-1214

Özsungur, F. (2021). Business Management and Strategy in Cybersecurity for Digital Transformation. In K. Sandhu (Ed.), (pp. 144–162). Advances in Information Security, Privacy, and Ethics. IGI Global. doi:10.4018/978-1-7998-6975-7.ch008

Razzaq, A., Hur, A., Ahmad, H. F., & Masood, M. (2013). Cyber security: Threats, reasons, challenges, methodologies and state of the art solutions for industrial applications. *2013 IEEE Eleventh International Symposium on Autonomous Decentralized Systems (ISADS)*, 1–6. 10.1109/ISADS.2013.6513420

Review, B. (2006). Book Review. *European Psychologist*, *11*(3), 244–245. doi:10.1027/1016-9040.11.3.244

Schneier, Schneier, & Bostelman. (2015). *Literature review of mobile robots for manufacturing*. Academic Press.

Ten, C.-W., Manimaran, G., & Liu, C.-C. (2010). Cybersecurity for Critical Infrastructures: Attack and Defense Modeling. *IEEE Transactions on Systems, Man, and Cybernetics. Part A, Systems and Humans*, *40*(4), 853–865. doi:10.1109/TSMCA.2010.2048028

Vardarlier, P. (2020). Digital Transformation of Human Resource Management: Digital Applications and Strategic Tools in HRM. In U. Hacioglu (Ed.), *Digital Business Strategies in Blockchain Ecosystems* (pp. 239–264). Springer International Publishing. doi:10.1007/978-3-030-29739-8_11

Vial, G. (2019). Understanding digital transformation: A review and a research agenda. *The Journal of Strategic Information Systems*, *28*(2), 118–144. doi:10.1016/j.jsis.2019.01.003

Watkins, L. (2016). *Enhancing Cybersecurity by Defeating the Attack Lifecycle*. ResearchGate. https://www.researchgate.net/publication/294142649_Enhancing_Cybersecurity_by_Defeating_the_Attack_Lifecycle

Weimann, G. (2005). Cyberterrorism: The Sum of All Fears? *Studies in Conflict and Terrorism*, *28*(2), 129–149. doi:10.1080/10576100590905110

Wiese, L., Waage, T., & Brenner, M. (2020). CloudDBGuard: A framework for encrypted data storage in NoSQL wide column stores. *Data & Knowledge Engineering*, *126*, 101732. doi:10.1016/j.datak.2019.101732

Chapter 14
Transformational Leadership and Innovative Work Behavior of Employees:
Two Sides of the Story

Jana Deprez
https://orcid.org/0000-0001-8862-574X
KU Leuven, Belgium

Wouter Robijn
KU Leuven, Belgium

Martin Euwema
KU Leuven, Belgium

ABSTRACT

Organizations need to innovate to stay relevant, for example, through the innovative work behavior of employees. Previous studies highlighted how different innovative phases may require other leadership behavior. In the present study, the authors aim to discover which type of transformational leadership behaviour best encourages employees in which innovative phase, both from the perspective of the manager and the employee. They conducted interviews with 42 leaders and 43 followers within four innovative companies in the e-tailing sector. They use thematic analysis and quantisization of the data. The results show that not every subcomponent of transformational leadership has the same influence on each phase of innovative work behavior, nor with the same magnitude. The most prevalent relationship is between intellectual stimulation and idea generation. They report specific actions by leaders that promote innovative work behavior in followers.

DOI: 10.4018/978-1-6684-6732-9.ch014

Copyright © 2023, IGI Global. Copying or distributing in print or electronic forms without written permission of IGI Global is prohibited.

INTRODUCTION AND BACKGROUND

Our world is changing due to evolutions in technology, economic struggles, and global competition. This has led to changes in the nature of work (Burke & Ng, 2006). One-way companies can surpass this changing world and maintain their competitiveness is by being innovative (Dess & Pickens, 2001; Deprez, Peeters, & Gorgievski, 2021). Research has shown that organizations which engage in technological change, grow faster than organizations which do not and that profit margins in organizations are related to creativity and innovation (Nystrom, 1990). Thus, the more innovative organizations are, the better they perform and grow and the more profitable they are. De Jong and Den Hartog (2007) pointed out that, instead of focusing all their effort on their R&D departments, organizations can be more innovative if they also invest in their employees' innovative capabilities. Employees can help their organizations move in a new and innovative direction by generating ideas and implementing them in the form of new products or services. Innovation cannot happen without the creation of new ideas, and these ideas are created, shaped, promoted, and implemented by people (Van de Ven, 1986). This view, stating that individual innovative effort leads to more organizational innovativeness, is proclaimed by several researchers (e.g., Amabile, 1988; Unsworth & Parker, 2003). Therefore, it is important to understand what influences the emergence of such innovative work behavior. In this study we investigate how leaders can promote innovative work behavior in their followers through transformational leadership.

Leaders play a crucial role in the life of their followers (Robijn et al., 2020). Leadership is found to have an influence on innovative efforts of employees (Mumford, Scott, Gaddis, and Strange, 2002; Deprez, Euwema, 2017). However, in their meta-analysis, Rosing et al. (2011) find support for the hypothesis that transformational leadership in particular has a positive effect on innovative work behavior. In spite of the high positive correlation, they point out the high degree of variation in the results, depending on the dependent variable, level of analysis and so on. Therefore, they stress the importance of further research into these variables, like the specific influence of transformational leadership on the sub-dimensions of innovative work behavior. In this study we follow Scott and Bruce (1994) stating that innovative work behavior constitutes of three distinct tasks: idea generation, idea promotion and idea implementation. Individual innovative work behavior starts with the formation of a novel idea, the idea generation phase. This is most of the time in response to something that is not going well in the workplace, possible problems or incongruities. The next phase is described as the promotion of this novel idea. To make it happen, sponsors are needed to provide the necessary support for the innovation (Galbraith, 1982). To finalize the innovative work behavior process, idea implementation is in place where the novel idea is implemented in a role, group or organization. Each of these subphases should have appropriate leadership behaviors addressing them, to best aid employee innovative behaviors. However, which exact behaviors these are, is still unclear.

In this chapter we will use the most used leadership model, transformational leadership, which consists of four types of behavior i.e. idealized influence, individual consideration, intellectual stimulation and inspirational motivation. The first one, idealized influence encompasses behavior the leader displays when he "envisions a desirable future, articulates how it can be reached, sets an example to be followed, sets high standards of performance, and shows determination and confidence" (Bass, 1999, p. 11). Second, when demonstrating individual consideration, the leader behaves in a way that considers the personal needs of his employees and coaches them with their personal career paths and in achieving their goals. When displaying individual consideration, the leader takes into account that every person is different and shows that they accept that fact by treating them according to their preferences (Bass

& Riggio, 2006). Third, intellectual stimulation is where the leader encourages his followers to act in a more innovative and creative way. His followers are encouraged to look at problems from a different point of view and figure out creative solutions for them. These ideas for solutions are not criticized by others or by the leader (Bass & Riggio, 2006). Last, inspirational motivation happens when leaders try to convince, persuade, and inspire their followers to act out a specific vision and believe in their ability to perform better. This is done by setting clear expectations for workers and energizing them to move into the future (Bass & Riggio, 2006).

In the present study we aimed to identify which type of transformational leadership behavior best encourages each of the three innovative work behaviors. The present study took place in the e-tailing sector as it is one of the first sectors that comes to mind when we think about innovation (Amit and Zott, 2001).

METHODS

Procedure

Four online retailers located in The Netherlands were selected (ranging from 30 to 650 employees – information on each organization below in Table 1). Data was collected from three different sources: direct observation, analysis of secondary documents and in-depth semi-structured interviews with 42 employees and 43 leaders) to assure data triangulation (Yin, 2009). All employees who were asked gave their consent to participate in the interviews, so the response rate was 100%. Different aspects were covered during the interview in a non-directive way (McCracken, 1988). This is the case when the researcher asks broad questions where only clarifications or examples are used to elaborate on the different topics quoted. Specifically important for this study were the questions that covered the topics 'leadership' and 'innovative work behavior'. The interviewers used an interview guide that was made upfront. Interviewees were asked what kind of leadership they displayed in their daily tasks and asked to give examples to support their answers and create a more vivid understanding for the researchers. Also were they asked to assess the type of leadership styles their bosses displayed and what feelings this evoked on their account in the context of innovative work behavior. The interviewer was the same person for all 85 interviews. The length of the interviews varied from 28 minutes to four hours and 15 minutes, with a mean of approximately one hour and forty minutes.

Table 1. Overview of the four case organizations

	Cases/Companies			
	Company 1	Company 2	Company 3	Company 4
Employees	±650	160	±30	78
Turnover	€ 548 million	€49 million	± €40 million	N/A*
Date of foundation	1952	2003	1991	1960
Number of interviewees	42	11	11	21
Number of leaders interviewed	24	5	7	6
Number of followers interviewed	18	6	4	15
*Because this is a service offering company this information is irrelevant.				

Participants

The most important source of data for this study was in depth interviews with members of the different enterprises, conducted by the researchers. Since all of the companies were founded and based in The Netherlands, the majority of the employees were native Dutch. All of the participants where Dutch-speaking. 42 people were asked from Company 1, 11 from Company 2, 11 from Company 3 and 21 from Company 4. At first a select number of people were asked to participate. In the next step people were added according to the snowball effect (Atkinson and Flint, 2001). In the sample were 55 men and 30 women. The tenure of the employees varied a lot, from people who had worked for the company their whole life to people who recently joined. This tenure had an average of ten years and three months and ranged from one month to 40 years. They were selected from the different layers of the organizations, ranging from line workers to top management.

Analyses

In the first step we performed a thematic analysis (using Nvivo) to investigate the obtained data (Braun & Clarke, 2006). In a second step quotes were assigned to the codes that fit the data best. When using Nvivo these quotes are grouped together to give an overview of the coverage of the codes. This phase was conducted by two researchers. To ensure the validity of the coding the interrater reliability was measured, which was .71 a fair to good agreement. In our results we first summarized the data into quantitative tables, as is also done in recent qualitative research by is Sucozhañay Calle (2014). This transformation of qualitative data into quantitative results is referred to as quantizing (Happ, 2009; Tashakkori & Teddlie, 2010). In order to this correctly we analyzed the different quotations and contrasted them to the specific context. We then assigned the outcomes to a rating scale that allowed comparison between the different cases. The rating scale was the following: high (3), medium (2), low (1) and (0) when no quotations were found in the data. The method used to appoint the different labels to the rating scale, consisted of counting the number of quotes and comparing the percentage with a predefined scale.

RESULTS

Our objective was to investigate which specific actions of leaders may lead to innovative work behavior in their followers. And what leadership behaviors are perceived as stimulating by their followers. We focus on the actions of transformational leaders. When we examine the quantitative literature review, we notice that a lot of components of transformational leadership relate to workers displaying more innovative work behaviors. Here we will examine what behaviors underlie this relationship. What is it that leaders in our organizations do exactly to make this happen? We will discuss each component in relation to what effects it produces. We now try to understand the underlying attitudes to define in depth this relationship. In this study we focus on the individual level.

As we noted above, transformational leadership consists of four components: idealized influence, individual consideration, intellectual stimulation, and inspirational motivation. We will discuss these different components in relation to innovative work behavior. In the next section we will depict the results of our analysis. We will first elaborate on the quantization results before analyzing the data in depth. We must note, based on the explanation of our methodology, that these results are not statistically tested, they are merely a summary of the qualitative data. By adding quotes, we try to make the data more vivid and practical.

Transformational Leadership Behaviors

In Table 2 we provide the results of our search for transformational leadership behaviors in the four companies. By following a quantization process, we could conclude which types of transformational leadership behavior were displayed in which companies. This is very different for each company. As an example, we see that leaders in company 2 show a lot of individual consideration but almost no idealized influence, whereas in company 3 we see quite the opposite. To compare, we provided the different scores for leaders and followers. In most cases this score is similar for leaders and followers. Nevertheless, for some scores, there is a big difference (1 vs 3) i.e., idealized influence for company 1, individual consideration and inspirational motivation for company 3. Quotes are added to set examples of what we define under the different categories.

Table 2. Transformational leadership category examples

Company			Transformational Leadership Behaviors*		
		IC	IM	IS	II
Company1	E.g.	"I think I am very consciously busy complimenting people when something goes right, but also thinking about, e.g. when someone points out that he wants to do more, he wants to develop himself, what is possible." (Leader)	"Everything is very informal, also with feedback, everything can be said, in two ways [...] I never have to think before saying something that they will take things the wrong way. It's very open and that motivates me. They give you the freedom to perform the best you can in your function." (Follower)	"I often set examples, show how things can be done differently. By asking them, making them see how things can be more effective, not only the output, but also their work, effort, making them see what is possible for them." (Leader)	"I think I give a lot of freedom. I have a clear vision, a clear goal, something I want to strive to achieve. I think I put a lot of energy in the feeling of being at home, not threatened, but feeling an open culture." (Leader)
L**		2	1	2	1
F**		2	2	2	3
Company 2	E.g.	"[...] I try to see what they find important, what their points of improvement are, where they can grow, if they like it, I try to discover if I communicate well with them." (Leader)	N/A	"During the cluster meeting, he asks if we already looked into something. He offers us a new perspective, it makes us think about possibilities." (Follower)	N/A
L**		3	0	1	0
F**		3	0	1	0
Company3	E.g.	"He often asks me if everything is alright, if I have any problems. [...] He gives me the opportunity to say what I think." (Follower)	"[...] he knows how to stimulate people, to put them to work. Honest, sincere, open, a counselor. You can consult him with private matters, and know he keeps them for himself. I find that important [...]" (Leader)	"In the monthly meetings there's always the question if there's something we can improve, something we can do better. I strongly encourage that, can we change something, why do we do it like that?" (Leader)	"[...] unwillingness is not an option for us, inability is, I want to think with them a lot, I want to assist them, I want include them in growth[...]" (Leader)
L**		1	1	2	2
F**		3	3	3	3
Company4	E.g.	"[...] my development is important to me, [...]. He takes that into account by giving me particular tasks and projects. He knows what I am doing and what motivates me." (Follower)	"He really made sure that there was a positive energy. He created a culture. [...] he has trust in professionalism and guides us, he likes to work in teams. It's important to deliver a group result!" (Follower)	"Our boss has told us multiple times to wonder why we do the things we do in that particular manner. You're being listened to and things get followed up, that motivates me to work that way." (Follower)	"I really like him. He has a lot of confidence, he stands behind you, he is honest, he doesn't take anyone down, he is the culture actually." (Follower)
L**		3	1	1	1
F**		3	1	2	2

Note. *Transformational Leadership Behaviors: IC: Individual Consideration; IM: Inspirational Motivation; IS: Intellectual Stimulation; II: Idealized Influence. Rating scale: high (3), medium (2), low (1) or (0) when no quotations regarding that topic were found. **L: Leader; F: Follower.

Transformational Leadership and Innovative Work Behavior

Next, we tried to quantize the relation between transformational leadership and innovative work behavior. We did this by analyzing how many transformational leadership quotes had outcomes that triggered or were related to innovative work behavior. The results are displayed in Table 3. The percentages of Total show us that within the transformational quotes, intellectual stimulation leads the most to innovative work behavior (64.00%) followed by inspirational motivation (38.88%), individual consideration (28.57%) and idealized influence (15.91%). These numbers oblige us to notice that according to Table 1, followers notice idealized influence as a transformational leadership behavior (44 quotes). Nevertheless, they do not directly connect this to their innovative work behavior. Employees do certainly appreciate this kind of behavior in their leader, and it might impact their attitude at work, however they do not connect this to more innovative work behavior. For example, an employee might be more motivated to work overtime, which does not directly stimulate creativity. Within the phases of innovative work behavior, we see that transformational leadership behaviors most of time lead to idea generation and to a lesser extent to idea promotion and idea implementation. We provided some quotes to set an example for what we understand as fitting quotes displaying this relationship.

Table 3. Relationship of transformational leadership and innovative work behavior

IWB phases			**Transformational Leadership Behavior**		
IC			**IM**	**IS**	**II**
Idea Generation		"He said what I was doing is OK, but he really wanted me to act proactive, take care of things and show interest in new things and pick them up, that's what he said to me in the first years. […] And then I got that attitude and he said *This is exactly what I wanted to achieve for you*." (Follower)	"We didn't say, we will make the plan. I find it relevant that *they* are motivated as pioneers in the department to shape it […]. And therefore *they* needed a vision, that *they* would implement." (Leader)	"We can always share our opinion and are being listened to. What we show in innovative work is being taken seriously and is being implemented, it (innovative behavior) is being encouraged." (Follower)	"My boss is visionary. He doesn't care much for details and says literally *OK, I have 10 ideas and if only one works, than that is that*. He's all about trying and experimenting." (Follower)
# 2			2	3	3
Idea Promotion		N/A	Let's say, I am very convinced that costs in marketing can be cut by 5M without any negative effects on turnover. […] Than I try to trigger people, give them perspective, try to persuade them of the idea and trigger them." (Leader)	"I try to stimulate them by saying Go ahead, do it and make a move to make sure that the organization is triggered by it to install it." (Leader)	"I try to be a sounding board […] And when a presentation needs to be given, they're the ones who have to give it preferably […] create ownership. Invite them to come with solutions and not just questions." (Leader)
# 0			2	2	2
Idea Implementation		"I really coach them and give them responsibilities and give them things to take up." (Leader)	"He knows how to motivate people, he really does and he triggers people by saying *Well, if you think that's a good idea, you should just operate on it then*." (Follower)	I organize meetings where I ask for innovative ideas, points of improvement in their domains […] I want them to actively think with me about improving our processes, our customer service,..." (Leader)	"The confidence and persuasion with which he brought the idea, didn't make people think otherwise […] You think, he will have thought it through, it will be correct, so yes, that's it, let's do it." (Follower)
# 2			1	1	2
Total**		**28.57%**	**38.88%**	**64.00%**	**15.91%**

Note. *Transformational Leadership Behaviors: IC: Individual Consideration; IM: Inspirational Motivation; IS: Intellectual Stimulation; II: Idealized Influence. Rating scale: high (3), medium (2), low (1) or (0) when no quotations regarding that topic were found. **Total: gives an indication of the percentage of people giving Transformational Leadership quotes relate that to Innovative Work Behavior.

In the following section, we will elaborate on table 4. We will discuss the different subcomponents of transformational leadership and their outcomes, especially focusing on the relationship with innovative work behavior in the three phases of the process, i.e., idea generation, idea promotion and idea implementation.

Idealized Influence

Transformational leaders display idealized influence in their attributes and behaviors. As has been mentioned in the literature review above, charisma is one of the aspects that best describes idealized influence. When a leader acts as an inspiring role model who leads the way, this emboldens the employees to act accordingly. It leads to organizational commitment and organizational citizenship behavior. Eleven employees (26%) of all four companies state that they get energized to do more, work harder, or support the company if a leader with idealized influence takes the lead. An example is given by an employee who points out that this kind of behavior "makes people get more committed to the company which makes them work harder, which causes better results, and these are being celebrated again." (Employee, Marketing, Company 1)

When my boss hadn't been at the office for three consecutive weeks because he was abroad for other business, finally came back and saw that it was busy and that everybody was busy and left work only at seven or eight, then he would go clean the warehouse. That feeling alone made everyone stay. Because when the manager champions it and screams: 'Well done, boys!' […] and asks if I can help him with something, then I am willing to do that for him. (Follower, Operations, Company 3)

This enthusiasm is a very appealing attribute of transformational leaders which speaks to the imagination of employees. In 23 interviews we noticed employees calling onto this inspiring attitude of their leaders and how it influences them in a positive way. "Our bosses' enthusiasm, you get drawn by that and it makes you equally enthusiastic!" (Follower, Management administration, Company 3) and "He (the boss) succeeded at getting everybody on board to jointly build this new culture. He really created our culture; he is our culture." (Follower, Bim, Company 4) are just a couple of examples that show this effect on employees. Please note that this is great and energizing, however this does not mean any form of innovative work behavior.

When leading a team it is important to know what your employees are doing in their daily job lives. This way they can better relate and understand what they experience. The manager of company 3 thinks it is a useful practice to act as a co-worker from time to time and work with his employees in the different departments. This way he gets a feeling of what happens in the workplace.

A year and a half ago I deliberately sat at customer service for a week. Sometimes I sit by the welcome desk and help them a little bit. Or I go help in the warehouse for a couple of days […] I get a feeling of what happens in the workplace. For example, when they complained that they needed a new truck, I said: 'Don't whine so much, you can just take the one from the other boys!'. But then I figured out that that was not the case. Because when you stand with your feet in the mud, then you get that feeling. (Leader, Board, Company 3)

In response to this kind of actions, three out of four followers of that company report that they like and appreciate it when their leader is interested in their person and work. It is important that leaders build a relationship with their staff. People need to see their leader set an example and identify with him as a person and not just as their boss. On top of that, all the leaders in our sample walk around in their offices. They do this to be close to their people and see what gets them going. These leaders do not stay locked away in their offices, far away from what is happening on the floor. They all state that their door is always open and that in most cases they do not even have a door. This stimulates the equality between leaders and followers. And this is regularly noticed and mentioned by followers.

We see that idealized influence can, in some cases, lead to innovative work behavior. But as stated in Table 4 over all four companies this is not very common (15.91%). In company 1, nine of the eighteen employees indicate that the idealized behavior of a top manager of the company led to them being persuaded and triggered to implement a new and innovative structure in the company. In addition to that for some followers idealized influence can also stimulate idea generation and idea promotion but only in 7 cases over all four companies.

Individual Consideration

The concept of individual consideration refers to the coaching role of transformation leaders. It is used to underline the diversity between employees. Not every person is the same and so is not every employee. Followers need different management styles, motivational actions, tasks, goals… Leaders should focus on the overlap between the goals of a follower and the vision of the organization. Repetitive feedback is needed to ensure that these two aspects are aligned.

A good way to achieve this individual consideration is to discuss the feelings of followers towards the current job and future perspectives with them. Leaders need to try to monitor if they are content and functioning well in their current situation. They must give their followers the tools to pursue their interests and keep them motivated. In our sample seven leaders indicate that they organize feedback meetings where they discuss the follower's functioning and career options and plans. A leader explains that the goal of these meetings is to "[…] see what they find important, what their points of improvement are, where they can grow, if they like it, […] and follow up on these points of discussion." (Leader, Online Marketing, Company 2). From a follower's perspective the meeting discusses his or her feelings towards the current tasks, job and company.

As their coach it is also the leader's job to give followers tips and tricks, they can use to get their job done in the best possible way. It is important that these tips are optional; the follower needs to decide if he or she will act in the proposed way. When these tips are given in the right way, followers do not feel forced to follow them. Rather they see them as possible solutions they can use if they feel the need as expressed by one employee: "[…] she gives me tips, but she does not say that that is the way I have to do it." (Follower, Sales, Company 1).

In team meetings you can jointly search for possibilities for the follower to develop himself or herself. Trainings can be helpful for the employee to unlock his or her full potential. As a surplus the organization can benefit from these newly educated skills. An additional advantage to this strategy is that it encourages commitment to the organization.

[…] I get the chance to follow another training. […] the fact that you can learn new knowledge which you can use in your function, that motivates me a lot. They really give you the freedom to perform in your function the best you can. (Follower, HR, Company 1)

When the leader gives this kind of attention to the aspirations of followers and clearly discusses with them what is feasible and what is not, they will understand and feel grateful if one of their wishes eventually gets realized. The follower mentioned above, together with eight other employees, states that this indeed motivates her a lot because she can learn a lot and use the newly learned information to perform better at her job.

As we noted above, in reference of Reuvers et al. (2008), the act of highlighting the different qualities of employees and their diverse talents, encourages employees to behave innovative. Asking for their different opinions not only creates a feeling of being respected by your employees, it also stimulates the creative process and idea generation.

Leaders (20.83%) show that they value their followers' opinions. They give them access to participate in decision making. This way they let them know that their inputs and ideas are appreciated. People are encouraged to share their thoughts, and this can be of benefit to the company. Followers in the sample (30.95%) in our interviews mention that they like it when their opinion is asked and taken into consideration. It gives them the feeling that they are taken seriously, which is valuable to them. A follower tries to explain the feeling this gives her: "It is very nice when your opinion is asked for [...]. Question about what you think, what you like, what you see happening in the future, it's just very pleasant. It gives you to feeling of being taken seriously." (Follower, Operations, Company 1).

We see that individual consideration encourages idea generation and idea implementation equally, but not idea promotion. Six followers point out that their leaders give them specific tasks they find pleasant or indicated that they wanted to do in their feedback meetings. This leads to idea implementation, because they perform the specific innovative tasks and try to implement them in the organization. In the next example leaders from one company put in place a box for possible ideas. People could suggest ideas, anonymously if they wished to do so. This way, novel and interesting ideas that would have never come to light, are now ready to be conducted. We can conclude that this stimulates idea generation and idea promotion.

[...] And there they put a box for ideas and said that we could throw in whatever we wanted. I did not put in just one card; I think I put in 26 cards with ideas (laughs). There were small ideas but also a lot of big ones. You could ask for personal wishes and I also put it mine, my own project and in the end, I was allowed to do that, the whole thing. [...] They're open for input. (Follower, Operations, Company 1)

Intellectual Stimulation

As noted above intellectual stimulation prompts followers to reassess their current situation and detect areas for improvement (Hater and Bass, 1988). We can see this as an attempt to make followers generate new ideas and take initiative. We see that it is useful to encourage followers to see their current situation from a different point of view. By forcing them to rethink this situation leaders activate innovative thinking. Eight transformational leaders state that they regularly ask this kind of questions in interviews and meetings with their followers. They specifically point out where a different viewpoint can be adopted in order to perform better or make better decisions.

I often set examples, show how things can be different. By asking them, making them see how things can be more effective, not only the output, but also their work, effort, by making them see what is possible for them. (Leader, Finance, Company 1)

Another trick six leaders use, is to give followers hints on interesting and innovative topics to pick up and generate ideas on. They propose subjects or points of interest to trigger certain initiative taking behaviors. When they do this from the beginning on, followers understand that this is part of the job and in the long run, will come up with ideas of their own.

Our boss tries to inspire us, trigger us to think about the question 'why don't we do it this way' or he tries to feed us information during a meeting or novel ideas he encounters in the market, [...]. (Follower, sales, Company 2) or He is a very smart man and now and then he reads something and asks us if we want to do something with what he just read. So in that way he tips me with subjects that might be interesting. (Follower, Support, Company 4)

Two leaders find it particularly important that their followers are up to date with the current developments in their field. Therefore, they want them to read the most recent publications in their sphere of activity. In addition to that, one leader organizes a reading session every two weeks where they analyze a book about the latest trends in their field of expertise. He does this in his spare time to show his followers it's important.

[…] what I really find important is that they read or learn by themselves, that's why I say that if they need books or want to attend certain events, the company will pay for them. […] I really stimulate them to follow certain people, professionals, blogs, and twitter, I also forward that sort of information when I find something fun or useful […] I really get energetic when I see they like their job […] (Leader, Online Marketing, Company 2)

Another leader recently organizes a two-weakly academy session, where followers come together to discuss a specific topic. During these meetings, a member of the team comes to speak about a new and innovative topic that is not yet known in the team, but that can have potential impact or importance.

We see that it is particularly interesting to discuss different problems within your team in order to generate a more thorough idea on how to improve the status quo. One leader states that a good content rich discussion where different parties wholeheartedly disagree can cause a moment of innovation where creation of new knowledge and ideas is stimulated. These team meetings are interesting because through simple team processes a higher level of output can be reached.

It is important that leaders arouse their followers to take the wheel and discover how they can solve a problem on their own. This type of intellectual stimulation forces them to take ownership and initiative, stimulating them to be more creative and innovative.

I encourage them to try new things, and then I say something like 'Go make that call on your own'. If they're at my desk asking for something, I can give them my answer but if they have to figure it out for themselves, they get wiser from that. […] (Leader, Management, Company 3) and I try to give them as much independence as possible without being distant. […] I try to be a sounding board, but it is still their thing. (Leader, Finance, Company 1)

All these leaders use different techniques, group meetings, reading sessions, innovation academies or discussions, with the same goal of triggering generation of new ideas. Eleven followers report that this encourages them to generate more ideas, promote these ideas to leaders and peers and implement them. Quotes like "My boss regularly asks me to think about PR campaigns. I have to be innovative and pick up things on my own as well. […] I am being asked to participate in thinking and asked to think further on ideas. That stimulates me to be creative and put in extra effort" (Follower, Support, Company 1) show this effect on innovative work behavior.

Inspirational Motivation

Our last subdivision of transformational leadership contains inspirational motivation. Leaders need to persuade their followers that their vision is a good one to follow. Followers have to be intrinsically motived to trust and publicize the mission statement of their leader. They should be inspired and enthused to sing from the same hymn sheet. With this in mind, leaders can outspread a vision on innovation in your organization.

You want to stimulate each other, bring out the best in each other. [...] When you're innovative and you bring forward new ideas, you inspire other people to do the same. Doing things slightly different can make them function slightly better and by bringing forward these ideas you can make improvements in the process flow of your company. (Leader, Support, Company 1)

To inspire and motivate followers, leaders must exert their propelling vision. In combination with displaying the effort they put in leading the firm to success, this can be seen as an important fashion to pass on the vision. Three followers cited about a presentation their boss gave to the company about the vision and mission. Its effect can be unclear but very persuasive "I don't know exactly how he persuaded people; it was mostly his own persuasion he projected upon us that made us think like *Waaw!* (Follower, Marketing, Company 1). Not a lot of leaders display the kind of behavior. Nevertheless, the high percentage (38.88%) indicates that a lot of these behaviors lead to followers displaying innovative work behavior. An example of how this leads to idea implementation can be found in "[...] he triggers people saying *if you think that's a good idea, maybe you have to roll in out then, show them the idea is yours."* (Follower, Sales, Company 1). Next to this, inspirational motivation leads to idea generation and idea implementation as well as quotes exemplify in table 4.

CONCLUSION

Theoretical Contribution

This study contributes to the current research literature on the influence of transformational leadership on innovative work behavior in the sense that we used qualitative techniques to investigate the effect on the different phases of innovative work behavior. By collecting qualitative data and using thematic analysis to investigate it, we could uncover which transformational leadership behaviors influence which phases of the innovative work behavior process. In our results we see that different transformational leadership behaviors influence different phases of innovative work behavior. When we dig deeper into the different combinations, we see for example that individual consideration promotes both idea generation and idea implementation but not in any case idea promotion. Another example is given by intellectual stimulation which is the most efficient behavior to stimulate innovative work behavior in our sample. This leads to a lot of idea generation, to a lesser extent to idea promotion and almost to no idea implementation. On the contrast idea implementation can be stimulated by inspirational motivation.

The most prevalent relationship we found was indeed the influence of intellectual stimulation on idea generation. This is in line with the literature we explored before executing our study (Scott & Bruce, 1994; Shalley & Gilson, 2004). It seems that when leaders act out behaviors in line with intellectual stimulation this encourages idea generation the most, compared to other subcomponents of transformational leadership behaviors. These actions include challenging followers to research and discuss the most recent literature, seek media channels for novelty and so on. All these actions stimulate followers to contest the status quo and think about new ways to innovate on the level of process and product. All of these behaviors are also found to have a positive impact on innovative work behavior in research by Pearce and Ensley (2004).

During our analysis we noticed a strong link between transformational leadership and organizational citizenship behavior. This kind of behavior is called to life by Smith, Organ, and Near (1983) who define it as extra role behavior, behavior that is not part of the strict sense of the job description nor is it stimulated by the existing reward system in the company. The link between these two concepts had been advocated by Podsakoff, MacKenzie, Paine, and Bachrach (2000). They state that a transformational leadership style promotes organizational citizenship behavior in individuals. A more recent study by Euwema, Wendt, and Van Emmerik (2007) also supports the positive influence of supportive leadership styles on group organizational citizenship behaviors.

We must note that a lot of outcomes of transformational leadership could not be fit into our framework of innovative work behavior. This is in line with the research literature above which points out that transformational leadership is linked to a lot more outcomes in individuals than innovative work behavior alone.

Practical Contribution

In our sample we found the most frequently mentioned transformational leadership behavior is idealized influence (36.07%), followed by individual consideration (28.69%), intellectual stimulation (20.49%) and inspirational motivation (14.75%) as the least mentioned transformational leadership behavior. But, when we investigate which of these behaviors stimulate innovative work behavior, we notice quite the opposite line-up. Intellectual stimulation and to a lesser extent, inspirational motivation led to innovative work behavior. This means that the behaviors leaders use the most or followers notice the most in their leaders, idealized influence, and individual consideration, lead to less innovative work behaviors than less common behaviors, intellectual stimulation and inspirational motivation. So instead of focusing on providing vision, setting good examples and pamper their followers, leaders should intellectually stimulate and inspirationally motivate their followers to increase their innovative work behavior.

In the companies where we found a lot of transformational leaders, evidence on this is especially given by followers. In company 3 followers provide us with a lot of quotes on transformational leadership behaviors of their leaders, even though the leaders do not speak of themselves in that extreme transformational way. These findings are especially interesting when discussing the perspectives of leaders and followers on the transformational actions of the leaders. This could lead to the conclusion that; however followers perceive their leaders as displaying idealized influence, this is not purposefully done. On top of this, a lot of evidence is found on the innovative influence certain behaviors of leaders have on followers. These influences are clearly stated by followers in our interviews. Nevertheless, not all these actions are cited by the leaders for the exact purpose of being innovative. When we take the example of idealized influence we notice when analyzing the data that leaders do not act out transformational leadership, they behave in a way that feels natural to them, stimulate the things that are important to them, and do the things that they feel are right. All of these things are mostly done without the purpose of being transformational or encouraging innovation. This does not leave out the effect is having on followers, who clearly state that all these actions do have an effect on their innovative work behavior.

Another thing that struck us when analyzing the data is that transformational leadership behaviors lead mostly to idea generation. Therefore, it is important for leaders to upscale their effort of stimulating idea promotion and idea implementation. This way, good ideas are not only generated, but actually promoted and implemented to make a change within the company.

ACKNOWLEDGMENT

We acknowledge the work of student Marie Pieters, without whom this research would not have been possible.

REFERENCES

Amabile, T. M. (1988). A model of creativity and innovation in organizations. *Research in Organizational Behavior*, *10*(1), 123–167.

Amit, R., & Zott, C. (2001). Value creation in e-business. *Strategic Management Journal*, *22*(6-7), 493–520. doi:10.1002mj.187

Bass, B. M. (1999). Current developments in transformational leadership. *The Psychologist Manager Journal*, *3*(1), 5–21. doi:10.1037/h0095852

Bass, B. M., & Riggio, R. E. (2006). Transformational leadership. Lawrence Erlbaum Associates, Inc. doi:10.4324/9781410617095

Braun, V., & Clarke, V. (2006). Using thematic analysis in psychology. *Qualitative Research in Psychology*, *3*(2), 77–101. doi:10.1191/1478088706qp063oa

Burke, R. J., & Ng, E. (2006). The changing nature of work and organizations: Implications for human resource management. *Human Resource Management Review*, *16*(2), 86–94. doi:10.1016/j.hrmr.2006.03.006

De Jong, J. P., & Den Hartog, D. N. (2007). How leaders influence employees' innovative behavior. *European Journal of Innovation Management*, *10*(1), 41–64. doi:10.1108/14601060710720546

Deprez, J., & Euwema, M. (2017). You can't always get what you want? Leadership expectations of intrapreneurs. *Journal of Managerial Psychology*, *32*(6), 430–444. doi:10.1108/JMP-04-2016-0107

Deprez, J., Peeters, E., & Gorgievski, M. J. (2021). Developing intrapreneurial self-efficacy through internships? Investigating agency and structure factors. *International Journal of Entrepreneurial Behaviour & Research*, *27*(5), 1166–1188. doi:10.1108/IJEBR-09-2020-0642

Dess, G. G., & Picken, J. C. (2001). Changing roles: Leadership in the 21st century. *Organizational Dynamics*, *28*(3), 18–34. doi:10.1016/S0090-2616(00)88447-8

Euwema, M. C., Wendt, H., & Van Emmerik, H. (2007). Leadership styles and group organizational citizenship behavior across cultures. *Journal of Organizational Behavior*, *28*(8), 1035–1057. doi:10.1002/job.496

Galbraith, J. R. (1982). Designing the innovating organization. *Organizational Dynamics*, *10*(3), 5–25. doi:10.1016/0090-2616(82)90033-X

Kanter, R. (1988). When a thousand flowers bloom: Structural, collective, and social conditions for innovation in organizations. *Research in Organizational Behavior, 10, 169–211.*

McCracken, G. (1988). *The long interview*. Sage.

Mumford, M. D., Scott, G. M., Gaddis, B., & Strange, J. M. (2002). Leading creative people: Orchestrating expertise and relationships. *The Leadership Quarterly*, *13*(6), 705–750. doi:10.1016/S1048-9843(02)00158-3

Nystrom, H. (1990). Organizational innovation. In M. S. West & J. L. Farr (Eds.), *Innovation and creativity at work: psychological and organizational strategies* (pp. 143–162). Wiley.

Pearce, C. L., & Ensley, M. D. (2004). A reciprocal and longitudinal investigation of the innovation process: The central role of shared vision in product and process innovation teams (PPITs). *Journal of Organizational Behavior*, *25*(2), 259–278. doi:10.1002/job.235

Podsakoff, P. M., MacKenzie, S. B., Paine, J. B., & Bachrach, D. G. (2000). Organizational citizenship behaviors: A critical review of the theoretical and empirical literature and suggestions for future research. *Journal of Management*, *26*(3), 513–563. doi:10.1177/014920630002600307

Robijn, W., Schaufeli, W. B., Deprez, J., & Euwema, M. C. (2020). Leaders, teams and work engagement: A basic needs perspective. *Career Development International*, *25*(4), 373–388. doi:10.1108/CDI-06-2019-0150

Rosing, K., Frese, M., & Bausch, A. (2011). Explaining the heterogeneity of the leadership- innovation relationship: Ambidextrous leadership. *The Leadership Quarterly*, *22*(5), 956–974. doi:10.1016/j.leaqua.2011.07.014

Scott, S. G., & Bruce, R. A. (1994). Determinants of innovative behavior: A path model of individual innovation in the workplace. *Academy of Management Journal*, *37*(3), 580–607. doi:10.2307/256701

Shalley, C. E., & Gilson, L. L. (2004). What leaders need to know: A review of social and contextual factors that can foster or hinder creativity. *The Leadership Quarterly*, *15*(1), 33–54. doi:10.1016/j.leaqua.2003.12.004

Sucozhañay Calle, D. (2014). *Leading Change in Higher Education: The role of transformational leadership and stakeholder management* [Unpublished doctoral dissertation]. University of Leuven.

Tashakkori, A., & Teddlie, C. (2010). *Sage handbook of mixed methods in social & behavioral research.* Sage. doi:10.4135/9781506335193

Unsworth, K., & Parker, S. K. (2003). Promoting a proactive and innovative workforce for the new workplace. In D. Holman, T. D. Wall, C. W. Clegg, P. Sparrow, & A. Howard (Eds.), *The new workplace: a guide to the human impact of modern working practices*. John Wiley & Sons.

Van de Ven, A. H. (1986). Central problems in the management of innovation. *Management Science*, *32*(5), 590–607. doi:10.1287/mnsc.32.5.590

Yin, R. (2009). *Case study research. Designing and Methods, 4(5).*

KEY TERMS AND DEFINITIONS

Idea Generation: One of the subphases of innovative work behavior. Consists of the initial steps taken in the innovative process, in which people come up with new ideas in a creative way.

Idea Implementation: One of the subphases of innovative work behavior. Is the final phase of the innovative process in which an idea is put into practice/use in an organization.

Idea Promotion: One of the subphases of innovative work behavior. After new ideas are generated, an employee will take his/her best ideas and try to gather support for them throughout the organization. This process will ensure sufficient resources to be able to progress to the implementation phase.

Idealized Influence: One of the factors of transformational leadership. Describes those who are acting like exemplary and ethical role models for their followers. These leaders instill pride, and gain respect and trust.

Individual Consideration: One of the factors of transformational leadership. Depicts the level of personal attention that a leader has for their followers. More specifically, leaders scoring high on this will listen to concerns and needs and work at addressing them.

Innovative Work Behavior: The behavior that employees demonstrate at work, which results in the creation of new or improved products, processes and/or procedures.

Inspirational Motivation: One of the factors of transformational leadership. These leaders are seen as charismatic, they can create an enticing picture of the future and strategic plans and as such give a big sense of purpose to their followers.

Intellectual Stimulation: One of the factors of transformational leadership. The degree to which a leader challenges and encourages creativity and critical thinking in their followers. Leaders scoring high on this will often ask their followers to reflect on their work.

Transformational Leadership: One of the most well-known leadership styles globally. Views a leader as being charismatic, inspiring and motivating, and providing intellectual stimulation and attention to individual followers.

Chapter 15
Artificial Intelligence in Human Resource Management:
The Next Generation of Technology for Business Excellence

Rajwinder Kaur
https://orcid.org/0000-0003-3494-8054
Chandigarh University, India

ABSTRACT

Artificial intelligence in human resources plays an important and crucial role in the 21st century. It is helpful in gathering, analysing, and presenting data in such a way that is more helpful for the HR professional to use. As technological advancements happen in the era, artificial intelligence helps to fulfil organisational demands as well as employee demands. Artificial intelligence eases the work of HR as well as effectively provides efficient work. Therefore, the present study explores the implementation of artificial intelligence in human resource functions. It further explores the various benefits and challenges of artificial intelligence in human resource functions. Finally, the study concludes that the work of artificial intelligence can be used in all areas of the HR functions. No doubt in the initial stage of artificial intelligence implementation the HR professionals and organization can face some challenges, but after its successful implementation, it is considered the best tool for HR functions.

INTRODUCTION

Artificial Intelligence (AI) refers to the use of digital computers and computer-based intelligence to perform various organisational tasks. Technology has changed all around the world and now people and many organisations use updated technology to work rather than a traditional mode of working (Wamba-Taguimdje et al., 2020). Leading organisations are aware of the benefits and usages of artificial intelligence in organisational systems. Artificial intelligence is used in various business functions such as human resources, marketing, customer experience and business models, etc. The use of artificial intelligence is

DOI: 10.4018/978-1-6684-6732-9.ch015

Copyright © 2023, IGI Global. Copying or distributing in print or electronic forms without written permission of IGI Global is prohibited.

transforming the business operations and functions of organisations (Di Vaio et al., 2020). According to the report and forecast by McKinsey, artificial intelligence will greatly impact the global economy and it will generate $13 trillion by the year 2030 in the global economy (albertchristopherr.medium.com).

Now a day's many leading organisations perceive that artificial intelligence will play a great role in human resource functions. HR professionals use artificial intelligence to improve the work and efficiency of the workforce. Integration of artificial intelligence in HR enhances the experience of the workforce and makes HR able to hire talented people (Eubanks, 2022). It simplifies the processes of human resource professionals which further contributes to innovative work and better decision-making (www.inc42.com).

Artificial intelligence automation supplies efficient instruments to human resource management to be able to retain and motivate a capable workforce that can increase value and leads to the achievement and expansion of the organization (Kshetri, 2021). One of the trends that have recently occurred in human resources is the implementation of artificial intelligence in hiring. Human resource activities are being automated because of the implementation of artificial intelligence and no direct dealings with third parties in recruitment and this has helped organizations to select or recruit the best talent in less time and money. With the automation and use of artificial intelligence in recruitment, organizations can reach the best talent in less time and money (www.strammer.com).

In today's time of the 21st-century artificial intelligence is a tool to reduce biases in systems and processes, retain people for a long time, hire suitable people for organization and recruit the best people (www.hrexchangenetwork.com). Human resource is one of the departments which takes care of the organization and employees. It works as a bridge between employer and employee. The human resource department improves the functioning of an organization using artificial intelligence. The improved functions of human resources include talent acquisition, onboarding, performance analysis and training, etc. Artificial intelligence enables HR professionals to improve the results and monitor the progress of employees in more effective ways (bigdata-madesimple.com).

The success of any business organization depends on basically two things i.e. efficient and skilled workforce and effective business strategies. Technology in the business world is always in demand. In the changing world, human resources face many challenges in day-to-day life (Zahidi et al., 2020). But artificial intelligence is one of the ways in the modern business world to manage HR-related tasks more efficiently and effectively than the previous times. Artificial intelligence has reached a new level and provides unbelievable benefits to human resources. HR executives believe that artificial intelligence in human resources will provide an improved experience so that business organizations can function smoothly (www.usmsystems.com).

LITERATURE REVIEW

Advancement in technology has made human life easier as well as more viable to face competition in the marketplace. Many researchers and authors have explored transformations as they change the working style of people. Artificial intelligence (AI) is one of the areas of technological transformation. Research in artificial intelligence is not much explored and is restricted only to the theoretical contributions (Jatobá and Snandes et al., 2019). Artificial intelligence contributes to many almost every aspect such as human resources, finance management and marketing etc. In the field of human resources, artificial intelligence has positive contributions. Indian companies are also slowly moving towards the use of artificial intelligence. Numbers of functions are integrated with the concept of artificial intelligence in

HR. It is also seen that AI in HR influences employee engagement practices and other related practices (Premnath and Chully, 2019).

Earlier there was a very big misconception in the minds of people that artificial intelligence will replace HR managers but the reality is that AI is introduced to make human jobs easy to perform. It is a supporting aspect in all the HR functions like recruitment, staffing and training, etc. AI is very much useful in gaining a competitive advantage for screening and sourcing (Merlin and Jayam, 2018). AI in today's time is not only supportive of basic HR functions but also an emphasis on rewards and recognition programs of the organization. It adds value to every aspect of human resource activity (Reddy, Jagadeesan and Rao, 2020). Artificial intelligence provides multiple solutions to the problem and provides the best and most effective solutions to the problems (Ahmed, 2018).

In today's time, everyone wants transparency and advancements in the systems, therefore it becomes essential to introduce advanced technological systems to overcome the challenges of the organizations. Artificial intelligence is one of the upcoming solutions to all the problems of the functions of the organization. It helps to improve systems of human resource management and overcome various challenges other than HR like strategy formulation, executing functions, etc (Barboza, 2019). With all such facilitation of AI in human resources, there are automatically improvements in the profitability of the organizations. The field of HR is very wide and the continuous developments help to improve the systems of human resources (Berhil, Benlahmar and Labani, 2020; Nawaz, 2019). In HR, AI was initially used for recruitment and related functions. To smoothen the work of HR professionals to securitize applications, identity matching and skill set matching, etc. (Geetha and Reddy, 2018; Nawaz, 2019; Nawaz and Gomes, 2019).

Artificial intelligence plays a significant role in all HRM processes. It is one of the fundamental steps toward the success of transforming human knowledge into organizational knowledge. It enhances the effectiveness of human resource management in the organization (Tandon, Joshi and Rastogi, 2017; Yawalkar, 2019). Human resources systems combined with artificial intelligence technologies, data mining, human resource strategy and planning can build a strong decision support system to assist organizations and people. Furthermore, employee relationship systems can also be better managed through artificial technologies (Jia, Guo, Li, Li and Chen, 2018). According to the study, the successful implementation of AI in the future will take 85% of manual work under control (Parveen and Palaniammal, 2019).

Some researchers have proved that employees in HR feel positive aspects of artificial intelligence. Employees are agreed and feel that it's a positive approach toward attaining a competitive edge (Kumari and Hemalatha, 2019). Failure in developing AI with HR practices can create big problems and issues in the organization. It could be very difficult for organizations to survive and grow in the competitive business environment (Matsa and Gullamajji, 2019). Organizations must consistently focus on implementing AI in the best way (Kumari and Hemalatha, 2019; Abdeldayem and Aldulaimi, 2020). Artificial intelligence should be integrated into all the human resource processes and functions by all organizations for better and more effective work (George and Thomas, 2019). Although this process cannot be done in one-night continuous improvements in the systems will bring big changes (Jiang, Du, Fu and Xiao, 2019).

Significance of Study

The present study is very important in today's rapidly growing technological world. Artificial intelligence is transforming the world with its advancements and helps human beings to be more perfect. It positively contributes to the various aspects of business organization. HR is one of the major important departments in every organization. It deals with the practical as well as the emotional aspect of employees. Therefore,

HR needs to take care of employees as they are the major contributors to any organization. They are the real assets of the organization. Therefore, artificial intelligence is gaining much more importance in the HR department. It is focusing on simpler, effective, and efficient work. Not just effective decision-making helps to create value for the organization but artificial intelligence too. Hence, the present study is an attempt to know the deeper insights into artificial intelligence and human resource functions.

Research Gaps

- From the review of literature, it is seen that artificial intelligence is an emerging concept. It is significantly important for human resource management and adding value to the organizations. By studying the existing literature, it is seen that there is a need to develop an integrated approach toward human resource functions and artificial intelligence. Most of the studies talk about the significance of artificial intelligence in human resource management. But the present study is an in-depth attempt to know the actual implementation of artificial intelligence in human resource functions.
- Based on past literature it is also seen that many studies are based on the secondary type of sources. They put a light in terms of more qualitative aspects. But the present study will put light on artificial intelligence in human resources by conducting in-depth interviews with people.
- Some or the other way, past studies are unable to recognize the actual implementation of artificial intelligence in human resource functions.
- There is a need to closely recognize the various benefits and challenges while implementing artificial intelligence in organizations.

RESEARCH OBJECTIVES

Based on the above research gaps identified, the present study fulfills the following objectives:

- To explore the implementation of artificial intelligence in human resource functions.
- To explore various benefits of artificial intelligence in HR.
- To explore various challenges while implanting artificial intelligence in HR.

RESEARCH METHODOLOGY

Research Methodology is a sequence of procedures and practices which is used to carry research study.
For the present study, both primary and secondary data are used.

Type of Research

The present study is a descriptive type of study which explores artificial intelligence in human resource functions as well as various benefits and challenges of artificial intelligence.

Period of Study

The period for the study is 2 months. During these 2 months, in-depth interviews of HR people are conducted, analysis was done, and a conclusion is drawn.

Data Collection

For the study, primary as well as secondary data are used.

Primary Data

Primary data for the study is collected through in-depth interviews of 15 HR professionals belonging to the different service sectors. The service sector includes the telecom sector, IT sector, banking sector, education sector, financial services, and communication services, etc.

Data from HR professionals is collected through an in-depth interview method. Some of the interviews are done face-to-face and some are done through the telephonic method.

Following are some of the questions which are asked during the interview of HR professionals:

Q1: In human resource management what are the functions where artificial intelligence is used?
Q2: How this artificial intelligence is used in human resource functions?
Q3: Do you feel any benefits of implementing artificial intelligence in human resource management?
Q4: What type of challenges does an organization face while implementing artificial intelligence?

Secondary Data

Secondary data is also used for the present study. In secondary data, various secondary sources are used like websites, reports, journals, research papers by researchers/university professors, etc. Many authenticated databases are explored to get secondary data. Databases for the study include Google Scholar, Research gate, Science Direct, Ebsco Host and JStor, etc. All the secondary data is taken from authenticated and reliable sources.

Study Area Selected for the Research

For the present research the service sector is selected. It includes the telecom sector, IT sector, banking sector, education sector, financial services and communication services, etc. HR professionals are selected based on the convenient sampling for interviews from India.

ANALYSIS AND INTERPRETATION

Implementation of Artificial Intelligence in Human Resource Functions

Recruitment Process

Recruitment is a process where the pool of candidates is invited for the vacant position in the organization to apply for the job. In this process many eligible and non-eligible candidates apply for the job, therefore it is very difficult for the HR professionals to manually find the appropriate person which is best suited for the job (Keller, 2018). So here artificial intelligence plays a big role and helps HR professionals to choose the best suitable candidate for the position. Through artificial intelligence, the process becomes very easy and quick. Before going into the further process of selecting a candidate virtual platforms and chat boards are used to screen the potential employees (Meyer, 2018). The process is not only beneficial for HR professionals but also assists potential employees. Eligible candidates can apply online to the vacant position which saves the cost and energy on the candidates. To locate the best resumes and match them with interviews, artificial intelligence searches job descriptions using algorithms and can search millions of websites (Garg, Srivastav and Gupta, 2018). To acquire talent throughout domains, a lot of MNCs have begun using AI. To fulfill available positions in one of its offices in Russia, PepsiCo, a manufacturer of food and beverages, is employing AI to identify and evaluate applicants (Garg, Srivastav and Gupta, 2018).

"During the interview of one of the respondents (Mr. Nupur), he said as an HR professional it's big convenience for us to use AI and recruit people. Otherwise, the manual process is too time-consuming as well as an extra cost for the organization. Chatbot-based AI helps a lot in the entire process. Now within the fraction of seconds, we select the application of eligible candidate and if suited then process further".

Hiring and on-Boarding Employees

After receiving the poll of applications from the candidates, prospects candidates are selected for the vacant positions according to the job position requirements. In the entire selection and hiring process, artificial intelligence plays a great role. Collection of all the required documents and proofs are collected through the means of artificial technology. Newly selected employees get all the essential information like job profile, duties on the job, organizational policies, etc. are communicated through the apps of the organization. The entire job-related data is provided through the laptop and digital media. If any newly hired employee has any query, then they can make use of artificial intelligence media to get information (Yawalkar, 2019).

Additionally, the HRM activities can successfully integrate the smart HR 4.0 into the hiring, developing, and off-boarding of employees (Pillai and Sivathanu, 2018). On the smartphone device, a chatbot can provide you with an itinerant and personalized schedule of the procedures to follow on the first day, boosting your self-assurance and making you seem good about yourself. If you are interested in learning more about the new company, chatbots will be happy to provide you with the details you want (He, 2018).

"According to one respondent (Ms. Kiran); at the time of selection and onboarding of employees artificial intelligence helps to ease the systems and processes as well as helps to familiarize employees with

the organizational policies. All the documents of employees are verified and checked whether they are all legal or not. Employees are making familiar with the important contacts of the organization and all this process is done with the help of artificial intelligence".

Training and Development Programs

Every employee who joins any new organization require training to perform the task in the way the organization wants. Training and development help the employees to get ready for the new roles, adapt to the culture of the organization, etc. Therefore, human resource professionals run artificial intelligence to help the employees to know the procedures and protocols of the organization. It helps us with a tool to provide information to the candidate without any restriction on time (Matsa and Gullamajji, 2019). Through the tools of artificial intelligence real-time training for the employees is very easy and employees feel more confirmable. It reduces the personal meeting stress of employees with a trainer. Virtual platforms provide the access to files and training materials at any time.

With the aid of AI, learning is motivated by the idea of simulation activities for a variety of tasks. As a leader of human resources, you might theoretically use AI to bring what-if evaluation to competitive analysis, valuation, product differentiation, and hiring selections. As a result, a variety of trainings will improve your cognitive, selection, and behavioral skills. Relying on an employee's preferred learning method, AI systems also suggest more customized/individualized learning (Merlin and R, 2018).

"One HR professional shared the experience and said that by the use of artificial intelligence in training and development it is easy for us to arrange trainings for employees. Otherwise, it is a big headache to invite a trainer and arrange all the necessary arrangements and facilities for trainers and after that, there is big doubt that employees are retaining things or not. But now if any employee wants to recall things then artificial intelligence is a big help for them. AI is also very much helpful in providing real-time answers to frequently asked questions" says Mr. Anuj).

Employee Engagement

An Engagement process is one where an employee can be automated for personal experience and real-time interaction. This process can involve keeping the employees updated regarding the status of an application and maintaining relationships to reduce stress and anxiety during the period of waiting (Ahmed, 2018). Artificial intelligence tools help to update records, gather information & perform tasks that involve fewer interactions. These tools can be used as a source of information through the means of virtual platforms or chatbots. Artificial intelligence helps to maintain internal communication, update information, providing timely information, filing various reports and issuing timely notices (Bibi, 2019; Maity, 2019). All this work helps to serve the organization and save the time and effort of HR professionals. Also, keep the employees engage in all the processes and provide the facility to not to miss any information by employees.

"According to one HR professional (Mr. Anantjeet Singh), AI helps to engage employees by providing them the timely information which saves the efforts of HR professionals".

Maintaining Workforce Data

In today's time, artificial intelligence is more helpful in maintaining workforce data. It is also useful in reducing biases in the systems and it brings uniformity to the systems. An organization with high transparency is liked by its stakeholders so artificial intelligence is helpful to bring transparency to the organization.

Based on the data maintenance by artificial intelligence, HR professionals can predict the trend and take corrective decisions for the future. Taking corrective decisions for the betterment of the organization is very important so artificial intelligence maintains corrective workforce data and makes able HR to take real-time decisions.

"One HR professional (Ms. Reema) shared that artificial intelligence is a useful tool in maintaining all HR records and data. It brings proper records maintenance system in the organization and builds HR functions smooth".

Improved Employee Retention

Finding outstanding workers is the most challenging task, and retaining skillful employees in the organization is even tougher. Employee retention is considered the hardest and most vital task by most firms (Wassan et al. 2021; Sharma, Chandwani, and Kothari, 2021; Jatobá et al. 2019). Artificial intelligence (AI) could be utilized to tackle problems in a variety of sectors, including human resources management. Using AI to handle the problem of keeping unsatisfied top talent can be done in a couple of ways, depending on the demands of the company and its workers (Zahidi et al. 2020; Bibi, 2019). Artificial intelligence (AI) could be capable to overcome this barrier, as its application may be equipped to predict specific employee demands and actions. HR personnel may now be preventive and implement the necessary precautions before an incident happens, thanks to the new technology (Merlin and Jayam, 2018; Rathi, 2018).

"According to one HR professional (Mr. Hardev), artificial intelligence helps leaders to know their capabilities and weak points. Dashboards and other tools are useful for leaders to improve the areas where they are lacking for effective employee retention".

Various Benefits of Artificial Intelligence in HR

Following are some of the benefits of artificial intelligence in HR:

- Artificial intelligence in human resource management helps to streamline the processes and functions of HR.
- It helps to reduce human biases and ambiguity in the HR processes.
- AI in HR helps to make recruitment and selection processes easy and more reliable with better candidate experience.
- Training and development of the employees become easier and more efficient through artificial intelligence. It improves the training processes also.

- The automation of administrative tasks reduces the burden on human resource professionals therefore they can focus on other areas and make better HR systems.
- Organizations that are using artificial intelligence in their organizations are far better than those that are not using it. The market reputation of artificial intelligence using organizations is more than the organizations not using AI.
- Artificial intelligence is one of the boosters of employee engagement. Because engagement of employees is necessary for quality and productive work.

Challenges While Implementing Artificial Intelligence in HR

Following are some of the challenges while artificial intelligence in HR:

- In India, some HR professionals are not much familiar with the aspect of artificial intelligence properly. Therefore, they find it difficult to implement in the organization.
- People in the organization are not having the appropriate skills they can properly utilize the use of artificial intelligence.
- Except for the HR professionals, employees also be afraid using new technology in the organization.
- For the better implementation of artificial intelligence in any organization, it requires a good number of finances for better results. But lack of funds creates a big challenge in the implementation of AI in the organization.
- Due to the limited proven applications of artificial intelligence sometimes organizations are not able to trust artificial intelligence.

CONCLUSION

No doubt artificial intelligence eases the working of human resources and better the functioning of an organization in terms of working and quality output. In today's time, artificial intelligence transforms many functions of human resources and almost in every function it contributes. In all the functions such as recruitment, hiring, on-boarding the employees, training, development and decisions making; artificial intelligence is used. Artificial intelligence enables HR to improve its functioning and take better decisions for the present as well as for the future. But to implement AI in organizational setup requires a more focused approach. HR professionals and employees need to have good knowledge of how decisions are to be made for the successful implementation of artificial intelligence.

LIMITATIONS OF THE STUDY

The present study has some limitations which are listed below:

- The study can be done by considering the quantitative data into consideration. For the study set of questions can be prepared and data can be collected through the questionnaire method.
- For better results, more HR professionals can be interviewed.

- The present study considers the interview method to get results so there may be a possibility of personal biases in the opinion of respondents.

AUTHOR BIOGRAPHY

Rajwinder Kaur is a research scholar at Chandigarh University. She is B.com (Hons.) and MBA (Banking, Finance, and HR) and now pursuing a PhD from Chandigarh University. She is interested in the areas of HR and Finance. She has done internships in Banks and under Charted Accountant and successfully completed various research projects. She has also done online courses from reputed online websites. As far as her publications are concerned, she has published more than 7 research papers in international and national journals. She has also published research papers in Scopus Journal and ABDC-indexed journals. She has also presented more than 8 research papers at national and international conferences. She has actively participated in various activities and is very much interested in research-related projects.

REFERENCES

Abdeldayem, M. M., & Aldulaimi, S. H. (2020). Trends and Opportunities of Artificial Intelligence in Human Resource Management: Aspirations for Public Sector in Bahrain. *International Journal of Scientific & Technology Research*, *9*(1), 3867–3871.

Ahmed, O. (2018). Artificial Intelligence in HR. *International Journal of Research and Analytical Reviews*, *5*(4), 971–978.

Barboza, C. (2019). Artificial Intelligence and HR: The new wave of Technology. *Journal of Advances in Social Science and Humanities*, *5*(4), 715–720.

Berhil, S., Benlahmar, H., & Labani, N. (2020). A review paper on artificial intelligence at the service of human resources management. *Indonesian Journal of Electrical Engineering and Computer Science*, *18*(1), 32–40. doi:10.11591/ijeecs.v18.i1.pp32-40

Bibi, M. (2019). Execution of Artificial Intelligence Approach in Human Resource Management Functions: Benefits and Challenges in Pakistan. *Sarhad Journal of Management Sciences*, *5*(1), 113–124. doi:10.31529jms.2018.5.1.8

Di Vaio, A., Palladino, R., Hassan, R., & Escobar, O. (2020). Artificial intelligence and business models in the sustainable development goals perspective: A systematic literature review. *Journal of Business Research*, *121*, 283–314. doi:10.1016/j.jbusres.2020.08.019

Eubanks, B. (2022). *Artificial intelligence for HR: Use AI to support and develop a successful workforce*. Kogan Page Publishers.

Garg, V., Srivastav, S., & Gupta, A. (2018). Application of artificial intelligence for sustaining green human resource management. *2018 International Conference on Automation and Computational Engineering (ICACE)*, 113-116. 10.1109/ICACE.2018.8686988

Geetha, R., & Reddy, B. S. (2018). Recruitment through Artificial Intelligence: A Conceptual Study. *International Journal of Mechanical Engineering and Technology*, *9*(7), 63–70.

George, G., & Thomas, M. R. (2019). Integration of Artificial Intelligence in Human Resource. *International Journal of Innovative Technology and Exploring Engineering*, *9*(2), 5069–5073. doi:10.35940/ijitee.L3364.129219

He, E. (2018). Can artificial intelligence make work more human? *Strategic HR Review*, *17*(5), 263–264. doi:10.1108/SHR-10-2018-146

Jatobá, M., Santos, J., Gutierriz, I., Moscon, D., Fernandes, P. O., & Teixeira, J. P. (2019). Evolution of Artificial Intelligence Research in Human Resources. *Procedia Computer Science*, *164*, 137–142. doi:10.1016/j.procs.2019.12.165

Jia, Q., Guo, Y., Li, R., Li, Y., & Chen, Y. (2018). A Conceptual Artificial Intelligence Application Framework in Human Resource Management. *Proceedings of The 18th International Conference on Electronic Business*, 106–114.

Jiang, F., Du, C., Fu, T., & Xiao, R. (2019). Research on the Application of Artificial Intelligence in Human Resource Management. *Journal of Social Sciences Studies*, *4*, 258–262.

Keller, J. R. (2018). Posting and slotting: How hiring processes shape the quality of hire and compensation in internal labor markets. *Administrative Science Quarterly*, *63*(4), 848–878. doi:10.1177/0001839217736045

Kshetri, N. (2021). Evolving uses of artificial intelligence in human resource management in emerging economies in the global South: Some preliminary evidence. *Management Research Review*, *44*(7), 970–990. doi:10.1108/MRR-03-2020-0168

Kumari, P. B., & Hemalatha, A. (2019). Perception towards Artificial Intelligence in Human Resources Management Practices – with Reference to IT Companies in Chennai. *International Journal of Recent Technology and Engineering*, *8*(4S3), 61–65.

Maity, S. (2019). Identifying opportunities for artificial intelligence in the evolution of training and development practices. *Journal of Management Development*, *38*(8), 651–663.

Matsa, P., & Gullamajji, K. (2019). To Study Impact of Artificial Intelligence on Human Resource Management. *International Research Journal of Engineering and Technology*, *6*(8), 1229–1238.

Merlin, R. P., & Jayam, R. (2018). Artificial Intelligence in Human Resource Management. *International Journal of Pure and Applied Mathematics*, *119*(17), 1891–1895.

Meyer, D. (2018). Amazon Reportedly Killed an AI Recruitment System Because It Couldn't Stop the Tool from Discriminating Against Women. *Fortune*. https://fortune.com/2018/10/10/amazon-ai-recruitment-bias-women-sex

Nawaz, N. (2019). Artificial Intelligence interchange human intervention in the recruitment process in Indian Software Industry. *International Journal of Advanced Trends in Computer Science and Engineering*, *8*(4), 1433–1442. doi:10.30534/ijatcse/2019/62842019

Nawaz, N. (2019). How far have we come with the study of artificial intelligence for recruitment process. *International Journal of Scientific & Technology Research*, *8*(7), 488–493.

Nawaz, N., & Gomes, A. M. (2019). Artificial Intelligence Chatbots are New Recruiters. *(IJACSA). International Journal of Advanced Computer Science and Applications*, *10*(9), 1–5. doi:10.14569/IJACSA.2019.0100901

Parveen, N. A., & Palaniammal, V. S. (2019). A Study on Artificial Intelligence in Human Resource Management today and tomorrow. *International Journal of Research and Analytical Reviews*, *6*(1), 513–516.

Pillai, R., & Sivathanu, B. (2020). Adoption of artificial intelligence (AI) for talent acquisition in IT/ITeS organizations. *Benchmarking*, *27*(9), 2599–2629. doi:10.1108/BIJ-04-2020-0186

Premnath, E., & Chully, A. A. (2019). Artificial Intelligence in Human Resource Management: A Qualitative Study in the Indian Context. *Journal of Xi'an University of Architecture & Technology*, *11*(12), 1193–1205.

Rathi, D. R. (2018). Artificial intelligence and the future of HR practices. *International Journal of Applied Research*, *4*(6), 113–116.

Reddy, K. V. S., Jagadeesan, D., & Rao, T. S. (2020). A Study on Artificial Intelligence Rewards and Recognition and its Effectiveness on Employees. *Journal of Critical Reviews*, *7*(18), 1345–1349.

Sharma, R., Chandwani, J., & Kothari, J. (2021). Computer Aided HR in the Era of Artificial Intelligence. *Turkish Journal of Computer and Mathematics Education*, *12*(9), 735–745.

Tandon, L. S., Joshi, P., & Rastogi, R. K. (2017). Understanding the Scope of Artificial Intelligence in Human Resource Management Processes – A Theoretical Perspective. *International Journal of Business and Administration Research Review*, *1*(19), 62–66.

Wamba-Taguimdje, S. L., Wamba, S. F., Kamdjoug, J. R. K., & Wanko, C. E. T. (2020). Influence of artificial intelligence (AI) on firm performance: The business value of AI-based transformation projects. *Business Process Management Journal*, *26*(7), 1893–1924. doi:10.1108/BPMJ-10-2019-0411

Wassan, S., Gulati, K., Pallathadka, H., Suhail, B., Kuhar, P., & Gupta, A. (2021). How artificial intelligence transforms the experience of employees. *Turkish Journal of Computer and Mathematics Education, 12*(10), 7116-7135. doi:.v12i10.5603 doi:10.17762/turcomat

Yawalkar, V. V. (2019). A Study of Artificial Intelligence and its role in Human Resource Management. *International Journal of Research and Analytical Reviews*, *6*(1), 20–24.

Zahidi, F., Imam, Y., Hashmi, A. U., & Baig, M. M. (2020). Impact of Artificial Intelligence on HR Management – A Review. *Dogo Rangsang Research Journal*, *10*(6), 92–101.

Chapter 16
Airbnb in the Local Neighbourhood:
Innovaiton vs. Disruption

Vipin Nadda
https://orcid.org/0000-0002-2970-3709
University of Sunderland in London, UK

Markéta Pospíšilová
University of Sunderland in London, UK

ABSTRACT

Airbnb is a platform allowing a peer-to-peer accommodation option for people sharing their own extra space. As simple it sounds, there are many challenges behind its implementation. It is crucial to look at both sides of the coin to understand not only what it brings but what it causes as well. Airbnb is a comparatively new phenomenon of the modern times and changes the traditional tourist behaviour as well as accommodation situation in the market. Initially, the general perception was that Airbnb is not a threat to the traditional accommodation as it attracts completely new customers. It is a big part of sharing economy and brings both advantages and disadvantages. The sharing economy is a new dimension of economy, and the classic structure is rapidly changing. It is a sustainable form of service provision and contributes to inclusive destination development. On the other hand, as Airbnb lies in providing accommodation by non-commercial residents, there is an overall lack of control of whether the host is reliable and if it is secure.

USE OF ROBOTICS AND AI IN TOURISM AND HOSPITALITY MARKETING

Artificial intelligence applications are stated as the most important technological innovation that came with the Industry 4.0 revolution (Bayuk and Demir, 2019: 781). Artificial intelligence; is a technology that has started to be used in the fields of business administration, medicine, automotive, and education. Artificial intelligence, which is the focus of attention of professional groups such as engineers, informa-

DOI: 10.4018/978-1-6684-6732-9.ch016

Copyright © 2023, IGI Global. Copying or distributing in print or electronic forms without written permission of IGI Global is prohibited.

tion technology experts, and analysts, has also started to be used in social sciences (Jarek and Mazurek, 2019: 47). Usage areas of artificial intelligence technologies; It is possible to summarize it as systems that think and act like humans, expert systems, natural language processing, robots, image processing, and machine learning (Adalı, 2017: 10-11). Artificial intelligence is defined as "human intelligence technology created with the help of computer programs" (Tsaih and Hsu, 2018: 127).

The use of artificial intelligence systems in solving large and complex problems of enterprises is one of the biggest advantages of analyzing data with the help of artificial intelligence and doing more work with less effort. By using this data, it is possible to offer appropriate products and services at the right time and in the right place. Such services will be effective in customers' decision to choose the business and purchase. Businesses that want to take advantage of these opportunities should use artificial intelligence technologies (Yeğin, 2020: 491-492). It is stated that artificial intelligence and robotic technology applications, which are also being used in the tourism and hospitality industry, can provide new opportunities for customers in the travel decision-making process, customer relations, purchasing decisions, payment systems, travel consultancy services such as artificial intelligence (Zlatanov and Popesku, 2019: 84). Artificial intelligence and robotic applications in the tourism and hospitality industry benefit from the detection of possible customer behaviors by making use of customer data (Bayuk and Demir, 2019: 781; Shahid and Li, 2019: 30-31).

It is stated that it is possible to provide uninterrupted instant services in tourism 24 hours a day, 7 days a week by using the natural language processing and feature identification functions of artificial intelligence. (Tsaih and Hsu, 2018: 127). Artificial intelligence and robotic applications in the tourism and hospitality sector; It is used in hotels, restaurants, and airports for cleaning rooms, delivering goods, carrying luggage, cooking, and cleaning (Ivanov, Webster, & Berezina, 2017; Devitt, 2019; Ibiş, 2019; Osawa et al., 2017; Ohlan, 2018; Trejos, 2016; Tuyed, 2016; Trejos, 2014; Yalçın Kayıkçı and Kutluk Bozkurt, 2018; Social Tables, 2019).

In this research, Rogers's (1995) Diffusion of Innovation and Davis (1989) technology acceptance model regarding use of robotics and AI in tourism and hospitality marketing were used. The Diffusion of Innovation Theory aims to collect data about people's adaptation processes towards innovations and to eliminate uncertainties. Davis (1989)'s Technology Acceptance Model is stated as individuals' intentions to accept the use of technology. In this context, the aim of this study is to examine the use of artificial intelligence and robotic technologies in tourism marketing conceptually and to reveal application examples. The fact that the use of artificial intelligence in the tourism industry is one of the new topics in the related literature, and the limited number of studies on artificial intelligence applications in terms of tourism marketing made it necessary to conduct this study. When the relevant literature is examined, the limited number of studies on the use of artificial intelligence and robotic technologies in the field of tourism marketing and the increase in the use and importance of new technologies in the tourism and hospitality industry necessitated this study. In this context, first of all, the concept of artificial intelligence and its applications will be discussed in this section. Then, the use of artificial intelligence as a marketing tool, the importance of artificial intelligence in the tourism industry and tourism marketing, and finally the examples of artificial intelligence in tourism marketing will be given.

REFERENCES

Adalı, E. (2017). Yapay zeka. *İTÜ Vakfı Dergisi, 75*, 8-13.

Bayuk, M. N. (2019). Endüstri 4.0 kapsamında yapay zeka ve pazarlamanın geleceği. Journal Of Social. *Humanities and Administrative Sciences*, *5*(19), 781–799. doi:10.31589/JOSHAS.163

Davis, F. D. (1989). Perceived Usefulness, Perceived Ease of Use and User Acceptance of Information Technology. *Management Information Systems Quarterly*, *13*(3), 319–340. doi:10.2307/249008

Devitt, M. (2019). *How can I help you? The emergence of robots in hotels and restaurants.* https://www.robotshop.com/community/blog/show/how-can-i-help you-the-emergence-of-robots-in-hotels-and-restaurants/

İbiş, S. (2019). Turizm endüstrisinde robotlaşma. *Türk Turizm Araştırmaları Dergisi*, *3*(3), 403–420. doi:10.26677/TR1010.2019.169

Ivanov, S., Webster, C., & Berezina, K. (2017). Adoption of robots and service automation by tourism and hospitality companies. *Revista Turismo & Desenvolvimento*, *27*(28), 1501–1517.

Jarek, K., & Mazurek, G. (2019). Marketing and artificial ıntelligence. *Central European Business Review*, *8*(2), 46–55. doi:10.18267/j.cebr.213

Ohlan, R. (2018). Role of information technology in hotel industry. International Journal of Scientific Research in Computer Science. *Engineering and Information Technology*, *3*(2), 277–281.

Osawa, H., Akiya, N., Koyama, T., Ema, A., Kanzaki, N., Ichise, R., & Kubo, A. (2017). What is real risk and benefit on work with robots? From the analysis of a robot hotel. *IEEE International Conference on Human-Robot Interaction*. 10.1145/3029798.3038312

Rogers, E. M. (1995). *Diffusion of Innovations*. Simon & Schuster Press.

Shahid, M. Z., & Li, G. (2019). Impact of artificial intelligence in marketing: a perspective of marketing professionals of Pakistan. *Global Journal of Management and Business Research: E Marketing*, *19*(2), 26-33.

Socialtables. (2019). *Robots in hotels: 6 hotel brands leading the way*. Retrieved from https://www.socialtables.com/blog/hospitality-technology/hot el-brands-robot/

Trejos, N. (2014). *Ready for the hotel industry's first robotic butler?* Retrieved from https://www.usatoday.com/story/travel/hotels/2014/08/12/alof t-hotels-starwoodroboticbultler/13954231/

Trejos, N. (2016). *USA Today, introducing Connie, Hilton's new robot concierge*. https://www.usatoday.com/story/travel/-roadwarriorvoices/201 6/03/09/introducing-connie-hiltons-new-robot-con cierge/8152 5924/

Tsaih, R.-H., & Hsu, C. C. (2018). Artificial intelligence in smart tourism: a conceptual framework. *The 18th International Conference on Electronic Business*, 124-133.

Tuyed. (2016). *İnsansı robotlar devri*. Retrieved from http://www.tuyed.org.tr/turizmde-insansi-robotlar-devri/

Yalçın Kayıkçı, M., & Kutluk Bozkurt, A. (2018). Dijital çağda Z ve Alpha kuşağı, yapay zeka uygulamaları ve turizme yansımaları. *Sosyal Bilimler Metinleri, 1*, 54–64.

Yeğin, T. (2020). The place and future of artificial intelligence in marketing strategies. *Ekev Akademi Dergisi, 24*(81), 489–506.

Zlatanov, S., & Popesku, J. (2019, April). Current applications of artificial intelligence in tourism and hospitality. *International Scientific Conference on Information Technology and Data Related Research*, 84-90.

Chapter 17
Managing the Service in a Small Hotel by Self-Service Technology Adoption:
The Customer Perspective From Thailand

Kannapat Kankaew
https://orcid.org/0000-0003-1127-5627
College of Hospitality Industry Management, Suan Sunandha Rajabhat University, Thailand

Thanasit Suksutdhi
https://orcid.org/0000-0003-4787-6491
School of Management Technology, Suranaree University of Technology, Thailand

Theppaluk Komolvanij
College of Hospitality Industry Management, Suan Sunandha Rajabhat University, Thailand

Korawin Kungwol
College of Hospitality Industry Management, Suan Sunandha Rajabhat University, Thailand

Rojanard Waramontri
College of Hospitality Industry Management, Suan Sunandha Rajabhat University, Thailand

Kanittha Charernnit
https://orcid.org/0000-0002-3016-9451
College of Hospitality Industry Management, Suan Sunandha Rajabhat University, Thailand

ABSTRACT

Modern technology is creating customer experience. Its algorithm could remember, predict, and provide customized needs of customers. The self-service technology (SST) is a service innovation that communicates with users through either internet-based social media or applications. Yet, the hotels in Thailand are like other businesses that applied SST. The employees could better communicate, create human relationship, and understand profoundly customer needs than technology. Therefore, the adoption technology in hotels, especially small hotels, must be efficient and effective. This study aims to assess the SST components that serve the small hotel customers' needs and evaluate electronic service quality and technology adoption leading to satisfaction and repurchase intention. This study mainly used quantitative method by structural equation modelling. The scope of the study is customers who experienced using small hotel in Nakhon Ratchasima Province in Thailand. Nakhon Ratchasima is the fifth biggest province in Thailand and one of the top destinations of Thai people.

DOI: 10.4018/978-1-6684-6732-9.ch017

Copyright © 2023, IGI Global. Copying or distributing in print or electronic forms without written permission of IGI Global is prohibited.

INTRODUCTION

The advancement of technology goes swiftly and was employed in all business sectors for creating customer experiences. Further, the algorithm of technology could remember, predict, and provide customize needs of customers. In addition, the application of technology is widely adopted as well as the number of internet users rose dramatically from 4.5 billion people in 2020 to 4.9 billion persons in 2021. In Thailand, the number of internet users ranked number 8 in Asia Pacific and expected to reach more than 61 million people in 2025 (Statista, 2021). This reflects the internet and application services would become more common in the service industry. More than a decade, (Taneja, 2011) shed the light on information technology adoption in airline business that passenger has gone digital and mobile. The passenger behavior has shifted from personal contact in the service processes to the usage of information technology, such as booking the ticket, payment, and check-in (Kankaew, 2022). Sophisticatedly, scholars employed technology to collect data for the research from the social media sources, like (Herjanto et al, 2021) administered netnography approach to review and analyze passenger's negative feedback on airline services. The netnography is technology-based to study the groups, communities, or individual in their own environment in specific time (Dawson, 2020). Today, specifically, amid the pandemic we have witnessed that the e-commerce was significantly success. The self-service technology (SST) is a service innovation. It communicates with users or customer through the internet and applications. The SST was extensively in myriad sectors including services, such as hotel for checking-in and out, airline check-in, travel booking, left baggage at the airport, purchasing, and buying goods in department store, food ordering, and mobile banking (Hanks, Line, & Mattila, 2015; Huang, Lee, & Chen, 2019; Myra, Ringgold, Atienza, Susilo, & Len, 2020).

Yet, the hotels in Thailand are like other businesses that applied SST. Howbeit, the adoption of self-service technology in the hotel shall consider the importance of high service quality. It is a key element which distinct the hotel from one another. Moreover, the service that creates value and positive customer experience shall come deliver from the hotel workforces. Since, the employees could better communicate and understand profoundly of customer needs than technology (Hallin, 2018). It should be underlined that the readiness and prompt to serve the customer smoothly and expectedly are crucial. Nevertheless, the majority of big hotels and chained hotels are promptly aligned the implication of information technology for guest services and resilience to the changes. On the contrary, small hotels are mostly own and managed as a family business. Notably, the small hotels which located outside the capital city of Thailand (Bangkok) and surrounding areas. It is where the technology infrastructures are in the development phases in some areas.

Hence, this study aims to assess the SST components that serve the small hotel customers' needs and evaluate electronic service quality leading to satisfaction and repurchase intention. Therefore, the adoption technology in hotel especially small hotels must be efficient and effective. That is the customers' perspectives are considered, their requirements are met resulting to service quality, satisfaction and return intention. This study mainly used quantitative method by structural equation modelling. The scope of study are customers who experienced small hotel in Nakhon Ratchasima Province in Thailand. Nakhon Ratchasima which is the fifth biggest province in Thailand and one of the top destinations of Thai people. In the past period there were various investors outlay in hotel business in Nakhon Ratchasima. There are 706 grand, medium, and small hotels. Nakhon Ratchasima province landscape composes of mountain valleys, plain and high land with 255 kilometers from the capital city 'Bangkok' Thailand. It is the gate province connecting to the northeastern. Thai government is now investing mega project in this province, such as high-speed train, toll road, road expansion. The city itself aims to be smart city, MICE city, art city, and safe city. (Nakhon Ratchasima Provincial Statistical Office, 2017). In this study, we aim to assess small hotels since the grand and medium hotels have service standards that rather meet the guests' needs. In the meantime, the grand and medium hotels financial could support for further development, especially modern information technology align in the services.

BACKGROUND OF THE STUDY

Self-Service Technology (SST)

In 1980, the concept of self -service derived from the study of Toffler, who defined the self-service words rooted from *prosumer*. It was explained as the production by consumers, where there is an ambiguity of interactions between service provider and service receiver through the use of self-service technology -SST. The SST was adopted to resolve organization's labor cost and to serve the customers' behavior that changed to autonomy in service consumption (Suwannakul, 2019). The SST was defined as the technological interaction of customers in receiving service without the service workforce's interaction. It is the technology that organization provide that enable customers' engagement in their own service (Huang et al., 2019; Muhammad et al., 2018). Consequently, the self-service technology allows organization performing speedy, easy, accuracy, and less communication with the frontline officers (Shahril et al., 2021). Then, it can be concluded that the self-service concept was employed as an extra choice of services offered to customer and communication mechanism. The integration of technology with self-service allows customer access to the service easier and more comfortable. Through its automatic system, technology facilitating and resulting to a positive impact toward users' mindset. Obviously, the time of customer is vital as well as the traditional services by service provider may not create novel and exciting experience to some specific guests. On the other hand, the customer who are technology savvy tend to use self-service rather than waiting in the queue for human services.

Though, scholars (Schumann et al., 2012) segregated the services into two types namely, self-services and delivered services. The first camp 'self-service' emphasizes on the processes and the role of customers. Contrastingly, the delivered services stresses on the importance of employees. Lay this on the line, the following table 1 compares the characteristics of self-services and delivered services.

Table 1. Characteristics of self-services and delivered-services

Characteristics	Delivered-Services	Self-Services
Role	Service provider or Customer and service provider	Customer
Customers' Participation	Customer is part of service delivery	Customer interaction with system
Human Interaction	High	Low
Service Processes Conformity	Yes	No
Automatic System	No	Yes
Process Complexity	High	Low
On-demand Service	Pre-determined	Standardization
Organization Representative	Employees	Information technology system

Sources: Adapted from Schumann et al (2012)

The adoption of SST, howbeit, organization should consider the system function properly and its benefit to users. The retail banking service is the first adopter of self-service technology (Li & Huang, 2019). Obviously, the automatic telling machine-ATM which is successfully SST of retail bank. It offers simply various money transactions and myriad locations of ATM can be found. Currently, it is not necessary that the bank's customer has to be at the ATM site but using mobile or internet banking instead. Form this statement, we can assume that people rely on the banking service technology. In other words, the symbiosis and connection with the main infrastructure of service organization is essential. For instance, the self-ordering system of restaurant should link with the point-of-sale system (POS), and the warehouse for the purpose of inventory and pricing. Whereas the check-in kiosk of the hotel should integrate with property management system (PMS) (Considine and Cormican, 2016). Further study from (Jakranukul, 2015), the SST facilitates customer in service delivery faster than human being. It is also become more popular among Thai new generations.

The rise of smartphone, addedly, enhances the development of application which people can purchase, sell, navigate, select, and pay at once. Today, the innovation of SST platform is designed in vary form i.e., website, application, stand-alone kiosk, and social media which is accessible to everyone. The SST was applied widely in businesses and services industries, such as restaurant, airlines, hotels, department store etc., Literal, the scholars (Jakrnukul, 2015; Alsiehemy, 2019; Carreirao, 2019, Huy et al., 2019) broadly conceptualized the SST into three features including; technology interfaces, direct transactions, and self-service or self-help. The technology interfaces refer to the technology which require intermediaries to communicate and transaction with users. It composes of automatic telephone answering machine, automatic kiosk communication, online and video record. While, the direct transactions determine as a technology which allows customer purchase or exchange resources without the interaction with service provider. However, it is sometimes still required assistant from service provider. Given as example, hotel's guest check-in/ out, self-ordering technology in restaurant technology need service workforces in some process like cleaning the room. The self-help refers to sophisticated technology which allows customer to learn, acquire knowledge, and practice how to use. This type of technology feature enables users to serve own self, such as self-service gas station, ATMs, and supermarket kiosk.

In Thailand, Phunphanasakul and Lalitasasivimol (2019) reviewed the implication of information technology in hotel business creating the competitive edges. This is correspondent with Samani (2019) cited that service innovation is one of differentiate strategy in hotel industry. The four types of service innovation namely, administration, communication, services, and support system require information technology in designing and development. In parallel with Maopraman and Jaroenwisan (2022) suggested to improve the hotel service quality and competitiveness through the use of information technology in digital economy. While Phuthong and Mangsungnoen (2017) examined the factors affecting the use and adoption of mobile technology health services consist of the expectation on efficiency, positive social influence, negative attitude of oneself to the changes, and the intention to use. This is consistent to Vongtharawat & Pasunon (2017) examined the factors impact online check-in of airline's passenger. The study illustrated the intention to use, social influence, perceive risk affect the use of online self-service check-in. Further study by Imthammaporn (2018) revealed that technology perception in terms of reliability and social conformity, convenience, and the promotion through e-marketing were the attributes affecting the use of self-service technology. Nevertheless, other scholars (Huang et al., 2019; Huy et al., 2019, and Kasavana, 2008) identified the factors affecting SST usage in hospitality industry composes of user interface, information, product display, architecture, payment processing, marketing, products, and services as compiled in table 2.

Table 2. Factors Affecting SST Usage in Hospitality Industry

Factors	Descriptions
User interface	The system's efficiency, quick response and no technical interruption.
Information	Abundant of products/ services information, no complication to search for information. The right information provided.
Product Display	Clear, concise, interesting, attracting customer to find out more information.
Architecture	The design of self-service kiosk, or equipment for the services. The infrastructure of the system should accommodate various service program.
Payment Processing	Safe, and securely store customers' data, accommodate multiple currencies, credit card, debit card or other type of payment.
Marketing	Dynamic marketing that tailor made package for customer individually.
Products	Selling kiosk may have space limit for goods presentation. The seller should use monitor to link with website presentation.
Services	The customer should always can contact with service provider according to their needs.

Compiled by authors.

Theory and Concept Relating to Technology Adoption

Technology adoption is a process of decision toward innovation. There are five phases including (1) knowledge is the first stage of the user that the existing of innovation, how to use the innovation, and principle and benefit of the innovation; (2) persuasion phase is the attitude of user toward innovation after the knowledge acquired. The attitude could either be positive or negative; (3) decision phase refers to the process on making decision whether to adopt or ignore the innovation; (4) implementation phase determines as a process occurring after the decision made that is to cease or continue adoption; (5) confirmation phase occurs when the user search for further information on the innovation to confirm or neglect the use of technology (Roger, 2003). Theoretically, there were some theories elucidate human behavior and technology adoption, such as theory of reasoned action-TRA. In 1975 and 1980 Ajzen and Fishbein illuminated TRA that explicate the relationship of belief and attitude to behavior. The TRA reflected the human behavior changed deriving from their belief and behave logically. At a later date, theory of reasoned action was applied in the study of (Davis, 1989) technology adoption phenomenon. Albeit the factors incorporate the human behavior exposed come from individual decision. Though, the key factor that influence behavior is the intention to behave inclusive of the attitudes towards behavior and subjective norm. These two factors are the key driving forces of human behavior to conduct or omit specific action. Despite that, the subjective norm is the belief of individual to social needs and reflection to his/her actions. Specifically, the important people who live closely to the individual such as family members, employer. Conceptualizing, the TRA signifies technology adoption in individual through attitudes, belief, and social norm reasonably. Later, the TRA has evolved by (Ajzen, 1991) to theory of planned behavior (TPB). Since, the TRA could not explain a complex behavior in specific situation that uncontrollable. Therefore, the TPB reflexed the perceived behavioral control which could filling the gap and limitation of TRA. The theory of planned behavior could annotate technology adoption of everyone arising from their intention. There are three elements impact the behavior intention namely, mindset toward the action, social norm, and perceived of self-control in the actions.

On the flip side, TPB still has limitation on the context of social norms, knowledge, as well as the consequence result whether positive or negative. It can be apprehended that both internal and external conditions influence to one behavior. For instance, the facilities which accommodate the usage of technology might enhance user's comfort and convenience. On the other hand, the unaccountable system in term of safety and security that one encounter during using technology can be barriers to technology adoption. Nevertheless, TPB was further developed (Davis, 1989) to technology acceptance model (TAM). The TAM was widely employed in the study in technology adoption. TAM concept has ignored the attitude which leads to behavior in explanation of technology adoption in the individual. The perceived usefulness and accessibility were administered to assess individual technology adoption (Davis et al., 1989). Although, the capable of TAM in explanation of technology adopt sounds effective, but scholars found some limitations still exist (Bayrataroglu et al., 2019). In addition, Huy et al (2019) highlighted the only factor of individual in technology adopt is the intention. Henceforth, TAM was expanded with other attributes in the study of the intention on technology adoption. The four additional attributes are demographic, perceived usefulness, perceived ease of use, and attitude toward technology adoption. The demographic also refers to previous experiences of individual that inspire the beneficial from using technology. The second attribute, perceived usefulness deals with the perception of each person to technology adoption could cherish job performance. Whereas the perceived ease of use is the expectation of user-friendly technology (Venkatesh and Davis, 2000). In the meantime, scholars promulgated that perceived usefulness has direct impact to technology adoption, in contrast perceived ease of use has indirect impact. Moreover, the perceived ease of use divided into two camps (Venkatesh and Bala, 2008) encompass with primary attribute or the anchors that disclose the computer competencies i.e., computer self-efficiency, perception of external control, computer playfulness or anxiety. The other camp is amendable attribute relate to the changed belief from direct experience on using technology. That contains of perceiving of joyfulness, objective of usability. To be more precise, the TAM2 has been developed and investigated (Venkatesh and Davis, 2000) by widening the TAM with extra variables. The results found the influence affecting technology adoption compose of social and norms, willingness, image. Over and above, the cognitive process does affect the technology adoption, such as job related, output quality, objective outcome, and user-friendly.

Whilst, in the 20th century, Rogers and Shoemaker (1971) identified factors affecting the technology adoption were:

(1) Receiver characteristics include gender, educational level, career, age, member of specific group, news and information he/she receives
(2) Society system refers to economic, social, culture, and geographical area, for example, the different economic situations impact to different technology adoption or ignorance.
(3) Technology characteristics form user's perspective are all form of noticeable benefits, such as technology helps to reduce cost of operation.
(4) Individual behavioral communication means the communication channel ex. radio, television, poster, or thinkers. The types of communication channel can influence technology adoption on people through logic, speed, emotional etc.,

Obviously, in Thailand, from the study of Chouyboonchoo et al (2019) disclosed the technology adoption in banking industry comprises of the expectation on attempt new technology, facilitation in using, joyfulness, value of the fee, and individual characteristics. Wisuttisaeng Piyathasanan (2017) highlighted the factors of choosing technology adoption in organization concern with return on investment, readiness of organizational resources, new system aligns with existing system, and the resilience in technology adaptation of rivals. Tychachoonhakij and Iamratanakul (2019) cited the perception of technology usefulness, user-friendly technology, attitude toward technology, quality of technology, result-oriented of using technology, system capability, and efficiency have influence on technology adoption in public sector in Thailand. There, still, were other issues to be considered on SST adoption in organization, for instance the lack of low-skilled and high-skilled labor in service job, and the lack of human relation in services. Suwannakul (2019) emphasized SSTs limitation in service business that compete in high service quality, when the system failure organization may not correct the problem promptly and efficiently. Additionally, if organization relies and focus only on technology, it will lose the opportunity to bond with customer. Therefore, the service quality has to be well-recognized while employing SST. The organization shall usually evaluate the SST service quality from the customer properly for further improvement.

Electronic Service Quality and Satisfaction

Electronic Service Quality

Service quality, generally, has been studied and discussed over three decades (Suwannakul, 2019). The service quality is the organization providing the service that meet or over the customer expectation. The customer is also comparing the perceived information with actual services they received (Suksutdhi, 2022). Since the sophisticated technology penetrates and adopt in several businesses. Then, Parasuraman et al (2005) created E-S-Qual which expanded from the original SQUAL. The new model, E-S-Qual and the sub model E-RecS-Qual, examine the service quality through website and the dealing with service problems and queries. The aim of these two models is to assess the electronic service quality. There are seven aspects of the services coupled with efficiency, privacy, system availability, fulfillment, responsiveness, compensation, and contact. Shared (2019) cited there are three elements on E-service assessment with traditional services. Firstly, there is no frontline personnel serve and interact with the customer. Secondly, the E-service context is virtual reality. This could result to missing real experience from personnel service situation. And lastly, the customer can access and purchase the service without the interaction with employee. The various models for assessing electronic service quality were created (Rahahleh et al., 2020) such as, Web Qual, E-Squall, Site Qual, and E-Tail Q. The Web Qual model made up with three dimensions comprising of service interaction quality, information quality, and usability. Where, the E-Squall exists eleven measurements on electronic services quality embracing with; reliability, reach ability, responsiveness, privacy, flexibility, knowledge, security, customization, and graphic style. On the one hand, the Site Qual consists of processing speed, ease of use, security and safety, and total design (Yoo and Donthu, 2001). Whilst the E Tail Q investigate electronic service quality in four aspects. Those are customer service, website design, reliability, and safety and privacy (Wolfinbarger and Gilly (2002). The electronic service quality has impact on customer engagement behavior and loyalty as confirm by the study of (Vo et al., 2019), the customers were satisfied with website of luxury hotels which bonding to the relationship between the hotel and guests. Rotchanakitumnuai (2013) added the electronic service quality including; ease of use, internet of things and security.

Satisfaction

The satisfaction reflects the customer perspectives toward the products or services received. When the products and services meet the customers' needs, Tentatively, they would return intention to purchase and use the services again. This is because of the satisfaction occurred. Or it can be said that the customer satisfied with the services. Scholars determined the satisfaction as a personal feeling or attitude to the products or services positively. It emanates from the previous information and expectation before using the services. Therefore, if the service provided lower than expectation, the dissatisfaction occurred. In contrast, if the service is beyond expectation the customer will be satisfied (Kotler & Armstrong, 2018; Keskosol & Merakate, 2019). Further definition of satisfaction toward electronic self-service was defined as the satisfaction in administering technology or the primary intention to use electronic self-service in particular context. The satisfaction may reduce from the usage that array positive attitude of electronic user. It is also obtained from direct experience of electronic used, and resulting to continuously adoption (Tychachoonhakij and Iamratanakul, 2019).

Concretely, it is not only the services and products that satisfied the customer, instead there are other elements assimilated. We have interpreted and summarized in table 2 as follows.

Table 3. Satisfaction components

Satisfaction Components	Description of Components
Express the positive behavior of feeling toward the services	-location of service; easy access -positive word of mount and organization provided as promise -service provider well-organized on providing the services to service receiver, and willing to assist -service environment, design of service atmosphere, colors, and spacious -service processes run effectively, speedy, adoption of technology to provide the service, automatic answering phone with adequate and proper information
The satisfaction of customer to the service received	-comfortable of parking lot, cleanliness, equipment and tools function properly -service provider grooming and personality, tone of voice and language used, courtesy -service received response to the needs, follow up and feedback to service receiver -timely service and promptly recovering the problem issues -general information provided as customer request, up-to-date
Other related components	-equitability service, fair policy, no discrimination -on time service delivery as promise -consistency of service delivery, show interest on customer, continuous training and development of employee -progressive service that is the advancement of the service provided in term of quality, outcome, and administer modern technology

Source: Adapted from Kenaphoom et al (2020)

Besides, the service provider can retrieve the service satisfaction feedback in many ways. As refer to Panthawee (2018) suggested the approaches to survey the degree of customer's satisfaction to maintain the service standard. The evaluation can be done by using questionnaire, interview, and observe systematically from quest behavior. Likewise, Kotler and Armstrong (2018) mentioned that each organization has its own methodology to assess the customer satisfaction. That depends on the objective of the assessment. The survey approaches that commonly used, for instance, complaint and suggestion system, customer satisfaction systems, ghost shopping, lost customer analysis.

Return Intention

Return intention to use the service was resulted from the customer awareness on value for money, usefulness, and benefit of goods and services received. Sometimes, the repeat of service use is not come from the inner feeling assurance of the customer or feeling specialty of the products or services. This kind of repeat use, then, unsustainable and it is not called loyalty. Since, the chance of churn customer to other organization that offers more attractive benefits (Ashton, 2015; Ibzan et al 2016). The return intention, for this reason, is the intention of individual to return using the same services in the same organization that he/she experienced. It is because of the benefit, value for money, and the satisfaction that meet or over expectation (Ibzan et al., 2016; Nilsson & Wall, 2017). The definition of return intention was also covered the repeat purchasing of individual more than once. There are variation types of return intention, such as marketing activities, pricing strategies, and branding (Tusakunee and Inkaew, 2016), and image value (Worasuwannarak & Kankaew, 2022). While the phenomenon of frequent return intention using service in long-term called loyalty. The customer loyalty, on that account, is as valuable resources of organization. They are not only repurchasing instead they tell and invite others (Sinpattarachat & Sangruengrob, 2018). In conclusion, the return intention is the planned to repurchase the products/services of customer from the same vendors due to positive experiences received.

Anywise, the purchasing behavior of individual underlines with two key reasons (1) logic, which is people will find information, compare, and analyze before using services. This logical purchasing is mostly found in male rather than female customer, because of the stability of mood toward the temptation. In contrast, (2) emotional purchase occurs in women rather than men. The customer tends to buy immediately when they were emotionally aroused (Kotler and Armstrong, 2018). What is more in the hospitality industry, the buying decision processes concern with two elements (1) stimulus is the factor attracting visitors' desired and buy the services, (2) determinant factor is the extent determines the goods and services that visitors desire to buy (Swarbrooke & Horner, 2007). More importantly, the post-purchase behavior has to be examined whether the customer may or may not return that depending on the value of service received and satisfaction (Kotler and Armstrong, 2018). Shoosanuk et al (2017) studied the factors affecting return intention in Thai restaurant. They found two key factors including satisfaction and trust. While the return intention using hotel services of Thais (Bunrangsee & Pasunon, 2018) were security and safety, rooms, services, and employees. Even thought, the winning reward hotel has less significant influence on customer return intention. Concurrently, Boon et al (2018) found tangibility, reliability, and responsiveness have significant impact on the customer return intention in hotel business. In addition, the good service quality enhances the hotel image and flourish relationship between customer and hotel. Consistently to Seetanah et al (2018) added that the service quality affects the satisfaction and return intention of the airport's passengers. Another study of Ranjbarian and Khazaei (2015) disclosed the perceived value and service quality influence travelers' satisfaction and return intention. In brief, the return intention of customer in hospitality industry bases on the good service quality, safety and security, perceived value, satisfaction, and good experiences. However, the organization should aware the purchasing behavior of individual both logical and emotional. To highlight, the customer who frequently repeat of use has immense value to organization.

Small Hotel, the Concept

Thai Hotels Association (2022) defines 'hotel' is a building constructed with the purpose for travelers paid to stay temporarily. According to Thailand's Hotel Act 2004 section 4, the hotel business composes of a range of services that are available to customers including; accommodation, food and beverages, as well as providing services for recreation and business travelers. Whilst, Suwannaphong (2020) mentioned hotel business is the accommodation service for tourists that is the room, meal and beverages associating to the needs of guests in exchange for money. As a consequence of the tourism dramatically growth, all related business, such as hotel has relatively developed from business to industry. It heightens managing hotel being more systematically. On that ground, the Thai Hotels Association (2022) concluded the characteristic of hotel as; (1) guests must pay in exchange for stay; (2) food and drink provided for guests; (3) short-term or long-term stay but no more than one month; (4) a large building that requires a lot of labors and cost. So that, it must be well-managed, standardized operating system to create the customers' trust to stay. The types of hotels were identified including; (1) Inn is small accommodation located near the road in countryside. There is usually no meal and beverage services; (2) Tavern is the accommodation for guests who traveling by horses; (3) Guest House is the house that the owner rent to guests in cheap price; (4) Motel is small hotel located near the main road serving for guests who travel by car; (5) Lodge is an accommodation that looks like small home located in countryside, having activities for guests to enjoy; (6) Resort is a place for recreation located in nice location outside the city or in touristic sites with scenery, natural resources, and full range of services provided (Kerdpiam, 2014; Thai Hotels Association, 2022).

Likewise, the Department of Tourism (2014) mentioned the hotel is business that providing accommodation with plenty of rooms and equipped with facilities to comfort the customers. The small hotels refer to the accommodation services having less than a hundred bedroom. The basic room facilities provided, for example; television, phone. The management system consists of administration, front office, housekeeping, and repairs and maintenance. Whereas, in the USA defined small hotels are the accommodation service having 79 bedrooms but not over 149 rooms (Thai Hotel Associations, 2022). Tanongphaeng & Na Thalang (2017) reflected another aspect of small hotel by its investment value and laboring. The scholars stressed small hotel having fixed assets no exceed 50 million Thai baht, and no more than 50 employees. Based on the literature, henceforth, small hotel is the accommodation business that provide room for guests to stay overnight. The number of rooms is not over 100 rooms. While, the basic facilities provide to comfort for guests and the room rate is rather cheap. What is more, the management of small hotel is high competence in every aspect of management and administration. Since, the management has to oversee all hotel operations and performance for service quality standard. In the final analysis, the questions of this study are;

1. What are the perceptions of customer toward SST;
2. What are the factors affecting electronic service quality;
3. Are self-service technology, technology adoption, and electronic service quality influence on customers' satisfaction;

METHODOLOGY

The quantitative research was administered by using structural equation modelling. The questionnaire with 5 Likert's scale rating was employed as a tool to collect the data. The sample group were people who experienced staying in small hotel in Nakhon Ratchasima province. Precisely, the respondents must also experience the information technology system of the hotel in any facets i.e., application and website. The questionnaires were distributed both online and onsite. We used google form and share through social media ex. Facebook, Twitter. Finally, there were 412 respondents return the questionnaires. The confirmatory factor analysis was implemented to investigate the correlation of variables. The results of model fit indices testing were as CMIN/DF 1.166, GFI 0.997, CFI 0.999, NFI 0.996, RFI 0.988, and RMSEA 0.020. Meanwhile, the descriptive analysis was used to explain the demographic information, mean, percentage, and standard deviation.

Scope of the study

In this study, population are people who used to purchase and consume the small hotels in Nakhon Ratchasima province. We, concisely, we have specified only those who experienced using information technology for booking, payment, check-in, and search for the hotel information whether from the application, hotel website, or intermediaries' websites. In terms of the study area, certainly, all small hotels which the number of rooms not exceeding 100 rooms provided, and the number of workforces less than or equal to 50 persons. The majority of the hotel in our study situated in Muang District, Nakhon Ratchasima.

SOLUTIONS AND RECOMMENDATIONS

The 412 returned questionnaires were analyzed of respondents' demographic as shown in figure 1. It is our intention to separate respondents' demographic into three categories for crystalized view. As shown in figure 1, the majority number of respondents are female accounted for 64 percent and male 36 percent. Interestingly, in figure 1 the percentage of generation Y or the millennials and generation Z respondents are rather high equal to 37 percent and 30 percent respectively. It is worth noticing that these two generations are accustomed with computer and technology. According to Espinoza et al (2010) stated that technology was presented earlier in 1965-1977, and more advancement during the generation Y that is technology-based social networking was widely utilized. It is consistent to the National Statistical Office of Thailand (2020) disclosed the majority age of internet users are generation Y accounted for 98.4 percent. This data reveals that people age around 21–38 years-old tend to use internet searching and booking the hotel rather than other groups.

Figure 1. Respondents demographic

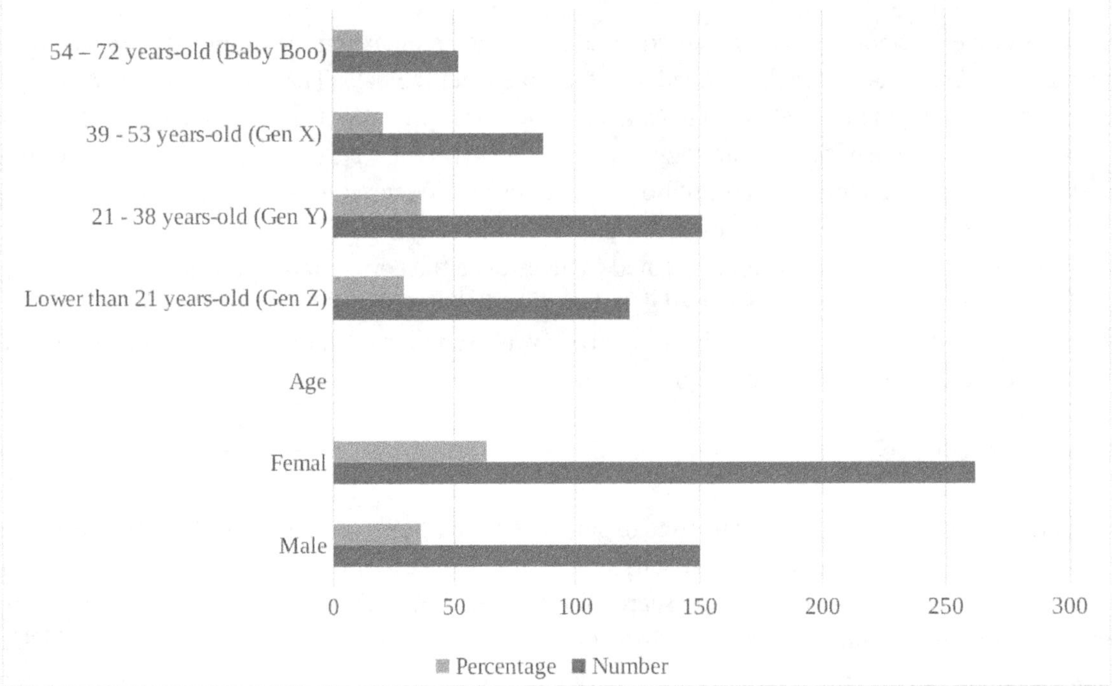

In sum, the other information of respondents on marital status, education, and occupation. As it can be seen that more than 50 percent of respondents are single. Whereas, the vast majority education has bachelor degree 71 percent, and working in private organization 38 percent follow by student 21 percent, and government officer 20 percent. The monthly income of respondents between THB 15,000-25,000 ranked highest, and followed by 25,001- 40,000. The perception of customer using SST of small hotel has been examined by structural equation modelling.

Table 4. Perception of customer toward SST

Components	Standardized estimate	Nonstandardized estimate	S.E.	C.R.	SMC
PSI	.870	2.13	.232	9.16***	.761
SSC	.830	2.02	.222	9.10***	.685
VPS	.700	1.67	.194	8.58***	.490
STC	.461	1.00	.043	6.23***	.213

***sig. 0.001

The results illustrated four guests' perception on using SST namely, the hotel products and services interesting (PSI), the SST system capability (SSC), variety of hotels' products and services (VPS), SST connectivity fast and efficient (STC). As refer to table 4, the products and services interesting has highest impact with $\beta = 0.87$, C.R. = 9.16 with p value less than 0.001, and the statistic explanation power is over 76 percent. It follows by the SST system capability with β = 0.83, C.R. = 9.10 with *p* value less than 0.001, and the statistic explanation power is over 68 percent. The third important factor is variety of products and services offered by hotel. The statistic shown β = 0.70, C.R. = 8.58 with *p* value less than 0.001, and the statistic explanation power is over 49 percent. And the SST connectivity fast and efficient ranked number four with β = 0.46, C.R. = 6.23 with *p* value less than 0.001, and the statistic explanation power is over 21 percent.

The measurement of technology adoption, later, was performed to assess the elements influencing the customer on technology adoption. The results shown two key elements have impact on technology adoption including perceived of usefulness (PU) and perceived ease of use (PE). The PU has higher explanation power than PE, statically, as shown in table 5. The PU has β = 0.97, C.R. = 10.16 with *p* value less than 0.001, and the statistic explanation power is 95 percent. Whereas, the PE has β = 0.82, C.R. = 9.19 with *p* value less than 0.001, and the statistic explanation power is over 67 percent.

Table 5. Perception of customer toward technology adoption

Components	Standardized estimate	Nonstandardized estimate	S.E.	C.R.	SMC
PU	.977	1.18	.066	10.16***	.954
PE	.823	1.14	.049	9.19***	.677

***sig. 0.001

Further, the four components of electronic service quality were investigated. The perspective of Thai customers toward electronic service quality (ESQ) in small hotel demonstrated that; system availability (SA) has highest score loading, follow by privacy (PV), fulfillment (FM), and efficiency (EF). According to table 6, the results portrayed the system availability has explanation power 89 percent with β = 0.94, C.R. = 9.59 with *p* value less than 0.001. Secondly, the privacy has β = 0.909, C.R. = 9.30 with *p* value less than 0.001, and the explanation power 82 percent. The FM, thirdly, has β = 0.898, C.R. = 9.25 with *p* value less than 0.001, and explanation power 80 percent. The EF ranked in last order with explanation power 68 percent and the β = 0.826, C.R. = 8.23 with *p* value less than 0.001.

Table 6. Perception of customer toward ESQ

Components	Standardized estimate	Nonstandardized estimate	S.E.	C.R.	SMC
SA	.948	1.09	.070	9.59***	.899
PV	.909	1.13	.064	9.30***	.826
FM	.898	1.14	.070	9.25***	.806
EF	.826	1.00	.056	8.23***	.682

***sig. 0.001

After everything, the SST, TA, and ESQ variables were evaluated the impact toward customer's satisfaction (SF). As well as we investigate the satisfaction, technology adoption, and self-service technology affecting on return to use intention (RUI), as shown in table 7.

Table 7. Perception of customer on SST, TA and ESQ toward SF

	Standardized Regression Weights	S.E.	C.R.	P	Results
SF < - - -TA	.689	.168	4.07	***	Supported
SF < - - - ESQ	.469	.051	8.39	***	Supported
SF < - - - SST	.453	.216	1.73	.401	Weak
RUI < - - -TA	.882	.450	2.78	.005	Supported
RUI < - - -SST	.296	.480	1.27	.226	Weak
RUI < - - -SF	.578	.328	2.07	.005	Supported

Sig. *0.5, **0.05, *** 0.001

Evidently, from table 7, the technology adoption has highest impact on customer satisfaction with the factor loading 68 percent. While the electronic service quality has lower impact on satisfaction with loading factor 46 percent. And the self-service technology has rather weak impact on satisfaction at 45 percent. On the other hand, the technology adoption has also high impact relating to return intention of customer with loading factor 82 percent. It is followed by the satisfaction with loading factor 57 percent. Whereas the self-service technology has lowest influence on return intention at 29 percent.

Recommendation

The findings of this study can contribute a better understanding of Thais perception on self-service technology, technology adoption, electronic service quality, and their satisfaction and return intention using small hotel. As it can be noticed that the majority of guests are generation Y aging in between 21-38 years old. This group of people are technology savvy (Espinoza, 2010). What is more, today, all generations are much more forced to use technology in daily life especially during the pandemic. That means more people in different generations are accustomed to technology usage. As of the income level of respondents, it is reflecting to the price of small hotels which is affordable, while the service is simple. Therefore, the small hotel owner should consider developing and improving technology to implement in the business.

More importantly, the presentation of hotel's products and services attracting the customers, the stability of self-service system with fast and efficient connectivity are crucial. According to the result, the hotel business owner should create and entrust the benefit of using information technology along with user-friendly design system. Whilst, the accessibility to the hotel's information technology, such as application is recommended. So that, it would allow more customer connect and reserve the room directly. As the present results highlight the detrimental effects that technology adoption loading factor has on return to use intention at highest level. It is also having highest impact on customer satisfaction, in which the satisfaction affects return to use intention over 50 percent. As a result of these investigations, suggestions were identified for future research in other types of hotel or businesses.

CONCLUSION

In summary, it has been shown from the results that self-service technology is vital for small hotel to acquire more customer, and reaching out new customer. However, attracting more user/customer the hotel must present its information technology that is accessible to everyone. In Thailand, presently, there are more people using technology specifically social media as (Statista, 2021) reported Thailand ranked in number 8 of internet users in Asia Pacific. Yet, the system must be user-friendly, the convergence of system capability, safe and secure have to be communicated to customer. Into the bargain, the design of products and services presented in the information technology must be attractive. Likewise, the perception of system usefulness enhances more user's adoption. This means that the hotel having more chance to get higher number of customers.

Meanwhile, it is vital to train hotel workforces on self-service technology system. Since, they can assist the customer promptly when the problem occurred. Nevertheless, the electronic service quality seems less significant comparing to technology adoption. In fact, it should not be neglected since it entails to other elements, such as responsiveness, efficiency, fulfillment, and privacy. These capabilities of SST system would, particularly, create positive guests' attitude toward technology adoption. That leading to the satisfaction and return to use intention. Finally, it is remarkable that the correlation of self-service technology with satisfaction and return intention on this study (table 7) are rather weak. It reminded that the information technology system of small hotel should be improved. The hotel business owner has to examine the system availability that can response to serve the customer needs.

REFERENCES

Ajzen, I. (1991). The Theory of Planned behavior. *Organizational Behavior and Human Decision Processes*, *50*(2), 179–211. doi:10.1016/0749-5978(91)90020-T

Ajzen, I., & Fishbein, M. (1980). *Understanding Attitudes and Predicting Social Behavior*. Prentice-Hall.

Alsiehemy, A. (2019). An Assessment of Customer Retention with Self-Service Technologies: A Model Development. *Business Management and Strategy*, *10*(1), 78–92. doi:10.5296/bms.v10i1.14686

Ashton, A. S. (2015). Developing a Tourist Destination Brand Value: The Stakeholders' Perspectives. *Tourism Planning & Development*, *12*(4), 398–411. doi:10.1080/21568316.2015.1013565

Bayraktaroglu, S., Kahya, V., Atay, E., & Ilhan, H. (2019). Application of Expanded Technology Acceptance Model for Enhancing the HRIS Usage in SMEs. *International Journal of Applied Management and Technology*, *18*(1), 48–66. doi:10.5590/IJAMT.2019.18.1.04

Boon, L. K., Fern, Y. S., & Siang, Y. Y. (2018). A Study of Revisit Intention to Boutique Hotels in Melaka. *European Proceedings of Social & Behavioural Sciences,* 793-805.

Bunrangsee, P., & Pasunon, P. (2018). Factors Affecting Hotel Selection of Thai Tourists in Bangkok. *Journal of Thonburi University*, *12*, 193–205.

Carreirão, P. (2019). *Top 10 self-service technologies that we all love to use*. Available https://asksuite.com/blog/top-10-self-service-technologies/

Chouyboonchoo, N., Sirichote, O., & Noknoi, C. (2019). Effects of Technology Acceptance and Service Quality on Customer Loyalty for Electronic Banking. *Economics and Business Administration Journal Thaksin University*, *11*(1), 31–52.

Considine, E., & Cormican, K. (2016). Self-service technology adoption: An analysis of customer to technology interactions. *Procedia Computer Science*, *100*, 103–109. doi:10.1016/j.procs.2016.09.129

Davis, F. D. (1989). Perceived Usefulness, Perceived Ease of Use and User Acceptance of Information Technology. *Management Information Systems Quarterly*, *13*(3), 319–339. doi:10.2307/249008

Davis, F. D., Bangozzi, R. P., & Warshaw, P. R. (1989). User Acceptance of Computer Technology: A Comparison of two Theoretical Models. *Management Science*, *35*(8), 982–1002. doi:10.1287/mnsc.35.8.982

Dawson, C. (2020). *A-Z of Digital Research Methods*. Routledge.

De Leon, Atienza, & Susilo. (2020). Influence of self-service technology (SST) service quality dimensions as a second-order factor on perceived value and customer satisfaction in a mobile banking application. Cogent Business & Management, 7(1). doi:10.1080/23311975.2020.1794241

Department of Tourism. (2014). Accommodation Standard for Tourism (Hotel) Part 2: 1-4 Stars. Ministry of Sport and Tourism. Bangkok: WVOThaiPrinting.

Espinoza, C., Ukleja, M., & Rusch, C. (2010). *Managing the Millennials*. John Wiley & Son.

Hallin, E. (2018). Seminar in Hotel Management and Leadership, 10 February 2018. Bangkok: Graduate School of Tourism Management. National Institute of Development Administration.

Hanks, L., Line, N., & Mattila, A. (2015). The Impact of Self-Service Technology and The Presence of Others on Cause-Related Marketing Programs in Restaurants. *Journal of Hospitality Marketing & Management*, *25*(5), 547–562. Advance online publication. doi:10.1080/19368623.2015.1046536

Herjanto, H., Amin, M., Okumus, F., & Cobanoglu, C. (2021). Airline Service: Low-Cost Carriers (LCCs) Failure and Passenger Emotional Expereince. *Tourism Review*. Advance online publication. doi:10.1108/TR-01-2021-0025

Huang, P. L., Lee, B. C. Y., & Chen, C.-C. (2019). The influence of service quality on customer satisfaction and loyalty in B2B technology service industry. *Total Quality Management & Business Excellence*, *30*(13-14), 1449–1465. doi:10.1080/14783363.2017.1372184

Huy, L. V., Hoan, N. P. T., Pham, L., & Berry, R. (2019). Technology readiness and satisfaction in Vietnam's luxury hotels. *International Journal of Management and Decision Making*, *18*(2), 183–208. doi:10.1504/IJMDM.2019.098648

Ibzan, E., Balarabe, F., & Jakada, B. (2016). Consumer Satisfaction and Repurchase Intentions. *Developing Country Studies*, *6*(2), 96–100.

Imthammaporn, W. (2018). *Technology Acceptance, Service Conveneince, and Social Media Marketing Affecting Decision to Use Food Order Service Applications of Generation Y Consumers in Bangkok* [MBA Thesis]. Graduate School, Bangkok University.

Jakranukul, C. (2015). *Perspectives of Self-Service Technology (SSTS) from Emerging Economy* [Master Thesis]. Thammasat University.

Kankaew, K. (Ed.). (2022). *Global Air Transport Management and Reshaping Business Models for the New Era*. IGI Global Publishing. doi:10.4018/978-1-6684-4615-7

Kasavana, M. L. (2008). The Convergence of Self-service Technology. *Hospitality Upgrade*, (Spring), 122–128.

Kenaphoom. (2020). *Survey Satisfaction of People to the Service of Sub-district Administration Organization, Songyang*. Research and Development Institute, Mahasarakham Rajabhat University.

Kerdpiam, K. (2014). *The Container Hotel Project: Art of Materials Hotel* [Master of Business Administration Thesis]. Bangkok University.

Keskosol, P., & Merakate, J. (2019). The Influence of Service Quality and Customer Satisfaction Towards Customer Loyalty in Hotel and Resort at Moosi Sub-District, Pak Chong District, Nakhon Ratchasima Province. *Journal of Humanities and Social Sciences*, *4*(3), 102–114.

Kotler, P., & Armstrong, G. (2018). *Principles of Marketing Management.* Pearson Prentice Hall.

Li, M., & Huang, S. (2019). Understanding Customers' Continuance Intentions Toward In-Lobby Self-Service Technologies. *Frontiers in Psychology*, *332*(10), 332. doi:10.3389/fpsyg.2019.00332 PMID:30837925

Maopraman, N., & Jaroenwisan, K. (2022). Technology Application and Innovation for Digital Era Hotel Industry. *Western University Research Journal of Humanities and Social Science*, *8*(1), 251–266.

Muhammad, S. I., Masood, U. H., & Ume, H. (2018). Impact of self-service technology (SST) service quality on customer loyalty and behavioral intention: The mediating role of customer satisfaction. *Cogent Business & Management*, *5*(1), 1. Advance online publication. doi:10.1080/23311975.2018.1423770

Nakhon Ratchasima Provincial Statistical Office. (2017, December 20). *Accommodation establishment in Nakhon Ratchasima Province*. Retrieved from https://www2.nakhonratchasima.go.th

National Statistical Office. (2020). *Summary of Household Technology Survey Results 2020*. Ministry of Digital Economy and Society.

Panthawee, R. (2018). The User's Satisfaction with the Service System of the Dean Office of the Faculty of Humanities and Social Sciences. Research Report, Chiang Mai Rajabhat University.

Parasuraman, A., Zeithaml, A. V., & Malhotra, A. (2005). E-S-QUAL: A Multiple-Item Scale for Assessing Electronic Service Quality. *Journal of Service Research*, *7*(3), 213–233. doi:10.1177/1094670504271156

Phuaphanasakul, J., & Lalitsasivimol, W. (2019). Creating Competitive Advantgae with Information Technology and Innovation of Hotel Business in Thailand: Literature Review. *MUT Journal of Business Administration*, *16*(2), 19–39.

Phuthong, T., & Mangsungnoen, N. (2017). Factors Influencing the Elderly Intention to Use and Adopt Mobile Health Services. *Veridian E-Journal Silpakorn University, 10*(3), 548–566.

Rahahleh, A., Al-Nsour, S., Moflih, M., Alabaddi, Z., Al-nassar, B., & Al-Nsour, N. (2020). The Influence of Electronic Service Quality on Relationship Quality: Evidence from Tourism Industry. *Management Science Letters, 10*, 2759–2768. doi:10.5267/j.msl.2020.4.034

Ranjbarian, B., & Khazaei, P. J. (2015). The Impact of Perceived Quality and Value on Tourists' Satisfaction and Intention to Revisit Nowshahr City of Iran. *Journal of Quality Assurance in Hospitality & Tourism, 16*(1), 103–117. doi:10.1080/1528008X.2015.966295

Rogers, E. M. (2003). *Diffusion of Innovations* (5th ed.). Free Press.

Rotchanakitumnuai, S. (2013). Electronic Service Quality for the Development of Tourism. *Creative Business and Sustainability Journal, 35*(3), 86–99.

Samani, T. (2019). Service Innovation of Hotel Industry in Thailand. *Journal of Thai Hospitality and Tourism, 14*(1), 103–110.

Seetanah, B., Teeroovengadum, V., & Nunkoo, R. S. (2018). Destination Satisfaction and Revisit Intention of Tourists: Does the Quality of Airport Services Matter? *Journal of Hospitality & Tourism Research*, 1–15. doi:10.1177/1096348018798446

Shahril, Z., Zulkafly, H. A., Ismail, N. S., & Sharif, N. U. N. M. (2021). Customer Satisfaction Towards Self-Service Kiosks for Quick Service Restaurants (QSRs) in Klang Valley. *International Journal of Academic Research in Business & Social Sciences, 11*(13), 24–72. doi:10.6007/IJARBSS/v11-i13/8502

Shared, H. A. (2019). The Relationship between E-service Quality and E-customer Satisfaction: An Empirical Study in Egyptian Banks. *International Journal of Business and Management, 14*(5), 171–182. doi:10.5539/ijbm.v14n5p171

Shoosanuk, A., & Jansiriluck, P., Utantada, S., Sakuna, J., & Sringkan, B. (2017). Influence of Service Quality on Perceived Value, Satisfaction and Customer Loyalty of Kathi Krua Thai Restaurant. *Journal of Rangsit Graduate Studies in Business and Social Sciences, 3*(2), 176–188.

Sinpattarachat, C., & Sangruengrob, T. (2018). Comparison Study on Revisiting Budget Hotel and Hostel at the Major Tourist Destinations in Thailand. *Dusit Thani College Journal, 13*(1), 139–154.

Statista. (2021). *Internet usage in Thailand - Statistics & Facts*. Available https://www.statista.com/topics/6140/internet-usage-in-thailand/

Suksuthi, T. (2022). Self-Service Technology (SST) Implication toward Intention to Revisit in Small Hotels: A Case Study of Nakhon Ratchasima Province, Thailand. *Geo Journal of Tourism and Geosites, 41*(2), 523–530. doi:10.30892/gtg.41225-859

Suwannakul, E. (2019). Applications of the SSTQUAL Scale for Self-Service Technology Quality Assessment: A Case of Airline Business in Thailand. *Journal of International and Thai Tourism, 15*(2), 106-120.

Suwannaphong, K. (2020). *Service Quality of Hotels in Muang District*. Phuket Province to Cater Special Interest Tourists.

Swarbrooke, J., & Horner, S. (2007). *Consumer Behavior in Tourism* (2nd ed.). Elsevier: Oxford Press. doi:10.4324/9780080466958

Taneja, K. N. (2011). *The Passenger Has Gone Digital and Mobile*. Ashgate.

Tanongphaeng, W., & Na Thalang, C. (2017). Management of Models for Small Hotel Trad Province Area. *Dusit Thani College Journal*, *11*(3), 1–17.

Tusakunee, K., & Inkaew, S. (2016). Factors Influencing the Repurchase Intentions of Female Customers of Wacoal Lingerie at Department Stores in Bangkok. *EAU Heritage Journal Social Science and Humanity*, *6*(2), 54–65.

Tychachoonhakij, P., & Iamratanakul, S. (2019). Technology Acceptance and Quality of Electronic Service Affect e-Government Procurement System. *Journal of the Association of Researchers*, *24*(3), 306–321.

Venkatesh, V., & Davis, F. D. (2000). A Theoretical Extension of the Technology Acceptance Model: Four Longitudinal Field Studies. *Management Science*, *46*(2), 186–204. doi:10.1287/mnsc.46.2.186.11926

Vo, N., Chovancova, M., & Tri, H. (2019). The Impact of E-service Quality on the Customer Satisfaction and Consumer Engagement Behaviors Toward Luxury Hotels. *Journal of Quality Assurance in Hospitality & Tourism*, *21*, 1–25.

Vongtharawat, M., & Pasunon, P. (2017). Factors Affecting Airline Passengers' Online Check-in Services Usage. *MUT Journal of Business Administration*, *17*(2), 1–14.

Wisuttisaeng, Y., & Piyathasanan, B. (2017). Executive Perspectives towards Self-Service Technology (SST) in Thailand's Service Sectors. *Journal of Business Administration*, *40*(156), 2–33.

Wolfinbarger, M., & Gilly, M. C. (2003). eTailQ: Dimensionalizing, Measuring, and Predicting Etail Quality. *Journal of Retailing*, *79*(3), 183–198. doi:10.1016/S0022-4359(03)00034-4

Worasuwannarak, B., & Kankaew, K. (2022). The Image Value of Southeast Asia Airlines: A Study of Attribute that Led to Image Value of Choosing Southeast Asia Airlines by Mean-End Theory Approach. In K. Kankaew (Ed.), *Global Air Transport Management and Reshaping Business Models for the New Era*. IGI Global Publishing. doi:10.4018/978-1-6684-4615-7.ch009

Yoo, B., & Donthu, N. (2001). Developing a Scale to Measure the Perceived Quality of an Internet Shopping Site (SITEQUAL). *Quarterly Journal of Electronic Commerce*, *2*(1), 31–45.

Compilation of References

Abdallah, A. (2022, April). Reviving a Collapsing Country's Economy Through Cultural Heritage: A Case Study of Tourism in Lebanon. *Journal of Hospitality and Tourism Management*, *6*(1), 1–7. doi:10.11648/j.ijhtm.20220601.11

Abdeldayem, M. M., & Aldulaimi, S. H. (2020). Trends and Opportunities of Artificial Intelligence in Human Resource Management: Aspirations for Public Sector in Bahrain. *International Journal of Scientific & Technology Research*, *9*(1), 3867–3871.

Abdelillah, H., & Esther, S. (2001). *The dynamic nature of innovation within mobile phone service providers in France.* doi:10.1108/EUM0000000005670

Adalı, E. (2017). Yapay zeka. *İTÜ Vakfı Dergisi*, *75*, 8-13.

Afuah, A. (2009). *Strategic innovation.* Routledge. doi:10.4324/9780203883242

Aguilera-Caracuel, J., & Ortiz-de-Mandojana, N. (2013). Green innovation and financial performance: An institutional approach. *Organization & Environment*, *26*(4), 365–385. doi:10.1177/1086026613507931

Ahmed, O. (2018). Artificial Intelligence in HR. *International Journal of Research and Analytical Reviews*, *5*(4), 971–978.

Ajide, F. (2016). Financial innovation and sustainable development in selected countries in West Africa. *Journal of Entrepreneurship, Management, and Innovation*, *12*(3), 85–112. doi:10.7341/20161234

Ajzen, I. (1991). The Theory of Planned behavior. *Organizational Behavior and Human Decision Processes*, *50*(2), 179–211. doi:10.1016/0749-5978(91)90020-T

Ajzen, I., & Fishbein, M. (1980). *Understanding Attitudes and Predicting Social Behavior.* Prentice-Hall.

Akandere, G., & Zerenler, M. (2017). Yeşil otellerde yeşil tedarik zinciri yönetimi ve işletme performansına etkisi. *Uluslararası Turizm ve Sosyal Araştırmalar Dergisi*, *2*, 77–98.

Akhgar, B. (2014). *Cyber crime and cyber terrorism investigator's handbook.* Elsevier.

Akın, H. B. (2005). *Yeni ekonomi: strateji, rekabet, teknoloji yonetimi.* Çizgi Kitabevi.

Aksoy, R. (2009). *İnternet Ortamında Pazarlama.* SeçkinYayıncılık.

Alan, A. K., Kabadayı, E. T., & Erişke, T. (2018). İletişimin yeniyüzü: Dijital pazarlama ve sosyal medya pazarlamasi. *Electronic Journal of Social Sciences*, *17*(66), 123–134.

Alavi, M., & Leidner, D. E. (2001). Review: Knowledge Management and Knowledge Management Systems: Conceptual Foundations and Research Issues. *Management Information Systems Quarterly*, *25*(1), 107. doi:10.2307/3250961

Albort-Morant, G., Henseler, J., Leal-Millán, A., & Cepeda-Carrión, G. (2017). Mapping the field: A bibliometric analysis of green innovation. *Sustainability*, *9*(6), 1011. doi:10.3390u9061011

Ali, I., Hatta, Z. A., & Azman, A., & Islam. (2017). Microfinance as a development and poverty alleviation tool in rural Bangladesh: A critical assessment. *Asian Social Work and Policy Review*, *11*(1), 4–15.

Ali, M., Upadhyay, A., & Kumar, V. (2017). Issues in Service Marketing in Emerging Economies. In V. Nadda, S. Dadwal, & R. Rahimi (Eds.), *Promotional Strategies and New Service Opportunities in Emerging Economies* (pp. 130–143). IGI Global. doi:10.4018/978-1-5225-2206-5.ch006

Allen, F., Demirgüç-Kunt, A., Klapper, L. F., & Martinez Peria, M. S. (2012). *The foundations of financial inclusion: Understanding ownership and use of formal accounts*. Policy Research Working Paper, 6290.

Allen, F., & Gale, D. (1994). *Financial innovation and risk sharing*. MIT Press.

Almehida, F., Santos, J. D., & Monteiro, J. A. (2020). The challenges and opportunities in the digitalization of companies in a post-COVID-19 World. *IEEE Engineering Management Review*, *48*(3), 97–103. doi:10.1109/EMR.2020.3013206

Al-Rahmi, W. M., Yahaya, N., Aldraiweesh, A. A., Alamri, M. M., Aljarboa, N. A., Alturki, U., & Aljeraiwi, A. A. (2019). Integrating technology acceptance model with innovation diffusion theory: An empirical investigation on students' intention to use E-learning systems. *IEEE Access: Practical Innovations, Open Solutions*, *7*, 26797–26809. doi:10.1109/ACCESS.2019.2899368

Alsiehemy, A. (2019). An Assessment of Customer Retention with Self-Service Technologies: A Model Development. *Business Management and Strategy*, *10*(1), 78–92. doi:10.5296/bms.v10i1.14686

Amabile, T. M. (1983). The social psychology of creativity: A componential conceptualization. *Journal of Personality and Social Psychology*, *45*(2), 357–376. doi:10.1037/0022-3514.45.2.357

Amabile, T. M. (1988). A model of creativity and innovation in organizations. *Research in Organizational Behavior*, *10*(1), 123–167.

Amabile, T. M. (1996). *Creativity in Context*. Westview Press.

Amin, S., Rai, A. S., & Topa, G. (2003). Does microcredit reach the poor and vulnerable? Evidence from Northern Bangladesh. *Journal of Development Economics*, *70*, 59–82.

Amit, R., & Zott, C. (2001). Value creation in e-business. *Strategic Management Journal*, *22*(6-7), 493–520. doi:10.1002mj.187

Anand, D., Bharti, V., & Singh, S. (2021, December). Systematic review on the smart energy transmission through "SMART GRID" - An application of IoT. In *3rd International Conference on Advances in Computing, Communication Control and Networking (ICAC3N)* (pp. 563-568). IEEE. 10.1109/ICAC3N53548.2021.9725663

Anderson, P., & Tushman, M. L. (1990). A cyclical model of how technological change occurs, with an emphasis on technological discontinuities and dominant designs. Administrative Science Quarterly.

Anderson, R. (2013). *Chris Barton, et al.* Measuring the Cost of Cybercrime. doi:10.1007/978-3-642-39498-0__12

Andersson, G., Gustaf, O., & Zalamans, D. (2012). Community engagement by an academic tourism department. Advances in Food. *Hospitality and Tourism*, *2*(1), 52–75.

Andreoli, R., Corolla, A., Faggiano, A., Malandrino, D., Pirozzi, D., Ranaldi, M., Santangelo, G., & Scarano, V. (2017). A framework to design, develop, and evaluate immersive and collaborative serious games in cultural heritage. *Journal on Computing and Cultural Heritage*, *11*(1), 1–22. doi:10.1145/3064644

Anyanwu, J. C., & Anyanwu, J. C. (2017). The key drivers of poverty in Sub-Saharan Africa and what can be done about it to achieve the poverty sustainable development goal. *Asian Journal of Economic Modelling*, *5*(3), 297–317. doi:10.18488/journal.8.2017.53.297.317

Apanasovich, N., Heras, H. A., & Parrilli, M. D. (2016). The impact of business innovation modes on SME innovation performance in post-Soviet transition economies: The case of Belarus. *Technovation*, *57*, 30–40. doi:10.1016/j.technovation.2016.05.001

Apriana, D., Kristiawan, M., & Wardiah, D. (2019). Headmaster's competency in preparing vocational school students for entrepreneurship. *International Journal of Scientific & Technology Research*, *8*(8), 1316–1330.

Arduengo, M., & Sentis, L. (2019). Robot economy: ready or not, here it comes. Retrieved from: https://arxiv.org/abs/1812.01755

Arfi, W. B., Hikkerova, L., & Sahut, J. M. (2018). External knowledge sources, green innovation and performance. *Technological Forecasting and Social Change*, *129*, 210–220. doi:10.1016/j.techfore.2017.09.017

Arıkuşu, S. (2017). Yapay Zeka İle Neler Yapabilirsiniz? *Techstar*, *3*(18), 67.

Arnett, D. B., Laverie, D. A., & McLane, C. (2002). Using job satisfaction and pride as internal-marketing tools. *The Cornell Hotel and Restaurant Administration Quarterly*, *43*(2), 87–96. doi:10.1177/001088040204300209

Arsenijevic, U., & Jovic, M. (2019). Artificial ıntelligence marketing: chatbots. *International Conference on Artificial Intelligence: Applications and Innovations*, 19-22.

Arundel, A., Lorenz, E., Lundvall, B. A., & Valeyre, A. (2006). The Organization of Work and Innovative Performance: A comparison of the EU-15. In *Druid Working Papers* (pp. 12-48). Aalborg University.

Ashton, A. S. (2015). Developing a Tourist Destination Brand Value: The Stakeholders' Perspectives. *Tourism Planning & Development*, *12*(4), 398–411. doi:10.1080/21568316.2015.1013565

Asksuite. (2021). *The Recruitment Challenge in The Hospitality Industry*. https://www.youtube.com/watch?v=yghavmrG2Kg

Astonmartinlagonda.com. (2021). *Aston Martin Lagonda Annual Report*. Available at: https://www.astonmartinlagonda.com/investors/annual-report

Astuti, E. S., Arifin, Z., Wilopo, W., & Iqbal, M. (2022). Effects of trading partner relationships and knowledge complementarity on innovation performance. *Journal of Asia Business Studies*, *16*(1), 53–79. doi:10.1108/JABS-01-2019-0012

Atrek, B., & İlter, B. (2017). Social Innovation Practices in Services for Sustainable Consumption: The Case of Turkey. In V. Nadda, S. Dadwal, & R. Rahimi (Eds.), *Promotional Strategies and New Service Opportunities in Emerging Economies* (pp. 32–65). IGI Global. doi:10.4018/978-1-5225-2206-5.ch002

Auernhammer, J., & Hall, H. (2014). Organizational culture in knowledge creation, creativity and innovation: Towards the Freiraum model. *Journal of Information Science*, *40*(2), 154–166. doi:10.1177/0165551513508356

Avgeli, V., Dahlan, M. A., Bakir, A., & Wickens, E. (2020). 4IR impacts on tourism education and industry. Journal on Tourism & Sustainability, 4 (1), 06–15.

Axel, J. (1999). Innovation on the market that is successful. *European Journal of Innovation Management*, *2*(1), 6–11. doi:10.1108/14601069910248838

Aydın, Ç., & Aydın, C. (2016). Konaklama sektöründe enerji kullanımı ve sıfır enerjili binalar kavramı. In 8. lisansüstü turizm öğrencileri araştırma kongresi bildiri kitabı (pp. 34-47). Bizim Büro Matbaacılık ve Basımevi.

Ay, L. (2009). Bilgi Teknolojisindeki Gelişmelerin Seyahat Acentalarına Yansımaları; Onlıne Seyahat Acentacılığı. *Sosyal Ekonomik Araştırmalar Dergisi*, *9*(17), 117–136.

Backhaus, K., & Tikoo, S. (2004). Conceptualizing and researching employer branding. *Career Development International*, *9*(5), 501–517. doi:10.1108/13620430410550754

Bağcı, E., & İçöz, O. (2019). Z ve alfa kuşağı ile dijitalleşen turizm. *Güncel Turizm Araştırmaları Dergisi*, *3*(2), 232–256. doi:10.32572/guntad.578926

Bahmani-Oskooee, M., & Oyolola, M. (2009). Poverty reduction and aid: Cross-country evidence. *The International Journal of Sociology and Social Policy*, *29*(5-6), 264–273. doi:10.1108/01443330910965796

Banet, J., & Lebeau, L. (2022). *Central Bank Digital Currency: Financial Inclusion vs. Disintermediation.* Working Paper 2218.

Barboza, C. (2019). Artificial Intelligence and HR: The new wave of Technology. *Journal of Advances in Social Science and Humanities*, *5*(4), 715–720.

Barclays. (2010). *Banking for billions, report on improving access to financial services and expanding microfinance.* Available at: www.newsroom.barclays.com/Media-Library/Banking-for-Billions-report-165f.aspx

Barney, J. (1991). Firm Resources and Sustained Competitive Advantage. *Journal of Management*, *17*(1), 99–120. doi:10.1177/014920639101700108

Barutçugil, İ. (1981). *Teknolojik yenilik ve araştırma geliştirme yönetimi.* Bursa Üniversitesi Yayınları.

Bass, B. M., & Riggio, R. E. (2006). Transformational leadership. Lawrence Erlbaum Associates, Inc. doi:10.4324/9781410617095

Bass, B. M. (1999). Current developments in transformational leadership. *The Psychologist Manager Journal*, *3*(1), 5–21. doi:10.1037/h0095852

Basu, P., & Srivastava, P. (2005). Exploring possibilities: Micro finance and rural credit access for the poor in India. *Economic and Political Weekly*, *40*(17), 1747–1756.

Batista, L., Dora, M., Toth, J., Molnár, A., Malekpoor, H., & Kumari, S. (2019). Knowledge management for food supply chain synergies–a maturity level analysis of SME companies. *Production Planning and Control*, *30*(10–12), 995–1004. doi:10.1080/09537287.2019.1582104

Bayraktaroglu, S., Kahya, V., Atay, E., & Ilhan, H. (2019). Application of Expanded Technology Acceptance Model for Enhancing the HRIS Usage in SMEs. *International Journal of Applied Management and Technology*, *18*(1), 48–66. doi:10.5590/IJAMT.2019.18.1.04

Bayuk, M. N., & Demir, B. N. (2019). Endüstri 4.0 kapsamında yapay zeka ve pazarlamanın geleceği. *Journal Of Social. Humanities and Administrative Sciences*, *5*(19), 781–799. doi:10.31589/JOSHAS.163

Beedie, P., & Hudson, S. (2003). Emergence of mountain-based adventure tourism. *Annals of Tourism Research*, *30*(3), 625–643. doi:10.1016/S0160-7383(03)00043-4

Belanche, D., Casalo, L. V., Flavian, C., & Schpers, J. (2020). Service robot implementation: A theoretical framework and research agenda. *Service Industries Journal*, *40*(3-4), 203–225. doi:10.1080/02642069.2019.1672666

Ben-Asher, N., & Gonzalez, C. (2015). Effects of cyber security knowledge on attack detection. *Computers in Human Behavior*, *48*, 51–61. doi:10.1016/j.chb.2015.01.039

Bendovschi, A. (2015). Cyber-Attacks – Trends, Patterns and Security Countermeasures. *Procedia Economics and Finance, 28*, 24–31. doi:10.1016/S2212-5671(15)01077-1

Benjamin, M. P., Jr. (1994). *Credit Schemes For Microenterprises: Motivation, Design, and Viability* [PhD dissertation]. Georgetown University.

Benjamin, L., Sass Rubin, J., & Zielenbach, S. (2004). Community development financial institutions: Current issues and future prospects. *Journal of Urban Affairs, 26*(2), 177–195. doi:10.1111/j.0735-2166.2004.00196.x

Bergendahl, M., & Magnusson, M. (2015). Creating Ideas for Innovation: Effects of Organizational Distance on Knowledge Creation Processes. *Creativity and Innovation Management, 24*(1), 87–101. doi:10.1111/caim.12097

Berger, P. L., & Luckmann, T. (2008). *Gerçekliğin Sosyal İnşâsı* (çev. Vefa Saygın Öğütle), İstanbul. *Paradigma (Maracay).*

Berhil, S., Benlahmar, H., & Labani, N. (2020). A review paper on artificial intelligence at the service of human resources management. *Indonesian Journal of Electrical Engineering and Computer Science, 18*(1), 32–40. doi:10.11591/ijeecs.v18.i1.pp32-40

Bernasek, A. (2003). Banking on social change: Grameen Bank lending to women. *International Journal of Politics Culture and Society, 16*(3), 369–385. doi:10.1023/A:1022304311671

Bharti, V., & Anand, D. (2021, September). The Empirical study and analysis of the Blockchain Technology. In *Third International Conference on Inventive Research in Computing Applications (ICIRCA)* (pp. 728-734). IEEE. 10.1109/ICIRCA51532.2021.9544657

Bhattacharya, A. K. (2001). *Community participation and sustainable forest development, global perspective.* Concept Publishing.

Bhattacharya, A. K. (2005). *Ecotourism and Livelihoods.* Concept Publishing.

Bhattacharya, A. K. (2005). *Training Manual on People's Bio-diversity Register.* Concept Publishing.

Bhattacharya, A. K. (2007). *Public People Private Partnership for Sustainable Forest Development.* Concept Publishing.

Bhattacharya, A. K. (2007a). *Forestry for Next Decade: Managing Thrust Areas (Set of 2 Vols).* Concept Publishing.

Bibi, M. (2019). Execution of Artificial Intelligence Approach in Human Resource Management Functions: Benefits and Challenges in Pakistan. *Sarhad Journal of Management Sciences, 5*(1), 113–124. doi:10.31529jms.2018.5.1.8

Birasnav, M. (2014). Knowledge management and organizational performance in the service industry: The role of transformational leadership beyond the effects of transactional leadership. *Journal of Business Research, 67*(8), 1622–1629. doi:10.1016/j.jbusres.2013.09.006

Bodenhausen, C., & Curtis, C. (2016). Transformational leadership and employee involvement: Perspectives from millennial workforce entrants. *Journal of Quality Assurance in Hospitality & Tourism, 17*(3), 371–387.

Boeke, S. (2018). National cyber crisis management: Different European approaches. *Governance: An International Journal of Policy, Administration and Institutions, 31*(3), 449–464. doi:10.1111/gove.12309

Bohle, P., Knox, A., Noone, J., Mc Namara, M., Rafalski, J., & Quinlan, M. (2017). Work organisation, bullying and intention to leave in the hospitality industry. *Employee Relations, 39*(4), 446–458. doi:10.1108/ER-07-2016-0149

Bojanc, R., & Jerman-Blažič, B. (2008). An economic modelling approach to information security risk management. *International Journal of Information Management, 28*(5), 413–422. doi:10.1016/j.ijinfomgt.2008.02.002

Bolboli, S. A., & Reiche, M. (2013). A model for sustainable business excellence: Implementation and the roadmap. *The TQM Journal*, *25*(4), 331–346. doi:10.1108/17542731311314845

Bolton, A. D., Goosen, L., & Kritzinger, E. (2022b). Emerging Technologies for Innovation and Productivity Management in the Automotive Industry: Impact of Digital Transformation on Communication. In Emerging Technologies for Innovation Management in the Software Industry (pp. 60-85). IGI Global. doi:10.4018/978-1-7998-9059-1.ch003

Bolton, A., Goosen, L., & Kritzinger, E. (2021c). The Integration and Implementation of the Internet of Things Through Digital Transformation: Impact on Productivity and Innovation. In P. Tomar (Ed.), Integration and Implementation of the Internet of Things Through Cloud Computing (pp. 85-112). IGI Global. doi:10.4018/978-1-7998-6981-8.ch005

Bolton, T., Goosen, L., & Kritzinger, E. (2020a). Security Aspects of an Empirical Study into the Impact of Digital Transformation via Unified Communication and Collaboration Technologies on the Productivity and Innovation of a Global Automotive Enterprise. Communications in Computer and Information Science, 1166, 99-113. doi:10.1007/978-3-030-43276-8_8

Bolton, A. D., Goosen, L., & Kritzinger, E. (2021a). Unified Communication Technologies at a Global Automotive Organization. In M. Khosrow-Pour (Ed.), *Encyclopedia of Organizational Knowledge, Administration, and Technologies* (pp. 2592–2608). IGI Global. doi:10.4018/978-1-7998-3473-1.ch179

Bolton, A. D., Goosen, L., & Kritzinger, E. (2022a). Impact of Digital Transformation via Unified Communication and Collaboration Technologies: Productivity and Innovation at a Global Enterprise. In M. Rodrigues & J. Proença (Eds.), *Impact of Digital Transformation on the Development of New Business Models and Consumer Experience* (pp. 271–298). IGI Global. doi:10.4018/978-1-7998-9179-6.ch014

Bolton, A. D., Goosen, L., & Kritzinger, E. (2022c). Challenges and Emerging Strategies for a Global Automotive Enterprise Towards a Post-COVID-19 Era: The Impact of Digital Transformation. In A. Pego (Ed.), *Handbook of Research on Global Networking Post COVID-19* (pp. 76–109). IGI Global. doi:10.4018/978-1-7998-8856-7.ch005

Bolton, A., Goosen, L., & Kritzinger, E. (2016). Enterprise Digitization Enablement Through Unified Communication and Collaboration. *Proceedings of the Annual Conference of the South African Institute of Computer Scientists and Information Technologists*. Johannesburg: ACM. 10.1145/2987491.2987516

Bolton, A., Goosen, L., & Kritzinger, E. (2020b). The Impact of Unified Communication and Collaboration Technologies on Productivity and Innovation: Promotion for the Fourth Industrial Revolution. In S. B. Buckley (Ed.), *Promoting Inclusive Growth in the Fourth Industrial Revolution* (pp. 44–73). IGI Global. doi:10.4018/978-1-7998-4882-0.ch002

Bolton, A., Goosen, L., & Kritzinger, E. (2021b). An Empirical Study into the Impact on Innovation and Productivity Towards the Post-COVID-19 Era: Digital Transformation of an Automotive Enterprise. In L. C. Carvalho, L. Reis, & C. Silveira (Eds.), *Handbook of Research on Entrepreneurship, Innovation, Sustainability, and ICTs in the Post-COVID-19 Era* (pp. 133–159). IGI Global. doi:10.4018/978-1-7998-6776-0.ch007

Boon, L. K., Fern, Y. S., & Siang, Y. Y. (2018). A Study of Revisit Intention to Boutique Hotels in Melaka. *European Proceedings of Social & Behavioural Sciences,* 793-805.

Boons, F., & Lüdeke-Freund, F. (2013). Business models for sustainable innovation: State-of-the-art and steps towards a research agenda. *Journal of Cleaner Production, 45*, 9–19. doi:10.1016/j.jclepro.2012.07.007

Bordo, M. D., & Levin, A. T. (2017). Central bank digital currency and the future of monetary policy (No. w23711). National Bureau of Economic Research.

Botega, L. F. de C., & da Silva, J. C. (2020). An artificial intelligence approach to support knowledge management on the selection of creativity and innovation techniques. *Journal of Knowledge Management*, *24*(5), 1107–1130. doi:10.1108/JKM-10-2019-0559

Boyes, H., Hallaq, B., Cunningham, J., & Watson, T. (2018). The industrial internet of things (IIoT): An analysis framework. *Computers in Industry*, *101*, 1–12. doi:10.1016/j.compind.2018.04.015

Bozkurt Uzan, Ş., & Sevimli, Y. (2020). Gastronomideki robotik uygulamalar ve yapay zekâ. *Tourism and Recreation*, *2*(2), 46–58.

Bradac, Z., Marcon, P., Zezulka, F., Arm, J., & Benesl, T. (2019). Digital Twin and AAS in the Industry 4.0 Framework. *IOP Conference Series. Materials Science and Engineering*, *618*(1), 012001. doi:10.1088/1757-899X/618/1/012001

Braun, V., & Clarke, V. (2006). Using thematic analysis in psychology. *Qualitative Research in Psychology*, *3*(2), 77–101. doi:10.1191/1478088706qp063oa

Brenner, M. (2019). *How to improve customer segmentation with AI*. Retrieved from: https://marketinginsidergroup.com/artificial-intelligence/how-to-improve-customer-segmentationwith-ai/

Brewer, R. (2016). Ransomware attacks: Detection, prevention and cure. *Network Security*, *2016*(9), 5–9. doi:10.1016/S1353-4858(16)30086-1

Brien, A. (2004). December. Do I want a job in hospitality? Only till I get a real job. In *Proceedings of the New Zealand tourism and hospitality research conference* (35-42). Wellington, New Zealand: Victoria University of Wellington.

Briner, R. B., Denyer, D., & Rousseau, D. M. (2009). Evidence-Based Management: Concept Cleanup Time? *The Academy of Management Perspectives*, *23*(4), 19–32. doi:10.5465/AMP.2009.45590138

Buckley, R. (2006). Adventure tourism research: A guide to the literature. *Tourism Recreation Research*, *31*(2), 75–83. doi:10.1080/02508281.2006.11081265

Buckley, R. (2013). Social-benefit certification as a game. *Tourism Management*, *37*, 203–209. doi:10.1016/j.tourman.2013.01.004

Buhalis, D., & O'connor, P. (2005). *Information Communication Technology Revolutionizing Tourism*. Academic Press.

Bulunmaz, B. (2016). Gelişen teknolojiyle birlikte değişen pazarlama yöntemleri ve dijital pazarlama. *TRT Akademi*, *1*(2), 348–365.

Bulut, C., Kaya, T., Mehta, A. M., & Danish, R. Q. (2022). Linking incremental and radical creativity to product and process innovation with organisational knowledge. *Journal of Manufacturing Technology Management*, *33*(4), 763–784. doi:10.1108/JMTM-01-2021-0037

Bulut, E., & Akçacı, T. (2017). Endüstri 4.0 ve İnovasyon Göstergeleri Kapsamında Türkiye Analizi. *ASSAM Uluslararası Hakemli Dergi*, *4*(7), 55–77.

Bunrangsee, P., & Pasunon, P. (2018). Factors Affecting Hotel Selection of Thai Tourists in Bangkok. *Journal of Thonburi University*, *12*, 193–205.

Burke, P. (2014). Tarih ve Toplumsal Kuram. Tarih Vakfı Yurt Yayınları.

Burke, R. J., & Ng, E. (2006). The changing nature of work and organizations: Implications for human resource management. *Human Resource Management Review*, *16*(2), 86–94. doi:10.1016/j.hrmr.2006.03.006

Buyukkeklik, A., Ozoglu, B., & Kemer, E. (2014). Buyer-supplier relationship in tourism supply chains: A research in Cappadocia Region in Turkey. *Journal of Applied Sciences*, *14*(7), 660–668. doi:10.3923/jas.2014.660.668

Büyükkeklik, A., Toksarı, M., & Bülbül, H. (2010). Çevresel duyarlılık ve yenilikçilik üzerine bir araştırma. *Süleyman Demirel Üniversitesi İktisadi ve İdari Bilimler Fakültesi Dergisi*, *15*(3), 373–393.

Caiazza, R., Richardson, A., & Audretsch, D. (2015). Knowledge effects on competitiveness: From firms to regional advantage. *The Journal of Technology Transfer*, *40*(6), 899–909. doi:10.100710961-015-9425-8

Calinaud, V., Kokkranikal, J., & Gebbels, M. (2021). Career advancement for women in the British hospitality industry: The enabling factors. *Work, Employment and Society*, *35*(4), 677–695. doi:10.1177/0950017020967208

Canlas, A., & Williams, M. (2022). Meeting belongingness needs: An inclusive leadership practitioner's approach. *Advances in Developing Human Resources*, *24*(4), 225–241. doi:10.1177/15234223221118953

Cao, X., Ali, A., Pitafi, A. H., Khan, A. N., & Waqas, M. (2021). A socio-technical system approach to knowledge creation and team performance: Evidence from China. *Information Technology & People*, *34*(7), 1976–1996. doi:10.1108/ITP-10-2019-0536

Carboni, N., & de Luca, L. (2016). Towards a conceptual foundation for documenting tangible and intangible elements of a cultural object. *Digital Applications in Archaeology and Cultural Heritage*, *3*(4), 108–116. doi:10.1016/j.daach.2016.11.001

Carbo, S., Gardener, E. P. M., & Molyneux, P. (2005). *Financial Exclusion*. Palgrave Macmillan. doi:10.1057/9780230508743

Carl, G., Kesidis, G., Brooks, R. R., & Suresh Rai. (2006). Denial-of-service attack-detection techniques. *IEEE Internet Computing*, *10*(1), 82–89. doi:10.1109/MIC.2006.5

Carreirão, P. (2019). *Top 10 self-service technologies that we all love to use*. Available https://asksuite.com/blog/top-10-self-service-technologies/

Carrillo-Hermosilla, J., Del Río, P., & Könnölä, T. (2010). Diversity of eco-innovations: Reflections from selected case studies. *Journal of Cleaner Production*, *18*(10-11), 1073–1083. doi:10.1016/j.jclepro.2010.02.014

Carvalho, L., & Costa, T. (2011). A literature review accompanied by research on case studies focusing on innovations in the tourism industry. *Tourism & Management Studies*, 23–33.

Cass, S. (2001). Anatomy of malice [computer viruses]. *IEEE Spectrum*, *38*(11), 56–60. doi:10.1109/6.963235

Castaneda, D. I., & Cuellar, S. (2020). Knowledge sharing and innovation: A systematic review. *Knowledge and Process Management*, *27*(3), 159–173. doi:10.1002/kpm.1637

CDFA. (2005). *Inside Out: The State of Community Development Finance 2004*. CDFA.

Central Bank of Sri Lanka. (2020). Economic and Social Statistics. Central Bank Annual Report.

Çetinkaya, F. Ö. (2019). *Sosyal medya ve Turizm 4.0*. Detay Yayıncılık.

Chalmers, A., Parkins, J., Webb, M., & Debattista, K. (2021). Realistic Humans in Virtual Cultural Heritage. *International Conference on Emerging Technologies and the Digital Transformation of Museums and Heritage Sites*, 156–165. 10.1007/978-3-030-83647-4_11

Chanana, N., & Sangeeta. (2021). Employee engagement practices during COVID-19 lockdown. *Journal of Public Affairs*, *21*(4), e2508. doi:10.1002/pa.2508 PMID:33041656

Chandra, N. S. (2011, September 2). *Reserve for Hornbills near Dandeli*. Retrieved from https://www.deccanherald.com/state/reserve-for-hornbills-near-dandeli-181997.html

Chang, C. H. (2011). The influence of corporate environmental ethics on competitive advantage: The mediation role of green innovation. *Journal of Business Ethics*, *104*(3), 361–370. doi:10.100710551-011-0914-x

Change.org. (n.d.). *Citizens: Retain IFS Officer Manojkumar #WeNeedManoj Back as Member Secretary KSPCB*. Retrieved from https://www.change.org/p/cm-of-karnataka-citizens-retain-ifs-officer-manoj-kumar-weneedmanoj-back-as-member-secretary-ks
pcb

Charlton, E. (2021). *4 things workers want implemented by their bosses' post-pandemic*. World Economic Forum. https://www.weforum.org/agenda/2021/05/employers-pandemic-covid-19-mental-health/.r

Charness, N., & Boot, W. R. (2016). Technology, gaming, and social networking. In *Handbook of the Psychology of Aging* (pp. 389–407). Academic Press. doi:10.1016/B978-0-12-411469-2.00020-0

Chatterjee, D. (1995). Book Reviews: Peter M. Senge, The Fifth Discipline: The Art and Practice of the Learning Organ ization. New York: Doubleday, 1990, pp. viii + 424, Rs 415. *Journal of Human Values*, *1*(1), 146–149. doi:10.1177/097168589500100115

Chaubey, A., & Sahoo, C. K. (2021). The drivers of employee creativity and organizational innovation: A dynamic capability view. *Benchmarking*. Advance online publication. doi:10.1108/BIJ-06-2021-0316

Chaudhuri, A., Datta, P. P., Fernandes, K. J., & Xiong, Y. (2021). Optimal pricing strategies for manufacturing-as-a service platforms to ensure business sustainability. *International Journal of Production Economics*, *234*, 108065. doi:10.1016/j.ijpe.2021.108065

Cheer, J. M., Reeves, K. J., & Laing, J. H. (2013). Tourism and traditional culture: Land diving in vanuatu. *Annals of Tourism Research*, *43*(xx), 435–455. doi:10.1016/j.annals.2013.06.005

Chen, S., Law, R., Xu, S., & Zhang, M. (2020). Bibliometric and visualized analysis of mobile technology in tourism. In Sustainability (Switzerland) (Vol. 12, Issue 19, pp. 1–16). MDPI. doi:10.3390u12197975

Cheng, C. C., Yang, C. L., & Sheu, C. (2014). The link between eco-innovation and business performance: A Taiwanese industry context. *Journal of Cleaner Production*, *64*, 81–90. doi:10.1016/j.jclepro.2013.09.050

Chen, L., Yue, D., Dou, C., Chen, J., & Cheng, Z. (2020). Study on attack paths of cyber attack in cyber-physical power systems. *IET Generation, Transmission & Distribution*, *14*(12), 2352–2360. doi:10.1049/iet-gtd.2019.1330

Chen, Y. S. (2008). The driver of green innovation and green image–green core competence. *Journal of Business Ethics*, *81*(3), 531–543. doi:10.100710551-007-9522-1

Chen, Y. S., Lai, S. B., & Wen, C. T. (2006). The influence of green innovation performance on corporate advantage in Taiwan. *Journal of Business Ethics*, *67*(4), 331–339. doi:10.100710551-006-9025-5

Chen, Y., Xu, Y., & Zhai, Q. (2019). The knowledge management functions of corporate university and their evolution: Case studies of two Chinese corporate universities. *Journal of Knowledge Management*, *23*(10), 2086–2112. doi:10.1108/JKM-04-2018-0228

Chen, Z. (2022). Visualizing experiencescape–from the art of intangible cultural heritage. *Current Issues in Tourism*, *25*(4), 559–578. doi:10.1080/13683500.2021.1892040

Cherubini, A., Passama, R., Crosnier, A., Lasnier, A., & Fraisse, P. (2016). Collaborative manufacturing with physical human–robot interaction. *Robotics and Computer-integrated Manufacturing*, *40*, 1–13. doi:10.1016/j.rcim.2015.12.007

Chibba, M. (2008). Poverty reduction in Developing countries. *World Economy*, *9*(1), 197–200.

Chiou, T. Y., Chan, H. K., Lettice, F., & Chung, S. H. (2011). The influence of greening the suppliers and green innovation on environmental performance and competitive advantage in Taiwan. *Transportation Research Part E, Logistics and Transportation Review*, *47*(6), 822–836. doi:10.1016/j.tre.2011.05.016

Choi, L., Lee, & Yoo. (2010). The Impact of Information Technology and Transactive Memory Systems on Knowledge Sharing, Application, and Team Performance: A Field Study. *Management Information Systems Quarterly*, *34*(4), 855. doi:10.2307/25750708

Chouyboonchoo, N., Sirichote, O., & Noknoi, C. (2019). Effects of Technology Acceptance and Service Quality on Customer Loyalty for Electronic Banking. *Economics and Business Administration Journal Thaksin University*, *11*(1), 31–52.

Chowdhury, A. (2009). *Microfinance as a poverty reduction tool: a critical assessment.* DESA Working Paper No. 89.

Cicerale, V. (2020). Turnover rates in the hospitality industry and the factors contributing to employee loss or retention. *Hospitality Graduate Student Scholarship*. https://scholarsarchive.jwu.edu/hosp_graduate/5

CIPD. (2022). *Resourcing and talent planning report 2022*. Chartered Institute of Personnel and Development. https://www.cipd.co.uk/Images/resourcing-and-talent-planning-report-2022-1_tcm18-111500.pdf

Clair, D. S. (2008). *An investigation into new approaches to teaching business at the university level.* Pepperdine University.

Coff, R. (2003). Bidding Wars Over R&D intensive firms: Knowledge, opportunism and the market for corporate control. *Academy of Management Journal*, *46*(1), 74–85. doi:10.2307/30040677

Coles, M., & Landrum, R. (2009). Asymmetric Encryption. In Expert SQL Server 2008 Encryption (pp. 73–110). Apress. doi:10.1007/978-1-4302-3365-7_4

Collier, P., & Dollar, D. (2002). Aid allocation and poverty reduction. *European Economic Review*, *46*(8), 1475–1500. doi:10.1016/S0014-2921(01)00187-8

Collin, B. (1997, March). Future of Cyberterrorism. *The Physical and Virtual Worlds Converge.*, *13*(2), 15–18.

Concept. (n.d.). *Book details, The Wildlife Memoirs, a forester recollects.* Retrieved from www.conceptpub.com/servlet/Detail?bookno=00001081

Considine, E., & Cormican, K. (2016). Self-service technology adoption: An analysis of customer to technology interactions. *Procedia Computer Science*, *100*, 103–109. doi:10.1016/j.procs.2016.09.129

Coombs, R., & Hull, R. (1998). Knowledge management practices and path-dependency in innovation. *Research Policy*, *27*(3), 237–253. doi:10.1016/S0048-7333(98)00036-5

Craig, C. J., JeongAe, Y., & Zou, Y. (2016). *The narrative nature of embodied knowledge: A cross-study analysis of teaching, learning, and living*. Academic Press.

Cukierman, A. (2020). Reflections on welfare and political economy aspects of a central bank digital currency. *Manchester School*, *88*(S1), 114–125. doi:10.1111/manc.12333

Dadwal, S. S., & Hassan, A. (2015). The augmented reality marketing: A merger of marketing and technology in tourism. In Mobile Computing and Wireless Networks: Concepts, Methodologies, Tools, and Applications (Vols. 1–4, pp. 63–80). IGI Global. doi:10.4018/978-1-4666-8699-1.ch005

Dangelico, R. M., & Pujari, D. (2010). Mainstreaming green product innovation: Why and how companies integrate environmental sustainability. *Journal of Business Ethics*, *95*(3), 471–486. doi:10.100710551-010-0434-0

Danneels, E. (2002). The dynamic relationship between product innovation and the competencies of a company. *Strategic Management Journal, 23*(12).

Das Gupta, M., Bongaarts, J., & Cleland, J. (2011). *Population, poverty, and sustainable development: A review of the evidence.* World Bank Policy Research Working Paper, (5719).

Daskon, C., & McGregor, A. (2012). Cultural Capital and Sustainable Livelihoods in Sri Lanka's Rural Villages: Towards Culturally Aware Development. *The Journal of Development Studies*, *48*(4), 549–563. doi:10.1080/00220388.2011.604413

Dassanayaka, D. M. C., Weerasinghe, I. M. S., Dahanayaka, S. N. S., Dedunu, H. H., Athurupana, K., & Muthuweera, N. K. G. (2022). Academics' attitudes towards online education amidst the Covid-19 outbreak. *International Journal of Educational Management*, *36*(5), 661–677. Advance online publication. doi:10.1108/IJEM-10-2021-0414

Davis, F. D. (1989). Perceived Usefulness, Perceived Ease of Use and User Acceptance of Information Technology. *Management Information Systems Quarterly*, *13*(3), 319–340. doi:10.2307/249008

Davis, F. D., Bangozzi, R. P., & Warshaw, P. R. (1989). User Acceptance of Computer Technology: A Comparison of two Theoretical Models. *Management Science*, *35*(8), 982–1002. doi:10.1287/mnsc.35.8.982

Davoodalhosseini, S. M. (2021). Central bank digital currency and monetary policy. *Journal of Economic Dynamics & Control*, 104150.

Dawson, C. (2020). *A-Z of Digital Research Methods*. Routledge.

De Jong, J. P., & Den Hartog, D. N. (2007). How leaders influence employees' innovative behavior. *European Journal of Innovation Management*, *10*(1), 41–64. doi:10.1108/14601060710720546

De Leon, Atienza, & Susilo. (2020). Influence of self-service technology (SST) service quality dimensions as a second-order factor on perceived value and customer satisfaction in a mobile banking application. Cogent Business & Management, 7(1). doi:10.1080/23311975.2020.1794241

De Marchi, V. (2012). Environmental innovation and R&D cooperation: Empirical evidence from Spanish manufacturing firms. *Research Policy*, *41*(3), 614–623. doi:10.1016/j.respol.2011.10.002

de Sancho, A. L., Dominguez, C., Macho, A. S. C., Alvarez, V. P., & Martire, F. (2013). Sustainable Innovation. Institute for Innovation and Technology.

Demirci, A. E. (2012). Yenilik yönetimi. In Temel kavramlar (pp. 2-15). Açıköğretim Fakültesi Yayınları.

Demir, K. (2006). Rogersın Yeniliğin Yayılması Teorisi ve Ġnternetten Ders Kaydı. *Kuram ve Uygulamada Egitim Yonetimi Dergisi*, *12*(3), 367–392.

Demirsoy, C. (2005). *Yeniliğin Yayılması Modellerinin Yeniliği Benimseyen Kategorilerinin İnternet Bankacılığı Ürünü Üzerinde Bir İncelemesi*. Hacettepe Üniversitesi.

Denning. (2001). Activism, Hacktivism, and Cyberterrorism: The Internet as a Tool for Influencing Foreign Policy. In *Networks and Netwars The Future of Terror, Crime, and Militancy* (pp. 239–288). RAND Corporation. https://www.rand.org/pubs/monograph_reports/MR1382.html

Department of Tourism. (2014). Accommodation Standard for Tourism (Hotel) Part 2: 1-4 Stars. Ministry of Sport and Tourism. Bangkok: WVOThaiPrinting.

Deprez, J., & Euwema, M. (2017). You can't always get what you want? Leadership expectations of intrapreneurs. *Journal of Managerial Psychology*, *32*(6), 430–444. doi:10.1108/JMP-04-2016-0107

Deprez, J., Peeters, E., & Gorgievski, M. J. (2021). Developing intrapreneurial self-efficacy through internships? Investigating agency and structure factors. *International Journal of Entrepreneurial Behaviour & Research*, *27*(5), 1166–1188. doi:10.1108/IJEBR-09-2020-0642

Dess, G. G., & Picken, J. C. (2001). Changing roles: Leadership in the 21st century. *Organizational Dynamics*, *28*(3), 18–34. doi:10.1016/S0090-2616(00)88447-8

Devi, R., & Bharti, V. (2021, December). Analysis of Network IDS using Data Analysis tool With Python. In *3rd International Conference on Advances in Computing, Communication Control and Networking (ICAC3N)* (pp. 1357-1360). IEEE. 10.1109/ICAC3N53548.2021.9725784

Devitt, M. (2019). *How can I help you? The emergence of robots in hotels and restaurants*. https://www.robotshop.com/community/blog/show/how-can-i-help you-the-emergence-of-robots-in-hotels-and-restaurants/

Devitt, M. (2019). *How can I help you? The emergence of robots in hotels and restaurants*. Retrieved from: https://www.robotshop.com/community/blog/show/how-can-i-help you-the-emergence-of-robots-in-hotels-and-restaurants/

Di Vaio, A., Palladino, R., Hassan, R., & Escobar, O. (2020). Artificial intelligence and business models in the sustainable development goals perspective: A systematic literature review. *Journal of Business Research*, *121*, 283–314. doi:10.1016/j.jbusres.2020.08.019

Didenko, A. N., & Buckley, R. P. (2021). *Central Bank Digital Currencies: A Potential Response to the Financial Inclusion Challenges of the Pacific*. UNSW Law Research Paper, No- 63.

Dipietro, R. B., & Condly, S. J. (2007). Employee turnover in the hospitality industry: An analysis based on the CANE model of motivation. *Journal of Human Resources in Hospitality & Tourism*, *6*(1), 1–22. doi:10.1300/J171v06n01_01

Dippelreiter, B., Grün, C., Pöttler, M., Seidel, I., Berger, H., Dittenbach, M., & Pesenhofer, A. (2009). Online Tourism Communities on the Path to Web 2.0: An Evaluation. *Information Technology & Tourism*, *10*(4), 329–353. doi:10.3727/109830508788403132

Dodds, R., & Butler, R. (2019). The phenomena of overtourism: A review. *International Journal of Tourism Cities*, *5*(4), 519–528. doi:10.1108/IJTC-06-2019-0090

Donaldson, L. (2001). The contingency theory of organizations. *Sage (Atlanta, Ga.)*.

Dowla, A. (2006). In credit we trust: Building social capital by Grameen Bank in Bangladesh. *Journal of Socio-Economics*, *35*(1), 102–122. doi:10.1016/j.socec.2005.12.006

Dowla, A. U. (1998). *Micro Leasing: The Grameen Bank Experience*. St. Mary's College of Maryland.

Downey, J. (2007). *Innovation management*. The Chartered Institute of Management Accountants.

Drazin, R., & Van de Ven, A. H. (1985). Alternative forms of fit in contingency theory. *Administrative Science Quarterly*, *30*(4), 514–539. doi:10.2307/2392695

Drejer, I. (2004). A Schumpeterian approach is taken to the problem of spotting innovative trends in service provider surveys. *Research Policy*, *33*(3), 551–562.

Drucker, F. P. (1985). *Innovation and entrepreneurship, practice and principles*. Perfect Bound.

Duncan, R. D. (2019). Why the 'identity' of your organization really matters. Forbes. https://www.forbes.com/sites/rodgerdeanduncan/2019/10/03/why-the-identity-of-your-organization-really-matters/?sh=41396be15892

Dutta, D., & Mishra, S. K. (2021). Predictors of applicant attraction among Gen-X and millennials: Evidence from an emerging economy. *International Journal of Manpower*, *42*(8), 1479–1499. doi:10.1108/IJM-04-2020-0169

Dzhabdzhugazova, E., Blinova, E., & Orlova, L. (2016). The hospitality industry's most cutting-edge developments. *International Journal of Environmental and Science Education.*

Ekong, U. M., & Ekong, C. N. (2022). Digital currency and financial inclusion in Nigeria: Lessons for development. *Journal of Internet and Digital Economics*, *2*(1), 46–67. doi:10.1108/JIDE-11-2021-0018

Elidemir, S. N., Ozturen, A., & Bayighomog, S. W. (2020). Innovative behaviors, employee creativity, and sustainable competitive advantage: A moderated mediation. *Sustainability (Switzerland)*, *12*(8), 3295. Advance online publication. doi:10.3390u12083295

Engert, W., & Fung, B. S. C. (2017). *Central bank digital currency: Motivations and implications.* Bank of Canada Staff Discussion Paper No 16.

Erceg, A., Sekuloska, J. D., & Kelic, I. (2020). Blockchain in the tourism industry - A review of the situation in Croatia and Macedonia. In Informatics (Vol. 7, Issue 1). MDPI Multidisciplinary Digital Publishing Institute. doi:10.3390/informatics7010005

Erdoğan, B. Z. (2013). Pazarlama İletişimi Kavramı ve Öğeleri. Anadolu Üniversitesi Yayınları.

Eriş, H., & Kemer, E. (2020). Medical Tourism Awareness of Health Workers. *Indian Journal of Forensic Medicine & Toxicology*, *14*(4), 7884–7889.

Erkmen, B., & Gönenç Güler, E. (2020). Turizm ve dijitalleşme: 'Haskovo-Edirne Kültürel ve TarihiDestinasyonlar Projesi' örneği. *Tourism and Recreation*, 111-118.

Esemu, T., & Wood, E. (2013). Innovation and the Creation of Value in Emerging Commercial Agricultural Sectors in Africa: Evidence From the Ugandan Flower Export Sector Quality Innovation: Knowledge, Theory, and Practices. IGI Global.

Eskiler, E., Ozmen, M., & Uzkurt, C. (2011). Bilgi Yonetimi Pazar Odaklılık ve Pazarlama Yeniliği ĠliÇkisi: Mobilya Sektoründe Bir AraÇtırma. *Eskişehir Osmangazi Üniversitesi İİBF Dergisi*, *6*(1), 31–69.

Espinoza, C., Ukleja, M., & Rusch, C. (2010). *Managing the Millennials*. John Wiley & Son.

Esquivel, V., & Sweetman, C. (2016). Gender and the sustainable development goals. *Gender and Development*, *24*(1), 1–8. doi:10.1080/13552074.2016.1153318

Esty, D. C., & Winston, A. S. (2007). *Yeşilden altına akıllı şirketler çevreci stratejiler ile nasıl avantaj yaratır?* Mediacat.

Eubanks, B. (2022). *Artificial intelligence for HR: Use AI to support and develop a successful workforce*. Kogan Page Publishers.

Euwema, M. C., Wendt, H., & Van Emmerik, H. (2007). Leadership styles and group organizational citizenship behavior across cultures. *Journal of Organizational Behavior*, *28*(8), 1035–1057. doi:10.1002/job.496

Evans, C. (2021). *Covid and jobs: Why are hospitality workers leaving the industry?* BBC News. https://www.bbc.co.uk/news/uk-wales-57241370

Expeditions, I. (n.d.). *Embracing the Sustainable Tourism Criteria of India for the Tour Operator Segment, Mandip Singh Soin, FRGS*. Retrieved from https://webunwto.s3.eu-west-1.amazonaws.com/imported_images/38173/mandip_singh_soin_ecotourism_society_of_india.pdf

Feenberg, A. (2010). Eleştirel Teknoloji Teorisi: Genel Bir Bakış. In Teknoloji ve toplum: Yıkıcı bir direniş ve yeniden yapılanma. Kalkedon Yayınları.

Feenberg, A. (2017). Critical theory of technology and STS. *Thesis Eleven, 138*(1). 3-12.

Fei, J., Wang, Y., Yang, Y., Chen, S., & Zhi, Q. (2016). Towards eco-city: The role of green innovation. *Energy Procedia, 104*, 165–170. doi:10.1016/j.egypro.2016.12.029

Fenwick, M., & Vermeulen, E.P. (2020). Banking and regulatory responses to FinTech revisited-building the sustainable financial service 'ecosystems' of tomorrow. *Singapore Journal of Legal Studies*, 165-189.

Ferdig, A. M. (2009). *Sustainability Leadership Relational Model and Practices*. Retrieved from https://www.sustainabilityleadershipinstitute.org/downloads/SLI_model_download.pdf

Ferdig, A. (2007, March). Sustainability Leadership: Co-creating a Sustainable Future. *Journal of Change Management, 7*(1), 25–35. doi:10.1080/14697010701233809

Ferreira, J., Coelho, A., & Moutinho, L. (2020). Dynamic capabilities, creativity and innovation capability and their impact on competitive advantage and firm performance: The moderating role of entrepreneurial orientation. *Technovation, 92–93*, 102061. Advance online publication. doi:10.1016/j.technovation.2018.11.004

Ferris, K., Cameron, D., Jenkins, A., & Marson, J. (2018). The consequences of the BREXIT vote on management attitudes to recruitment in the hospitality industry. *Business Law Review, 39*(4).

Financial Times. (2022). *UK hospitality industry loses nearly 200,000 overseas workers*. https://www.ft.com/content/027ea2e9-d6c3-4a18-a735-87f92ace95a4

Finnan, C. (2006). *Practicing Modernity: Female Creativity in the Weimar Republic*. Königshausen & Neumann.

Firoiu, D., & Croitoru, A. G. (2013). Tourism and tourism infrastructure from the perspective of technological changes. *Romanian Economic & Business Review, 8*(2), 93-103.

Flammini, A., Ferrari, P., Marioli, D., Sisinni, E., & Taroni, A. (2009). Wired and wireless sensor networks for industrial applications. *Microelectronics Journal, 40*(9), 1322–1336. doi:10.1016/j.mejo.2008.08.012

Florida, R., & Mellander, C. (2010). There goes the metro: How and why bohemians, artists and gays affect regional housing values. *Journal of Economic Geography, 10*(2), 167–188. doi:10.1093/jeg/lbp022

Fondevila Gascón, J. F., Marqués-Pascual, J., Muñoz González, M., & Polo López, M. (2019). The impact of robotics on the tourism sector: The case of Barcelona. *Harvard Deusto Business Research, VIII*(1), 49–61. doi:10.3926/hdbr.225

Fovino, I. N., Carcano, A., Masera, M., & Trombetta, A. (2009). Design and Implementation of a Secure Modbus Protocol. In C. Palmer & S. Shenoi (Eds.), *Critical Infrastructure Protection III* (Vol. 311, pp. 83–96). Springer Berlin Heidelberg. doi:10.1007/978-3-642-04798-5_6

Freeman, C. (1982). *Innovation and long cycles of economic development. Seminário Internacional*. Universidade Estadual de Campinas.

Frishammar, J., Richtnér, A., Brattström, A., Magnusson, M., & Björk, J. (2019). Opportunities and challenges in the new innovation landscape: Implications for innovation auditing and innovation management. *European Management Journal, 37*(2), 151–164. doi:10.1016/j.emj.2018.05.002

Frye, W. D., Kang, S., Huh, C., & Lee, M. J. M. (2020). What factors influence Generation Y's employee retention in the hospitality industry? An internal marketing approaches. *International Journal of Hospitality Management, 85*, 102352. doi:10.1016/j.ijhm.2019.102352

Fu, K., Cheng, D., Tu, Y., & Zhang, L. (2016). Credit Card Fraud Detection Using Convolutional Neural Networks. In A. Hirose, S. Ozawa, K. Doya, K. Ikeda, M. Lee, & D. Liu (Eds.), *Neural Information Processing* (Vol. 9949, pp. 483–490). Springer International Publishing. doi:10.1007/978-3-319-46675-0_53

Galbraith, J. R. (1982). Designing the innovating organization. *Organizational Dynamics, 10*(3), 5–25. doi:10.1016/0090-2616(82)90033-X

Gamble, J. R. (2020). Tacit vs explicit knowledge as antecedents for organizational change. In Journal of Organizational Change Management (Vol. 33, Issue 6, pp. 1123–1141). Emerald Group Holdings Ltd. doi:10.1108/JOCM-04-2020-0121

Gan, G. C., Chong, C. W., Yuen, Y. Y., Yen Teoh, W. M., & Rahman, M. S. (2021). Executive coaching effectiveness: Towards sustainable business excellence. *Total Quality Management & Business Excellence, 32*(13-14), 1405–1423. do i:10.1080/14783363.2020.1724507

Ganguly, A., Talukdar, A., & Chatterjee, D. (2019). Evaluating the role of social capital, tacit knowledge sharing, knowledge quality and reciprocity in determining innovation capability of an organization. *Journal of Knowledge Management, 23*(6), 1105–1135. doi:10.1108/JKM-03-2018-0190

Gao, X., Guo, X., & Lo, T. (2021). Digital infrastructure - A potential method for rural revitalization through digitization of rural information. *Projections - Proceedings of the 26th International Conference of the Association for Computer-Aided Architectural Design Research in Asia, CAADRIA 2021, 2*, 699–708.

Garau, C. (2015). Perspectives on cultural and sustainable rural tourism in a smart region: The case study of Marmilla in Sardinia (Italy). *Sustainability (Switzerland), 7*(6), 6412–6434. doi:10.3390u7066412

Garg, V., Srivastav, S., & Gupta, A. (2018). Application of artificial intelligence for sustaining green human resource management. *2018 International Conference on Automation and Computational Engineering (ICACE)*, 113-116. 10.1109/ICACE.2018.8686988

Geetha, R., & Reddy, B. S. (2018). Recruitment through Artificial Intelligence: A Conceptual Study. *International Journal of Mechanical Engineering and Technology, 9*(7), 63–70.

Geisler, E., & Wickramasinghe, N. (2015). *Principles of Knowledge Management: Theory, Practice, and Cases*. Routledge. doi:10.4324/9781315686448

George, G., & Thomas, M. R. (2019). Integration of Artificial Intelligence in Human Resource. *International Journal of Innovative Technology and Exploring Engineering, 9*(2), 5069–5073. doi:10.35940/ijitee.L3364.129219

George, P., Coleman, B., & Barnoff, L. (2010). Stories from the field: Practicing structural social work in current times: Practitioners' use of creativity. *Critical Social Work, 11*(2), 13–27.

Ghadeer, M., Badr, E., & Aboul-Ela, G. (2016). Employer branding: What constitutes An Employer of choice? *The Journal of Business and Retail Management Research, 11*(1), 154–166.

Ghani, B., Zada, M., Memon, K. R., Ullah, R., Khattak, A., Han, H., Ariza-Montes, A., & Araya-Castillo, L. (2022). Challenges and strategies for employee retention in the hospitality industry: A review. *Sustainability, 14*(5), 2885. doi:10.3390u14052885

Ghasemaghases, M., & Callic, G. (2020). Assessing the impact of big data on firm innovation performance: Big data is not always better data. *Journal of Business Research, 108*, 147–162. doi:10.1016/j.jbusres.2019.09.062

Giglitto, D., Ciolfi, L., & Bosswick, W. (2022). Building a bridge: Opportunities and challenges for intangible cultural heritage at the intersection of institutions, civic society, and migrant communities. *International Journal of Heritage Studies, 28*(1), 74–91. doi:10.1080/13527258.2021.1922934

Giritlioğlu, İ., & Güzel, M. O. (2015). Otel işletmelerinde yeşil yıldız uygulamaları: Gaziantep ve Hatay bölgesinde bir araştırma. *Journal of International Social Research, 8*(40), 889–904. doi:10.17719/jisr.20154013968

Giudici, E., Melis, C., Dessì, S., & Francine Pollnow Galvao Ramos, B. (2013). Is intangible cultural heritage able to promote sustainability in tourism? *International Journal of Quality and Service Sciences, 5*(1), 101–114. doi:10.1108/17566691311316275

Giustiniano, L., Lombardi, S., & Cavaliere, V. (2016). How knowledge collecting fosters organizational creativity. *Management Decision, 54*(6), 1464–1496. doi:10.1108/MD-04-2015-0111

Glinik, M., Poandl, E. M., & Mueller, C. (2019). Searching for the ideal business model: Challenges for start-ups. *ISPIM Conference Proceedings*, 1-11.

Goosen, L. (2015). Educational Technologies for Growing Innovative e-Schools in the 21st Century: A Community Engagement Project. In D. Nwaozuzu, & S. Mnisi (Ed.), *Proceedings of the South Africa International Conference on Educational Technologies* (pp. 49 - 61). Pretoria: African Academic Research Forum.

Goosen, L. (2016, February 18). *"We don't need no education"? Yes, they DO want e-learning in Basic and Higher Education!* Retrieved from https://uir.unisa.ac.za/handle/10500/20999

Goosen, L. (2018a). Sustainable and Inclusive Quality Education Through Research Informed Practice on Information and Communication Technologies in Education. In L. Webb (Ed.), *Proceedings of the 26th Conference of the Southern African Association for Research in Mathematics, Science and Technology Education (SAARMSTE)* (pp. 215 - 228). University of Botswana.

Goosen, L., & Mukasa-Lwanga, T. (2017). Educational Technologies in Distance Education: Beyond the Horizon with Qualitative Perspectives. In U. I. Ogbonnaya, & S. Simelane-Mnisi (Ed.), *Proceedings of the South Africa International Conference on Educational Technologies* (pp. 41 - 54). Pretoria: African Academic Research Forum.

Goosen, L., & Van der Merwe, R. (2015). e-Learners, Teachers and Managers at e-Schools in South Africa. In C. Watson (Ed.), *Proceedings of the 10th International Conference on e-Learning (ICEL)* (pp. 127 - 134). Nassau: Academic Conferences and Publishing International.

Goosen, L. (2004). *Criteria and Guidelines for the Selection and Implementation of a First Programming Language in High Schools*. Potchefstroom Campus: North West University. Retrieved from http://hdl.handle.net/10394/226

Goosen, L. (2018b). Trans-Disciplinary Approaches to Action Research for e-Schools, Community Engagement, and ICT4D. In T. A. Mapotse (Ed.), *Cross-Disciplinary Approaches to Action Research and Action Learning* (pp. 97–110). IGI Global. doi:10.4018/978-1-5225-2642-1.ch006

Goosen, L. (2018c). Ethical Data Management and Research Integrity in the Context of e-Schools and Community Engagement. In C. Sibinga (Ed.), *Ensuring Research Integrity and the Ethical Management of Data* (pp. 14–45). IGI Global. doi:10.4018/978-1-5225-2730-5.ch002

Goosen, L. (2018d). Ethical Information and Communication Technologies for Development Solutions: Research Integrity for Massive Open Online Courses. In C. Sibinga (Ed.), *Ensuring Research Integrity and the Ethical Management of Data* (pp. 155–173). IGI Global. doi:10.4018/978-1-5225-2730-5.ch009

Goosen, L. (2022). Augmented/Virtual Reality Technologies and Assistive/Humanoid Robots: Students With Autism Spectrum Disorders. In S. Dhamdhere & F. Andres (Eds.), *Assistive Technologies for Differently Abled Students* (pp. 239–267). IGI Global. doi:10.4018/978-1-7998-4736-6.ch012

Goosen, L., & Naidoo, L. (2014). Computer Lecturers Using Their Institutional LMS for ICT Education in the Cyber World. In C. Burger, & K. Naudé (Ed.), *Proceedings of the 43rd Conference of the Southern African Computer Lecturers' Association (SACLA)* (pp. 99-108). Nelson Mandela Metropolitan University.

Göral, R., Akgöz, E., & Topuz, Ç. (2014). *Turizm işletmelerinde yeşil iş modeli inovasyonu yönetim aracı olarak yeşil inovasyon radarı. In Ulusal Turizm Kongresi Bildiriler Kitabı.* Detay Yayıncılık.

Gordon, L. A., Loeb, M. P., & Zhou, L. (2016). Investing in Cybersecurity: Insights from the Gordon-Loeb Model. *Journal of Information Security*, *07*(02), 49–59. doi:10.4236/jis.2016.72004

Gordon, S., & Ford, R. (2006). On the definition and classification of cybercrime. *Journal in Computer Virology*, *2*(1), 13–20. doi:10.100711416-006-0015-z

Grameen Annual Report, . (2005). *Grameen Bank scholarship program.* Grameen Bank.

Grameen Bank. (2004). Opening Speech by Muhammed Yunus. *30th Zonal Manager Conference.* Grameen Ban.

Grameen Bank. (2005). Opening Speech by Muhammed Yunus. *30th Zonal Manager Conference.* Grameen Bank.

Grameen Shakka Bartta. (2006). *Grammen Shikka Activities.* Grameen Shikka.

Grameen Shikka Bartta. (2008). *Proud mothers from the borrowers of GB.* Department Administration, Grameen Bank.

Grameen Shikka Bartta, . (2009). *Five highest scholars' faces from the children of GB members in 2009.* Grameen Bank.

Grameen Shikka Bartta. (2014). *Grameen Bank talented Scholars.* Department Administration, Grameen Bank.

Grameen Shikka Bartta, . (2014). *Talented children stories.* Grameen Bank.

Grameen Shikka Bartta. (2019). *Arsenic mitigation program in Bangladesh.* Grameen Shikka.

Grant, R. M. (1991). The Resource-Based Theory of Competitive Advantage: Implications for Strategy Formulation. *California Management Review*, *33*(3), 114–135. doi:10.2307/41166664

Green, K. (2019). *Competitive People Strategy How to attract, develop and retain the staff you need for business success.* Kogan Page.

Gretzel, U., Werthner, H., Koo, C., & Lamsfus, C. (2015). Conceptual foundations for understanding smart tourism ecosystems. *Computers in Human Behavior*, *50*(1), 558–563. doi:10.1016/j.chb.2015.03.043

Grönroos, C. (2006). On defining marketing: Finding a new roadmap for marketing. *Marketing Theory*, *6*(4), 395–417. doi:10.1177/1470593106069930

Güle, Ģ. H. K., & Bülbül, H. (2004). Yenilikcilik: İşletmeler İcin Stratejik Rekabet Aracı. Ankara: Nobel Yayıncılık.

Güne, Ç. S. (2010). *Yenilik Yayılımı: Bir Araştırma*. Ġstanbul Üniversitesi.

Güneş, G. (2011). Konaklama sektöründe çevre dostu yönetimin önemi. *Karamanoğlu Mehmetbey Üniversitesi Sosyal ve Ekonomik Araştırmalar Dergisi, 13*(20), 45–51.

Gupta, S. K., Rout, P. C., & Tyagi, P. (2019). Community Based Tourism Development Amid Complex Mountain Issues: A Strategic Analysis of Chakrata Region of Uttarakhand. *International Journal of Hospitality and Tourism Systems, 12*(1), 47–55.

Gürdin, B. (2020). Robonomi ve müşteri memnuniyeti: Hizmet robotlarına ilişkin literatür taraması. *Ekonomi Maliye İşletme Dergisi, 3*(1), 85–100. doi:10.46737/emid.732024

Gursoy, D., Maier, T. A., & Chi, C. G. (2008). Generational differences: An examination of work values and generational gaps in the hospitality workforce. *International Journal of Hospitality Management, 27*(3), 448–458. doi:10.1016/j.ijhm.2007.11.002

Gurteen, D. (1998). Knowledge Creativity and Innovation. *Journal of Knowledge Management, 2*(1), 5–13. doi:10.1108/13673279810800744

Haamann, T., & Basten, D. (2019). The role of information technology in bridging the knowing-doing gap: An exploratory case study on knowledge application. *Journal of Knowledge Management, 23*(4), 705–741. doi:10.1108/JKM-01-2018-0030

Habash, R. (2017). *Green Engineering: Innovation, Entrepreneurship and Design*. CRC Press. doi:10.4324/9781315116389

Hallin, E. (2018). Seminar in Hotel Management and Leadership, 10 February 2018. Bangkok: Graduate School of Tourism Management. National Institute of Development Administration.

Hall, J. (2006). Environmental supply chain innovation. In *Greening the supply chain* (pp. 233–249). Springer. doi:10.1007/1-84628-299-3_13

Han, H., & Kim, Y. (2010). An investigation of green hotel customers' decision formation: Developing an extended model of the theory of planned behavior. *International Journal of Hospitality Management, 29*(4), 659–668. doi:10.1016/j.ijhm.2010.01.001

Hanks, L., Line, N., & Mattila, A. (2015). The Impact of Self-Service Technology and The Presence of Others on Cause-Related Marketing Programs in Restaurants. *Journal of Hospitality Marketing & Management, 25*(5), 547–562. Advance online publication. doi:10.1080/19368623.2015.1046536

Haque, A. U., Faizan, R., Zehra, N., Baloch, A., Nadda, V., & Riaz, F. (2015). Leading Leadership Style to Motivate Cultural-Oriented Female Employees in IT Sector of Developing Country: IT Sectors' Responses from Pakistan. *International Journal of Academic Research in Business & Social Sciences, 5*(9), 280–302. doi:10.6007/IJARBSS/v5-i9/1836

Harber, C. (2002). Education, democracy, and poverty reduction in Africa. *Comparative Education, 38*(3), 267–276. doi:10.1080/0305006022000014133

Harrington, T. S., Srai, J. S., & Kumar, M. (2019). Knowledge management in SMEs and MNCs: Matching knowledge mobility mechanisms to supply network configuration profiles. *Production Planning and Control, 30*(10–12), 971–994. doi:10.1080/09537287.2019.1582103

Hashemi, S. M. (1997). Building up Capacity for Banking with the Poor: The Grameen Bank of Bangladesh. In H. Schneider (Ed.), *Microfinance for the Poor?* (pp. 109–128). OECD.

Hayat, M., Shakeel, M., & Chen, B. (2021). Impact of work ethics and work environment on project success with the moderating role of job engagement. *Science Journal of Business and Management, 9*(1), 15. doi:10.11648/j.sjbm.20210901.12

Hbr.org. (2018). *When Empowering Employees Works*. Available at: https://hbr.org/2018/03/when-empowering-employees-works-and-when-it-doesnt

Heap, J. (1989). *The Management of Innovation and Design*. Academic Press.

He, E. (2018). Can artificial intelligence make work more human? *Strategic HR Review*, *17*(5), 263–264. doi:10.1108/SHR-10-2018-146

Heidegger, M. (1977). *The Question Concerning Technology And Other Essays*. Garland Publishing.

Heise, U. K. (2004). Science, Technology And Postmodernism. In The Cambridge companion to postmodernism içinde (pp. 136-167). Cambridge University Press. doi:10.1017/CCOL0521640520.008

Helfat, C. E., & Peteraf, M. A. (2003). The dynamic resource-based view: Capability lifecycles. *Strategic Management Journal, 24*(10), 997–1010. doi:10.1002/smj.332

Hellström, T. (2007). Critical infrastructure and systemic vulnerability: Towards a planning framework. *Safety Science, 45*(3), 415–430. doi:10.1016/j.ssci.2006.07.007

Herjanto, H., Amin, M., Okumus, F., & Cobanoglu, C. (2021). Airline Service: Low-Cost Carriers (LCCs) Failure and Passenger Emotional Expereince. *Tourism Review*. Advance online publication. doi:10.1108/TR-01-2021-0025

Hines, P. (1993). Integrated Materials Management: The Value Chain Redefined. *International Journal of Logistics Management, 4*(1), 13–22. doi:10.1108/09574099310804920

Hjalager, A. M. (2002). Repairing innovation defectiveness in tourism. *Tourism Management, 23*(5), 465–474. doi:10.1016/S0261-5177(02)00013-4

Hjalager, A. M. (2010). A review of innovation research in tourism. *Tourism Management, 31*(1), 1–12. doi:10.1016/j.tourman.2009.08.012

Hjalager, A.-M. (2010). An examination of the research done on innovative tourist practises. *Tourism Management, 31*(1), 1–12.

Hofer, C. W. (1990). Toward a contingency theory of business strategy. In *Strategische Unternehmungsplanung/Strategische Unternehmungsführung* (pp. 151–175). Physica. doi:10.1007/978-3-662-41484-2_7

Hoffmann, J., Ivcevic, Z., & Brackett, M. (2016). Creativity in the age of technology: Measuring the digital creativity of millennials. *Creativity Research Journal, 28*(2), 149–153. doi:10.1080/10400419.2016.1162515

Holsapple, C. W., & Joshi, K. D. (2004). A formal knowledge management ontology: Conduct, activities, resources, and influences. *Journal of the American Society for Information Science and Technology, 55*(7), 593–612. doi:10.1002/asi.20007

Honohan, P. (2004). *Financial sector policy and the poor.* World Bank Working Paper No. 43.

Horbach, J., Rammer, C., & Rennings, K. (2012). Determinants of eco-innovations by type of environmental impact-The role of regulatory push/pull, technology push and market pull. *Ecological Economics, 78*, 112–122. doi:10.1016/j.ecolecon.2012.04.005

Hospitality Training Foundation. (2000). *Getting the basics right in the hospitality industry: integrating the basic skills standards into the occupational standards of the Hospitality Training Foundation.* https://www.worldcat.org/title/1166630477 https://www.gov.uk/skilled-worker-visa/if-you-work-in-healthcare-or-education

Hospitality, U. K. (2018). *UK Hospitality Workforce Commission 2030 report: The changing face of hospitality September 2018*. https://www.youthemployment.org.uk/dev/wp-content/uploads/2018/09/UK-Hospitality-Workforce-Commission-2030.pdf

Hossain, D. M. (2013). Social Capital and Microfinance: The Case of Grameen Bank, Bangladesh. *Middle East Journal of Business, 8*(4).

Hotel Restaurant Magazine. (2022a). *Turizm sektöründe yükselen trend yeşil oteller*. https://www.hotelrestaurantmagazine.com/turizm-sektorunde-yukselen-trend-yesil-oteller/

Hotel Restaurant Magazine. (2022b). *Türkiye'nin en çevreci beş yıldızlı oteli Renaissance İstanbul Bosphorus Hotel*. https://www.hotelrestaurantmagazine.com/turkiyenin-en-cevreci-bes-yildizli-oteli-renaissance-istanbul-bosphorus-hotel/

Hou, Y., Kenderdine, S., Picca, D., Egloff, M., & Adamou, A. (2022). Digitizing Intangible Cultural Heritage Embodied: State of the Art. *Journal on Computing and Cultural Heritage, 15*(3), 1–20. doi:10.1145/3494837

Huang, M.-H., & Rust, R. (2018). Artificial Intelligence in Service. *Journal of Service Research, 21*(2), 155–172. doi:10.1177/1094670517752459

Huang, P. L., Lee, B. C. Y., & Chen, C.-C. (2019). The influence of service quality on customer satisfaction and loyalty in B2B technology service industry. *Total Quality Management & Business Excellence, 30*(13-14), 1449–1465. doi:10.1080/14783363.2017.1372184

Hübscher, M. (2021). Megaprojects, gentrification, and tourism. A systematic review on intertwined phenomena. *Sustainability (Switzerland), 13*(22), 12827. Advance online publication. doi:10.3390u132212827

Hui, W., & Nadda, V. (2015). Interactivity: The concept and its dimensions. In Computer-mediated marketing strategies: Social media and online brand communities (pp. 157-184). IGI Global.

Huitsing, P., Chandia, R., Papa, M., & Shenoi, S. (2008). Attack taxonomies for the Modbus protocols. *International Journal of Critical Infrastructure Protection, 1*, 37–44. doi:10.1016/j.ijcip.2008.08.003

Hulme, D. (2008). *The story of the Grameen Bank: From subsidised microcredit to market-based microfinance*. Brooks World Poverty Institute Working Paper, (60).

Hulme, D., & Mosley, P. (1996). *Finance Against Poverty*. Routledge.

Hulme, D., Mosley, P., Wood, G. D., & Sharif, I. A. (1997). Finance for the poor or poorest? Financial innovation, poverty, and vulnerability. In *Who needs credit? Poverty and finance in Bangladesh*. Zed Books.

Hussain, M., Maskooki, M., & Gunasekaran, A. (2001). Implications of Grameen banking system in Europe: Prospects and prosperity. *European Business Review, 13*(1), 26–41.

Hutchinson, D., & Warren, M. (2003). Security for Internet banking: A framework. *Logistics Information Management, 16*(1), 64–73. doi:10.1108/09576050310453750

Huy, L. V., Hoan, N. P. T., Pham, L., & Berry, R. (2019). Technology readiness and satisfaction in Vietnam's luxury hotels. *International Journal of Management and Decision Making, 18*(2), 183–208. doi:10.1504/IJMDM.2019.098648

İbiş, S. (2019). Turizm endüstrisinde robotlaşma. *Türk Turizm Araştırmaları Dergisi, 3*(3), 403–420. doi:10.26677/TR1010.2019.169

Ibrahim, N., & Ali, N. M. (2018). A conceptual framework for designing virtual heritage environment for cultural learning. *Journal on Computing and Cultural Heritage, 11*(2), 1–27. doi:10.1145/3117801

Ibzan, E., Balarabe, F., & Jakada, B. (2016). Consumer Satisfaction and Repurchase Intentions. *Developing Country Studies, 6*(2), 96–100.

iCraze. (2021). *Grape County by Green Spaces. iCraze, January-February 2021.* Retrieved from https://www.magzter.com/stories/Lifestyle/iCraze/GRAPE-COUNTY-BY-GREEN-SPACES

Iğık, C., Akoğul, E., TaÇ, S., Uyrun, A., Hajiyeva, T., Turan, B., & Dırbo, A. H. (2018). Turizm ve Ġnovasyon ĠliÇkisi: Literatür Taraması. *Journal of Tourism Intelligence and Smartness*, 34–74.

Ihde, D. (2010). Heidegger on technology: One size fits all. *Philosophy Today, 54*(Supplement), 101–105. doi:10.5840/philtoday201054Supplement53

Imthammaporn, W. (2018). *Technology Acceptance, Service Conveneince, and Social Media Marketing Affecting Decision to Use Food Order Service Applications of Generation Y Consumers in Bangkok* [MBA Thesis]. Graduate School, Bangkok University.

Inauen, M., & Schenker-Wicki, A. (2011). The impact of outside-in open innovation on innovation performance. *European Journal of Innovation Management, 14*(4), 496–520. doi:10.1108/14601061111174934

India at Expo. (2022, January 9). *Expo 2020 Dubai, India Pavilion, Mainstreaming Sustainability for Future of Tourism.* YouTube. https://www.youtube.com/watch?v=Iq_z2Z2CzV4

Indian Express. (2011). The Boss of Heritage Holidays. *The New Indian Express.* Retrieved from. https://www.newindianexpress.com/lifestyle/2011/jul/31/the-boss-of-heritage-holidays-276867.html

International Organization for Standardization. (2012). Retrieved from: https://www.iso.org/obp/ui/#iso:std:iso:8373:ed-2:v1:e

İpar, M. S., & Aksu, M. (2022). Turistlerin yeşil otel tercihlerine yönelik algıları, çevreci davranış eğilimleri ve davranışsal niyetlerle ilişkisi. *Journal of Gastronomy, Hospitality and Travel, 5*(1), 440–463.

Ir.tesla.com. (2020). *Tesla Investor Relations.* Available at: https://ir.tesla.com/

Irfan, M., Ahmad, M., Fareed, Z., Iqbal, N., Sharif, A., & Wu, H. (2022). On the indirect environmental outcomes of COVID-19: Short-term revival with futuristic long-term implications. *International Journal of Environmental Health Research, 32*(6), 1271–1281. doi:10.1080/09603123.2021.1874888 PMID:33448868

Isa, W. M. W., Zin, N. A. M., Rosdi, F., & Sarim, H. M. (2018). Digital preservation of intangible cultural heritage. *Indonesian Journal of Electrical Engineering and Computer Science, 12*(3), 1373–1379. doi:10.11591/ijeecs.v12.i3.pp1373-1379

Işık, C., & Barlak, S. (2018). Otel yöneticilerinin yeşil inovasyon algıları: İstanbul ili örneği. *Journal of Tourism Intelligence and Smartness, 1*(1), 14–26.

Işik, C., Kasımatı, E., & Ongan, S. (2017). Analyzing the causalities between economic growth, financial development, international trade, tourism expenditure and/on the CO2 emissions in Greece. *Energy Sources. Part B, Economics, Planning, and Policy, 12*(7), 665–673. doi:10.1080/15567249.2016.1263251

Islam, J., & Hu, H. (2012). A review of literature on contingency theory in managerial accounting. *African Journal of Business Management, 6*(15), 5159–5164.

Ismail, M., Shaaban, M. F., Naidu, M., & Serpedin, E. (2020). Deep Learning Detection of Electricity Theft Cyber-Attacks in Renewable Distributed Generation. *IEEE Transactions on Smart Grid, 11*(4), 3428–3437. doi:10.1109/TSG.2020.2973681

Ismail, N. N. H. M., Nasir, M. K. M., & Rahman, R. S. A. R. A. (2021). Factors that influence women to be involved in entrepreneurship: A case study in Malaysia. *Creative Education, 12*(04), 837–847. doi:10.4236/ce.2021.124060

Ivanović, S., Milojica, V., & Roblek, V. (2016). A Holistic Approach to Innovations in Tourism. *International Conference on Economic and Social Studies (ICESoS'16)*, 367–380. Retrieved from https://www.researchgate.net/publication/301295108

Ivanov, S., Seyitoğlu, F., & Markova, M. (2020). Hotel managers' perceptions towards the use of robots: A mixed-methods approach. *Information Technology & Tourism, 22*(4), 505–535. doi:10.100740558-020-00187-x

Ivanov, S., Webster, C., & Berezina, K. (2017). Adoption of robots and service automation by tourism and hospitality companies. *Revista Turismo & Desenvolvimento, 27*(28), 1501–1517.

Ivanov, S., Webster, C., & Garenko, A. (2018). Young Russian adults' attitudes towards the potential use of robots in hotels. *Technology in Society, 55*, 24–32. doi:10.1016/j.techsoc.2018.06.004

Iverson, R. D., & Deery, M. (1997). Turnover culture in the hospitality industry. *Human Resource Management Journal, 7*(4), 71–82. doi:10.1111/j.1748-8583.1997.tb00290.x

Ivkov, M., Bleši´c, I., Dudi´c, B., Pajtinková Bartáková, G., & Dudi´c, Z. (2020). Are future professionals willing to implement service robots? Attitudes of hospitality and tourism students towards service robotization. *Electronics, 9*(1942), 1-16.

Jadhav, V. S., & Mundhe, S. D. (2011). Information technology in Tourism. *International Journal of Computer Science and Information Technologies, 2*(6), 2822–2825. http://www.maharashtratourism.gov.in

Jaiswal, A., Kumar, S., Kaiwartya, O., Kumar, N., Song, H., & Lloret, J. (2021). Secrecy Rate Maximization in Virtual-MIMO Enabled SWIPT for 5G Centric IoT Applications. *IEEE Systems Journal, 15*(2), 2810–2821. doi:10.1109/JSYST.2020.3036417

Jakranukul, C. (2015). *Perspectives of Self-Service Technology (SSTS) from Emerging Economy* [Master Thesis]. Thammasat University.

Jalaliyoon, N., Hamed Taherdoost, A., Lumpur, K., & Neda Jalaliyoon, M. (2014). Marketing vs E-Marketing Steganography View project E-Commerce Quality Assessment; Evaluation of the Quality of E-Service View project. *International Journal of Academic Research in Management, 3*(4). https://www.researchgate.net/publication/282654148

Jänisch, R. (2018). *Künstliche Intelligenz Revolutioniert Das Marketing*. Retrieved from: https://www.iox.bot/kunstliche-intelligenz-im-marketing

Jarek, K., & Mazurek, G. (2019). Marketing and artificial ıntelligence. *Central European Business Review, 8*(2), 46–55. doi:10.18267/j.cebr.213

Jatobá, M., Santos, J., Gutierriz, I., Moscon, D., Fernandes, P. O., & Teixeira, J. P. (2019). Evolution of Artificial Intelligence Research in Human Resources. *Procedia Computer Science, 164*, 137–142. doi:10.1016/j.procs.2019.12.165

Jiang, F., Du, C., Fu, T., & Xiao, R. (2019). Research on the Application of Artificial Intelligence in Human Resource Management. *Journal of Social Sciences Studies, 4*, 258–262.

Jia, Q., Guo, Y., Li, R., Li, Y., & Chen, Y. (2018). A Conceptual Artificial Intelligence Application Framework in Human Resource Management. *Proceedings of The 18th International Conference on Electronic Business*, 106–114.

Johnson, G., Whittington, R., Scholes, K., Angwin, D., & Regnér, P. (2010). *Exploring Strategy*. https://twitter.com/ExploreStrategy

Johnson, S., & Rogaly, B. (1997). *Microfinance and poverty reduction*. Oxfam. doi:10.3362/9780855988005

Jorde, T. M., & Teece, D. J. (1990). The implications of innovation and cooperation for both market competitiveness and antitrust laws. *The Journal of Economic Perspectives*, *4*(3), 75–96.

Joshi, C., Ranjan, R. K., & Bharti, V. (2021, April). ANN based Multi-Class classification of P2P Botnet. *International Journal Of Computing and Digital Systems*, *11*(1), 1319–1325. doi:10.12785/ijcds/1101107

Jurevičienė, D., & Ivanova, O. (2013). Behavioural Finance: Theory and Survey [Finansinė Elgsena: Teorija Ir Tyrimas]. *Mokslas - Lietuvos Ateitis*, *5*(1), 53–58. doi:10.3846/mla.2013.08

Kagermann, H., Wahlsterand, W., & Helbig, J. (2013). Recommendations for implementing the strategicinitiative industrie 4.0: Final report of the ındustrie 4.0 working group. *Securing the Future of German-Manufacturing Industry*. Retrieved from: https://www.researchgate.net/publication/357467063_Turizmde_Dijitallesme_Akilli_Turizm_Uygulamalari_Dijital_Turizm_ve_Tu rizm_40_Digitalization_in_Tourism_Smart_Tourism_Applications _Digital_Tourism_and_Tourism_40

Kamal, A. (2021). *The Grameen model and its applicability in developed countries*. University of London and Kings College London Press.

Kammarer, D. (2008) *Determinants of environmental product ınnovation a comparative study on manufacturers of electrical and electronic appliances in Germany and California*. (Publication No. 18057) [Doctoral dissertation, ETH Zurich]. ETH Zurich Research Collection.

Kankaew, K. (Ed.). (2022). *Global Air Transport Management and Reshaping Business Models for the New Era*. IGI Global Publishing. doi:10.4018/978-1-6684-4615-7

Kanter, R. (1988). When a thousand flowers bloom: Structural, collective, and social conditions for innovation in organizations. *Research in Organizational Behavior, 10, 169–211.*

Kao, T. Y., Chen, J. C., Wu, J. T. B., & Yang, M. H. (2016). Poverty reduction through empowerment for sustainable development: A proactive strategy of corporate social responsibility. *Corporate Social Responsibility and Environmental Management*, *23*(3), 140–149. doi:10.1002/csr.1365

Kasavana, M. L. (2008). The Convergence of Self-service Technology. *Hospitality Upgrade*, (Spring), 122–128.

Kaur, K., & Bharti, V. (2019). A Survey on Big Data—Its Challenges and Solution from Vendors. In *Big Data Processing Using Spark in Cloud* (pp. 1–22). Springer. doi:10.1007/978-981-13-0550-4_1

Keenan, S. F., & Mishra, P. (2016). Profiling scholars of creativity: Practicing the process with Dr. Michele Root-Bernstein. *TechTrends*, *60*(3), 200–203. doi:10.100711528-016-0055-2

Kelikume, I. (2021). Digital financial inclusion, informal economy, and poverty reduction in Africa. *Journal of Enterprising Communities: People and Places in the Global Economy*, *15*(4), 626–640. doi:10.1108/JEC-06-2020-0124

Keller, J. R. (2018). Posting and slotting: How hiring processes shape the quality of hire and compensation in internal labor markets. *Administrative Science Quarterly*, *63*(4), 848–878. doi:10.1177/0001839217736045

Kemer, E. (2021a, April). The Impact of Hotel Business Managers' Innovation Abilities on Perceptions of Industry 4.0. In *Proceedings of the Conference on Managing Tourism Across Continents* (p. 99). University of South Florida M3 Center Publishing. 10.5038/9781955833011

Kemer, E. (2021b). The Role of Agricultural Products in Establishing Gastronomic Identity. *Journal of Gastronomy. Hospitality and Travel*, *4*(2), 226–232.

Kemer, E. (2021c, December). The Moderating Role of Occupational Commitment in the Effect of Income Level on Job Satisfaction. *Journal of Social Sciences of Mus Alparslan University*, *9*(6), 1877–1890. doi:10.18506/anemon.1003065

Kemer, E. (2022). The Relationship Between Organizational Innovation and Mobile Applications in Hotel Businesses. In *Disruptive Innovation and Emerging Technologies for Business Excellence in the Service Sector* (pp. 164–185). IGI Global. doi:10.4018/978-1-7998-9194-9.ch008

Kemmerer, R. A. (2003). Cybersecurity. *25th International Conference on Software Engineering, 2003. Proceedings*, 705–715. 10.1109/ICSE.2003.1201257

Kenaphoom. (2020). *Survey Satisfaction of People to the Service of Sub-district Administration Organization, Songyang*. Research and Development Institute, Mahasarakham Rajabhat University.

Kenderdine, S., Yip, A., Oliver, C., Pather, N., Sammut, C., Djokic, T., Marcus, N., & Ong, A. (2021). Designing Multidisciplinary Interactive Virtual Environments for Next-Generation Immersive Learning Experiences: Case Studies and Future Directions in Astrobiology, Anatomy and Cultural Heritage. In Creative and Collaborative Learning through Immersion (pp. 49–67). Springer.

Kerdpiam, K. (2014). *The Container Hotel Project: Art of Materials Hotel* [Master of Business Administration Thesis]. Bangkok University.

Keskosol, P., & Merakate, J. (2019). The Influence of Service Quality and Customer Satisfaction Towards Customer Loyalty in Hotel and Resort at Moosi Sub-District, Pak Chong District, Nakhon Ratchasima Province. *Journal of Humanities and Social Sciences*, *4*(3), 102–114.

Khanal, B. P., & Shimizu, T. (2019). Strategies for Development of Yoga, Ayurveda, and Meditation-based Health Tourism in Nepal: Using SWOT Analysis. *Journal of Tourism & Adventure*, *2*(1), 85–107. doi:10.3126/jota.v2i1.25934

Khandker, S. R., Khalily, B., & Khan, Z. (1995). *Grameen Bank: Performance and Sustainability*. Discussion Paper No. 306. World Bank.

Khan, P. A., & Johl, S. K. (2019). Nexus of comprehensive green innovation, environmental management system-14001-2015 and firm performance. *Cogent Business & Management*, *6*(1), 1–12. doi:10.1080/23311975.2019.1691833

Khoo, H. H., & Tan, K. C. (2002). Using the Australian business excellence framework to achieve sustainable business excellence. *Corporate Social Responsibility and Environmental Management*, *9*(4), 196–205. doi:10.1002/csr.28

Kilibarda, P., & Fonda, N. (1997). Random Selection. *People Management*, *3*(24).

Kim, J., & Lee, J. (2020). An Investigation of Teachers' Stages of Concern and Levels of Use about SW Education Based on Concerns-Based Adoption Model. *The Journal of the Korea Contents Association*, *20*(8), 75–87.

Kim, S., & Lee, H. (2010). Factors affecting employee knowledge acquisition and application capabilities. *Asia-Pacific Journal of Business Administration*, *2*(2), 133–152. doi:10.1108/17574321011078184

Kiper, M. (2004). Teknoloji transfer mekanizmalari ve bu kapsamda üniversite– sanayi işbirliği. *Teknoloji, Türk Mühendis ve Mimar Odaları Birliği,* 59-122.

Kirici Tekeli, Ü. E., Kemer, Ü. E., & Kasap, G. (2022). A Process of Meaning Creation: An Analysis of Space Tourism Posters via Semiotic Analysis. *Journal of Travel & Hospitality Management/Seyahat ve Otel Isletmeciligi Dergisi, 19*(1), 81-98.

Klein, K. J., & Sorra, J. S. (1996). The challenge of innovation implementation. *Academy of Management Review, 21*(4), 1055–1080. doi:10.2307/259164

Korkmaz, H., & Atay, L. (2017). Otel işletmelerinde yeşil pazarlama ve çevre sertifikalarının değerlendirilmesi. *Aksaray Üniversitesi İktisadi ve İdari Bilimler Fakültesi Dergisi, 9*(4), 113–126.

Köse, B. (2012). *Tüketici Yenilikçiliği ve Yeniliklerin Benimsenmesi: Bir Yenilik Olarak Mobil\sİnternet*. Afyon Kocatepe Üniversitesi.

Kotera, Y., Adhikari, P., & Sheffield, D. (2021). Mental health of UK hospitality workers: Shame, self-criticism, and self-reassurance. *Service Industries Journal, 41*(15-16), 1076–1096. doi:10.1080/02642069.2020.1713111

Kotler, P., Wong, V., Saunders, J., & Armstrong, G. (2005). *Principles of Marketing* (4th ed.). Academic Press.

Kotler, P., & Armstrong, G. (2018). *Principles of Marketing Management.* Pearson Prentice Hall.

Kristensen, K., & Westlund, A. H. (2004). Accountable business performance measurement for sustainable business excellence. *Total Quality Management & Business Excellence, 15*(5-6), 629–643. doi:10.1080/1478336041000168011б

Krombholz, K., Hobel, H., Huber, M., & Weippl, E. (2015). Advanced social engineering attacks. *Journal of Information Security and Applications, 22*, 113–122. doi:10.1016/j.jisa.2014.09.005

Kshetri, N. (2021). Evolving uses of artificial intelligence in human resource management in emerging economies in the global South: Some preliminary evidence. *Management Research Review, 44*(7), 970–990. doi:10.1108/MRR-03-2020-0168

Küçükoğlu, M. T. (2014). *Sürdürülebilirlik ve yeşil yenilik perspektifinde Türk işletmelerin incelenmesi* [Yayınlanmamış Doktora Tezi]. İstanbul Üniversitesi.

Kumar, P. K. (2021, October 7). *We are a society of like-minded people working for a cause.* Retrieved from https://hospitality.economictimes.indiatimes.com/news/travel/we-are-a-society-of-like-minded-people-working-for-a-cause/86835984

Kumar, P. K. (2021a, October 7). *Industry should support RTSOI with CSR funds to spread the message of responsible tourism: Rakesh Mathur.* Retrieved from https://travel.economictimes.indiatimes.com/news/associations/industry-should-support-rtsoi-with-csr-funds-to-spread-the-message-of-responsible-tourism-rakesh-mathur/86834603

Kumari, P. B., & Hemalatha, A. (2019). Perception towards Artificial Intelligence in Human Resources Management Practices – with Reference to IT Companies in Chennai. *International Journal of Recent Technology and Engineering, 8*(4S3), 61–65.

Kumar, R., & Bharti, V. (2021, September). A Critical Review of Finger Vein Recognition Techniques for Human Identification. In *Third International Conference on Inventive Research in Computing Applications (ICIRCA)* (pp. 1-9). IEEE. 10.1109/ICIRCA51532.2021.9544906

Kuo, C. M., Chen, L. C., & Tseng, C. Y. (2017). Investigating an innovative service with hospitality robots. *International Journal of Contemporary Hospitality Management, 29*(5), 1305–1321. doi:10.1108/IJCHM-08-2015-0414

Kurtzman, J., & Zauhar, J. (2003). A Wave in Time – The Sports. *Journal of Sport Tourism, 8*(1), 35–47. doi:10.1080/1477508032000093443

Labanauskaitė, D., Fiore, M., & Stašys, R. (2020). Use of E-marketing tools as communication management in the tourism industry. *Tourism Management Perspectives, 34*, 1–8. doi:10.1016/j.tmp.2020.100652

Lai, M., Sun, L. H., & Chu, H. E. (2020). Emotional labor and service sabotage in the hospitality industry: The mediating role of emotional exhaustion. *Journal of Tourism and Hospitality Management, 8*(1), 120–132.

Lai, P. H., & Nepal, S. K. (2006). Local perspectives of ecotourism development in Tawushan Nature Reserve, Taiwan. *Tourism Management, 27*(6), 1117–1129. doi:10.1016/j.tourman.2005.11.010 PMID:32287717

Larsen, O. M. (2005). *Governing innovation for sustainable development: integration of environmental and innovation policies in Norway* [Unpublished Master's Thesis]. University of Oslo.

Lashley, C., & Chapman, A. (1999). Labour turnover: Hidden problem, hidden cost. *Hospitality Review, 1*(1), 49–54.

Latour, B. (2010). *The pasteurization of france*. Harvard University Press.

Lazim, C. S. L. M., Ismail, N. D. B., & Tazilah, M. D. A. K. (2021). Application of technology acceptance model (TAM) towards online learning during covid-19 pandemic: Accounting students perspective. *Int. J. Bus. Econ. Law, 24*(1), 13–20.

Lee, J. J., Gemba, K., & Kodama, F. (2006). Analyzing the innovation process for environmental performance improvement. *Technological Forecasting and Social Change, 73*(3), 290–301. doi:10.1016/j.techfore.2004.03.008

Lee, J. S., Hsu, L. T., Han, H., & Kim, Y. (2010). Understanding how consumers view green hotels: How a hotel's green image can influence behavioural intentions. *Journal of Sustainable Tourism, 18*(7), 901–914. doi:10.1080/09669581003777747

Lee, J., Kim, S., Lee, J., & Moon, S. (2019). Enhancing employee creativity for a sustainable competitive advantage through perceived human resource management practices and trust in management. *Sustainability (Switzerland), 11*(8), 2305. Advance online publication. doi:10.3390u11082305

Leenders, M. A., & Chandra, Y. (2013). Antecedents and consequences of green innovation in the wine industry: The role of channel structure. *Technology Analysis and Strategic Management, 25*(2), 203–218. doi:10.1080/09537325.2012.759203

Lee, Y. H., Hsieh, Y. C., & Hsu, C. N. (2011). Adding innovation diffusion theory to the technology acceptance model: Supporting employees' intentions to use e-learning systems. *Journal of Educational Technology & Society, 14*(4), 124–137.

Lenka, U., & Gupta, M. (2020). An empirical investigation of innovation process in Indian pharmaceutical companies. *European Journal of Innovation Management, 23*(3), 500–523. doi:10.1108/EJIM-03-2019-0069

Lenzerini, F. (2011). Intangible cultural heritage: The living culture of peoples. *European Journal of International Law, 22*(1), 101–120. doi:10.1093/ejil/chr006

Leyshon, A., & Thrift, N. (1995). Geographies of financial exclusion: Financial abandonment in Britain and the United States. *Transactions of the Institute of British Geographers, NS, 20*(3), 312–341.

Lezzi, M., Lazoi, M., & Corallo, A. (2018). Cybersecurity for Industry 4.0 in the current literature: A reference framework. *Computers in Industry, 103*, 97–110. doi:10.1016/j.compind.2018.09.004

Liberato, P., Liberato, D., Abreu, A., Alén-González, E., & Rocha, Á. (2018). Generation Y: The Competitiveness of the Tourism Sector Based on Digital Technology. *Advances in Intelligent Systems and Computing, 724*, 227–240. doi:10.1007/978-3-319-74980-8_21

Li, J. J., Bonn, M. A., & Ye, B. H. (2019). Hotel employee's artificial intelligence and roboticsawareness and its impact on turnover intention: The moderating roles of perceivedorganizational support and competitive psychological climate. *Tourism Management, 73*(1), 172–181. doi:10.1016/j.tourman.2019.02.006

Li, M., & Huang, S. (2019). Understanding Customers' Continuance Intentions Toward In-Lobby Self-Service Technologies. *Frontiers in Psychology, 332*(10), 332. doi:10.3389/fpsyg.2019.00332 PMID:30837925

Lin, Y. C., Pearson, E. T., & Cai, L. A. (2011). Food as a form of destination identitiy: A tourism destination brand perspective. *Tourism and Hospitality Research, 11*(1), 30–48. doi:10.1057/thr.2010.22

Li, P., Menon, M., & Liu, Z. (2019). Green innovation under uncertainty-a dynamic perspective. *International Journal of Services. Economics and Management, 10*(1), 68–88.

Liu, D., Chen, X.-P., & Yao, X. (2011). From autonomy to creativity: A multilevel investigation of the mediating role of harmonious passion. *The Journal of Applied Psychology, 96*(2), 294–309. doi:10.1037/a0021294 PMID:21058804

Liu, D., & Zeinaly, S. (2020). A new model for investigating the role of IT-based innovation in the pharmaceutical knowledge-sharing attitude: A study of marketing biotechnology firms. *Kybernetes*. Advance online publication. doi:10.1108/K-07-2019-0505

Liu, Y., Chan, C., Zhao, C., & Liu, C. (2019). Unpacking knowledge management practices in China: Do institution, national and organizational culture matter? *Journal of Knowledge Management, 23*(4), 619–643. doi:10.1108/JKM-07-2017-0260

Lo, F. Y., & Campos, N. (2018). Blending Internet-of-Things (IoT) solutions into relationship marketing strategies. *Technological Forecasting and Social Change, 137*, 10–18. doi:10.1016/j.techfore.2018.09.029

Lo, J. Y., Chan, W., & Zhang, C. X. (2014). Tools for benchmarking and recognizing hotels' green effort—Environmental assessment methods and eco-labels. *Journal of China Tourism Research, 10*(2), 165–185. doi:10.1080/19388160.2013.857626

Lo, P., Chan, H. H. Y., Tang, A. W. M., Chiu, D. K. W., Cho, A., See-To, E. W. K., Ho, K. K. W., He, M., Kenderdine, S., & Shaw, J. (2019). Visualising and revitalising traditional Chinese martial arts: Visitors' engagement and learning experience at the 300 years of Hakka Kungfu. *Library Hi Tech, 37*(2), 269–288. doi:10.1108/LHT-05-2018-0071

Lopa, J., & Gong, Z. (2020). Sexual harassment of hospitality interns. *Journal of Hospitality & Tourism Education, 32*(2), 88–101.

López-Cabarcos, M. Á., Srinivasan, S., & Vázquez-Rodríguez, P. (2020). The role of product innovation and customer centricity in transforming tacit and explicit knowledge into profitability. *Journal of Knowledge Management, 24*(5), 1037–1057. doi:10.1108/JKM-02-2020-0087

López-Torres, G. C., Garza-Reyes, J. A., Maldonado-Guzmán, G., Kumar, V., Rocha-Lona, L., & Cherrafi, A. (2019). Knowledge management for sustainability in operations. *Production Planning and Control, 30*(10–12), 813–826. doi:10.1080/09537287.2019.1582091

Lu, L., Zhang, P., & Zhang, T. (2021). Leveraging "human-likeness" of robotic service at restaurants. *International Journal of Hospitality Management, 94*, 1–9. doi:10.1016/j.ijhm.2020.102823

Lund, N. F., Holst-Beck, P., Pine, B. J. II, & Leask, A. (2022). Hamlet Live : The 7 I's Experiential Strategy Framework for heritage visitor attractions. *Journal of Heritage Tourism, 17*(2), 125–141. doi:10.1080/1743873X.2021.1951277

Luthans, F., & Stewart, T. I. (1977). A general contingency theory of management. *Academy of Management Review, 2*(2), 181–195. doi:10.2307/257902

Lynch, L. M. (2007). The adoption and diffusion of organisational innovation: evidence for the United States economy. National Bureau of Economic Research.

Lyotard, J. F. (1984). *The Postmodern Condition: A Report On Knowledge*. University of Minnesota Press.

MacDonald, R., & Jolliffe, L. (2003). Cultural rural tourism: Evidence from Canada. *Annals of Tourism Research, 30*(2), 307–322. doi:10.1016/S0160-7383(02)00061-0

Mackey, J., & Sisodia, R. (2014). *Conscious Capitalism: Liberating the Heroic Spirit of Business*. Harvard Business School Press.

Magazine, L. (2021, July 1). *Grape County Eco Resort, Get one with Nature*. Retrieved from https://www.luxpressomagazine.com/post/grape-county-eco-resort-get-one-with-nature

Mahmud, M., Otsuka, K., Sawada, Y., Tanaka, M., & Tanaka, T. (2017). *Women empowerment in Bangladesh: Household decisions under development of non-farm sectors and microfinance institutions*. JICA-RI Working Paper, 154.

Mahtab, N., Islam, M.D., Ahmed, S., & Ahmed, S.U. (2017). Social business and its sustainability: A case study on 'Aponjon 'Project of D. Net, Bangladesh. *International Journal of Economics, Commerce and Management, 5*(7).

Maier, D., Maftei, M., Maier, A., & Biţan, G. E. (2019). A review of product innovation management literature in the context of organization sustainable development. *Amfiteatru Economic, 21*(13), 816–829. doi:10.24818/EA/2019/S13/816

Mainga, W., Daniel, R. M., & Alamil, L. (2022). Perceptions of employability skills of undergraduate business students in a developing country: An exploratory study. *Higher Learning Research Communications, 12*(1), 28–63. doi:10.18870/hlrc.2022.v12i1.1257

Mainsah, E., Heuer, S. R., Kalra, A., & Zhang, Q. (2004). Grameen Bank: Taking capitalism to the poor. *Chazen Web Journal of International Business, 1*, 28.

Maity, S. (2019). Identifying opportunities for artificial intelligence in the evolution of training and development practices. *Journal of Management Development, 38*(8), 651–663.

Malek, K., Kline, S. F., & DiPietro, R. (2018). The impact of manager training on employee turnover intentions. *Journal of Hospitality and Tourism Insights, 1*(3), 203–219. doi:10.1108/JHTI-02-2018-0010

Malhotra, P. (2021, January 19). *Create an ecosystem where we can all co-exist*. Retrieved from https://bwhotelier.businessworld.in/article/Create-an-ecosystem-where-we-can-all-co-exist-Chavan/19-01-2021-367116/

Maloney Tichaawa, T., Mhlanga, O., & Sicwebu, S. (2017). The Impact of Information Communication Technologies (ICTs) on Tourism Businesses in East London, South Africa. In ACTA Universitatis Danubius (Vol. 13). Academic Press.

Manaf, N. A., & Ibrahim, K. (2017). Poverty reduction for sustainable development: Malaysia's evidence-based solutions. *Global Journal of Social Sciences Studies, 3*(1), 29–42. doi:10.20448/807.3.1.29.42

Management Association. (Ed.). (2018). Cyber Security and Threats: Concepts, Methodologies, Tools, and Applications. IGI Global. doi:10.4018/978-1-5225-5634-3

Manhart, M., & Thalmann, S. (2015). Protecting organizational knowledge: A structured literature review. *Journal of Knowledge Management, 19*(2), 190–211. doi:10.1108/JKM-05-2014-0198

Maopraman, N., & Jaroenwisan, K. (2022). Technology Application and Innovation for Digital Era Hotel Industry. *Western University Research Journal of Humanities and Social Science, 8*(1), 251–266.

Marak, Z. R., Tiwari, A., & Tiwari, S. (2019). Adoption of 3D printing technology: An innovation diffusion theory perspective. *International Journal of Innovation*, *7*(1), 87–103. doi:10.5585/iji.v7i1.393

Markopoulos, E., Aggarwal, V., & Vanharanta, H. (2019), September. Democratization of intrapreneurship and corporate entrepreneurship within the mckinsey's three horizons innovation space. In *International Conference on Human Systems Engineering and Design: Future Trends and Applications* (pp. 1007-1017). Springer.

Marriott International. (2019). *Marriott International Announces Expanded Wellbeing Certification Program*. https://news.marriott.com/news/2019/09/18/marriott-international-announces-expanded-wellbeing-certification-program

Marshall, J., Coleman, G., & Reason, P. (2011). Leadership for Sustainability: An Action Research Approach. Greenleaf Publishing. https://doi.org/10.4324/9781351278287.

Martins, E., Martins, N., & Terblanche, F. (2004). An organizational culture model to stimulate creativity and innovation in a university library. In *Advances in Library Administration and Organization* (Vol. 21, pp. 83–130). JAI Press., doi:10.1016/S0732-0671(04)21003-3

Mastny, L. (2001). *Traveling ligh new paths for international tourism*. Worldwatch Paper.

Matikiti, R., Mpinganjira, M., & Roberts-Lombard, M. (2018). Application of the Technology Acceptance Model and the Technology–Organisation–Environment Model to examine social media marketing use in the South African tourism industry. *South African Journal of Information Management*, *20*(1). Advance online publication. doi:10.4102ajim.v20i1.790

Matsa, P., & Gullamajji, K. (2019). To Study Impact of Artificial Intelligence on Human Resource Management. *International Research Journal of Engineering and Technology*, *6*(8), 1229–1238.

Matt, C., Hess, T., & Benlian, A. (2015). Digital Transformation Strategies. *Business & Information Systems Engineering*, *57*(5), 339–343. doi:10.100712599-015-0401-5

Ma, X., Wang, R., Dai, M., & Ou, Y. (2021). The influence of culture on the sustainable livelihoods of households in rural tourism destinations. *Journal of Sustainable Tourism*, *29*(8), 1235–1252. doi:10.1080/09669582.2020.1826497

McAlister, J. (2022). *Record Staff Shortages Causing Hospitality to Lose £21 billion in trade*. https://www.bighospitality.co.uk/Article/2022/06/23/record-staff-shortages-causing-hospitality-to-lose-21bn-in-trade

McCabe, S., Sharples, M., & Foster, C. (2012). Stakeholder engagement in the design of scenarios of technology-enhanced tourism services. *Tourism Management Perspectives*, *4*, 36–44. doi:10.1016/j.tmp.2012.04.007

McCracken, G. (1988). *The long interview*. Sage.

Mclaren.com. (2021). *Annual Results - McLaren Investors*. Available at: https://investors.mclaren.com/sites/mclaren-ir/files/report-document/mclaren-group-limited-2020-annual-report.pdf

McQuade, S. (2006). Technology-enabled Crime, Policing and Security. *The Journal of Technology Studies*, *32*(1). Advance online publication. doi:10.21061/jots.v32i1.a.5

Meghini, C., Bartalesi, V., & Metilli, D. (2021). Representing narratives in digital libraries: The narrative ontology. *Semantic Web*, *12*(2), 241–264. doi:10.3233/SW-200421

Mehrotra, N., Puhazhendhi, V., Nair, G.G., & Sahoo, B.B. (2009). *Financial Inclusion- An Overview*. Department of Economic Analysis and Research, NABARD.

Melewar, T. C., & Navalekar, A. (2002). Leveraging corporate identity in the digital age. In Marketing Intelligence & Planning (Vol. 20, Issue 2, pp. 96–103). doi:10.1108/02634500210418518

Melis, C., & Chambers, D. (2021). The construction of intangible cultural heritage: A Foucauldian critique. *Annals of Tourism Research*, *89*, 103206. doi:10.1016/j.annals.2021.103206

Mensah, I. (2004, May). *Environmental management practices in US hotels*. Hotel Online. https://www.hotel-online.com/News/PR2004_2nd/May04_EnvironmentalPractices.html

Mentz, E., & Goosen, L. (2007). Are groups working in the Information Technology class? *South African Journal of Education*, *27*(2), 329–343.

Merlin, R. P., & Jayam, R. (2018). Artificial Intelligence in Human Resource Management. *International Journal of Pure and Applied Mathematics*, *119*(17), 1891–1895.

Mesthene, E. G. (1971). *Technological Change-Its Impact on Man and Society*. Harvard University Press.

Meyer, D. (2018). Amazon Reportedly Killed an AI Recruitment System Because It Couldn't Stop the Tool from Discriminating Against Women. *Fortune*. https://fortune.com/2018/10/10/amazon-ai-recruitment-bias-women-sex

Michael, B., Koroleska, N., Tai, A., & Wong, D. W. H. (2022). A critical look at using financial technology policy to promote the sustainable development goals. *Sustainable Development*, *30*(6), 1911–1920. doi:10.1002d.2358

Mitchell, C. (2002). Selling the brand inside. Harvard Business Review. Available at: https://hbr.org/2002/01/selling-the-brand-inside

Mize, M., Trexler, C. J., Crump, A., Young, G. M., Buntong, B., & LeGrand, K. (2020). Piloting of the concerns-based adoption model: Farmer concerns about the participatory guaranteed system in Cambodia. *Journal of International Agricultural and Extension Education*, *27*(3), 75–87.

Morduch, J. (1999). The role of subsidies in microfinance: Evidence from the Grameen Bank. *Journal of Development Economics*, *60*(1), 229–248.

Morrison-Smith, S., & Ruiz, J. (2020). Challenges and barriers in virtual teams: A literature review. *SN Applied Sciences*, *2*(6), 1–33. doi:10.100742452-020-2801-5

MPEDB. (2005). *Madhya Pradesh State Forest Policy, 2005*. Retrieved from https://mpforest.gov.in/ecotourism/pdf/forestpolicy.pdf

Mrugalska, B., & Wyrwicka, M. K. (2017). Towards Lean Production In Industry 4.0. 7th International Conference on Engineering, Project, and Production Management. *Procedia Engineering*, *182*, 466–473. doi:10.1016/j.proeng.2017.03.135

Muhammad, S. I., Masood, U. H., & Ume, H. (2018). Impact of self-service technology (SST) service quality on customer loyalty and behavioral intention: The mediating role of customer satisfaction. *Cogent Business & Management*, *5*(1), 1. Advance online publication. doi:10.1080/23311975.2018.1423770

Mumford, M. D., & Gustafson, S. B. (1998). Creativity syndrome: Integration, application, and innovation. *Psychological Bulletin*, *103*(1), 27–43. doi:10.1037/0033-2909.103.1.27

Mumford, M. D., Scott, G. M., Gaddis, B., & Strange, J. M. (2002). Leading creative people: Orchestrating expertise and relationships. *The Leadership Quarterly*, *13*(6), 705–750. doi:10.1016/S1048-9843(02)00158-3

Muñoz-Pascual, L., & Galende, J. (2017). The impact of knowledge and motivation management on creativity: Employees of innovative Spanish companies. *Employee Relations*, *39*(5), 732–752. doi:10.1108/ER-05-2016-0096

MurakamiD.ShchapovI.Viswanath-NatrajG. (2022). CBDCs, Financial Inclusion, and Monetary Policy. *Available at* SSRN 4102397.

Murphy, J., Gretzel, U., & Pesonen, J. (2019). Marketing robot services in hospitality and tourism: The role of anthropomorphism. *Journal of Travel & Tourism Marketing*, *36*(7), 784–795. doi:10.1080/10548408.2019.1571983

Muthuveloo, R., Shanmugam, N., & Teoh, A. P. (2017). The impact of tacit knowledge management on organizational performance: Evidence from Malaysia. *Asia Pacific Management Review*, *22*(4), 192–201. doi:10.1016/j.apmrv.2017.07.010

Nabiyev, V. V. (2012). *Yapay Zekâ: İnsan-Bilgisayar Etkileşimi*. Seçkin Yayıncılık.

Nachmias, S. (2017). *Students' Attitude Towards Hospitality Education: An Anglo-Cypriot Critical Study*. http://irep.ntu.ac.uk/id/eprint/30577/1/8398_Nachmias.pdf

Nadda, V., Chaudhary, H. S., & Arnott, I. (2020). Cloud computing in tourism. In Digital Marketing Strategies for Tourism, Hospitality, and Airline Industries (pp. 141-155). IGI Global. doi:10.4018/978-1-5225-9783-4.ch007

Nadda, V., Rafiq, Z., & Tyagi, P. (2017, Mar 3). *Effectiveness and Challenges of Recruitment process outsourcing (RPO) in the Indian Hotel Sector*. Retrieved from Munich Personal RePEc Archive: https://mpra.ub.uni-muenchen.de/77164/

Nadda, V. K., Dadwal, S. S., & Firdous, A. (2015). Social media marketing. In *Handbook of Research on Integrating Social Media into Strategic Marketing* (pp. 359–379). IGI Global. doi:10.4018/978-1-4666-8353-2.ch021

Nadda, V. K., Dadwal, S. S., Mulindwa, D., & Vieira, R. (2015). Role of social media in tourism. In *Handbook of Research on Global Hospitality and Tourism Management* (pp. 142–162). IGI Global. doi:10.4018/978-1-4666-8606-9.ch009

Nadda, V., & Arnott, I. (2020). Marketing Innovation in Tourism. In *Handbook of Research on Innovations in Technology and Marketing for the Connected Consumer* (pp. 401–415). IGI Global. doi:10.4018/978-1-7998-0131-3.ch019

Nadda, V., Arnott, I., Sealy, W., & Delaney, E. (2022). *Employability and Skills Development in the Sports, Events & Hospitality Industries*. IGI Global. doi:10.4018/978-1-7998-7781-3

Nadda, V., Dadwal, S., & Rahimi, R. (Eds.). (2017). *Promotional Strategies and New Service Opportunities in Emerging Economies*. IGI Global. doi:10.4018/978-1-5225-2206-5

Nair, R. S., & Rajappan, S. (2021). The New-Normal in Education: Comprehending the Stages of Concern through the Concerns-based Adoption Model (CBAM). *Human Resource Management Practices for Industry*, *4*(0), 209.

Najda-Janoszka, M., & Kopera, S. (2014). Exploring Barriers to Innovation in Tourism Industry – The Case of Southern Region of Poland. *Procedia: Social and Behavioral Sciences*, *110*, 190–201. doi:10.1016/j.sbspro.2013.12.862

Nakhon Ratchasima Provincial Statistical Office. (2017, December 20). *Accommodation establishment in Nakhon Ratchasima Province*. Retrieved from https://www2.nakhonratchasima.go.th

National Statistical Office. (2020). *Summary of Household Technology Survey Results 2020*. Ministry of Digital Economy and Society.

Nawaz, N. (2019). Artificial Intelligence interchange human intervention in the recruitment process in Indian Software Industry. *International Journal of Advanced Trends in Computer Science and Engineering*, *8*(4), 1433–1442. doi:10.30534/ijatcse/2019/62842019

Nawaz, N. (2019). How far have we come with the study of artificial intelligence for recruitment process. *International Journal of Scientific & Technology Research, 8*(7), 488–493.

Nawaz, N., & Gomes, A. M. (2019). Artificial Intelligence Chatbots are New Recruiters. *(IJACSA). International Journal of Advanced Computer Science and Applications, 10*(9), 1–5. doi:10.14569/IJACSA.2019.0100901

Neff, D. J., & Moss, R. C. (2011). *The future of nonprofits: Innovate and thrive in the digital age*. John Wiley & Sons. doi:10.1002/9781118386781

Nesheim, T., Olsen, K. M., & Tobiassen, A. E. (2011). Knowledge communities in matrix-like organizations: Managing knowledge towards application. *Journal of Knowledge Management, 15*(5), 836–850. doi:10.1108/13673271111174357

Neuhofer, B., Buhalis, D., & Ladkin, A. (2014). A Typology of Technology-Enhanced Tourism Experiences. *International Journal of Tourism Research, 16*(4), 340–350. doi:10.1002/jtr.1958

Nguyen, K. T., Laurent, M., & Oualha, N. (2015). Survey on secure communication protocols for the Internet of Things. *Ad Hoc Networks, 32*, 17–31. doi:10.1016/j.adhoc.2015.01.006

Nidhi, B. (2022, July) *Heaven on Earth! 2nd home amidst nature. Place to be in your checklist.* Retrieved from https://www.tripadvisor.in/Hotel_Feature-g303883-d11880822-zft1-Grape_County_Resort.html

Niewöhner, N., Asmar, L., Wortmann, F., Röltgen, D., Kühn, A., & Dumitrescu, R. (2019). Design fields of agile innovation management in small and medium sized enterprises. *Procedia CIRP, 84*, 826–831. doi:10.1016/j.procir.2019.04.295

Nonaka, I. (1994). A Dynamic Theory of Organizational Knowledge Creation. *Organization Science, 5*(1), 14–37. doi:10.1287/orsc.5.1.14

NSJ. (2017) *Chief Conservator of Forests Manojkumar (IFS), "Connect with Nature" and "The Role of Media in Conservation".* https://www.facebook.com/nsojbangalore/videos/chief-conservator-of-forests-manoj-kumar-ifs/1542730205785597/

Nystrom, H. (1990). Organizational innovation. In M. S. West & J. L. Farr (Eds.), *Innovation and creativity at work: psychological and organizational strategies* (pp. 143–162). Wiley.

O'Neill, M. (2014). The Internet of Things: Do more devices mean more risks? *Computer Fraud & Security, 2014*(1), 16–17. doi:10.1016/S1361-3723(14)70008-9

O'Reilly, C., & Binns, A. J. (2019). The three stages of disruptive innovation: Idea generation, incubation, and scaling. *California Management Review, 61*(3), 49–71. doi:10.1177/0008125619841878

Obermayer, N., Csizmadia, T., & Hargitai, D. M. (2022). Influence of Industry 4.0 technologies on corporate operation and performance management from human aspects. *Meditari Accountancy Research, 30*(4), 1027–1049. doi:10.1108/MEDAR-02-2021-1214

Odabaşı, Y., & Oyman, M. (2005). Pazarlama İletişimi Yönetimi. MediaCat Kitapları.

OECD/EU. (2006). *Oslo Kılavuzu: Yenilik Verilerinin Toplanması ve Yorumlanması İcin İlkeler.* Ekonomik ĞÇbirliği ve Kalkınma Orgütü Avrupa Birliği Ġstatistiği Ofisi.

Ogun, T. P. (2010, August). Infrastructure and poverty reduction: Implications for urban development in Nigeria. In *Urban Forum* (Vol. 21, No. 3, pp. 249-266). Springer Netherlands.

Ohlan, R. (2018). Role of information technology in hotel industry. *International Journal of Scientific Research in Computer Science, Engineering, and Information Technology, 3*(2), 277–281.

Ohlan, R. (2018). Role of information technology in hotel industry. International Journal of Scientific Research in Computer Science. *Engineering and Information Technology*, *3*(2), 277–281.

Ohlin, J. B., & West, J. J. (1994). An analysis of the effect of the fringe benefit offerings on the turnover of hourly workers in the hotel industry. *International Journal of Hospitality Management*, *12*(4), 323–336. doi:10.1016/0278-4319(93)90049-F

Oke, A., Munashi, N., & Walumbwa, F. O. (2009). The Influence of Leadership on Innovation Processes and Activities. *Organizational Dynamics*, *38*(1), 64–72. doi:10.1016/j.orgdyn.2008.10.005

Olander, H., Vanhala, M., & Hurmelinna-Laukkanen, P. (2014). Reasons for choosing mechanisms to protect knowledge and innovations. *Management Decision*, *52*(2), 207–229. doi:10.1108/MD-11-2012-0791

Osawa, H., Akiya, N., Koyama, T., Ema, A., Kanzaki, N., Ichise, R., & Kubo, A. (2017). What is real risk and benefit on work with robots? From the analysis of a robot hotel. *Proceedings of HRI2017 Companion of the 2017 ACM/IEEE International Conference on Human-Robot Interaction.* 10.1145/3029798.3038312

Oslo Kılavuzu. (2005). *Yenilik verilerinin toplanması ve yorumlanması için ilkeler.* OECD/Eurostat Ortak Yayımı.

Otley, D. (2016). The contingency theory of management accounting and control: 1980–2014. *Management Accounting Research*, *31*, 45–62. doi:10.1016/j.mar.2016.02.001

Ottenbacher, M. C. (2007). The management of innovation in the hospitality business, including the various approaches that can be taken to achieve success. *Journal of Hospitality & Tourism Research*, *31*(4), 431–454.

Özar Berksü, Z. (2020, June 2). *Türkiye'nin en iyi çevre dostu otelleri.* Oggusto. https://www.oggusto.com/surdurulebilir-yasam/turkiyenin-en-iyi-cevre-dostu-otelleri

Özgürel, G., & Kılınç-Şahin, S. (2021). Turizmde robotlaşma: Yiyecek-içecek sektöründe robot şefler ve robot garsonlar. *OPUS–Uluslararası Toplum Araştırmaları Dergisi*, *18*, 1849–1882.

Ozili, P. K. (2022b). Central bank digital currency in Nigeria: opportunities and risks. In The New Digital Era: Digitalisation, Emerging Risks and Opportunities (Vol. 109, pp. 125-133). Emerald Publishing Limited. doi:10.1108/S1569-37592022000109A008

Ozili, P. K. (2022d), Can Central Bank Digital Currency Increase Financial Inclusion? Arguments for and Against. In Big Data Analytics in the Insurance Market (Emerald Studies in Finance, Insurance, and Risk Management). Emerald Publishing Limited. doi:10.1108/978-1-80262-637-720221013

Ozili, P. K. (2022e). Embedded finance: assessing the benefits, use case, challenges and interest over time. *Journal of Internet and Digital Economics.*

Ozili, P. K. (2022f). Circular Economy and Central Bank Digital Currency. *Circular Economy and Sustainability*, 1-16.

Ozili, P.K. (2022a). Central bank digital currency research around the world: a review of literature. *Journal of Money Laundering Control.*

Ozili, P. K. (2018). Impact of digital finance on financial inclusion and stability. *Borsa Istanbul Review*, *18*(4), 329–340. doi:10.1016/j.bir.2017.12.003

OziliP. K. (2022c). Central bank digital currency can lead to the collapse of cryptocurrency. *Available at* SSRN 3850826.

Özkoç, A. G., & Kemer, E. (2017). The Strategic Role of Institutionalization for Accommodation Enterprises in Terms of Organizatıonal Innovation. *Gaziantep University Journal of Social Sciences*, *16*(2), 568–578.

Özmen, Ş. (2013). *Ağ Ekonomisinde Yeni Ticaret Yolu: E-Ticaret*. İstanbul Bilgi Üniversitesi Yayınları.

Özsungur, F. (2021). Business Management and Strategy in Cybersecurity for Digital Transformation. In K. Sandhu (Ed.), (pp. 144–162). Advances in Information Security, Privacy, and Ethics. IGI Global. doi:10.4018/978-1-7998-6975-7.ch008

Pai, C. K., Liu, Y., Kang, S., & Dai, A. (2020). The role of perceived smart tourism technology experience for tourist satisfaction, happiness, and revisit intention. *Sustainability (Switzerland), 12*(16), 6592. Advance online publication. doi:10.3390u12166592

Palomares, X. (2008). *Innovation Typology in the Tourism Industry* [Master's thesis]. Universitat de Girona.

Panthawee, R. (2018). The User's Satisfaction with the Service System of the Dean Office of the Faculty of Humanities and Social Sciences. Research Report, Chiang Mai Rajabhat University.

Parasuraman, A., Zeithaml, A. V., & Malhotra, A. (2005). E-S-QUAL: A Multiple-Item Scale for Assessing Electronic Service Quality. *Journal of Service Research, 7*(3), 213–233. doi:10.1177/1094670504271156

Parveen, N. A., & Palaniammal, V. S. (2019). A Study on Artificial Intelligence in Human Resource Management today and tomorrow. *International Journal of Research and Analytical Reviews, 6*(1), 513–516.

Pathirage, C. P., Amaratunga, D. G., & Haigh, R. P. (2007). Tacit knowledge and organisational performance: Construction industry perspective. *Journal of Knowledge Management, 11*(1), 115–126. doi:10.1108/13673270710728277

Paul, S. K., & Roy, S. (2017). Tourism-based heritage conservation in Murshidabad: An appraisal. *Journal of Heritage Tourism, 12*(2), 139–154. doi:10.1080/1743873X.2016.1159685

Pearce, C. L., & Ensley, M. D. (2004). A reciprocal and longitudinal investigation of the innovation process: The central role of shared vision in product and process innovation teams (PPITs). *Journal of Organizational Behavior, 25*(2), 259–278. doi:10.1002/job.235

Pehlivan, B. (2018). *Yapay Zeka ile Dijital Pazarlama Dönüşümü*. Retrieved 08/10/22 from: Marketing Türkiye, Retrieved from: https://www.marketingtr.net/tr/blog/detay/Yapay-Zeka-ile-Dijital-PazarlamaDonusumu/6/160/0

Pels, H. (2018). *The Complete Guide to AI Marketing in 2018*. Retrieved from: Emarsy:https://www.emarsys.com/resources/blog/complete-guide-to-ai-marketing/

Perakakis, E., Mastorakis, G., & Kopanakis, I. (2019). Social Media Monitoring: An InnovativeIntelligent Approach. *Designs, 3*(24), 1–12.

Peters, M., & Pikkemaat, B. (2006). The application of innovation in tourism. *Journal of Quality Assurance in Hospitality and Tourism.*

Petković, G., Pindţo, R., & Molnar Agić, M. (2018). Digital Economy and (non) IncrementalChanges in Tourism and Retail Business Model. *Ekonomika Preduzeća, 1*(2), 151–165. doi:10.5937/EKOPRE1802151P

Phuaphanasakul, J., & Lalitsasivimol, W. (2019). Creating Competitive Advantgae with Information Technology and Innovation of Hotel Business in Thailand: Literature Review. *MUT Journal of Business Administration, 16*(2), 19–39.

Phuthong, T., & Mangsungnoen, N. (2017). Factors Influencing the Elderly Intention to Use and Adopt Mobile Health Services. *Veridian E-Journal Silpakorn University, 10*(3), 548–566.

PIB. (2016, March 14). *Sustainable Tourism Criteria for India.* Press Information Bureau, Government of India, Ministry of Tourism. Retrieved from https://pib.gov.in/newsite/PrintRelease.aspx?relid=137882#:~:text=The%20Ministry%20of%20Tourism%20has,been%20adopted%20by%20the%20stakeholders

Pillai, R., & Sivathanu, B. (2020). Adoption of artificial intelligence (AI) for talent acquisition in IT/ITeS organizations. *Benchmarking, 27*(9), 2599–2629. doi:10.1108/BIJ-04-2020-0186

Pine, J. B. II, & Gilmore, J. H. (2011). *The experience economy.* Harvard Business Review Press., doi:10.1163/9789004495012_003

Pinho, C., Franco, M., & Mendes, L. (2021). Application of innovation diffusion theory to the E-learning process: Higher education context. *Education and Information Technologies, 26*(1), 421–440. doi:10.100710639-020-10269-2

Plowman, J. (2019). *Unreal Engine Virtual Reality Quick Start Guide: Design and Develop Immersive Virtual Reality Experiences with Unreal Engine 4.* Packt Publishing Ltd.

Podsakoff, P. M., MacKenzie, S. B., Lee, J. Y., & Podsakoff, N. P. (2003). Common Method Biases in Behavioral Research: A Critical Review of the Literature and Recommended Remedies. In Journal of Applied Psychology (Vol. 88, Issue 5, pp. 879–903). doi:10.1037/0021-9010.88.5.879

Podsakoff, P. M., MacKenzie, S. B., Paine, J. B., & Bachrach, D. G. (2000). Organizational citizenship behaviors: A critical review of the theoretical and empirical literature and suggestions for future research. *Journal of Management, 26*(3), 513–563. doi:10.1177/014920630002600307

Poon, A. (1988). Innovation and the future of Caribbean tourism. *Tourism Management, 9*(3), 213-220.

Porter, M. E. (1990). The competitive advonioge of notions. *Harvard Business Review*, 73–93.

Porter, M. E., & Linde, C. V. D. (1995). Green and competitive: Ending the stalemate. *Harvard Business Review*, 120–134.

Pratton, J.D. (2003). The training and retention of chefs. *International Journal of Contemporary Hospitality Management, 15*(4), 237-242.

Premnath, E., & Chully, A. A. (2019). Artificial Intelligence in Human Resource Management: A Qualitative Study in the Indian Context. *Journal of Xi'an University of Architecture & Technology, 11*(12), 1193–1205.

PWC. (2011). *Millennials at work Reshaping the workplace.* Available at: https://www.pwc.com/co/es/publicaciones/assets/millennials-at-work.pdf

Qiu, Q., & Zhang, M. (2021). Using content analysis to probe the cognitive image of intangible cultural heritage tourism: An exploration of Chinese social media. *ISPRS International Journal of Geo-Information, 10*(4), 240. Advance online publication. doi:10.3390/ijgi10040240

Rafique, H., Almagrabi, A. O., Shamim, A., Anwar, F., & Bashir, A. K. (2020). Investigating the acceptance of mobile library applications with an extended technology acceptance model (TAM). *Computers & Education, 145*, 103732. doi:10.1016/j.compedu.2019.103732

Rahahleh, A., Al-Nsour, S., Moflih, M., Alabaddi, Z., Al-nassar, B., & Al-Nsour, N. (2020). The Influence of Electronic Service Quality on Relationship Quality: Evidence from Tourism Industry. *Management Science Letters, 10*, 2759–2768. doi:10.5267/j.msl.2020.4.034

Rahimi, R., Nadda, V. K., & Wang, H. (2018). CRM in tourism: Customer relationship management (CRM). In Digital Marketing and Consumer Engagement: Concepts, Methodologies, Tools, and Applications (pp. 928-955). IGI Global.

Rahimi, R., Nadda, V., Hyseni, B., & Mulindwa, D. (2016). Motivations of South Asian students to study tourism and hospitality in the United Kingdom. *Tourism and Hospitality Management, 12*, 223–234.

Rahman, A. (1999). Micro-credit Initiatives for Equitable and Sustainable Development: Who Pays? *World Development, 27*(1), 67–82.

Rangarajan, C. (2008). *Report of the Committee on Financial Inclusion.* Government of India.

Ranjan, A., & Chaturvedi, P. (2022). Digital Technologies and the Intangible Cultural Heritage of the Rural Destination. In *Disruptive Innovation and Emerging Technologies for Business Excellence in the Service Sector* (pp. 196–218). IGI Global. doi:10.4018/978-1-7998-9194-9.ch010

Ranjbarian, B., & Khazaei, P. J. (2015). The Impact of Perceived Quality and Value on Tourists' Satisfaction and Intention to Revisit Nowshahr City of Iran. *Journal of Quality Assurance in Hospitality & Tourism, 16*(1), 103–117. doi:10.1080/1528008X.2015.966295

Rantala, O., Rokenes, A., & Valkonen, J. (2018). Is adventure tourism a coherent concept? A review of research approaches on adventure tourism. *Annals of Leisure Research, 21*(5), 539–552. doi:10.1080/11745398.2016.1250647

Rasheed, M. I., Okumus, F., Weng, Q., Hameed, Z., & Nawaz, M. S. (2020). Career adaptability and employee turnover intentions: The role of perceived career opportunities and orientation to happiness in the hospitality industry. *Journal of Hospitality and Tourism Management, 44*, 98–107. doi:10.1016/j.jhtm.2020.05.006

Rathi, D. R. (2018). Artificial intelligence and the future of HR practices. *International Journal of Applied Research, 4*(6), 113–116.

Ratten, V. (2020). Tourism entrepreneurship research: A perspective article. *Tourism Review, 75*(1), 122–125. doi:10.1108/TR-06-2019-0204

Rayport, J. F., & Sviokla, J. (1995). Exploiting the Virtual Value Chain. *Harvard Business Review, 73*(6), 75–85.

Razzaq, A., Hur, A., Ahmad, H. F., & Masood, M. (2013). Cyber security: Threats, reasons, challenges, methodologies and state of the art solutions for industrial applications. *2013 IEEE Eleventh International Symposium on Autonomous Decentralized Systems (ISADS)*, 1–6. 10.1109/ISADS.2013.6513420

Reddy, K. V. S., Jagadeesan, D., & Rao, T. S. (2020). A Study on Artificial Intelligence Rewards and Recognition and its Effectiveness on Employees. *Journal of Critical Reviews, 7*(18), 1345–1349.

Reed, D. (2002). Poverty and the environment: Can sustainable development survive globalization? *Natural Resources Forum, 26*(3), 176–184. doi:10.1111/0165-0203.00019

Rennings, K. (2000). Redefining innovation-eco-innovation research and the contribution from ecological economics. *Ecological Economics, 32*(2), 319–332. doi:10.1016/S0921-8009(99)00112-3

Rennings, K., Ziegler, A., Ankele, K., & Hoffmann, E. (2006). The influence of different characteristics of the EU environmental management and auditing scheme on technical environmental innovations and economic performance. *Ecological Economics, 57*(1), 45–59. doi:10.1016/j.ecolecon.2005.03.013

Revfine. (2020). *How Artificial Intelligence is Changing the Travel Industry*. Retrieved from: https://www.revfine.com/artificial-intelligence-travel-industry/

Review, B. (2006). Book Review. *European Psychologist, 11*(3), 244–245. doi:10.1027/1016-9040.11.3.244

Richardson, S. (2008). Undergraduate tourism and hospitality students' attitudes toward a career in the industry: A preliminary investigation. *Journal of Teaching in Travel & Tourism, 8*(1), 23–46. doi:10.1080/15313220802410112

Richtnér, A., & Åhlström, P. (2010). Top management control and knowledge creation in new product development. *International Journal of Operations & Production Management, 30*(10), 1006–1031. doi:10.1108/01443571011082508

Riordan, O. (2006). *Using the VRIO framework in practising firms taking the resource-based view (RBV).* Academic Press.

Rizvic, S., Boskovic, D., Okanovic, V., Sljivo, S., & Zukic, M. (2019). Interactive digital storytelling: Bringing cultural heritage in a classroom. *Journal of Computers in Education, 6*(1), 143–166. doi:10.100740692-018-0128-7

Roberts, M. (2012). *Transformational Leadership.* www.world viewthinking.com

Robertson, T. S. (1967). The actions that go into creating new things and the ways in which those new things spread. *Journal of Marketing, 31*(1), 14–19.

Robijn, W., Schaufeli, W. B., Deprez, J., & Euwema, M. C. (2020). Leaders, teams and work engagement: A basic needs perspective. *Career Development International, 25*(4), 373–388. doi:10.1108/CDI-06-2019-0150

Roffe, I. (1999). Innovation and creativity in organisations: A review of the implications for training and development Competition and change. *Journal of European Industrial Training, 23*(4/5), 224–237. doi:10.1108/03090599910272103

Rogers, E. M. (1983). *Spreading of new ideas and practises.* The Free Press.

Rogers, E. M. (1995). *Diffusion of Innovations.* Simon & Schuster Press.

Rosegger, G. (1996). *The economics of production and innovation.* Butterworth-Heinemann Inc.

Rosete, A., Soares, B., Salvadornho, J., Reis, J., & Amorım, M. (2020). service robots in the hospitality ındustry: an exploratory literature review. Lecture Notes in Business Information Processing, 377.

Rosing, K., Frese, M., & Bausch, A. (2011). Explaining the heterogeneity of the leadership- innovation relationship: Ambidextrous leadership. *The Leadership Quarterly, 22*(5), 956–974. doi:10.1016/j.leaqua.2011.07.014

Rotchanakitumnuai, S. (2013). Electronic Service Quality for the Development of Tourism. *Creative Business and Sustainability Journal, 35*(3), 86–99.

Roult, R., Gaudette, M., Auger, D., & Adjizian, J.-M. (2016). Site Management and Use of social media by Tourism Businesses: The Case of Quebec. *Czech Journal of Tourism, 5*(1), 21–34. doi:10.1515/cjot-2016-0002

Roxo, P. (2020). Transmedia storytelling as a potential employer branding strategy: Participatory culture and recruitment. *U. Porto Journal of Engineering, 6*(1), 66–77. doi:10.24840/2183-6493_006.001_0007

RTSOI. (2018). *Sustainable Tourism Criteria for India (STCI), Practicing Responsible Tourism.* Regional Workshop, Ahmedabad. Retrieved from https://www.rtsoi.org/wp-content/upoads/2019/11 /Ahmedabad-Nov18-Report.pdf

RTSOI. (2021, August 20). *Rakesh Mathur, President, RTSOI talks about his approach of being a responsible traveller* [Video]. YouTube. https://www.youtube.com/watch?v=1c_RSPq0CpE 01:08

RTSOI. (2022). *Just another day in the office of Mr. Rakesh Mathur.* https://m.facebook.com/ResponsibleTourismSocietyOfIndia/videos/just-another-day-in-the-office-for-mr-rakesh-mathur-president-and-founding-membe/267810335525306/

Rudan, E., & Stipanović, C. (2021). Music in the tourism offering of rural regions (the case of eastern croatia). *European Countryside, 13*(3), 685–696. doi:10.2478/euco-2021-0036

Ryan, D. (2016). *Understanding digital marketing: marketingstrategies for engaging the digital generation.* Kogan Page Publishers.

Sachs, J. D., Schmidt-Traub, G., Mazzucato, M., Messner, D., Nakicenovic, N., & Rockström, J. (2019). Six transformations to achieve the sustainable development goals. *Nature Sustainability, 2*(9), 805–814. doi:10.103841893-019-0352-9

Saçılık, M. Y., & Çevik, S. (2014). Çevreye duyarlı otelcilik kapsamında yeşil yıldız uygulaması: Antakya Güngör Palace örneği. In E. Koç, H. Abdioğlu, & R. Kılıç (Eds.), *The 9th international conference: New perspectives in tourism and hospitality* (pp. 404-414). Academic Press.

Şahin, A., & Şen, S. (2017). Hizmet kalitesinin müşteri memnuniyeti üzerine etkisi. *Uluslararası Sosyal Araştırmalar Dergisi, 10*(52), 1176–1184.

Saint Simon, H. (1964). *Social organization, the science of man, and other writings.* Harper & Row.

Saint Simon, H. (1975). *Henri de Saint Simon, 1760-1825: Selected writings on science, industry and social organization.* Holmes and Meier Publishers.

Salloum, S. A., Alhamad, A. Q. M., Al-Emran, M., Monem, A. A., & Shaalan, K. (2019). Exploring students' acceptance of e-learning through the development of a comprehensive technology acceptance model. *IEEE Access: Practical Innovations, Open Solutions, 7*, 128445–128462. doi:10.1109/ACCESS.2019.2939467

Samani, T. (2019). Service Innovation of Hotel Industry in Thailand. *Journal of Thai Hospitality and Tourism, 14*(1), 103–110.

Sarabdeen, El-Rakhawy, & Khan. (2011). Employer branding in selected companies in UAE. *Communications of IBIMA.*

Sarstedt, M., Ringle, C. M., & Hair, J. F. (2017). Partial Least Squares Structural Equation Modeling. In *Handbook of Market Research* (pp. 1–40). Springer International Publishing. doi:10.1007/978-3-319-05542-8_15-1

Saulais, P., & Ermine, J. L. (2012). Creativity and knowledge management. In VINE (Vol. 42, Issue 3, pp. 416–438). doi:10.1108/03055721211267521

Saunila, M., Ukko, J., & Rantala, T. (2018). Sustainability as a driver of green innovation investment and exploitation. *Journal of Cleaner Production, 179*, 631–641. doi:10.1016/j.jclepro.2017.11.211

Schleicher, J., Schaafsma, M., & Vira, B. (2018). Will the Sustainable Development Goals address the links between poverty and the natural environment? *Current Opinion in Environmental Sustainability, 34*, 43–47. doi:10.1016/j.cosust.2018.09.004

Schneier, Schneier, & Bostelman. (2015). *Literature review of mobile robots for manufacturing.* Academic Press.

Schoonhoven, C. B. (1981, September). Problems with contingency theory: Testing assumptions hidden within the language of contingency "theory". *Administrative Science Quarterly, 26*(3), 349–377. doi:10.2307/2392512 PMID:10252610

Schumpeter, J. (1939). *Business cycles: A theoretical, historical, and statistical analysis of the capitalist process.* McGraw-Hill Book Company.

Scott, S. G., & Bruce, R. A. (1994). Determinants of innovative behavior: A path model of individual innovation in the workplace. *Academy of Management Journal, 37*(3), 580–607. doi:10.2307/256701

Sealy, W. (2023). Working Paper: The good, the bad & the ugly of event management initiatives in a regional business school.

Sealy, W. (2020). A commentary on risk and resilience in the hospitality, tourism, aviation and events Industry: Responses to COVID –19 and lessons learned. *Journal on Tourism & Sustainability.*, *4*(1), 82–93.

Seasons, F. (2022). *Jobs at Four Seasons LTD.* https://jobs.fourseasons.com/home/working-at-fs/

Seetanah, B., Teeroovengadum, V., & Nunkoo, R. S. (2018). Destination Satisfaction and Revisit Intention of Tourists: Does the Quality of Airport Services Matter? *Journal of Hospitality & Tourism Research*, 1–15. doi:10.1177/1096348018798446

Seger-Guttmann, T., & Medler-Liraz, H. (2018). Hospitality service employees' flirting displays: Emotional labor or commercial friendship? *International Journal of Hospitality Management*, *73*, 102–107. doi:10.1016/j.ijhm.2018.02.008

Selgin, G. (2021). Central Bank Digital Currency as a Potential Source of Financial Instability. *The Cato Journal*, *41*, 333.

Selmanović, E., Rizvic, S., Harvey, C., Boskovic, D., Hulusic, V., Chahin, M., & Sljivo, S. (2020). Improving Accessibility to Intangible Cultural Heritage Preservation Using Virtual Reality. *Journal on Computing and Cultural Heritage*, *13*(2), 1–19. Advance online publication. doi:10.1145/3377143

Şenocak, B., & Mohan, Y. B. (2018). İşletmelerde çevresel sürdürülebilirlik bilinci ve yeşil işletmecilik uygulamaları ile işletme başarısı arasındaki ilişki. *Süleyman Demirel Üniversitesi İktisadi ve İdari Bilimler Fakültesi Dergisi*, *23*(1), 161–183.

Seo, K. H., & Lee, J. H. (2021). The Emergence of Service Robots at Restaurants: Integrating Trust. *Perceived Risk, and Satisfaction, 13*(8), 1-16.

Shahid, M. Z., & Li, G. (2019). Impact of artificial intelligence in marketing: a perspective of marketing professionals of pakistan. *Global Journal of Management and Business Research: E Marketing, 19*(2), 26-33.

Shahid, M. Z., & Li, G. (2019). Impact of artificial intelligence in marketing: a perspective of marketing professionals of Pakistan. *Global Journal of Management and Business Research: E Marketing*, *19*(2), 26-33.

Shahril, Z., Zulkafly, H. A., Ismail, N. S., & Sharif, N. U. N. M. (2021). Customer Satisfaction Towards Self-Service Kiosks for Quick Service Restaurants (QSRs) in Klang Valley. *International Journal of Academic Research in Business & Social Sciences*, *11*(13), 24–72. doi:10.6007/IJARBSS/v11-i13/8502

Shalley, C. E., & Gilson, L. L. (2004). What leaders need to know: A review of social and contextual factors that can foster or hinder creativity. *The Leadership Quarterly*, *15*(1), 33–54. doi:10.1016/j.leaqua.2003.12.004

Shared, H. A. (2019). The Relationship between E-service Quality and E-customer Satisfaction: An Empirical Study in Egyptian Banks. *International Journal of Business and Management*, *14*(5), 171–182. doi:10.5539/ijbm.v14n5p171

Sharma, M. (2008). *Index of financial inclusion.* Working Paper 215, Indian Council for Research on International Economic Relations.

Sharma, M., Ranjan, R. K., & Bharti, V. (2021, July). A new image encryption algorithm using a bit shifted logistic map. In *12th International Conference on Computing Communication and Networking Technologies (ICCCNT)* (pp. 1-5). IEEE. 10.1109/ICCCNT51525.2021.9580146

Sharma, R., & Bharti, V. (2021, December). A Review Towards Machine Learning Spectrum for Bioinformatics. In *3rd International Conference on Advances in Computing, Communication Control and Networking (ICAC3N)* (pp. 199-202). IEEE. 10.1109/ICAC3N53548.2021.9725652

Sharma, R., Chandwani, J., & Kothari, J. (2021). Computer Aided HR in the Era of Artificial Intelligence. *Turkish Journal of Computer and Mathematics Education, 12*(9), 735–745.

Sharratt, M., & Usoro, A. (2003). Understanding Knowledge-Sharing in Online Communities of Practice. *Electronic Journal of Knowledge Management, 1*(2), 187–196. www.ejkm.com

Sheth, J. N., & Sharma, A. (2005). International e-marketing: Opportunities and issues. *International Marketing Review, 22*(6), 611–622. doi:10.1108/02651330510630249

Shoosanuk, A., & Jansiriluck, P., Utantada, S., Sakuna, J., & Sringkan, B. (2017). Influence of Service Quality on Perceived Value, Satisfaction and Customer Loyalty of Kathi Krua Thai Restaurant. *Journal of Rangsit Graduate Studies in Business and Social Sciences, 3*(2), 176–188.

Shuai, H., & Yu, W. (2021). Discussion on the application of computer digital technology in the protection of intangible cultural heritage. *Journal of Physics: Conference Series, 1915*(3), 032048. Advance online publication. doi:10.1088/1742-6596/1915/3/032048

Singh, A. K., Tyagi, P. K., & Tyagi, P. (2021). Evaluation of sustainable tourism practices in the state of Bihar, India. *E3S Web of Conferences. 296.* doi:10.1051/e3sconf/202129605013

Singh, A. K., Tyagi, P. K., Jain, E., Tyagi, P., Singh, A. K., & Sharma, N. (2022, March). Robotics and Artificial Intelligence in Hospitality Sector: A Descriptive Bibliometric Analysis and Future Research Directions. In *International Conference on Electronics and Renewable Systems (ICEARS)* (pp. 1484-1491). IEEE. 10.1109/ICEARS53579.2022.9752272

Sinpattarachat, C., & Sangruengrob, T. (2018). Comparison Study on Revisiting Budget Hotel and Hostel at the Major Tourist Destinations in Thailand. *Dusit Thani College Journal, 13*(1), 139–154.

Sismondo, S. (1993). Some Social Constructions, Social Studies of Science. *Sage Publication, 23*(3), 515–553.

Sismondo, S. (2010). *An introduction to science and technology studies.* Blackwell Publishing.

Skublewska-Paszkowska, M., Milosz, M., Powroznik, P., & Lukasik, E. (2022). 3D technologies for intangible cultural heritage preservation—Literature review for selected databases. *Heritage Science, 10*(1), 1–24. doi:10.118640494-021-00633-x PMID:35003750

Smartinsight. (2022). *Artificial Intelligence.* Retrieved from: https://www.smartinsights.com/tag/artificial-intelligence-ai-for-marketing/

Smith, E. A. (2001). The role of tacit and explicit knowledge in the workplace. *Journal of Knowledge Management, 5*(4), 311–321. doi:10.1108/13673270110411733

Socialtables. (2019). *Robots in hotels: 6 hotel brands leading the way.* Retrieved from https://www.socialtables.com/blog/hospitality-technology/hotel-brands-robot/

Song, M., Fisher, R., & Kwoh, Y. (2019). Technological challenges of green innovation and sustainable resource management with large scale data. *Technological Forecasting and Social Change, 144*, 361–368. doi:10.1016/j.techfore.2018.07.055

Sood, S. (2009, March 1). *From bandits to birds like sonchiriya: The Story of Chambal.* Retrieved from https://www.cntraveller.in/story/bandits-birds-like-sonchiriya-real-story-chambal/

Sørensen, B. M. (2008). 'Behold, I am making all things new': The entrepreneur as savior in the age of creativity. *Scandinavian Journal of Management, 24*(2), 85–93. doi:10.1016/j.scaman.2008.03.002

Srikalimah, S., Wardana, L. W., Ambarwati, D., Sholihin, U., Shobirin, R. A., Fajariah, N., & Wibowo, A. (2020). Do Creativity and Intellectual Capital Matter for SMEs Sustainability? The Role of Competitive Advantage. *Journal of Asian Finance. Economics and Business*, *7*(12), 397–408. doi:10.13106/jafeb.2020.vol7.no12.397

Stamboulis, Y., & Skayannis, P. (2003). Innovation strategies and technology for experience-based tourism. In Tourism Management (Vol. 24). doi:10.1016/S0261-5177(02)00047-X

Starčević, K., Vojinović, Ž., & Glavaš, J. (2022). Intangible cultural heritage and their influence on financial results in rural tourism. *Ekonomika Poljoprivrede*, *69*(2), 483–496. doi:10.5937/ekoPolj2202483S

Statista. (2021). *Internet usage in Thailand - Statistics & Facts*. Available https://www.statista.com/topics/6140/internet-usage-in-thailand/

Stubbs, W. (2019). Strategies, practices, and tensions in managing business model innovation for sustainability: The case of an Australian BCorp. *Corporate Social Responsibility and Environmental Management*, *26*(5), 1063–1072. doi:10.1002/csr.1786

Sucozhañay Calle, D. (2014). *Leading Change in Higher Education: The role of transformational leadership and stakeholder management* [Unpublished doctoral dissertation]. University of Leuven.

Süklüm, N. (2018). Yeşil otellerin maliyetler açısından değerlendirilmesi. *Hitit Üniversitesi Sosyal Bilimler Enstitüsü Dergisi*, *11*(1), 375–394.

Suksuthi, T. (2022). Self-Service Technology (SST) Implication toward Intention to Revisit in Small Hotels: A Case Study of Nakhon Ratchasima Province, Thailand. *Geo Journal of Tourism and Geosites*, *41*(2), 523–530. doi:10.30892/gtg.41225-859

Sun, C., Chen, H., & Liao, R. (2021). Research on incentive mechanism and strategy choice for passing on intangible cultural heritage from masters to apprentices. *Sustainability (Switzerland)*, *13*(9), 5245. Advance online publication. doi:10.3390u13095245

Suwannakul, E. (2019). Applications of the SSTQUAL Scale for Self-Service Technology Quality Assessment: A Case of Airline Business in Thailand. *Journal of International and Thai Tourism*, *15*(2), 106-120.

Suwannaphong, K. (2020). *Service Quality of Hotels in Muang District*. Phuket Province to Cater Special Interest Tourists.

Suyidno, S., Susilowati, E., Arifuddin, M., Sunarti, T., Siswanto, J., & Rohman, A. (2020, March). Barriers to scientific creativity of physics teacher in practicing creative product design. *Journal of Physics: Conference Series*, *1491*(1), 012048. Advance online publication. doi:10.1088/1742-6596/1491/1/012048

Swarbrooke, J., & Horner, S. (2007). *Consumer Behavior in Tourism* (2nd ed.). Elsevier: Oxford Press. doi:10.4324/9780080466958

Tandon, L. S., Joshi, P., & Rastogi, R. K. (2017). Understanding the Scope of Artificial Intelligence in Human Resource Management Processes – A Theoretical Perspective. *International Journal of Business and Administration Research Review*, *1*(19), 62–66.

Taneja, K. N. (2011). *The Passenger Has Gone Digital and Mobile*. Ashgate.

Tang, M., Walsh, G., Lerner, D., Fitza, M. A., & Li, Q. (2018). Green innovation, managerial concern and firm performance: An empirical study. *Business Strategy and the Environment*, *27*(1), 39–51. doi:10.1002/bse.1981

Tanongphaeng, W., & Na Thalang, C. (2017). Management of Models for Small Hotel Trad Province Area. *Dusit Thani College Journal, 11*(3), 1–17.

Tan, Y. S., & Wright, A. S. (2022). Exploring "smart and green" concepts: A new synergy for Irish hospitality. *Tourism and Hospitality, 3*(1), 276–296. doi:10.3390/tourhosp3010019

Tarter, C. J., & Hoy, W. K. (1998). Toward a contingency theory of decision making. *Journal of Educational Administration, 36*(3), 212–228. doi:10.1108/09578239810214687

Tashakkori, A., & Teddlie, C. (2010). *Sage handbook of mixed methods in social & behavioral research.* Sage. doi:10.4135/9781506335193

Tejada, P., & Moreno, P. (2013). Patterns of innovation in tourism "Small and Medium-size Enterprises.". *Service Industries Journal, 33*(7–8), 749–758. doi:10.1080/02642069.2013.740469

Tekeli, M., & Kırıcı Tekeli, E. (2020). Sustainable gastronomic tourism. In F. Türkmen (Ed.), *Selected academic studies from Turkish tourism sector* (pp. 113–133). Peter Lang.

Ten, C.-W., Manimaran, G., & Liu, C.-C. (2010). Cybersecurity for Critical Infrastructures: Attack and Defense Modeling. *IEEE Transactions on Systems, Man, and Cybernetics. Part A, Systems and Humans, 40*(4), 853–865. doi:10.1109/TSMCA.2010.2048028

TERI. (2018). *AK Bhattacharya.* Retrieved from https://wsds.teriin.org/2018/bio/AK-Bhattacharya.pdf

Testa, M. R., & Sipe, L. (2012). Service-leadership competencies for hospitality and tourism management. *International Journal of Hospitality Management, 31*(3), 648–658. doi:10.1016/j.ijhm.2011.08.009

Tidd, J., & Bessant, J. (2018). Innovation management challenges: From fads to fundamentals. *International Journal of Innovation Management, 22*(05), 1840007. doi:10.1142/S1363919618400078

Tideman, S. (2013). Sustainable Leadership: Towards a Workable Definition. *Journal of Corporate Citizenship, 49.* https://www.researchgate.net/publication/263604448_Sustainable_Leadership_Towards_a_Workable_Definition

Tien, N.H., Phu, P.P., & Chi, D.T.P. (2019). The role of international marketing in international business strategy. *International Journal of Research in Marketing Management and Sales, 1*(2), 134-138.

Tilak, J. B. (2002). Education and poverty. *Journal of Human Development, 3*(2), 191–207. doi:10.1080/14649880220147301

Ting, I. W. K., Sui, H. J., Kweh, Q. L., & Nawanir, G. (2021). Knowledge management and firm innovative performance with the moderating role of transformational leadership. *Journal of Knowledge Management, 25*(8), 2115–2140. doi:10.1108/JKM-08-2020-0629

Tjepkema, L. (2019). *What Is Artificial Intelligence Marketing & Why Is It So Powerful?* Retrieved 08/10/22 from: Emarsys:https://www.emarsys.com/resources/blog/artificial-intelligence-marketing-solutions/

Today, G. K. (2014, August 27). *Comprehensive Sustainable Tourism Criteria India (STCI) Launched.* Retrieved from https://www.gktoday.in/topic/comprehensive-sustainable-tourism-criteria-india-stci-launched/

Topsakal, Y., Yüzbaşıoğlı, N., & Bahar, M. (2018). Endüstri 4.0 çağında 'akıllı' olma yolunda oteller için öneriler, 2. In Uluslararası Turizmin Geleceği; İnovasyon, Girişimcilik ve Sürdürebilirlik Konferansı (pp. 252-256). Mersin.

Tortella, B. D., & Tirado, D. (2011). *The amount of water consumed by hotels in a seasonal destination with a large number of tourists*. Academic Press.

Tosi, H. L. Jr, & Slocum, J. W. Jr. (1984). Contingency theory: Some suggested directions. *Journal of Management*, *10*(1), 9–26. doi:10.1177/014920638401000103

Tracy, B., & Swart, M. P. (2019). Training and development research in tourism and hospitality: A perspective paper. *Tourism Review*, *75*(1), 256–259. doi:10.1108/TR-06-2019-0206

Trapani, B., & Annunziato, A. (2019). Crossing the Bridge of Change: Measuring Instructional Change Using the Concerns Based Adoption Model. *Journal for Leadership and Instruction*, *18*(1), 12–16.

Travassos, J. M., Martins, S. S., Simões, J. C., & Mansur, W. J. (2018). Radar diffraction horizons in snow and firn due to a surficial vertical transfer of mass. *Brazilian Journal of Geophysics*, *36*(4), 507–518. doi:10.22564/rbgf.v36i4.1978

Trejos, N. (2014). *Ready for the hotel industry's first robotic butler?* Retrieved from https://www.usatoday.com/story/travel/hotels/2014/08/12/aloft-hotels-starwoodroboticbultler/13954231/

Trejos, N. (2016). *Introducing Connie, Hilton's new robot concierge*. Retrieved from: https://www.usatoday.com/story/travel/roadwarriorvoices/2016/03/09/introducing-connie-hiltons-new-robot-concierge/815259
24/

Trejos, N. (2016). *USA Today, introducing Connie, Hilton's new robot concierge*. https://www.usatoday.com/story/travel/-roadwarriorvoices/2016/03/09/introducing-connie-hiltons-new-robot-con cierge/81525924/

Triguero, A., Moreno-Mondéjar, L., & Davia, M. A. (2013). Drivers of different types of eco-innovation in European SMEs. *Ecological Economics*, *92*, 25–33. doi:10.1016/j.ecolecon.2013.04.009

TripAdvisor. (2022). *Grape County Resort Rooms: Pictures & Reviews* - Tripadvisor; www.tripadvisor.in

Tsaih, R.-H., & Hsu, C. C. (2018). Artificial intelligence in smart tourism: a conceptual framework. *The 18th International Conference on Electronic Business*, 124-133.

Tsaih, R.-H., & Hsu, C. C. (2018). *Artificial intelligence in smart tourism: A conceptual framework*. The 18th International Conference on Electronic Business, Guilin, China.

Tüfekci, N., & Tüfekci, O. K. (2014). *Pazarlama Yeniliği ile Pazarlama Performansı ĠliĢkisini Acıklamaya Yonelik Bir Vaka ÇalıĢması: Süleyman Demirel Üniversitesi Olimpik Yüzme Havuzu Orneği ve Bir Model Onerisi*. Academic Press.

Tusakunee, K., & Inkaew, S. (2016). Factors Influencing the Repurchase Intentions of Female Customers of Wacoal Lingerie at Department Stores in Bangkok. *EAU Heritage Journal Social Science and Humanity*, *6*(2), 54–65.

Tussyadiah, I. (2020). A review of research into automation in tourism: Launching the annals of tourism research curated collection on artificial intelligence and robotics in tourism. *Annals of Tourism Research*, *81*(3), 1–13. doi:10.1016/j.annals.2020.102883

Tuyed. (2016). *İnsansı robotlar devri*. Retrieved from http://www.tuyed.org.tr/turizmde-insansi-robotlar-devri/

Tyagi, P. K., & Gupta, S. K. (2019, March). Recruitment and Selection Process in Travel Trade Organisations of Chandigarh: An Evaluation. *Journal of Emerging Technologies and Innovative Research*, *6*(3), 787–794.

Tyagi, P. K., Singh, A. K., Singh, D. V., & Tyagi, P. (2021). The Role of Social Crowdsourcing in Mobile Tourism. *Journal of Contemporary Issues in Business and Government, 27*(3), 149–161.

Tyagi, P. K., Singh, A. K., Tyagi, P., & Singh, V. (2021). A Study on Tourist Perception Towards Usage of Mobile Wallet. *Turkish Journal of Computer and Mathematics Education, 12*(13), 1–8.

Tyagi, P. K., & Tyagi, P. (2022). Customer Perception and Brand Image Through Sensory Marketing. In *Disruptive Innovation and Emerging Technologies for Business Excellence in the Service Sector* (pp. 41–68). IGI Global. doi:10.4018/978-1-7998-9194-9.ch003

Tyagi, P., Tyagi, P. K., Singh, A. K., Jain, E., & Singh, A. K. (2022, March). Tourist Experiences Through Mobile Augmented Reality. In *International Conference on Electronics and Renewable Systems (ICEARS)* (pp. 1605-1610). IEEE. 10.1109/ICEARS53579.2022.9752325

Tychachoonhakij, P., & Iamratanakul, S. (2019). Technology Acceptance and Quality of Electronic Service Affect e-Government Procurement System. *Journal of the Association of Researchers, 24*(3), 306–321.

Tzima, S., Styliaras, G., Bassounas, A., & Tzima, M. (2020). Harnessing the potential of storytelling and mobile technology in intangible cultural heritage: A case study in early childhood education in sustainability. *Sustainability (Switzerland), 12*(22), 1–22. doi:10.3390u12229416

UNESCO. (2003). *Intangible Heritage - 2003 Convention*. https://ich.unesco.org/en/intangible-heritage-domains-00052

Unsworth, K., & Parker, S. K. (2003). Promoting a proactive and innovative workforce for the new workplace. In D. Holman, T. D. Wall, C. W. Clegg, P. Sparrow, & A. Howard (Eds.), *The new workplace: a guide to the human impact of modern working practices*. John Wiley & Sons.

Van de Ven, A. H., & Drazin, R. (1984). *The concept of fit in contingency theory*. Retrieved from Minnesota University Minneapolis strategic management research center: https://apps.dtic.mil/sti/pdfs/ADA152603.pdf

Van de Ven, A. H. (1986). Central problems in the management of innovation. *Management Science, 32*(5), 590–607. doi:10.1287/mnsc.32.5.590

Vardarlier, P. (2020). Digital Transformation of Human Resource Management: Digital Applications and Strategic Tools in HRM. In U. Hacioglu (Ed.), *Digital Business Strategies in Blockchain Ecosystems* (pp. 239–264). Springer International Publishing. doi:10.1007/978-3-030-29739-8_11

Vatan, A., & Doğan, S. (2021). What do hotel employees think about service robots? A qualitative study in Turkey. *Tourism Management Perspectives, 37*, 1–10. doi:10.1016/j.tmp.2020.100775

Vatan, A., & Zengin, B. (2014). Çevresel inovasyon ve konaklama işletmelerindeki uygulamalar üzerine bir araştırma. *The Journal of Academic Social Science, 2*(8), 511–530. doi:10.16992/ASOS.458

Vaughan, L. (2016). Performance, practice and presence: Design parameters for the living archive. *Performing Digital: Multiple Perspectives on a Living Archive*, 51–62. doi:10.4324/9781315599960

Veen, R. V. D., & Preece, J. (2005). Poverty reduction and adult education: Beyond basic education. *International Journal of Lifelong Education, 24*(5), 381–391. doi:10.1080/02601370500169723

Venkatesh, V., & Davis, F. D. (2000). A Theoretical Extension of the Technology Acceptance Model: Four Longitudinal Field Studies. *Management Science, 46*(2), 186–204. doi:10.1287/mnsc.46.2.186.11926

Vial, G. (2019). Understanding digital transformation: A review and a research agenda. *The Journal of Strategic Information Systems, 28*(2), 118–144. doi:10.1016/j.jsis.2019.01.003

Viederyte, R. (2016). The significance of organisational and operational innovations in international logistics organisations, as well as the anticipated advantages of these advancements. *Studies on Regional Formation and Development, 20*(3), 134-146.

Villis, U., Strack, R., Bruysten, S., & Yunus, M. (2013). *The Power of Social Business: Lessons from Corporate Engagements with Grameen.* Available at: http://socialbusinesspedia.com/CaseStudy Report_PDF/BCG_Report_2013.pdf

Vinuesa, R., Azizpour, H., Leite, I., Balaam, M., Dignum, V., Domisch, S., Felländer, A., Langhans, S. D., Tegmark, M., & Nerini, F. F. (2020). The role of artificial intelligence in achieving the Sustainable Development Goals. *Nature Communications, 11*(1), 1–10. doi:10.103841467-019-14108-y PMID:31932590

Von Nordheim, G., Boczek, K., & Koppers, L. (2018). Sourcing the Sources: An analysis of the use of Twitter and Facebook as a journalistic source over 10 years in The New York Times, The Guardian, and SüddeutscheZeitung. *Digital Journalism, 6*(7), 807-828.

Vo, N., Chovancova, M., & Tri, H. (2019). The Impact of E-service Quality on the Customer Satisfaction and Consumer Engagement Behaviors Toward Luxury Hotels. *Journal of Quality Assurance in Hospitality & Tourism, 21*, 1–25.

Vongtharawat, M., & Pasunon, P. (2017). Factors Affecting Airline Passengers' Online Check-in Services Usage. *MUT Journal of Business Administration, 17*(2), 1–14.

Vosinakis, S., Avradinis, N., & Koutsabasis, P. (2018). Dissemination of Intangible Cultural Heritage Using a Multi-agent Virtual World. Lecture Notes in Computer Science, 10754, 197–207. doi:10.1007/978-3-319-75789-6_14

Wahid, A. N. M. (1999). The Grameen Bank and women in Bangladesh. *Challenge, 42*(5).

Walsh, P. R., & Dodds, R. (2017). Measuring the choice of environmental sustainability strategies in creating a competitive advantage. *Business Strategy and the Environment, 26*(5), 672–687. doi:10.1002/bse.1949

Wamba-Taguimdje, S. L., Wamba, S. F., Kamdjoug, J. R. K., & Wanko, C. E. T. (2020). Influence of artificial intelligence (AI) on firm performance: The business value of AI-based transformation projects. *Business Process Management Journal, 26*(7), 1893–1924. doi:10.1108/BPMJ-10-2019-0411

Wang, Y. (2018). Intelligent customer service system design based on natural language processing. In *5th International Conference On Electrical & Electronics Engineering And Computer Science (ICEEECS)* (pp. 374-379). Francis Acad Press.

Wang, C.-J. (2020). Managing emotional labour for service quality: A cross-level analysis among hotel employees. *International Journal of Hospitality Management, 88*, 102396. doi:10.1016/j.ijhm.2019.102396

Wassan, S., Gulati, K., Pallathadka, H., Suhail, B., Kuhar, P., & Gupta, A. (2021). How artificial intelligence transforms the experience of employees. *Turkish Journal of Computer and Mathematics Education, 12*(10), 7116-7135. doi:.v12i10.5603 doi:10.17762/turcomat

Watkins, L. (2016). *Enhancing Cybersecurity by Defeating the Attack Lifecycle*. ResearchGate. https://www.researchgate.net/publication/294142649_Enhancing_Cybersecurity_by_Defeating_the_Attack_Lifecycle

Weber, M. (1975). Science as a vocation. In From Max Weber: Essays in sociology (pp. 129-159). Oxford University Press.

Weerasinghe, I. M. S., & Dedunu, H. H. (2020a). Contribution of academics to university–industry knowledge exchange: A study of open innovation in Sri Lankan universities. *Industry and Higher Education*. Advance online publication. doi:10.1177/0950422220964363

Weerasinghe, I. M. S., & Dedunu, H. H. (2020b). Do demographic factors matter in university-industry knowledge exchange? A study based on Sri Lankan university system. *Journal of Knowledge Management, 25*(5), 973–988. doi:10.1108/JKM-02-2020-0092

Weiermair, K. (2006). *Product Improvement or Innovation: What is the key to success in tourism?* OECD Publishing.

Weimann, G. (2005). Cyberterrorism: The Sum of All Fears? *Studies in Conflict and Terrorism, 28*(2), 129–149. doi:10.1080/10576100590905110

Wernerfelt, B. (1984). *A Resource-based View of the Firm.* Academic Press.

Wiese, L., Waage, T., & Brenner, M. (2020). CloudDBGuard: A framework for encrypted data storage in NoSQL wide column stores. *Data & Knowledge Engineering, 126*, 101732. doi:10.1016/j.datak.2019.101732

Williams, A. (2008). *Innovation and tourism go hand in hand.* Routledge.

Wirtz, J., Patterson, P. G., Kunz, W. H., Gruber, T., Lu, W. N., Paluch, S., & Martins, A. (2018). Brave new world: Service robots in the frontline. *Journal of Service Management, 29*(5), 907–931. doi:10.1108/JOSM-04-2018-0119

Wisuttisaeng, Y., & Piyathasanan, B. (2017). Executive Perspectives towards Self-Service Technology (SST) in Thailand's Service Sectors. *Journal of Business Administration, 40*(156), 2–33.

Wolfinbarger, M., & Gilly, M. C. (2003). eTailQ: Dimensionalizing, Measuring, and Predicting Etail Quality. *Journal of Retailing, 79*(3), 183–198. doi:10.1016/S0022-4359(03)00034-4

Worasuwannarak, B., & Kankaew, K. (2022). The Image Value of Southeast Asia Airlines: A Study of Attribute that Led to Image Value of Choosing Southeast Asia Airlines by Mean-End Theory Approach. In K. Kankaew (Ed.), *Global Air Transport Management and Reshaping Business Models for the New Era.* IGI Global Publishing. doi:10.4018/978-1-6684-4615-7.ch009

World Bank. (2006). *World Bank World Development Indicators.* World Bank.

World Bank. (2008). Finance for All - Policies and Pitfalls in Expanding Access. World Bank Policy Research Report.

Wratten, E. (1995). Conceptualizing urban poverty. *Environment and Urbanization, 7*(1), 11–38. doi:10.1177/095624789500700118

Wu, L. W., & Lin, J. R. (2013). Knowledge sharing and knowledge effectiveness: Learning orientation and co-production in the contingency model of tacit knowledge. *Journal of Business and Industrial Marketing, 28*(8), 672–686. doi:10.1108/JBIM-04-2011-0050

Xie, J. (2022). Innovative Design of Artificial Intelligence in Intangible Cultural Heritage. *Scientific Programming, 2022*(1). doi:10.1155/2022/6913046

Xie, X., Huo, J., & Zou, H. (2019). Green process innovation, green product innovation, and corporate financial performance: A content analysis method. *Journal of Business Research, 101*, 697–706. doi:10.1016/j.jbusres.2019.01.010

Yağcı, O. (2017). Turizm ĠÇletmelerinde Yenilik Yonetimi. In F. Okumuĝ & U. Avcı (Eds.), Turizm İşletmelerinde Çağdaş Yonetim Teknikleri. Ankara: Detay Yayıncılık.

Yalçın Kayıkçı, M., & Kutluk Bozkurt, A. (2018). Dijital çağda Z ve Alpha kuşağı, yapay zeka uygulamaları ve turizme yansımaları. *Sosyal Bilimler Metinleri, 1*, 54–64.

Yang, J., & Rui, M. (2009). Turning knowledge into new product creativity: An empirical study. *Industrial Management & Data Systems, 109*(9), 1197–1210. doi:10.1108/02635570911002270

Yang, Z., Chen, H., Du, L., Lin, C., & Lu, W. (2021). How does alliance-based government-university-industry foster cleantech innovation in a green innovation ecosystem? *Journal of Cleaner Production, 283*, 1–17. doi:10.1016/j.jclepro.2020.124559

Yan, W. J., & Chiou, S. C. (2021). The safeguarding of intangible cultural heritage from the perspective of civic participation: The informal education of chinese embroidery handicrafts. *Sustainability (Switzerland), 13*(9), 4958. Advance online publication. doi:10.3390u13094958

Yaron, J., Benjamin, M., & Piprek, G. (1997). *Rural Finance: Issues, Design, and Best Practices*. World Bank.

Yawalkar, V. V. (2019). A Study of Artificial Intelligence and its role in Human Resource Management. *International Journal of Research and Analytical Reviews, 6*(1), 20–24.

Yeğin, T. (2020). The place and future of artificial intelligence in marketing strategies. *Ekev Akademi Dergisi, 24*(81), 489–506.

Yelkikalkan, N., Özcan, S., & Temel, K. (2019). Endüstri 4.0 Farkındalığının Belirlenmesi: Çanakkale Onsekiz Mart Üniversitesi Örneği. *Journal of Entrepreneurship and Development, 14*(1), 31–44.

Yıldız, S. (2018). Profesyonel turist rehberlerinin teknolojik rehber algısını belirlemeye yönelik bir araştırma: İstanbul örneği. *Journal of Social and Humanities Sciences Research, 5*(31), 4686–4697.

Yılmaz, O., & Atik, K. (2022). Çanakkale kent merkezindeki leed sertifikalı yeşil binalar üzerine araştırmalar: Çanakkale Esas 17 Burda Avm örneği. *Kırklareli Üniversitesi Mühendislik ve Fen Bilimleri Dergisi, 8*(1), 88–108.

Yin, R. (2009). *Case study research. Designing and Methods, 4(5).*

Yin, S., & Li, B. (2019). Academic research institutes-construction enterprises linkages for the development of urban green building: Selecting management of green building technologies innovation partner. *Sustainable Cities and Society, 48*, 1–23. doi:10.1016/j.scs.2019.101555

Yonah, Z. O., & Salim, B. A. (2008). *ICTs as tools for poverty reduction*. Academic Press.

Yoo, B., & Donthu, N. (2001). Developing a Scale to Measure the Perceived Quality of an Internet Shopping Site (SITE-QUAL). *Quarterly Journal of Electronic Commerce, 2*(1), 31–45.

Yücel, D. (2021). İnovasyonun yeni yüzü: Açık yeşil inovasyon. *Ekonomik ve Sosyal Araştırmalar Dergisi, 17*(2), 419–441.

Yunus, M. (2010). *Seven principles of social business*. Available at: www.yunuscenter.ait.asia/social-business

Yunus, M. (2004). Grameen Bank, microcredit and millennium development goals. *Economic and Political Weekly*, 4077–4080.

Yunus, M., Dalsace, F., Menasce, D., & Faivre-Tavignot, B. (2015). Reaching the Rich World's Poorest consumers. *Harvard Business Review, 3*(1), 46–53.

Zahidi, F., Imam, Y., Hashmi, A. U., & Baig, M. M. (2020). Impact of Artificial Intelligence on HR Management – A Review. *Dogo Rangsang Research Journal, 10*(6), 92–101.

Zailani, S., Govindan, K., Iranmanesh, M., Shaharudin, M. R., & Sia Chong, Y. (2015). Green innovation adoption in automotive supply chain: The Malaysian case. *Journal of Cleaner Production, 108*, 1115–1122. doi:10.1016/j.jclepro.2015.06.039

Zhang, D., Rong, Z., & Ji, Q. (2019). Green innovation and firm performance: Evidence from listed companies in China. *Resources, Conservation and Recycling, 144*, 48–55. doi:10.1016/j.resconrec.2019.01.023

Zhang, L., & Sun, Z. (2019). The application of artificial intelligence technology in the tourism industry of Jinan. *Journal of Physics: Conference Series*, *1302*(3), 032005. doi:10.1088/1742-6596/1302/3/032005

Zhang, W., & Zhang, W. (2018). Knowledge creation through industry chain in resource-based industry: Case study on phosphorus chemical industry chain in western Guizhou of China. *Journal of Knowledge Management*, *22*(5), 1037–1060. doi:10.1108/JKM-02-2017-0061

Zhang, Y., Han, M., & Chen, W. (2018). The strategy of digital scenic area planning from the perspective of intangible cultural heritage protection. *EURASIP Journal on Image and Video Processing*, *2018*(1), 130. Advance online publication. doi:10.118613640-018-0366-7

Zhang, Y., & Lee, T. J. (2022). Alienation and authenticity in intangible cultural heritage tourism production. *International Journal of Tourism Research*, *24*(1), 18–32. doi:10.1002/jtr.2478

Zhang, Y., Liu, S., Tan, J., Jiang, G., & Zhu, Q. (2018). Effects of risks on the performance of business process outsourcing projects: The moderating roles of knowledge management capabilities. *International Journal of Project Management*, *36*(4), 627–639. doi:10.1016/j.ijproman.2018.02.002

Zhao, S., Jiang, Y., Peng, X., & Hong, J. (2020). Knowledge sharing direction and innovation performance in organizations: Do absorptive capacity and individual creativity matter? *European Journal of Innovation Management*, *24*(2), 371–394. doi:10.1108/EJIM-09-2019-0244

Zhao, Y., & Ko, J. (2020). How do teaching quality and pedagogical practice enhance vocational student engagement? A mixed-method classroom observation approach. *International Journal of Educational Management*, *34*(6), 987–1000. doi:10.1108/IJEM-11-2019-0393

Zhou, J., & George, M. (2001). When job dissatisfaction lead to creativity. *Academy of Management Journal*, *44*(4), 682–696. doi:10.2307/3069410

Zhou, X., Yu, Y., Yang, F., & Shi, Q. (2021). Spatial-temporal heterogeneity of green innovation in China. *Journal of Cleaner Production*, *282*, 1–10. doi:10.1016/j.jclepro.2020.124464

Zlatanov, S., & Popesku, J. (2019). Current Applications of Artificial Intelligence in Tourism and Hospitality. Paper presented at Sinteza 2019 - International Scientific Conference on Information Technology and Data Related Research. doi:10.15308/Sinteza-2019-84-90

Zlatanov, S., & Popesku, J. (2019, April). Current applications of artificial intelligence in tourism and hospitality. *International Scientific Conference on Information Technology and Data Related Research*, 84-90.

Zsarnoczky, M. (2017). How does artificial intelligence affect the tourism ındustry? *Vadyba Journal of Management*, 2(31), 85–90.

Zsarnoczky, M. (2017). Social sciences How Does Artificial Intelligence Affect The Tourism Industry? *Journal of Management*, *31*(2), 84–90.

About the Contributors

Vishal Bharti is currently working as Additional Director, in dept. of CSE. Previously he has worked as Professor and Head in Department CSE, School of Computing at DIT University, Dehradun. He has also worked as Professor and Head in AIT-CSE at Chandigarh University, Mohali, Punjab, Associate Prof. and; Head, Department of CSE at Dronacharya College of Engineering Gurgaon. He completed his Ph.D. in 2016. He did his M.Tech. and B.E. from Birla Institute of Technology, Mesra. Ranchi. He also holds Doctorate in Management Studies in addition to MBA in IT and E-MBA in S&M. He is having a mixed bag of experience of 14+ Years in both Academia and IT Industry He have five filed patents out of which two are in the process of Granting and Commercialization, Twenty-Seven copyrights and 13 Govt. Grants (SERB, DST, NSTEDB, EDI etc.) to his credit. He published more than Seventy-Eight research works at both National and; International domain like IEEE, Springer, Taylor and; Francis, Elsevir and was awarded with Best Faculty Award in 2010, Best Computer Teacher in 2019, Academic Leadership Award in 2019, Best Young HoD of the Year Award 2019. He is a member of more than 80+ International and National Societies/Conferences/Journals as Advisory Board.

* * *

Gaurav Bathla is working with LPU as an associate professor. He has written many papers and participated in conferences.

Anthony Bolton obtained his PhD from the School of Computing at the University of South Africa. He is also Chief Information Officer (CIO) and Chief Technical Officer (CTO) Global Telecom, End User Infrastructure & Services, Immersive Technology Development and Engineering at General Motors in Ireland.

Priya Chaturvedi is a Senior Research Fellow working on Intangible Cultural Heritage. She has written a chapter for an edited book and has presented ideas at various national and international conferences. She has also contributed manuscripts on various terms in the upcoming Encyclopedia of Tourism Management and Marketing. She has taught various tourism-related subjects in bachelor and master programmes.

Jana Deprez is a postdoctoral research fellow in Organizational Psychology. Her area of expertise consists of intrapreneurship, entrepreneurship and innovation as well as polynomial regression analyses.

Darshana Dewapriya is a Professor of Information Systems at the Southern Cross University in Gold Coast, Australia. He is also the Associate Dean (Research) in the Faculty of Business, Law and Arts and serves as the Director of the Digital Enterprise Lab. Professor Sedera has published over 200 peer-reviewed publications in major refereed journals and conferences. His publications have appeared in The Journal of the AIS, The Academy of Management, The Journal of the Strategic Information Systems, Information and Management, IT and People and the Communications of the AIS. Professor Sedera has substantial experience in working with the industry and academia. He has served as a chief investigator of several ARC grants (both Linkage and Discovery) and has received direct industry funding leading to funding over $1.5 million. Professor Sedera also serves at several ABDC A* and A-ranked journal editorial boards. Prior to joining the Southern Cross University, Professor Sedera has worked as a Professoriate staff at the Swinburne University of Technology, Monash University, and Queensland University of Technology.

Martin Euwema is full professor in Organizational Psychology, and chair of the research group Occupational and Organizational Psychology and Professional Learning, at KU Leuven. his main interests are leadership, conflict management, and family businesses.

Leila Goosen is a full professor in the Department of Science and Technology Education of the University of South Africa. Prof. Goosen was an Associate Professor in the School of Computing, and the module leader and head designer of the fully online signature module for the College for Science, Engineering and Technology, rolled out to over 92,000 registered students since the first semester of 2013. She also supervises ten Masters and Doctoral students, and has successfully completed supervision of 43 students at postgraduate level. Previously, she was a Deputy Director at the South African national Department of Education. In this capacity, she was required to develop ICT strategies for implementation. She also promoted, coordinated, managed, monitored and evaluated ICT policies and strategies, and drove the research agenda in this area. Before that, she had been a lecturer of Information Technology (IT) in the Department for Science, Mathematics and Technology Education in the Faculty of Education of the University of Pretoria. Her research interests have included cooperative work in IT, effective teaching and learning of programming and teacher professional development.

Manish Kumar Hooda has joined Semi-Conductor Laboratory, Department of Space (GOI) in May, 2004 after completing his Master's Degree from Kurukshetra University Haryana & obtained PhD in 2007 from Kurukshetra University Haryana. During his initial assignments he was responsible in process development activities for Micro-Electro Mechanical Systems (MEMS) Devices. In his initial days he has developed the key technology enabler processes required for MEMS Device Fabrications. He has been associated with many projects responsibilities in different capacities for various Space Applications: ASIC developments for satellite Payloads, ASIC for Launch Vehicle control, Sensors Such for measuring: Pressure, Temperature, Humidity, Micro thrusters, and Micro-igniters for microsatellite and space craft Application, Gyroscope, Varactor, Accelerometer etc. He played a vital role in process integration for 180nm CMOS technology on 200mm silicon wafer at SCL (one of its kind facility in country). Presently, he is Head of Technology Development Division at SCL. Under His Present Capacity he is responsible for establishing exotic Compound Semiconductor Manufacturing Facility in country at SCL for devices development based on new technologies such as: III-V and II-VI Compound Semiconductors materials, for High Power switching and detector applications for futuristic India's space mission.

Sadeque Imam Shaikh is having 22 years of teaching experience in different Universities of UK and abroad. At present ha has been working as Lecturer of MBA and Computing at University of Wales Trinity Saint David London. Sadeque is a DBA Researcher at UCAM (Catholic University of Murcia, Spain) and has completed MPhil in Management (UCAM), MSc (Learning and Technology), Glyndwr University UK, MSc Computer Network, University of Bedfordshire UK and MSc Computer Science, BSc (Hon's) Computer Science. Sadeque is also having prestigious fellowships with different organizations of UK such as FHEA, FBCS, FRSA and FRAS. Sadeque has also published research papers in different Journals and conference proceedings at home and abroad and worked as an Executive editor of Multi discipline journal of University of Science and Technology Chittagong. He also received Graduate of The Year Award (University of Bedfordshire), UK IT Industry awards (BCS), He was also the Former Dean, University of Science & Technology Chittagong & Senior Lecturer and Curriculum Leader, Glyndwr University London.

Alice Jalley currently lives in West Sussex and attended the University of Chichester where she gained a first-class degree in BA (Hons) Event Management. Alice's event management experience started in the wedding industry where she worked as a venue coordinator at a barn wedding venue helping couples plan their special day. During Alice's time working at a wedding venue, she became passionate about sustainability and finding ways to lessen the impact of events whilst also making the event unforgettable. To delve deeper into the environmental impacts of weddings, Alice focused her final year University dissertation on how to reduce waste at weddings. After University, Alice moved on to working in pharmaceutical events where she now travels the world delivering conferences for big name pharmaceutical companies. Alice is enjoying the different areas of the event industry and expanding her skills by working with different people and clients. Doing events around the world has opened Alice's eyes to different cultures and how to be flexible within the different environments. In her spare time Alice enjoys walking her dogs along the beach, reading books, and watching different series on Netflix. Alice also enjoys playing netball and exploring the different countries she gets to travel too within her job and trying the local food dishes.

Paula Jenkins is a Business School Academic and HR consultant and Learning Designer with 30 years' experience of developing people in organisations in leadership, people management and personal mastery capability, providing management and leadership development and People Management consultancy in learning design, facilitation and the integration of psychometric profiles into development programmes. She has worked in HR roles nationally and internationally in both the private and public sectors in a variety of strategic positions with a focus on organisation development, providing HR and learning needs analysis, development and facilitation of organisation development programmes, leadership and management programme design and delivery and DiSC® profiling for management development. Her private sector HR experience includes industry giants such as British Airways, Cathay Pacific Airways Ltd Hong Kong and SMES such as COVE Communities. Her public sector clients through the University of Chichester include The Pensions Regulator and the Education sector. Paula has also worked in the Education sector internationally with the British Council and The Hong Kong Polytechnic University and in the UK with Northbrook Further Education College (now Brighton MET) and Bell Education Trust. Paula has Post graduate qualifications in Human Resource Management and Adult Education and is a licensed practitioner of DiSC psychometrics and MBTI. She is a member of the CIPD, The British Academy of Management and The Chartered Management Institute. She is Chief Examiner for the University of Northumbria HRM modules and an External Examiner for HRM at Leeds Beckett University.

Kannapat Kankaew is currently entitled as Assistant Professor and Deputy Dean in Research and Academic Services at College of Hospitality Industry Management; Suan Sunandha Rajabhat University. He received Doctor of Public Administration degree in Human Resources Management. Prior his academic professional, he used to work in the aviation industry for more than 13 years. He has published and participated in International Conferences more than 30 papers in reputed journals. And he has dedicated as an editorial board and reviewer for various journals both domestic and international. He did published chapters in edited book, being a book editor, and examiner for PhD and Master students both national and international institutions. His latest edited book is Global Air Transport Management and Reshaping Business Models for the New Era.

Rajwinder Kaur is a research scholar at Chandigarh University. She is B.com (Hons.) and MBA (Banking, Finance, and HR) and now pursuing a Ph.D. from Chandigarh University. Her interest areas are HR and Finance. She has done internships in Banks and under Charted Accountant and successfully completed various research projects. She has also completed online courses from reputed online websites. As far as her publications are concerned, she has published more than 7 research papers in international and national journals. She has also published research papers in Scopus, WoS and ABDC indexed journals. She has also presented many research papers at national and international conferences. She has actively participated in various activities and is very much interested in research-related projects.

Shaheed Khan, academically qualified in the areas of and armed with Post Graduate Degrees in History, Tourism, Business Administration and Law and a Research Degree in Tourism Management, focuses on Tourism, Ecotourism, Mergers and Acquisitions and Human Resources. He also has a Micro-specialization in Strategy Management from Indian Institute of Management Kozhikode and a Corporate Program in Leadership Management from Harvard School of Publishing. He brings to the table multiple facets of functioning that supports in any area of academics and practice in the corporate world. Having worked in the Government, Private and Social Sectors, Shaheed has got to broad understanding of Tourism, Travel and Hospitality (TTH)., Shaheed currently is the Head, Research, Training and Advocacy with Dharthi NGO and Dharthi Learning Centre, Pondicherry. Dharthi has its Headquarters in Bangalore and works with Private and Government organizations in the domain of Environment, Forests, Communities and Tourism. Shaheed had worked in the states of Karnataka, Tamil Nadu, Pondicherry, Maharashtra, and Madhya Pradesh for Dharthi. He is also an Adjunct Faculty in the domain of Tourism, General Management, M&A in Educational Institutions (Central and State University, Deemed to be and Private Universities), and engages Class session for Corporates in Leading IT and manufacturing Companies of India. He has authored over 15 articles in Journals of repute and contributed to Chapters in Edited Books as well. He has worked with other stakeholders to ensure for the Ecotourism segment and has been supporting the cause of Sustainable Tourism.

Theppaluk Komolvanij is a head of airline business program, College of Hospitality Industry Management, Suan Sunandha Rajabhat University.

Elmarie Kritzinger joined the University of South Africa's College of Science, Engineering and Technology (CSET) in 2000 and currently holds the position of Professor in the School of Computing. Prof Kritzinger completed her PhD in 2006 and Post Graduate Certificate in Education in 2012. She also successfully completed her Master's in Education (Online Technology). Her research primarily focuses on Cyber Safety awareness, training and education for school learners, teachers, and schools. The main aim is to establish and promote social responsibilities within communities to establish and grow a cyber-safety culture within South Africa. Prof Kritzinger has established herself as a mature researcher and has published in accredited national and international journals, contributed to a chapter in a book and presented at peer-reviewed conferences across the globe. Prof Kritzinger currently hold a NRF C3 rating within her research field.

Anupam Mazumdar has been working as a Business & Computing lecturer at the London campus of the University of Wales Trinity Saint David (UWTSD) since October 2018. Before joining UWTSD, Anupam was a visiting lecturer at UK College of Business and Computing (UKCBC) since April 2018. He has been working as a visiting lecturer (part time) in various UK Higher Education institutions since 2009 and has taught different modules from the Institute for the Management of Information Systems (IMIS) and Association of Computer Professionals (ACP) awarding bodies. After completing his bachelor's degree in computer science from the University of Madras, Chennai, India, he worked in an education establishment in Bangladesh as a supporting lecturer. Upon completion of his master's degree in Computer Systems & Network Engineering from the University of Greenwich, UK, he has worked for couple of years within the IT industry as well as a lecturer in various UK Higher Education institutions. In February 2014, he started his doctoral journey researching Cloud Computing Adoption in SMEs and successfully completed his Doctoral degree (DBA) in May 2019. He has been a Fellow of the Higher Education Academy since April 2021. He is an active member of British Computer Society (BCS), Skills for FE and HE in the UK, and Cloudready Skills supported by Microsoft. Over the last 3 years, he has been supervising a few numbers of Cloud Computing students on their final project. In addition, he has been supervising MBA students on their final dissertation as well as Postgraduate Research students (Doctorate) on their research. He has been an active researcher in the field of computing and business.

Panch Ramalingam with almost close to four decades of teaching and administrative experience, professes his first love for research and augmenting a better thought process for the teaching community across levels. He is an another for more than 80 publications as author and editor. His books have won awards and accolades as well. His most recent, publication, School Psychology, in the Indian Context has been translated into 13 Indian languages already. His ideation about the psyche of individuals and the way they work, is something that one needs to admire. he and his work have ensured, that the outreach for a larger outlook is always there for the organization to benefit. He carries with his work, and ensures success to one and all.

Aditya Ranjan is the Head of Consulting at Bakri Chhap Agro Tourism and Natural Product Pvt. Ltd. He is Ph.D. in "Deconstructing Rural Tourism in India" from the Department of Tourism and Hospitality Management, Jamia Millia Islamia. His research interest is in Rurality, Rural Tourism, and Destination marketing. He has published research papers and has presented ideas at various national and international conferences. He has edited a book titled "Rurality, Ruralism and Rural tourism: Challenges and Coping Strategies" and has written chapters for different edited books. He has also contributed manuscripts on various terms in the upcoming Encyclopedia of Tourism Management and Marketing. He has completed an advanced tourism research course from Mid-Sweden University. His advisory work involves helping state government, students, researchers, and stakeholders answer difficult tourism questions, specifically about rural tourism. Previously, he taught various tourism-related courses as Assistant Professor at the University Institute of Tourism and Hospitality Management, Chandigarh University.

Wouter Robijn is a research fellow in Organizational Psychology, at KU Leuven. His primary focus is on leadership behavior, team dynamics, and well-being.

Wendy Sealy has considerable work experience in the hospitality, events, marketing and public relations, having worked in the sector for over 22 years for Marriott International Hotels and Resorts, Almond Beach Resorts and Bougainvillea Beach Resorts. Dr. Sealy has been lecturing since 2005. Before joining the University of Chichester, she taught at the undergraduate and post-graduate level in Tourism Management at Buckinghamshire New University and at the postgraduate level in Sport and Event Management at the University of the West-Indies. Dr. Sealy graduated from the University of the West Indies with a first class honours degree in History and Sociology. She later completed her masters degree in Tourism Marketing with distinction at the University of Surrey and her Doctor of Philosophy degree with Brunel University, London. Dr. Sealy is Reader in Graduate Employability in the Business School at the University of Chichester and is responsible for coordinating the teaching, learning and research activities for the BA (Hons) Event Management. She is responsible for employer-student engagement activity and the co-ordination of live event projects under the provision of the event management degree programme. Wendy is particularly interested in the experiences of event management students in higher education and has spent a considerable amount of time conducting research and publishing work in this area. She is the creator of the Event Management Body of Skills (EMBOS) model for event management education, published in Event Management – an International Journal. Her other interest involves experimenting with different ways to embed employability into the students' higher education experiences in order to ensure that they can compete for jobs at graduation. She is also the Associate Editor of the Journal of Tourism and Sustainability and a member of the editorial committee of the Journal of International Tourism and Hospitality. Dr. Sealy has published her research in several academic journals and books including the Journal of Travel and Tourism Marketing, the Journal of Travel Research and The International Journal on Tourism and Sustainability. She is also an advocate for Inclusivity and Diversity in research.

Disha Sharma is a Finance Faculty, Presently working as an Assistant Professor at Amity Business School, Amity University Chhattisgarh. She has done qualified UGC-NET & SET, did master in three subjects, and completed her Ph.D. from Pt. Ravi Shankar Shukla University, Raipur. She has five years of teaching experience. She has published many papers on her credit of national and international repute. She has also written many book chapters in International and Scopus indexed books. She also has experience as Co-Principal Investigator in ICSSR Project and currently working on many other projects. She has presented various research papers at national and international conferences. She is a lifetime member of the All Indian Commerce Association and All India Accounting Association.

Amrik Singh is working with Lovely Professional University, Punjab, India. He is PhD in Hospitality Management from Kurukshetra University, India. His area of expertise in tourism and hospitality, human resource management, sustainability, waste management, green practices, restaurant and resort management. He has published more than 35 research papers including peer reviewed, ugc indexed and scopus indexed research articles and book chapters. He is associated as editorial board members and reviewers with reputed and Scopus-indexed journals.

Gurinder Pal Singh is working as Senior Technician 'A' in Semiconductor Laboratory (SCL), Ministry of Electronics and Information Technology (MeitY), Mohali, Punjab. Previously the Semiconductor Laboratory was under Department of Space (DoS). He completed his M.Tech (CSE) in 2020 from Rayat-Bahra University. He did his M.Sc IT from Punjab Technical University in 2002. He completed Cisco Certified Network Associate (CCNA) in 2008. His specialties are Cyber Security, Network Security, Web Management, and Development. He has developed many SCL websites and has managed Intranet and Spacenet. He is having experience of 26+ Years in IT Industry. He played an important role in the 2018 Cyber Security Exercise organized by the Indian Space Organization (ISRO). He has published five research papers at both National & International domain like UGC Care, Apple Academic Press. He received an award from S.A.S.Nagar Administration on 15 August 2004 for developing Mohali Web Portal.

Freeda Maria Swarna M. has over 15 years of experience in the Sustainability, Conservation Science, Environment, Communities and Tourism domains. With Post Graduate Degrees in Tourism and Ecology & Environment, and a Research Degree in Tourism Management; her strength lies in combining Applied Sciences and the integration of sound research with a robust implementation. As Director, Dharthi NGO was nominated to the Karnataka Ecotourism Development Board as a member of the General Body, where during her three-year tenure, she was instrumental in conducting Cumulative Impact assessment (CIA) studies, having consultations with stakeholders for a robust Ecotourism Policy for the State of Karnataka. Freeda is in the process of authoring two books, one on Ecotourism, and has published articles and papers to her credit. With a penchant for writing, she is in the process of putting up her blogsite called , which will contain impactful stories of her travels, people and places.

Mehmet Tekeli graduated from Nevşehir Hacı Bektaş Veli University, Faculty of Tourism, Department of Tourism Management (2014). He received his master's degree from Nevşehir Hacı Bektaş Veli University Tourism Management Department (2016), and his doctoral degree from Nevşehir Hacı Bektaş Veli University Tourism Management Department (2021). He is an Assistant Professor Dr. at Karamanoğlu Mehmetbey University, School of Applied Sciences. His main fields of study are tourism and tourism management.

Index

A

B

C

D

E

F

G

H

I

K

M

N

P

Q

R

S

T

U

Recommended Reference Books

IGI Global's reference books are available in three unique pricing formats: Print Only, E-Book Only, or Print + E-Book.

Order direct through IGI Global's Online Bookstore at **www.igi-global.com** or through your preferred provider.

ISBN: 9781799887096
EISBN: 9781799887119
© 2022; 413 pp.
List Price: US$ **250**

ISBN: 9781799874157
EISBN: 9781799874164
© 2022; 334 pp.
List Price: US$ **240**

ISBN: 9781668440230
EISBN: 9781668440254
© 2022; 320 pp.
List Price: US$ **215**

ISBN: 9781799889502
EISBN: 9781799889526
© 2022; 263 pp.
List Price: US$ **240**

ISBN: 9781799885283
EISBN: 9781799885306
© 2022; 587 pp.
List Price: US$ **360**

ISBN: 9781668455906
EISBN: 9781668455913
© 2022; 2,235 pp.
List Price: US$ **1,865**

Do you want to stay current on the latest research trends, product announcements, news, and special offers?

Join IGI Global's mailing list to receive customized recommendations, exclusive discounts, and more.
Sign up at: **www.igi-global.com/newsletters.**

Publisher of Timely, Peer-Reviewed Inclusive Research Since 1988

IGI Global
PUBLISHER of TIMELY KNOWLEDGE

www.igi-global.com Sign up at www.igi-global.com/newsletters facebook.com/igiglobal twitter.com/igiglobal linkedin.com/igiglobal

Ensure Quality Research is Introduced to the Academic Community

Become an Evaluator for IGI Global Authored Book Projects

The overall success of an authored book project is dependent on quality and timely manuscript evaluations.

Applications and Inquiries may be sent to:
development@igi-global.com

Applicants must have a doctorate (or equivalent degree) as well as publishing, research, and reviewing experience. Authored Book Evaluators are appointed for one-year terms and are expected to complete at least three evaluations per term. Upon successful completion of this term, evaluators can be considered for an additional term.

If you have a colleague that may be interested in this opportunity,
we encourage you to share this information with them.

Easily Identify, Acquire, and Utilize Published Peer-Reviewed Findings in Support of Your Current Research

IGI Global OnDemand

Purchase Individual IGI Global OnDemand Book Chapters and Journal Articles

For More Information:
www.igi-global.com/e-resources/ondemand/

Browse through 150,000+ Articles and Chapters!

Find specific research related to your current studies and projects that have been contributed by international researchers from prestigious institutions, including:

Massachusetts Institute of Technology
HARVARD UNIVERSITY
COLUMBIA UNIVERSITY IN THE CITY OF NEW YORK
Australian National University

- Accurate and Advanced Search
- Affordably Acquire Research
- Instantly Access Your Content
- Benefit from the InfoSci Platform Features

"*It really provides an excellent entry into the research literature of the field. It presents a manageable number of highly relevant sources on topics of interest to a wide range of researchers. The sources are scholarly, but also accessible to 'practitioners'.*"

- Ms. Lisa Stimatz, MLS, University of North Carolina at Chapel Hill, USA

Interested in Additional Savings?

Subscribe to
IGI Global OnDemand *Plus*

Learn More

Acquire content from over 128,000+ research-focused book chapters and 33,000+ scholarly journal articles for as low as US$ 5 per article/chapter (original retail price for an article/chapter: US$ 37.50).

IGI Global
PUBLISHER of TIMELY KNOWLEDGE

7,300+ E-BOOKS. ADVANCED RESEARCH. INCLUSIVE & AFFORDABLE.

IGI Global e-Book Collection

- **Flexible Purchasing Options** (Perpetual, Subscription, EBA, etc.)
- Multi-Year Agreements with **No Price Increases** Guaranteed
- **No Additional Charge** for Multi-User Licensing
- No Maintenance, Hosting, or Archiving Fees
- Continually Enhanced & Innovated **Accessibility Compliance Features** (WCAG)

Handbook of Research on Digital Transformation, Industry Use Cases, and the Impact of Disruptive Technologies
ISBN: 9781799877127
EISBN: 9781799877141

Handbook of Research on New Investigations in Artificial Life, AI, and Machine Learning
ISBN: 9781799886860
EISBN: 9781799886877

Handbook of Research on Future of Work and Education
ISBN: 9781799882756
EISBN: 9781799882770

Research Anthology on Physical and Intellectual Disabilities in an Inclusive Society (4 Vols.)
ISBN: 9781668435427
EISBN: 9781668435434

Innovative Economic, Social, and Environmental Practices for Progressing Future Sustainability
ISBN: 9781799895909
EISBN: 9781799895923

Applied Guide for Event Study Research in Supply Chain Management
ISBN: 9781799889694
EISBN: 9781799889717

Mental Health and Wellness in Healthcare Workers
ISBN: 9781799888130
EISBN: 9781799888147

Clean Technologies and Sustainable Development in Civil Engineering
ISBN: 9781799898108
EISBN: 9781799898122

Request More Information, or Recommend the IGI Global e-Book Collection to Your Institution's Librarian

For More Information or to Request a Free Trial, Contact IGI Global's e-Collections Team: eresources@igi-global.com | 1-866-342-6657 ext. 100 | 717-533-8845 ext. 100

Are You Ready to

Publish Your Research ?

IGI Global
PUBLISHER of TIMELY KNOWLEDGE

IGI Global offers book authorship and editorship opportunities across 11 subject areas, including business, computer science, education, science and engineering, social sciences, and more!

Benefits of Publishing with IGI Global:

- Free one-on-one editorial and promotional support.
- Expedited publishing timelines that can take your book from start to finish in less than one (1) year.
- Choose from a variety of formats, including Edited and Authored References, Handbooks of Research, Encyclopedias, and Research Insights.
- Utilize IGI Global's eEditorial Discovery® submission system in support of conducting the submission and double-blind peer review process.
- IGI Global maintains a strict adherence to ethical practices due in part to our full membership with the Committee on Publication Ethics (COPE).
- Indexing potential in prestigious indices such as Scopus®, Web of Science™, PsycINFO®, and ERIC – Education Resources Information Center.
- Ability to connect your ORCID iD to your IGI Global publications.
- Earn honorariums and royalties on your full book publications as well as complimentary content and exclusive discounts.

Join Your Colleagues from Prestigious Institutions, Including:

Australian National University

Massachusetts Institute of Technology

Johns Hopkins University

Harvard University

Tsinghua University

Columbia University in the City of New York

Learn More at: www.igi-global.com/publish

or Contact IGI Global's Aquisitions Team at: acquisition@igi-global.com

Individual Article & Chapter Downloads

US$ 29.50/each

Easily Identify, Acquire, and Utilize Published Peer-Reviewed Findings in Support of Your Current Research

- Browse Over ***170,000+ Articles & Chapters***
- ***Accurate & Advanced*** Search
- Affordably Acquire ***International Research***
- ***Instantly Access*** Your Content
- Benefit from the ***InfoSci® Platform Features***

THE UNIVERSITY
of NORTH CAROLINA
at CHAPEL HILL

"It really provides an excellent entry into the research literature of the field. It presents a manageable number of highly relevant sources on topics of interest to a wide range of researchers. The sources are scholarly, but also accessible to 'practitioners'."

\- Ms. Lisa Stimatz, MLS, University of North Carolina at Chapel Hill, USA

Interested in Additional Savings?

Subscribe to

IGI Global OnDemand *Plus*

Learn More

Acquire content from over 137,000+ research-focused book chapters and 33,000+ scholarly journal articles for as low as US$ 5 per article/chapter (original retail price for an article/chapter: US$ 29.50).

CPSIA information can be obtained
at www.ICGtesting.com
Printed in the USA
LVHW060022030423
743149LV00014B/1294

9 781668 467336